Scandinavian Defense

The Dynamic 3...Qd6

Second Edition

by

Michael Melts

Foreword by
Ian Rogers

2009
Russell Enterprises, Inc.
Milford, CT USA

Scandinavian Defense
The Dynamic 3...Qd6

Second Edition

© Copyright 2009

Michael Melts

ISBN: 978-1-888690-55-2

Published by:
Russell Enterprises, Inc.
PO Box 5460
Milford, CT 06460 USA

http://www.chesscafe.com
info@chesscafe.com

Cover design by Janel Lowrance
Editing and Proofreading: Hanon Russell
Production: Mark Donlan

Printed in the United States of America

Table of Contents

Foreword to the First Edition

When choosing an opening, chessplayers tend to be extremely fashion-conscious. Yet the Scandinavian Defence is such an ugly duckling that even Viswanathan Anand's adoption of the defence in his world title contest against Garry Kasparov in 1995 was not enough to push the opening into the mainstream.

The lack of popularity of the Scandinavian Defence is difficult to fathom as the opening is easy to adopt without extensive study and is fun to play. A clash of forces occurs at the start of the game, putting both sides under pressure to find good moves far earlier than in trendy theoretical openings.

The subject of this book – 1.e4 d5 2.exd5 ♕xd5 3.♘c3 ♕d6!? – is something of a curiosity even among regular exponents of the Scandinavian. A belief that the queen is unstable on d6, and vulnerable to ♘b5 or ♗f4, leads most to believe that the queen would be more safely placed on a5, or even back home on d8. There is not even a recognised main line in the 3...♕d6 variation, with some books quoting a thirty-year old Karpov-Lutikov game as their model for White.

Yet in the comparative analysis contained here – which in some chapters turns into a mini-masterclass on the Scandinavian – the author has gone a long way towards demonstrating that 3...♕d6 should not be regarded as a poor relation to 3...♕a5 and 3...♕d8.

With Melts' demonstration of the difficulty White has in conveniently chasing away the Black queen on d6, the advantages of 3...♕d6 over 3...♕d8 are easy to understand.

Melts also attempts to perform a demolition job on 3...♕a5. Even to this sceptical writer, who has used 3...♕a5 on and off for more than two decades, Melts manages to show that in certain lines the queen on a5 is so vulnerable to b4 and ♗d2 ideas that the liabilities of the queen on d6 seem mild in comparison.

Apart from 3...♕d6 pioneer David Bronstein, the reader will find few illustrative games featuring big names but will soon realise that there is a sizeable number of highly competent crossboard, correspondence and internet players (including the author himself) who trust 3...♕d6 and are willing to use it as more than just a surprise weapon.

Like all variations of the Scandinavian, it is impossible to play 3...♕d6 without due care and attention. Black is taking a risk with his early queen development and a single misstep can be fatal. Yet such a danger is true of any sharp opening – the potential pitfalls just start earlier in the Scandinavian than in most lines of the Sicilian Defence.

In fact someone who studies this book carefully and employs Melts' ideas will be equally likely to find their opponent struggling for good moves. Few players currently know much about 3...♛d6, and plans which succeed in other Scandinavian lines can sometimes fall flat against 3...♛d6.

No doubt as the analysis in this book is tested at higher levels, new problems will arise for Black which may require new strategies for Black. Yet the foundation Melts has built should be sufficient to ensure that 3...♛d6 remains playable, whatever surprises the new edition of Chess Informant will bring.

Alexey Shirov recently expressed his regret that he was not able to use the King's Gambit because it was "not a serious opening." Shirov meant that, with accurate play by Black, White is struggling for equality and it was therefore not worth trying the King's Gambit even as a surprise weapon. For the world's top players, the 3...♛d6 Scandinavian has never been considered a 'serious opening' but perhaps after the publication of this book, that attitude may gradually begin to change.

It may be too much to expect the ugly duckling to be transformed immediately into a beautiful swan and become the opening of choice for the world's best. However, thanks to Melts, 3...♛d6 can now be seen as a useful extra string to the bow of any player seeking a sharp defence to 1.e4.

Ian Rogers
Sydney, Australia
June 2001

Foreword to the Second Edition

In 2001 I wrote that the 3...♕d6 Scandinavian was not considered a 'serious opening' by the world's top players. The situation began to change in 2005 when Sergey Tiviakov, a Russian/Dutch Grandmaster then rated close to 2700, began to test the line at the highest level. Three years later, the 3...♕d6 Scandinavian is still part of Tiviakov's repertoire. Tiviakov's success has induced other world class players, such as Gata Kamsky who Tiviakov defeated with the line, to experiment with the opening.

As a result of the rise in popularity of the 3...♕d6 Scandinavian, the second edition of this book is vastly changed from the first. Though I have to say that I enjoyed Melt's analytical demolition of the 3...♕a5 Scandinavian in the first edition, there is no longer any need for an inferiority complex when 3...♕d6 is compared to 3...♕a5. Statistics and practice leave 3...♕a5 as the (new) poor cousin of the Scandinavian and Melts has no need to put the boot in.

With a multitude of games played in the line since 2001, there can now be an entertaining chapter on the many opening disasters which may befall both White and Black after 3...♕d6. The opening traps make up just part of a new section of the book designed to explain the 3...♕d6 Scandinavian to club players. These chapters could almost stand alone as a 'How to Play the 3...♕d6 Scandinavian' book but Melts wants to do better – he wants to prove that 3...♕d6 can stand up to rigorous theoretical scrutiny.

As in the first edition, Melts demonstrates the main lines though forty illustrative games but the games in the new edition are mostly very recent. Though there is often a temptation to lose oneself in a thicket of variations and sub-variations, there is always a main game to follow which explains the themes well.

But how well does Melts' book stand up analytically? I conducted a test.

One of Tiviakov's heaviest defeats in the 3...♕d6 Scandinavian came against Peter Svidler in Wijk aan Zee 2006. Tiviakov was forced from a sharp line of the opening into a depressing endgame and never recovered. Surely many players with White would seek to play this way? However to Melts this is just a minor concern. Svidler-Tiviakov is only given as a sub-variation, since Melts convincingly shows that Tiviakov could have at least equalised with an improvement on move 19. No fanfare, no fuss – for Melts there are more difficult lines to concentrate on – but also no worries for Black.

No doubt there will be lines found in coming years to test Black in the 3...♕d6 Scandinavian. However Melts' serious study of a serious opening shows that at

the moment not much need scare Black. Easy to play and theoretically sound –
how many openings can boast that?

Ian Rogers
Sydney, Australia
September, 2008

Preface to the First Edition

The Scandinavian Defense (also called the Center Counter) is one of the oldest of chess openings, first recommended by Lucena in the 15th century. Since the seventh game of the Morphy-Anderssen match, Paris 1858, chess players have known the 3...♛a5 line (1.e4 d5 2.exd5 ♛xd5 3.♘c3 ♛a5), and modern theory considers this the best line for Black after 3.♘c3.

The variation 1.e4 d5 2.exd5 ♛xd5 3.♘c3 ♛d6 is not well known to most chess players, making it very often an unpleasant surprise for White. It offers Black good chances to gain an equal position with counterplay.

But this variation is not popular in modern chess theory. Why? Various negative opinions can be found: "The queen is unfavorably placed on d6, compared to a5. First, there is no useful pin on the c3-knight, second the queen can be harassed by ♗f4" (John Emms in *The Scandinavian*, 1997), or similarly "The position of the black queen on d6 is vulnerable in view of the eventual threats ♘b5 and ♗f4. Therefore, this line is inferior for Black." ("Two letters on the Center Counter Defense," by Leonid Shamkovich, *Chess Life*, February 1998).

Yet this logic can be turned on in its head! The position of the black queen on a5 is vulnerable in view of the eventual threats b2-b4 and ♗d2, but this is never mentioned by theorists. Why not?

Why do we see the 3...♛d6 line in the opening repertoire of legendary grandmaster David Bronstein, not to mention other fine players, for example J. Magem, L. Fressinet, E. Dizdarevic, D. Donchev, R. Dzindzichashvili, E. Gausel, Kiril Georgiev, L. Gofshtein, A. Hauchard, C. Horvath, Ye Jiangchuan, M. Jirovsky, B. Kurajica, E. Mozes, C. Mann, Ye Rongguang, D. Sermek, A. Sygulski, T. Utasi, V. Zaitsev, most of whom have FIDE ratings in the 2450-2550 range? Do they use this variation only for its surprise value, or do they have a more informed opinion which differs from today's mainstream chess theory?

Will modern theoretical opinion about this variation change? Only future chess practice and analysis can answer that, but the search for a verdict will be highly interesting!

Preface to the Second Edition

The first edition of this book was published in 2001. It took the chess world by surprise, especially club chess players. In one of the oldest (!) openings, on the third (!) move, Black has a **paradoxical** continuation! As you will see, the 3...♕d6 line is not at all bad for Black, and statistically even has slightly better results than usual 3...♕a5!

Some club players regarded the first edition skeptically, thinking that there were too few games played by strong players. Well...

During next few years there were a lot of games played with 3...♕d6 – in my database there are 573 games from 1965 to March 2001 and about 4,000 games from April 2001 to August 2008.

Looking in the *New in Chess Yearbook* #48, 1998, page 71, we see for the Scandinavian Defense (1.e4 d5 2.e×d5 ♕×d5 3.♘c3) the following information: for 3...♕d6 Black's score is 43.5% (out of 261 games) and for 3...♕a5 Black's score is 41.5% (out of 2,085 games). Of great interest are the statistics found at the website *www.365chess.com*: for 3...♕d6 Black's score is 46.2% (out of 3,754 games) and for 3...♕a5 Black's score is 44.55% (out of 19,504 games). Even after ten years, the 3...♕d6 line has produced slightly better results for Black than 3...♕a5.

When in 2002 Bojan Kurajica (2548) won a game as Black against Judit Polgar (2685) using the 3...♕d6 weapon, perhaps the world's top players only smiled a little. But grandmaster Sergey Tiviakov's advocacy of the move 3...♕d6 worked wonders for its popularity. In 2006 Sergey had the following results against players with Elo ratings of 2600 and above: Al Modiahki (2564) 0-1; Nijboer (2584) 0-1; Kamsky (2686) 0-1; Grischuk (2719) ½-½; Svidler (2743) ½-½; Anand (2792) ½-½. Tiviakov scored 4½ out of 6 with Black (!) against this field. In 2007 grandmaster Liviu-Dieter Nisipeanu (2690) defeated Veselin Topalov (2770) with the 3...♕d6 line. Adherents of 1.e4 had a problem: "How to play against the Scandinavian after 3...♕d6 ?"

Now you can find 3...♕d6 in the opening repertoire of chess players rated 2600 and above (e.g., Tiviakov, Nisipeanu, Ye Jiangchuan, Almasi, Dreev, Gashimov, Bauer) as well as other strong grandmasters rated 2500 and higher.

This book has a lot of fragments from games played with 3...♕d6 before August 1, 2008. Readers with the first edition will notice many differences in the second edition. I wanted to make the book more interesting for club players, while I also think some of my comments on opening phase of many games may even surprise some grandmasters.

Acknowledgments

It is very hard to write a book without help. I would like to thank everyone who has helped me in preparing this one, in particular my chess friends Hugh Myers and Larry Waite (USA), Timothy Harding (Ireland), Samion Borisovich Gubnitsky (Ukraine), Krzysztof Pytel (France) and Jerzy Konikowski (Germany).

This book contains forty annotated chess games, but the annotations include fragments from hundreds of additional games. My favorite chess books have complete games with verbal annotations. This book is relatively short on words and long on my analysis. There may well be mistakes (is there a chess book without them?), but I hope any such may be "fruitful errors" providing players with food for thought.

I have enjoyed the creative efforts of all those who have played games with the 3...♕d6 variation of the Scandinavian Defense, and am very appreciative of all those who have sent me their games from the USA and other countries.

Michael Melts
West Hartford
January 2009

About the Author

Michael Melts (born 1950 in Kharkov, Ukraine) is an International Correspondence Chess Master. He served as editor-in-chief for the first three volumes of the *Correspondence Chess Informator* series (Ukraine/Germany), and for the correspondence chess almanac *Chess Secrets* (ChessBase, Germany). His games and opening articles have been published in *Chess in the USSR*, *Chess Informant* (Yugoslavia), *New in Chess Yearbook* (Netherlands), *Fernschach International* (Germany), *Correspondence Chess Yearbook* (Italy), *The Chess Correspondent* (USA), *Check!* (Canada), *Chess Post* (England), *Chess Mail* (Ireland) and *Scottish Correspondence Chess* (Scotland).

Melts is a discoverer of many chess novelties. His innovation in the Evans Gambit, 1.e4 e5 2.♘f3 ♘c6 3.♗c4 ♗c5 4.b4 ♗xb4 5.c3 ♗e7 6.d4 ♘a5 7.♗e2 exd4 8.♕xd4!?, first played in the game Melts-Gayevsky, Dnepropetrovsk 1981, was employed by Kasparov in his famous game against Anand at Riga 1995, and was named one of the best novelties of 1995.

Michael Melts emigrated from the Ukraine to the USA in 1994. He lives with his wife in West Hartford, Connecticut.

Annotation Symbols

1-0	White won
0-1	Black won
½-½	draw
!	strong move
!!	excellent move
?	poor move
??	blunder
!?	interesting move
?!	dubious move
=	equal game
±	White stands slightly better
∓	Black stands slightly better
±	White is clearly better
∓	Black is clearly better
+−	White has a decisive advantage
−+	Black has a decisive advantage
∞	unclear position
∞	with compensation for material
⇄	with counterplay
×	captures
+	check
#	checkmate
corr.	correspondence game

Introduction

A Little History

The variation 1.e4 d5 2.exd5 ♕xd5 3.♘c3 ♕d6

was first recommended by the Englishman William Norwood Potter (1840-1895) in the late 19th century. Mr. Potter was a very strong chess player, as shown by his scores in the matches Potter-Zukertort 1875 (+2 –4 =8) and Potter-Mason 1879 (+5 –5 =11). At the London tournament of 1876, Potter scored +5 –3 =2 to finish 3rd, behind Blackburne and Zukertort but ahead of MacDonnell, Janssens and Minchin. He won handicap tournaments in 1875 and 1878, and served as editor of *The City of London Chess Magazine* 1874-76. He is mentioned in Emanuel Lasker's *Manual of Chess*: "I heard in London that a London master, Mr. Potter, who loved unusual and strange moves, had influenced Steinitz greatly. They were friends, and Steinitz somehow began to copy Potter's style." Potter and Steinitz were partners in the 1872-1873 correspondence match between the London and Vienna chess clubs, won by London 1½-½.

However, Potter's recommendation of 3...♕d6 was ignored by the chess world for many years. His analysis of the line 3...♕d6 4.♘b5 ♕e5+ 5.♗e2 ♘a6 6.♘f3 ♕f6 7.d4 h6, which appeared in the magazine *Land and Water*, was in fact not very good, and failed to answer many questions, such as how to play after 4.d4. The 3...♕d6 line was not mentioned in the 19th century opening "bibles" of Bilguer, Staunton, Mason, Gunsberg and others. This continued in the first half of the 20th century (for example Bilguer's *Handbuch* by Schlechter, Mieses, Tarrasch, Teichmann et al). Even works from early in the second half of the 20th century (for example by Euwe, Keres, Pachman and others) show no line, no note, no comment! Despite extensive research, involving databases totaling several million games, I did not find any with 3...♕d6 before 1965!

Starting about 1965, Samion Borisovich Gubnitsky, a correspondence master from Kharkov, Ukraine, began to use the 3...♕d6 variation with success. The game

Introduction

Turishchev-Gubnitsky, USSR 1968 (½-½, 27), was published in the magazine *Chess in the USSR* (6/1968) and in *Chess Informant* (5/109).

Sometimes you will see the name "Pytel variation" applied to 3...♕d6, based on Polish master Krzysztof Pytel's analysis of nine games in *The Chess Player* (#13/ 1977). In a letter to this writer dated August 12, 1998, Krzysztof wrote: "My wife Bozena began to play 3...♕d6 because, one, at the time everyone knew we played 1.e4 e6 or 1.e4 c5 2.♘f3 d6 3.d4 cxd4 4.♘xd4 ♘f6 5.♘c3 a6, complicated openings, and two, by 3...♕d6 we found a way to play solidly and simply (in the strategic sense), and to avoid opponent's preparation (nobody could find any theory for this variation!)."

In *Chess Informant* #28 (1979) there appeared the game Karpov-Lutikov, USSR 1979, with annotations by Parma. This was the first instance of the line 3...♕d6 4.d4 ♘f6 5.♘f3 a6. As a result of this game, the move 5...a6 had a dubious reputation for many years (one sees 5...a6?! even in the 1997 edition of *ECO*). But in the 1990s, David Bronstein sometimes used the move, which led to its being called the "Bronstein Variation" in some publications.

This next anecdote will be interesting for many chess players."Everything started in August 20005. I was playing in an open tournament in Solsona (Spain). I was White against a Cuban player Omar Almedia, and after a mere 11 moves I was lost. Luckily for me my draw offer on move 12 was accepted by my opponent. **1.e4 d5 2.exd5 ♕xd5 3.♘c3 ♕d6 4.d4 ♘f6 5.♘f3 a6 6.g3 ♗g4 7.h3 ♗h5 8.♗g2 ♘c6 9.0-0 0-0-0 10.♗f4?!** (After the correct 10.♗e3 e5 an equal ending arises almost by force.) **10...♕b4 11.d5?** (After this mistake White loses material) **11...e6 12.a3 ½-½.** Well, this was a very useful experience for me. I thought, if I can get a lost position with white so quickly (and I have to admit that I had even studied this variation regularly before as White) then why could the same thing not happen to other strong players?! So, I decided to work on this line to incorporate the Scandinavian Defence into my repertoire." Sergey Tiviakov,"Scandinavian with 3...Qd6," *Secrets of Opening Surprises*, Volume 6, New In Chess, 2007.

By now the move 3...♕d6 has been played at all levels of chess practice, including strong grandmaster events. For opening theoreticians, the 3...♕d6 line is no longer just a minor byway, but a system with its own main lines and variations.

For the Skeptics

There are basically three kinds of skeptical reactions to the move 3...♕d6:

1. "3...♕d6 is certainly playable, but when the queen comes out to the center so soon, well, that is too extravagant."

2. "The queen is unfavorably placed on d6, compared to a5. First, there is no useful pin on the c3 knight, second the queen can be harassed by ♗f4." (John Emms in *The Scandinavian*, 1997). Or similarly "The position of the black queen on d6 is vulnerable in view of the eventual threats ♘b5 and ♗f4. Therefore, this line is inferior for Black." ("Two Letters on the Center Counter Defense" by Leonid Shamkovich, *Chess Life*, February 1998).

3. "It is hard to find any merit in this maneuver over the normal 3...♛d8 or 3...♛a5."

If the reader is similarly skeptical, the following reasoning may be of interest:

1. Often we see in chess books and articles the words "this is a theoretical move," "chess theory," "theory of chess openings," etc. But most grandmasters would counter that there really is no such thing as "chess theory." "Theory" in the scientific sense defines a set of laws, whereas chess, as Lasker once remarked, is beautiful precisely because of its *exceptions*.

For example, in chess books for beginners we see rules for the opening:
A) "Do not bring your queen out too early. Keep your queen safe." (Fine).
B) "Do not move any piece twice in the opening, but put it at once on the right square." (Lasker).

1.e4 e5 2.♛h5 – this move breaks all known opening axioms."A few years ago I wrote an article for the Chesscafe, *Jake, Joe and Garry*, in which I quoted Nigel Short, who had written that Vladimir Kramnik had prepared the move 2.♛h5 to use against Kasparov...Kramnik had told Short that in the main variation after 1.e4 e5 2.♛h5 ♘c6 3.♗c4 g6 4.♛f3 ♘f6 5.♘e2 he considered the position to be equal." (From Hans Ree's *Dutch Treat* column at *ChessCafe.com*, April 2005). Are you OK?

In many chess books we read that one of the main principles of the opening is "Don't move your queen into the center," and that is generally correct. However,"Here we will talk mainly about exceptions, or, more precisely, about a different interpretation of the rules as applied to dynamic variations. Very characteristic of certain modern opening variations is the active role of the heavy pieces, if their maneuvers disrupt the opponent's plans and assist the favorable coordination of one's own forces." (Alexei Suetin, *Plan Like A Grandmaster*, 1988). For example, consider the following more or less established opening lines:

1.e4 e5 2.d4 exd4 3.♛xd4 ♘c6 4.♛e3
1.e4 e5 2.♘f3 ♘c6 3.♗b5 a6 4.♗xc6 dxc6 5.0-0 ♛d6
1.e4 d5 2.exd5 ♘f6 3.d4 ♗g4 4.♘f3 ♛xd5 5.♘c3 ♛f5
1.e4 c6 2.c4 d5 3.exd5 cxd5 4.cxd5 ♛xd5 5.♘c3 ♛d6
1.e4 e6 2.d4 d5 3.♘d2 c5 4.exd5 ♛xd5 5.♘f3 cxd4 6.♗c4 ♛d6
1.e4 c5 2.♘f3 d6 3.d4 cxd4 4.♛xd4 ♘c6 5.♗b5 ♛d7 6.♛d3
1.e4 c5 2.c3 ♘f6 3.e5 ♘d5 4.d4 cxd4 5.♛xd4 e6 6.♘f3 ♘c6 7.♛e4

1.c4 ♘f6 2.♘c3 e6 3.e4 c5 4.e5 ♘g8 5.d4 c×d4 6.♕×d4 ♘c6 7.♕e4
1.d4 ♘f6 2.c4 g6 3.♘c3 d5 4.♘f3 ♗g7 5.♕b3 d×c4 ♕×c4

In each case the last move posts the queen in the center at an early stage, yet these lines do not have the reputation of being "extravagant."

2. The move 3...♕d6 has its pluses and minuses, as does 3...♕a5. To evaluate the lines objectively requires weighing their respective pluses and minuses by analyzing many games. To Emms' objection above, one can by analogy counter that the position of the black queen on a5 is vulnerable in view of the eventual threats b2-b4 and ♗d2. Yet no one concludes from this that one should not play 3...♕a5 in the Scandinavian Defense!

3. There are very important objective factors in favor of 3...♕d6. The black queen is more active on d6 than on d8 or a5, and Black is able to castle queenside with ease. These factors help Black to equalize and obtain counterplay.

Part I Information for Club Players

This book has many variations annotated with Informant-like chess symbols. Many stronger players with ratings of 2000 and higher are comfortable with this approach. However, I have designed Part I for club players with lower ratings in the 1400-2000 range. It is hoped that it will help these players better understand the rationale behind this opening.

1. Why is 3...♕d6 good for you?

Perhaps the most difficult choice when creating an opening repertoire is how to answer 1.e4. The basic choice is between the open and semi-open games.

A) Open games (1.e4 e5) give White many good possibilities. Playing Black, you need to be ready a variety of second moves: 2.c3, 2.d4, 2.f4, 2.♗c4, 2.♘c3 and 2.♘f3. There are many books about open games. But you must also not forget about possible surprises as early as White's second move! For example, 2.♕h5, 2.♕f3, 2.♗b5, 2.♗e2, 2.a3, 2.b3 and 2.g3 have all appeared in games played by strong grandmasters. The possibilities are almost endless.

B) Semi-open games (e.g., 1...c6, 1...c5, 1...e6, 1...d6, 1...g6, 1...♘c6 or 1...♘f6) may appeal to you. You would like to get a playable middlegame. But to accomplish this, you need to know a lot about these semi-open games. Otherwise, Black may face serious problems, perhaps even a lost game, before getting out of the opening. So what can you do? Play **1...d5!**

B1) After 2.d3 d×e4 3.d×e4 (White does not have good compensation for the pawn after 3.♘c3 e×d3 4.♗×d3) 3...♕×d1+ 4.♔×d1 Black's king is smiling at his counterpart;

B2) 2.e5 is bad – after 2...♗f5, 3...e6, and 4...c5 Black is essentially playing a French without the locked-in bishop;

B3) After 2.♘c3 Black (!) has choice between 2...d4 3.♘ce2 ♘c6 or 2...d×e4 3.♘×e4 ♘c6 (3...♗f5) – in all cases with a good game;

B4) After 2.d4 d×e4 3.♘c3 (or 3.f3) we have the unclear Blackmar-Diemer Gambit. If you do not want to play against the Blackmar-Diemer Gambit, 2...c6 (the Caro-Kann Defense), 2...e6 (the French Defense) or 2...♘c6 (the Nimzovitch Defense) may be played. But you can also have some fun with the unusual 2...c5, 2...♘f6 or even 2...g6. For example, after 2...g6 3.e×d5 (if 3.e5 or 3.♘c3 Black is playing a line of the Pirc/Modern that is not very dangerous) 3...♕×d5 4.♘c3 (4.c4 ♕a5+ or 4...♕d8) 4...♕d6!? and Black has transposed to more familiar lines (see 1.e4 d5 2.e×d5 ♕×d5 3.♘c3 ♕d6 4.d4 g6 in Game 37). It is important that after 2.d4 you (and not your opponent!) have a large choice from some usual continuations, while you can also surprise your opponent by selecting from some more unusual moves!

B5) After **2.e×d5 ♕×d5**, the main line is reached after most popular continuation **3.♘c3**. White however has a couple of other possibilities on the third move which we will look at briefly. They are the moves 3.d4 and 3.♘f3 with the idea of refraining, at least for the time being, from blocking the c-pawn with the knight.

B5a) After 3.d4 e5, Black has no difficulties:

B5a1) 4.d×e5 (or 4.♘c3 ♕×d4 5.♕×d4 e×d4 6.♘b5 ♘a6 7.♘×d4 ♘f6 8.♗g5 ♘e4 with equal chances) 4...♕×d1+ 5.♔×d1 ♘c6 6.f4 ♗f5 7.c3 0-0-0+ 8.♔e1 f6, De Firmian, N. (2575) – Granda Zuniga, J. (2610), Amsterdam 1996 or 6.♘f3 ♗g4 7.♗f4 0-0-0+ 8.♘bd2 ♗c5, Jaenig, R. (2110) – Bakhmatov, E. (2273), Wiesbaden 2000 with sufficient compensation for the pawn.

B5a2) 4.♘f3 e×d4 5.♕×d4 (5.♘×d4 ♗b4+ 6.♘c3 ♘e7 or 6.c3 ♗c5) 5...♘f6 6.♘c3 ♕×d4 7.♘×d4 ♗c5 8.♘db5 ♘a6 9.♗f4 0-0 10.♗e2 (10.♘×c7 ♘×c7 11.♗×c7 ♖e8+ 12.♗e2 ♗b4 with sufficient compensation for the pawn) 10...c6 11.♘d6 ♘b4 with counterplay or 8.♗e3 0-0 9.0-0-0 (9.♘db5 ♗×e3 10.♘×c7 ♗f4 11.♘×a8 ♘c6 with sufficient compensation) 9...♘c6 with counterplay.

B5a3) 4.♗e3 ♘c6 5.♘c3 ♗b4 6.♕d2 ♕a5 7.d×e5 ♘ge7, Drazic, S. (2480) – Tiviakov, S. (2645), Trieste 2007 with sufficient compensation for the pawn or 5.♘f3 ♗g4 6.♘c3 (6.♗e2 e4) 6...♗b4 7.♗e2 (7.d×e5 ♗×f3 8.♕×f3 (Toma, A. (2225) – Ardelean, G. (2490), Predeal 2007) 8...♗×c3+ 9.b×c3 ♕×e5 with a counterplay) 7...e4 8.♘d2 ♗×c3 9.b×c3 (9.♗×g4 ♗×d4) 9...♗×e2 10.♕×e2 ♘f6 with counterplay.

B5b) After 3.♘f3, Black may choose from several interesting continuations.

B5b1) If you prefer to play aggressively, you can use a plan with ♗c8-g4, ♘b8-c6 and 0-0-0. You need to be prepared for a very tactical game where both sides need to be cautious; for example, 3...♗g4 4.♗e2 ♘c6 5.d4 (5.0-0, 5.♘c3, 5.h3) 5...0-0-0 6.c4 (6.c3, 6.♗e3) 6...♕d7 7.♗e3 ♗×f3 8.♗×f3 ♘×d4 9.♗g4 (9.♗×d4) 9...♘c2+ 10.♕×c2 ♕×g4 11.0-0 a6 12.b4 e6 13.b5 a×b5 14.c×b5 ♗d6 15.♘d2 ♕h5 16.h3 ♕×b5 17.♖ab1 ♕c6 18.♕b3 ♘e7 19.♖fc1 ♕a6 20.♖c4 b5 21.♖g4 ♖hg8 22.a4 b4 23.♖c4 ♘c6 24.♖cc1 ♘a5 25.♕c2 f5 26.♖×b4 ♔d7 27.♖b5 g6 28.♘f3 ♘c6 29.♖b6 c×b6 30.♕×c6+ ♔e7 31.♗g5+ ♔f7 32.♖d1 1-0, Timofeev A. (2650) – Ovechkin R. (2555), Krasnoyarsk 2007.

B5b2) If you prefer to play more positionally, I recommend 3...♘f6 (this is more flexible than other moves, though 3...c6, 3...♘c6, 3...♗f5, 3...♗g4, 3...g6 are also not bad). 4.d4 (4.g3?! ♗g4 5.♗g2 ♕e4+; 4.♘c3 ♕d6 see Game 40) 4...c6 5.♗e2 (5.♘c3 ♕d6 see Games 13-17), and then keeping in mind the discussion of pawn structures (see *Typical Pawn Structures* in the Section 4 of Part I, *General Ideas and Game Plans*) Black may select:

1. A classical Caro-Kann pawn structure with pawns at c6 and e6; for example, 5...♗f5 (5...♗g4 6.h3 ♗h5 7.0-0 e6 8.c4 ♕d6 9.♘c3 ♗e7 10.♗e3 0-0 11.♕d2 ♕c7 12.♖fd1 ♖d8 13.♘e5 ♗×e2 14.♕×e2 ♘bd7 15.♗f4 ♗d6 16.♘×d7 ♖×d7 17.♗e5 ♘e8 18.♖ac1 ♖ad8 with equal chances, Spoljar, M. (2210) – Savic, M. (2535), Bizovac 2008) 6.0-0 e6 7.c4 (7.♗f4 ♕e4) 7...♕a5 8.♘c3 ♗e7 9.♗e3 ♘bd7 10.a3 (Jakubiec A. (2495) – Heinzel O. (2403), Neckar 2007 10...♘e4 11.♘×e4 ♗×e4 with equal chances.

2. A pawn structure with g6- and c6-pawns; for example, 5...g6 6.c4 ♛d6 7.♘c3 c6 8.0-0 0-0 9.h3 ♞a6 10.♗e3 ♗f5 11.a3 ♞e4 12.♛b3 ♞c7 13.♖ad1 b5 14.c×b5 ♞×c3 15.♛×c3 c×b5 with counterplay, Dumpor A. (2401) – Hrvacic P. (2284), Bosnia 2007 or 9.♗g5 ♗f5 10.♛d2 ♞bd7 11.♗f4 ♛b4 12.h3 (12.a3 ♛b3 13.d5 c5 14.♖fe1 ♞b6 with counterplay) 12...♞b6 13.♞e5 ♖fd8 14.a3 ♞e4 15.♞×e4 ♛×d2 16.♞×d2 ♖×d4 17.♗e3 ♗×e5 18.♗×d4 ♗×d4 with sufficient compensation for the lost material.

3.d4, 3.♞f3, or even 3.c4 or 3.♛f3 may or may not be bad for White, but almost every "guru" tell us in his chess opening bible that 3.♞c3 is the best move because Black needs to lose a tempo. I believe most of your opponents will think the same. After **3 ♞c3 ♛d6**, the following position is reached:

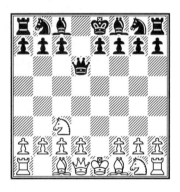

• After 1.e4 d5, you have reduced the number of possible white continuations on the second move, already saving you time on the clock!
• Most of your opponents will know something about the moves 3...♛a5 and 3...♛d8, while they will probably not have a high opinion of the move 3...♛d6. This is very good for you (be-cause "Any opening is good enough if its reputation is bad enough." Tartakower)!
• There are very important objective factors in favor of 3...♛d6. The black queen is more active on d6 than on d8 or a5, and Black is able to castle queenside more easily. These factors help Black to equalize and obtain counterplay. Later in this book you will see that Black, after 3...♛d6, will have a choice between solid positional plans with kingside castling or riskier but more aggressive plans with queenside castling.

These are just some of the reasons why the 3...♛d6 Scandinavian Defense might be ideal for you!

2. Opening Catastrophes for White

Every chess player loves to win quickly. I think that White has more chances to make go wrong in the 3...♛d6 lines than after 3...♛d8 or 3...♛a5. Black's queen on d6 can be a very dangerous monster! Take a look at the following games.

Degebuadze, A. (2560) – Pytel, K. (2440), Amiens 2000: 4.d4 ♞f6 5.♞f3 c6 6.♗c4 ♗g4

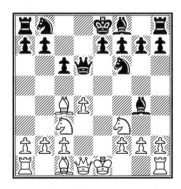

7.♗×f7+? (this move works after 3...♕d8 4.d4 ♘f6 5.♗c4 c6 6.♘f3 ♗g4? but not here) 7...♔×f7 8.♘e5+ ♕×e5+ 9.d×e5 ♗×d1 10.e×f6 ♗×c2 0-1

Muzychuk, A. (2456)–Gara, A. (2349), Szeged 2006: 4.d4 ♘f6 5.♗c4 c6 6.♘ge2 ♗g4

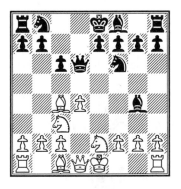

7.♗f4?! ♗×e2 8.♕d2 (8.♘×e2? ♕b4+ and 9...♕×c4−+; 8.♗×d6?! ♗×d1 9.♗×b8 ♗×c2∓) 8...♗×c4 9.♗×d6 e×d6 with better chances for Black.

4.d4 ♘f6 5.♗c4 ♗g4 6.f3 ♗f5 7.♘ge2 e6 8.0-0 c6

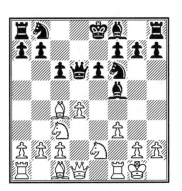

9.♘g3?! (Michalek, J. (2323) – Cempel, J. (2263), Czechia 2000) 9...♗×c2! 10.♕×c2 ♕×d4+ 11.♔h1 ♕×c4 with an extra pawn.

Kozlov, Y. (2292) – Shkola, V., Alushta 2004: 4.d4 c6 5.♗c4 ♘f6 6.♘ge2 ♗g4 7.f3 ♗f5 8.♗f4 ♕b4 9.♗b3 e6 10.a3 ♕a5 11.g4 ♗g6 12.♕d2 ♘bd7 13.0-0-0?

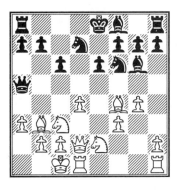

13...♗×a3 14.♔b1 (14.b×a3 ♕×a3+ 15.♔b1 ♕×b3+) 14...♗b4 with an extra pawn.

Roiz Baztan, D. (2344) – Mellado Trivino, J. (2451), Spain 2001: 4.d4 ♘f6 5.♗e3 a6 6.♘f3 ♘c6 7.♕d2 ♗g4 8.♘g5 e6 9.f3 ♗h5 10.♗e2 0-0-0 11.0-0-0 h6 12.♘ge4 ♕b4 13.a3 ♕a5 14.♘×f6 g×f6 15.d5 ♗g6

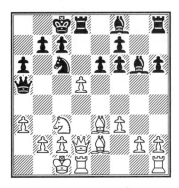

16.♗c4?! (16.♔b1) 16...♗×a3 17.♘a2 (17.b×a3 ♕×a3+ 18.♔b1 ♕b4+ 19.♔c1 ♕×c4∓) 17...♗b4 18.c3 ♗e7 19.b4 ♘×b4 0-1

4.d4 ♘f6 5.♘f3 a6 6.♗e3 ♘c6 7.♗d3
♗g4 8.0-0 e6 9.h3 ♗h5 10.♕e2 ♗e7

11.♘e4?! ♘xe4 12.♗xe4 (Ponkratov, P.
(2360) – Lysyj, I. (2470), Chalkidiki
2003) 12...f5 13.♗xc6+ ♕xc6∓ 14.g4?!
fxg4 15.♘e5 ♕g2+! 16.♔xg2 gxh3+
17.♔xh3 ♗xe2∓.

Hoarau, J. – Lorans, S. (2160), L'Etang
2001: 4.♗c4 ♘f6 5.d4 a6 6.♘ge2 b5
7.♗d3 ♗b7 8.♗f4 ♕b6 9.0-0 e6 10.a3
c5 11.dxc5 ♗xc5

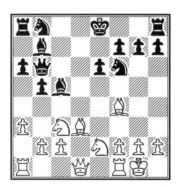

12.b4?? ♕c6 0-1

Hedzic, H. – Wulfmeyer, J. Bayern
1997: 4.♘f3 a6 5.d4 ♘f6 6.♗c4 ♘bd7
7.♗b3 e6 8.♕e2 ♗e7 9.♗g5 0-0
10.♖d1 c6 11.0-0 b5 12.♘e5 c5
13.♘xd7 ♕xd7 14.dxc5 ♕c6 15.♗e3
♗b7 16.f3 ♗xc5

17.♕f2? ♘g4! with a winning position.

Hamman, S. (1570) – Bismuth, L.,
France 2003: 4.d4 ♘f6 5.♗e3 a6 6.♘f3
♗g4 7.♗e2 ♘c6 8.♕d2 0-0-0 9.0-0-0
e6 10.h3 ♗xf3 11.♗xf3 ♘a5

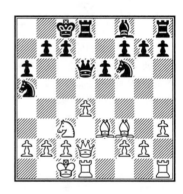

12.♖he1? ♘c4 13.♕d3 ♕b4 0-1

Daurelle, H. (2187) – Bratanov, Z.
(2432), La Fere 2002: 4.♘f3 ♘f6 5.d4
a6 6.♗g5 ♘c6 7.♕d2 ♗f5 8.0-0-0
0-0-0 9.♗c4 e6 10.♖he1 ♕b4 11.♕e2
♗e7 12.d5 exd5 13.♘xd5?! (13.♗xd5)
13...♘xd5 14.♗xd5 (14.♖xd5 ♗g5+
15.♘xg5 ♘d4∓) 14...♖he8
(14...♗xg5+ 15.♘xg5 ♗xc2 16.♔xc2
♕c5+ 17.♔b1 ♖xd5∓) 15.♕c4? ♗g5+
0-1

4.d4 ♘f6 5.♘f3 c6 6.♘e5 ♗f5 7.♕f3
e6 8.♗f4 ♕xd4 9.♖d1 ♕c5

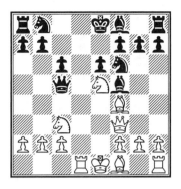

10.♘b5? (Michalczak, T. (2374) – Pytel, K. (2377), Skanderborg 2005) 10...c×b5 11.♕×b7 ♕b4+ 12.c3 ♕e4+ 13.♕×e4 ♗×e4 14.♗×b5+ ♔e7∓.

4.d4 ♘f6 5.♘f3 a6 6.g3 ♗g4 7.♗g2 ♘c6 8.h3 ♗×f3

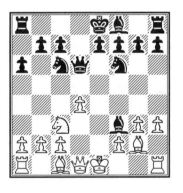

9.♗×f3?! 0-0-0 10.d5 (Vasilkova, S. (2355) – Danielian, E. (2480), Moscow 2008) 10...♕e5+! 11.♕e2? ♘d4; 11.♗e3 e6 12.0-0 e×d5∓; 11.♔f1 e6 12.♔g2 ♘b4∓.

Saiboulatov, D. (2410) – Grafl, F. (2410), Belgium 2007: 4.d4 ♘f6 5.♘f3 a6 6.g3 ♗g4 7.h3 ♗h5 8.♗g2 ♘c6 9.0-0 0-0-0 10.d5?! ♘×d5 11.♘×d5 ♕×d5 12.♕×d5 ♖×d5 In the position with the bishop on g4 White, after ♘f3-g5, gets a better game (hitting the f7-pawn). Now White does not have

sufficient compensation for the pawn. 13.g4 ♗g6 14.♘h4 ♖d8 15.♘×g6 h×g6 16.c3 e6∓.

4.d4 ♘f6 5.♘f3 a6 6.g3 ♗g4 7.h3 ♗h5 8.♗g2 ♘c6 9.0-0 0-0-0 10.♗f4 ♕b4 11.d5 e5 (Khairullin, I. (2533)–Lysyj, I. (2523), Cheboksary 2006)

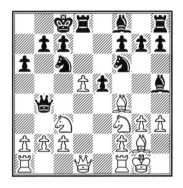

12.a3?! ♕×b2 13.♕d2 (13.♕d3 ♗g6) 13...♗×f3 14.♖fb1 (14.♗×f3 ♘d4∓) 14...♕×a1 15.♖×a1 ♗×g2 16.♔×g2 e×f4∓.

Potze, R. (2124) – Van Beek, A. (2276), Hoogeveen 2003: 4.d4 ♘f6 5.♘f3 a6 6.g3 ♗g4 7.♗g2 ♘c6 8.♗f4 ♕b4 9.0-0 0-0-0

10.♕e1?! ♗×f3 11.♗×f3 ♘×d4 12.♗g2 e6∓.

Longson, A. (2225) – Hanley, C. (2387), Edinburgh 2003: 4.d4 ♘f6

5.♘f3 a6 6.g3 ♗g4 7.♗g2 ♘c6 8.♗f4 ♛b4 9.d5 0-0-0 10.0-0 e5

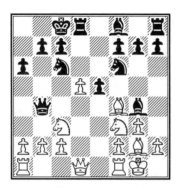

11.♗d2?! ♘d4 12.♘e2 (12.h3 ♗xf3 13.♗xf3 ♛xb2∓, Klinova, M. (2407) – Gofshtein, L. (2513), Hoogeveen 2001) 12...♗xf3 13.♗xb4 ♘xe2+ 14.♔h1 ♘xg3+ 15.hxg3 ♗xd1 16.♗xf8 ♖hxf8 17.♖axd1∓.

4.d4 ♘f6 5.♘f3 a6 6.♘e5 ♘c6 7.♗f4 ♗f5

Now moving the ♘e5 is bad for White; for example, 8.♘g6? ♛xd4 9.♛xd4 (9.♘xh8 ♛xf4∓) 9...♘xd4 10.0-0-0 hxg6 11.♖xd4 c6∓ or 8.♘xf7? ♛xf4 9.♘xh8 ♘e4 10.♘xe4 ♛xe4+ 11.♛e2 ♛xe2+ 12.♗xe2 ♘xd4 13.♗d1 g6∓.

4.d4 ♘f6 5.♗e3 a6 6.♘f3 b5 7.♗d3 ♗b7 8.♛e2 e6 9.0-0-0 ♗e7 10.♘e5 c5

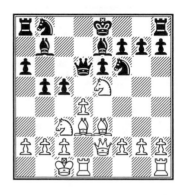

11.♗f4?! (Deinert, W. (1951) – Stahl, M. (2165), Recklinghausen 2005) 11...cxd4 12.♘g6 (12.♖he1 dxc3 13.♗xb5+ axb5 14.♖xd6 ♗xd6 15.♛xb5+ ♗c6 16.♘xc6 ♗xf4+ 17.♔b1 0-0∓) 12...♛c6 13.♘xe7 (13.♘xb5 hxg6 14.♘c7+ ♔f8 15.♘xa8 ♗d6∓) 13...♔xe7 14.♘b1 ♛d5∓.

4.d4 ♘f6 5.♘f3 a6 6.♘e5 ♘c6 7.♗f4 ♗f5 8.♗c4 ♘xe5

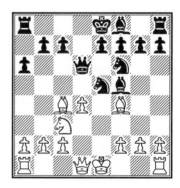

9.dxe5?! (Arakhamia Grant, K. (2425) – Mashinskaya, I. (2300), Varna 2002) and after 9...♛b4 White has problems; for example, 10.♛d2 ♛xc4 11.exf6 ♖d8 12.♛e3 gxf6 13.♛f3 e5 14.♗d2 ♗c2 15.♛xf6 (15.♖c1 ♛d3∓) 15...♖g8 16.♛xe5+ ♗e7∓ or 10.♛e2 ♛xb2 11.0-0 ♛xc3 12.exf6 gxf6 13.♖ab1 ♛xc2 14.♛xc2 ♗xc2 15.♖xb7

22

e5 16.♖×c7 (16.♗e3 ♗d6∓) 16...♔d8 17.♖×f7 e×f4 18.♖×f6 ♗g7 19.♖×f4 ♖e8∓.

4.♘f3 ♘f6 5.d4 a6 6.♘e5 e6 7.♗f4 ♘c6 8.♗e2 (Weber, M. (2305) – Schindler, W. (2300), Germany 1992) 8...♘×d4

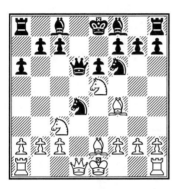

9.♘g6?! ♕b4 10.♘×h8 ♘×e2 11.♗×c7 (11.♕×e2 ♕×f4 12.0-0 ♗d7 13.♖ad1 ♗d6 14.g3 ♕f5∓ or 12.g3 ♕h6 13.♖d1 ♗d7∓) 11...♗d7 12.a3 (12.♕×e2 ♕×b2 13.0-0 ♕×c3 14.♗e5 ♕c5∓) 12...♕c5 13.♕×e2 ♕×c7 14.0-0 (14.0-0-0 ♗×a3) 14...g6 15.♖ad1 16.♘×f7 ♔×f7∓.

4.d4 g6 5.♗c4 ♗g7 6.♘f3 ♘f6 7.h3 a6 8.♘e5 0-0

9.♗f4?! (Ermenkov, E. (2462) – Rowe, P. (2049), Turin 2006) 9...♘c6 10.♘×g6 (10.0-0 ♘h5 11.♗h2 ♘×e5 12.d×e5

♗×e5; 10.♘×c6 ♕×c6 11.♗e2 ♖d8 12.0-0 ♗f5∓) 10...♕b4 11.♘e5 ♕×b2 12.♗d2 ♘×d4∓.

Safonov, A. – Melts, M., Kharkov 1971: 4.d4 ♘f6 5.♘f3 ♘c6 6.d5 ♘b4 7.♘b5 ♕c5 8.c4 ♘g4 9.♕d2 ♗d7 10.a3 ♘×d5 11.b4?! (11.c×d5) 11...♕b6

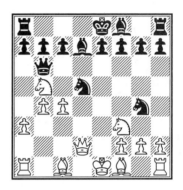

12.♕×d5? (12.♘bd4 e5) 12...♕×f2+ 13.♔d1 0-0-0 14.♗d2 ♗×b5 15.♕×b5 ♖×d2+! 16.♘×d2 ♘e3+ 17.♔c1 ♕e1+ 18.♔b2 ♕×d2+ 19.♔b3 ♕c2#.

4.d4 ♘f6 5.♗g5 a6 6.♕d2 ♗f5 7.♗f4 ♕d7 8.♘f3 ♘c6 9.d5 ♘b4 10.0-0-0 ♗×c2

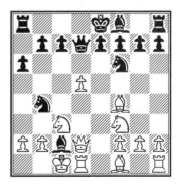

11.♘e5?! (Krug, S. (2114) – Jirovsky, P. (2348), Bayern 2003) 11...♕f5 12.♖e1 ♘f×d5 13.♗c4 ♕×f4∓.

4.d4 ♘f6 5.♗d3 ♗g4 6.f3 ♗h5 7.♘ge2 ♘c6 8.♘e4 ♘xe4 9.♗xe4 0-0-0 10.c3 e5 11.♗e3 ♗g6

12.♕a4?! exd4 13.♗xc6 (13.♘xd4 ♘xd4 14.♗xd4 ♗xe4 15.fxe4 ♕f4∓, Schwarz, D. (2203) – Lipka, J. (2432), Slovakia 2003) 13...dxe3 14.♘d4 (14.♗b5 ♕d2+ 15.♔f1 a6 16.♗c4 ♗c2–+) 14...e2 15.♗b5 ♕b6∓ or 15.♔xe2 ♕c5∓.

Gullaksen, E. (2354) – Guerrero, C. (2073), Catalan Bay 2003: 4.d4 ♘f6 5.♗g5 ♗g4 6.f3 ♗f5

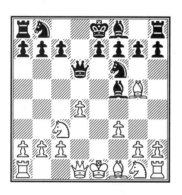

7.♕d2?! ♘c6 8.♘b5 (8.0-0-0 0-0-0 9.♘ge2 e5 10.dxe5 (10.♘g3 ♘xd4 11.♘xf5 ♘xf5 12.♗c4 ♕xd2+ 13.♖xd2 ♖xd2 14.♔xd2 ♘d6, and Black has an extra pawn, Landa, K. (2542) – Hasangatin, R. (2458), St. Petersburg

1999) 8...♕e6+ 9.♔f2 0-0-0 10.c3 ♕d7 11.♗c4 a6 12.♘a3 e5∓.

3. Typical Mistakes for Black

Of course, you would be wrong if, after reading Opening Catastrophes for White, you think Black wins automatically after 3...♕d6. Each side can make mistakes! You will benefit by learning typical mistakes made by Black.

Korneev, O. (2475) – Hettler, W., Hamburg 1993: 4.d4 a6 5.♘ge2 b5 6.♗f4

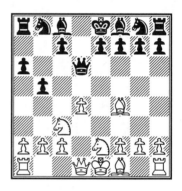

6...♕b6? 7.♘d5 1-0

Clawitter, C. – Van Meter, L. (2262), Los Angeles 2003: 4.d4 ♘f6 5.♘f3 a6 6.♗c4 b5 7.♗b3 ♗b7 8.0-0 c5 9.dxc5

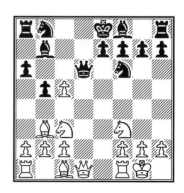

9...♕c6 10.♗xf7+ 1-0

Short, N. (2676) – Sulava, N. (2526), Ohrid 2001: 4.d4 ♘f6 5.♗e3 ♗f5? 6.♕f3 ♗c8 7.0-0-0 c6 8.♗f4 ♕b4 9.♘ge2

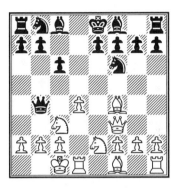

9...♗e6?! 10.♗c7 ♘a6? 11.a3 with a winning position.

Manik, M. (2460) – Garancovsky, P. (2150), Tatranske Zruby 2006: 4.d4 ♘f6 5.♘f3 ♗g4 6.h3 ♗h5 7.g4 ♗g6 8.♘e5 c6 9.♗f4

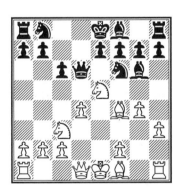

9...♕b4? 10.♘c4 ♘e4 11.a3 ♘xc3 12.axb4 ♘xd1 13.♘b6 1-0

Sanchez Abad, R. – Vela Villares, I., Spain 2002: 4.d4 ♘f6 5.♘f3 a6 6.g3 ♗g4 7.h3 ♗h5 8.g4 ♗g6 9.♗g2 ♘c6 10.a3 0-0-0 11.♗e3 e5 12.♘xe5 ♘xe5

13.dxe5 ♕xe5?! 14.♗xb7+ ♔xb7 15.♕xd8±.

Debray, T. (2042) – Fillaudeau, E. (1850), Val d'Isere 2002: 4.♘f3 ♘f6 5.d4 ♗g4 6.♗e3 e6 7.h3 ♗h5 8.g4 ♗g6 9.♘e5

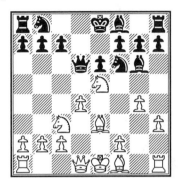

9...♘bd7? (9...♘c6) 10.♘b5 ♕b6 11.d5 ♗c5 (11...♕a5+ 12.♗d2 ♕b6 13.♘c4) 12.♘c4 1-0

4.d4 ♘f6 5.♗c4 ♗g4 6.f3 ♗f5 7.♕e2 (Al Modiahki, M. (2569) – Danielian, E. (2415), Dubai 2005) 7...♕xd4?

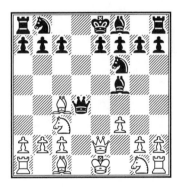

8.♘b5 ♕b6 (8...♕d7 9.♗f4 ♘a6 10.♖d1 ♕c8 11.♗xc7±) 9.♗e3 ♕c6 (9...♕a5+ 10.♗d2 ♕b6 11.♕e5+−) 10.♘xa7±.

Chervonov, I. – Gubnitsky, S., Kiev 1967: 4.d4 c6 5.♗c4 ♘f6 6.♘ge2 ♗g4

7.f3 ♗f5 8.♗f4 ♕b4 9.♘b3 e6 10.a3 ♕a5 10.a3 ♕a5 11.0-0 ♗e7 12.♘g3 0-0? (12...♗g6)

13.d5! ♘xd5 14.♘xd5 cxd5 15.♘xf5 exf5 16.♗xd5±.

Petrosian, S. (2424) – Velicka, P. (2439), Norderstedt 2003: 4.d4 c6 5.♗c4 ♘f6 6.♘ge2 ♗f5 7.♗f4 ♕b4 8.♗b3 e6 9.0-0 ♕a5? 10.d5!

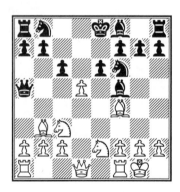

10...cxd5 (10...exd5 11.♘d4 ♗e6 12.♕e2±; for 10...♘xd5 see analysis in Game 4) 11.♘d4 ♗g6 12.♘cb5 ♘a6 13.c4 ♗e7 (13...dxc4 14.♗a4±) 14.cxd5 ♘xd5 15.♗xd5 exd5 16.♖e1 ♔f8 17.♖xe7! ♔xe7 18.♗d6+ with a very strong attack.

Lanka, Z. (2521) – Michaelis, N. (2145), Germany 1999: 4.d4 ♘f6

5.♗c4 a6 6.♘f3 e6 7.0-0 b5 8.♗b3 ♗b7 9.♖e1 ♗e7 10.♗g5 0-0 11.♕e2 ♘bd7?! 12.d5! ♘xd5 13.♗xd5 1-0

Nagy, J. (2260) – Outioupine, V., Pecs 1998: 4.d4 ♘f6 5.♘f3 c6 6.♘e5 ♗f5 7.♗c4 e6 8.♗f4 ♕d8?! 9.g4 ♗e4?! (9...♗g6) 10.♘xe4 ♘xe4 11.♕e2 ♕a5+? (11...♘d6)

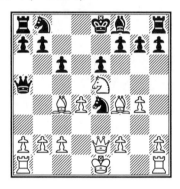

12.♔f1 ♘d6 13.♘xf7 ♘xc4 14.♕xe6+ ♗e7 15.♖e1 1-0

Petrik, T . (2413) – Pisk, P. (2322), Czechia 2004: 4.d4 ♘f6 5.♘f3 a6 6.♗e3 ♗f5 7.♗c4 e6 8.♕e2 ♗e7 9.0-0-0 ♘d5 10.♗xd5 exd5 11.♖he1 0-0 12.♘e5 ♗e6 13.♗f4 ♕d8? (13...♘c6!? 14.♘g6 ♗g5)

14.♘xf7 ♗xf7 15.♕xe7 ♕xe7 16.♖xe7 ♘c6 17.♖xc7 ♗h5 18.g4 ♗xg4 19.♗d6 ♖xf2 20.♖g1±.

Bastian, H. (2360)–Mueller, G., Bad Neuenahr 1982: 4.d4 ♘f6 5.♗e2 c6 6.♘f3 ♗g4 7.0-0 e6 8.♘e5 ♗xe2 9.♕xe2 ♘bd7 10.♗g5 ♕xd4 11.♗xf6 gxf6?

12.♘xf7 ♔xf7 13.♖ad1 ♕c5 14.♖xd7+ ♗e7 15.♘e4 1-0

Khachian, M. (2473) – Serpik, I., Costa Mesa 2003: 4.d4 ♘f6 5.♘f3 a6 6.♗c4 b5 7.♗b3 ♗b7 8.0-0 e6 9.♖e1 ♗e7 10.♘g5 0-0? 11.♘xe6 ♖e8 12.♗f4 1-0

Stuart, K. – Beratti, H., Internet 2003: 4.d4 e5? 5.♘f3 exd4 6.♘xd4

6...c6 7.♕e2+ ♗e7 8.♗e3 ♘f6 9.0-0-0 ♕c7 10.g3 0-0 11.♗f4 ♗d6 12.♗xd6 ♕xd6 13.♘db5 +−

Farago, S. (2255) – Persson, R. (2150), Budapest 1997: 4.g3 ♘f6 5.♗g2 ♗g4

6.♘ge2 c6 7.h3 ♗f5 8.d4 ♘bd7 9.♗f4 e5?

10.dxe5 ♘xe5 11.♕xd6 ♗xd6 12.0-0-0 0-0-0 13.♖xd6 ♖xd6 14.♗xe5 ±.

Antonio, R. (2521) – Goh, Koong Jong J. (2314), Ho Chi Minh City 2003: 4.d4 ♘f6 5.♘f3 a6 6.h3 ♘c6 7.♗d3 e5?! 8.dxe5 ♘xe5 9.♕e2 ♘fd7 10.♗f4 f6 11.0-0-0 ♕c5

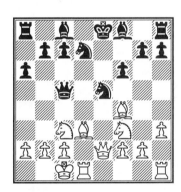

12.♘d4! ♗e7 13.♘e6 ♕d6 14.♕h5+ g6 15.♗xg6+ hxg6 16.♕xh8+ ♔f7 17.♖xd6 ♗xd6 18.♘d8+ 1-0

Ehlvest, J. (2640) – Handoko, E. (2440), Dubai 2007: 4.d4 ♘f6 5.♗g5 a6 6.♕d2 e5?! 7.dxe5 ♕xe5+ 8.♗e2 ♗b4 9.♘f3 ♗xc3 10.bxc3 ♕e7 11.0-0 ♘e4 12.♕d4 f6? (12...♘xg5 13.♕xg7 ♘xf3+ 14.♗xf3 ♖f8 15.♖fe1 ♗e6

16.♗xb7 ♖a7 17.♘d5 with a strong initiative) 13.♖fe1

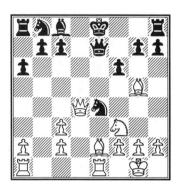

13...♘c6 14.♕d5 ♘c5 (14...♘xg5 15.♘xg5 ♘e5 16.♗c4±) 15.♘d4 ♘e5 16.♗h5+ (16...♔f8 17.♖xe5 +- or 16...g6 17.♗xf6 +-) 1-0

Berescu, A. (2400)– Gerencer, J. (2176), Szombathely 2003: 4.d4 ♘f6 5.♘f3 a6 6.g3 e6 7.♗g2 ♗e7 8.0-0 0-0 9.♖e1 c5?

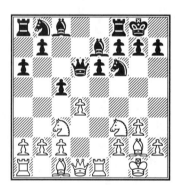

10.♗f4 ♕b6 11.♘a4 ♕a5 12.♘xc5 ♗xc5 13.dxc5 ♖d8 14.b4 ♖xd1 15.♖axd1 ♕b5 16.♖d8+ ♘e8 17.♘d4 ♕a4 18.♗c6 1-0

4.d4 ♘f6 5.♘f3 a6 6.♗e3 ♘bd7 7.♗e2 e6 8.0-0 c5?! (8...♗e7) 9.♕d2 cxd4 10.♘xd4 ♕c7?! (10...e5)

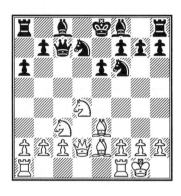

11.♗f4 ♕b6?! (11...e5) 12.♗f3 ♗e7 13.♖fe1 ♘f8? (13...0-0 14.♘a4 ♕b4 15.♕xb4 ♗xb4 16.c3 ♗a5 17.♘b3 ♗d8 18.♖ad1 ± or 14...♕d8 15.♕c3 e5 16.♘f5±) 14.♘a4 ♕d8 (14...♕b4 15.♕xb4 ♗xb4 16.♘b6 ♗xe1 17.♖xe1 +-) 15.♕c3 ♗d6 16.♗xd6 ♕xd6 17.♘f5 1-0, Nijboer, F. (2540) – Sulava, N. (2486), Metz 2000.

4.d4 ♘f6 5.♘f3 a6 6.g3 ♗g4 7.♗g2 ♘c6 8.0-0 0-0-0 9.♗f4 ♕b4 10.a3 ♕c4 11.d5 e6?!

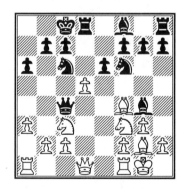

12.dxc6! ♖xd1 13.cxb7+ ♔b8 14.♖fxd1 ♗d6 15.♖xd6 (or 15.♗xd6 cxd6 16.♖xd6 ♕c7 17.♖ad1 ♘d5 18.♘xd5 ♕xd6 19.♘e3 ♕b6 20.♘xg4 with a material advantage and better position, Muzychuk, A. (2456) – Gara, A. (2349), Szeged 2006) 15...♗xf3

(15...c×d6 16.♗×d6+ ♔a7 17.♘e5 +−)
16.♗×f3 c×d6 17.♗×d6+ ♔a7 18.♖d1
with a very strong initiative; for example,
18...♘d7 19.♗f4 ♘b6 20.♗e3 +−, or
18...♖e8 19.♗f4 ♘d5 20.♘×d5 e×d5
21.b8♕+ ♖×b8 22.♗e3+ ♖b6
23.♖×d5 +−, or 18...♘d5 19.♘×d5
e×d5 20.♖×d5 ♕×c2 21.♖c5 ♕×b2
22.♖c8 +−.

San Martin, J. (2113) − Arrieta
Gonzalez, A., San Sebastian 2002: 4.d4
♘f6 5.♘f3 a6 6.♗e3 ♘c6 7.h3 ♗f5
8.♗d3 ♗g6 9.♕e2 ♗×d3 10.♕×d3

10...0-0-0? 11.♘g5 1-0

Kreiman, B. (2515) − Tare, M., Agios
Nikolaos 1997: 4.d4 ♘f6 5.♘f3 a6 6.g3
♗g4 7.♗g2 ♘c6 8.♗f4 ♕d7 9.h3 ♗h5?

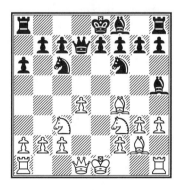

10.g4 ♗g6 11.♘e5 ♕×d4 (11...♕e6

12.d5 +−; 11...♕d6 12.♘×g6 ♕e6+
13.♘e5 +−; 11...♘×e5 12.d×e5 ♕×d1+
13.♖×d1 +−) 12.♗×c6+ 1-0

Bromberger, S. (2495) − Nagatz, F.
(2275), Dresden 2007: 4.d4 ♘f6 5.♘f3
♗g4 6.h3 ♗h5 7.g4 ♗g6 8.♘e5 c6
9.♗g2 e6? (9...♘bd7)

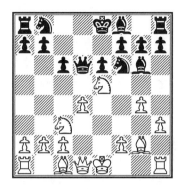

10.h4 ♗×c2 (10...h5 11.♘×g6 f×g6
12.g5 ±; 10...♘bd7 11.♘×d7 ♕×d7
12.h5 ±) 11.♕×c2 ♕×d4 12.f4 ±.

Thorhallsson, T. (2460) − Koskinen, V.
(1975), Copenhagen 2007: 4.d4 ♘f6
5.♘f3 a6 6.♗e2 ♗g4 7.h3 ♗h5 8.g4
♗g6 9.♘e5 ♘d5?! (9...♘c6) 10.♗f3 c6
11.h4 (11.0-0!? ♘d7?! 12.♘×d5 c×d5
13.♗f4 ±; 11...♘×c3!? 12.b×c3 ♘d7)
11...♘×c3 12.b×c3

12...h6? (12...♘d7!? 13.♘×d7 ♕×d7

14.h5 ♛e6+) 13.♖b1 ♖a7 14.♗f4 ♗h7 15.0-0 ♛d8 16.d5 f6 17.♘×c6 ♘×c6 18.d×c6 ♛×d1 19.♖f×d1 1-0

Godena, M. (2487) – Giua, F. (2138), France 2000: 4.d4 ♘f6 5.♘f3 a6 6.♗e3 ♗g4 7.h3 ♗h5 8.g4 ♗g6 9.♘e5 ♘d5?! (9...♘c6) 10.♛f3 c6? (10...♘×e3!? 11.f×e3 ♘c6 12.♗g2 ♘a5)

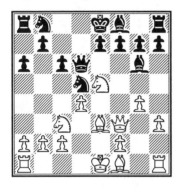

11.♗d3 ♛f6 12.♘×d5 ♛×f3 13.♘c7+ ♔d8 14.♘×f3 ♔×c7 15.♗×g6 f×g6 16.♗f4+ ♔d8 17.0-0-0 ♘d7 18.♖he1 h6 19.♘e5 ♘×e5 20.d×e5+ ♔e8 21.e6 1-0

Ponomariov, R. (2616) – Fressinet, L. (2440), Batumi 1999: 4.♘f3 ♘f6 5.d4 a6 6.♗c4 ♘bd7 7.0-0 b5 8.♗b3 ♗b7? (8...e6) 9.♘g5! e6 (9...♘d5 10.♘×f7!) 10.♖e1 ♗e7

(in the game Nakamura H. (2601) – Stripunsky A. (2553), New York 2004 there was 10...♘d5, and White could have won after 11.♘ge4 ♛b6 12.♘×d5 ♗×d5 13.♗×d5 e×d5 14.♘d6+ ♔d8 15.♖e8# as per Lane, G.) 11.♘×e6 f×e6 12.♖×e6 ♛b4 13.a3 ♛a5 14.♗d2 b4 15.a×b4 ♛f5 16.♛e2 ♘g8 17.♖a5! ♛f8 18.♘d5 ♔d8 (18...♗×d5 19.♗×d5 ♖b8 20.♗c6 ♔d8 21.♖×a6 ♘gf6 22.b5+−) 19.b5 ♗d6 (19...a×b5 20.♛×b5 ♖b8 21.♘×e7 ♘×e7 22.♗g5+−) 20.b×a6 ♗c6 21.♘b4 ♘b8 1-0

4. General Ideas and Game Plans

After 3...♛d6, White has many good continuations. I think the best is **4.d4** (for 4.g3, 4.♗c4 and 4.♘f3 see Games 38-40; practice indicates that without d2-d4 Black has many chances for equality and counterplay; that is why White sooner or later plays d2-d4). After **4.d4** Black's best move (in my opinion) is **4...♘f6** (see Game 37 for other moves).

White has many logical continuations after 4...♘f6. Playing Black, what is the best continuation and the best plan after each of these moves by White? The truth is, I don't know! Nobody knows! Why? Because the correct decision (for you!) will depend upon the evaluation of some of Black's continuations and how they mesh with your own style of play. We return to these questions later in the Recommendations section.

Typical Pawn Structures

Pawns are the most enduring feature of a position. Pawn structure can determine strategy in the opening and middlegame. In positions with 3...♛d6,

Black can create different pawn structures. We will concentrate, from Black's perspective, on plans which are common for such positions.

The pawn structures that arise in the 3...♛d6 system usually belong to one of three groups:

A) Black's c-pawn is on c6;
B) Black's a-pawn is on a6; and
C) Black's g-pawn is on g6.

In addition, virtually any of White's fifth moves (except 5.♘b5) gives Black the following possibilities:

• With 5...♘c6 (5...♘bd7, 5...♗g4, 5...♗f5 or even 5...♗e6) to create a position which does not neatly fit into one of these groups – see the Recommendations;
• With 5...c6 (5...a6 or 5...g6) to create a position which may have characteristics of more than one group and therefore possibly transpose from one group to another.

A) Black's c-pawn is on c6

This group has some different pawn structures: pawn structures with Black's c6-pawn; pawn structure with Black's c6- and e6-pawns, etc. The most important among them is the classical Caro-Kann pawn structure.

The pawn formation where White's d4-pawn is facing the Black's e6- and c6-pawns often occurs in positions that arise from the Caro-Kann Defense. In this book you can see this pawn structure in Games 1-4, 12-17, and 32-38.

Here you see the classical Caro-Kann pawn structure with both sides having castled on the kingside. Unlike the French Defense, the 3...♛d6 system in the Scandinavian Defense usually does not force the Black's bishop to remain at c8. It has an open road to the kingside, and is usually developed there quite early in the game. This pawn structure gives one of the most solid defenses available to Black. Even though players often castle on opposite wings, Black's position with this pawn structure cannot usually be defeated by direct attacks. The nature of this pawn structure limits the advantage of the bishop-pair, so White must find a strategy that permanently secures an advantage in space (for example by d4-d5), but that often is not easy.

In positions with the classical Caro-Kann pawn structure, c6-c5 is Black's most natural source of counterplay because:

A) if, after c2-c3 c5×d4 White recaptures with a pawn (c3×d4), then Black can blockade the isolated d-pawn with a knight on d5;
B) if, after c2-c4 c5×d4 White recaptures on d4 with a piece, then Black has obtained the use of the c5- and e5-

squares for minor pieces. For example, Brkic, A. – Benkovic, P., Subotica 2003: 4.d4 ♘f6 5.♘f3 c6 6.g3 ♗g4 7.♗g2 ♘bd7 8.0-0 e6 9.h3 ♗h5 10.a3 ♕c7 11.♘e2 ♗g6 12.♘f4 ♗e7 13.♘×g6 h×g6 14.♕e2 0-0 15.c4 ♖fe8 16.♗d2 ♗d6 17.♖fe1 a5 18.♘c3 a4 19.♖ad1 ♗f8 20.♘e5 c5

21.♘×d7 ♘×d7 22.♕f3 c×d4 23.♖×d4 ♘c5 24.h4 ♖ad8 25.♖×d8 ♖×d8 26.h5 ♖d3 27.♕g4 g×h5 28.♕×h5 ♕d8 29.♔h2 b6 30.♗f3 ♗e7 31.♔g2 ♗f6 32.♖h1 ♔f8 33.♗b4 g6 34.♗×c5+ b×c5 35.♕×c5+ ♔g7 36.♕c6 ♗×b2 37.♕×a4 ♗×a3 38.♖d1 ♖×d1 39.♕×d1 ♕×d1 40.♗×d1 ♗c5 ½-½

But this plan (with c6-c5) also has its drawbacks. After c6-c5 White often has the possibility to play d4-d5 with the initiative or after d4×c5, White may have an advantage in both the middlegame and endgame thanks to the queenside majority (and then try to take advantage of this majority in the endgame by playing a2-a3, b2-b4 and c2-c4).

Our discussion of some typical plans for the classical Caro-Kann pawn structure is relevant even with castling on opposite wings. The game Matanovic,

A. – Petrosian, T., Kiev 1959, illustrates this strategy well:

12...♘d5 13.♗×e7 (13.♗d2 b5 14.♗b3 a5 with an attack) **13...♕×e7 14.♖he1 0-0 15.♔b1 ♖ad8 16.♗b3 ♕f6 17.♕e2 ♖d7**

Petrosian begins regrouping his army, provoking c2-c3 with the doubling of rooks on the d-file.

18.c3

18...b5!?

This move is the beginning of a standard plan in such positions. Black intends ...b7-b5-b4, which will result in the undermining of the d4-pawn if White takes on d4, or, if Black exchanges on c3, in hanging pawns (i.e., pawns on c3 and d4) which can be attacked with either ...c6-c5 or ...e6-e5. In the end, White will end up with an isolated pawn. White's king will also be in a less secure position.

19.g3 ⃞fd8 20.f4?!

After 20.⃞×d5 ⃞×d5, Black has a small edge.

20...b4

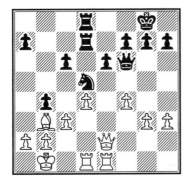

21.⃞f3?! (here 21.⃞×d5 ⃞×d5 22.c×b4 was better, and if 23...⃞×d4 24.⃞×d4 ⃞×d4, then 25.a3 leads to a defensible position) **21...b×c3 22.b×c3 c5!** (White has problems with his pawns.) **23.⃞e5**

After 23.c4 ⃞b4 24.d×c5 ⃞d3 25.⃞e2 ⃞×c5 28.⃞×d7 ⃞×d7, Black has a better game because of the superiority of the knight over the bishop, as well as a better pawn structure.

23...c×d4 24.⃞×d5 ⃞×d5 25.⃞×d5 e×d5! (25...⃞×d5 26.⃞×d4! ⃞×d4 27.c×d4 with an unclear ending) **26.⃞×d4 h6 27.g4 ⃞e7! 28.⃞f2** (28.⃞×d5? ⃞b7+) **28...⃞b8+ 29.⃞a1 ⃞a3 30.⃞c2 ⃞e8! 31.⃞b4** (31.⃞d2 ⃞e2 32.⃞×e2 ⃞c1#) **31...d4! 32.⃞×d4 ⃞e1+ 33.⃞d1 ⃞×d1+**

34.⃞×d1 ⃞×c3+ 35.⃞b1 ⃞×h3 36.a4 h5! 37.g×h5 ⃞f5+ 38.⃞b2 ⃞×f4 39.⃞b3 ⃞f5 40.⃞c4 ⃞h7 41.⃞d2 0-1

Note:

1. White had the bishop-pair.
2. After **12...⃞d5 13.⃞×e7 ⃞×e7**, White had a queen, two rooks and the light-squared bishop versus queen, two rooks and knight.
3. Putting some pressure on the d4-pawn, Black provoked **18.c3**.
4. With **18...b5 and 20...b4** Black initiated an attack on the c3-pawn.
5. After **21...b×c3 22.b×c3 c5**, Black had a strong initiative in the center.

There are occasions when Black castles queenside.

Huschenbeth, N. (2305) – Stark, L. (2430), Pardubice 2007: 4.d4 ⃞f6 5.⃞f3 c6 6.⃞c4 ⃞g4 7.⃞e3 ⃞bd7 8.⃞d2 e6 9.⃞f4 ⃞b4 10.⃞b3 ⃞d5 11.⃞e5 ⃞×f4 12.⃞×f4 ⃞×e5 13.⃞×e5 0-0-0

14.h3 ⃞d6 15.⃞e3 ⃞h5 16.⃞g5 ⃞g6 17.0-0-0 ⃞e7 18.⃞f4 ⃞f6 19.a3 ⃞b6 20.⃞a4 ⃞c7 21.⃞e3 ⃞b8 22.f4 h5 23.g3 ⃞f5 24.⃞c5 ⃞hg8 25.h4 ⃞a5 26.⃞c4 g6 27.b4 ⃞c7 28.c3 ⃞e7 ½-½

Manolaraki, Y. (2118) – Papadopoulou, V. (2217), Ermioni 2006: 4.d4 c6 5.♞f3 ♞f6 6.♝c4 ♝g4 7.♝e3 e6 8.h3 ♝h5 9.g4 ♝g6 10.♞e5 ♞d5 11.♞×d5 e×d5 12.♞×g6 h×g6 13.♝b3 ♞d7 14.♛d2 ♞f6 15.0-0-0 0-0-0

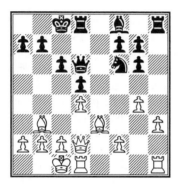

16.♝f4 ♛d7 17.f3 ♝d6 18.c3 ♜de8 19.♝c2 ♛c7 20.♝×d6 ♛×d6 21.♛h2 ♛×h2 22.♜×h2 g5 23.♚d2 g6 24.♜e1 ♜×e1 25.♚×e1 ♞d7 26.♚f2 ♞f8 27.♚g3 ♞e6 28.h4 g×h4+ 29.♜×h4 ♜×h4 30.♚×h4 ♚c7 31.g5 b6 32.♚g4 c5 33.d×c5 b×c5 34.f4 ♞g7 35.f5 g×f5+ 36.♝×f5 ♚d6 37.♝h7 ♚e7 ½-½

B) Black's a-pawn is on a6

This group has a few different pawn structures. The most important of them are:

B1) pawn structure with Black's a6-pawn;
B2) pawn structure with Black's a6-, b5- (and c5-) pawns.

B1) Pawn structure with Black's a6-pawn

After 4.d4 ♞f6, virtually and fifth move by White (except 5.♞b5) allows Black to play 5...a6 thereby creating a pawn

structure that belongs in this group; for example, after 5.♝c4 a6.

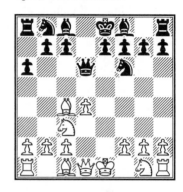

The move 5...a6 looks a bit extravagant. What is the reason for moving the a-pawn?

Usually after 5...a6:

1. White cannot attack the queen on d6 by ♞c3-b5 or (after ♛d6-c6) White cannot pin the queen with ♝b5.
2. Black can bring the knight on b8 to the active c6-square; after ♞b8-c6 Black attacks the d4-pawn and can carry out e7-e5 more easily, looking for counterplay in the center.
3. Black can easily activate the ♞b8 and ♝c8, and then play 0-0-0 – one of the most aggressive (and sometimes riskier) plans in the 3...♛d6 system.
4. Black can play b7-b5; see "Pawn structure with Black's a6-, b5- (and c5-) pawns."

You can see this pawn structure in Games 5-8 (after 5.♝c4), Games 10, 18-28 (after 5.♞f3), and Games 30-36 (after other continuations by White). Black has several ways to respond, depending on what exactly White plays. For example, after 5.♝c4 a6 6.♞ge2, if the idea of playing a gambit (after 6...♛c6 and 7...♛×g2) does not appeal to you,

you may play 6...b5 (Game 6). After 6.♘f3, it is better to play 6...♗g4 (Game 26), and after 6.♗b3, 6...♘c6 (Game 7).

Now some examples of the pawn structure with Black's a6-pawn.

Dragojlovic, A. (2400) – Milanovic, D. (2515), Bizovac 2007: 4.d4 ♘f6 5.♘f3 a6 6.♗g5 ♗g4 7.h3 ♗h5 8.♕d2 ♘bd7 9.♗e2 e6 10.0-0-0 0-0-0

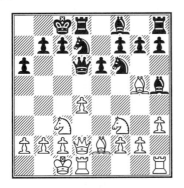

11.g4 ♗g6 12.♕e3 ♕b6 13.♘e5 ♘xe5 14.dxe5 ♕xe3+ 15.♗xe3 ♖xd1+ 16.♖xd1 ♘d7 17.f4 h5 18.♖f1 hxg4 19.hxg4 ♖h3 20.♗f3 ♗b4 21.♘e2 ♗e4 22.♗xe4 ♖xe3 23.♗f3 g5 24.c3 ♗c5 0-1

Jaracz, P. (2485) – Vatter, H. (2327), Dresden 2006: 4.d4 ♘f6 5.♘f3 a6 6.♗d3 ♗g4 7.♘e4 ♘xe4 8.♗xe4 ♘c6

9.c3 f5 10.♗c2 g6 11.h3 ♗xf3 12.♕xf3 e5 13.dxe5 ♕xe5+ 14.♕e3 0-0-0 15.♕xe5 ♘xe5 16.♗g5 ♖e8 17.0-0-0 ♗e7 18.♗e3 ♖hf8 19.♗h6 ♖h8 20.♗b3 ♗f6 21.f4 ♘d7 22.g4 ♘c5 23.gxf5 ♘xb3+ 24.axb3 gxf5 25.♖d5 ♖e6 26.♗g5 ♗xg5 27.fxg5 ♖f8 28.♖f1 ½-½

Van Eijk, S. (2203) – Hertig, T., Groningen 2004: 4.d4 ♘f6 5.♘f3 a6 6.h3 ♘c6 7.♗g5 ♗f5 8.♕d2 0-0-0 9.0-0-0 ♘e4 10.♘xe4 ♗xe4 11.♗f4 ♕b4

12.♘e5 ♕a4 13.♘xc6 ♕xc6 14.f3 ♖xd4 15.♕f2 ♖xd1+ 16.♔xd1 ♗g6 17.g4 e6 18.♔c1 ♗c5 19.♕e2 ♖d8 20.♗g2 ♕a4 0-1

Zozulia, A. (2360) – Weisenburger, H. (2140), Bad Wiessee 2006: 4.d4 ♘f6 5.♘f3 a6 6.♗e2 ♗f5 7.♘e5 ♘c6 8.♘xc6 ♕xc6 9.♗f3 ♕b6 10.0-0 0-0-0

11.♗e3 ♕×b2 12.♕e1 ♕a3 13.♖b1 c6 14.♗f4 ♗×c2 15.♖c1 ♗d3 16.d5 g5 17.♗e5 g4 18.♕e3 g×f3 19.♕b6 ♖d6 20.♖b1 ♗b5 21.♘×b5 a×b5 22.♗×d6 ♘×d5 23.♕d4 ♕×d6 24.♕×h8 ♕h6 25.♖b3 f×g2 26.♖e1 ♘f6 1-0

Tiviakov, S. (2700) – Almeida, O. (2462), Solsona 2005: 4.d4 ♘f6 5.♘f3 a6 6.g3 ♗g4 7.h3 ♗h5 8.♗g2 ♘c6 9.0-0 0-0-0

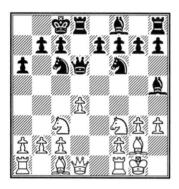

This is one of main positions of the variation 4.d4 ♘f6 5.♘f3 a6 6.g3 (see Game 18). This position is a minefield for both sides–one bad move by either side could cost the game! My opinion of some of these lines differs from those put forward by some grandamsters. We will investigate them later. Note: 10.♗f4 (?! Tiviakov) 10...♕b4 11.d5 (?) "After this mistake White loses material" Tiviakov) 11...e6 12.a3 ½-½. You will be interested to see my analysis of this position after 12.a3 in Game 18.

B2) Pawn structure with Black's a6-, b5- (and c5-) pawns

This pawn structure will normally arise from the with a6-pawn structure. Black can play b7-b5 with the idea (as in the Sicilian Defense) seeking more control in the center with ♗c8-b7 and/or b5-b4 with a possible attack on the ♘c3. A dynamic game for both sides is typical for this pawn structure (especially after c7-c5 and the exchange of the c5-pawn for the d4-pawn like in the Sicilian Defense). Games 6, 7, 18-28 provide many examples of this pawn structure.

Very often this pawn structure will give Black good chances for equality and counterplay. For example, if, after b7-b5, Black is able to play c7-c5, White usually will not get any advantage in the ending after d×c5 ♕×d1. Some examples of this pawn structure:

Medvegy, Z. (2456) – Heinzel, O. (2402), Austria 2005: 4.d4 ♘f6 5.♗c4 a6 6.♗b3 e6 7.♘f3 b5 8.♕e2 ♗b7 9.♗g5 ♘bd7 10.0-0-0

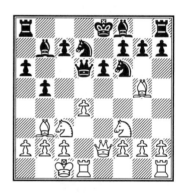

10...♘d5 11.♘e4 ♕b6 12.♘e5 ♘×e5 13.d×e5 h6 14.♗h4 ♗e7 15.♗×e7 ♘×e7 16.♖he1 ♖d8 17.♖×d8+ ♔×d8 18.g3 ♔c8 19.c3 ♘g6 20.f4 ♖d8 21.♗c2 ♘e7 22.♕e3 ♕×e3+ 23.♖×e3 ♗×e4 24.♗×e4 c6 25.♖d3 ½-½

Kalaitzoglou, P. (2160) – Andronis, V. (2069), Kalithea 2006: 4.d4 ♘f6 5.♗c4

a6 6.♘ge2 b5 7.♗b3 ♗b7 8.♗f4 ♕b6
9.0-0 e6 10.a4 c5

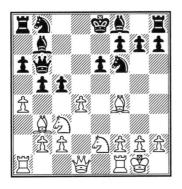

11.a×b5 a×b5 12.♗×b8 ♖×b8 13.♘×b5
♗e7 14.♘bc3 0-0 15.d×c5 ♗×c5
16.♕d3 ♖fd8 17.♕g3 ♗d6 18.♕h3
♖bc8 19.♖fd1 h5 ½-½

Ramesh, R. (2443) – Mellado Trivino,
J. (2493), Andorra 2000: 4.d4 ♘f6
5.♗c4 a6 6.♘f3 b5 7.♗b3 ♗b7 8.♘e5
e6 9.♗f4 c5

10.d×c5 ♕×d1+ 11.♖×d1 ♗×c5 12.0-0
♘c6 13.♘×c6 ♗×c6 14.♗d6 ♗×d6
15.♖×d6 ½-½

Boe Olsen, M. (2362) – Fries Nielsen,
J. (2425), Koge 2004: 4.d4 ♘f6 5.♘f3
a6 6.♗c4 b5 7.♗b3 ♗b7 8.0-0 e6
9.♗g5 c5

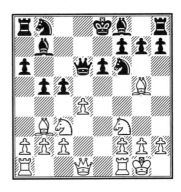

10.d×c5 ♕×d1 11.♖a×d1 ♗×c5 12.♘e5
♘bd7 13.♘×d7 ♘×d7 14.♖fe1 ♘f6
15.♗×f6 g×f6 16.♘d5 ½-½

Boehnisch, M. (2354) – Jirovsky, M.
(2450), Germany 2002: 4.d4 ♘f6 5.♗c4
a6 6.♘f3 b5 7.♗b3 ♗b7 8.0-0 e6 9.♖e1
c5 10.a4

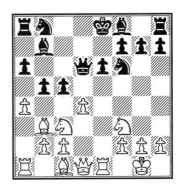

10...c4 11.♗a2 ♕c6 12.♗g5 ♘bd7
13.♕e2 ♗b4 14.♗d2 ♘b6 15.a×b5
a×b5 16.♕e5 ♗×c3 17.♗×c3 0-0
18.♗b4 ♖fe8 19.c3 ♘fd5 20.♗a3 ♘×c3
21.♗b1 ♘×b1 22.♖a×b1 ♘d7 23.♕g3
♕b6 24.♘e5 ♘×e5 25.♗c5 ♘f3+
26.g×f3 ♕c6 27.♖e3 ♖ad8 28.♖be1
♖d5 29.♖e4 ♖f5 30.♖1e3 ♕a6 31.♖g4
♕a1+ 32.♔g2 g6 33.♕c7 ♗d5 34.♕d7
♖a8 35.♕×b5 ♕d1 36.♖g3 h5 37.♔h3
♕f1+ 38.♔h4 ♕×f2 0-1

C) Black's g-pawn is on g6

Thanks to the games of some grandmasters (especially Bojan Kurajica), fianchettoing Black's king's bishop has become popular. The idea of a kingside fianchetto is not new in the Scandinavian Defense. However, with the black queen on d6, Black has more chances to equalize and obtain counterplay (e.g., castling on either wing, double fianchetto, etc.)

This pawn structure includes:
C1) pawn structure with g6-pawn;
C2) pawn structure with g6- and c6-pawns;
C3) pawn structure with g6- and a6-pawns;
C4) pawn structure with g6-, a6- and b5-pawns;
C5) pawn structure with g6-, a6-, b5- and c5-pawns.

Note that in the first three categories, if Black castles kingside, White can initiate an attack with h2-h4-h5 after castling queenside. This set-up is unpretentious (but solid and flexible). It often provokes very aggressive (but sometimes antipositional) continuations from White, resulting in strong counterplay for Black.

These pawn structures may also arise from other openings of course:

1.e4 d5 2.exd5 ♕xd5 3.♘c3 ♕d6 4.d4 g6 or 4...♘f6 5.♘f3 g6;
1.e4 g6 2.♘f3 d5 3.exd5 ♕xd5 4.♘c3 ♕d6;
1.e4 c6 2.d4 g6 3.♘f3 d5 4.exd5 ♕xd5 5.♘c3 ♕d6;
1.♘f3 g6 2.d4 ♗g7 3.e4 d5 4.exd5 ♕xd5 5.♘c3 ♕d6;

1.d4 g6 2.e4 ♗g7 (or 1.e4 g6 2.d4 ♗g7) 3.♘f3 d5 4.exd5 ♕xd5 5.♘c3 ♕d6.

Let's take a look at some games with this pawn structure:

Vouldis, A. (2528) – Kurajica, B. (2557), Plovdiv 2003: 4.d4 ♘f6 5.♘f3 a6 6.g3 g6 7.♗g2 ♗g7 8.0-0 0-0 9.♗f4 ♕d8 10.♕d2 ♘bd7 11.♗h6 ♘b6 12.♗xg7 ♔xg7 13.♖fe1 c6

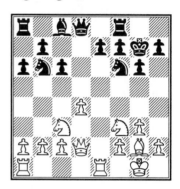

14.♘e4 ♘c4 15.♕e2 ♘d6 16.♘xf6 exf6 17.b3 ♗g4 18.♕d2 ♗xf3 19.♗xf3 ♕b6 20.h4 h5 21.c3 ♖fe8 22.♔g2 a5 23.♕c2 ♕c7 24.♖ad1 ♕b6 25.♕d2 ♖ad8 26.♕f4 ♖xe1 27.♖xe1 ♕c7 28.♕d2 ♖d7 29.♕b2 c5 30.dxc5 ♕xc5 31.♖e3 ♘b5 32.c4 ♘d4 33.♗e4 0-1

Braun, P. (2305)–Nilsson, S. (2200), Marianske Lazne 2008: 4.d4 ♘f6 5.♘ge2 ♗f5 6.♗f4 ♕d8 7.♘g3 ♗e6 8.♕d2 c6 9.♗e2 ♘bd7 10.0-0 g6 11.♖fe1 ♗g7 12.♖ad1 0-0 13.♗h6 ♘b6 14.♗xg7 ♔xg7 15.♕c1 ♗c4 16.b3 ½-½

Pogonina, N. (2460) – Kurajica, B. (2550), Solin 2007: 4.d4 ♘f6 5.♘f3 g6 6.♘b5 ♕b6 7.c4 c6 8.♘c3 ♗g7

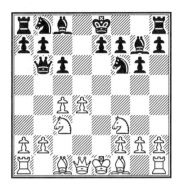

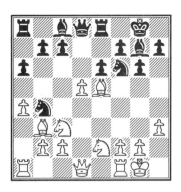

9.c5 ♕d8 10.♗c4 b5 11.c×b6 a×b6 12.♘e5 0-0 13.0-0 ♗a6 14.♗×a6 ♖×a6 15.♕e2 ♖a7 16.♖d1 ♘d5 17.♗e3 e6 18.♖ac1 ♕d6 19.♘c4 ♕d8 20.♘e5 ♕d6 21.♘c4 ♕d8 22.♘e5 ½-½

Parligras. M. (2490) – Epishin, V. (2550), Seville 2007: 4.d4 ♘f6 5.♘f3 g6 6.♘b5 ♕b6 7.c4 c6 8.♘c3 ♗g4 9.♗e2 ♗g7 10.0-0 0-0 11.a3 ♖d8 12.♗e3 ♘bd7 13.b4 ♕c7

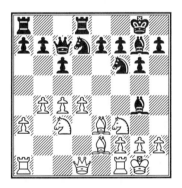

14.h3 ♗×f3 15.♗×f3 ♘e8 16.♕b3 ♘d6 17.♖ad1 ♘f5 18.♘e2 ½-½

Krstic, U. (2350) – Martinovic, S. (2182), Bosnjaci 2006: 4.♗c4 ♘f6 5.d4 g6 6.♘ge2 ♗g7 7.♗f4 ♕d8 8.0-0 0-0 9.h3 a6 10.a4 ♘c6 11.d5 ♘b4 12.♗b3 ♖e8 13.♗e5 e6

14.d×e6 ♗×e6 15.♕×d8 ♖a×d8 16.♗×c7 ♖d2 17.♗×e6 ♖×e6 18.♖fd1 ♖e×e2 19.♘×e2 ♖×e2 20.♔f1 ♖e8 21.c3 ½-½

Galego, L. (2467) – Sulava, N. (2531), Lisbon 2001: 4.♘f3 ♘f6 5.h3 g6 6.♗c4 ♗g7 7.0-0 0-0 8.d3 ♘c6 9.a3 b6 10.♖e1 ♗b7 11.♗g5 ♖ae8 12.♕e2 e5 13.♗×f6 ♕×f6 14.♗d5 ♘d8 15.♗×b7 ♘×b7 16.♖ad1 ♘d6 ½-½

Krstic, U. (2360) – Kurajica, B. (2541), Zadar 2004: 4.♘f3 ♘f6 5.h3 g6 6.d4 ♗g7 7.♗d3 0-0 8.0-0 ♘c6 9.♘b5 ♕d8 10.c3 a6 11.♘a3 b5 12.♘c2 ♘d5

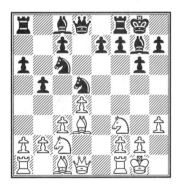

13.a4 b4 14.c4 b3 15.♘ce1 ♘db4 16.♗e4 ♖b8 17.♗e3 ♘a5 18.♕e2 ♕d6 19.♖d1 ♗d7 20.♗g5 ♕e6 21.d5 ♕d6 22.♗e3 ♗×a4 23.♖a1 ♕d7 24.♗c5

39

♘a2 25.♗d3 c6 26.♕×e7 ♖fd8 27.♕×d7 ♖×d7 28.♗a3 c×d5 29.c×d5 ♗b5 30.d6 ♘c4 31.♖d1 ♘×a3 32.b×a3 ♖×d6 0-1

Brkic, A. (2428) – Kurajica, B. (2557), Solin 2003: 4.d4 g6 5.♘f3 ♗g7 6.g3 ♘f6 7.♗f4 ♕b6 8.♕d2 0-0 9.0-0-0 c5 10.d×c5 ♕×c5 11.♗g2 ♘c6 12.♖he1 ♗f5

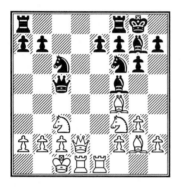

13.h3 ♘b4 14.♘d4 ♖ad8 15.♕e3 ♖×d4 16.♕×d4 ♕×d4 17.♖×d4 ♘×c2 18.♖dd1 ♘×e1 19.♖×e1 ♖e8 20.g4 ½-½

Radulski, J. (2501) – Kurajica, B. (2541), Zadar 2004: 4.d4 g6 5.♘f3 ♗g7 6.♘b5 ♕d8 7.♗f4 ♘a6 8.♗e5 ♘f6 9.♘c3 ♘b8 10.♗c4 0-0 11.♕e2 a6 12.0-0-0 b5 13.♗b3 ♘c6 14.♖he1 ♘a5 15.♘e4

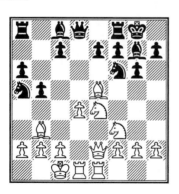

15...♗b7 16.♘c5 ♘×b3+ 17.a×b3 ♕c8 18.♔b1 b4 19.d5 ♖d8 20.♗×f6 e×f6 21.♕c4 ♗f8 22.♘×b7 ♕×b7 23.g4 a5 24.g5 a4 25.g×f6 a×b3 26.c×b3 ♖a5 27.♖e7 ♔c8 28.♕e4 ♗×e7 29.f×e7 ♖e8 30.♘d4 ♕a6 31.♔c2 ♖c5+ 32.♔b1 ♕d6 0-1

Kovacevic, A. (2556) – Kurajica, B. (2541) Zadar 2004: 4.d4 g6 5.♘f3 ♗g7 6.♘b5 ♕d8 7.♗f4 ♘a6 8.♗e2 c6 9.♘a3 ♘f6 10.0-0 ♘c7 11.♘c4 0-0 12.h3 ♘cd5 13.♗h2 ♗h6 14.♖e1 ♗e6 15.♗f1 c5

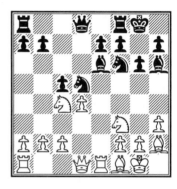

16.d×c5 ♖c8 17.♘d4 ♗d7 18.♘b3 ♗e6 19.c3 ♘d7 20.c6 b×c6 21.♘d4 ♘c5 22.♘×e6 ♘×e6 23.♕a4 ♕e8 24.♕×a7 ♖a8 0-1

Avdic, A. (2304) – Kurajica, B. (2539), Neum 2005: 4.d4 g6 5.♘f3 ♗g7 6.g3 ♗f5 7.♗g2 ♕a6

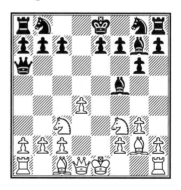

8.♘e5 ♘d7 9.♘×d7 ♗×d7 10.♘e4 b6
11.c3 ♖c8 12.a4 ♘f6 13.♘×f6+ ♗×f6
14.♗h6 c5 15.d5 ♕c4 16.♕e2 ♗×c3+
0-1

Kennaugh, C. (2310) – Bronstein, D.
(2445), Hastings 1995: 4.d4 ♘f6 5.♗c4
a6 6.♘ge2 b5 7.♗b3 ♗b7 8.♗f4 ♕d8
9.0-0 ♘bd7 10.♕e1 g6 11.♖d1 ♗g7
12.♘g3 0-0 13.a4 c5

14.d×c5 ♕c8 15.a×b5 a×b5 16.♕×e7
♘×c5 17.♗d5 ♘×d5 18.♘×d5 ♘e6
19.♗c1 ♗×d5 20.♖×d5 ♕×c2 21.♖×b5
♖a1 22.♗e3 ♖×f1+ 23.♘×f1 ♘d4
24.♗×d4 ♗×d4 25.♕h4 ♗×b2 26.♕b4
♗g7 ½-½

Silva F. (2007)–Silva A. (2194), Vila
Nova de Gaia 2004: 4.h3 ♘f6 5.♘f3 a6
6.d4 ♗f5 7.♗d3 ♗×d3 8.♕×d3 ♘c6
9.0-0 g6 10.♗g5 ♗g7 11.♕d2 0-0-0

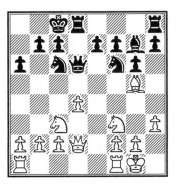

12.♖fd1 ♕d7 13.♕e2 ♕f5 14.♗e3 h6
15.♘a4 ♘e4 16.c4 ♘g5 17.♗×g5 h×g5
18.d5 ♘e5 19.♘×e5 ♗×e5 20.♕g4
♕×g4 21.h×g4 ♖h4 22.g3 ♖×g4
23.♖ac1 b5 24.♘c5 ♖×c4 25.♖×c4
b×c4 26.♘a4 e6 0-1

5. Recommendations

It is always somewhat risky (and definitely thankless) to recommend specific opening lines. Basically, you will not be able to please everyone all the time. To those who may find fault with my recommendations, I apologize in advance. But for those who are looking for some guidance, read on…

How to use this book

1. If you do not have the time to go through this book thoroughly, I suggest you focus on this Part I. This should allow you to begin to play the 3...♕d6 system in your games. Good luck!

2. With a little more time available, go through the main moves of each game, but skip the variations. For example, do not read about the variation 4.d4 ♘f6 5.♘f3 a6 6.g3 b5?! in Game 18 because 6...b5?! is bad for Black.

Recommendations for Black (Part I)

1. When first using the 3...♕d6 system, take your time and do not move very quickly. You will be facing new positions and you want to try to avoid making mistakes.

2. At first, White usually has better piece development. Try to finish the development of your pieces as quickly as possible.

3. Avoid "aggressive" moves, such as advancing a pawn to c5 or e5 too early because White has a lead in development.

4. Very often taking the b2-pawn with the queen can be dangerous for Black. Always check the white possibilities carefully before making this move.

5. Sometimes winning the d4-pawn by ♛d6×d4 (for example, after ♛d1×f3 ♛d6×d4) can be dangerous for Black (especially if White may play ♘c3-b5). Always check this possibility before playing ♛d6×d4.

6. Remember the move d4-d5 can be sometimes very unpleasant for Black even with pawns on c6 and e6.

7. If Black has played the bishop to h5 or f5, and then drops it back to g6 after g2-g4 by White, watch out for ♘e5, followed by h2-h4 etc. The best way for Black to counter this is to try to eliminate the e5-knight as quickly as possible.

8. When you have pawns on e6 and f7 be alert to White's possibility of sacrificing a knight by ♘e5×f7, ♘g5×e6 or ♘g5×f7.

9. Occasionally, after Black has castled queenside, the f7-pawn becomes vulnerable to ♘f3-e5 or ♘f3-g5 and this can be dangerous for Black. White's initiative may continue even if Black can cover f7 with ♗f5-g6. White can challenge the bishop with; for example, ♗e2-d3. Always check this possibility before castling queenside.

10. After Black has castled queenside, White may be able to move the queen

to a7 and this could be very dangerous for Black. Always check this possibility before and after castling queenside.

Recommendations for Black (Part II)

Now I would like to give some recommendations for Black after 4.d4 ♘f6.

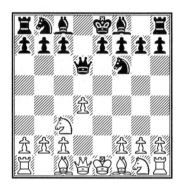

White has many logical possibilities in this position:

A) 5.♗c4 (Games 1-9)
B) 5.h3 (Game 30)
C) 5.♘b5 (Game 31)
D) 5.♘ge2 (Game 32)
E) 5.♗d3 (Game 33)
F) 5.♗e2 (Game 34)
G) 5.♗e3 (Game 35)
H) 5.♗g5 (Game 36)
I) 5.♘f3 (Games 10-29)

Black has a number of alternatives, depending on how White plays after 4...♘f6 and what your own style of play is.

1. If you are a positional player (or you want to avoid aggressive or tactical complications) I recommend you play the 3...♛d6 system with the classical Caro-Kann pawn structure. Almost any fifth move by White (except 5.♘b5) allows you the possibility of playing **5...c6** (and after ♗c8-f5 or ♗c8-g4, playing e7-e6). Actually, White has only one aggressive response after **5.♘f3 c6**, and that is **6.♘e5**. After 6...♗f5 (Game 16), White gets a strong initiative by 7.♗c4 or 7.♗f4 with an early g2-g4.

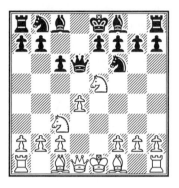

But Black has two other continuations, both safe enough and usually leading to positional play (Game 17). The first of these is **6...♘bd7**, with the goal of removing White's knight from the active e5-square. The usual continuations after 6...♘bd7 are:

A) 7.♗f4 ♘d5 8.♘×d5 ♛×d5, which practice and analysis show is not dangerous for Black;
B) 7.♘c4 ♛c7, which experience in the 3...♛a5 variation shows is not dangerous for Black either; and
C) 7.f4 ♘b6 8.g4 h5 9.g5 ♘fd7, which analysis shows is not dangerous for Black.

Brkic, A. (2575) – Gallagher, J. (2495), Crete 2007: 6...♘bd7 7.♘c4 ♛c7 8.♛f3 ♘b6 9.♗f4 ♛d8 10.♗e5 ♗g4 11.♛g3 h5 12.h3 h4 13.♛f4 ♗e6 14.♘e3 ♘bd5 15.♘e×d5 ♘×d5 16.♛d2 ♘×c3 17.b×c3 ♛d5 18.f3 (18.♛e3 ♗f5!? Tiviakov, S.) 18...♖h5 19.♗f4 ♖d8 ½-½

The second continuation is **6...♗e6**. An important consideration here is that the bishop cannot be attacked by ♘f3-g5 because this knight is already on e5. But e6, blocking the e7-pawn, seems an unusual post for the bishop, and one might wonder how to develop the ♗f8. The answer is that after 6...♗e6 Black plans to develop the kingside by g7-g6, ♗f8-g7 and then 0-0.

Popovic, P. (2495)–Muse, D. (2410), Germany 2006: 6...♗e6 7.♗f4 ♛d8 8.♗e2 ♘bd7 9.0-0 g6 10.♘×d7 ♛×d7 11.♗e5 ♗g7 12.♘e4 0-0 (12...♘×e4!? 13.♗×g7 ♖g8 14.♗e5 0-0-0) 13.♘c5 ♛c8 14.♖e1 ♖d8 15.c3 ♗d5 16.♗f1 b6 17.♘a6 ♖d7 18.♛a4 ♛b7 19.♘b4 a5 20.♘d3 ♖ad8 21.♘f4 ♗h6 22.h3 b5 23.♛c2 ♗c4 24.♘d3 ♗×d3 25.♛×d3 a4 26.a3 ♘e8 27.♛f3 ♘d6 28.h4 ½-½

After **5.♘b5**, I recommend **5...♛d8**

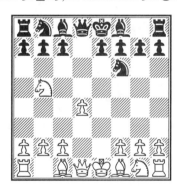

White usually plays here 6.c4 or 6.♗f4.

A) After 6.c4 c6 7.♘c3 ♗f5 8.♘f3 e6 or 7...g6 8.♘f3 ♗g7, Black has a normal game with counterplay.

B) After 6.♗f4 ♘d5 7.♛f3 (if 7.♗g3 c6 8.♘c3 ♗f5 chances are equal) 7...c6 8.♘c3 ♘×f4 ♛d6 10.♛d2 g6 11.♘f3 ♗g7 12.♗c4 0-0, Black has a good game. If White wants to continue to play aggressively with 8.♗c4, Black is still fine; after 8...♘xf4 White will be worse; for example, 9.♕xf4 (9.♗xf7+ ♔xf7 10.♕xf4+ ♔g8 11.♘c7 e5! 12.♕xe5 ♗d6 13.♕e8+ ♕xe8+ 14.♘xe8 ♗b4+ 15.c3 ♗a5) 9...cxb5 10.♕xf7+ ♔d7 11.♗xb5+ ♘c6 12.0-0-0 ♘c7 13.♘f3 ♕d6 14.♖he1 ♕f6 15.♕b3 e6 or 10.♗xf7+ ♔d7 11.♕f5+ ♔c7 12.♕c5+ ♘c6.

2. If you prefer to play aggressively with tactical tricks, and you are not afraid to sacrifice a pawn for the initiative, I can recommend several plans:

2A) If White plays **5.♗c4**, I recommend **5...a6**.

After 6.♘ge2 (if 6.♗b3, play 6...♘c6 as in Game 7; if 6.♘f3 play 6...♗g4, Game 26 or 6...b5, Game 27), play 6...b5 (Game 6) 7.♗b3 (if 7.♗d3 b5 8.♗f4 ♕d7 9.f3 e6 10.♕d2 c5 11.dxc5 ♗xc5 with a good game for Black) 7...♗b7 and now:

2A1) 8.0-0 c5 9.dxc5 (9.♗f4 ♕c6 10.d5 ♕d7) 9...♕c6 10.♘f4 e6 11.♖e1 ♗e7 12.♕e2 ♘bd7 13.a4 b4 14.♘cd5 ♗xc5 with counterplay.

2A2) 8.♗f4 ♕d7 9.0-0 (9.d5 c5; 9.f3 e6, followed by c7-c5 or 9.♕d3 ♗xg2

10.♖g1 ♗b7) 9...e6 and then c7-c5 with a good game.

2B) After **5.h3**, play **5...a6**. This move is the most flexible continuation here. White now has many different possibilities but Black's plan would be to continue as follows: g7-g6, ♗f8-g7, 0-0. Then (depending how White plays) Black can continue ♘b8-c6, ♗c8-e6; b7-b5, ♗c8-b7 or c7-c5. In any event Black has good counterplay. In response to White's plan to attack with the h-pawn (one of the most dangerous of White's plan after g6, ♗g7 and 0-0) White will need an extra tempo. See examples of games in the g6-pawn structure group.

2C) After **5.♘b5**, play **5...♕b6**. Here White usually moves 6.c4 (6.♗f4 ♘d5 7.♕f3 c6 with better chances for Black), and after 6...a6 7.♘c3 Black has a good choice between 7...♗g4, 7...♘c6 and even 7...e5 with counterplay.

2D) After **5.♘ge2**, play **5...a6**.

Here White usually moves 6.♕d3 or 6.♗f4.

After 6.♕d3 ♘c6 7.♗f4 ♘b4 8.♕d2 ♕c6 9.♘g3 (9.a3 ♘bd5 10.♗e5 ♗d7

11.0-0-0 0-0-0 12.♘×d5 ♘×d5) 9...♗e6 10.a3 ♘bd5 11.♘×d5 ♘×d5 or 11.♘f4 0-0-0 12.♘c×d5 ♘×d5 13.0-0-0 ♘×f4 14.♗×f4 e6 Black has an equal game with counterplay.

After 6.♗f4 ♕b6 7.g3 (7.d5 c6 8.♗e3 ♕a5) 7...♘c6 8.♗g2 (8.d5?! ♘g4 9.d×c6 ♕×f2+ 10.♔d2 e5 11.♔c1 e×f4 12.♘×f4 ♗d6) 8...♗g4 9.0-0 0-0-0 7.♕d2 ♗f5 8.0-0-0 ♘c6 9.♘g3 ♗g6 10.♗d3 0-0-0 11.♗e3 ♕a5, Black has a good game.

2E) After **5.♗d3**, I recommend **5...♘c6**. After 6.♘ge2 (6.♘f3 ♗g4 7.h3 ♗×f3 8.♕×f3 0-0-0 with a good game for Black; 6.♗e3 e5!? or 6...g6!?) 6...e5

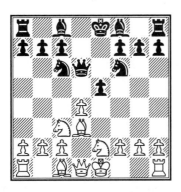

we have a position with the following possibilities for White:

2E1) 7.♘b5 (7.d×e5?! ♘×e5 8.♗b5+ c6 9.♕×d6 ♗×d6) 7...♕d8 or 9...♕e7 with counterplay;

2E2) 7.0-0 ♘×d4 8.♘×d4 ♕×d4 9.♘b5 (9.♖e1 ♗g4 10.♗e3 ♕×c3 11.b×c3 ♗×d1 12.♖a×d1 ♗e7∓) 9...♕b6 10.♕e2 ♗d6 11.♗e3 ♕a5 12.♗c5 (12.c4 a6) 12...♗g4 13.♕e3 0-0-0 and now:

2E2a) 14.♗×a7 b6 15.a4 e4 16.♘c4 ♗e6 or 15.♗c4 ♖he8 with counterplay;

2E2b) 14.♘×d6+ c×d6 15.♗×a7 ♘d5 16.♕g3 h5 or 16.♕g5 ♗e6 with counterplay.

F) After **5.♗e2**, play **5...♘c6**.

White's best continuation here is 6.♗e3 (after 6.♘b5 ♕d7 7.♗f4 ♘d5 8.♗g3 a6 9.♘a3 e6 Black has fine game) 6...♗f5 7.♘f3 e6 8.0-0 ♗e7 9.♘b5 ♕d7 10.c4 a6 11.♘c3 0-0-0 or 7...0-0-0 8.0-0 a6 with counterplay. For 6.♘f3 a6 see 6.♗e2 ♘c6, Game 23.

If White wants to play more aggressively (and with more risk!), Black need not be afraid:

F1) 6.d5 ♘b4 7.♘b5 ♕d8 8.c4 (8.♘f3 a6; 8.♗f3 a6) 8...c6

F1a) 9.♕a4?! e5 10.d×c6 b×c6 11.♘a3 ♘e4 12.♗e3 ♘c5 13.♗×c5 ♗×c5 14.♘f3 (14.♖d1 ♕f6∓) 14...e4 15.♘d2 ♗×f2+ 16.♔×f2 ♕×d2∓;

F1b) 9.d×c6 b×c6 10.♕×d8+ ♔×d8 11.♘a3 (11.♘d4?! e5) 11...♘e4 (11...♗f5 12.♘f3 e6 13.♗e3 ♗d6 14.0-0 ♔e7⇄) 12.♗f4 (12.♗e3 e5

13.♘f3 f6∓) 12...g5 13.♖d1+ ♗d7 14.♗e5 ♖g8 15.♗g4 e6⇄; 11...e5 12.♘f3 e4 ♗e6 14.♗f4 ♚c8 15.0-0 ♚b7∓.

G) After **5.♗e3**, play **5...a6**; for example, 6.♛d2 (6.♗d3 ♘c6 7.♛d2 e5 8.d×e5 ♘×e5 9.♗e2 ♛×d2+ 10.♗×d2 ♗e6∓ or 8.♘f3 e×d4 9.♘×d4 ♘×d4 10.♗×d4 ♗e6 11.0-0-0 0-0-0 with counterplay) 6...b5 7.♗f4 (7.♘f3 ♗b7; 7.♗d3 ♗b7; 7.♗e2 ♗b7 8.♗f3 ♘c6) 7...♛b6 8.♘f3 ♗b7 9.♘e5 (or 9.♗e2 e6 10.0-0 ♗d6 11.♘e5 ♘bd7=) 9...e6 10.0-0-0 (10.a4 b4 11.♘e2 ♘d5=) 10...♘c6 11.a3 ♗d6 with an equal position.

H) After **5.♗g5**, play **5...h6**. If 6.♗h4 (after 6.♗e3 we have position from the line 5.♗e3 with Black's pawn on h6) 6...♛b6 (6...♘c6!?) and Black should be fine; for example, 7.a3?! ♘c6 8.d5 ♛×b2 9.♘ge2 ♘d8 10.♗g3 c6 11.♗c7 ♘×d5 12.♗a5 ♗g4∓ or 12.♖a2 ♛×a2 13.♘×a2 ♘×c7∓; 7.♛d2 ♗f5 8.0-0-0 ♘bd7 9.♘f3 e6 10.♗d3 ♗×d3 11.♛×d3 0-0-0 with counterplay; 7.♗c4 ♛×b2 8.♘ge2 ♛b4 9.♛d3 ♘c6 10.♖b1 ♗f5 11.♛×f5 ♛×c4 12.♗×f6 (12.♖×b7?! ♘×d4) 12...e×f6 13.0-0 b6 with counterplay.

I) **5.♘f3** This move is more flexible than any other, in keeping with Lasker's old rule for the opening,"Bring out knights before bishops," because after 5.♘f3 White keeps open the option of playing the ♗f1 to b5, c4, d3, e2 or g2. The position of this bishop can often influence the plans of both sides. After **5.♘f3**, I recommend **5...g6** or **5...a6**.

IA) **5...g6** After this move, the position belongs to the g6-pawn structure group.

This position may arise several ways; for example, 1.♘f3 g6 2.e4 d5 3.e×d5 ♛×d5 4.d4 ♘f6 5.♘c3 ♛d6 or 1.d4 g6 2.e4 d5 3.e×d5 ♛×d5 4.♘c3 ♛d6 5.♘f3 ♘f6.

White has now many continuations (see Game 29), but Black always has counterplay:

IA1) 6.g3 ♗g7 7.♗g2 (7.♗f4 ♛b6 8.♛d2 0-0) 7...♛a6 (7...♘c6!?) 8.♗f4 c6 9.♛d2 0-0 10.0-0-0 b5;

IA2) 6.♘b5 ♛b6 7.c4 (7.♗f4 ♘a6; 7.♘a3 ♗e6) 7...a6 8.♘c3 ♗g7 9.c5 ♛a7 10.♗e2 0-0 11.0-0 b6;

IA3) 6.♘e5 ♗g7 (6...♗e6!?) 7.♗f4 ♘h5 (7...♘d5!?) 8.♘b5 ♛d8 9.♛f3 0-0 10.0-0-0 c6 11.♘c3 ♘×f4 12.♛×f4 ♗e6 13.h4 ♘d7 14.h5 ♘×e5 15.d×e5 ♛a5 16.♖e1 (16.♗c4 ♗×e5 17.♛h4 ♗f6∓; 16.h×g6 h×g6 17.♗c4 ♗×c4 18.♛×c4 ♛×e5∓) 16...♗×a2 17.h×g6 h×g6 18.♛h4 (18.♛h2 ♖fd8 19.♗d3 ♗e6∓; 18.♖e3 ♗e6 19.♗c4 ♗×c4 20.♛×c4 ♗×e5∓) 18...♖fe8 19.♗d3 ♗e6∓ or 17.♗d3 ♗e6 18.♛h4 ♖fe8 19.f4 ♛a1+ 20.♘b1 (20.♚d2 ♛×b2 21.♖b1 ♛a3 22.♖×b7 ♖ad8 23.♘e4 ♗c4∓) 20...♖ad8 21.h×g6 h×g6 22.g4 ♗a2 23.♚d2 ♛×b2∓;

IB) 5...a6 After this move (see Games 18-29), the position belongs to the a6-pawn structure group.

After 6.h3, play 6...♘c6 (Game 19).
After 6.♘e5, play 6...♘c6 (Game 20).
After 6.♗e2, play 6...♘c6 (Game 23).
After 6.♗d3, play 6...♘c6 (Game 25).
After 6.♗c4, play 6...♗g4 (Game 26) or 6...b5 (Game 27).
After 6.♗e3, play 6...♘c6 (Game 21) or 6...b5 (Game 22).

The move **6.g3** (Game 18) is the most principled and dangerous way for White to fight for an opening advantage. White prepares the fianchetto of the ♗g2 and takes control of the f4-square for ♗c1-f4. After **6.g3 ♘c6** (not 6...b5 because after 7.♗g2 ♗b7 8.0-0 Black may have problems) **7.♗g2** (after 7.♗f4 ♕d8 8.d5 ♘b4 9.♗c4 b5 or 8.♗g2 e6 9.0-0 ♗e7 Black has a good game with counterchances).

7...♗g4. After this move, White has a wide selection of moves, but Black always has counterplay; for example, 8.0-0 0-0-0; 8.♗e3 0-0-0 9.♕e2 (9.h3 ♗h5; 9.0-0 e5) 9...e5; 8.d5 ♘e5 9.♗f4 ♘xf3+ 10.♗xf3 e5; 8.h3 ♗xf3 9.♕xf3 (or 9.♗xf3) 9...0-0-0. Many of these and other lines are minefields for both sides–one slip and it is lights out!

Part II 3.♘c3 ♛d6 4.d4 ♘f6 5.♗c4

Games 1-9 cover lines beginning **1.e4 d5 2.e×d5 ♛×d5 3.♘c3 ♛d6 4.d4 ♘f6 5.♗c4**.

White delays the development of ♘g1, which may decide to go to f3 or to e2 (for 5.♘f3, see Part III and for 5.♘ge2, see Game 32, Part IV).

This position is one of the most common in the 3...♛d6 system, and can be regarded as the first main line. For some time theoreticians thought that the aggressive and natural move 5.♗c4 was the best after 4...♘f6, intending ♘g1-e2 and ♗c1-f4 to attack the queen. But since then, analysis and Black's practical results have improved the assessment of Black's position after 5.♗c4. Black has several good replies: 5...c6 (Games 1-4), 5...a6 (Games 5-8), 5...♗g4, 5...♘c6 or even 5...♘bd7 (Game 9).

The moves 5...c6 and 5...a6 are the most popular continuations for Black after 5.♗c4. But the lesser known alternatives 5...♗g4, 5...♘c6 and 5...♘bd7 can create interesting counterplay for Black too.

Game 1
Charbonneau, P. (2500) –
Kamsky, G. (2715)
Montreal 2007

1.e4 d5 2.e×d5 ♛×d5 3.♘c3 ♛d6 4.d4 ♘f6 5.♗c4 c6 6.♘f3

6...♗e6

For 6...♗f5 see Game 29. The move 6...♗g4 is a mistake in an analogous position of the 3...♛d8 line, but is good here and after 3...♛a5. Not 7.♗×f7+??, which works after 3...♛d8 4.d4 ♘f6 5.♗c4 c6 6.♘f3 ♗g4? 7.♘e5! ♗e6 8.♗×e6 f×e6± or 7.♗×f7+! ♚×f7 8.♘e5+ ♚g8 9.♘×g4±. After 3...♛d6 the moves 7.♘e5 and 7.♗×f7+ are mistakes, e.g., 7.♗×f7+ ♚×f7 8.♘e5+ ♛×e5+ 9.d×e5 ♗×d1–+. After 6...♗g4, we examine **A)** 7.h3; **B)** 7.0-0 and **C)** 7.♗e3.

A) 7.h3?! leads to positions similar to certain lines of the Caro-Kann Defense (e.g., 1.e4 c6 2.♘f3 d5 3.♘c3 ♗g4 4.h3 ♗×f3 5.♛×f3 e6 6.d4 d×e4 7.♘×e4 ♛×d4 or 6...♘f6 7.♗d3 d×e4 8.♘×e4

♕×d4). 7...♗×f3 8.♕×f3 ♕×d4. We see similar situations in some variations in Games 10, 12, 13 and 25, when White has the initiative for the d-pawn. But in this case White must use a tempo defending the ♗c4, which can cause the initiative to slip:

A1) 9.♗d3 e6 10.♗e3 ♕b4 (10...♕d8 11.0-0-0 ♘bd7 12.♕g3 ♕a5 13.♔b1 ∞) 11.0-0-0 ♘bd7 12.♗f4 ♘d5 13.♗d2 ♕b6 14.♖he1 (14.♘e4 ♘e5∓) 14...♗e7∓;

A2) 9.♗b3 e6

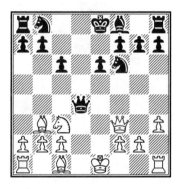

10.♗e3 (10.♗f4 ♗b4 11.♖d1 ♕e4+ or 11.0-0 ♗×c3 12.b×c3 ♕e4∓) 10...♕d8 (10...♕b4 11.0-0-0 ♘bd7 12.♖he1 ♗e7 13.♖d4 ♕a5 14.♖a4 ♕e5 15.♗d2 ♕c5 16.♗e3 ♕e5 17.♗d2 ♕c5=) 11.♖d1 ♘bd7 12.♕g3 ♗e7 13.0-0 (13.♕×g7 ♖g8 14.♕h6 ♖×g2∓) 13...0-0 14.♗h6 ♘e8 15.♘e4 ♕c8∓;

B) 7.0-0 ♗×f3?! (7...♘bd7!?; 7...e6 8.♗g5 ♗e7 9.♕d3 ♗f5 10.♕e2 0-0⇄, Witt, H. – Mook, K., Frankfurt 2005 or 9.h3?! ♗×f3 10.♕×f3 ♕×d4 11.♗b3 ♘bd7 12.♖ad1 ♕e5 13.♗f4 ♕h5∓; 8.♗e3 ♘bd7±) 8.♕×f3 ♕×d4? 9.♘b5! with a dangerous initiative:

B1) 9...c×b5 (9...♕×c4 10.♘c7+ ♔d8 11.♘×a8 ♘bd7 12.♗e3±) 10.♗×b5+ (10.♕×b7?! ♕×c4 11.♕×a8 ♕c7) 10...♘bd7 11.♕×b7 ♖d8 12.♗e3 ♕d5 13.♗c6 (13.♕×d5!? ♘×d5 14.♗×a7 e6 15.c4) 13...♕f5 14.♗×a7 e6 15.♗b6 ♗d6 16.♗×d8 ♔×d8 17.♕a8+ ♗b8 18.♖ad1 ♔e7 19.♕b7 ♖d8 20.♖d3 ♕a5 21.♗×d7 ♘×d7 22.♖×d7+ ♖×d7 23.♕×b8±;

B2) 9...♕d8 10.♗f4 c×b5 (10...♘a6 11.♖ad1 ♕c8 12.♖fe1 e6 13.♘d6+ ♗×d6 14.♗×d6±) 11.♕×b7 ♘bd7 (11...b×c4 12.♗c7 ♕d7 13.♖ad1 +− or 12...♘bd7 13.♗×d8 ♖×d8 14.♕×a7±) 12.♗×b5 ♖c8 13.♖ad1 ♖c5 14.♗a4 ♖c4 15.b4 ♕c8 (15...♖×f4 16.♖×d7 ♘×d7 17.♖d1 e5 18.♖×d7+−) 16.♕×c8+ ♖×c8 17.♖×d7 ♘×d7 18.♖d1 ♖d8 19.♗c7±;

C) 7.♗e3

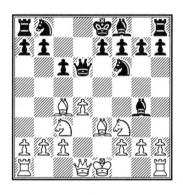

There are two main alternatives here, **C1)** 7...e6 and **C2)** 7...♘bd7.

C1) 7...e6 8.h3 ♗h5 (8...♗×f3 9.♕×f3 ♘bd7 10.0-0 ♕c7 11.♖ad1 ♗d6 12.♘e4 ♘×e4 13.♕×e4 0-0 14.♗d3 g6 15.c3 ½-½ Marciano, D. (2522) – Moldovan, D. (2411), Cannes 2005) 9.g4 (9.0-0 ♘bd7 10.♗e2 ♕c7 11.♖e1

49

♗d6 12.♘d2 ♗g6 13.♗f3 0-0 14.♘c4 ♗f4 15.g3 ♗×e3 16.♘×e3 ♖ad8∓, Traldi, P. – Melts, M., USA 1999) 9...♗g6 10.♘e5

C1a) 10...♘d5 11.♘×d5 e×d5 12.♘×g6 h×g6 13.♗b3 (13.♗d3 ♕b4+ 14.♔f1 ♕×b2 15.♖b1 ♕×a2 16.♖×b7⩱; 13...♘d7 14.c3 0-0-0=) 13...♘d7 14.♕d2 ♘f6 15.0-0-0 0-0-0 16.♗f4 ♕d7 17.f3 ♗d6 18.c3 ♖de8 19.♗c2 ♕c7 20.♗×d6 ♕×d6 21.♔h2 ♕×h2 22.♖×h2 g5=, Manolaraki, Y. (2118) – Papadopoulou, V. (2217), Ermioni 2006;

C1b) 10...♘bd7 11.f4?! ♕b4 12.♘×d7 (12.♗b3?! ♘×e5 13.d×e5 ♘e4 14.♕d4 ♖d8 15.♕×b4 ♗×b4 16.a3 ♗c5 17.♗×c5 ♘×c5∓, Fernandez Torre, I. (2183) – Vigil Alvarez, L. (2300), Oviedo 2005) 12...♕×c4 13.♘×f6+ g×f6 14.a3 h5∓, Fusi, C. (2317) – Kreindl, H. (2200), Vienna 2006;

C2) 7...♘bd7 8.h3 (8.0-0-0!?; 8.♕d2 e6 9.♗f4 ♕b4 10.♗b3 ♘d5 11.♘e5?! ♘×f4 12.♕×f4 ♘×e5 13.♕×e5 0-0-0∓, Huschenbeth, N. (2305) – Stark, L. (2430), Pardubice 2007; 11.a3 ♕b6 12.0-0-0 ♘×f4 13.♕×f4 ♘f6 14.♘e4 ♘×e4 15.♕×e4 ♗×f3 16.♕×f3 ♗e7=) and now:

C2a) 8...♗×f3 9.♕×f3

C2a1) 9...e6 10.0-0 ♘b6 11.♗b3 ♗e7 12.♘e4 ♘×e4 13.♕×e4 ♘d5 14.♗d2 ♘f6 (14...0-0-0!?; 14...0-0!?) 15.♕d3 ♖d8 16.c3 0-0 (16...e5!?) 17.♕f3 ♕c7 18.♗f4 (Sedina, E. (2371) – Hernandez Penna, S. (2158), Basel 2006) 18...♗d6 19.♗g5 ♗e7 20.♖fe1 ♘d5=;

C2a2) 9...♘b6 10.♗b3 (10.♗e2 ♕b4 11.0-0-0 ♘c4 12.♗×c4 ♕×c4 13.d5

c×d5 14.♘×d5 ♖c8⇄) 10...e6 (10...♘bd5?! 11.♘×d5 c×d5? 12.♗a4+ ♘d7 13.0-0 e6 14.c4 ♖d8 15.♖ac1 ♗e7 16.c×d5 e×d5 17.♖c5 0-0 18.♖×d5 ♕e6 19.♗b3 ♕b6 20.♖c1 ♘f6 21.♖×d8 ♖×d8 22.g4 h6 23.♕f5 a5 24.h4±, Duschek, V. (2235) – Lentrodt, T. (2285), Germany 1997; 11...♘×d5!?) 11.0-0-0 (11.♗f4 ♕×d4 12.♖d1 ♕c5∓) 11...♗e7 (11...0-0-0!?) 12.♗f4 ♕d7⇄;

C2b) 8...♗h5 9.g4 ♗g6

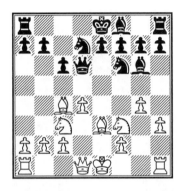

Now we examine **2b1)** 10.♕e2, **C2b2)** 10.♕d2 and **C2b3)** 10.♘h4.

C2b1) 10.♕e2 e6 11.0-0-0 ♗e7 (11...♕c7!? 12.d5 c×d5 13.♗×d5 ♖c8 14.♗b3 a6 15.♘d4 ♘c5⇄; 14.♘d4 ♘×d5 15.♘×d5 ♕a5±)

C2b1a) 12.♖he1 ♘d5 13.♗×d5?! (13.♘×d5 c×d5 14.♗b5!?) 13...c×d5 14.♕d2 (14.♘b5 ♕c6 15.♗f4 0-0 16.h4 ♖fc8∓; 14.h4 h5∓) 14...0-0 (Machalova, V. (2212) – Kantorik, M. (2330), Banska Stiavnica 2006) 15.h4 (15.♗f4 ♕a6∓) 15...♘f6 16.h5 ♗e4 17.♗f4 ♕a6 18.♘g5 ♗b4∓;

C2b1b) 12.♗b3 0-0-0 13.♘d2 ♘d5 (13...♕c7!? 14.h4 h5 15.g5 ♘d5=)

14.♘ce4 ♛c7 15.h4 (Blanco Sisniega, J. – Septien Lopez, V., Pamplona 2001) 15...h5=;

C2b2) 10.♛d2 e6 11.0-0-0 (11.♗f4 ♛b4 12.♗b3 ♗d6 13.a3 ♗xf4 14.♛xf4 ♛e7⇄) 11...♗e7 (11...♘b6!?; 11...♛b4!? 12.♘e5 ♘e4 13.♘xe4 ♗xe4 14.c3 ♛a5 15.♖he1 ♘xe5 16.dxe5 ♗d5 17.♗b3 0-0-0 18.♛d4 ♗xb3 19.♛xd8+ ♛xd8 20.♖xd8+ ♔xd8 21.axb3 ♔c7=, Rafiei, A. (2164) – Darban, M. (2397), Iran 2005)

C2b2a) 12.♗f4 ♛b4 13.♗b3 ♘b6 14.♘e5 (14.a3 ♛a5 15.♖he1? ♗xa3!∓; 15.♘e5 ♘fd5 16.♘xd5 ♛xd2+ 17.♖xd2 cxd5 18.♘xg6 hxg6=) 14...♘fd5 15.♘xd5 ♛xd2+ 16.♖xd2 cxd5 (16...exd5 17.♖e1) 17.♘xg6 hxg6=;

C2b2b) 12.♘e5 ♘xe5 (12...♘b6!?) 13.dxe5 ♛xd2+ (13...♛xe5 14.f4!? ♛c7 15.f5 exf5 16.♗f4) 14.♖xd2 ♘d5 15.♘xd5 cxd5!? (15...exd5 16.♗e2∞, Knudsen, J. –Woodworth, R., corr. 1995) 16.♗b5+ ♔d8∞;

C2b3) 10.♘h4 ♘d5 (10...♘b6!? 11.♗b3 ♘bd5 12.♘xg6 hxg6 13.♘xd5 ♘xd5 14.♛f3 e6=) 11.♘xg6 hxg6 12.♛f3 (12.♘xd5 cxd5 13.♗b3 e6 14.c3 ♛c6=) 12...e6 13.♗d2 ♘xc3 (13...♘b4!? 14.0-0-0 ♛xd4) 14.♗xc3 ♗e7 15.0-0-0 ♗g5+ 16.♗d2 (16.♔b1 ♘b6 17.♗b3 ♛f4=) 16...♗xd2+ 17.♖xd2 ♘b6 18.♗b3 ♘d5 19.♗xd5 ♛xd5=, Abdul, M. (2242) – Kulicov, O. (2407), Dubai 2006.

We return now to Charbonneau – Kamsky.

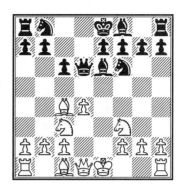

With 6...♗e6 Black plans to exchange light-squared bishops.

7.♗xe6

7.♗d3 (7.♗b3!?; for 7.♘e5 see 4.d4 ♘f6 5.♘f3 c6 6.♘e5 ♗e6 7.♗c4, Game 17) 7...♘bd7 (Schallueck, H. – Klawitter, B., Hamburg 2004) 8.0-0±; 7...♗g4 – Game 13; 7...♘a6!? 8.a3 g6.

7...♛xe6+ 8.♘e5

8.♗e3!? ♛f5 9.0-0.

7...♘bd7 9.♛e2 g6

9...♘xe5 10.dxe5 ♘d7 11.♗f4 (11.f4 g5!? 12.fxg5 ♗g7) 11...g6 12.0-0-0 ♗g7 13.♖he1 0-0-0⇄.

10.0-0

10.♗f4 0-0-0 11.♘xd7 ♛xe2+ 12.♔xe2 ♖xd7 13.♗e5 ♗g7=.

10...♗g7

10...0-0-0!? 11.♘d3 ♛xe2 12.♘xe2 ♗g7 13.♗e3 ♘d5 14.c4 ♘5b6 15.b3 e5⇄.

11.♖e1

51

11.♘xd7 ♕xd7 12.♗g5 0-0 13.♖ad1 ♖fe8 14.♖fe1 ♖ad8=.

11...0-0 12.♗g5

12...♘xe5 13.♕xe5 (13.dxe5 ♘d5 14.♘xd5 cxd5 15.♖ad1 ♖ac8 16.c3=) **13...♕xe5 14.dxe5 ♘g4 15.♗f4** (15.♗xe7?! ♖fe8 16.♗d6 ♘xe5∓) **15...f6 16.f3?!** (16.e6 f5 17.h3 ♗xc3 18.bxc3 ♘f6∞; 16.exf6 ♗xf6 17.♗g3 ♗xc3 18.bxc3 ♔f7=) **16...♘xe5 17.♖ad1 ♖fd8 18.♗xe5 fxe5∓19.♖xd8+ ♖xd8 20.♘e4 ♗h6 21.♔f2 ♔f7 22.♔e2 ♖d5 23.♖d1 ♔e8 24.♖d3 ♖a5 25.♖b3 ♖xa2?!** (25...b6∓) **26.♖xb7 ♗c1 27.b3 ♗b2 28.♖c7 ♗d4 29.♖xc6 ♗b6 30.♔d3 ♔d7 31.♖c4 ♖a1 32.♖a4 ♖d1+ 33.♔e2 ♖g1 34.g3 ♖g2+ 35.♔d3 ♖xh2 36.c4 a5 37.c5 ♗c7 38.♔c4 ♖b2 39.b4 ♖xb4+ 40.♖xb4 axb4 41.♔xb4 ♔c6 42.♔c4 ♗a5 43.♘g5 h5 44.♘f7 ♔c7 45.♔d3 ♗e1 46.♘xe5 g5 47.♘f7 ♗xg3 48.♘xg5 ♔c6 49.♔e2 ♗f4 50.♘e4 h4 51.♔f1 h3 52.♘f2 ½-½**

Summary: After 1.e4 d5 2.exd5 ♕xd5 3.♘c3 ♕a5 (or ♕d8) 4.d4 ♘f6, the natural and aggressive arrangement for White's kingside pieces is ♗c4 and ♘f3;

for example, 5.♗c4 c6 6.. ♘f3 (5.♘f3 c6 6.♗c4). The move 6...♗g4 here is good for White, but in the 3...♕d6 system, 6...♗g4 forces upon White an unwelcome choice: a) to offer an unclear gambit with 7.h3 (7.0-0) 7...♗xf3 8.♕xf3 ♕xd4; or b) to give Black, after 7.♗e3 e6 (7...♘bd7), an equal game with counterplay.

In this game **6...♗e6** was played and after **7.♗xe6 ♕xe6+**, Black had no problems. White needs to play 7.♗b3, 7.♗d3 or 7.♘e5.

Game 2
Renet, O. (2507) – Marcelin, C. (2481)
Besancon 2006

1.e4 d5 2.exd5 ♕xd5 3.♘c3 ♕d6 4.d4 ♘f6 5.♗c4 c6 6.h3

As we have seen in Game 1, after 6.♘f3 ♗g4, Black equalizes. Therefore here White tries the prophylactic h2-h3 before ♘g1-f3.

6...♗e6

With 6...♗e6 (as after 6.♘f3 ♗e6 in Game 1) Black hopes to exchange light-squared bishops to gain control of the light squares. More popular is 6...♗f5, and after 7.♘f3 we examine **A)** 7...e6 and **B)** 7...♘bd7.

A) 7...e6

A1) 8.♘h4

A1a) 8...♗g6 9.0-0 (9.a4!?) 9...♗e7 10.♘e2 (10.♘×g6 h×g6 11.a4 ±) 10...0-0 (10...♗h5!?) 11.♘×g6 h×g6 12.c3 ± , Lahno, K. (2465) – Sirotkina, N. (2275), Sochi 2007;

A1b) 8...♗×c2 9.♕×c2 ♕×d4 10.♕b3 (10.♗×e6 f×e6 11.♘f3 ♕c4 12.b3 ∞ ; 10...♕e5+?! 11.♗e3 ♕×e6 12.0-0-0) 10...b5 11.♘×b5 (11.♗×e6?! ♕e5+ 12.♗e3 ♕×e6) 11...c×b5 12.♗×b5+ ♘bd7 13.♘f3 ♕e4 ± ;

A2) 8.0-0 ♗e7 9 ♖e1 (9.♕e2 ♘bd7 10.♗g5 0-0=) 9...0-0 10. Ce2 ♕c7 (10...c5 11.c3 ♖d8 12.♗f4 ♕b6 ⇄ , Baier, S. – Bruhn, B. (2190), Berlin 1996) 11.♗f4 ♗d6 12.♗×d6 ♕×d6 13.♘g3 ♗g6 14.♕e2 ♘bd7=, Kadziolka, B. (2301) – Papadopoulou, V. (2227), Heraklio 2004);

B) 7...♘bd7.Now White should postpone the decision where to castle.

B1) 8.0-0 Both analysis and practical play indicate that kingside castling causes Black little problem. For example, 8...e6 9.a4 ♗e7 10.a5 0-0 11.♘h4 (11.♘e2 ♕c7) 11...♗g6 12.♘×g6 h×g6 13.♖e1 b5 14.♗b3 ♖fe8 15.♗g5 ♕c7 16.♕f3 ♖ac8 ⇄ , Gara, A. (2377) – Papadopoulou, V. (2267), Szombathely 2004 or 9.♖e1 ♗e7 10.♗e3 0-0 (Dichkovskij, A. (1942) – Makarevich, V. (2062), Alushta 2006; 10...♘d5!?) 11.♘h4 ♗g6 12.♘×g6 h×g6 13.♕f3 ± ;

B2) 8.♕e2

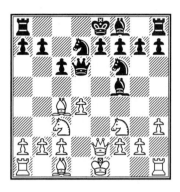

8...e6 (9...♘b6!?; 9...0-0-0? 10.♗×f7 e6 11.g4 ±) and now:

B2a) 9.♗b3 ♕c7 (9...0-0-0 10.0-0 ♗e7 11.♘e5 ♗g6 12.♖d1 ± ; 9...♗e7 10.g3 0-0 11.♗f4 ♕b4 12.g4 ♗g6 13.0-0-0 ±) 10.♗d2 ♗d6 11.0-0-0 0-0-0 (11...0-0!? 12.g4 ♗g6 13.♖dg1 b5 14.h4 b4 15.♘d1 h5 ⇄) 12.♖he1 (12.♘h4 ♗g6 13.♘×g6 h×g6 14.♕f3 ♘b6 15.♗g5 ±) 12...♘d5 (13.♘e5?! ♘×c3 14.♗×c3 ♘×e5 15.d×e5 ♗c5 ∓ , Holzhaeuer, M. (2325) – Mann, C. (2440), Germany, 1991) 13.♗×d5 e×d5 (13...c×d5?! 14.♘h4 ♗g6 15.♘×g6 h×g6 16.♘b5) 14.♘h4 ♗g6 15.♘×g6 h×g6 16.♕f3 ♘b6 17.♘e2 ♘c4 18.♗f4=;

B2b) 9.♗g5 sets Black more problems than 9.♗b3. With it White envisions a potentially dangerous plan of 0-0-0, followed by g2-g4 or ♘f3-e5. But if Black plays with caution (always useful in chess) it need not be feared. Some samples lines after 9.♗g5:

B2b1) 9...♗e7 (10...0-0-0?! 11.♘e5 ♗g6 12.♗f4 ♕b4? 13.♘×c6! +– ; 10...0-0?! 11.g4 ♗g6 12.♘e5 ♘b6 13.h4) 10.0-0-0 ♘b6 11.♘h4 (11.♘e5 h6 12.♗f4 ♘×c4 13.♕×c4 ♕b4=)

11...♘×c4 12.♕×c4 (12.♘×f5? ♕b4−+)
12...♗g6 (12...♗e4 13.♘×e4? ♘×e4
14.♗×e7 ♕×e7∓) 13.♘×g6 h×g6=;

B2b2) 9...h6 10.♗h4 (10.♗×f6 ♘×f6
11.d5 c×d5 12.♗b5+ ♔d8 13.♘e5
♕c7∞) 10...♘d5 11.♘×d5 (11.♗×d5!?
c×d5 12.0-0) 11...c×d5 12.♗b5
(12.♗b3!?) 12...a6 13.♗×d7+ ♕×d7=,
Brustkern, J. (2215) – Muse, D. (2315),
Berlin 1995;

B2b3) 9...♕c7 10.♘h4 (10.0-0-0 b5
11.♗d3 ♗×d3 12.♖×d3 ♗d6=)
10...♗g6 11.♘×g6 h×g6 12.0-0-0 0-0-0
13.♘e4 ♘b6 14.♗b3 (14.♘×f6 g×f6
15.♗×f6? ♕f4+ 16.♔b1 ♕×f6−+)
14...♗e7=.

We return now to Renet – Marcelin.

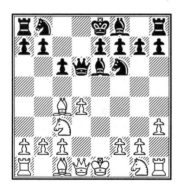

7.♗b3

After 7.♗×e6 ♕×e6+ Black equalizes
as in Game 1.

7...♘bd7

7...♘a6 8.♘f3 ♗×b3 (8...g6 9.0-0 ♗×b3
10.a×b3 ♗g7 11.♗g5 0-0 12.♕d2±)
9.a×b3 e6 10.♗g5 ♗e7 11.0-0 ♘b4
12.♗×f6 (12.♘e5 0-0 13.♗×f6 g×f6
14.♘c4 ♕c7 15.♕d2 ♔h8 16.♘e3

♖fd8 17.♖fe1 f5⇄) 12...g×f6 13.♘e4
♕f4 14.♖e1 (Buchal, S. (2295) – Alber,
H. (2335), Hessen 1992) 14...♖g8⇄.

8.♘f3 ♗×b3

8...g6 9.0-0 ♗×b3 10.a×b3 ♗g7
11.♗g5 0-0 12.♖e1 ♘b6 13.♕d2±.

9.a×b3 e6 10.0-0 ♕c7

10...♗e7 11.♕d3 0-0 12.♖e1 ♕c7±.

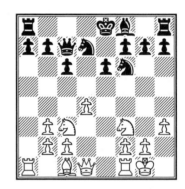

11.♕e2

11.♕d3 ♗d6 12.♘g5 (12.♗g5 0-0
13.♖fe1 ♖fe8 ⇄) 12...0-0 13.♗d2 h6
(13...♖fd8!?) 14.♘ge4 ♗e7 15.♖fe1
a5⇄.

11...♗d6 12.♘e4

12.♘d2 0-0 13.♘c4 ♗f4 14.♗×f4 ♕×f4
15.♕e3 ♕c7 16.♖fd1 ♘d5 17.♕d3
♘7b6=.

12...♗f4 (12...♘×e4 13.♕×e4 ♘f6
14.♕h4 h6 15.♗g5 ♘d7 16.♗d2 0-0
17.♖fe1 ♖fd8 18.c4±; 14...0-0!?)
13.♘×f6+ ♘×f6 14.♗×f4 (14.♘e5
♗×c1 15.♖f×c1 0-0 16.c3 ♘d7 17.♘×d7
♕×d7 18.♖a5±) **14...♕×f4 15.b4**
(15.♖a4!? ♕d6 16.♘e5) **15...0-0**

16.♕e5 ♕e4 (16...♞d5 17.♕×f4 ♞f4
18.♖fe1 ♖fd8 19.g3 ♞d5 20.c3±)
**17.♕×e4 ♞×e4 18.♖fe1 ♞d6
19.♞e5 ♖fd8 20.c3 a6 21.f3 ♖ac8
22.♔f2 ♖c7 23.♖e2 ♖e7 24.♖ae1
g6 25.g4 ♔g7 26.♔g3 ♖a8 27.♖a1
♖c7 28.h4 ♖h8 29.♞d3 ♖e7
30.♖h1 h6 31.h5 g5 32.♞e5 ♞e8
33.♖f1 ♞f6 34.f4 g×f4+ 35.♖×f4
♞d7 36.♞f3 ½-½**

Summary: After **1.e4 d5 2.e×d5
♕×d5 3.♞c3 ♕d6 4.d4 ♞f6
5.♗c4 c6**, White sometimes plays the
prophylactic 6.h3, followed by ♞g1-f3.
After 6.h3 Black has two good possibilities: 6...♗f5 and 6...♗e6.

After 6...♗f5 7.♞f3 the move 7...♞bd7
is more flexible than 7...e6. White then
has two alternatives: 8.0-0 or 8.♕e2.
After 8.0-0 Black usually has an equal
game. 8.♕e2, intending 0-0-0, is the
more aggressive move. Also important
is the fact that by 8.♕e2 White defends
the ♗c4 and gains extra control of e5
for an eventual ♞f3-e5.

With 6...♗e6 (as after 6.♞f3 ♗e6 in
Game 1) Black hopes to gain control of
the light squares, and has an equal
game.

In sum, the prophylactic 6.h3 is not very
dangerous for Black (a tempo is a
tempo!), but Black must play actively
and not assume equality will come by
itself!

Game 3
Prlac, V. (2115) – Jukic, Z. (2315)
Sibenik 2007

**1.e4 d5 2.e×d5 ♕×d5 3.♞c3 ♕d6
4.d4 ♞f6 5.♗c4 c6 6.♞ge2**

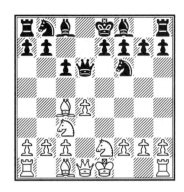

6...♗g4

6...♗f5 – Game 4. Other interesting alternatives are **A)** 6...♞bd7 and **B)**
6...♗e6.

A) 6...♞bd7?! 7.♗f4 ♕b4 8.♗b3
(Carstensen, T. – Wichmann, D., Hamburg 2005) 8...♞b6 9.0-0 ♗f5?!
(9...♞bd5 10.♞×d5 ♞×d5 11.c3 ♕a5
12.♗e5±) 10.♞g3 ♗g6 11.a3 ♕a5
12.♗d2 ♕a6 (12...0-0-0? 13.♞ce4 ♕b5
14.a4 ♕a6 15.♞c5+−) 13.f4 e6 14.f5
♗×f5 (14...e×f5 15.♕e1+ ♔d7
16.♞×f5±) 15.♞×f5 e×f5 16.♕e1+ ♗e7
(16...♔d7 17.♗×f7±) 17.♖×f5±;

B) 6...♗e6 7.♗f4 ♕d7 8.♗×e6 ♕×e6

B1) 9.0-0 ♕d7 10.♞g3 e6 11.♞ce4
♗e7 12.♞×f6+ g×f6 13.♕g4 ♞a6
14.♕g7 0-0-0 (14...♖f8? 15.♖ad1 0-0-0
16.c4 ♞c7 17.♕×h7±, Nedev, T. (2480)
– Zatonskih, A. (2417), USA 2003)
15.c3 ♖df8∞; 12...♗×f6!?

B2) 9.♕d3 ♞bd7 10.0-0-0 ♞b6
11.♖he1 0-0-0 12.♞g1 ♕g4
(12...♞d7!? 13.♞f3 e6 14.♞e5 ♕e8±)
13.♗g3 e6 14.♞f3 ♗d6?! (Oral, T.
(2565) – Nedela, V. (2374), Czechia

2005) 15.♗×d6 ♖×d6 16.♘e5 ♕h5 (16...♕f4+ 17.♕e3 ♕×e3+ 18.♖×e3 ♖f8 19.♖g3 ♘e8 20.♘e4 ♖d5 21.♘g5±; 19...g6 20.♖f3±) 17.♕g3 ♘e8 18.♘e4 ♖d5 (18...♖d8 19.♕g5±) 19.♕a3 ♔b8 (19...a6 20.♘×c6±) 20.c4 ♖d8 21.♕e7±; 14...♘fd5?! 15.♘e5 ♕h5 16.♘×d5 ♖×d5 17.♘×c6± or 16...e×d5?/16...♖×d5? 17.♕f3±; 14...♕h5≠.

Back to Prlac – Jukic.

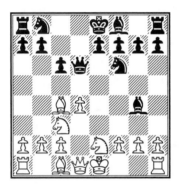

7.f3

7.♗f4?! ♗×e2 8.♕d2 ♗×c4 9.♗×d6 e×d6 10.0-0-0 ♗e7 11.♖he1 ♗e6∓; 7.0-0!?; 7.♕d3!?.

7...♗f5

An interesting alternative is 7...♗h5 (7...♗e6?! 8.♗f4 ♕d7 9.♗×e6 ♕×e6 10.0-0 with the better game for White, Quadrio, A. (2210) – Correia, M., Lisbon 1996; 10.♕d3!?)

A) 8.0-0 ♘bd7 9.♗f4

A1) 9...e6 10.♘×h5 ♘×h5 11.♘e4 ♕c7 12.♕e1 ♘b6 (12...0-0-0? 13.♘g5 ♘b6 14.♘×f7±) 13.♗b3 ♗e7 (13...0-0-0?! 14.♕a5) 14.♕a5 ♘d5 15.♕×c7 ♘×c7 16.c4 with the better ending;

A2) 9...♗g6 10.♘×g6 h×g6 11.g3. White has a better game thanks to the two bishops and the f3-pawn which controls e4.Note that if Black becomes overly aggressive, White could get a serious advantage; for example, 11...e5?! 12.♗e3 ♘b6 13.d×e5 ♕×d1 (13...♕×e5? 14.♗×b6) 14.♖a×d1 ♘×c4 15.e×f6 ♘×e3 (15...g×f6 16.♖fe1 or 16.♗d4) 16.♖fe1 ♗c5 17.f×g7 ♖g8 18.♘a4± or 11...♘h5?! 12.♘e4 ♕c7 13.♕e2 e6 14.a4 0-0-0 15.♘g5 ♘c5 (15...♘b6 16.♘×f7±) 16.c3 (16.d×c5? ♘×g3±) 16...f6 17.b4±;

B) 8.♗f4 and now:

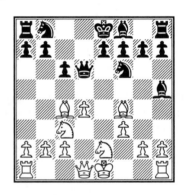

B1) 8...♕b4 9.♗b3 e6

B1a) 10.a3 (10.♕d2 ♘bd7 11.0-0-0 (Checiak, K. – Liszka, Z. (2250), Warsaw 1999) 11...0-0-0⇄; 11.♗c7!?) 11...♘bd7 12.0-0-0 ♗g6 13.♔b1 (13.g4? ♗×a3!, Srebrnic M. (2196) – Kovac L., Slovenia 2002) 13...0-0-0⇄;

B1b) 10.0-0 ♘bd7 11.♗c7 ♘b6 12.♘f4 ♗g6 13.♖e1 ♗e7 14.a3 ♕a5 15.♕e2 0-0 (15...♖c8!? 16.♗e5 0-0) 16.♘×e6 ♖fe8 (Cornette, M. (2409) – Debray, T. (2088), Reims 2004) 17.♘d8 ♕h5 (17...♗×d8? 18.♕×e8+ ♘×e8 19.♖×e8#; 17...h6? 18.♘×b7±;

17...♗d6 18.♕xe8+ ♘xe8 19.♖xe8+
♗f8 20.♗d6±) 18.♘xb7 ♗xa3 19.♕d2
♗xb2 20.♖ab1=;

B2) 8...♕d8

B2a) 9.♗e5 ♘bd7 10.♘f4 e6 11.♕e2
♕a5 (Mengarini, A. – Schiller, E., New
York 1980) 12.♗xf6 (12.0-0-0 0-0-0 ⇄)
12...♘xf6 13.♘xe6 fxe6 14.♕xe6+ ♗e7
15.0-0-0 ♖f8 16.♖he1 ♕c7∞;

B2b) 9.0-0 (9.♕d2!?; 9.h4!?) 9...e6
10.♖e1 ♗d6 11.♕d2 0-0 12.♖ad1 ♘d5
(12...♗g6!?) 13.♗xd6 ♕xd6 14.♘e4
♕e7 15.♗b3 ♘d7 16.c4 ♘5b6 17.♘f4
♗g6 (Sammalvuo, T. – Lampen, T.,
Vantaa 1991) 18.c5 ♘d5 19.♗xd5 cxd5
20.♘d6±.

We return now to Prlac – Jukic.

8.♗b3

Other interesting possibilities are **A)**
8.0-0 and **B)** 8.♗f4.

A) 8.0-0 e6 9.♗f4 (9.♘g3? ♗xc2;
9.♗d3 ♗xd3 10.♕xd3 ♘bd7 11.♗f4
♕b4 12.♘e4 0-0-0? 13.a3 ♕a5 14.♘g5
♘c5 15.♕d1±, Ochoa, A. – Stuart, K.,
Internet 2003; 12...♘xe4=) 9...♕d8
10.♕d2 ♗d6 11.♘g3?! ♗xc2!;

10...♘bd7 11.♘g3 ♗g6 12.♗b3 ♗e7
13.♘ce4 ♘xe4 14.♘xe4 (Rolletschek,
H. (2320) – Weiss, C. (2290), Linz
1996) 14...♘f6 15.♖ae1 0-0 16.♗e5
♕b6⇄;

B) 8.♗f4

B1) 8...♕b4 9.♗b3

B1a) 9...♘bd7 10.0-0 e6 11.a3
(11.♗c7 ♕e7 12.♘g3 ♗g6 13.♕d2
♘c5 14.♗e5 0-0-0 15.♕f4 ♘xb3
16.axb3 a6 17.♘a4 ♕b4 18.c4 h5⇄;
18...♕xb3?! 19.♗c7) 11...♕a5 (11...♕b6!?
12.♘g3 ♗g6 13.♘ge4 0-0-0) 12.♘g3
♗g6 13.♕e2 0-0-0 14.♗c4 ♕b6⇄,
Berry, F. – McCartney, P. (1997),
Charleston 2004;

B1b) 9...e6

B1b1) 10.a3 ♕a5 11.0-0 (11.♕d2 ♘a6
12.♘g3 ♗g6 13.♘ge4 ♖d8 14.♘xf6+
gxf6 15.♘e2 ♕b6 16.♗e3 ♕b5 17.♘c3
♕a5⇄, Zelenika, S. (2286) – Muse, D.
(2372), Pula 1999) 11...♗e7
(11...♘bd7 12.♔h1 ♘d5 13.♗d2 ♕c7
14.♘e4 ♗e7 15.c4 ♘5f6 16.♗f4±,
Ewald, M. – Gergs, F., Germany 1996)
12.♘g3 0-0? (12...♗g6) 13.d5!
(13.♘xf5 ♕xf5=) 13...♘xd5 14.♘xd5
cxd5 15.♘xf5 exf5 16.♗xd5±,
Chervonov, I. – Gubnitsky, S., Kiev
1967;

B1b2) 10.0-0 ♕a5 (10...♘d5? 11.♘xd5
cxd5 12.♘g3 ♗g6 13.♗xb8! ♖xb8
14.f4 ♗e7 15.f5 exf5 16.c3 ♕d6
17.♘xf5 ♗xf5 18.♖xf5±,
Solodovnichenko, Y. (2507) –
Blanchard, J. (2236), Haarlem 2004;
10...♗e7 11.♘g3 ♗g6 12.♘ce4 0-0
13.c3 ♕a5 14.♕e2 ♘d5 15.♗d2 ♕c7
16.f4 ♖e8=, Lacasa Diaz, J. (2335) –

De la Riva Aguado, J. (2345), Spain 1994) 11.♘g3 ♗g6 12.♘ce4 (Westerinen, H. (2386) – Fries Nielsen, J. (2356), Gausdal 2006) 12...♘bd7 13.♘d6+ ♗×d6 14.♗×d6 0-0-0 15.c3 ♘b6=;

B1b3) 10.♕d2

B1b3a) 10...♗e7 11.♗c7 (11.g4 ♗g6 12.0-0-0 ♘bd7 13.h4 h5⇄, Ayas Fernandez, A. (2325) – De la Riva Aguado, J. (2280), Spain 1996) 11...b6 12.g4 ♗g6 13.h4 h6?! (13...h5 ⇄) 14.♘f4 ♗h7 (14...♘d5 15.a3 ♕a5 16.♘×g6 f×g6 17.♗×d5 c×d5 18.♕e3±) 15.g5 ♘d5 16.♘f×d5 c×d5 17.g×h6 g×h6 18.0-0-0 ♘d7 19.♕f4 (19.♕×h6 ♖c8 20.♕f4 ♕a5 21.♗×d5 ♗b4∞) 19...♕a5 (19...♖c8 20.♖he1±) 20.♖de1 ♖c8 (20...♘f6 21.♗e5) 21.♘×d5±;

B1b3b) 10...♗d6 11.a3 (11.g4!? ♗g6 12.a3 ♗×f4 13.♘×f4 with the idea h2-h4-h5) 11...♗×f4 12.♕×f4 (12.♘×f4!? ♕d6 13.g4 ♗g6 14.h4±) 12...♕b6!? (12...♕a5 13.♘g3 ♗g6 14.♘ge4 ♘×e4 15.f×e4±, Homuth, M. – Mueller, R., Germany 1990) 13.0-0-0 (13.♘g3 ♗×c2 14.♗×c2 ♕×b2∞) 13...0-0 14.♘g3 ♗g6 15.♘ge4 ♘bd7=;

B1b4) 10.g4 ♗g6 11.h4 h6 (11...h5!?) 12.♗d2 (12.♗c7 ♘a6 13.a3 ♕e7

14.♗g3 0-0-0 15.♕d2 ♕d7 16.0-0-0 ♘c7=) 12...♕d6 13.♘f4 ♗h7 14.♕e2 ♗e7 15.0-0-0 ♘d5? (15...♘bd7 16.g5 ♘d5 17.♘f×d5 c×d5 18.g×h6 g×h6⇄) 16.♘h5 ♘×c3 17.♗×c3 ♗f6 18.f4 ♗g6 19.♘×f6+ g×f6 20.f5 1-0, Olsson, A. (2416) – Jaderberg, B. Sweden 2005;

B2) 8...♕d8

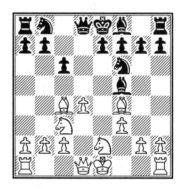

B2a) 9.♕d2 e6

B2a1) 10.h4 (10.0-0-0 – 8.0-0 e6 9.♗f4 ♕d8 10.♕d2) 10...h5 11.a3 ♘bd7 12.0-0-0 ♘b6 13.♗d3 ♗×d3 14.♕×d3 ♘bd5 15.♗g5 ♗e7 16.♔b1 ♕a5 17.♗d2 ♕c7 18.♘e4 b5⇄, Litvin, G. – Gubnitsky, S., Kharkov 1971;

B2a2) 10.0-0-0 ♘bd7 11.g4 ♗g6 12.h4 h5 (12...h6 13.♗g3 14.♗b3 ♘bd5 15.a3 ♗d6∞, Kosikov, A. (2420) – Gergel, V. (2305), Smolensk 1991 or 14.♗d3 ♗×d3 15.♕×d3 ♗d6 16.g5 ♘fd5 17.♘e4 ♗×g3 18.♘2×g3 ♕c7 19.♘h5 ♘f4=) 13.♗g5 h×g4 14.f×g4 b5 15.♗b3? (15.♗d3) 15...b4 16.♘a4 ♘e4 17.♕e3 ♘×g5 18.h×g5 ♖×h1 19.♖×h1 ♗e7∓, Rotshtein, E. – Gubnitsky, S., Berdiansk 1970;

B2b) 9.♘g3 ♗g6

B2b1) 10.h4 h5 (10...h6!?) 11.♕d2 e6

12.0-0-0 (Low, S. – Fletcher, J., Perth, 1994) 12...♗b4 13.a3 ♗×c3 (13...♗a5 14.♗g5±; 13...♗e7!?) 14.♕×c3 ♘d5 15.♗×d5 c×d5 16.♕b4 ♕d7 17.♗×b8 ♖×b8 18.♘e2 f6 19.♘c3±.

B2b2) 10.0-0 e6 (10...♗×c2 11.♗×f7+ ♔×f7 12.♕×c2 ♕d4+ 13.♔h1 e6 14.♘ce4⩲ or 13...♕×f4 14.♕b3+ e6 15.♕×b7+ ♘bd7 16.♕×a8±) 11.♕d2 (11.♘ce4!?)

B2b2a) 11...♗×c2 12.♘b5 c×b5 13.♗×b5+ ♘c6 14.♗×c6+ (14.♖ac1 ♗g6 15.♖×c6 b×c6 16.♗×c6+♘d7−+) 14...b×c6 15.♕×c2 ♕d4+ 16.♔h1 ♖c8∞;

B2b2b) 11...♗d6 12.♗×d6 ♕×d6 13.f4 (13.♘ce4!? ♘×e4 14.f×e4 ♘d7 15.♕f2 0-0-0 16.e5 ♕c7 17.c3 ♘b6=) 13...♗×c2 (13...0-0 14.f5 e×f5 15.♘×f5 ♗×f5 16.♖×f5 ♘bd7=) 14.♖ac1 ♗f5 15.♘×f5 e×f5 16.♕e1+ ♔f8 (16...♕e7 17.d5) 17.♕e5⩲;

Back to Prlac – Jukic.

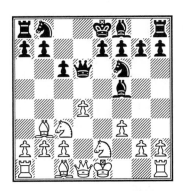

8...e6

8...♘bd7 9.♗f4 ♕b4 – 8.♗f4 ♕b4 9.♗b3 ♘bd7

9.♗f4 ♕d8

9...♕d7!? 10.h4 (10.♘g3 ♗g6 11.0-0 ♘a6 12.♕d2 0-0-0 13.♖ad1 ♗d6⇄) 10...h5 11.♘g3 ♗g6 12.♕d2 ♘a6 13.0-0-0 0-0-0 14.a3 ♘d5⇄.

10.♘g3 ♗g6 11.♘ce4

11.0-0 ♗d6 12.♗×d6 (12.♕d2 ♗×f4 13.♕×f4 0-0 14.♖ad1 ♘d5⇄) 12...♕×d6 13.♘ge4 ♕e7 14.a4 ♘bd7 15.a5 0-0 16.♕e2 ♖fd8 17.a6 b6=.

11...♘d5

11...♘bd7!? 12.0-0 h5 13.♘d6+ ♗×d6 14.♗×d6 ♘b6 15.♗e5 (15.♗c5 h4 16.♘e2 ♕c7 17.♕d2 h3 18.g3 0-0-0 ⇄) 15...♘bd7 16.f4?! (16.♗f4=) 16...h4 17.♘e2 h3 18.g3 ♕e7∓.

12.♗d2 ♘d7

12...♗e7 13.♕e2 h5 14.0-0-0 b5 (14...♕c7 15.♔b1 h4 16.♘f1 ♘d7=)

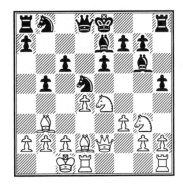

A) 15.a4 a6 16.h4 0-0 17.f4 ♕b6 (17...♗×h4?! 18.♘×h5 ♘d7 19.♖h3 ♗e7 20.♖dh1 ±) 18.f5 (18.♘×h5? b×a4 19.♗×d5 c×d5 20.♘c5 a3 21.b×a3 ♘c6∓) 18...e×f5 19.♘g5?! (19.♘c3 ♘×c3 20.♗×c3⇄) 19...♖e8 20.♕f2 (20.♘×h5 b×a4 21.♗×a4 ♘c3∓) 20...b×a4 21.♗×a4 f4 22.♘e2 (22.♗×f4 ♕a5∓) 22...♗f6∓;

B) 15.h4 ♘d7 (15...♗xh4? 16.♖xh4
♛xh4 17.♗g5 ♛h2 18.♖h1±) 16.f4
♘7b6 (16...♗xh4?! 17.f5) 17.♖df1 0-0
18.f5 (18.♘xh5?! a5 19.a3 a4 20.♗a2
b4⯑) 18...exf5 19.♘xf5 ♖e8 (19...a5?!
20.g4) 20.♛f3 a5 21.a3 a4 22.♗a2
♘c4⇄.

**13.♛e2 ♗e7 14.c4 ♘5f6 15.♗c3
♛c7 16.0-0**

16.h4 0-0-0 (16...h5!? 17.0-0-0 0-0-0)
17.h5 ♘e4 18.♘xe4 ♗f5 19.0-0-0
h6⇄.

16...0-0 (16...h5!?) **17.♖ad1 ♖fe8
18.♖fe1 ♖ad8 19.♗c2 ♘f8?!**

19...♘xe4 20.♘xe4 (20.fxe4 ♗h4
21.♛g4 ♗e7 22.♖f1 b5=) 20...♘f6
21.b3 ♘xe4 22.♗xe4 (22.fxe4 b5
23.cxb5 cxb5∓) 22...♗xe4 23.♛xe4
♗d6 24.g3 ♛e7 25.♔g2 ♛f6 26.f4
h5⇄.

20.♘xf6+ ♗xf6 21.♘e4 ♗xe4
(21...♘d7 22.♘xf6+ ♘xf6±) **22.♛xe4**
(22.fxe4!? e5 23.d5 ♗e7 24.♖f1 ♛b6+
25.♔h1) **22...♘g6 23.g3 ♘f8?!**
(23...c5 24.d5 ♗xc3 25.bxc3 ♖e7
26.♛d3 ♖d6 27.f4± or 26...exd5
27.cxd5 ♖xe1+ 28.♖xe1 c4 29.♛e3
♛a5=; 29.♛d4 ♘e7 30.f4 b5 31.♗e4±)
24.♔g2 g6 25.♛e3 ♗g7 (25...b5

26.cxb5 cxb5 27.♗d3 ♛b6 28.♛d2
♖d5 29.♗e4 ♖d7 30.a3 ♖c8⇄ or
26.c5 a5 27.a3 ♘d7 28.♛f2 ♗g7⇄)
26.b3 c5 (26...♘d7 27.♗b4 ♗f8
28.♗d2 ♗g7 29.♛f2 b5?! 30.♗f4 e5
31.dxe5 ♗xe5 32.♗g5; 29...♘f6± or
27.h4 h5 28.♖d2 ♔h7 29.♖ed1 ♗h6
30.f4 ♗g7 31.♗d3 ♔g8 32.♗e4 ♘f6
33.♗f3 ♛b6±; 29.♖de2!?) **27.dxc5
♗xc3 28.♛xc3 ♛xc5 29.b4 ♛c7
30.f4?!** (30.c5±) **30...♖xd1
31.♗xd1** (31.♖xd1 e5 32.f5 e4
33.fxg6 hxg6⇄; or 32.fxe5 ♖xe5
33.♔f2 b6 34.a3 ♘e6⇄) **31...♖c8
32.♗e2 ♘d7 33.♖c1?!** (33.♖d1±)
33...♘b6?! (33...e5 34.fxe5 ♘xe5
35.c5 ♛c6+ 36.♗f3 ♘xf3 37.♛xf3 ♖d8
38.♛xc6 bxc6 39.a4 a6=) **34.a3 ♘d5
35.♛d4 b6 36.♗f3 ♘e7 37.c5
♘f5?!** (37...♖d8!? 38.♛c3 bxc5)
**38.♛c3 ♖d8 39.♖d1 ♖xd1
40.♗xd1 h5 41.♗f3 bxc5 42.bxc5**
½-½

Summary: After **1.e4 d5 2.exd5
♛xd5 3.♘c3 ♛d6 4.d4 ♘f6
5.♗c4 c6 6.♘ge2**, there are two natural replies that provide Black with
counterplay, 6...♗f5 (Game 4), and
6...♗g4. After 6...♗g4, White's best
alternative is **7.f3**, controlling e4. Black
can reply either 7...♗f5 or 7...♗h5.

On h5 the bishop is out of play; even if
it is not threatened Black will eventu-
ally have to spend a tempo bringing it
to g6. One of White's dangerous plans
consists of ♗f4, then ♘e2-f4, g2-g4,
h2-h4-h5 etc.

After 7...♗f5 8.♗f4, Black must choose
between 8...♛d8 and the more adven-
turous 8...♛b4. In both cases White has
an edge in development and Black must
play very precisely, especially on

8...♛b4, when the queen can sometimes be vulnerable.

6...♗e6 is playable, but White has better chances after 7.♗f4 ♛d7 8.♗×e6 ♛×e6.

Game 4
Jenni, F. (2540) – Ekstroem, R. (2465)
Samnaun 2008

1.e4 d5 2.e×d5 ♛×d5 3.♘c3 ♛d6 4.d4 ♘f6 5.♗c4 c6 6.♘ge2 ♗f5

7.♗f4

The main alternative is 7.0-0. After 7...e6 (7...♘bd7 8.♗f4 ♛b4 9.♗b3 e6 – 7.♗f4 ♛b4 8.♗b3 e6 9.0-0 ♘bd7) 8.♘g3 (8.♗f4 ♛d8 9.♘g3 ♗g6 – 7...♛d8 8.♘g3 ♗g6 9.0-0 e6) 8...♗g6 9.f4 (9.♘ce2 ♘bd7 10.♗b3 0-0-0 11.♗f4 ♛b4⇄, Del Rio Angelis S. (2489) – Pinheiro J. (2339), Leon. 2001; 11...e5!?), we examine the following possibilities: **A)** 9...♛d7 and **B)** 9...♗×c2.

A) 9...♛d7 10.f5 e×f5 11.♗g5 (11.♛d3!? f4 12.♘ge4) 11...♗e7 12.♗×f6 ♗×f6 13.♛e1+ ♛e7 (13...♚f8!? 14.♖d1 ♘a6) 14.♘×f5 ♗×f5 15.♖×f5 ♗×d4+ (15...♘d7!?) 16.♚h1 f6

17.♘e4 ♗e5 18.♖×e5 (18.♖d1 ♘d7 19.♛a5 with a strong initiative, Al Modiahki, M. (2528) – Cicak, S. (2490), Benasque 1999) 18...♛×e5 (18...f×e5 19.♖d1 ♘d7 20.♘d6+ ♚d8 21.♗a6!) 19.♛b4 ♘d7 20.♘d6+ ♚e7 21.♖d1 with an attack or 10...♗×f5 11.♘×f5 e×f5 12.♛d3 g6 (12...♘a6!? 13.♖×f5 ♗e7 14.a3 ♘c7 15.♗e3 0-0 16.♖af1 ♘cd5±) 13.♗g5 (13.♖e1+!?) 13...♗e7 14.♖ae1 0-0 15.g4⊞, Hoffmann, M. (2435) – Cicak, S. (2490), Sitges 1999;

B) 9...♗×c2 10.♛d2 ♗f5 (10...♘bd7!? 11.f5 0-0-0 12.f×e6 f×e6 13.♗×e6 ♛×e6 14.♛×c2 ♛c4⇄) 11.♘×f5 e×f5 12.♖e1+ ♗e7 (Iliopoulos, A. (2084) – Nikolaidis, I. (2516), Korinthos 2004) 13.♖e5 (13.♛e2!? ♛×d4+?! 14.♗e3; 13...0-0∞) 13...♘bd7 14.♖×f5 0-0⇄ or 10.♛e2 ♗e7 11.f5 ♛×d4+ (11...b5 12.♘×b5 c×b5 13.♗×b5+ ♘bd7 14.♛×c2 ♛×d4+ 15.♚h1±) 12.♗e3 (12.♚h1 ♛g4 13.♖f3 e5∞, Charbonneau, P. (2485) – Zatonskih, A. (2436), Reykjavik 2004) 12...♛e5 (12...♛g4? 13.♛×c2 ♛×c4 14.♖f4 ♛a6 15.♖a4+−) 13.f×e6 f×e6 14.♖ae1 ♗g6 15.♛d1∞.

We return now to Jenni – Ekstroem.

7...♕b4

After 7...♕d8 we have **A)** 8.♘g3; **B)** 8.d5 and **C)** 8.0-0.

A) 8.♘g3 ♗g6 9.h4 (9.0-0 e6 – 8.0-0 e6 9.♘g3 ♗g6; 9.♕e2!? ♕xd4 10.♗e3 ♕g4 11.f3 ♕c8 12.0-0-0 ♘bd7 13.f4 ♘b6 14.♗xb6 axb6 15.♘b5 e6 16.♕e5 with a very strong initiative, Llaneza Vega, P. (2280) – Schmidt, R. (2160), Budapest 2008; 9...e6 10.0-0-0 ♘d5±) 9...h6 (9...h5!?) 10.h5 (10.♕e2!?) 10...♗h7

A1) 11.♕e2 e6 (11.♕e2!? ♕xd4 12.♗e5⩲) 12.0-0-0 ♘d5 13.♘xd5 cxd5 14.♗d3 ♗xd3 15.♖xd3 ♗d6 16.♗d2 0-0 17.♕g4 ♔h8 18.f4 f5 19.c4 ♗xf4 20.♕e2 ♗d6 21.♕g4 f4=, Jordanova, S. (2230) – Gheorghe, C. (2257), Vratsa 2006;

A2) 11.♗e5 ♘bd7 12.♕e2 e6 13.0-0-0 ♕a5 14.f4 (14.♗xf6 ♘xf6 15.♗xe6 fxe6 16.♕xe6+ ♗e7 17.♖he1 ♕c7 18.♖d2∞) 14...0-0-0 15.f5 ♘xe5 16.dxe5 ♘d5 17.♗xd5 (17.♘xd5 cxd5 18.♗b3 ♗e7 19.♔b1 ♗g5 20.♕g4 ♖he8 21.♖d4 ♔b8⇄, Gerber, P. (2245) – Braun, G. (2330), Germany 1996) 17...exd5 (17...cxd5 18.fxe6 fxe6 19.♕g4±) 18.♕g4 ♔b8 19.♖he1 ♖g8⇄;

A3) 11.d5 cxd5 (11...b5?! 12.♗b3 b4 13.dxc6 ♘xc6 14.♗a4 ♕b6 15.♘d5 ♘xd5 16.♕xd5 ♖c8 17.0-0-0) 12.♘xd5 ♘xd5 13.♗xd5 ♘c6 14.0-0 e6 15.♗e4 ♕xd1 (15...♕f6 16.♕f3 ♗xe4 17.♘xe4 ♕xb2 18.♖ab1 ♕a3 19.♖b3 ♕a6 20.♖d1 ♖d8 21.♗d6⩲) 16.♖fxd1 ♗xe4 17.♘xe4 ♖d8 18.♗d6 (18.♘d6+ ♗xd6 19.♗xd6±) 18...♗e7 19.c4 0-0 20.♗xe7 ♘xe7±;

B) 8.d5 cxd5 9.♘xd5 ♘xd5 10.♕xd5 ♕xd5 11.♗xd5 ♘c6 12.0-0-0

B1) 12...♖c8 13.♗xc6+ (Wach, M. (2381) – Velicka, P. (2464), Bayen 2000) 13...bxc6 14.♖he1 ♗g6 15.♘d4 e6± or 14.♘d4 ♗d7 15.♖he1 c5±; 13.♘g3 ♗g6 14.♖he1 ♘b4 15.c3± or 14.c3 e6±;

B2) 12...e6 (13...f6 14.♘d4 ♘xd4 15.♖xd4 e5 16.♗xb7 ♖b8 17.♗c6+ ♔f7 18.♗d5+ ♔g6 19.g4∞, Medvegy, N. (2388) – Johansson, T. (2212), Cork 2005) 13.♗xc6+ (13.♗f3 ♗c5 14.♘g3 ♗g6 15.♖d2 ♖d8 16.♖hd1 ♖xd2 17.♖xd2±) 13...bxc6 14.♘d4 ♗g6 15.♖he1±.

C) 8.0-0

8...e6 9.♘g3 (9.♗d3 ♗xd3 10.♕xd3 ♗e7 11.♖fe1 0-0 12.♗g5 ♘bd7 13.♘g3 ♖e8 14.♖ad1 ♕b6 15.♗d2 ♖ad8 16.♘a4 ♕c7 17.c4 a6⇄, Montheard, X. (2220) – Pytel, K. (2380), Saint Quentin 1998; 13...♕b6!? 14.♘f5 exf5 15.♖xe7 ♖fe8⇄) 9...♗g6.

Now we examine **C1)** 10.♗e5; **C2)** 10.♕d2 and **C3)** 10.♖e1.

C1) 10.♗e5 ♘bd7 11.♕e2 ♗b4 (11...♗e7 12.♗b3 0-0 13.f4 ♕a5 14.f5 e×f5 15.♘×f5 ♗b4 ⇄, Sperdokli, E. (2129) – Papadopoulou, V. (2217), Athens 2006) 12.♘ce4 (12.♖ad1!?) 12...♘×e4 13.♘×e4 ♘×e5 14.d×e5 ♛d4 15.♘g5 ♛f4 16.♘f3 ♗h5=, Holzschuh, S. (2257) – Jakel, W. (2260), Germany 2005; 10.♛e2!? ♛×d4 11.♗c7;

C2) 10.♛d2 ♗e7 (10...♘bd7!?) 11.♖ae1 (11.♖ad1!?) 11...0-0 12.♗e5 ♘bd7 13.f4. All White's pieces are developed, each is more active than its black counterpart, and White has a space advantage to boot. After Krzysztof Pytel's 1977 article, chess theoreticians assessed this position as ± or even ±, e.g., 13...♘b6 14.♗b3±, Sieberg – Pytel, B., Biel 1976. 13...♘g4 is an interesting improvement for Black. However in 1999, Krzysztof Pytel wrote me about his new idea: 13...♘×e5 14.f×e5 ♘g4!! (∓ Pytel).

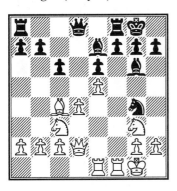

I began to analyze. Black threatens 15...♗×c2 (16.♛×c2 ♛×d4+). If 15.♔h1 (or 15.♖d1), then 15...♗g5, with advantage to Black. After 15.♘ge4, 15...c5 is very unpleasant. 15.♘ce4 ♛b6 16.♔h1 is nice for Black who can play 16...♖ad8 or even 16...♛×b2. After 15.♛f4 h5, Black threatens ♗e7-g5 and what can White do? A very difficult position for White! White's only reasonable move seems to

be 15.♛d1, and after 15...h5 16.h3 (16.♘ce4 ♛b6∓) 16...♗h4 we arrive at this position.

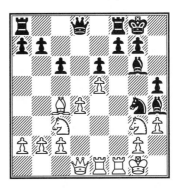

Having analyzed this position at considerable length, I will share some of my findings:

C2a) 17.♖f3

C2a1) 17...♗×c2 18.♛×c2 (18.♛d2 ♘h6∓) 18...♛×d4+ 19.♔h1 ♘×e5 (19...♛×c4 20.h×g4∞) 20.♖e4 ♘×f3 (20...♛d6? 21.♖×h4 ♘×f3 22.♘ce4 ♛d8 23.♖×h5 g6 24.♛c1! g×h5 25.♛h6+−) 21.♖×d4 ♘×d4∞;

C2a2) 17...♗×g3 18.♖×g3 ♛h4 19.♘e2 (19.♖f3 ♗×c2 20.♛d2 ♘h6 21.♖f4 ♛g5 22.♗×e6! ♗g6 23.♗b3 ♖ad8∓) 19...♘×e5 20.♗b3 (20.♗×e6 f×e6 21.d×e5 ♖ad8∓) 20...♖ad8 (20...♖fd8!?) 21.♛d2 (21.♛c1 ♖×d4∓) 21...♔h7 (21...♘d7 22.♗×e6) 22.♛a5 ♘d7 23.♛×a7 ♘f6 24.♖d1 ♘e4 25.♖f3 ♖d7∓;

C2b) 17.♘ce4 ♗×e4 18.♘×e4 ♗×e1 19.h×g4 (19.♖×e1 ♘h6∞) 19...♗h4 20.g×h5 (20.c3!? h×g4 21.♛×g4) 20...♗g5 (18.♖×e4 ♗×g3 19.h×g4 ♛h4 20.♖f3 h×g4∓) 21.♛d3 (21.♖f3 ♗h6∞) 21...♗h6 22.♖f6!! (22.c3 ♛h4

23.♕f3 b6 24.♘d6 ♕e7∞) 22...c5 23.c3 (23.♖xh6?? ♕xd4+ 24.♕xd4 cxd4–+) 23...cxd4 (23...♖c1 24.h6 g6 25.♘d6+–) 24.♖xh6+–.

C3) 10.♖e1

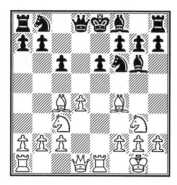

10...♗e7

C3a) 11.a4 0-0 12.h4 (Paulet, I. (2240) – Moldovan, D. (2435), Predeal 2007) 12...h5 13.♗d3 (13.♗e2!?) 13...♘g4!? (13...♗xd3 14.♕xd3±) 14.♗e2?! (14.♗xg6 fxg6⇄) 14...♗xh4 15.♗xg4 hxg4 16.♕xg4 ♗xc2∓ or 16.♘ge4 ♘a6∓;

C3b) 11.♕e2 ♕xd4 (11...0-0 12.♖ad1 ♘d5⇄, Pavelka, J. – Buran, J. (2208), Moravia 2003) 12.♗e5 ♕b6 13.h4 h5 14.♘a4 ♕a5 15.♗xe6 fxe6?! (15...0-0 16.♗b3 ♘bd7 17.♗c3 ♗b4=) 16.♗xf6 with a strong attack; for example, 16...gxf6 17.♕xe6 ♕c7 18.♕xf6 ♖g8 19.♘f5 ♗xf5 20.♕xf5 ♘d7 21.♖ad1 or 16...♗xf6 17.♕xe6+ ♔f8 18.♕c8+ ♕d8 19.♕xb7 ♘d7 20.♖ad1;

C3c) 11.♘ce4

C3c1) 11...♘bd7 (11...♘d5 12.♗d2 ♘d7 13.♗b3 0-0 14.c4 ♘5f6=, Sermier, G. (2269) – Pytel, K. (2380), Besongon

1999) 12.a4 (12.♘d6+? ♗xd6 13.♗xd6 ♘b6∓) 12...0-0 13.a5 ♘d5⇄;

C3c2) 11...♘xe4 12.♘xe4 0-0 13.c3 (13.a4!?) 13...♘d7 14.♕e2 (Larghi, R. – Marelli, M., Robecchetto 1992) 14...♘b6 15.♗d3 ♘d5 16.♗d2 (16.♗e5?! f6 17.♗g3 f5 18.♘d2 f4) 16...♕b6⇄;

C3c3) 11...0-0 12.♘xf6+ ♗xf6 13.c3 ♘d7 14.♘e4 (14.♗d3 ♗xd3 15.♕xd3± or 14...♘b6 15.♗xg6 hxg6 16.♘e4±) 14...♗e7 15.♗b3 a5 16.h3 ♘b6 17.♘c5 (17.a3 a4⇄, Le Guang, K. – Pytel, K. (2385), Le Havre 2000) 17...♘d5 18.♗xd5 cxd5 19.♕b3 (19.♘xb7 ♕b6 20.♕b3 ♕c6 21.♘c5 ♗xc5 22.dxc5 ♕xc5=) 19...♖c8 (19...b6?! 20.♘b7) 20.♕b5 ♗xc5 21.dxc5 ♕c6 22.a4±.

Back to Jenni – Ekstroem.

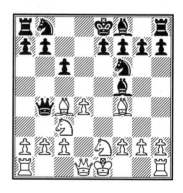

8.♗b3

8.♗d3 ♗xd3 9.♕xd3 e6 10.0-0-0 ♘bd7=, Birk, S. (2260) – Unrath, H (2320), Germany 1990.

8...e6

8...♘bd7 9.♘g3 ♗g6 10.a3 ♕b6 11.0-0 h5 12.♖e1 h4 13.♘ge4 ♘xe4 14.♘xe4

♗xe4 15.♖xe4 ♞f6 16.♖e3 e6 17.c3
0-0-0⇄, Nabours, A. – Schiller, E.,
Internet, 1990.

9.0-0

We now examine White's alternatives
A) 9.♛d2 and **B)** 9.♗c7.

A) 9.♛d2 ♞bd7 10.0-0-0 (10.f3!? 0-0-0
11.a3 ♛a5 12.0-0 e5 13.♗g3 ♗g6
14.♖ad1 exd4 15.♞xd4 ♗c5⇄, Hall,
J. (2487) – Gausel, E. (2525), Malmo
2003) 10...♛a5 11.♔b1 (11.a3? ♗xa3
12.bxa3 ♛xa3+ 13.♔b1 ♛xb3+)
11...♗b4 12.a3 (12.f3 ♞d5 13.♗xd5
cxd5∓) 12...♞e4 13.♛e3 ♗xc3
14.♞xc3 ♞xc3+ 15.♛xc3 ♛xc3
16.bxc3 ♞f6=, Olsson, A. (2337) –
Fries Nielsen, J. (2454), Stockholm
2002;

B) 9.♗c7 ♞a6 (9...♛e7 10.♗g3 ♞a6
11.0-0 0-0-0 12.♛d2 ♛d7=) 10.a3
♛e7 11.♗e5 0-0-0 12.♞g3 (12.♛d2
♞c5 13.♗c4 ♞cd7⇄, Langer, M.
(2269) – Zatonskih, A. (2460) Okla-
homa 2004)

B1) 12...♗g6 13.♛e2 ♞d5 (13...♛d7
14.0-0-0±) 14.h4 f6 15.h5 ♗f7
(15...♞xc3 16.bxc3 ♗f7 17.♗f4 ♞c7
18.0-0 ♞d5 19.♗d2 ♛c7 20.♖fe1±)
16.♞xd5 exd5 17.♗f4 ♛d7 18.0-0-0±
or 17...♛xe2+ 18.♔xe2±;

B2) 12...♞g4 13.♛e2 (13.♗f4?! ♛f6)
13...♞xe5 14.♛xe5 (14.♞xf5?! exf5
15.dxe5 ♞c5 16.♗c4 g5 17.0-0 ♗g7
18.♖fe1 ♞e6∓ or 14.dxe5?! ♗g6
15.♗c4 ♞c5 16.b4? ♛h4 17.bxc5 ♛d4
18.0-0 ♛xc3∓; 16.0-0 h5∓) 14...♗g6
15.h4 h5 16.0-0-0 ♞c7=.

We return now to Jenni – Ekstroem.

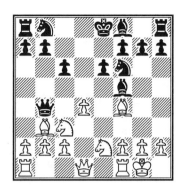

9...♞bd7

Also worth consideration are **C1)**
9...♗e7; **(C2)** 9...♛a5 and **(C3)**
9...♞a6.

C1) 9...♗e7?! 10.♗c7 ♗d8 (10...♞d5?
11.a3 ♞xc3 12.♞xc3+–; 10...♞a6?
11.a3+–, Lehmann, A. (2250) –
Eschmann, P. (2190), Winterthur 2007)
11.♗xd8 ♔xd8 12.♗g3 ♛a5 13.d5 ♔c7
(13...cxd5 14.♞xf5±) 14.♞xf5 exf5±,
Roederer, K. (2205) – Lentrodt, T.
(2280), Germany 1998 or 10...b6
11.♞g3 ♗g6 12.h4 ♛a5 13.♖e1 ♞bd7
(13...0-0 14.♖e5 c5 15.d5 ♞bd7
16.♖e1±) 14.♛f3 ♖c8 15.♛xc6 0-0
16.♛b7 ♗b4 17.♖e3±;

C2) 9...♛a5?! 10.d5! (10.♞g3 ♗g6
11.♛e2 ♗e7 12.♖ad1 ♞bd7 13.d5
cxd5 14.♗xd5 ♞xd5 15.♞xd5 exd5
16.♗d6 0-0 17.♛xe7 (Kraft, K. –
Ruehr, W., Germany 1981) 17...♛b6⇄
or 14...♛b4 15.♗d2 0-0 16.♗xe6 fxe6
17.♞d5 exd5 18.♗xb4 ♗xb4⇄)

C2a) 10...cxd5 11.♞d4 ♗g6 12.♞cb5
♞a6 13.c4 ♗e7 (13...dxc4 14.♗a4±)
14.cxd5 ♞xd5 15.♗xd5 exd5 16.♖e1
♔f8 17.♖xe7! ♔xe7 18.♗d6+ ♔d7
(18...♔d8 19.b4 ♛b6 20.♛f3 ♖e8

21.♕xd5 ♗e4 22.♕xf7 +−) 19.b4 ♘xb4
20.♕b3 ♘d3 21.♕xd5 ♔c8 22.♗g3
with very strong attack, Petrosian, S.
(2424) – Velicka P. (2439), Norderstedt
2003;

C2b) 10...♘xd5 11.♘xd5 cxd5 12.♘d4
♗e4 (12...♗g6 13.c4 ♘d7 14.cxd5 e5
15.♗xe5 ♘xe5 16.f4 ♗c5 17.fxe5±)
13.c4 ♘c6 14.♘b5 ♖c8 15.♕e2 a6
(16...♗f5 17.g4 a6 18.gxf5 axb5
19.♗xb5± or 16...♗g6 17.♗xe6 fxe6
18.♕xe6+ ♗e7 19.♘d6+ ♔f8
20.♕xc8+±) 16.cxd5 ♗xd5 17.♘c7+
♖xc7 18.♗xc7 ♕xc7 19.♗xd5±,
Autenrieth, M. (2360) – Schmid, G.,
Abensberg 1987;

C3) 9...♘a6 10.♘g3 (10.a3 ♕b6
11.♕d2 ♗e7 12.♖fe1 0-0 ⇄) 10...♗g6
11.♘ce2 (11.a3 ♕a5 12.♕e2 ♗e7
13.♖fe1 0-0 14.♘ge4 ♖ad8 ⇄,
Birjulin, A. – Melts, M.,corr. 1988-90)
11...0-0-0 (11...♗e7 12.♗e5 0-0-0
13.c3 ♕b6 14.♘f4 ♘b8 ±, Koch, C.
(2221) – Cade, S. (2250), Internet 2001)
12.a4 (12.♗e5 ♗d6 13.c3 ♕b6 14.f4?!
♗xe5 15.fxe5 ♘g4!) 12...♗d6 13.c3
♕a5 14.♗xd6 ♖xd6 15.♘f4 ♘c7
16.♕f3 c5=.

Let's return to Jenni – Ekstroem.

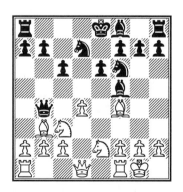

10.♖e1

10.♘g3 (10.a3 ♕a5 11.♘g3 ♗g6
12.♕f3 ♗e7 13.♖fe1 ♘b6± Wolfram,
D. (2102) – Arwanitakis, M. (2242),
Hartberg 2004; 10...♕b6!? 11.♕d2
0-0-0) 10...♗g6 11.♗c7 (11.♖e1 0-0-0
⇄, Klanten, C. – Wittal, W., Internet
2002) 11...♘d5 (11...♕e7 12.♕e2
♘b6±) 12.♘xd5 cxd5 13.♖e1 ♖c8
14.c3 (14.♗f4 ♗d6=) 14...♕b5 15.♗f4
♗e7±.

10...♗e7

One alternative way to play is 10...♘b6
(another interesting possibility is
10...0-0-0; for example, 11.a3 ♕b6
12.♘g3 ♗g6 ⇄ or 11.♘g3 ♗g6 12.h4
e5 ⇄) 11.a3.

A) 11...♕a5 12.♘g3 ♗g6 13.♗c7 ♖c8
(13...♗e7 14.♖e5 ♕a6 15.♘a2 ♘fd5
16.♘b4 ♗xb4 17.axb4 ♕b5 18.♕e1
♘c4 19.♗a4 ♕xb4 20.♖xd5 ♕xe1+
21.♖xe1 ♘xb2 22.♖a5 ♘xa4 23.♖xa4
♗xc2 24.♖a3 with better chances for
White) 14.♗e5 (14.♖e5?! ♕a6)
14...♗e7 15.h4 h6 (15...h5 16.♘ce2)
16.♘ce4 ♘xe4 (16...♘bd5 17.c4 ♘xe4
18.♘xe4 ♘f6 19.♗xf6 gxf6 20.d5±)
17.♘xe4 0-0 18.♕g4 h5 19.♕g3 with
better chances for White;

B) 11...♕e7 12.♘g3 ♗g6 13.♗g5
(13.a4!?) 13...0-0-0 14.a4 (14.♘ge4 h6
15.♗f4 ♕d7 ⇄) 14...h6 15.♗h4
♕b4 ⇄, Nemeth, F. (2450) – Schmidt,
R. (2160), Cluj 2008.

11.♗c7

Also possible is 11.a3 ♕a5 (11...♕b6
12.♘g3 ♗g6±) 12.♕d2 ♕d8 (12...0-0-0?
13.♘d5; 12...0-0?! 13.♘d5 ♕d8
14.♘xe7+ ♕xe7 15.c4; 12...♘b6!?)
13.d5 (13.♘g3 ♗g6 14.♘ce4 ♘xe4

15.♘xe4 ♗xe4 16.♖xe4±) 13...cxd5
14.♘d4 ♗g6?! 15.♖xe6 fxe6 16.♘xe6
♕a5 17.♘c7+ ♔f7 18.♖e1; 14...♗e4
(Timoshenko, G. (2536) – Mateuta, G.
(2469), Kavala 2004) 15.♘db5 0-0
16.♗c7 ♕c8 17.♗d6 ♗xd6 (17...♖e8
18.♗g3 ♖d8 19.♗c7=) 18.♘xd6 ♕c6
(18...♕c7!?) 19.♘dxe4 dxe4 20.♗a4
♕c7 21.♘xe4 ♖fd8=.

11...♗d8

11...♘b6?! is a very dangerous continuation for Black; for example, 12.♘g3
♗g6 13.a3 ♕a5 14.♖e5; 11...b6?!
12.♘g3 ♗g6 13.a3 ♕a5 14.♕f3 ♖c8
15.♕xc6 ♗d8 16.♖xe6+ fxe6
17.♕xe6+ ♗e7 18.♗d6 ♘g8 19.♗xe7
♘xe7 20.♘d5±; 14...♘d5 15.♗xd5
cxd5 16.♕e2 0-0 17.b4 ♗xb4 18.axb4
♕xb4 19.♘b5±.

12.a3 ♕e7 13.♗g3

Other interesting possibilities:

A) 13.♘g3 ♗xc7 (13...♗xc2 14.♕xc2
♗xc7 15.♘f5 ♕f8 16.d5 cxd5 17.♘xd5
♘xd5 18.♗xd5 ♕c5 19.♕b3⯀)
14.♘xf5 ♕f8 15.♘e3 0-0-0⇄;

B) 13.♗f4 ♘b6 (13...0-0 14.♘g3 ♗g6
15.♕f3 ♗a5⇄) 14.♘g3 ♗g6 15.♘ce4

♘xe4 (15...♗c7?! 16.♘xf6+ gxf6
17.♗xc7 ♕xc7 18.♕f3 with strong pressure, Karlovich, A. (2160) –
Makropoulou, M. (2237), Athens 2005)
16.♘xe4 ♗xe4 17.♖xe4 ♘d5
18.♗d2±.

C) 13.♗xd8

C1) 13...♖xd8?! 14.♘g3 g6 (14...♗g6
15.f4±) 15.♕d2 ♕d6 (15...0-0 16.♘xf5
gxf5 17.♕g5+ ♔h8 18.♕xf5±) 16.♘xf5
gxf5 with better chances for White;

C2) 13...♕xd8 14.♘g3 (14.f3 0-0
15.♘g3 ♗g6 16.♘ce4 ♕b6⇄)
14...♗g6 15.♕f3 (15.h4 h6⇄) 15...0-0
16.♖ad1 (16.♘ce4 ♘xe4 17.♘xe4
♗xe4 18.♖xe4 ♘f6=) 16...♕c7 17.h4
h6 18.♘ce2 ♖fe8 19.♘f4 ♗h7⇄.

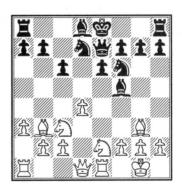

13...0-0 14.♘f4 ♘b6 15.♕f3

15.d5 (15.h3 ♗c7 16.♘h5 ♗xg3
17.♘xg3 ♗g6⇄ or 16...♘xh5
17.♕xh5 ♗xg3 18.♕xf5 ♗c7 19.g3 a5
20.a4 ♖fd8 21.♖ad1 ♕b4⇄)
15...cxd5 16.♘fxd5 ♘bxd5 17.♘xd5
(17.♗xd5 ♘xd5 18.♘xd5 ♕g5 19.♘e3
♗e4∓) 17...♘xd5 18.♗xd5 ♗c7
19.♕f3 (19.♗xb7 ♖ab8 20.♗e4 ♗xe4
21.♖xe4 ♗xg3 22.hxg3 ♖xb2 23.♖b4
♖xb4 24.axb4 ♕xb4 25.♖xa7 g6∓)

19...♗×g3 20.h×g3 ♗×c2 21.♗×b7
♖ab8 22.♖e2 ♗g6 23.♗e4 ♗×e4
24.♛×e4 ♛f6 25.♛f4 ♛×f4 26.g×f4
g6=.

**15...♗c7 16.h3 ♖ad8 17.♖ad1
♖fe8**

17...h6 18.♘d3 ♗×g3 19.♛×f5 ♛c7
20.♛f3 ♗d6 21.♘e4 ♘×e4 22.♖×e4
♘d5 ⇄.

18.♘fe2 (18.♗h4!? ♗×f4 19.♛×f4 h6
20.♛f3 ♖d7 21.♗g3±) **18...♗×g3**
(18...♘bd5 19.♗e5 ♘×c3 20.♘×c3
h6⇄) **19.♘×g3 ♗g6 20.♘ce2 ♛c7**
(20...e5!? 21.♘f4 e4 22.♘×g6 h×g6
23.♛f4 ♘bd5) **21.h4 h6 22.♘f4
♗h7= 23.♘gh5 ♘×h5 24.♘×h5
♘d5 25.c3** (25.c4 ♘e7 26.g3 ♛a5
27.♘f4?! ♖×d4; 27.♖e5!? ♛c7
28.♖ee1=) **25...♗g6 26.♗×d5**
(26.♗c4 a5=) **26...♗×h5 27.♛×h5
♖×d5 28.♖e5 ♖ed8 29.♖de1?!**
(29.♖×d5 ♖×d5 30.♛e2 a5 31.c4=;
29...c×d5 30.♖d3 ♛f4?! 31.♛f3 ♛c1+
32.♔h2 ♖d7 33.♛e5 ♔h7 34.♖g3 g6
35.h5 g5 36.♖f3 ♛×b2 37.♖f6 ♛d2
38.♖×h6+ ♔×h6 39.♛h8# or 37...♛c2
38.f4 g×f4 39.♛×f4+–; 30...♔h7!?)
29...c5 30.♖×d5?! (30.d×c5 ♛×c5
31.g3 ♛b5 32.♖×d5 ♖×d5 33.♛e2
♛d7∓) **30...♖×d5 31.♖e5 c×d4
32.♖×d5 e×d5 33.♛×d5** (33.c×d4
♛c1+ 34.♔h2 ♛f4+ 35.♔h3 ♛×d4∓)
**33...d×c3 34.b×c3 ♛×c3∓
35.♛×b7 ♛e1+ 36.♔h2 ♛×f2
37.♛a8+ ♔h7 38.♛e4+ f5 39.♛c4
♛e3 40.a4 ♛e4 41.♛×e4 f×e4
42.♔g3 ♔g6** (42...g5–+) **43.♔g4
a5** (43...e3 44.♔f3 ♔h5 45.g3 g5–+)
**44.g3 e3 45.♔f3 ♔h5 46.♔×e3
♔g4 47.♔f2 ♔f5?** (47...♔h3 48.♔f3
g5–+) **48.♔e3 h5 49.♔f3 g6**

50.g4+ ♔e5 51.g×h5 g×h5 52.♔e3
♔f5 53.♔f3 ♔e5 ½-½

Summary: After **1.e4 d5 2.e×d5
♛×d5 3.♘c3 ♛d6 4.d4 ♘f6
5.♗c4 c6 6.♘ge2 – 6...♗f5**. This
move is better than 6...♗g4. After
6...♗f5, White has two main possibilities, 7.0-0 and 7.♗f4.

If 7.0-0 ♘bd7 (7...e6 8.♘g3 ♗g6, and
here White has the aggressive move
9.f4), Black should have an equal game.
More popular against 6...♗f5 is 7.♗f4.
White develops his bishop in the center and attacks Black's queen – what
could be more natural? Black can reply
7...♛d8 or 7...♛b4.

After 7...♛d8, White has a choice between the popular 8.0-0, 8.♘g3, and the
little-known but very interesting 8.d5.

I believe that after 7...♛b4 (this looks
riskier than 7...♛d8) Black can more
easily equalize and gain counterplay
than after 7...♛d8. My preference is for
7...♛b4, for several reasons:
1. After 7...♛b4 8.♗b3 (or 8.♗d3
♗×d3 9.♛×d3) Black moves, while after 7...♛d8, White moves.compared to
some lines, e.g., 1.e4 d5 2.e×d5 ♛×d5
3.♘c3 ♛d8 4.d4 ♘f6 5.♗f4 c6 6.♗c4
♗f5 7.♘ge2, this is like giving White
an extra move.
2. After 7...♛b4 White's choice of replies is greatly restricted compared to
7...♛d8.
3. After 7...♛b4 Black can more easily
castle queenside than after 7...♛d8.

But I cannot say that 7...♛d8 is bad;
White can still get into trouble after this
move.

Game 5
Calizaya, M. (2125) – Uria, J. (2300)
Callao 2007

1.e4 d5 2.e×d5 ♕×d5 3.♘c3 ♕d6 4.d4 ♘f6 5.♗c4 a6 6.♘ge2 ♕c6

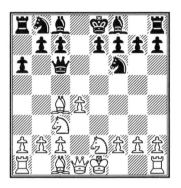

Black forces White to play an unclear gambit. Beginners' books always tell us that pawn-grabbing with the queen in the opening is very dangerous. However sometimes (for example Fischer's favorite "Poisoned Pawn" variation of the Najdorf Sicilian Defense with 7...♕b6) matters are not so clear!

7.♗b3

The main alternative is 7.♕d3 ♕×g2 8.♖g1, after which Black has **A)** 8...♕×h2; **B)** 8...♕c6 and **C)** 8...♕h3.

A) 8...♕×h2 The second pawn-grab is very dangerous here for Black; for example, 9.♗f4 ♕h3 10.♘g3 (10.♕d2 ♕d7 11.0-0-0 b5 12.♗b3 ♘c6 13.♗e5 ♗b7∓, Kornilov, I. (2371) – Rodchenkov, V. (2417), Essentuki 2003), and now:

A1) 10...b5 11.♗b3 c6 (11...g6 12.♘ce4 ♗g7 13.♗×f7+ ♔f8 14.♗b3± or 11...♘bd7 12.a4 b4 13.♘ce4 ♘×e4

14.♕×e4 ♖a7 15.0-0-0 ♘f6 16.♕e3 h5 17.d5 with a strong attack) 12.0-0-0 ♘bd7 13.♕e2 ♕g4 14.♕e3 e6 15.♘ge4 ♕h5 16.♖h1 ♕f5 17.♘g3 ♕g6 18.♖dg1 ♘g4 19.♕f3±, Burchert, W. (2187) – Dubois, M. (2012), Italy 1999;

A2) 10...♕d7 11.♘ge4 (11.0-0-0 g6 12.♗e5 ♘c6 13.♗×f6 e×f6 14.♘d5 ♗g7 15.♖de1+ ♔f8 16.♕a3+ ♔g8 17.♘h5 ♕d8 18.♘e7+ ♘×e7 19.♖×e7 +−, Asadpour, M. – Grun, S., Norrkoeping 1997) 11...b5 12.♗b3 ♘×e4 13.♘×e4 ♘c6 14.0-0-0 ♘a5 15.d5 g6 (15...♘×b3+ 16.♕×b3 ♕f5 17.♕e3 g6 18.♖g5 ♕h3 19.♘f6+ ♔d8 20.♕c5 +−) 16.♕c3 ♕f5 17.♗×c7 ♘×b3+ 18.♔b1!! (18.a×b3? ♗h6+) 18...f6 19.♕c6+ ♕d7 (19...♔f7 20.♕×a8 ♕×e4 21.♕×c8±) 20.♕×a8 ♕×c7 21.a×b3±;

A3) 10...h5 11.0-0-0 (11.♕d2 b5 12.♗b3 ♗b7∓, Ribshtein. N. (2329) – Kantsler, B. (2507), Tel Aviv 2001) 11...♘c6 12.d5 ♘b4 (12...♘a5 13.♗×c7 ♘×c4 14.♕×c4 g6 15.d6±) 13.♕d4 c6 14.d6 h4 15.♘ge4 ♕f5 16.♖d2 ♘×e4 (16...♕×f4? 17.♘×f6+ ♕×f6 18.d7+) 17.♘×e4±;

B) 8...♕c6 9.♗f4 ♕d7 (White also has good game with sufficient compensation for the pawn after 9...g6, 9...♘bd7 or 9...♕b6) 10.0-0-0 b5 11.♗b3 ♗b7 12.d5 g6 13.♘d4 c5 14.d×c6 ♘×c6 15.♘e6 (15.♘d×b5!? a×b5 16.♕e3) 15...f×e6 16.♕e3 ♘d5 (Gallo, E. (2113) – Scharrer, P. (2210), Verona 2006) 17.♖×d5! e×d5 18.♘×d5 ♗g7 19.♘c7+ ♔d8 (19...♔f8 20.♘e6+ ♔e8 21.♘×g7+ ♔f8 22.♗h6+−) 20.♘e6+ ♔c8 21.♘×g7 ♘d8 22.♖d1 +− or 10...♘c6 11.a3 g6 12.d5 ♘a5 13.♗b5a×b5 14.♘×b5 ♖b8 (14...e5

15.♗xe5 ♗h6+ 16.♔b1 0-0 17.♗xf6)
15.♘xc7+ ♔d8 16.♕c3+− ;

C) 8...♕h3

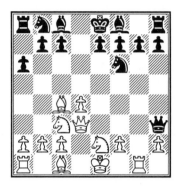

The main alternatives now for White are
C1) 9.♗e3; **C2)** 9.♘g3; **C3)** 9.♖g3; and
C4) 9.♕xh3.

C1) 9.♗e3

C1a) 9...b5 10.♗b3 (10.♗d5 ♘xd5
11.♘xd5 ♕d7 12.♕e4 ♖a7 13.♘df4
♕f5 14.♕xf5 ♗xf5 15.d5 ♖a8∞)
10...♗b7 (10...♗f5!?) 11.0-0-0 ♘c6
12.♘f4 ♕d7 (Lumongdong, L. (2150)
− Safar, A., Macau 2007) 13.a3 g6∞;

C1b) 9...♘c6 10.0-0-0 (10.♘f4!? ♕f5
11.♕d2) 10...♕d7 (10...b5 11.♗b3
♕f5 12.♕d2 ♘a5 13.♘g3 ♘xb3+
14.axb3 (Petrov, M. (2490) −
Panbukchian, V. (2325), Sofia 2003)
14...♕f3∓; 12.♘d5!?) 11.♗f4 ♘a5
12.♖g5 b5 13.♗d5 (13.♗xb5?! axb5
14.♘xb5 ♗a6 15.♘xc7+ ♕xc7 16.♗xc7
♗xd3 17.♖xd3 ♘c6∓, Shrestha, K.
(2145) − Wong Meng Kong (2445),
Macau 2007) 13...h6 (13...♖a7
14.♗f3≅) 14.♖e5 c6⇄;

C1c) 9...♕f5 10.♕d2 h6 (10...♘c6!?
11.0-0-0 ♕a5 12.♖g5 b5 13.♘f4
♗d7⇄) 11.0-0-0 (11.♗f4 ♕a5

12.0-0-0 g5 13.♗e5 ♘bd7 14.♔b1 e6
15.f4 ♗e7⇄) 11...♕a5 (11...♘c6!?
12.♗f4 b5) 12.♘f4 (12.♔b1 ♘c6
13.♗f4 ♗g4 14.d5≅, Broehl, S. (2205)
− Olbrisch, M., Lohmar 1998) 12...♘c6
13.♘cd5 ♕xd2+ 14.♖xd2 ♘xd5
15.♘xd5 ♔d7 16.♗f4 (16.♘c3!? f6
17.f4) 16...b5 17.♘xc7 ♖a7 18.d5 ♘e5
19.♗e2 ♘c4⇄;

C1d) 9...♗f5 10.♕d2 ♘c6 11.0-0-0 e6
12.♘f4 ♕h4 13.d5 (13.♕e2 ♗d6
14.♘fd5 (Madl, I. (2385) − Feher, G.
(2295), Hungary 1997) 14...0-0-0
15.♘xf6 gxf6 16.d5 ♘e5 17.♗xa6 bxa6
18.♕xa6+ ♔d7 19.dxe6+ ♗xe6∓)
13...♘e5 14.♗e2 0-0-0 15.♘g2
(15.♕d4 ♘c6 16.♕c4 exd5 17.♘cxd5
♘xd5 18.♖xd5 ♖xd5 19.♕xd5 ♕f6∓)
15...♕h3 16.♘f4 ♕h4 17.♘g2 ♕h3=;

C1e) 9...g6 10.0-0-0 ♗g7 (10...♕f5
11.♕d2 ♗g7 12.♘g3 ♕a5 13.♗h6
♗xh6 14.♕xh6 ♘c6 15.♖he1≅;
13...0-0 14.♗xg7 ♔xg7 15.♕e2≅,
Labroche, J. − Raffeneau, F. (1995),
Internet 2001) 11.♘f4 ♕f5 12.♕d2
♕d7 13.h4 b5 14.♗b3 ♘c6 15.♘d3 0-
0 16.♘c5 ♕d8⇄, Gongora Reyes, M.
(2427) − Narciso Dublan, M. (2469),
Havana 1999;

C2) 9.♘g3 ♘c6 10.♗f4

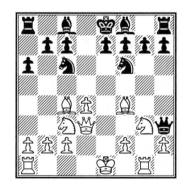

C2a) 10...b5 11.♗b3 (11.♗d5? ♘b4 12.♕f3 ♘×c2+ 13.♔d2 ♘×d4 14.♕e3 c6 15.♕×d4 ♘×d5 16.♘×d5 c×d5∓) 11...♗b7 12.0-0-0 ♘a5 13.♗×c7 ♘×b3+ 14.a×b3 ♖c8 15.♗e5 ♘d5 16.♖de1 e6 17.♘×d5 ♗×d5∓;

C2b) 10...♗g4 11.f3 (Kornilov, I. (2281) – Agapov, S. (2254), Serpukhov 2002) 11...0-0-0 (11...♘b4 12.♕e2 ♗f5 13.♘ge4 0-0-0 14.0-0-0 e6∓) 12.♗×f7 (12.f×g4 ♖×d4∓; 12.♕e3 ♗e6 13.♗×e6+?! ♕×e6 14.♕×e6+ f×e6∓; 13.♗f1!?) 12...♖×d4 13.♕e3 ♗d7 14.♗e5 ♘×e5 15.♕×e5 ♖d6 16.♘ge4 e6 17.♘×d6+ (17.♘×f6 ♕h4+) 17...♗×d6∓;

(C3) 9.♖g3 ♕f5 (9...♕×h2 10.♗f4 ♕h1+ 11.♖g1 ♕h3 reaches the same position as after 7.♕d3 ♕×g2 8.♖g1 ♕×h2 9.♗f4 ♕h3) 10.♗e3 ♕×d3 11.♗×d3 g6 12.♘f4 (12.♗f4!?) 12...c6 13.d5 (13.♔f1!?) 13...♗g7 14.♘a4 (14.0-0-0!?) 14...♘bd7 15.d×c6 b×c6 16.c4?! (16.0-0-0) 16...0-0 17.0-0-0 e5 18.♘e2 e4 19.♗c2 ♘e5∓, Kuzmin, I. (2251) – Zaitsev, V. (2426), Novosibirsk 2001;

C4) 9.♕×h3 ♗×h3 10.♘f4 ♗f5 11.♘fd5

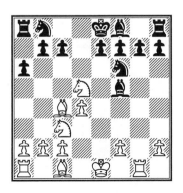

The main alternatives now are **C4a)** 11...♔d7; **C4b)** 11...♔d8 and **C4c)** 11...♘×d5.

C4a) 11...♔d7 12.♗f4 ♘×d5 13.♗×d5 ♘c6 14.♗×f7 (14.0-0-0!?) 14...♗×c2 15.d5 (15.♖g5 e6 16.d5 e×d5 17.♖×d5+ ♗d6 18.♗×d6 c×d6 19.♗h5 (Bukacek, E. (2240) – Hangweyrer, M. (2347), Austria 2005) 19...♖af8 20.♗g4+ ♔c7 21.♔f1 ♗g6 22.♖ad1 ♖f4 23.♗e2 ♖d8∓) 15...♘d8 16.♗h5 ♗f5 17.♘a4 g6 18.♗e5 (18.♘c5+ ♔e8 19.♗e5 ♖g8 20.♗g4 ♗g7 21.♗×g7 ♗×g4 22.♖×g4 22...♖×g7∓) 18...♖g8 19.♖c1 ♖c8 20.♗g4 ♗×g4 21.♖×g4 ♘f7 22.♘c5+ ♔e8 23.f4∞;

C4b) 11...♔d8 12.♘×f6 (12.♗f4!? ♘e8 13.♘e3) 12...e×f6 13.♗f4 (13.♗×f7 ♗×c2 14.♘d5 g5 15.f4 h6 16.♗e3 ♗d6 17.♔d2 ♗a4 18.h4∞; 13...♘c6 14.♗e3 ♘b4 15.♔d2 ♘×c2 16.♖ac1 ♘×e3 17.f×e3 g6 18.♖cf1 c5 19.e4 ♗d7∓) 13...g5 (13...♘c6!?) 14.♗g3 (Rodriguez, A. (2479) – Galego, L. (2518), Sao Paulo 2005) 14...♗×c2 15.♖c1 ♗g6 16.♘d5 ♘c6 17.♗×c7+ ♔d7 18.♗g3 ♖e8+ 19.♔d2∞;

C4c) 11...♘×d5 12.♘×d5 ♔d7 13.♗f4 ♘c6

C4c1) 14.♘×c7? ♖c8 15.♘d5 ♘d4 16.0-0-0 ♖×c4 17.♘b6+ (17.♘e3 ♔e8 18.♘×c4 ♘e2+ 19.♔b1 ♘×f4–+) 17...♔e8 18.♘×c4 ♘e2+ 19.♔b1 ♘×f4–+ or 16.♘b6+ ♔e8 17.♘×c8 (17.0-0-0 ♖×c4 18.♘×c4 ♘e2+ 19.♔b1 ♘×f4–+) 17...♘×c2+ 18.♔e2 ♘×a1 19.♖×a1 ♗×c8 20.♗d5 e6 21.♖c1 ♔d8 22.♗e4 ♗b4 23.♗c7+ (23.♖c7 e5! 24.♗×e5 ♖e8 25.f4 ♗g4+ 26.♔d3 ♖×e5–+) 23...♔e7 24.♗e5 ♗d6 25.♗×g7 ♖g8∓;

C4c2) 14.♗×c7 (14.0-0-0!?) 14...♖c8 15.♗b6 (after 15.♗f4?! we have same position as after 14.♘×c7 ♖c8 15.♘d5) 15...♗×c2 16.♗c5 ♔e8 17.♘b6 ♖d8 18.♗d5 e6 19.♗×f8 ♖×f8 20.♗×c6+ b×c6 21.♖c1 ♗e4 22.f3 ♗×f3 23.♔f2 ♖b8 (23...♗e4 24.♔e3) 24.♔×f3 ♖×b6 25.♖×g7 ♖×b2 26.♖×c6 ♖×a2 27.♖×h7∓.

We return now to Calizaya – Uria.

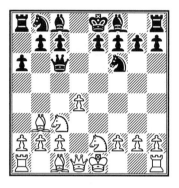

7...♕×g2 8.♖g1 ♕×h2

Also coming under consideration are **A)** 8...♕c6; **B)** 8...♕f3 and **C)** 8...♕h3.

A) 8...♕c6

A1) 9.d5 ♕d6 (9...♕b6 10.♗e3 ♕a5 11.♕d4 g6 12.0-0-0 ♗g7∞; 10...♕b4!?) 10.♗g5 (10.♗f4 ♕b6 11.♕d4 ♘bd7 12.♔c4 ♕c5 13.♗×c7 ♕×c4 14.♗×c4 b5 15.♗b3 ♘c5=) 10...♗f5 (10...♘bd7!? 11.♕d4 ♘c5) 11.♕d2 e5 12.♘g3 (Peredun, A. (2306) – Arencibia, W. (2522), Toronto 2003) 12...♗g6∞;

A2) 9.♕d3 b5 (9...♘bd7!? 10.♗f4 ♘b6 11.0-0-0 ♗g4 12.h3 ♗h5 13.♕g3 0-0-0∞) 10.♗f4 ♕b7 (10...♘bd7!? 11.0-0-0 ♗b7 12.♔b1 ♖d8∞) 11.0-0-0 g6 12.♘g3 ♗g7 13.♖de1 ♘c6∞, Hussein,

N. (2334) – Wong Meng Kong (2459), Turin 2006;

B) 8...♕f3 9.♗f4

B1) 9...b5 10.♗×c7 ♗b7 11.♕d2 (11.d5!? ♘bd7 12.♕d4 ♖c8 13.♗f4 ♘c5 14.0-0-0) 11...♘bd7 12.0-0-0 ♖c8 13.♗g3 b4 14.♘a4 ♗d5 15.♘c5 ♗×b3 16.a×b3 ♘d5 17.♘f4 ♘7b6∞, Feletar, D. (2376) – Kurajica, B. (2536), Pula 1999;

B2) 9...♗g4 10.♕d2 (10.♗×c7 ♘bd7 11.♕d2 ♖c8 12.♗f4 e6 13.a3 ♖d8 14.0-0-0 ♘c5∞) 10...♘bd7 11.0-0-0 e6 12.♗×c7 ♖c8 13.♗e5 (13.♗g3 ♗b4 14.♕d3 0-0 15.a3 ♕×d3 16.♖×d3 ♗e7=) 13...♗b4 14.♗×f6 ♘×f6 15.d5 e5 16.♕g5 (16.d6 0-0 17.♕g5 h6 18.♕g6∞) 16...0-0 17.♖d3 ♕f5∞, Burkett, M. (2182) – Fels, B. (2113), Internet 2003;

C) 8...♕h3 9.♗f4 ♕d7

C1) 10.d5 g6 (10...b5? 11.♕d4±; 10...c5? 11.♘a4±) 11.♕d2 b5 (11...♗g7 12.0-0-0 0-0 13.♗h6 e5 14.h4 ♕e7 15.♕g5 ♗×h6 16.♕×h6 ♘g4∓, Santoro, A. (2056) – Zaitsev, V. (2411), Italy 1999) 12.♕d4 (12.0-0-0 c5 13.d×c6 ♘×c6) 12...♗g7 13.♕c5 0-0 14.♗×c7 ♗b7⇄;

C2) 10.♛d3 ♘c6 11.a3 (11.d5 ♘a5 12.0-0-0 g6? 13.♗a4 b5 14.♘xb5 axb5 15.♗xb5 c6 16.dxc6 ♛xd3 17.♖xd3 ♗a6 18.♗xa6 ♖xa6 19.c7 ♖a8 20.♖gd1 ♘c6 21.♖c3 +– ; 12...♘xb3+) 11...♘h5 (11...e6?! 12.0-0-0 ♘e7 13.♗e5 ♘g6 14.♗xf6 gxf6 15.d5 e5 16.♗a4 b5 17.♘xb5 ♗h6+ 18.♔b1 0-0 19.♘bc3 ♛h3 20.♛c4±, McShane, L. (2568) – Lalic, B. (2547), Catalan Bay 2003; 11...♘a5?! 12.♗a2 b5 13.0-0-0 ♗b7 14.d5 g6 15.♘g3 ♗g7 16.♘ce4 ♘c4 17.♘xf6+ ♗xf6 18.♗xc4 bxc4 19.♛xc4 0-0?! 20.♘e4 ♗g7 21.♘c5 ♛c8 22.♖ge1±, Gormally, D. (2472) – Plaskett, J. (2490), London 2005) 12.♛c4 e6 (12...♛f5?! 13.♖g5) 13.d5 ♘a5 14.♛xc7 ♘xb3 15.cxb3 ♛xc7 (15...♘xf4 16.♛xf4 ♗d6 17.♛g5) 16.♗xc7 ♗d7 17.dxe6 ♗xe6 18.♘d4 ♖c8 19.♘xe6 fxe6 20.♗e5 ♗e7=.

Back to Calizaya – Uria.

9.♗f4 ♛h5

9...♛h3 10.♗xc7 (10.♛d2 ♛d7 11.0-0-0 b5∞, Garcia, S. – Fonseca, J. (2220), Panama 2006)

A) 10...g6 (10...♘c6 11.d5 ♘a7 12.♛d4⩲, Vera, R. – Utasi, T., Havana 1986) 11.♛d2 ♗g7 12.0-0-0 0-0

13.♖h1 ♛d7?! (13...♛f3!?∞) 14.♗f4 ♘g4 (14...♘c6 15.♗h6) 15.♘d5⩲ ; 13.d5!?;

B) 10...♗g4 11.♛d2 ♘bd7 12.0-0-0 ♖c8

B1) 13.♗e5 e6 (13...♛f3 14.♘f4 ♖xc3 15.bxc3 ♘e4 16.♗d5 ♘xd2 17.♗xf3 ♘xf3 18.♖xg4±) 14.♖g3 ♛h6 15.♗f4 ♛h5 16.♛e3 (16.♖e3 ♗b4 17.d5 e5∓) 16...♘a5 17.d5 ♗c5 18.♛d2 e5∞;

B2) 13.♗g3 ♛h5 14.♖de1 ♗xe2?! (14...♛a5) 15.♖xe2 e6 16.d5 ♘c5 17.dxe6 ♘xb3+ 18.axb3 fxe6 19.♖xe6+ ♔f7 20.♖b6 ♛f3 21.♗e5 ♗c5 22.♖xg7+ ♔xg7 23.♛g5+ 1-0, Honfi, K. (2325) – Neurohr, S. (2325), St. Ingbert 1990.

10.♗xc7

10.♛d2 g6 (10...♘c6 11.♗xc7 ♘a5 12.0-0-0 ♘xb3+ 13.axb3 ♗g4 14.♘f4 ♛f5 15.♖de1 g6∞) 11.0-0-0 ♛a5 (11...♗g7 12.♗xc7 0-0 13.d5 ♘bd7 14.♖h1 ♛g4 15.d6 e6 16.♖dg1 ♛b4∞) 12.♔b1 ♗g7 (12...♘c6?! 13.d5 with a strong initiative, Lindfeldt, J. M. (2326) – Drenchev, P. (2357), Bulgaria 2000) 13.♘d5 ♛xd2 14.♘xc7+ ♔f8 15.♖xd2 ♖a7∞.

10...♗g4 (10...♘c6!?) **11.♕d3**

11.♕d2 ♘bd7 (11...♗×e2?! 12.♘×e2 e6 13.0-0-0⩱, Thomas, V. – Al Khelaifi, S., Turin 2006) 12.0-0-0 ♖c8 13.♗g3 (13.♗e5 e6 14.♘g3 ♕g6 15.♘ce2 h5∓, Nyysti, S. (2245) – Karttunen, M. (2429), Helsinki 2002) 13...♕a5 (Govbinder, M. – Melts, M., Internet 1998) 14.♕e3 h5 15.f3 ♗f5 16.♗h4 g6 17.♔b1 ♗h6 18.f4∞.

11...♘bd7

11...♘c6!? 12.♕e3 (12.0-0-0 ♖c8 13.♗b6 e6 14.♕e3 ♕h6 15.f4 ♗e7 16.d5 e×d5∞ or 15.♕×h6 g×h6 16.d5 e×d5∞) 12...♗×e2 (12...e6?! 13.d5; 12...♖c8 13.♗e5⇄) 13.♘×e2 ♘d5 14.♗×d5 ♕×d5 15.0-0-0 ♘b4 (15...♖c8 16.♘c3 ♕e6 17.♕f4 g5∞) 16.♘c3 (16.♖g5?! ♕×a2 17.♖a5 ♕e6) 16...♘×a2+ 17.♘×a2 ♕×a2 18.d5∞.

12.0-0-0 ♖c8 13.♗f4

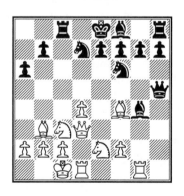

13...♕a5?!

A) 13...e6?! 14.f3! ♗×f3 (14...♗f5 15.♕e3 ♗g6 16.♖g5±) 15.♖g5 ♗×e2 16.♘×e2 ♕h4 (16...♕h6 17.♖c5 ♘×c5 18.d×c5±) 17.♕f3 ♗d6 18.♖×g7 ♗×f4+ (18...♕h5 19.♕×b8 ♖b8 20.♕g2±) 19.♘×f4 ♕h6 20.♖dg1 ♕f8

21.♗×e6! f×e6 22.♔b1 ♔e8 23.♕a3 ♘g8 24.♕d6 ♘f8 25.♘d5 ♕h4 26.♖f1 1-0, Rodriguez, A. (2460) – Giaccio, A. (2517), Italy 2002;

B) 13...♕f5! 14.♕e3 ♗×e2 15.♘×e2 ♘d5 16.♕d2 (16.♕f3?! ♘×f4 17.♘×f4? g5; 17.♕×f4 ♕×f4+ 18.♘×f4 g6±) 16...♘×f4 (16...e6?! 17.♖g5; 16...♘7b6!?) 17.♘×f4 e6 18.♖de1 (18.d5 e5⇄) 18...g6 19.♘d5 ♗d6 20.♘e3 ♕f6 21.♗d5 ♖c7∓ or 21.d5 ♗f4∓.

14.♖×g4! ♘×g4 15.♕f3 ♘gf6 16.♕×b7 ♔d8 (16...♕d8 17.♘d5 ♘×d5 18.♗×d5 g6 19.♕×a6 ♗g7 20.♗b7±; 18...e6 19.♗c6 ♗e7 20.d5± or 19...♖×c6 20.♕×c6 ♕b6 21.♕c8+ ♕d8 22.♕×a6±; 18.♕d5!? e6 19.♕b7 ♗e7 20.♗a4 ♖c4 21.♕×a6 ♕c8 22.♕a7; 17.♕×a6!? g6 18.♘b5 ♗g7 19.♘a7 ♖a8 20.♕b7 0-0 21.♘c6) **17.♗×f7 ♕b6** (17...g5 18.♗g3 ♗g7 19.d5 ♕b6 20.♘d4±; 19...♘c5 20.♕a7 ♖f8 21.♘d4±; 20...♘fd7 21.♗e6 ♕b6 22.♕×b6+ ♘×b6 23.♗×c8±; 21...♖f8 22.d6 ♖e8 23.♗×d7 ♘×d7 24.d×e7+ ♖×e7 25.♖d5± or 18...♕b6 19.♕f3 h5 20.♘a4 g4 21.♕e3 ♗h6 22.♗f4 ♕c6 23.♘c5 ♗×f4 24.♘×f4±; 19...♗g7 20.♘a4 ♕a5 21.♘c5+−; 20...♕c6 21.♘c5 e6 22.♕e3 ♘×c5 23.d×c5+ ♔e7 24.♗h5±) **18.♕×b6+** (18.♕g2!? e6 19.♗e3) **18...♘×b6 19.d5 g5** (Black has problems completing development: A) 19...h5 20.♘d4 ♘c4 21.♘e6+ ♔d7 22.♘a4 h4 23.b3±; 20...♖c4 21.♘c6+ ♔c8 22.♗e6+ ♘fd7 23.♗e3 ♔b7 24.♗×b6±; 22...♘bd7 23.♗g5 h4 24.♘e5±; 23...♔c7 24.d6+ e×d6 25.♗×c4 ♔×c6 26.♗×a6±; B) 19...g6 20.♘d4 ♖c4 21.♘c6+!?; 21.d6!?; 21.♗e5 ♔c8 22.♗e6+ ♔b7 23.d6 ♖c5 24.f4±;

21...♗h6+ 22.♔b1 ♔d7 23.♗e6+
♔e8 24.d6 ♖c5 25.♗×f6 e×f6
26.♘e4± or 21...♘bd7 22.♘c6+ ♔c8
23.♗d4 ♔c7 24.d6+; 23...♔b7
24.♘a5+; 24.♔b1± or 23.♗h6+ e5
24.d×e6±) **20.♗×g5 h5 21.♔b1
♗h6 22.♗h4 ♖f8** (22...♘c4
23.♘d4±) **23.♗e6 ♖c4 24.♘d4
♘a4** (24...♔e8 25.d6 e×d6 26.♘f5±)
25.♘×a4 ♖×a4 26.♗×f6 (26.d6
e×d6 27.b3±) **26...♔e8?!** (26...♖×f6
27.b3 ♖×d4 28.♖×d4 ♖×f2 29.♖a4±)
**27.b3 ♖b4 28.a3 ♖b6 29.♗e5
♖×f2 30.♖h1 1-0**

Summary: After **1.e4 d5 2.e×d5
♛×d5 3.♘c3 ♛d6 4.d4 ♘f6
5.♗c4 a6 6.♘ge2**, the move **6...♛c6**
forces White to play a gambit line that
is not for the faint-hearted. We see from
the analysis of this game that the bound-
ary between a correct and an incorrect
sacrifice can be very fine, and that perhaps the counterattack 6...♛c6 should
not be regarded as "mere pawn-grabbing."

After 7.♛d3 ♛×g2 8.♖g1, Black has
only one good reply, 8...♛h3. 8...♛×h2
or 8...♛c6 is dangerous for Black.

After 7.♗b3 (7.♗d3 may be playable,
but this bishop is more active on the a2-
g8 diagonal) 7...♛×g2 8.♖g1, we have
an unclear position where Black has
four reasonable possibilities: 8...♛c6,
8...♛f3, 8...♛h3 and 8...♛×h2.

Game 6
Ardeleanu, A. (2424) –
Malaniuk, V. (2539)
Arad 2006

**1.e4 d5 2.e×d5 ♛×d5 3.♘c3 ♛d6
4.d4 ♘f6 5.♗c4 a6 6.♘ge2 b5**

6...♘c6!? 7.♗f4 (7.0-0 ♗f5?! 8.♗f4 ♛b4
(Shabala, S. (2255) – Kernazhitsky, L.
(2370), Kiev 2007) 9.b3 0-0-0 10.a3
♛b6 11.♗e3 or 8...♛d7 9.d5 ♘a5
10.♗d3; 7.e5!?) 7...e5 8.d×e5 ♘×e5
9.♗b3 ♛×d1+ 10.♖×d1 ♗d6⇄,
Badev, K. (2310) – Solomunovic, I.
(2440), Nis 2008.

7.♗b3

7.♗d3 ♗b7 8.♗f4 (8.f3 ♘bd7 9.♗f4
(Langer, M. (2308) – Braunlich, T.
(2178), USA 2006) 9...e5 10.♗g3 h5
11.h4 ♗e7∓) 8...♛b6 9.f3 (Buckley,
M. (2147) – Conlon, J. (2170), London
2002) 9...♘c6 10.♛d2 e6 11.a3 ♖d8⇄
or 8...♛d7 9.f3 e6 10.♛d2 c5 11.d×c5
♗×c5 (Veber, B. (2120) – Nikolov, S.
(2392), Portoroz 2003) 12.0-0-0 ♘c6=.

7...♗b7

7...♘c6 (For 7...e6 or 7...e5 see Game
7; 7...♗g4 – Game 8) 8.♗f4 ♛d7 9.♛d3
♗b7 10.f3 (10.0-0 ♘a5 11.♘g3 ♘×b3
12.a×b3 e6 13.♘ge4 ♗e7⇄) 10...e6
(10...g6!?) 11.0-0-0 ♘b4 12.♛e3 a5
13.a4 b×a4 14.♘×a4 (14.♗×a4 ♗c6∓,
Zhelnin, V. (2430) – Gorshkov, Y.
(2240), Kaluga 2007) 14...♘bd5= or
9.♛d2 g6 (9...♗b7 10.0-0 ♘a5 11.♘g3
♘×b3 12.a×b3 e6 13.♗e5 ♗e7 14.♛e2

75

0-0 15.♖ad1 ♖fd8 16.♘ce4 ♘×e4 17.♘×e4 f6 ½-½, Bokros, A. (2260) – Jirovsky, P. (2360), Komarno 1997) 10.0-0 ♗g7 (11...♘a5!?) 11.♗h6 0-0 12.♗×g7 ♔×g7 13.f3±.

8.♗f4

8.0-0

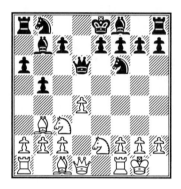

A) 8...♘bd7 9.♘g3 (9.♗f4!?) 9...g6 (9...c5!?) 10.♕e2 ♗g7 11.♗e3 c5 12.d×c5 ♕c6 13.f3 ♘×c5 (Matsuo, T. (2205) – Jirovsky, M. (2435), Rotterdam 1998) 14.♗d4 ♘×b3 15.a×b3=;

B) 8...e6 9.♕d3 (9.♗f4 – 8.♗f4 ♕b6/♕d7/♕d8 9.0-0 e6) 9...c5 10.d×c5 ♕×d3 11.c×d3 ♗×c5 12.♗e3 (Ostrovsky, A. (2372) – Rozenvaser, D., Odessa 2000) 12...♘bd7 ⇄ or 10...♕c6 11.♕h3 ♗×c5 12.♗e3 ♗×e3 13.f×e3=, Crepan, M. (2250) – Nikolov, S. (2399), Bled 2003;

C) 8...c5 9.d×c5 (9.♗f4 ♕c6 10.d5 ♕d7∞) 9...♕c6 10.♘f4 ♘bd7 (10...e6 11.♖e1 ♗e7 12.♕e2 (Aigner, M. (2260) – Braunlich, T. (2195), Stillwater 2007) 12...♘bd7 13.a4 b4 14.♘cd5 ♗×c5 ⇄) 11.a4 (11.♘cd5 g5 12.♘b4 ♕×c5 13.♘fd5 ♘×d5 14.♗×d5 ♗×d5

15.♘×d5 ♖g8 16.♕f3 ⇄, Braun, V. (2189) – Eismont, O. (2431), Germany 2003) 11...♘×c5 12.a×b5 a×b5 13.♖×a8+ ♗×a8 14.♗a2 b4 15.♗d5 ♘×d5 16.♘c×d5 e5 17.♕e2 ♘e6 18.♘×e6 f×e6∞.

Returning to Ardeleanu – Malaniuk.

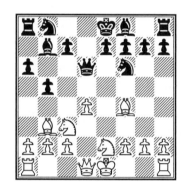

8...♕d7

Also coming under consideration are **A)** 8...♕d8 and **B)** 8...♕b6.

A) 8...♕d8 9.0-0 (9.♕d3 ♗×g2 10.♖g1 ♗b7 11.0-0-0 ♘bd7 12.♘g3 g6∞ or 9.♕d2 e6 10.0-0 ♗d6 11.♗g5 ♘bd7 12.♖fe1 0-0 13.♖ad1 1/2-1/2, Susterman, A. (2299) – Gheorghe, C. (2222), Bucharest 2004; 10...♗e7!? 11.♖ad1 b4 12.♘a4 ♘bd7 ⇄; 9...b4!? 10.♘a4 ♗×g2 11.♖g1 ♗d5∞)

A1) 9...c5 (9...b4!? 10.♘a4 e6; 9...g6!? 10.♕d3 ♘c6) 10.d×c5 ♕×d1 (10...♘bd7 11.c6 ♗×c6 12.♘d4 ♗b7 13.♕e2 e6 14.♘f5 ♕b6 15.♖ad1±) 11.♖a×d1 e6 12.♖fe1 ♘bd7 (12...♗×c5 13.♘g3 ♘bd7 14.a4 b4±) 13.c6 ♗×c6 14.♘d4 ♗b7±;

A2) 9...♘bd7 10.a4 (10.♖e1 c5 11.d×c5 ♘×c5 12.♘d4 e6 13.♕d2

♘×b3 14.a×b3 ♗c5 15.♖ad1 0-0=)
10...b4 11.♘a2 e6 12.♕d2 (12.c3 a5
13.c×b4 a×b4 14.♘ac1 ♘h5=) 12...a5
13.c3 b×c3 14.♘e×c3 ♘b6 15.♖ac1
♗d6 16.♘b5± , Zeller, F. (2434) –
Slobodjan, R. (2539), Heringsdorf 2000
or 10.♕e1 g6 (10...c5 11.d×c5 ♘×c5
12.♖d1 ♕b6 13.♘d5±) 11.♖d1 ♗g7
12.♘g3 0-0 13.a4 (Kennaugh, C.
(2310) – Bronstein, D. (2445), Hastings
1995) 13...b4 14.♘ce4 a5 15.♕e2
♘d5=;

A3) 9...e6

A3a) 10.d5

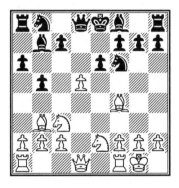

A3a1) 10...e×d5 11.♘g3 (11.♖e1 ♗e7
12.♘d4 0-0 13.♘f5 ♗c5 14.♕f3 ♘e4?
15.♘×e4 d×e4 16.♕c3 +– , Vallejo
Pons, F. (2528) – Magem Badals, J.
(2529), Leon 2000) 11...♗e7 12.♘f5 0-0
(12...♔f8 13.♘×e7 ♔×e7≊) 13.♘×d5
♘×d5 14.♗×d5 ♗×d5 15.♕×d5 c6
(Moiseenko, V. (2400) – Bazarov, K.
(2230), Sochi 2007) 16.♕×d8 ♗×d8
17.♗d6 ♖e8 18.♖fe1± ;

A3a2) 10...c5 11.d×c6 (11.d×e6? ♕×d1
12.♖a×d1 c4∓ , Moreda, L. (2336) –
Garcia Palermo, C. (2464), Buenos
Aires 2001; 11.a4 c4 12.♗a2 ♘×d5
13.♘×d5 ♕×d5 14.♕×d5 ♗×d5

15.a×b5 a×b5 16.♘c3 ♘c6 17.♘×b5
♔d7∓) 11...♘×c6 12.♕e1 (12.a4 b4
13.♘a2 ♘a5∓ or 13.♘b1 ♗c5∓)
12...♗c5 (12...♕b6!?) 13.♘g3 0-0
14.♘ce4 ♘×e4 15.♘×e4 ♕b6=;

A3b) 10.a4 b4 11.♘a2 a5 (11...♗e7
12.♕d3 0-0 13.c4 (13.♖ad1 (Tissir M.
(2426) – Saud M. (2198), Caleta 2005)
13...♘c6 14.c4 ♘a5∓) 13...♘c6
14.♗c2 ♗d6 15.♗g5 g6=) 12.♘ac1
♗d6 13.♘d3 ♗×f4 14.♘d×f4 0-0 15.c4
(Alexikov, A. (2390) – Boricsev, O.
(2330), Alushta 2003) 15...♘c6∓ or
15.♕d3 ♕d6 16.♖fe1 ♘c6 17.f3
♗a6∓;

A3c) 10.♘g3

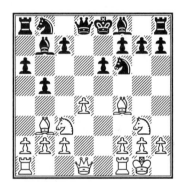

A3c1) 10...♗e7 11.d5 (11.♖e1 0-0
12.♕d2 c5 13.d×c5 ♕×d2 14.♗×d2
♘bd7 15.♘ce4 ♘×e4 16.♘×e4 ♗×e4
17.♖×e4 ♘×c5 18.♖e2 ♖fd8 ½-½,
Pavlov, M. (2451) – Hasangatin, R.
(2503), Alushta 2004) 11...♗×d5
12.♘×d5 ♘×d5 (12...e×d5? 13.♘f5 0-0
14.♗×d5 ♘×d5 15.♕×d5 c6 16.♕×d8
♗×d8 17.♗d6 ♖e8 18.♖fe1 +–)
13.♗×d5 ♕×d5 14.♕×d5 e×d5
15.♗×c7±;

A3c2) 10...♗d6 (10...c5 11.d×c5 ♕×d1
12.♖a×d1 ♗×c5 13.♖fe1 0-0 14.a4 b4

15.♘ce4 ♘xe4 16.♘xe4±, Skytte, R. (2215) – Jensen, V. (2270), Aarhus 1998; 15...♘bd7!?) 11.♗xd6 (11.♗g5 ♗e7 12.♖e1 0-0 13.d5 c5 14.dxc6 ♘xc6 15.♘ce4 ♘d4∓, Parligras, M. (2498) – Svetushkin, D. (2501), Bucharest 2002) 11... Cxd6 (or 11...♕xd6) 12.d5±;

B) 8...♕b6

B1) 9.♕d2 e6 (9...♗xg2 10.♖g1 ♗b7 11.0-0-0 ♘c6 12.a3 g6 13.♗e5 ♘a5 14.♗a2 ♖d8 15.♘g3⩲; 11...♘bd7 12.♔b1 e6 13.d5 e5 14.♗e3 ♘c5∞) 10.0-0-0 ♘bd7 11.f3 (11.d5 e5 12.♗e3 ♗c5=) 11...c5 12.dxc5 ♗xc5 13.♘g3 (13.♗g5? h6–+ (Jakubowski, K. (2483) – Szwed, J. (2215), Warsaw 2005) 13...0-0 14.♔b1 ♖fd8 15.♕e2 ♗d4 16.♘ce4 ♘d5 17.♗xd5 ♗xd5 18.c3 ♗e5 19.♘h5=;

B2) 9.♕d3 ♘bd7 (9...♗xg2 10.♖g1 ♗b7 11.♕g3 ♘h5 12.♗xc7 ♘xg3 13.♗xb6 ♘xe2 14.♘xe2 ♘d7 15.♗a5±) 10.a4 ♕a5 (10...b4!? 11.a5 ♕a7 12.♘a4 ♗xg2) 11.0-0 b4 12.♘d1 e6 13.♘e3 0-0-0 14.♗g3 ♘e4 15.♘c4 ♕f5 16.♕e3 h5⇄, Repkova, E. (2359) – Kaps, D. (2237), Punat 2003;

B3) 9.0-0

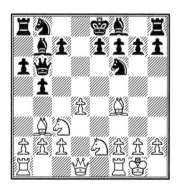

9...e6 (9...♘bd7 10.d5 c5 11.a3 c4 12.♗a2∞; 10...♘c5 11.♗e3±) and now:

B3a) 10.d5 c5 (10...exd5? 11.♘xd5 ♘xd5 12.♗xd5 ♗c5 13.b4 ♗e7 14.♗e3 c5 15.bxc5±, Zhang, E. – Petursson, M. (1915), Singapore 2007 or 13...♗xb4 14.♗xb7 ♕xb7 15.♕d4 ♘c6 16.♕xg7 0-0-0 17.♕xf7±) 11.a4 (11.♗e3 ♕d6 12.a3 c4 13.♗a2 ♘xd5 14.♘xd5 ♕xd5 15.♕xd5 ♗xd5∓) 11...c4 12.♗a2 ♘xd5 13.♘xd5 ♗xd5∞;

B3b) 10.a4 c5 (10...♘bd7 11.axb5 axb5 12.♕d3 ♖xa1 13.♖xa1 b4 14.♘b5 with a strong pressure) 11.axb5 axb5 12.♗xb8 ♖xb8 13.♘xb5 ♗e7 14.♘bc3 0-0 15.dxc5 ♗xc5⩲, Kalaitzoglou, P. (2160) – Andronis, V. (2069), Kalithea 2006; 10...b4 11.a5 ♕a7 12.♘a4 ♘bd7 13.♕d3 ♗c6 (13...♗e7!?) 14.♖fe1 (14.c4 bxc3 15.♘exc3 ♕b7 16.d5 exd5 17.♖fe1+ ♗e7 18.♗c2 ♔f8∞) 14...♕b7 15.♕h3 (15.f3!? ♗e7 16.♗c4) 15...♗e7 16.♘g3 0-0 17.♘f5 (Peredy, F. (2200) – Mozes, E. (2370), Szeged 1997) 17...♗d8=.

Back to Ardeleanu – Malaniuk.

9.d5 (9.♕d3 ♗xg2 10.♖g1 ♗b7∞)

Other alternatives are **A)** 9.f3 and **B)** 9.0-0.

A) 9.f3 e6 (9...♘c6!?) 10.♗e3 ♗e7 11.0-0 0-0 12.♘f4 ♘c6 13.♘e4 ♘b4 14.♘xf6+ ♗xf6 15.c3 ♘d5 16.♘xd5 ♗xd5 17.♗c2 ♖fd8=, Girya, O. (2335) – Beridze, T. (2030), Kemer 2007 or 11.♘g3 ♘c6 12.♘ce4 0-0-0 13.c3 ♘d5 ⇄, Valenta, V. (2285) – Jirovsky, M. (2445), Litomysl 1996;

B) 9.0-0 e6

B1) 10.a4 (10.♔h1 c5 11.dxc5 ♕c6 12.f3 ♗xc5 13.♘g3 0-0 14.♘ge4 ♗e7 15.♕e2 b4 16.♘xf6+ ♗xf6 17.♘a4 (Bjeloglav, M. (2005) – Vojinovic, J. (2215), Zlatibor 2007) 17...♘d7=) 10...b4 11.♘b1 ♗e7 12.♘d2 (Rodriguez, A. (2511) – Ryan, J. (2330), Sants 2006) 12...0-0 13.♖e1=;

B2) 10.♕d3 c5 11.dxc5

B2a) 11...♕xd3 12.cxd3 ♗xc5 13.d4 (13.♖ac1 ♘bd7=, (Kleinschroth, R. (2175) – Eismont, O. (2433), Dortmund 2004) 13...♗e7 (13...♗b6!? 14.a4 b4 15.a5 ♗d8±) 14.d5 ♘xd5 15.♘xd5 ♗xd5 16.♗xd5 exd5 17.♘c3 (17.♖ad1 ♘c6 18.♖xd5 0-0=) 17...d4 18.♘d5 ⯑;

B2b) 11...♗xc5 12.♕g3 (12.♖ad1 ♕xd3 13.♖xd3 ♘c6=, Chovanec, M. (2135) – Vojtek, V. (2275), Slovakia 2002) 12...0-0 (12...♕c6 13.♖ad1 ♘bd7 14.♘d4±) 13.♖ad1 ♕c6 14.♗e5 ♔h8 15.♘d4 (15.♘f4?! ♘bd7⯑, Wegener, D. (2305) – Mozes, E. (2365), Budapest 1993) 15...♕c8 16.♗xf6 gxf6 17.♕h4 ♘d7±.

Returning to Ardeleanu – Malaniuk.

9...c5 10.dxc6 ♕xc6

10...♘xc6 11.♕xd7+ ♘xd7 12.a4 bxa4 13.♗xa4 0-0-0 14.f3 e6 15.0-0-0 ♗e7 16.♘e4 ♘b6 17.♗xc6 ♗xc6 18.♗d6±.

11.f3 ♘bd7 12.♕d2?!

12.♕d4 (12.♘d4 ♕b6 13.♗e3 e6 14.♕e2 ♗c5 15.0-0-0 0-0 16.♖he1∞) 12...e6 (12...♕c5 13.♕d2 e5 14.♗e3 ♕d6 15.♕xd6 ♗xd6 16.♘g3 ♗c5 17.♗xc5 ♘xc5 18.0-0-0 0-0 19.♖he1±) 13.0-0-0 ♘c5 (13...♗c5 14.♕d3 e5 15.♗g5 0-0 16.♘g3±) 14.♕e5 ♘xb3+ 15.axb3 ♗e7 16.♖he1 ♕c5 17.♘g3 ♕xe5 18.♗xe5 ♖d8=.

12...e5∓ 13.♗e3 ♘c5 14.0-0-0 (14.♖d1 ♘xb3 15.axb3 ♗b4 16.♔f2 0-0 ∓) **14...♘xb3+ 15.axb3 ♗b4 16.♗g5 0-0 17.♔b1 a5 18.♕d3** (18.♕e3!?) **18...♗xc3** (18...e4!?) **19.♗xf6 ♕xf6?!** (19...♗xb2 20.♗xg7? e4-+ or 20.♗e7 ♖fe8 21.♕d7 ♖ac8 22.♕xc6 ♗xc6∓) **20.♘xc3 b4 21.♘e4?!** (21.♘a4±) **21...♗xe4 22.fxe4 a4 23.bxa4?!** (23.♕d6!? ♕f2 24.♖d2 ♕a7 25.♕d7) **23...♖xa4 24.b3 ♖a3 25.♔b2 ♕f2 26.♖a1 ♕a7 27.♖hd1 h5 28.♖f1 ♖a8 29.♖ab1 ♖a2+ 30.♔c1 ♖c8**

31.♚d1 ♖c×c2 32.♛×c2 ♛d4+ 0-1

Summary: In the line **1.e4 d5 2.e×d5 ♛×d5 3.♘c3 ♛d6 4.d4 ♘f6 5.♗c4 a6 6.♘ge2**, we saw in Game 5 how after 6...♛c6 both sides are forced into an unclear gambit. Recalling the words of Aron Nimzovitch from *My System*. The win of a pawn anywhere on the side of the board brings no happiness in its train," one might well ask "Why play 6...♛c6 and 7...♛×g2, and risk giving White a strong initiative, if I can have a normal game after 6...♘c6 or 6...b5?" And one may be right.

After **6...b5** (this move is more popular than 6...♘c6), we will see in later games (27 and 28) the same position but with ♘g1-f3. The position of this game, with ♘g1-e2, is more favorable for Black than with ♘f3. **7.♗b3 ♗b7 8.♗f4** Here Black has three possibilities: 8...♛b6, 8...♛d8 and 8...♛d7.

After 8...♛b6 the plan of d4-d5 or a2-a4-a5 can be unpleasant for Black in some lines. After 8...♛d8 the same is true of the plan of a2-a4 with the idea of a4×b5. Safer than either of these is 8...♛d7, because from d7 the queen can control the important squares b5, c6, d5, e6 and f5 (on e6×d5, after d4-d5).

In different lines of Game 6 Black uses the standard method for counterplay. Typical for this method is the move c7-c5 in positions with White's ♗b3, ♘c3, pawns on a2, b2, c2, d4 (or d5) and Black's pawns on a6, b5. After c7-c5, Black threatens c5-c4, and to save the bishop White must play a2-a3 (a2-a4) or d4×c5 (d5×c6). In the first instance,

after c5-c4, White may have a problem activating the bishop. In the second instance, Black usually has a good game (no problems with White's pawn in then center as well as the possibility, after ♘b8-d7-c5, to capture the ♗b3, gaining the bishop-pair). We will also see this pattern in other lines, for example in Games 7, 26, 27, 28.

Game 7
Fercec, N. (2470) – Milanovic, D. (2510)
Nova Gorica 2008

1.e4 d5 2.e×d5 ♛×d5 3.♘c3 ♛d6 4.d4 ♘f6 5.♗c4 a6 6.♗b3

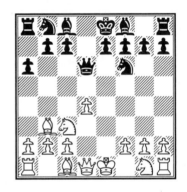

Anticipating b7-b5. Moving the bishop before it is attacked can be useful if Black plays imprecisely.

6...♘c6 (6...♗f5?! 7.♛f3; 6...♗g4 see Game 8).

Also coming under consideration are **A)** 6...b5; **B)** 6...g6 and **C)** 6...e6.

A) 6...b5?! 7.♛f3 (for 7.♘ge2 see Game 6; 7.♘f3 – Games 27 and 28) 7...c6 8.♘ge2 ♗g4 (8...e6 9.♗f4±, Paehtz, T. (2406) – Schlesinger, O. (2230), Germany 2005) 9.♛d3 e6 (9...c5?! 10.d×c5 10.f3 (10.♗f4!?; 10.♘g3!?) 10...♗f5

11.♘e4 ♛d8 12.0-0 with better chances for White or 7...♘c6 8.♘e4 ♛d7 (8...♛×d4 9.♘g5±) 9.♘e2 (9.♘c5 ♛d6 10.♗f4 ♗g4±; 9.c3!?) 9...♖b8 (9...e6 10.♛×f6± or 9...♗b7 10.♘c5±) 10.0-0 with a strong initiative;

B) 6...g6 7.♘ge2 ♗g7 8.♗f4 ♛d8 9.♛d2 0-0 (9...♘c6!?) 10.0-0-0 (10.♗h6 ♗×h6 11.♛×h6 ♘c6 12.0-0-0 ♘g4⇄) 10...♘c6 11.♗h6 (11.a3!?) 11...e5 (11...♗×h6!?) 12.♗×g7 ♔×g7 13.d5 ♘a5 14.f3 (14.♘g3 c5 15.d×c6 ♛×d2+ 16.♖×d2 ♘×c6 17.♖e1 ♗f5±) 14...♘×b3+ (14...c5 15.d×c6 ♛×d2+) 15.a×b3±, Nyysti, S. (2297) – Karttunen, M. (2434), Oulainen 2002;

C) 6...e6 7.♘ge2 (7.♘f3 – Game 28) and now:

C1) 7...c5 (7...♘c6 – 6...♘c6 7.♘ge2 e6) 8.♗f4 ♛d8 9.d5 (9.0-0 b5; 9.d×c5 ♛×d1+ 10.♖×d1 ♗×c5 11.0-0 b5 12.♗d6 ♘bd7 13.♖fe1 ♗b7⇄, Janev, E. (2413) – Kurajica, B. (2534), Mondariz 2000) 9...b5 10.d×e6 ♛×d1+ 11.♖×d1 c4 12.♘a4 c×b3 13.♘b6 ♗b7 14.♘×a8 ♗×a8 15.a×b3 ♘c6 16.e×f7+ ♔×f7 17.0-0 ♗c5⇄;

C2) 7...b5 8.♗f4 (8.0-0 ♗b7 – 7.♗b3 ♗b7 8.0-0 e6, Game 6; 8...c5!?)

C2a) 8...♛b6

C2a1) 9.♛d3 c5 10.d×c5 ♗×c5 11.0-0 ♗b7⇄; 9.♛d2 ♗b7 – 7.♗b3 ♗b7 8.♗f4 ♛b6 9.♛d2 e6, Game 6; 9...c5!?; 9.0-0 ♗b7 – 7.♗b3 ♗b7 8.♗f4 ♛b6 9.0-0 e6, Game 6; 9...c5 10.a4!?; 9...♘bd7 10.♗e3!?;

C2a2) 9.a4 b4 (9...♗b7 10.♛d3 b4 11.a5 ♛a7 12.♘d1 ♗×g2 13.♖g1

♗e4∞, Almagro Llanas, P. (2373) – Garcia Albarracin, F. (2308), Spain 2004; 10.0-0!? or 10.a×b5!?) 10.a5 (10.♘b1 ♗d6 11.a5 ♛a7 12.0-0 0-0-0=) 10...♛a7 (10...♛b7!?) 11.♘a4 ♘c6⇄ or 11.♘a2 ♘c6⇄;

C2b) 8...♛d8

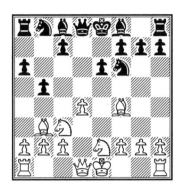

9.0-0 ♗b7 – 7.♗b3 ♗b7 8.♗f4 ♛d8 9.0-0 e6, Game 6; 9.♛d2 ♗b7 – 7.♗b3 ♗b7 8.♗f4 ♛d8 9.♛d2 e6, Game 6. Now we examine 9.♛c1, 9.♛d3 and 9.d5.

C2b1) 9.♛c1 c5 10.d×c5 ♗×c5 11.♗×b8?! (11.0-0 0-0=) 11...♖×b8 12.♛g5 ♛e7 13.0-0-0 (13.♛×g7?! ♖g8 14.♛h6 ♗×f2+) 13...0-0 (13...♗×f2 14.♖hf1?! h6 15.♛e5 ♗a7∓, Urbina, R. (2290) – Juarez Flores, C. (2365), Panama 2006; 14.♘d4!?∞) 14.♘g3 ♗b7∓;

C2b2) 9.♛d3 ♗b7 (9...c5?! 10.♛f3±; 9...♘bd7!? 10.♛f3 ♖b8) 10.0-0-0 (10.0-0 c5 11.d×c5 ♛×d3 12.c×d3 ♗×c5⇄; 10...♘bd7!?)

C2b2a) 10...♘c6?! 11.d5 ♘b4 12.♛g3 ♘b×d5 13.♘×d5 ♘×d5 (13...♗×d5 14.c4⊞, Moeller, D. (2175) – Buechmann, O. (2109), Kiel 2005;

13...e×d5 14.♖he1 ♗e7 15.♗×c7 ♕d7 16.♘d4±) 14.♗×d5 ♗×d5 15.♗×c7 ♕f6 16.♘f4 ♗b7 17.♖he1 ♖c8 18.♔b1 ♗b4 19.♗e5 ♕f5 20.♕×g7 ♖f8 21.♘×e6+– ; 18...h5 19.h4 ♗b4 20.♖e2± ;

C2b2b) 10...c5 11.d×c5 (11.d5?! c4 12.♕e3 ♕c8 13.d×e6 ♗c5 14.♕g3 0-0 15.♗h6 ♘h5 16.e×f7+ ♖×f7 17.♕h4 ♘f6 18.♕g5 c×b3 19.♗×g7 ♖×g7 20.♕×f6 ♗e7 0-1, Solovjov, S. (2457) – Kokarev, D. (2495), St. Petersburg 2004) 11...♕×d3 12.c×d3 ♗×c5 13.d4 ♗b6 14.d5 e×d5 15.♘×d5 ♘×d5 16.♗×d5 ♗×d5 17.♖×d5 ♘c6 18.f3 0-0= ;

C2b3) 9.d5 c5 10.d×c6 ♕×d1+ 11.♖×d1 ♘×c6 12.0-0 ♗b7 13.♘g3 ♘a5 14.♖fe1 ♗b4 15.♘f5 (15.♗d6 ♗×d6 16.♖×d6 ♖d8 17.♖×d8+ ♔×d8∓, Golubovic, B. (2426) – Sermek, D. (2571), Rabac 2003) 15...0-0 16.♗d6 ♗×d6 (16...♗×c3 17.♘e7+ ♔h8 18.b×c3 ♘e4⇄) 17.♘×d6 ♖fd8= or 14...♗e7 15.♘ce4 ♘×e4 16.♘×e4 ♘×b3 17.a×b3 ♗×e4 (17...♖c8 18.c3± , Vallejo Pons, F. (2630) – Kurajica, B. (2566), Villarrobledo 2001) 18.♖×e4 0-0= ;

C2c) 8...♕d7

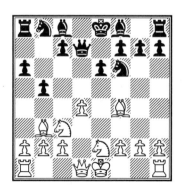

9.d5 (9.♕d2 ♗b7 – 7.♗b3 ♗b7 8.♗f4 ♕d7 9.♕d2 e6, Game 6; 9.0-0 c5 10.d×c5 ♗×c5 11.♕×d7+ ♘b×d7 12.♖ad1 ♗b7=, Fiebig, T. (2263) – Eismont, O. (2433), Dortmund 2004 or 9...♗b7 – 7.♗b3 ♗b7 8.♗f4 ♕d7 9.0-0 e6, Game 6) 9...c5 10.d×c6

C2c1) 10...♘×c6 11.0-0 ♗b7 12.♕×d7+ ♘×d7 13.♗d2 (13.♗e3 ♘a5∓, Petrov, M. (2441) – Bratanov, Z. (2398), Plovdiv 2004) 13...f5 (13...♗e7 14.♖ad1⇄) 14.♘g5 ♘c5⇄ ;

C2c2) 10...♕×c6

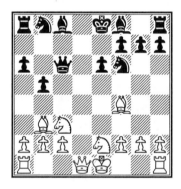

C2c2a) 11.a4 b4 12.a5 ♕×g2 (12...♘bd7!? 13.♘a4 ♕×g2 14.♖g1 ♕f3) 13.♖g1 ♕f3 14.♘a4 ♘c6?! (Pavlovic, S. (2379) – Benkovic, P. (2469), Dimitrovgrad 2003) 15.♘b6 ♗c5 16.♗e3 (16.♘×a8?! ♗×f2+ 17.♔d2 ♘d4∓) 16...♗×e3 (16...♗×b6 17.a×b6⩲) 17.f×e3 ♖b8 18.♕d6 ♗b7 19.♗a4⩲; 14...♘bd7 15.♖g3 ♕c6 16.♕d4 ♘h5∓ ;

C2c2b) 11.♕d2 ♗c5 (11...♕×g2 12.♖g1 ♕b7 13.0-0-0 ♘c6 14.♘g3⩲) 12.♗e3 (12.0-0-0 0-0 13.f3 ♗b7 14.♔b1 ♕b6 15.♘g3 ♘c6⇄) 12...♗b7 13. O-O-O O-O 14.f3 ♘bd7 15.h4 a5

82

16.a4⇄, Melia, S. (2362) – Ushenina, A. (2484), Moscow 2008.

Back to Fercec– Milanovic.

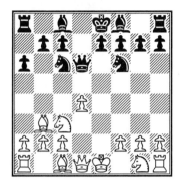

7.♘ge2

7.♗e3 (7.♘f3 ♗f5 8.♗g5 ♖d8 9.0-0 h6 10.♗e3 e6 11.h3 ♗e7 12.a3 0-0 13.♛e2 ♖fe8⇄, Szieberth, A. (2389) – Jirovsky, M. (2452), Tanta 2001) 7...e6 (7...♗g4!?) 8.♘f3 ♗e7 9.♛e2 0-0 10.0-0-0 b5⇄, Mai, P. – Von Alvensleben, W. (2235), Germany 1995.

7...e5

7...♗g4 – Game 8; 7...b5 – 5.♗c4 a6 6.♘ge2 b5 7.♗b3 ♘c6, Game 6.

Alternatives here are **A)** 7...♗f5; **B)** 7...♘a5 and **C)** 7...e6.

A) 7...♗f5 (!? Grefe & Silman) 8.♗f4

A1) 8...e5? 9.d×e5 ♘×e5 (9...♛×d1+ 10.♖×d1 ♘g4 11.e6±) 10.♛d4 (10.0-0!? 0-0-0 11.♘g3) 10...♘fd7 11.0-0-0 f6 (11...♛×d4 12.♘×d4±) 12.♛a4 ♛b4 13.♛×b4 ♗×b4 14.♘d4±;

A2) 8...♛d7 9.♛d2 (9.d5!? ♘a5 10.0-0) 9...e6 10.0-0 ♗b4 (10...0-0-0!?) 11.♛e3

(11.a3 ♗a5 12.♖ad1 0-0-0⇄) 11...0-0 (11...0-0-0!?) 12.♗g5 (12.♖ad1 ♖fe8 13.a3 ♗d6 14.♘g3=) 12...♗g4 13.♛d2 h6 14.♗h4 ♗e7⇄, Lanc, A. (2376) – Bombek, P. (2242), Slovakia 2002 or 10.a3 0-0-0 11.0-0-0 (11.♖d1 ♗d6 12.♗g5 h6 13.♗×f6 g×f6∓, Akopian, G. (2235) – Danielian, E. (2437), Yerevan 2004; 12.0-0!?) 11...♗d6 12.f3 (Kristjansson, S. (2374) – Danielsen, H. (2526), Reykjavik 2001) 12...♖he8⇄;

B) 7...♘a5 8.♗f4

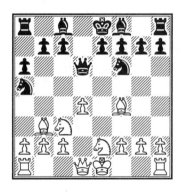

8...♛d7 (8...♛d8 9.♛d3 b5 10.♛g3 ♖a7 (Voloshin, L. (2468) – Londyn, R. (2152), Prague 2003) 11.0-0 ♘h5?! 12.♛e3 ♘×f4 13.♘×f4 ♗f5 14.♖fe1±; 11...♗f5 12.♖fe1±)

B1) 9.0-0 ♘×b3 (9...g6!? 10.♗e5 ♗g7 11.♘f4 0-0 12.♛f3 c6⇄) 10.a×b3 e6 11.d5 (11.♖e1 ♗e7= Hodges; 11.♛d3 b6?! (Solic, K. (2145) – Sermek, D. (2520), Sibenik 2007) 12.♛g3 ♖a7 13.♗e5± or 12...c6 13.♗e5±; 11...♗e7±) 11...♘×d5 (11...e×d5!? 12.♘d4 ♗c5 13.♖e1+ ♔f8∞) 12.♘×d5 e×d5 (12...♛×d5 13.♛×d5 e×d5 14.♗×c7±) 13.♘c3 c6 14.♖e1+ ♗e7 15.♘a4 ♛d8 16.♛d4 ♗e6 17.♛×g7 ♗f6 18.♛h6±;

B2) 9.♕d3 ♘xb3 (9...e6 10.0-0 ♗e7 11.♗e5 0-0 12.♕g3 ♘xb3 13.axb3 ♘e8 14.♖ad1±) 10.axb3 e6 11.h4 ♕c6 (11...♗e7 12.h5) 12.0-0-0 ♗d6 (12...♗d7 13.d5 ♘xd5 14.♘xd5 ♕xd5 15.♕xd5 exd5 16.♗xc7±) 13.♗e5 ♗d7 14.d5 ♘xd5 15.♘d4∞, Maiorov, O. (2446) – Rodchenkov. V. (2417), Krasnodar 2003;

C) 7...e6 8.♗f4 ♕d8 9.0-0 ♗d6 10.♕d2 0-0 11.♖ad1 ♘a5 12.♗xd6 ♕xd6 13.♘e4 (13.♘g3 b6 14.♘ge4 ♘xe4 15.♘xe4 ♕e7 16.♖fe1 ♗b7=) 13...♘xe4 14.♕xa5 b6 15.♕e5 ♗b7=, Rolletschek, H. (2325) – Schueller, E. (2255), Germany 1997 or 8...♕d7 9.♕d3 ♗e7 (9...♗d6!?) 10.0-0-0 ♘a5 (10...b5!?) 11.♗e5 0-0 12.♕g3 b5? (12...♘xb3+ 13.axb3 ♘h5 14.♕f3 f6) 13.♘f4 ♗b7 14.d5 ♘xb3+ 15.axb3 b4 16.♗xf6 ♗xf6 17.♘h5 +–, Krakops, M. (2440) – Kerek, K. (2305), Spain 1996.

Let's return to Fercec– Milanovic.

8.dxe5

Also worth consideration are **A)** 8.♗e3 and **B)** 8.d5.

A) 8.♗e3

A1) 8...♘g4 9.♕d2 ♘xe3 (9...♗e7 10.0-0 0-0=) 10.fxe3 ♗e7 (10...♘a5 11.0-0 ♘xb3 12.axb3±) 11.0-0 0-0 12.a3 ♕h6 (12...♗g4!?) 13.♕d3 ♗g5 14.♘d5 ♗g4 15.♘g3⇄, Karavaev, V. (2363) – Zaitsev, V. (2413), Smolensk 2000;

A2) 8...♗e7 (8...exd4 9.♘xd4 ♗g4 10.f3 0-0-0 11.♘ce2 ♘xd4 12.♕xd4 ♕xd4 13.♗xd4±, Parligras, M. (2497) – Moldovan, D. (2447), Bucharest 2003; 11...♕e5!?) 9.h3 (Blomstrom, L. (2195) – Joensen, J., Copenhagen 2007) 9...0-0 10.0-0 ♖d8 11.♕e1 ♗f5⇄ or 9.dxe5 ♕xe5⇄;

B) 8.d5 ♘a5 9.♗g5 ♗e7 10.♘g3 0-0 11.♘ge4?! (11.0-0 ♘xb3 12.axb3±) 11...♘xe4 12.♘xe4? (12.♗xe7 ♕xe7 13.♘xe4∓) 12...♕b4+ 13.♔f1 ♗xg5 14.♘xg5 (Rigo, G. (2059) – Boricsev, O. (2342), Venice 2003) 14...f6 15.♘f3 ♖d8∓ or 9.♗e3 ♘xb3 (9...♗e7!?) 10.axb3 ♗f5 (10...♗e7!?) 11.♘g3 ♗g6 12.f3 0-0-0 (12...♕d7!?) 13.♘ge4 ♕d7 (13...♘xe4!? 14.fxe4 f5)14.♘xf6 gxf6 15.♕e2±, Mitkov, N. (2515) – Nikolov, S. (2400), Skopje 1998.

8...♕xd1+

A) 8...♕xe5?! 9.♗f4 ♕a5 10.0-0 ♗g4 11.h3 ♗h5 12.g4 ♗g6 13.♖e1 ♗e7 14.♘d4 0-0-0 (14...♖d8 15.♘xc6) 15.♘xc6 bxc6 16.♕f3 with better chances for White; 10...♗c5 11.♗d2 ♗d6 12.♘g3 ♗xg3 13.♘d5± or 12...0-0 13.♘ce4±; 10...♗e7 11.♘d4 ♘xd4 12.♕xd4 0-0 13.♖ae1 ♗c5 (13...♗d8 14.♗xf7+ ♔xf7 15.♕c4+ ♔g6 16.♖e5±) 14.♕e5 ♗b6 15.♕xa5 ♗xa5 16.♖e7 with a better ending for White;

B) 8...♘xe5 9.0-0 ♕xd1 10.♖xd1 ♗g4 11.♖e1 ♗d6 (11...0-0-0!?) 12.♗g5 ♘fd7 13.♘e4 ♗b4 14.c3 ♗a5 (14...♗e7 15.♗xe7 ♔xe7 16.♘d4±) 15.h3 ♗f5 16.♘4g3 ♗g6?! (16...♗e6!? 17.♗xe6 fxe6 18.♘d4 0-0 19.♘xe6 ♖fe8 20.♘d4 ♘d3) 17.♘f4 0-0? (17...f6!? 18.♗h4 0-0-0 19.♘gh5 ♗xh5 20.♘xh5 g5) 18.♖ad1 ♗b6 19.♘d5±, Galkin, A. (2507) – Feoktistov, A. (2390), St. Petersburg 1999.

9.♘xd1 ♘xe5

10.♘dc3

Other alternatives are **A)** 10.0-0, **B)** 10.♗g5 and **C)** 10.♗f4.

A) 10.0-0 ♗d6 11.♘dc3 (11.h3 c5 12.♘e3 ♗e6 13.♗xe6 fxe6 14.b3 ♔f7 ½-½, Saravanan, V. (2393) – Sermek, D. (2595), Calcutta 2002) 11...0-0 (11...♘g6 12.♗g5 ♘g4 13.♘g3 0-0 14.♘ce4 ♗e5 15.c3 h6 16.♗d2±, Isanbaev, R. (2344) – Zaitsev, V. (2412), Moscow 1999) 12.♗g5 ♘h5 13.♘e4 h6 14.f4 (14.♗d2!?) 14...hxg5 15.fxe5 ♗xe5 16.♖xf7 ♖xf7 17.♘xg5 (17.♖f1? ♘f4 18.♘xf4 ♗xf4 19.♗xf7+ ♔xf7 20.g3 ♗f5–+) 17...♗xb2 (Holzke, F. (2471) – Pfretzschner, R. (2222), Germany 2004) 18.♗xf7+ 18...♔f8 19.♖f1 ♘f6 20.♘f4 ♔e7∓;

B) 10.♗g5 ♗e7 11.♘e3 ♗d7 (11...♘g6!?) 12.♖d1 ♖f8? (12...h6!?) 13.♘g3 g6 14.♗xf6! ♗xf6 15.♘d5 ♗d8 16.0-0 c6 17.♖fe1 f6 18.♘xf6+ ♗xf6 19.f4 ♗g4 20.♖d4±, Varga, Z. (2475) – Mozes, E. (2355), Hungary 1993;

C) 10.♗f4 ♗d6 11.0-0 (11.h3 0-0 12.♘dc3 ♗d7 13.0-0 h6 14.♖ad1 ♖fe8 15.♖fe1 ♖ad8⇄, Alonso, S. (2339) – Soppe, G. (2448), Mar del Plata 1999) 11...0-0 12.♘e3 (12.♖e1 ♖e8 13.♘e3 ♗d7 14.♘d5 (14.♗g5 ♘e4∓ Hodges, P.) 14...♘xd5 15.♗xd5 c6 16.♗b3 ♖ad8 17.♖ad1 ♗g4=, Fritz 2 (computer) – Hodges P.,1993) 12...♘h5 13.♗xe5 ♗xe5 14.c3 c6 15.♖ad1 ♗c7 16.♘d4 g6 17.♖fe1 ♘f6 18.h3 ♖e8 19.♘c4 ♗d7=, Stiri, A. (2186) – Dochev, D. (2353), Agios Kirykos 2004.

We return now to Fercec– Milanovic.

10...h6

We also examine **A)** 10...♗d7; **B)** 10...♗e6 and **C)** 10...♗d6.

A) 10...♗d7 11.♗g5 ♗e7 12.0-0-0 (12.0-0 a5 13.♘f4 a4 14.♖fe1 h6 15.♘fd5 ♘xd5 16.♘xd5 ♗d6 17.♗f4 f6=) 12...0-0-0 (12...h6? 13.♗xf6 ♗xf6

14.f4 ♘c6 15.♗×f7+ ♔e7 ±, Kuczynski, R. (2509) – Dischinger, F. (2241), Essen 2001) 13.♖he1 h6 14.♗×f6 ♗×f6 15.♘d5 ±;

B) 10...♗e6 11.♗×e6 f×e6 12.♘f4 (12.♗f4 ♗d6 13.♘d4 0-0-0 14.0-0-0 ♘d3+ 15.♖×d3 ♗×f4+ 16.♔b1 ♖he8=) 12...0-0-0 (12...♔f7!?) 13.0-0 (13.♘×e6? ♖e8 14.♘×f8 ♘f3+ 15.♔d1 ♖d8+ 16.♔e2 ♘d4+) 13...♔d7 14.♗e3 ♗d6=, Chambers, C. – Dehaybe, A., Internet 2003.

C) 10...♗d6 11.♗g5

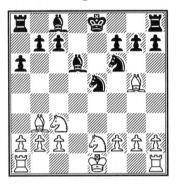

C1) 11...♗f5 12.♘g3 ♗g6 (12...♗e6!? 13.0-0-0 0-0-0 14.♗×e6+ f×e6 15.♖he1 ±) 13.0-0 (Kaminski, M. (2514) – Dubois, L. (2258), Cappelle la Grande 2000) 13...0-0-0 14.♗×f6 g×f6 15.f4 ♗c5+ 16.♔h1 ♘g4 17.f5 ♘f2+ 18.♖×f2 ♗×f2 19.♘ce4 ♗×g3 20.♘×g3 ♖he8 21.♔g1 ±;

C2) 11...♘ed7

C2a) 12.0-0-0 0-0 (½-½ Krejci, J. (2257) – Jirovsky, M. (2521), Czechia 2005) 13...♖e8 (13...h6 14.♗h4 ♖e8 15.♖he1 ±) 14.♖he1 b5 15.♘g3 (15.♗f4!?) 15...♖×e1 16.♖×e1 ♗b7=;

C2b) 12.♗f4 ♗×f4 13.♘×f4 0-0 14.0-0 (14.0-0-0 ♘c5 15.♘cd5 ♘×d5 16.♘×d5

c6 17.♘e7+ ♔h8 18.♘×c8 ♖a×c8 19.♖he1 ±) 14...c6 15.♖fe1 ♘c5 16.♗c4 b5 (16...♗f5? 17.♖e5 1-0, Balabaev, F. (2089) – Nikolov, S. (2376), Ljubljana 2000) 17.♘d3 ±.

Back to Fercec– Milanovic.

11.♗f4 (11.0-0 ♗d6 12.♘g3 0-0 13.♘ge4 ♘×e4 14.♘×e4 ♗b4 15.♗f4 ♖e8 16.c3 (Bon, M. (2148) – Mellado Trivino, J. (2447), Banyoles 2002) 16...♗f8 17.♗c2 f5 18.♘g3 g5 19.♗×e5 ♖×e5=; 12...♗e6!? 13.♘ge4 ♘×e4 14.♘×e4=) **11...♗d6 12.0-0-0 0-0 13.f3** (13.♖he1 ♖e8 ⇄) **13...♖e8 14.♔b1 ½-½**

Summary: After **1.e4 d5 2.e×d5 ♕×d5 3.♘c3 ♕d6 4.d4 ♘f6 5.♗c4 a6 6.♗b3**, Black has two good continuations, **6...e6** and **6...♘c6**.

After 6...e6 7.♘ge2 (7.♘f3 see Game 28), Black again has two good possibilities, 7...c5 and 7...b5.

The line **6...♘c6 7.♘ge2** affords Black a number of choices:

A) 7...♗f5 is considered fine for Black by Grefe and Silman, but analysis of 8.♗f4 indicates that Black may have problems after 8...e5 (8...♛d7 is better).

B) After 7...♘a5 8.♗f4 ♛d7 9.0-0 ♘xb3 10.axb3 e6 11.d5 White has interesting chances for the initiative.

C) After 7...e6 8.♗f4 ♛d8, followed by ♗f8-d6, Black may be able to equalize.

D) The line 7...g6 8.♗f4 ♛d8 9.d5 ♘a5 10.♛d4 is unpleasant for Black.

E) The game continuation **7...e5** is probably the most popular reply at this time. After **7...e5 8.dxe5** (8.d5 or 8.♗e3 gives Black an equal game) **8...♛xd1+ 9.♘xd1 ♘xe5** a very interesting queenless middle game has arisen. At first glance Black seems to have clear equality, but practice and analysis show that he must play this middle game very cautiously. After **9...♘xe5**, White has many alternatives, of which the best may be 10.♘dc3.

Game 8
Papadopoulos, I. (2285) –
Tzermiadianos, A. (2460)
Ermioni 2006

**1.e4 d5 2.exd5 ♛xd5 3.♘c3 ♛d6
4.d4 ♘f6 5.♗c4 a6 6.♗b3 ♗g4**

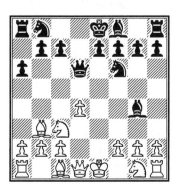

For 6...b5, 6...e6, 6...g6 and 6...♘c6 see Game 7.

7.♘ge2

After 7.f3 we examine **A)** 7...♗h5 and **B)** 7...♗f5.

A) 7...♗h5 8.♘ge2 ♘c6 9.♗f4 e5 (9...♛d7 10.d5 ♘a5 11.♛d4 ♘xb3 12.axb3 c6 13.0-0-0 ♘xd5 14.♘xd5 cxd5 15.♘c3 e6 16.♛e5 ♗g6 17.♘xd5 ♖c8 18.♖d2± or 14...♛xd5 15.♛b6 ♛b5 16.♛c7 c5 17.♖d5±) 10.dxe5 ♘xe5 11.♛d4 (11.♛xd6 ♗xd6 12.♗g3 0-0-0 13.0-0-0± , Bulski, K. (2260) – Bugalski, M. (2204), Polanica Zdroj 2005) 11...♛xd4 12.♘xd4 ♗d6 13.0-0 ♘xf3+ 14.♖xf3 ♗xf3 15.♗xd6± or 13...0-0-0 14.♘f5 ♗c5+ 15.♔h1 ♗g6 16.♘xg7 ♘ed7 17.g4±;

B) 7...♗f5 8.♘ge2

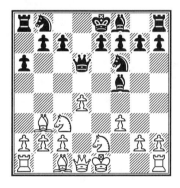

B1) 8...e6 9.♗f4 ♛d8 10.d5 exd5 11.♘xd5 ♘xd5 12.♗xd5 ♗xc2 13.♗xf7+ ♔xf7 14.♛xc2 ♗b4+ 15.♔f2 ♘c6 16.♖ad1 ♛e7 17.♛c4+ ♔f8 18.♖d5 ♛f7 19.♖hd1± , Borsavolgyi, T. (2315) – Boricsev, O. (2334), Hungary 2003; 9...♛b6 10.♛d2 (10.♘g3!? ♗g6 11.d5) 10...♘bd7 11.♘a4 ♛a7 12.0-0-0 b5 13.♘ac3 0-0-0 14.♘g3 ♗g6 15.♛e2 ♗b4 16.♘ce4 ♘d5

17.♗d2 ♖he8 18.♗xb4 ♘xb4 19.f4 ♕b6 20.c3 ♘c6 21.♕f3 ½-½, Bar, R. (2418) – Gofshtein, L. (2498), Israel 2002;

B2) 8...♘c6 9.♗f4 (9.d5!? Grefe & Silman) 9...♕d7

B2a) 10.a3 ♘a5 (10...e6!?) 11.♗a2 e6 12.d5 (12.b4 ♘c6 13.d5 exd5 14.♘xd5 ♘xd5 15.♕xd5 ♗xc2 16.♕xd7+ ♔xd7 17.♗xf7 (Kuczynski, R. (2450) – Sygulski, A. (2400), Wroslaw 1987) 17...♗e7 18.♖c1 ♗a4=) 12...exd5 13.♘xd5 ♘xd5?! (13...0-0-0!?) 14.♕xd5 ♕xd5 15.♗xd5 c6 16.0-0-0 cxd5 17.♖xd5 ♘b3+ (17...♗e6 18.♖xa5 b6 19.♖a4±) 18.cxb3 ♖c8+ 19.♔d2 ♗e6 (19...♖c2+ 20.♔d1 ♖c5 21.♖d2±) 20.♖d3±, Masserey, Y. (2374) – Vuckovic, B. (2497), Biel 2001;

B2b) 10.♕d2 (10.0-0!?)

B2b1) 10...♘a5 11.0-0 (11.♘e4?! ♘xb3 12.♘xf6+ gxf6 (Posch, W. (2250) – Brustkern, J. (2240), Austria 2006) 12...exf6 13.axb3 0-0-0∓) 11...0-0-0 12.♖fd1 e6 13.♘g3 ♗g6=;

B2b2) 10...e6 11.0-0-0 ♗b4 (11...0-0-0!? 12.d5 exd5 13.♘xd5 ♘xd5 14.♕xd5 ♕xd5 15.♖xd5 ♗e6 16.♖xd8+ ♘xd8=)

12.g4 (12.a3!?) 12...♗g6 13.h4 h5 14.d5 ♘xd5 (14...exd5?! 15.g5 ♘h7 16.♕e3+ ♕e7 17.♕xe7+ ♘xe7 18.♗xc7 ♖c8 19.♗b6±) 15.♗xd5 exd5 16.♕e3+ ♕e6 17.♘xd5=, Kuba, J. (2194) – Klima, L. (2432), Olomouc 2004.

We return now to Papadopoulos – Tzermiadianos.

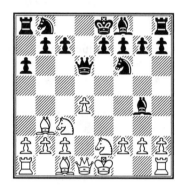

7...♘c6

Another interesting possibility is 7...e6:

A) 8.♗e3 ♗e7 (8...♘c6!?; 8...♘bd7!?; 8...♘d5!?) 9.♕d2 0-0?! (9...h5!?; 9...♘c6!?; 9...♘bd7!?; or 9...♘d5!?) 10.f3 ♗f5 11.g4 ♗g6 12.h4 h5 (12...h6 13.♘f4 ♗h7 14.g5±) 13.♘f4 hxg4 14.♘xg6 (14.♗xe6 ♗h7 15.♗xg4 ♘xg4 16.fxg4 ♘c6⩲) 14...fxg6 15.0-0-0 gxf3 (15...♘c6 16.♗f4 ♕d7 17.♕e3 ♘d5 18.♘xd5 exd5 19.fxg4±) 16.♖dg1 ♘c6 (Zatonsky, O. – Melts, M., Internet 1998) 17.♕d3!? (17.d5 ♘e5) 17...♘d5 (17...♘b4? 18.♕xg6 ♖f7 19.h5 f2 20.♗xf2 ♕f4+ 21.♔b1 ♘bd5 22.h6+−) 18.♕xg6 ♖f7 (18...♗f6 19.♘e4 ♕e7 20.♘g5±) 19.♘e4 with a strong attack;

B) 8.♗f4 (8.f3 ♗f5 – 6.f3 ♗f5 8.♘ge2 e6) 8...♕xf4 9.♘xf4 ♗xd1 10.♖xd1

♗b4 (10...♗d6!?) 11.♘fe2 ♘bd7 (11...♘c6 12.0-0 ♘a5 13.d5 e5=) 12.a3 ♗d6=, Tiviakov, S. (2599) – Christiansen, L. (2570), Moscow 2001.

8.h3 (8.f3 ♗f5 – 6.f3 ♗f5 8.♘ge2 ♘c6) **8...♗×e2 9.♘×e2 0-0-0** (9...e5!?) **10.c3**

10.♗f4!? ♛d7 (10...e5 11.d×e5 ♛c5 12.♛c1 ♘×e5 13.0-0 ♘c4 14.c3 ⇄ or 11...♘×e5 12.♛d6 ♗×d6 13.0-0 ⇄) 11.0-0 ♘×d4?! (11...e6 12.c3 ♔b8 13.♛c2 ⇄) 12.♘×d4 ♛×d4 13.♛×d4 ♖×d4 14.♗e3 ♖e4 (14...♖d6 15.♗×f7 e6 16.♖fe1 ♔d7 17.♗c5 ♖c6 18.♖ad1+ ♘d5 19.♗×f8 ♖×f8 20.♗×e6+) 15.♗×f7 e6 16.♖ae1 ♗b4 (16...♔d7 17.♗g5±) 17.f3 ♖e5 18.♗d2±.

10...e5 11.♗e3

11.0-0 e×d4 12.♘×d4 ♘×d4 13.c×d4 ♛×d4 14.♛×d4 ♖×d4 15.♗×f7=.

11...♘d5

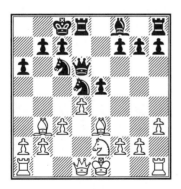

12.d×e5?! (12.0-0 ♔b8 13.♛d3 ♘×e3 14.f×e3 f6 15.♘g3 ♛d7±) **12...♛×e5** (12...♘×e5 13.♗×d5 ♛×d5 14.♛×d5 ♖×d5=) **13.♗×d5** (13.♗d4 ♛g5 14.0-0 ♘f4 ♗c5 15.h4 ♛g4 16.g3 ⇄;

15.♘×f4 ♘×d4 16.c×d4 ♛×f4∓) **13...♖×d5 14.♛c2 g5?!** (14...♗d6!? 15.♗f4 ♛e6 16.♗×d6 ♖×d6) **15.♖d1** (15.0-0!? ♗d6 16.♘g3 h5 17.c4 ♘b4 18.♛e4 ⇄) **15...♗d6** (15...♖×d1+!? 16.♛×d1 ♗c5 17.♗×c5 ♛×c5 18.0-0 ♖d8) **16.♖×d5 ♛×d5 17.0-0 h6** (17...♛e5 18.♘g3; 17...h5 18.♖d1 ♛e5 19.♘g3 h4 20.♛f5+ ♔b8 21.♛×e5 ♗×e5 22.♘e2±) **18.b3 f5 19.♖d1 ♛e5 20.g3 ♖f8 21.♛d3?** (21.♘d4 f4 22.♘×c6 b×c6 23.♗d4 ♛e6 24.g4 c5 25.♗g7 ♖g8∓; 24.♛d3 ♛b7 25.g4 c5 26.♗g7 ♖g8 27.♗f6 ⇄ or 24...♛×h3 25.♛×a6+ ♔d7 26.♛d3; 21...♖×d4 22.♗×d4 ♛e6 23.♛d3 f4 24.g4 ♖d8∓) **21...♛e8** (21...f4! 22.g×f4 g×f4 23.♘×f4 ♖×f4 24.♗×f4 ♛×f4∓ or 22.♗c1 ♛e6 23.g4 h5∓; 22.♗d4 ♛e6 23.g4 f3∓ or 23.g×f4 g×f4∓) **22.f4 ♛h5 23.♔g2 g×f4 24.♘×f4 ♗×f4 25.♛d7+ ♔b8 26.♗×f4 ♛e2+ 27.♔h1 ♔a8** (27...♘e5!? 28.♛d2 ♛e4+ 29.♔g2 ♘d3∓) **28.♗×c7 ♛h5 29.♔g2 ♛e2+ 30.♔h1 ♛f3+ 31.♔h2 ♛e2+ 32.♔h1 ½-½**

Summary: After **1.e4 d5 2.e×d5 ♛×d5 3.♘c3 ♛d6 4.d4 ♘f6 5.♗c4 a6 6.♗b3 ♗g4**, the popular move 6...♘c6 was considered. **6...♗g4** is another interesting (but little known!) possibility. After this move White has two main alternatives, 7.f3 and 7.♘ge2.

A) 7.f3 and now Black probably gets an equal game with counterplay with 7...♗f5.

B) The game continuation **7.♘ge2** is more flexible than 7.f3. Black has a choice between 7...♘c6 and 7...e6. In both cases Black sooner or later plays 0-0-0 or ♖d8 with counterplay.

Game 9
Zhelnin, V. (2430) – Kovalenko, I. (2410)
Kaluga 2007

1.e4 d5 2.e×d5 ♕×d5 3.♘c3 ♕d6 4.d4 ♘f6 5.♗c4 ♗g4

For 5...c6 see Games 1-4, 5...a6 – Games 5-8 and 26. Other interesting possibilities for Black are **A)** 5...♘c6 and **B)** 5...g6.

A) 5...♘c6

A1) 6.♘f3 (6.♘b5? ♕b4+ 7.c3 ♕×c4 8.♘×c7+ ♔d7∓) 6...♗g4 7.♗e3 e6 8.h3 (8.0-0 0-0-0⇄) 8...♗h5 9.0-0 0-0-0⇄;

A2) 6.♘ge2 ♗f5 (6...e5 7.0-0 a6 8.d×e5 ♘×e5 9.♗b3 – Game 7; 6...♗g4 – 5...♗g4 6.♘ge2 ♘c6) 7.d5 (7.♘b5 ♕b4+ 8.c3 ♕×c4 9.♘×c7+ ♔d7 10.b3 ♕d3∓; 7.0-0 e6 8.♘b5 ♕d7 9.♗f4 ♖c8 10.♘g3 ♗g6⇄) 7...♘b4

A2a) 8.♘d4 ♗g6 9.♗b5+ ♘d7 10.0-0 a6 11.♗e2 ♘×d5 12.♘×d5 ♕×d5 13.c4 ♕d6 (Constantin, D. (2106) – Thiriet, B. (2156), France 2003) 14.f4 e5 15.f×e5 ♘×e5 16.♕a4+ ♘d7 17.♖d1 0-0-0∓;

A2b) 8.0-0 0-0-0 (8...♗×c2 9.♕d4 ♕b6 10.♕h4∞) 9.♕d4 (9.♗f4?! e5; 9.♘d4

♗g6?! 10.♘db5) 9...♕b6 (9...c5 10.♕h4∞) 10.♗f4 ♗×c2 11.♗e3∞;

B) 5...g6

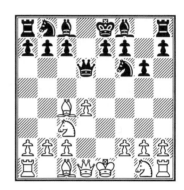

B1) 6.♘ge2 ♗g7 7.♗f4 ♕d8 8.0-0 0-0 9.h3 (9.♘g3!?) 9...a6 (9...♘c6!? 10.a4 ♘b4) 10.a4 ♘c6 11.d5± , Krstic, U. (2350) – Martinovic, S. (2182), Bosnjaci 2006 or 7...♕b6 8.0-0 (8.♕d2 0-0 9.0-0-0 ♘c6=) 8...0-0 9.a3 ♗f5 10.♘g3± ;

B2) 6.♘f3 ♗g7 7.0-0 0-0 8.h3 (8.♘b5 ♕d8 9.♗f4 c6) 8...a6 (8...c6 9.a4 ♘a6 10.♖e1 ♘b4 11.♕e2 ♖e8 12.♘g5 ♘bd5±) 9.a4 (9.♗g5 ♘c6 10.♖e1±) 9...c5 (9...♘c6!?) 10.d×c5 (10.♗g5!?) 10...♕×c5 11.♕e2 ♘c6± , Oral, T. (2540) – Schleifer, M. (2369), Quebec 2001.

We now return to Zhelnin – Kovalenko.

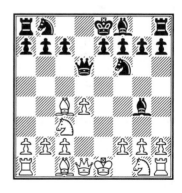

6.♘ge2

White's main alternative is 6.f3 (For 6.♘f3 c6 – Game 1; 6...a6 – Game 26; 6.♛d3 a6 7.♘ge2 ♘c6 8.♗f4 ♛d7 9.0-0-0 0-0-0⇄) 6...♗f5, and now we examine **A)** 7.♛e2 and **B)** 7.♘ge2.

A) 7.♛e2 a6 (7...♛×d4? 8.♘b5 ♛b6 9.♗e3 ♛a5+ 10.♗d2 ♛b6 11.♛e5+– or 9...♛c6 10.♘×a7±; 8...♛d7 9.♗f4 ♘a6 10.♖d1 ♛c8 11.♗×c7±; 7...c6!?) 8.g4!? (8.♗e3 ♘c6 9.0-0-0 (Al Modiahki, M. (2569) – Danielian, E. (2415), Dubai 2005) 9...♘b4 10.♗b3 ♘bd5 11.♘×d5 ♘×d5 12.♘h3 e6⇄) 8...♗g6 9.g5 ♘h5 (9...♘fd7?! 10.♘d5) 10.♗e3 ♘c6 11.0-0-0 0-0-0 12.♘e4±;

B) 7.♘ge2

B1) 7...a6

B1a) 8.♘g3 ♗g6 9.0-0 ♘c6 10.♗e3 0-0-0 (10...♛b4!?) 11.♘ce2?! (11.♘ge4!?) 11...e5 12.c3 h5 13.♗d3 ♗×d3 ♘d5 14.♗f2 (Godlewski, A. (2140) – Kania, P. (2255), Lublin 1999) 14...h4 15.♘e4 ♛d7∓ or 14.♛×d3 ♛d7∓, Aldokhin, I. – Glidzhain, G., Russia 2004;

B1b) 8.♗f4

B1b1) 8...♛d8 9.g4 ♗g6 10.♛d2 e6 11.0-0-0 ♗b4?! (11...♘bd7±) 12.h4 h5 (Kruchev, B. (2289) – Filippov, V. (2159), Voronezh 2004) 13.g5 ♘d5 14.♗×d5 e×d5 15.♛e3+ ♗e7 16.♗h2 0-0 17.♘f4±;

B1b2) 8...♛b6 9.♛d2 (Llaneza Vega, M. (2136) – Olea Perez, M. (2245), Oviedo 2003) 9...♘c6 (9...♛×b2 10.♖b1 ♛×c2 11.♛×c2 ♗×c2 12.♖×b7 e6 13.d5±) 10.0-0-0±;

B2) 7...e6 (7...c6 – Game 3; 6...♘c6 – 6.♘ge2 ♘c6 7.f3 ♗f5)

B2a) 8.0-0 ♘c6 (8...c6 – Game 3; 8...a6 9.♘g3? ♗×c2!) 9.♗f4 (9.♘b5 ♛d7 10.♗f4 ♖c8=) 9...♛b4 (9...♛d7!?) 10.♗b3 0-0-0⇄ (McGeary, W.) or 8.♗e3 ♘c6 9.♛d2 0-0-0 (9...♘d5 10.♘×d5 e×d5 11.♗b3±) 10.a3 ♘a5 11.♗d3 ♗×d3 12.♛×d3 ♛a6=;

B2b) 8.♗f4

B2b1) 8...♛d7 (8...♛b6!?) 9.♛d2 ♗d6 (9...♘c6 10.0-0-0 ♘b4=, Pachia, M. – Grunberg, M. (2445), Romania, 1999) 10.0-0-0 c6? (10...♘c6±) 11.g4 ♗g6 12.h4 h6 (12...h5 13.♗×d6 ♛×d6 14.♘f4) 13.♗×d6 ♛×d6 14.♘f4 ♗h7 15.g5±, Laznicka, V. (2319) – Kantorik, M. (2364), Roznov 2002;

B2b2) 8...♛d8 9.0-0 (9.♘g3 ♗g6 10.0-0 c6 11.♛d2 – Game 3; 9...♘c6 10.0-0-0±; 9.♛d2 ♘c6 10.0-0-0±; 9.d5!?) 9...c6 10.♛d2 (10.♖e1!?) 10...♘bd7 11.♘g3 ♗g6 (11...♛b6!?) 12.♗b3 ♗e7 13.♘ce4 ♘×e4 14.♘×e4 0-0 (Rolletschek, H. (2320) – Weiss, C. (2290), Linz 1996) 15.♘d6±;

B2b3) 8...♛b4 9.♗b3 ♗d6 (9...c6 – 6...♗g4 7.f3 ♗f5 8.♗f4 ♛b4 9.♗b3 e6,

Game 3) 10.a3 (10.♗a4+ ♘bd7 11.a3 ♕xb2?! 12.♖b1; 11...♕b6 12.♕d2 0-0 ⇄) 10...♕b6 11.♗e3 ♘bd7 (11...♘c6!?) 12.♕d2 0-0-0⇄, Rodriguez Gonzalez, I. – Pages de Garriga, B., Spain 2002.

Back to Zhelnin – Kovalenko.

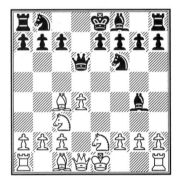

6...♘c6

6...♘bd7 7.f3 (7.♗f4?! ♗xe2 8.♘xe2? ♕b4+ or 8.♗xd6? ♗xd1 –+; 8.♕d2 ♗xc4 9.♗xd6 exd6∓; 7.♗e3?! ♕c6 8.♕d3 ♕xg2 9.0-0-0 0-0-0∓; 7.0-0 ♘b6 8.♗b3 c6 9.♗f4 ♕xf4 10.♘xf4 ♗xd1 11.♖axd1 e6=) 7...♗f5 8.♗f4 ♕b4 9.b3 c6 (9...♘b6? 10.a3 ♕a5 11.b4) 10.♗c7 (10.a3 ♕a5 11.b4 ♕d8 12.♘g3 ♗g6 13.0-0 ♘b6 14.♗b3 e6 ⇄) 11.a3 ♕e7 12.0-0 (12.♗d3 ♗xd3 13.♕xd3 ♘c5 14.dxc5 ♕xc7∓; 12.♗g3 ♘b6 13.♗d3 ♗xd3 14.♕xd3 ♕d7=; 12.♗a5 ♘b6 13.♗b4 ♕d7 14.♗xf8 ♖xf8 15.0-0 0-0-0 ⇄) 12...♘b6 13.♗e5 ♘fd7 ⇄, Kosnitsky, V. – Melts, M., Internet 1998.

7.f3 ♗f5 8.♗f4

8.♗b3 a6 – Game 8. We also examine **A)** 8.0-0; **B)** 8.♗e3 and **C)** 8.d5.

A) 8.0-0 0-0-0 9.♗e3 (9.♘b5 ♕d7 10.c3 a6 11.a4 (Deflesselle, T. (2072)

– Frayssinet, F. (2040), Paris 2003) 11...e5 12.♗e3 ♘d5 13.♗xd5 ♕xd5∓; 10.♗f4 a6 11.♘xc7 e5 12.♘a8 ♕e7 13.♗g3 ♗b8 14.♘b6 ♕b4∓) 9...e5 10.d5 ♕b4 11.♗d3 ♗xd3 12.dxc6 (12.♕xd3 ♗c5∓) 12...♗c4 13.cxb7+ ♔xb7∓, Panarin, M. (2475) – Nikolaidis, I. (2520), Moscow 2005;

B) 8.♗e3 0-0-0 9.♕d2 ♕b4 (9...♘a5 10.♗d3 ♗xd3 11.♕xd3 e6 12.0-0 ♕a6 13.♕xa6 bxa6=) 10.♗xf7 (10.♗b3 e5 11.0-0-0 ♖d7 12.♖he1 ♘a5∞; 11...♘c5!?) 10...♕xb2 (10...e6 11.g4 ♕e7 12.gxf5 ♕xf7 13.fxe6 ♕xe6 14.0-0-0±) 11.0-0 ♕xc2 (11...e6?! 12.g4; 11...h5?! 12.♘g3) 12.♕xc2 ♗xc2 13.d5 ♘e5 (13...♘b4 14.♘f4 e5 15.dxe6 ♘d3∞) 14.♗e6+ ♔b8 15.♖ac1⩱;

C) 8.d5 After this ambitious move the game becomes very tactical.

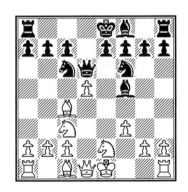

8...♘b4 (8...♘e5 9.♗f4 ♕c5?! 10.♗xe5 ♕xc4 11.♕d4; 9...g5!?; 8...♘a5!?)

C1) 9.♗b3 0-0-0 10.♗f4

C1a) 10...♕c5 11.♕d2 (11.♕d4 e6 12.♕xc5?! ♗xc5 13.♘a4 ♗d6∓, Jahn, C. (2140) – Brecht, A. (2280), Germany 1998; 12.♗e3!? ♕a5 13.0-0-0) 11...♘fxd5 (11...♘bxd5 12.0-0-0 ⇄)

12.0-0-0 e6 13.a3 ♘c6 14.♘×d5 e×d5 15.♗e3 ♛e7 16.♖he1 ⩱;

C1b) 10...e5 11.♗g5 ♛b6 (11...h6!?; 11...♗e7!?) 12.♘g3 (12.a3 ♘c6 13.♛d2 ♘d4 14.♘×d4 e×d4 15.♘e2?! d3! 16.♗e3 ♗c5 17.♗×c5 ♛×c5 18.c×d3 ♖he8⩱, Kovalenko, O. (2137) – Kovalenko, I. (2413), Dniepropetrovsk 2007; 15.♘a4⇄) 12...♗e6 13.♛e2 ♘b×d5 14.♘×d5 ♗×d5 15.0-0-0∞;

C2) 9.♘d4 ♗g6 (9...♘f×d5?! 10.♘×f5 ♛e5+ 11.♔f2! ♛×c3 12.b×c3 ♛×c3 13.♛d4 ♛×c2+ 14.♗e2±; 9...♘b×d5 10.♘×f5 ♛e5+ 11.♛e2 ♛×f5 12.♗×d5 ♘×d5 13.♛b5+ c6 14.♛×b7 ♔c8 15.♛×c8+ ♖×c8 16.♗d2±) 10.♛e2 (Sambuev, B. (2536) – Kholmov, R. (2434), Moscow 2005) 10...0-0-0!

C2a) 11.0-0 e5 12.♘db5 ♛b6+ 13.♗e3 ♗c5 14.♗×c5 ♛×c5+ 15.♔h1 ♘b×d5 16.♗×d5 ♘×d5 17.♛×e5 ♖he8 18.♛×g7? ♘e3 19.♖fe1 c6 20.♘a3 ♛g5 21.♖e2 ♘f5–+;

C2b) 11.♘cb5 (11.♘db5 ♛b6 12.♗b3 ♘f×d5 13.♘×d5 ♘×d5) 11...♛b6 12.a4 (12.♗e3 a6 13.♘c3 e5 14.♘f5 ♛a5⩱; 12.♗d2 e5 13.d×e6 a6⩲) 12...e5 13.d×e6 ♖×d4 14.♘×d4 ♛×d4⩱.

Let's return to Zhelnin – Kovalenko.

8...e5

8...♛d7!?; 8...♛b4?! is bad now: 9.b3! (9.♗b5 0-0-0 10.a3 ♛a5 11.♗×c6 b×c6⇄, Georgiev, K. (2516) – Panbukchian, V. (2325), Sofia 2003) 9...♛b6 (9...0-0-0 10.a3 ♛b6 11.♘a4±; 9...♘a5 10.♗d3 ♗×d3 11.♛×d3 ♛b6 12.a3 e6 13.b4±; 9...♛a5 10.a3 a6 11.b4 ♛b6 12.♔f2! e5 13.♗e3±; 9...e6 10.♗c7; 9...e5 10.d×e5 ♖d8 11.♛c1 ♘h5 12.a3 ♛e7 13.♘d5±) 10.♘a4 ♛b4+ 11.c3 ♛a5 12.♘c5 b5 13.♗d3 ♗×d3 14.♛×d3 ♛b6 15.a4 b4 16.a5 ♘×a5 17.c×b4 ♘c6 18.b5±.

9.d×e5 ♘×e5 10.♗b3

10.♗b5+!? ♗d7 (10...c6 11.♛d4 ♛×d4 12.♘×d4 ♘g6 13.♗g3 ♗d7 14.♗c4±) 11.♗×d7+ ♘f×d7 12.♛×d6 ♗×d6 13.♘b5 ♗b4+ 14.c3 ♗a5 15.0-0-0±.

10...0-0-0 11.♛×d6 ♗×d6 12.0-0-0 ♘fd7

12...a6!? 13.♗×e5 ♗×e5 14.♗×f7 ♖hf8 15.♗b3 b5⇄; 12...♖he8!? 13.♘b5 ♗c5 14.♖×d8+ ♔×d8⇄.

13.♘b5 ♗c5

14.♖d5

14.♘g3!? ♗g6 15.h4 h5 16.♖he1 ♖he8±.

14...♖he8 15.♖hd1 (15.♘g3!? ♗g6 16.h4⇄) **15...a6 16.♘bc3?!** (16.♘bd4!? ♗g6 17.♘g3) **16...♗e6 17.♖5d2** (17.♖×c5?! ♘×c5 18.♖×d8+ ♚×d8 19.♗×e5 ♗×b3∓) **17...♗×b3 18.c×b3** (18.a×b3 ♘g6∓) **18...♘g6 19.♘d5 ♘×f4 20.♘e×f4 c6 21.♖c2 ♗a7 22.♘d3** (22.♚b1 ♘f8 23.h4 ♘g6 24.♘×g6 h×g6 25.♚c1 ♖e5∓) **22...♘e5 23.♘×e5 ♖×e5 24.♘c3 ♗e3+ 25.♚b1 ♖×d1+ 26.♘×d1 ♗g1?!** (26...♗f4 27.g3 ♖e1∓) **27.h3 ♖e1 28.♖c1 ♗d4 29.♘c3 ♖×c1+ 30.♚×c1 f5 31.♚c2 ♚d7 32.♘e2 ♗e5 33.b4** (33.f4!? ♗f6 34.♘c3) **33...♚d6 34.b3 c5** (34...♚d5!?) **35.b×c5+ ♚×c5 36.a4 ♚d5 37.♚d3 g5 38.g4 ½-½**

Summary: After **1.e4 d5 2.e×d5 ♕×d5 3.♘c3 ♕d6 4.d4 ♘f6 5.♗c4**, in Games 1-8 we considered the most popular moves 5...c6 and 5...a6, but Black has other interesting possibilities, such as 5...♘c6, 5...g6 and 5...♗g4. These offer considerable scope for fantasy, innovation, and independent analysis, not to mention fun.

We see that Black can have an interesting, active game without using the better-known moves 5...c6 and 5...a6. This indicates 5.♗c4 may not be White's best move after 4...♘f6.

Part III 3.♘c3 ♕d6 4.d4 ♘f6 5.♘f3

Games 10-29 cover lines after **1.e4 d5 2.e×d5 ♕×d5 3.♘c3 ♕d6 4.d4 ♘f6 5.♘f3**

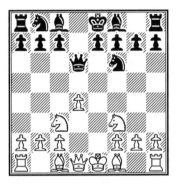

This can be considered the second main line. We will examine the following possibilities for Black: 5...♗g4 (Games 10-12), 5...c6 (Games 13-17), 5...a6 (Games 18-28), and 5...g6 with 5...♗f5 or 5...♘c6 (Game 29).

After the natural 5...♗g4, White has several possibilities, but only the move 6.h3 is dangerous for Black.

After 5...c6, White's main alternatives are 6.♗d3 (Game 13), 6.♗e2 (Game 14), 6.h3 (Game 15), and 6.♘e5 (Games 16, 17). Positions after 6.♗e3 and 6.♗g5 will be examined in Part IV, Games 35 and 36.

After 5...a6, White has many different continuations (Games 18-28), but no single one can be called a "main" or "best" line – in each case Black can achieve equality or significant counterplay. The move 5...a6 is very popular now (perhaps because of David Bronstein's games in 1995-

1996), but for a long time after the famous game Karpov – Lutikov, Moscow 1979 (see Game 21), it had a dubious reputation.

Other Black continuations, 5...g6, 5...♗f5, and 5...♘c6, will be examined in Game 29. In my opinion White, with best play, has slightly better chances than Black in these lines.

Game 10
Thorhallsson, T. (2460) –
Koskinen, V. (1975)
Copenhagen 2007

1.e4 d5 2.e×d5 ♕×d5 3.♘c3 ♕d6 4.d4 ♘f6 5.♘f3 ♗g4

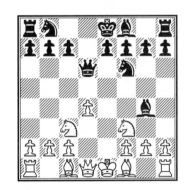

6.♗e2

After the natural 5...♗g4 White has several possibilities, but only the move 6.h3 is dangerous for Black, after which a choice must be made between 6...♗h5 (Game 11) and 6...♗×f3 (Game 12). For 6.♗d3 see Game 33 and for 6.♗g5, Game 36. Other interesting continuations here are **A)** 6.♘b5; **B)** 6.♗e3 and **C)** 6.g3.

A) 6.♘b5 ♕d8 7.♗c4 (7.♗f4 ♘a6 8.♗c4 c6? 9.♘e5±, Airumian, S. (2055) – Melnikov, N., St. Petersburg 2007; 7...♘d5 8.♗g3 c6 9.♘c3 ♘×c3 10.b×c3± , Priebe, V. (2082) – Chandler, P. (2245), Germany 2001) 7...e6 8.h3 ♗h5 9.♗f4 ♘a6 10.0-0 c6 11.♘c3 ♗d6⇄ or 9.0-0 c6 10.♘c3 ♗e7 11.♗f4 0-0⇄; 6...♕b6 7.c4 (7.♗f4!? ♘d5 8.♗d2) 7...c6 (7...a6!?) 8.♘c3 e6 9.♗e2 (9.c5!?) 9...♗e7 10.0-0 0-0± , Castany Pampalona, L. – De la Riva Aguado, J. (2250), St. Feliu 1994;

B) 6.♗e3 c6 (6...a6 – Game 21) 7.h3 (7.♗e2 – Game 14; 7.♗d3 – Game 13; ♗c4 – Game 1) 7...♗h5 (7...♗×f3 8.♕×f3 see Game 12) 8.g4 (8.♗e2 e6 9.♘e5 ♗×e2 10.♕×e2 ♘bd7 11.f4 ♕c7 12.0-0-0± , Zelcic, R. (2555) – Kovacevic, B. (2470), Zadar 2006) 8...♗g6 9.♘e5 ♘bd7

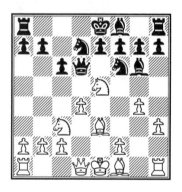

B1) 10.f4 e6 11.♕f3 (Kersten, U. (2318) – Alber, H. (2387), Offenbach 2005) 11...♗×c2 12.♖h2 ♗g6 13.h4 (13.0-0-0 ♕c7 14.♘×g6 h×g6 15.♖c2 ♕a5∓) 13...h5 (13...♕b4?! 14.a3 ♕a5 15.♘c4 ♗e4 16.♕e2 ♕c7 17.g5±) 14.g5 ♘g4 15.♖d2 ♘×e3 16.♕×e3 ♘×e5 17.d×e5 ♕b4 18.0-0-0 ♗c5∓;

B2) 10.♘c4 (10.♘×g6 h×g6 11.♕f3 ♘b6 12.0-0-0 e6 (Leskur, D. (2476) –

Muse, M. (2434), Sibenik 2005) 13.♗f4± ; 12.♗d3!? e6 13.0-0) 10...♕c7 11.♕f3 ♘b6 (11...e6 12.♗f4 ♕d8 13.0-0-0 ♘d5± , Zinchenko, Y. (2460) – Hasangatin, R. (2416), Alushta 2005; 11...♘d5 12.♘×d5 c×d5 13.♕×d5 e6 14.♕g2 ♗×c2 15.♖c1 ♗a4=) 12.♗f4 ♕d8 13.0-0-0 ♘bd5 14.♘e5 e6 15.h4 ♘×c3 16.♕×c3 ♗e4 (Sumaneev, D. (2452) – Nedela, V. (2385), Karvina 2001) 17.f3 ♗d5∞;

C) 6.g3 ♘c6 (6...a6 7.♗g2 – Game 18; 6...c6 7.♗g2 – Game 38) 7.♗g2 0-0-0

C1) 8.♗e3 ♕b4 9.♕c1 ♗×f3 10.♗×f3 ♘×d4 11.♗×d4 (11.♗g2 h5 12.a3 ♕b6∓) 11...♕×d4 12.0-0 (Lakos, N. (2372) – Kaps, D. (2237), Punat 2003) 12...♕e5 (12...e6? 13.♗×b7+ ♔×b7 14.♖d1) 13.♖e1 ♕f5 14.♕e3 e6∓;

C2) 8.h3 ♗h5 (8...♗×f3!? 9.♕×f3 ♕×d4) 9.0-0 (Sveshnikov, E. (2507) – Yegiazarian, A. (2537), Stepanakert 2005) 9...♘×d4 10.g4 (10.♕×d4 ♕×d4 11.♘×d4 ♖×d4 12.♗e3 ♖c4 13.♗×a7 e6 14.♗e3 ♗b4∓) 10...♗g6 11.♘×d4 ♕×d4 12.♕f3 c6 13.♗e3 (13.♖d1 ♕b6) 13...♕b4 14.♗×a7 e6 15.♖fc1 ♗d6 16.a3 ♕a5 17.♗e3 ♕e5∓.

We return now to Thorhallsson – Koskinen.

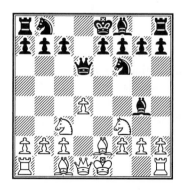

6...a6

6...♘c6 (6...c6 – Game 14) is dangerous for Black; for example, 7.d5
(7.♘b5!? ♕d7 8.♘e5) 7...♘b4 (7...♘e5
8.♘b5) 8.♘b5 ♕b6 9.c4 c6 10.♗e3
♕a5 (10...♕d8 11.♘c3±) 11.♘c3 cxd5
(11...♖d8 12.a3 ♘a6 13.0-0±) 12.a3
♘c6 13.cxd5 ♖d8 14.b4 ♕c7 15.♕b3±
or 8...♕d7 9.♘e5 ♗xe2 10.♕xe2 ♕d8
11.a3 ♘bxd5 (11...♘a6 12.♘c3 ♘xd5
13.♕f3±) 12.c4 c6 (12...♘b6 13.♗f4)
13.cxd5 cxb5 14.♕xb5+ ♘d7 15.0-0 a6
(15...f6 16.♘d3 ♕b6 17.♕a4±)
16.♕e2 ♘xe5 17.♕xe5 ♕d6 18.♕e4
♖d8 19.♖d1±.

7.h3

7.♗e3 ♘c6 – Game 23. White has two
other popular alternatives here: A)
7.♗g5 and B) 7.0-0.

A) 7.♗g5

A1) 7...e6 8.h3 ♗h5 (8...♗xf3!? 9.♗xf3
♘c6)

A1a) 9.♕d2 (9.♘e5!? ♗xe2 10.♕xe2
♕xd4 11.♖d1) 9...♗e7 (9...♘c6 10.♗f4
♕d7 11.g4 ♗g6 12.♘e5 ♘xe5 13.♗xe5
0-0-0 14.0-0-0⇄, Darmarakis, M.
(2174) – Tzermiadianos, A. (2447),
Greece 2005) 10.0-0-0 ♘c6?!
(10...♘bd7) 11.♗f4 ♕d7 (Santo Roman, M. (2385) – Hauchard, A. (2485),
St. Affrique 1997) 12.♘e5! ♘xe5
13.dxe5 ♗xe2 14.♕xe2 ♘d5 15.♕g4±;

A2) 7...♘bd7 8.h3 ♗h5 9.♕d2 e6
10.0-0-0 ♗e7

A2a) 11.♕e3 0-0 (11...♘b6!?) 12.g4
♗g6 13.♘e5 ♘b6 14.♗xf6 ♗xf6 15.h4
♘d5 16.♘xd5 exd5 17.h5 ♗e4 18.f3

h6 (18...c5? 19.♕a3±, Zilka, S. (2202)
– Trombik, K. (2263), Karvina 2002)
19.♔b1 ♗g5 20.♕b3 ♗h7⇄;

A2b) 11.♘e5 (11.♗f4 ♕b6 12.♘e5
♗xe2 13.♕xe2 0-0 14.♘xd7 ♘xd7
15.♘d5 exd5 16.♕xe7±) 11...♗xe2
12.♕xe2 0-0 13.f4 c6 14.♘c4 ♕c7 15.f5
♗b4 16.fxe6 (Kovacik, E. (2204) –
Kantorik, M. (2315), Slovakia 2002)
16...♖ae8 17.exf7+ ♖xf7∓;

B) 7.0-0 e6 (7...♘c6 – Game 23) 8.h3

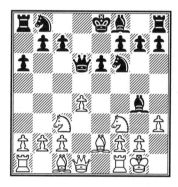

B1) 8...♗h5 9.♘e5 ♗xe2

B1a) 10.♕xe2 ♕xd4 (10...♘c6 11.♕f3
♘xd4 12.♕xb7 ♖d8 13.♗f4 ♕b6
14.♕xb6 cxb6 15.♖fd1 (Jobava, B.
(2616) – Gashimov, V. (2565), Dubai
2004) 15...♗e7±; 13...g5!?) 11.♕f3
(11.♖d1 ♕c5∞) 11...c6 12.♗f4 ♘bd7
13.♖fe1 ♕b6 14.♖ad1≅;

B1b) 10.♘xe2 ♘c6 (10...♗e7 11.♗f4
♕d8 12.c4 0-0 13.♕b3 with pressure,
Posazhennikov, A. (2256) – Goodger,
M. (2161), Telford 2004; 11...♕b6!?
12.a4 0-0) 11.♗f4 ♘xe5 12.♗xe5 ♕b6
(12...♗c6!?; 12...♕d7 13.♘f4 0-0-0±,
Breyther, R. (2370) – Hargens, T.
(2255), Germany 1990) 13.c4 0-0-0⇄,
Enjuto Velasco, R. (2080) – Narciso
Dublan, M. (2440), Zamora 1996;

B2) 8.♖e1 ♗e7 (8...♘c6 9.d5 ♘b4 10.d×e6 ♗×e6 11.a3 ♘c6 12.♘g5±) 9.♗g5 0-0 10.♗×f6 (10.♘e5!? ♗×e2 11.♕×e2 ♕×d4 12.♖ad1 ♕b4 13.♘e4⧸) 10...♗×f6 11.♘e4 (Fedorov, A. (2616) – Gashimov, V. (2565), Dubai 2004) 11...♕f4 12.♘×f6+ ♕×f6±.

Back to Thorhallsson – Koskinen.

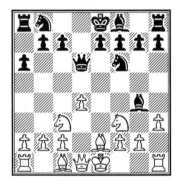

7...♗h5

7...♗×f3 is slightly unusual, but certainly possible. The only way to cause White problems is to maintain pressure on d4; for example, 8.♗×f3 ♘c6 and now:

A) 9.♗e3 0-0-0 10.♕e2 (10.d5 ♘e5 11.0-0 e6 12.d×e6 ♕e7 13.♕e2 ♕×e6= or 10...♘b4 11.♕e2 e6 12.d×e6 ♕×e6 13.0-0 ♘c6=) 10...h5 (10...e5 11.d×e5 ♘×e5 12.♖d1 ♕b4 13.♖×d8+ ♔×d8 14.0-0 ♗d6=) 11.0-0-0 g6 12.♕c4 e6 13.♗×c6 ♕×c6 14.♕×c6 b×c6 15.♗g5 ♗e7 16.♖he1±, Ljubic, J. (2246) – Balinov, I. (2453), Schwarzach 2000;

B) 9.0-0 0-0-0 10.d5 ♘b4 (10...♘e5?! 11.♗f4 ♘×f3+ 12.♕×f3 e5 13.♗g3) 11.♕e2 e6 (11...♘b×d5?! 12.♘×d5 ♘×d5 13.♖d1 ♘f4 14.♗×f4 ♕×f4 15.♗×b7+ or 13...c6 14.c4 ♘f4

15.♕c2±) 12.♗g5 ♘b×d5 (Koglin, A. (2279) – Steinbacher, C. (2120), Krefeld 2001) 13.♖ad1 ♗e7 14.♗×f6 ♗×f6 15.♘×d5 e×d5 16.♗×d5 ♕f4±.

8.g4

A) 8.♘e5 (8.♗e3 ♘c6 or 8.0-0 ♘c6 9.♗e3 – Game 23) 8...♗×e2 9.♘×e2 (9.♕×e2 ♘c6 10.♘c4 ♕×d4 11.♗e3 ♕d7 12.♖d1 ♕e6∞ or 9...♕×d4 10.♗g5 ♘bd7∞) 9...e6 10.0-0 (Posazhennikov, A. (2256) – Goodger, M. (2161), Telford 2004) 10...♘c6 11.♗f4 ♘×e5 12.d×e5 ♕×d1 13.♖f×d1 ♘d5=;

B) 8.g3 ♗g6 (8...♘bd7!?) 9.♘e5 (9.♗f4!?) 9...♘c6 (9...♕b6?! (Nagel, R. – Hofsommer, M., Internet 2005) 10.♘c4 ♕a7 11.d5 with strong pressure) 10.♗f4 ♕×d4 11.♘×c6 ♕d1+ 12.♖×d1 b×c6 13.♗f3 ♘d7 14.♗×c6 0-0-0 15.0-0± or 10...♘×e5 11.d×e5 ♕×d1+ 12.♖×d1 ♘d7±.

8...♗g6 9.♘e5

9.h4!? h5 (9...h6 10.♘e5 ♘c6 11.♗f4∞; 9...♘e4 10.h5 ♘×c3 11.b×c3 ♗e4 12.0-0±) 10.♘e5 ♘×g4 11.♘×g6 ♕×g6 12.♘d5 ♕d6 (12...♕c6 13.♗f3) 13.c4 c6 14.♗f4 e5 15.d×e5 ♘×e5∞.

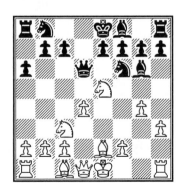

9...♞d5?!

It is best for Black is to eliminate the e5-knight as quickly as possible. To that end, Black's most popular choice here has been 9...♞c6! (9...♞bd7? 10.♞c4) 10.♞×c6 ♛×c6 11.♗f3 ♛e6+ (11...♛c4? 12.g5±; 11...♛b6!?) 12.♗e3 0-0-0 (12...♞e4? 13.d5 ♛e5 14.♗×e4 ½-½, Morito, H. – Bianchi, G. 2355, Buenos Aires 1985 14...♗×e4 15.f4+−) 13.♛e2 (Kozakov, M. (2420) – Hauchard, A. (2524), Frunze 1999) 13...♞e4 14.0-0 ♞×c3 15.b×c3 ♗e4⇄.

10.♗f3

10.♞×d5!? ♛×d5 11.0-0.

10...c6

10...♞×c3 11.b×c3 ♞c6 12.♗f4±.

11.h4?!

11.♞×d5!? c×d5 12.♗f4 (12.c4!?; 12.0-0!?)

A) 12...♛e6 (12...♛d8 13.♞×g6 h×g6 14.c4 ♛a5+ 15.♔f1±) 13.0-0 f6 (13...♞d7 14.♖e1±) 14.♞×g6 h×g6 15.c4 d×c4 (15...♖×h3 16.c×d5±) 16.♗×b7 ♖a7 17.♗g2±;

B) 12...♛b4+ 13.c3 (13.♛d2!?) 13...♛×b2 14.♗×d5 e6 15.♞×g6 h×g6 16.♖b1 ♛c3+ 17.♗d2 ♛×d4 18.♗×b7 ♗c5 (18...♖a7 19.♛c2 ♛c5 20.♛a4+ ♞d7 21.♗e3±) 19.♗e3 ♛c3+ (19...♛×d1+ 20.♔×d1±) 20.♔e2 ♛c4+ (20...♗×e3 21.♗×a8±) 21.♔f3 ♗×e3 22.f×e3 (22.♗×a8? ♛f4+ 23.♔e2 ♛×f2+ 24.♔d3 0-0−+) 22...♖a7 23.♛d6±.

11...♞×c3 12.b×c3

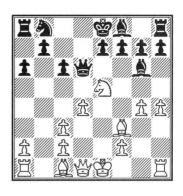

12...h6?!

12...♞d7!

A) 13.♞×d7 ♛×d7 14.h5 (14.0-0 h5⇄) 14...♛e6+ 15.♔f1 ♗e4 16.♛e2 ♗×f3 17.♛×f3 0-0-0⇄ or 13.♞c4 ♛e6+ (13...♛c7? 14.h5) 14.♛e2 ♛×e2+ 15.♔×e2 0-0-0⇄;

B) 13.♗f4 ♞×e5 14.d×e5 (14.♗×e5 ♛a3 15.d5 0-0-0 16.h5 f6 17.♗d4 ♗e8⇄ or 17.h×g6 f×e5⇄) 14...♛×d1+ (14...♛a3?! 15.♛d4 ♖d8 16.♛c4) 15.♖×d1 h5 16.g×h5 (16.e6 f×e6 17.g×h5 ♗×h5 18.♔e2 g6∓) 16...♗×h5 17.♔e2 ♗×f3+ 18.♔×f3 e6∓.

13.♖b1 ♖a7 (13...b5 14.0-0 ♗h7 15.♗f4 ♛f6 16.♗g3 ♖a7 17.♖e1± or 16...e6 17.♞×c6±)

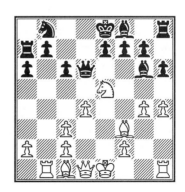

14.♗f4 ♗h7 (14...♞d7 15.0-0 ♛f6
16.♞×g6 ♛×g6 17.d5 e5 18.d×c6 b×c6
19.♗×e5 ♞×e5 20.♖b8+ ♚e7 21.♛d8+
♚e6 22.♗d5+ c×d5 23.♖b6+ or 17...c5
18.♖e1 b5 19.h5 ♛f6 20.♛d2 ±)
15.0-0 ♛d8 (15...♞d7 16.♖e1 ♞×e5
17.d×e5 ♛×d1 18.♖e×d1 e6
19.♗e3+−; 17...♛c5 18.♛d2 ♛c4
19.♖bd1 f6 20.♛d8+ ♚f7 21.e6+
♚g6 22.h5#; 17...♛c7 18.e6 ♞c8
19.♛d4 ♖a8 20.e×f7+ ♚×f7 21.♛c4+
e6 22.♖×b7+ ♛×b7 23.♛×e6#;
16...♛f6 17.♞×d7 ♚×d7 18.♗b8 ♖a8
19.♖×b7+ ♚c8 20.♛b1 ♛×f3 21.♛b6
♛×g4+ 22.♗g3+− or 17...♛×f4
18.♞e5 e6 19.♖×b7 ±) **16.d5 f6**
(16...c5 17.♖e1 b5 18.a4 f6 19.♞c4 ±)
**17.♞×c6 ♞×c6 18.d×c6 ♛×d1
19.♖f×d1 1-0**

Summary: After **1.e4 d5 2.e×d5
♛×d5 3.♞c3 ♛d6 4.d4 ♞f6
5.♞f3 ♗g4**, White has many different possibilities (see the comments to
6.♗e2).

6.♗e2 is a popular move but moves
such as 6.♞b5, 6.♗e3 (or 6.h3 in
Games 11 and 12) may present more
problems for Black. Only the move
6.h3 is dangerous for Black, after
which Black must decide between
6...♗h5 (Game 11) and 6...♗×f3
(Game 12). After **6.♗e2** Black has
good possibilities of equalizing and
obtaining counterplay: 6...c6 (Game
14) is a common and very solid move;
6...♗×f3 is not bad, but does yield
White the two bishops; 6...♞bd7 and
6...e6 are little known, but probably
safe enough; 6...a6 (with idea of ♞c6
and 0-0-0) is more active but also
more risky. 6...♞c6 is dangerous for
Black.

Game 11
Macieja, B. (2585) – Heberla, B. (2487)
Krakow 2006

**1.e4 d5 2.e×d5 ♛×d5 3.♞c3 ♛d6
4.d4 ♞f6 5.♞f3 ♗g4 6.h3 ♗h5
7.g4 ♗g6 8.♞e5**

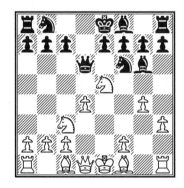

8...♞bd7

Typically pressuring the ♞e5 as quickly
as possible. Black has problems after
other moves:

A) 8...a6 9.♗g2 ♞c6 (Lazic, D. (2310)
– Petric, M. (2105), Mataruska Banja
2007) 10.♗f4 ♞×e5 11.d×e5 ♛b4
12.e×f6 ♛×f4 13.♗×b7+− or 9...c6
10.h4 ±;

B) 8...♛b6 9.g5 (9.♞c4 ♛e6+ 10.♞e5
♛b6 11.♗g2 (Stellwagen, R. (2208) –
Kantorik, M. (2330), Pardubice 2006)
11...♞bd7 ±) 9...♞fd7 (9...♞e4 10.♛g4
♞d6 11.♞c4 ±) 10.♞c4 ♛e6+ 11.♞e3
♞a6 12.h4 with the initiative;

C) 8...♞c6 9.♗b5 0-0-0 (9...a6 10.♗a4
b5 11.♛f3 b×a4 12.♞×c6 ♗×c2 13.0-0
♖c8 14.♖e1 e6 15.♗f4 ♛d7 16.♞e5 ±
or 12...♛e6 13.♗e3 ±) 10.♗×c6 b×c6
11.♛e2 (11.♛f3 ♛d5 ≡, Dorrington, C.
(2161) – Kolesnikov, E. (2361),

Chalkidiki 2001) 11...12.♗f4 ♕b4 13.0-0-0 e6 14.a3 ♕a5 15.♘c4 ♕a6 16.b4±;

D) 8...e6 9.♗g2 (9.♗f4!? ♕b4 10.♘xg6 hxg6 11.♕f3 ♘c6 12.♗b5; 9...♕d8 10.♕f3 c6 11.0-0-0; 9...♕b6 10.♕f3 ♗xc2 11.♖c1) 9...♕b6 (9...♘c6 10.♗f4 ♘xe5 11.dxe5 ♕xd1+ 12.♖xd1±; 9...c6 10.h4±; 9...♘d5 10.♗xd5 exd5 11.♕e2 ♗e7 12.♗f4±) 10.h4 ♗b4 11.♕e2 (11.0-0!? ♗xc3 12.bxc3) 11...c6 (11...♕xd4 12.0-0♾; 11...♘bd7 12.♘xd7 ♔xd7 13.h5±; 11...♘c6 12.♘xc6 bxc6 13.h5±) 12.a3 ♗xc3+ 13.bxc3±;

E) 8...c6

E1) 9.♗g2 ♘bd7 (9...e6? 10.h4±, Bromberger, S. (2495) – Nagatz, F. (2275), Dresden 2007; 9...♘d5 10.f4 f6 11.♘xg6 hxg6 12.♘xd5 cxd5 13.♕d3 ♔f7 14.♕b5±; 10.♘xd5!? cxd5 11.c4) 10.♗f4 (10.f4!? e6 (Labib, I. (2409) – Chahrani, I. (2337), Cairo 2001) 11.h4) 10...♕b4 (De Coverly, R. (2113) – Shepley, J. (2131), West Bromwich 2003) 11.♘xg6 hxg6 12.♕d2±;

E2) 9.h4 ♘bd7 10.♘xd7 (10.♘c4 ♕c7?! 11.h5 ♗e4 12.♘xe4 ♘xe4 13.♕f3, threatening 14.♗f4 practically winning, according to Emanuel Lasker. This situation can arise in the 3...♕a5 line also; 10...♕e6+ 11.♕e2 ⇄) 10...♕xd7 11.h5 ♗e4 12.♘xe4 ♘xe4 13.♕d3 (13.♗g2 ♘f6 14.g5 ♘d5±, Pinter, E. (2320) – Todor, R. (2220), Slovakia 2001) 13...♘f6 14.g5 ♘d5 15.♗d2 e6 16.0-0-0 0-0-0 17.♕f3 with strong pressure;

E3) 9.♗f4

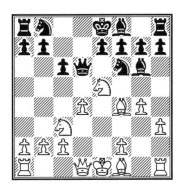

E3a) 9...♕b4 (9...♕d8 10.♗g2 ♘d5 11.♘xd5 cxd5 12.c4±, Potihoshkina, N. (2195) – Makogonova, N. (2134), Moscow 2000) 10.♘c4 ♘e4 (10...e6 11.♗d6 ♗xd6 12.a3+−) 11.a3 ♘xc3 12.axb4 ♘xd1 13.♘b6 1-0, Manik, M. (2460) – Garancovsky, P. (2151), Tatranske Zruby 2006;

E3b) 9...♘d5 10.♕d2!

E3b1) 10...♘xc3 (10...♕b4 11.♘xd5 ♕xd2+ 12.♔xd2 cxd5 13.♗b5+ ♔d8 14.♖ae1±) 11.♕xc3 11...♕d5 12.f3 e6 (12...♘d7? 13.♘xg6 hxg6 14.♗c4+−) 13.♗c4 (13.h4 f6 14.♗c4±) 13...♕d8 (Denny, K. (2365) – Chahrani, I. (2308), Turin 2006) 14.h4± or 11...♗e4 12.♖g1 ♘d7 (12...♕f6 13.♕e3 ♗xc2 14.♗c4 ♗g6 15.d5±) 13.0-0-0 ♗d5 (13...♘xe5 14.dxe5±) 14.♕e3 ♘xe5 15.dxe5 ♕b4 16.e6 0-0-0 17.♕e5 ♖d6 18.exf7±;

E3b2) 10...♘xf4 11.♕xf4

E3b2a) 11...♘d7 12.0-0-0 f6 (12...♘xe5 13.dxe5 ♕c7 14.♗d3 ♗xd3 15.♖xd3±, Psakhis, L. (2575) – Sygulski, A. (2410), Yurmala 1987; 12...0-0-0 13.♗c4 f6 14.♘xg6 hxg6 15.♕e3 e5 16.♘e4 ♕b4 17.♗e6±)

13.♘xg6 hxg6 14.♕e4 g5 15.♗c4 ♕f4+ (15...0-0-0 16.♗e6 ♕f4+ 17.♕xf4 gxf4 18.h4±) 16.♕xf4 gxf4 17.♗e6 g5 18.♘e4±;

E3b2b) 11...♕f6 12.♕e3

E3b2b1) 12...e6 13.0-0-0 h6 (13...♗b4 14.h4 ♗xc3 15.bxc3 h6 16.g5 ♕e7 17.♘xg6 fxg6 18.♗d3±) 14.h4 ♗h7 15.g5 ♕e7 16.g6 fxg6 17.♗d3 ♕f6 18.♘e4±;

E3b2b2) 12...♘d7 13.h4 h5 (13...h6 14.0-0-0 0-0-0 15.g5 ♕e6 16.♗c4 ♕f5 17.♗d3 ♕e6 18.♘xg6± or 15...♕d6 16.h5 hxg5 17.♗e2±) 14.g5 ♕d6 15.0-0-0 0-0-0 16.♗h3±.

Back to Macieja – Heberla.

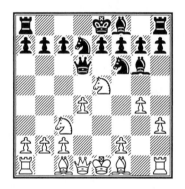

9.♗f4

We now examine the alternatives: **A)** 9.♘b5; **B)** 9.♘xg6 and **C)** 9.f4.

A) 9.♘b5 ♕b6 10.♘c4 (10.♘xd7 ♘xd7∓; 10.♗f4 ♘d5 11.♘xd7 ♔xd7 12.♗d2 c6∓ or 11.♘c4 ♕c6 12.♕f3 ♔d8 13.♘e5 ♘xe5 14.dxe5 e6 15.♗g5+ ♔c8∓) 10...♕e6+ (10...♕c6 11.d5) 11.♘e3 0-0-0 12.f4 ♗e4 (12...♘d5? 13.f5 ♘xe3 14.fxe6 ♘xd1 15.exd7+ ♖xd7 16.♔xd1±, Rigo, G.

(2060) – Scharrer, P. (2220), Trento 2007) 13.♗c4 ♕b6⇄;

B) 9.♘xg6 hxg6 10.♕f3 c6 (10...♕xd4? 11.g5 ♘h5 12.♗e3 ♕b4 13.0-0-0 e6 14.a3 ♕a5 15.♖xd7 ♔xd7 16.♕xf7+ ♗e7 17.♗c4+− or 13...c6 14.♖xd7 ♔xd7 15.♕xf7 ♖d8 16.a3 ♕a5 17.♗e2 ♔c8 18.♕xg6±) 11.♗e3 ♘b6 (11...e6 12.0-0-0±, Kosanovic, G. (2420) – Terzic, G. (2295) Nis 1996) 12.0-0-0 ♘bd5 13.♗d2 ♘xc3 14.♗xc3 ♕d5 15.♕xd5 ♘xd5 16.♗d2 0-0-0±;

C) 9.f4 e6 (9...0-0-0!? 10.♗g2 e6 11.h4 h5 12.♘xg6 fxg6 13.♕f3 c6 14.g5 ♘g4 15.♘e2 ♘b6⇄; 11.♕f3 ♕a6⇄) 10.h4 ♘d5 11.♗g2 h5 (11...♗b4?! 12.♘xg6 hxg6 13.♗xb7 ♖b8 14.♗f3 ♕xd4 15.a3 ♗c5 16.♕e2 with an unpleasant position for Black, Lagemann, T. – Hofsommer, M., Internet 2005 or 15...♕xd1+ 16.♔xd1 ♘a6 17.b4 with a better ending for White) 12.♘xg6 fxg6 13.♘xd5 exd5 14.♕e2+ ♗e7 15.♗d2 0-0-0 16.0-0-0±.

Let's return to Macieja – Heberla.

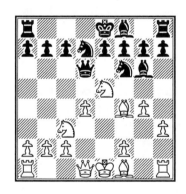

9...♘xe5

9...♕b6?! 10.♘c4 ♕e6+ 11.♘e3 ♘e4 (Ait Chaouche, S. – Jankowski, J., France 2000) 12.♘b5 0-0-0 13.♕f3±.

10.♗×e5

10.d×e5 ♕b4 11.♗d2 (11.♕d2 ♘e4 12.♗b5+ c6 13.♕d5 ♕c5 14.♕×c5 ♘×c5 15.♗e2 ♗×c2∓) 11...♘d7 (11...♘d5!?) 12.♕e2 (12.f4 e6∓; 12.e6!?) 12...0-0-0⇄.

10...♕b6 11.♕f3

11.♗g2 0-0-0 12.♕d2 e6 13.0-0-0 ♘d5=.

11...e6

11...♗×c2 12.♖c1 (12.♗c4!? e6 13.0-0) 12...♗g6 (12...♕×b2? 13.♗b5+ ♘d7 14.♕×b7 ♕×c3+ 15.♔e2 ♖d8 16.♗×c7+−) 13.♘b5 ♖c8 14.♗×c7 (14.♖×c7 ♖×c7 15.♘×c7+ ♔d8∞) 14...♕e6+ 15.♕e2 (15.♗e2? ♗e4∓) 15...a6 16.♕×e6 f×e6 17.♘a3 (17.♘a7 ♖a8 18.♗a5 ♗e4 19.♖h2 g6 20.g5 ♘d5∓) 17...e5 18.♗g2 ♔d7 19.d×e5 ♖×c7 20.♖×c7+ ♔×c7 21.e×f6 e×f6∓.

12.♗×f6

12.0-0-0 0-0-0 13.♔b1 ♘d5 14.♘×d5 e×d5 15.♗d3±.

12...g×f6 13.0-0-0 0-0-0 14.♗d3

14.♕×f6?! ♖g8 15.♗d3 (15.♘e2? ♕c6−+) 15...♗h6+ 16.♔b1 ♗g7 17.♕f3 ♗×d4∓.

14...♗e7

14...♗g7!? 15.♗e4 (15.d5 ♔b8 16.♖he1 a6 17.a3 ♖he8⇄) 15...c6 16.♘e2 ♖he8⇄.

15.d5 ♗b4

15...♔b8 16.♖he1 e5 17.a3 (17.♗f5 ♗b4) 17...a6 18.♗×g6 f×g6 19.♘e4 ♖hf8=.

16.♕×f6

16.♗×g6 f×g6 17.♕×f6 ♗×c3 18.♕×c3 e×d5

A) 19.♖×d5 ♖×d5 20.♕×h8+ ♖d8 21.♕×h7? (21.♕e5 ♕×f2=) 21...♕d4 22.c3 (22.a3 ♕d5−+) 22...♕f4+ 23.♔c2 ♕e4+, and Black wins;

B) 19.f4 d4 20.♕f3?! (20.♕g3 ♕d6 21.♖he1 ♖he8 22.♕f3 c5=) 20...♖he8 21.♖d3 (21.♖he1? ♖×e1 22.♖×e1 ♕a5) 21...c5 22.♖hd1 ♖d7∓.

16...♗×c3 17.♕×c3 e×d5 18.f4 ♕e3+ (18...d4 19.♕c4 ♗×d3 20.♖×d3 ♕f6 21.♖f1 ♖he8 22.g5 ♕f5 23.♖×d4 ♕×h3 24.♖×d8+ ♖×d8 25.b3 h5 26.g×h6 ♕×h6 27.♕×f7 ♕a6 28.♕f5+ ♔b8 29.♖e1 ♕×a2 30.♕f6± or 23...♖×d4 24.♕×d4 ♕×h3 25.♖d1 ♕e3+ 26.♕×e3 ♖×e3 27.♖d5±; 22...♕g7 23.h4 ♖e4=) **19.♕d2 ♕×d2+ 20.♔×d2 ♗×d3 21.♔×d3± ♖de8 22.♖de1 ♔d7 23.♖e5 ♖×e5 24.f×e5 ♖g8 25.♖f1 ♔e7 26.♖f5 ♖g6 27.♖h5 h6 28.♔d4 c6 29.♖f5 ♖e6 30.a4 b6?** (30...f6±) **31.b4 ♖g6 32.b5± ♖e6 33.♖f3 ♖g6 34.♖c3 c5+ 35.♔×d5 h5 36.♖c4 h×g4 37.♖×g4 ♖h6 38.h4 ♔d7 39.♖f4**

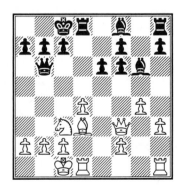

♚e7 40.♖g4 ♚d7 41.♖f4 ♚e7
42.c3 ♚e8 43.a5 b×a5 44.♚×c5
♖e6 45.♚d5 a6 46.c4 a4 47.h5
♖h6 48.♖h4 ♚d7 49.♖h3 ♚c7
50.♖f3 a×b5 51.♖×f7+ ♚b6
52.♖f6+ 1-0

Summary: After **1.e4 d5 2.e×d5
♕×d5 3.♘c3 ♕d6 4.d4 ♘f6 5.♘f3
♗g4 6.h3**, just as in Game 10 with
6.♗e2, Black usually does not have
problems in the opening. After
6...♗h5 (6...♗×f3 – Game 12) the
moves **7.g4 ♗g6 8.♘e5** commonly
create the potential for aggressive plans
involving moves as ♗c1-f4, ♗f1-g2,
♘e5-c4, and h3-h4-h5, separately or in
combination with each other.

After **8.♘e5** Black has many logical
continuations but as analysis shows,
Black's best move is **8...♘bd7**
(Black has difficulties after other
moves). We then examined White's
possibilities, 9.♘b5, 9.♘×g6, 9.f4 and
9.♗f4.

After 9.♘b5 ♕b6 Black has a good
game. After 9.♘×g6 h×g6 White stands
slightly better thanks to the bishop-pair.
After 9.f4 0-0-0 Black has a good game
with counterplay.

Thanks to the well-known game
Psakhis-Sygulski (with 8...c6 9.♗f4)
many chess theoreticians rated 6...♗h5
as a serious mistake. White's menacing
initiative in this game makes a very
strong impression, and it is hard to see
any way for Black to equalize. The
move **9.♗f4** looks good after
8...♘bd7, but as our analysis shows,
after **9...♘×e5**, Black has decent game
with counterplay.

Game 12
Baklan, V. (2615) – Loeffler, S. (2445)
Austria 2007

1.e4 d5 2.e×d5 ♕×d5 3.♘c3 ♕d6
4.d4 ♘f6 5.♘f3 ♗g4 6.h3 ♗×f3
7.♕×f3

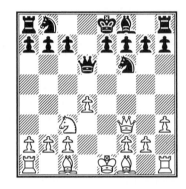

7...c6

7...♘c6 and now:

A) 8.♗b5 0-0-0 (8...e6 9.♗f4 ♕d7
10.0-0 ♗e7 11.♖ad1 0-0-0 12.♗e5±
or 10...♗d6 11.♗e5 ♗×e5 12.d×e5
♘d5 13.♖ad1±) 9.♗×c6 ♕×c6
10.♕×c6 b×c6 11.♗e3 e6 12.a3 ♘d5±,
Sale, S. (2440) – Muse, D. (2335),
Croatia 1996;

B) 8.♗e3 (8.♘b5!? ♕d7 9.♗f4 or
8...♕e6+ 9.♗e3) 8...e6 9.0-0-0 0-0-0
(9...a6?! 10.♗f4 ♕d7 11.d5) 10.a3
10...♗e7?! (10...♕d7 11.♚b1 ♘e7
12.♗c4 ♘ed5± or 11.♗c4 ♗d6
12.♖he1±) 11.♗c4 ♘a5 (11...♕d7!?)
12.♗a2 ♕a6 (12...♘d5 13.♗d2 ♘c6
14.♕×f7 ♘×d4 15.♗×d5 e×d5
16.♗e3±) 13.d5 ♘c4 14.♗×c4 ♕×c4
15.♖d4±, Lau, R. (2490) – Mann, C.
(2445), Germany 1995.

8.♗e3

The following game, played by two unknowns on the Internet in 2000, is an interesting instance of the d-pawn sacrifice: 8.♗g5 ♛xd4 9.♗e2 ♘bd7 10.0-0 e6 11.♖ad1 ♛c5 (11...♛b6!?) 12.♗e3 ♛a5 (12...♛b4!?) 13.♘e4 ♘xe4 14.♖xd7 ♔xd7 15.♛xf7+ ♗e7 16.♖d1+ ♘d6 17.♗f4? (17.♗g4∞) 17...e5? (17...♛e1+!) 18.♗g4+ 1-0 Main alternatives here are **A)** 8.♗f4 and **B)** 8.♗d2.

A) 8.♗f4 ♛xd4 9.♖d1 ♛b6 (9...♛b4!?; 9...♛c5!?) 10.♗c4

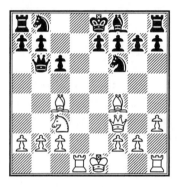

A1) 10...♛xb2?! 11.♖b1 with a very strong initiative; for example, 11...♛a3 12.♖xb7 ♘bd7 13.0-0 ♖c8 (13...♛c5 14.♖c7±) 14.♗xf7+ ♔xf7 15.♖xd7± or 11...♛c2 12.♖xb7 ♘bd7 13.0-0 ♖c8 14.♗a6 ♛f5 (14...e6 15.♖xd7±) 15.♖xa7 ♖d8 16.♗c7±;

A2) 10...e6 11.0-0 ♘bd7 (11...♗e7!?) 12.♖fe1 ♗e7 13.♗xe6? (13.b3=; 13.g4 0-0-0 14.g5 ♘e8 15.b3 ♘c5 16.a4⩲) 13...fxe6 14.♖xe6 ♘f8 15.♖ee1 ♘g6 16.♗d6 ♖d8 17.♛g3 (17.♛f5 ♖xd6 18.♖xd6 0-0∓) 17...0-0 18.♗xe7 (18.♖xe7 ♘xe7 19.♗xe7 ♖xd1+ 20.♘xd1 ♛d4∓) 18...♖xd1 19.♘xd1 ♖e8 20.♛a3 c5 21.♛a4 ♖xe7 0-1, Liedtke, M. (2280) – Braun, G. (2330), Germany, 1997;

B) 8.♗d2

B1) 8...♛xd4 9.0-0-0 ♘bd7 10.♗f4 ♛b6 (10...♛c5!?; 10...♛b4!? 11.♗c7 g6∞, Volkmann, F. (2420) – Walter, T. (2070), Austria 2006) 11.♗c4 e6 12.♖he1 ♗b4? (12...0-0-0; 12...♗e7) 13.♗xe6 fxe6 14.♖xe6+ ♔f7 (14...♔d8 15.♖xf6 gxf6 16.♛d3+−) 15.♖xd7+ ♔xe6 16.♖xg7 d4 17.♛e2+ ♘e4 (17...♔f5 18.♖g5+ ♔xf4 19.h4+−) 18.♘xe4 ♛xg7 19.♘c5+ ♔d5 20.♛h5+ ♔c4 21.♘e6 c5 22.♛e2+ ♔d5 23.♘c7+ ♛xc7 24.c4+ ♔d4 25.♗xc7+−. White has the initiative for the d-pawn in these two lines (8.♗f4 ♛xd4 and 8.♗d2 ♛xd4). Of course these lines are not forced after 8...♛xd4, but they illustrate the possibilities for both sides.

B2) 8...e6 (8...♘bd7 9.0-0-0 ♛xd4 – 8...♛xd4 9.0-0-0 ♘bd7; 9...0-0-0?! 10.♗f4 ♛b4 11.d5±) 9.0-0-0 ♛c7

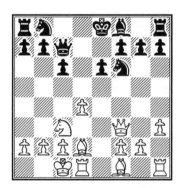

This position can arise after 3...♛a5 4.d4 ♘f6 5.♘f3 ♗g4 6.h3 ♗xf3 7.♛xf3 c6 8.♗d2 e6 9.0-0-0 ♛c7. White has better chances:

B2a) 10.♗c4

B2a1) 10...♗e7 11.♖he1 (11.g4!?) 11...♘d5?! (11...♘bd7!?) 12.♛g4 0-0

13.♗h6 ♗f6 14.♘e4 ♕e7 15.h4 ♚h8 16.♘xf6 ♕xf6 17.♗g5 ♕xf2 18.♗xd5 1-0, Wieczorek, O. (2204) – Molnar, J. (1921), Marianske Lazne 2008;

B2a2) 10...♘bd7 11.g4 (11.♖he1 0-0-0 12.♗b3 ♘b6 13.♘e2 c5 14.dxc5 ♗xc5 15.♗g5 ♕c6 16.♕xc6+ bxc6 17.f3±, Motylev, A. (2680) – Laylo, D. (2344), USA 2005) 11...♘b6 12.♗b3

B2a2a) 12...♘bd5 (12...0-0-0 13.g5 ♘fd5 14.♘e4± or 13...♘e8 14.♘e4±; 12...♗b4!? 13.g5 ♘fd5 ⇄; 13.♗f4 ♗d6 ⇄; 13.♚b1!?) 13.g5 ♘xc3 14.♗xc3 ♘d5 15.♗d2 b5 (15...a5!? 16.♖de1 ♕d7 or 16.c4 a4 17.♗c2 ♘b6) 16.h4 ♗d6 17.♚b1 g6 18.h5 ♖f8 19.hxg6 hxg6 20.♖c1 0-0-0 21.c4±, Yemelin, V. (2540) – Podinic, V. (2415), Neum 2005;

B2a2b) 12...h6 (12...♗d6 13.g5 ♘fd5 14.♘e4 ♗f4 15.c4 with pressure) 13.h4 0-0-0 14.g5 ♘e8 15.♘e4 (15.gxh6!? gxh6 16.♘e4) 15...♖xd4 16.♗f4 ♖xd1+ (16...♕d7 17.♖xd4 ♕xd4 18.♖d1 ♕b4 19.♗g3±) 17.♖xd1 e5 18.♗g3 f6 19.♕f5+ ♚b8 20.gxf6 gxf6 21.♘xf6 ♗d6 22.♕e6 1-0, Zambrana, O. (2511) – Salazar, C. (2215), Cali 2007;

B2b) 10.g4 ♘bd7 (10...h6 11.h4 ♘bd7 12.♗h3 ♘b6 13.g5 hxg5 14.hxg5 ♘fd5 15.g6 f5 16.♖he1±, Polgar J. (2550) – De Needleman, C. (2005), Novi Sad 1990) 11.♚b1 ♗e7 12.g5 ♘d5 (Brkic, A. (2477) – Podinic, V. (2415), Neum 2005) 13.♘xd5 cxd5 14.h4 ♖c8 (14...g6 15.h5 ♖f8 16.hxg6 hxg6 17.♖h7 ♖c8 18.♗d3 b5 19.c3 a5 20.♖xf7±) 15.c3 (15.♗d3!?) 15...♕a5 16.h5 b5 (16...0-0 17.♗d3 with a strong

initiative) 17.g6 hxg6 18.hxg6 ♖xh1 19.gxf7+ ♚f8 20.♕xh1 with a very strong attack.

We return now to Baklan – Loeffler.

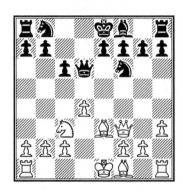

8...♘bd7

8...e6 (8...♘d5 9.♗c4 e6 10.0-0 ♗e7 11.♘e4 ♕c7 12.♗b3 ½-½, Teran Alvarez, I. (2400) – Epishin, V. (2575), Sevilla 2008; 12.♗d2!?)

A) 9.♗d3 (9.g3 ♗e7 10.♗g2 0-0 11.0-0 ♘bd7 12.♖ad1 ♘b6 13.♖fe1 ♖fe8 14.♘e4 ♘xe4 15.♕xe4 ♕d5 ⇄, Adamowicz, K. (2075) – Hasangatin, R. (2480), Cappelle La Grande 2008) 9...♗e7 10.0-0 ♘bd7 11.a3 ♕c7 12.♘e4 ♘xe4 13.♕xe4 ♘f6 14.♕f3 0-0=, Unzicker, W. (2450) – Lein, A. (2465), Bad Wildbad 1993; 9...♘bd7 10.0-0 ♕c7 11.♘a4 ♗d6 12.c4 0-0 ⇄, Volkmann, F. (2430) – Kantorik, M. (2345), Austria 2007 or 10.0-0-0 ♘b6 11.♘e4 ♘xe4 12.♗xe4 ♘d5 13.♗d2 ♕c7 14.c4 ♘f6 15.♗c2 0-0-0 16.♗c3 ♗e7 ⇄, Handke, F. (2467) – Mann, C. (2455), Germany 2004;

B) 9.0-0-0 (9.♗c4 – 5.♗c4 c6 6.♘f3 ♗g4 7.♗e3 e6 8.h3 ♗xf3 9.♕xf3, Game 1; 9.♗e2 ♘bd7 10.0-0 ♕c7 11.♘e4 ♘xe4 12.♕xe4 ♘f6 13.♕f3

♗d6 14.c4 0-0⇄, Talla, V. (2425) – Kantorik, M. (2330), Banska Stiavnica 2006)

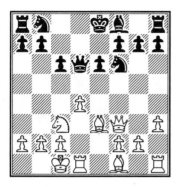

B1) 9...♗e7 (9...♘bd7 see 8...♘bd7 9.0-0-0 e6)

B1a) 10.g4 ♘bd7 11.♗g2 (11.♗f4!? ♛b4 12.♔b1) 11...♘d5 12.♘e4 ♛b4 (12...♛xd4!?∞) 13.♗d2 ♛a4 14.♛b3 ♛xb3 15.axb3 0-0-0±, Skoko, M. (2255) – Matovic, P. (2200), Stara Pazova 2007;

B1b) 10.♔b1 (10.♗d3 ♘bd7 11.g4 ♘b6 12.g5 ♘fd5 13.♘e4 ♛d8 14.♖hg1 ♘b4 15.c3 ♘xd3+ 16.♖xd3 ♛d5 17.♔b1 a5⇄, Kovalev, A. (2550) – Nedela, V. (2374), Czechia 2005 or 15.♔b1 ♛d5 16.b3 ♛a5 17.a4 ♘6d5 18.♗d2 b5⇄) 10...♘bd7 11.♗d3 0-0 (11...♘b6!? 12.♗f4 ♛d7) 12.g4 (12.♗f4 ♛b4 13.♗c7 ♘b6 14.a3 ♛a5∞) 12...♛b4 13.h4 ♘d5 14.♘xd5 cxd5 15.g5 f5 16.gxf6 ♘xf6 17.♛h3±, Vorobiov, E. (2543) – Hasangatin, R. (2460), Cappelle la Grande 2006;

B2) 9...♛c7

B2a) 10.♘e4 (10.g4!?; 10.♔b1 ♘bd7 – 8...♘bd7 9.0-0-0 e6 10.♔b1 ♛c7; 10.♗f4 ♗d6 11.♗xd6 ♛xd6 12.♘e4

♘xe4 13.♛xe4 ♘d7=, Priborsky, J. (2335) – Kantorik, M. (2330), Banska Stiavnica 2006; 12.g4 0-0 13.g5 ♘d5±) 11...♘xe4 11.♛xe4 ♘d7 12.c4 ♘f6 13.♛c2 ♗d6 14.g3±, Nikolenko, O. (2480) – Nagrocka, E. (2165), Katowice 1995 or 13.♛f3 0-0-0 14.g4 h6±;

B2b) 10.♗d3 ♘bd7 11.g4

B2b) 11...♘d5?! 12.♘xd5 cxd5 13.♔b1 a6 14.h4 (14.♛e2 ♘b6 15.f4 0-0-0 16.f5 with pressure, Afek, Y. (2328) – Fries Nielsen, J. (2356), Gausdal 2006) 14...♖c8 (14...♘b6 15.b3) 15.♗d2 b5 16.♖de1 ♘b6 17.b3 ♗d6 18.g5 with better chances for White;

B2b) 11...♘b6 12.g5 ♘fd5 13.♘e4 (13.♘xd5 ♘xd5 14.♗d2 ♘b4 15.♗c4 0-0-0 16.a3 ♘d5±) 13...♘xe3 14.fxe3 0-0-0 15.♖df1 ♖d7 16.h4 h6±.

Back to Baklan – Loeffler.

9.0-0-0

9.♗d3 e6 10.0-0-0 ♗e7 – 8...e6 9.♗d3 ♗e7 10.0-0 ♘bd7; 9.♗c4 – 5.♗c4 c6 6.♘f3 ♗g4 7.♗e3 ♘bd7 8.h3 ♗xf3 9.♛xf3, Game 1.

9...e6

A) 9...0-0-0?! 10.♗f4 ♕b4 11.a3 ♕a5 (11...♕b6 12.b4 a5 13.♘a4±) 12.d5! (Sigrist, A. – Ertl, R., Internet 2004) 12...c×d5 (12...c5 13.♘b5 ♘e8 14.♗d2±) 13.♘×d5 e5 (13...♘×d5? 14.♖×d5 ♕a4 15.♕c3+ ♔c6 16.♕×c6+ b×c6 17.♗a6#) 14.b4 ♕a4 15.♕c3+ ♕c6 16.♕×c6+ b×c6 17.♗a6+ ♔b8 18.♘×f6 g×f6 19.♗e3±;

B) 9...♘d5 10.♗d2 (10.♘e4!?) 10...♘7f6 (10...♘×c3 11.♗×c3 e6±) 11.g4 (11.♗c4 ♘×c3 12.♗×c3 e6±) 11...e6 (11...♘×c3 12.♗×c3 e6± or 12.♕×c3 ♘e4±) 12.g5 ♘×c3 13.♗×c3 ♕d5 14.♕×d5 ♘×d5= or 12.♘e2 (Gurcan, E. (1955) – Sitnic, A., Kemer 2007) 12...♘b6 13.g5 ♕d5±.

10.♔b1

A) 10.g4 (10.♗c4 0-0-0 11.g4 ♘b6 12.♗b3 ♕d7 13.♗f4 ♘fd5 14.♗g3 ♘×c3 15.♕×c3 ♗d6=, Zubarev, A. (2515) – Nosenko, A. (2500), Kharkov 2007) 10...♘b6 11.h4 (Manca, F. (2405) – Garcia Palermo, C. (2455), Italy 2007) 11...♘bd5 12.♘×d5 ♕×d5 13.♕×d5 ♘×d5±;

B) 10.♗f4 ♕b4

B1) 11.a3 (11.♗c7 ♘b6 12.a3 ♕e7 13.♗e5 0-0-0 14.♔b1±, Zdebskaja, N. (2344) – Gheorghe, C. (2234), Chisinau 2005; 12...♕a5!?) 11...♕a5 12.♗c4 ♗e7 (12...♘b6!? 13.♗b3 ♗e7±) 13.♖he1 0-0 14.♗b3 (Jansa, V. (2458) – Cicak, S. (2506), Passau 2000) 14...♘b6 15.♔b1 ♘bd5±;

B2) 11.♘b5 c×b5 12.♕×b7 ♘b6 13.♗c7 ♘fd7 14.d5 ♖c8 (14...e5!?; 14...♗e7?! 15.d×e6 f×e6 16.a3 ♗g5+ (Held, P. – Mann, C. (2305), Germany

1989) 17.f4 ♗×f4+ 18.♔b1 ♕e7 19.♗×f4±) 15.d×e6 f×e6 16.a3 ♕e7 (16...♕c5? 17.♖×d7!) 17.♗×b6 (17.♗×b5? ♕g5+) 17...♘×b6 18.♗×b5+ ♔f7∞.

Let's return to Baklan – Loeffler.

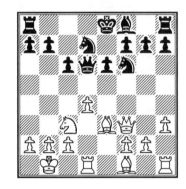

10...♕c7

10...♗e7 – 8...e6 9.0-0-0 ♗e7 10.♔b1 ♘bd7.

11.g4

11.♗c1!? ("White keeps the bishops on their original squares, where they can influence the game without becoming targets for the black knights. Meanwhile White is able to gain further ground by surging forward with the g- and h-pawns", Emms J.). 11...♘b6 12.g4 h6 13.h4 0-0-0 14.♗h3 (14.g5!? h×g5 15.h×g5 ♖×h1 16.♕×h1 ♘fd5 17.♘e4) 14...♗d6 15.♘e2 (15.g5!? h×g5 16.h×g5 ♘fd5 17.♘×d5 ♘×d5 18.c4 or 17...c×d5 18.g6; 15.b3!? ♘bd5 16.♘e2 or 15...♔b8 16.g5) 15...♘c4 (15...♘fd5?! 16.b3! c5 17.c4 ♘b4 18.♗b2±, Bologan, V. (2530) – Muse, D. (2325), Berlin 1995) 16.g5 ♘d5 17.g×h6 g×h6⇄ or 16.b3 ♘a3+ 17.♔b2 b5⇄.

11...♝b4?!

11...h6 12.♝d3 (12.h4 0-0-0 13.♖g1 ♘b6 14.g5 h×g5 15.h×g5 ♘fd5 16.♝c1 ♘×c3+ 17.♛×c3 ♝d6 18.g6 f5 19.♖e1 ♛e7 20.♛f3 ♖de8 21.♖h1 ♖hf8 22.♖h7 ♘d5=, Edouard, R. (2404) – Govciyan, P. (2397), Besancon 2006) 12...♘b6 13.h4 0-0-0 14.g5 ♘fd5 15.♘×d5 ♘×d5 16.g×h6 g×h6±.

12.g5 ♘d5

12...♝×c3 13.g×f6 ♛b6 14.♝c1 ♝×d4 15.f×g7 ♝×g7 16.♖×d7 +– or 15...♖g8 16.♛d3±.

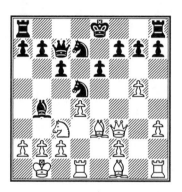

13.♘e4 (13.♘×d5 c×d5 14.h4 a6 15.h5 ♘b6 16.♝d3 0-0-0 17.b3♚b8 18.g6 h×g6 19.h×g6 f6 20.♖h7 ♖hg8 21.♝c1±; 16...♘a4!?; 14...♖c8?! 15.c3 ♝d6) **13...b5 14.h4 ♘7b6 15.♝c1** (15.h5 0-0-0 16.♖c1 ♘×e3 17.f×e3 ♖d5 18.h6 g6 19.♛f6 ♖g8 20.c3 ♝f8 21.♛f3 ♖f5±) **15...0-0-0 16.c3 ♝d6** (16...♝f8!? 17.b3 ♛b7 18.h5 a5) **17.b3** (17.♘×d6+!? ♖×d6 18.h5) **17...♝f4 18.♝b2 ♘e7** (18...h6 19.♝e2 h×g5 20.h×g5 with better chances for White.) **19.♖g1** (19.h5 or 19.♘c5 is also possible.) **19...h5 20.g×h6** (20.♘c5!? ♘f5 21.♘a6 ♛d6 22.♝a3) **20...♖×h6**

21.h5 (21.♖×g7!? ♘f5 22.♖g4 ♖×h4 23.♖×h4 ♘×h4 24.♛h5 ♘f5 25.♝d3.) **21...♖g8** (21...♘f5!?) **22.♝e2** (22.♘c5!? ♘f5 23.♝d3 ♘d5 24.♝×f5 e×f5 25.♖de1±) **22...g5 23.♝c1** (23.h×g6!? ♘×g6 24.♘c5 ♘d5 25.♝d3 ♛d6 26.♖de1 ♚c7 27.♝e4 with strong pressure.) **23...♘bd5! 24.♘×g5** (24.♖de1!? f6 25.c4 b×c4 26.b×c4 ♛b6+ 27.♝b2 with better chances for White; 24... ♝×c1 25.♖×c1 ♘f4 26.♝f1 f6 27.♘c5 ♘ed5±) **24...♝×c1 25.♖×c1 ♖f6**⩱

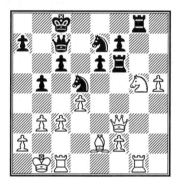

26.♛g3?! (26.♛e4 ♖f5 27.c4 b×c4 28.b×c4 ♘f4 29.♘f3 ♖×g1 30.♖×g1 ♖×h5=) **26...♛×g3 27.♖×g3 ♖×f2**⩱ **28.♝d1 ♘f5 29.♖f3** (29.♖g1!?) **29...♖d2?!** (29...♖h2! 30.♘×f7 ♖gg2 31.♖c2 ♘fe3 32.♖×g2 ♖×g2∓) **30.♘e4 ♖h2 31.♖f2 ♖h4 32.c4?!** (32.♝f3∓) **32...b×c4 33.b×c4 ♘de3**∓ **34.♘f6 ♖g1 35.♝e2** (35.♝d2 ♖hh1–+) **35...♖hh1?!** (35...♖×c1+ 36.♚×c1 ♘×d4 37.♝d3 ♘df5∓) **36.♖×g1 ♖×g1+ 37.♚b2 ♘×d4?!** (37...♚d8 38.♚c3 ♚e7 39.♘e4 ♖a1 40.♘d2 ♖×a2 41.♖h2 ♚f8∓; 38.♘e4 ♘g4 39.♖f4 ♖g2 40.♖×g4 ♖×e2+ 41.♚b1 ♚e7 42.♘g3 ♖h2 43.♘×f5+ e×f5∓) **38.h6 ♖h1?** (38...♘×e2 39.♖×e2 ♘c4+ 40.♚b3 ♖h1 41.♚×c4 ♖×h6±) **39.♝h5**

♘d1+ (39...♖h3 40.h7 ♘×c4+ 41.♔c1 ♖h1+ 42.♗d1 ♘e5∞; 40.♖c2! ♘d×c2 41.h7±) **40.♗×d1 ♖×h6 41.♗c2 ♖h4 42.♗d3 ♔d8 43.♔c3 e5 44.c5 ♘e6 45.♘e4 ♘f4 46.♗c4 ♘d5+ 47.♗×d5 c×d5 48.♘d6 ♔d7 49.♖f6 ♖h3+ 50.♔b4 e4 51.♘f5 a5+ 52.♔b5 ♖c3 53.c6+ ♔e8 54.♖d6 1-0**

Summary: 1.e4 d5 2.e×d5 ♕×d5 3.♘c3 ♕d6 4.d4 ♘f6 5.♘f3 ♗g4 6.h3 ♗×f3 is the alternative to 6...♗h5. After **7.♕×f3**, Black has two possibilities: 7...♘c6 and 7...c6.

After 7...♘c6 8.♗b5 0-0-0 9.♗×c6 ♕×c6 10.♕×c6 b×c6 11.♗e3, we have a position which is slightly better for White. I consider this ending difficult for both sides, with White's chances for victory no better than Black's chances for a draw. And, after 7...♘c6 8.♗e3 (or 8.♘b5), White is slightly better. That may explain why the more popular alternative is 7...c6.

After **7...c6**, White must decide what to do about the d-pawn. Usually it is defended by **8.♗e3**, but it may also be sacrificed to open the position for the bishops, clear the d-file, and use the advantage in development to attack Black's king. These lines (8.♗g5, 8.♗f4 and 8.♗d2) are unclear after 8...♕×d4.

Usually Black, after 7...c6 and then e7-e6, has a solid position without weaknesses, but a bit passive against White's bishops. Black often sets up pieces on the first three ranks, conceding White a spatial advantage. When Black and White both castle short, the chances are approximately even. With castling on

opposite wings, the situation can become complicated, giving Black more chances for counterplay. When both players castle long, White can plan a kingside pawn advance with g2-g4-g5 and h3-h4 with better chances.

Game 13
Mamedov, R. (2560) –
Vysochin, S. (2530)
St. Petersburg 2006

1.e4 d5 2.e×d5 ♕×d5 3.♘c3 ♕d6 4.d4 ♘f6 5.♘f3 c6 6.♗d3

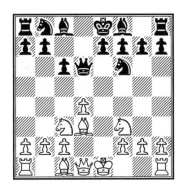

6...♗g4

The other alternative is 6...g6. This can be played with the idea of offering the exchange of light-squared bishops by ♗c8-f5; if White answers ♗d3×f5, Black intensifies control of the central light squares after g6×f5 and follows with e7-e6. Therefore White may wish to wait for Black to exchange bishops on d3, and after ♕d1×d3 try to compel the move e7-e6, after which the dark-square complex e5-f6-h6 can be weakened by an exchange of dark-squared bishops.

7.♗e3

Other possibilities:

110

A) 7.0-0 (7.♘e4 ♘xe4 8.♗xe4 ♘d7 9.0-0 ♘f6 10.♖e1 (Krivec, J. (2345) – Drazic, S. (2485), Nova Gorica 2008) 10...0-0-0=) 7...♗xf3 (7...♘bd7; 7...e6 8.♗e3 ♗e7 9.♗e2 0-0 10.♛d2 ½-½, Sebag, M. – Chiche, J., Montlucon 1997) 8.♛xf3 ♛xd4 (8...♘bd7!?; 8...e6!?) 9.♘b5 ♛d8 (9...cxb5?! 10.♛xb7 ♛d5 11.♗e4) 10.♗g5 cxb5 (10...♘bd7⩱) 11.♗xf6 ♘c6 12.♗xb5 (12.♗g5!?⩱) 12...♛b6 13.♗xc6+ ♛xc6 14.♛xc6+ bxc6 15.♗c3 0-0-0± or 9.♖d1 (9.♖e1!?) 9...♘bd7 (9...e6 10.♗e2 ♛c5 11.♗e3 ♛a5 12.a3⩱; 9...♛g4?! 10.♛xg4 ♘xg4 11.♗f5 ♘e5 12.♗c8 ♘bd7 13.♗xb7) 10.♗e2 ♛b6 (Thompson, P. – Blair, D., Internet 1999) 11.b4⩱;

B) 7.h3

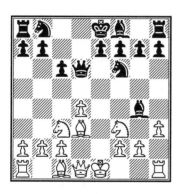

B1) 7...♗h5 8.♗e3 (8.g4 ♗g6 9.♗xg6 hxg6 10.♘e5 ♘bd7 11.♗f4 ♘d5=; 11.♘c4?! ♛e6+ 12.♘e3 0-0-0∓) 8...e6 9.♛d2 ♘bd7 10.♗g5 ♗g6 11.♗f4 ♛b4 12.0-0 ♗xd3 13.♛xd3 ♗e7 14.♘ce4 ♘xe4 15.♘xe4 0-0 16.c3 ♛b6±, Bitalzadeh, A. (2317) – Blanchard, J. (2219), Amsterdam 2005;

B2) 7...♗xf3 8.♛xf3 ♛xd4 (8...♘bd7 9.♗e3 e6 10.0-0-0 ♘b6 11.♘e4 ♘xe4 12.♗xe4 ♘d5 13.♗d2 ♛c7 14.c4 ♘f6

15.♗c2 0-0-0 16.♗c3 ♗e7 17.♖he1±, Handke, F. (2467) – Mann, C. (2455), Germany 2004)

B2a) 9.0-0 (9.♘b5? cxb5 10.♛xb7 ♛d5 11.♗xb5+ ♔d8!∓) 9...e6 (9...♘bd7!?) 10.♗e3 ♛h4 11.♘b5 (11.♖ad1 ♘bd7⩱) 11...♘a6 (11...♘d5? 12.c4) 12.♘xa7 ♘b4∞;

B2b) 9.♗e3 ♛b4 (9...♛e5 10.0-0-0 ♘bd7 11.♖he1⩱) 10.a3 ♛xb2? (10...♛a5 11.b4?! ♛e5; 11.0-0⩱) 11.♔d2! ♘d5 12.♘xd5 cxd5 (Salem, G. (2341) – Aryanejad, H. (2231), Abu Dhabi 2003) 13.♛xd5 ♘c6 14.♖hb1 ♛f6 15.♖xb7 ♖d8 16.♛b5±.

We return now to Mamedov – Vysochin.

7...♘bd7

Also coming under consideration is 7...e6 8.h3 (8.♛e2 ♗e7 9.0-0-0 ♘bd7 10.h3 ♗h5 11.♖he1 ♘d5 12.♘e4 ♛c7±, Foerster, R. – Hornung, T., Bad Homburg 2004) 8...♗h5 (8...♗xf3 9.♛xf3 see 7...c6 8.♗e3 e6 9.♗d3, Game 12) and now:

A) 9.♛e2 ♘bd7 10.g4 ♗g6 11.♗xg6 hxg6 12.0-0-0 0-0-0?! (12...♗e7⇄) 13.♘e5! (Rohit, G. (2397) – Foudzi, J.

(2033), Negombo 2003) 13...♕e7 14.♘×c6 b×c6 15.♕a6+ ♔b8 16.♗f4+ e5 17.d×e5 ♕b4 18.♗g3± or 9.♕d2 ♗e7 10.g4 ♗g6 11.♗×g6 h×g6 12.0-0-0 ♕d8 13.♔b1 ♗b4 14.♕d3 ♗×c3 15.♕×c3 0-0 16.♕a3 ♕d5 17.♘d2 b5 18.f3 ♘bd7 19.g5 ♘h5 20.♘e4 a5⇄, Sandehn, K. – Jonovic, P., Internet 2003;

B) 9.g4 ♗g6 10.♘e5 ♗×d3 (10...♘bd7!? 11.♘×g6 h×g6 12.♕f3 ♘b6 14.0-0-0 ♘bd5⇄) 11.♕×d3 ♘bd7 12.f4 ♗e7 13.0-0-0 0-0 14.g5 ♘d5 15.♘e4 ♕c7 16.c3 (16.♔b1 ♖fd8±) 16...♖fd8 17.h4 (Abovan, S. – Pytel, K. (2380), Le Havre 1998) 17...c5 18.♘×d7 (18.h5?! ♘×e5 19.f×e3 ♘×e3 20.♕×e3 c×d4∓; 18.g6 h×g6 19.h5 c×d4 20.h×g6 ♘×e5∓ or 19.♘g5 ♘×e5 20.f×e5 ♘×e3 21.♕×e3 c×d4∓) 18...c×d4 19.♕×d4 ♕×d7 20.♕e5 ♗d6=.

Back to Mamedov – Vysochin.

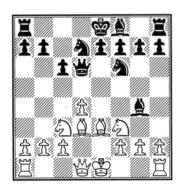

8.♕e2

Also possible is 8.h3; for example, 8...♗h5 (8...♗×f3 9.♕×f3 – 12) 9.♕e2 (9.♕d2!? ♗×f3 10.g×f3) 9...e6 10.0-0-0 and now:

A) 10...♕c7 11.♔b1 ♗b4 (11...♗d6!?) 12.♗d2 ♗×c3 13.♗×c3 ♘d5

(13...♗g6!?; 13...0-0-0!?) 14.♗d2 ♘f4 15.♗×f4 ♕×f4 16.g4 ♗g6 17.♗×g6 h×g6 18.d5 c×d5 19.♖×d5 (Ottenweller, W. – Law, S., Internet 2003) 19...0-0-0 20.♖d4 ♕f6 21.♕e3 ♘b6±;

B) 10...♗e7 11.g4 ♗g6 12.♗×g6 (12.♔b1 ♗×d3 13.♖×d3 0-0-0 14.♘g5 ♖hf8 15.♕f3 ♘b6 16.♗f4 ♕b4 17.a3 ♕a5±) 12...h×g6 13.g5 ♘d5 14.♘e4 ♕c7 15.c4 ♘×e3 16.f×e3 ♕a5 (16...0-0-0±) 17.♔b1 0-0-0 (17...♕f5?! 18.♘fd2 ♖×h3?! 19.♖hf1 ♕a5 20.c5 ♕a6 21.♘c4±) 18.♕g2±, Sandehn, K. – Klawitter, B., Internet 2003;

C) 11.g4 ♗g6 12.♗×g6 h×g6 13.d5 ♘×d5 14.♘×d5 c×d5 15.♖×d5 ♗e7 16.♖d3 a6 17.♔b1 ♖d8 18.♗d4 ♘f6 19.g5 ♘h5 20.♗e5 (Vysochin, S. (2530) – Varga, Z. (2505), Predeal 2006) 20...♕c6 21.♖hd1 (21.♖c3 ♕d5 22.♖c7 f6 23.♗h2 f×g5∞) 21...♖×d3 22.♖×d3 (22.♕×d3 0-0=) 22...0-0 23.♖c3 ♕b6±.

Let's return to Mamedov – Vysochin.

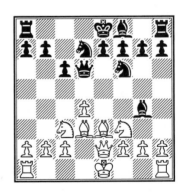

8...e6 (9...0-0-0 10.h3 ♗h5? 11.g4 ♗g6 12.♗×g6 h×g6 13.♘g5 ♕b4 14.0-0-0 ♘b6 15.a3±) **9.0-0-0 ♗e7** (9...♘d5!? 10.♘×d5 ♕×d5 11.♔b1

♕h5) **10.♔b1 0-0-0** (10...0-0!?)
11.h3 ♗h5 12.g4 ♗g6 13.♘×g6

13.♘g5 ♖hf8

A) 14.♕f3 ♘b6 (14...♗×d3!? 15.♖×d3
♘b6) 15.♗f4 ♕b4 ⇄;

B) 14.f4 ♘d5? (14...♘b6 15.♘ge4
♘×e4 16.♘×e4 ♕d5 17.♗f2 ♖fe8±)
15.♘×d5 ♕×d5 (15...c×d5 16.f5)
16.f5 e×f5 17.c4 ♕a5 18.♗d2 ♗b4
19.♗×b4 ♕×b4 20.g×f5 h6 21.a3 ♕b6
22.♘e4±.

13...h×g6 14.♘g5 ♖hf8 15.♗c1
(15.♕f3 ♘d5 16.♘ce4 ♕c7 17.c4 ♘×e3
18.f×e3±; 16...♕b4 17.♘×f7!?;
15...♘b6!?) **15...♘b6 16.a3 ♘bd5
17.♘ce4** (17.♘a4!? ♘d7 18.h4)
**17...♘×e4 18.♘×e4 ♕c7 19.c4
♘f6 20.♘c3 a6** (20...♖d7!? 21.♗e3
♕a5 22.g5 ♘h5 23.d5 ♖fd8 24.♕c2±)
**21.g5 ♘h5 22.♗e3 ♔b8 23.♕f3
f5?!** (23...♕d7 24.♖he1±) **24.g×f6
♘×f6** (24...♖×f6 25.♕g4 ♘f4 26.♖he1
♖f5 27.d5 with the initiative) **25.♕g2
♕a5?!** (25...c5!?) **26.c5 ♘d5
27.♘×d5** (27.♘e4!?) **27...♖×d5
28.♕×g6 ♖fd8** (28...♕d8!?)
29.♗f4+ ♔a7 30.♕×g7 ♗f8?
(30...♗×c5!? 31.♗c7 ♕b5 32.♗×d8
♗×a3 33.♖d2 ♖×d8) **31.♕f7?**
(31.♕g4±) **31...♗×c5 32.♗c7 ♕b5
33.♗×d8 ♗×a3 34.♖d2 ♗×b2?**
(34...♖×d8 35.♕×e6 ♗b4 36.♖dd1?!
♗c3 37.♕a2 ♕f5+ 38.♔a1 ♗×d4
39.♖d2 ♗d5 40.♖hd1 ♖a5 41.♖×d4
♖×a2+ 42.♔×a2∓; 36.♖c2) **35.♖×b2
♕d3+ 36.♔a2 ♕c4+ 37.♔a1 ♖b5
38.♕f3 ♕a4+ 39.♔b1 1-0**

Summary: After **1.e4 d5 2.e×d5
♕×d5 3.♘c3 ♕d6 4.d4 ♘f6
5.♘f3**, the move **5...c6** is one of the

most flexible alternatives. Now White
has many possibilities, some of which
transpose to other games. **6.♗d3** After 5...c6, White's bishop has only three
squares on the f1-a6 diagonal: d3 as
here, e2 (Game 14), and c4 (Game 1).

After **6...♗g4** (6...g6 is playable too),
White has two alternatives: to offer the
sacrifice of the d-pawn; for example,
after 7.0-0 ♗×f3 ♕×f3 ♕×d4 (or after
7.h3 ♗×f3 8.♕×f3 ♕×d4), or to defend
it by 7.♗e3. Usually, after 7.♗e3, Black
does not have difficulties in the opening. After 7.0-0 or 7.h3, Black is better
off declining the d-pawn. For example,
after 7.h3 ♗h5 8.g4 ♗g6 9.♗×g6 h×g6,
Black has a very solid position and
threatens 10...♘×g4.

Game 14
Hjartarson, J. (2619) –
Nevednichy, V. (2582)
Turin 2006

**1.e4 d5 2.e×d5 ♕×d5 3.♘c3 ♕d6
4.d4 ♘f6 5.♘f3 c6 6.♗e2** (the actual move order in the game was 4...c6
5.♘f3 ♘f6)

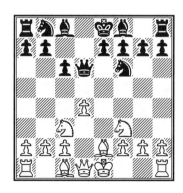

6...♗g4

After 6...♗f5 (6...g6!?) we examine **A)**
7.♗g5; **B)** 7.♘e5 and **C)** 7.0-0.

113

A) 7.♗g5 ♘bd7 (7...e6!?) 8.♕d2 ♘b6 (8...0-0-0!?) 9.♗f4 ♕d8 (9...♕b4!? 10.a3 +−) 10.0-0-0 (10.0-0 g6=) 10...♘bd5 11.♘xd5 ♕xd5± or 9.♘e5 e6 (9...h6!? 10.♗f4 g5 11.♗g3 ♕e6) 10.g4 ♘e4 11.♘xe4 ♗xe4 12.f3 ♗g6 13.♗f4 (13.h4 f6) 13...♕d8 14.c4 ♗e7 (14...♕h4!?+ 15.♗g3 ♕h6∞) 15.0-0-0 ♘d7 16.♘xg6 hxg6±, Obodchuk, A. (2423) − Kuntz, P. (2200), Bled 2002;

B) 7.♘e5 ♘bd7 (Black risks unnecessary problems after 7...e6?! 8.g4 ♗g6 9.h4 – see; for example, the line 6...♗g4 7.h3 ♗h5 8.g4 ♗g6 9.♘e5 e6 10.h4)

B1) 8.♗f4 ♘xe5 9.dxe5 ♕xd1+ (9...♕b4 10.♗d2 ♘e4 11.♘d5 ♕xd2+ 12.♕xd2 ♘xd2 13.♘c7+ ♔d7 14.♘xa8 ♘e4∞) 10.♖xd1 ♘d7 11.g4 ♗e6 (11...♗xc2 12.♖d2 ♗g6 13.e6∞ or 13.0-0∞) 12.♘e4 h6 (12...0-0-0? 13.♘g5 ♘c5 14.♖xd8+ ♔xd8 15.♗e3±) 13.h4 (13.♗g3 0-0-0 14.c4 g6 15.f4 f6 16.exf6 exf6∓) 13...g6 14.♗g3 ♗d5=;

B2) 8.♘c4 ♕c7 This position is well known after 3...♕a5 4.d4 ♘f6 5.♘f3 ♗f5 6.♘e5 c6 7.♗e2 ♘bd7 8.♘c4 ♕c7:

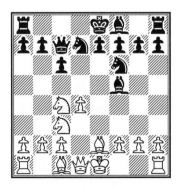

B2a) 9.♘e3 ♗e6 (9...♗g6!?) 10.a4 g6 11.♗f3 (11.0-0!? ♗g7 12.f4) 11...♘b6 12.a5 ♘bd5 13.♘exd5 ♘xd5 14.♘e4 ♗g7 15.♘c5 ♗f5 16.c3=, Nygren, D. (2196) – Jaderberg, B. (2307), Sweden 2001;

B2b) 9.♗g5 ♘b6 (9...e5!?) 10.♕d2 ♘xc4 11.♗xc4 e6 (11...0-0-0!? 12.♗f4 ♕b6 13.0-0-0 e6⇄) 12.0-0-0 (12.♗d3 ♗xd3 13.♕xd3=) 12...♗b4 (12...0-0-0!?) 13.♗xf6 gxf6 14.a3 ♗d6=, Lau, R. −De Greef, H., Leeuwarden 1993;

B2c) 9.0-0 e6 (9...0-0-0!?) 10.♗d3 (10.a4 ♘d5!?; 10.g3!? ♗e7 11.♗f4) 10...♗xd3 11.♕xd3 b5 12.♘d2 ♗e7 13.♘de4 0-0 14.♗g5 ♖fe8 15.♖ad1 ♖ad8=, Andres Gonzalez, I. (2330) – Cornette, M. (2448), Spain 2006;

C) 7.0-0 e6 (7...h6!?) 8.♘e5 (8.♘h4!?; 8.♗g5 ♘bd7 9.a3 ♕c7=, Brkic, A. (2565) − Sedlak, N. (2575), Vogosca 2007) 8...♘bd7 9.f4 ♗e7?! (9...h5) 10.g4 ♗g6 (10...♗xc2 11.♕xc2 ♕xd4+ 12.♔g2 ♘xe5 13.♖d1) 11.♘c4 ♕c7 12.f5±, Fedosenko, P. (2242) – Guenkine, E., Kiev 2003; or 7...♘bd7 8.♗e3 (8.♖e1 e6 9.♗e3 ♕c7 10.♕d2 ♗d6 11.h3 0-0 12.♘h4 ♗g6 13.♘xg6 hxg6⇄, Sadykov, R. (2160) − Ponkratov, P. (2495), Kazan 2008) 8...e6 9.♕d2 ♗e7 10.♗f4 ♕b4 11.♘h4 ♘e4 12.♘xe4 ♕xd2 13.♘xd2 ♗xh4±, Solomaha, A. (2376) − Guenkine, E., Kiev 2003; 8.♗g5 e6 9.♗h4 ♕c7 10.♗g3 ♗d6 11.♖e1 0-0 12.♘h4 ♗g6 13.♗f3 ♖fd8 14.♕e2 ♗xg3 15.hxg3±, Adzic, M. (2250) − Benkovic, P. (2430), Mataruska Banja 2007.

We return now to Hjartarson – Nevednichy.

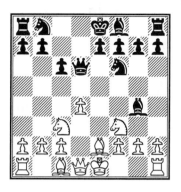

7.0-0

Alternatives are **A)** 7.♗g5; **B)** 7.♗e3 and **C)** 7.h3.

A) 7.♗g5 ♘bd7 (7...e6!?)

A1) 8.♕d2 e6 9.h3 (9.♗f4 ♛b4 10.0-0 ♗e7 11.a3 ♛a5 12.h3 ♗h5 13.♖fe1 0-0 14.g4 ♗g6⇄, Dhar, S. (2140) – Tiviakov, S. (2645), Vlissingen 2007) 9...♗h5 (9...♗×f3 10.♗×f3 ♛c7±) 10.♗f4 ♛b4 11.a3 (11.♘c7 ♗d6 12.a3 ♛×b2 13.♖a2 ♛×a2 14.♘×a2 ♗×c7∞) 11...♛b6 (11...♛×b2?! 12.0-0 ♗g6 13.♖a2 ♛b6 14.♖b1 ♛a5 15.♖×b7±) 12.0-0-0 ♘d5±;

A2) 8.0-0 e6 9.♗h4 ♗e7 10.♗g3 ♛b4 11.♕d2 ♛a5 12.♘e5 ♗×e2 13.♛×e2 0-0 14.♘c4 ♛a6 15.a4 (15.♗d6 ♗×d6 16.♘×d6 ♛×e2 17.♘×e2 b5 18.a4 a6±) 15...♘b6 16.♘e5 ♛×e2 17.♘×e2 a5±, Labib, I. (2305) – Surjadnij, A. (2420), Cairo 1998 or 9.♕d2 ♛c7 (9...♗×f3 10.♗×f3 0-0-0±) 10.♗f4 ♗d6 11.♗×d6 ♛×d6 12.♛e3 ♗f5±, Muratovic, A. (2376) – Ardelean, G. (2461), Obrenovac 2004;

B) 7.♗e3

B1) 7...e6 8.0-0 (8.♕d2 ♛c7) 8...♘bd7 (8...♗e7 9.♕d2 ♛c7 10.h3 ♗×f3

11.♗×f3 ♘bd7±; 10...♗h5!?) 9.♕d2 (9.h3 ♗×f3 10.♗×f3 ♗e7±) 9...♛c7 10.♗f4 ♗d6 11.♗×d6 ♛×d6 12.a3 0-0±, Janousek, P. (2191) – Kantorik, M. (2330), Tatranske Zruby 2006;

B2) 7...♘bd7 8.♕d2 e6

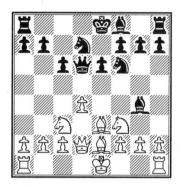

B2a) 9.0-0 (9.0-0-0 ♛c7 10.h3 ♗h5 11.g4 ♗g6±) 9...♗e7 (9...♛c7 10.h3 ♗×f3 11.♗×f3 ♗d6 12.♖fe1 0-0-0±, Hecht, H. (2425) – Mann, C. (2440), Germany 1990) 10.♗f4 11.♖fe1 0-0 (11...0-0-0? 12.a3 ♛a5 13.♘b5 ♛b6 14.♗c7+–) 12.♗c7 ♗d8 (12...♘b6 13.a3 ♛a5 14.♘e5 ♗×e2 15.♛×e2±) 13.a3 ♛e7 14.♗g3±;

B2b) 9.♗f4 ♛b4 10.♗c7 ♗d6!? (10...♘b6 11.a3 ♛e7 12.♗e5 ♛d7 13.0-0-0 0-0-0±) 11.♘b5 (11.a3 ♛×b2 12.♖a2 ♛×a2 13.♘×a2 ♗×c7∞) 11...c×b5 12.c3 ♛a4 13.♗×d6 ♘e4 14.♛f4 ♛c2 15.♛×g4 ♘×d6 16.♛f4 ♛×b2 17.0-0∞ or 10.a3 ♛a5 (10...♛×b2? 11.0-0 ♗f5 12.♖a2 ♛b6 13.♖b1±; 10...♛b6 11.0-0 ♗e7±) 11.0-0 ♗e7 12.♖fe1 0-0 13.h3 ♗h5 14.b4 ♛d8 15.♘a4 (Kovacevic, A. (2521) – Radibratovic, P. (2343), Herceg Novi 2001) 15...♘d5 16.♗h2 b5 17.♘c5 ♘×c5 18.b×c5 ♗f6±;

C) 7.h3

C1) 7...♗h5

C1a) 8.0-0 e6 9.♖e1 (9.♘e5 ♗xe2 10.♘xe2 ♗e7 11.♗f4 ♕b4 12.c3 ♕b6 13.♘c4 ♕d8 14.♕b3 b5 15.♘e5 0-0 16.a4 ♕b6 17.axb5 cxb5 18.c4 b4 19.c5 ♕b7 20.♖a4 ♘d5∞, Litvin, G. – Gubnitsky, S., Kharkov 1966) 9...♘bd7 10.♘e5 (10.♗e3!?) 10...♗xe2 11.♖xe2 (11.♕xe2 ♕xd4 12.♘xd7 ♕xd7 13.♗g5 0-0-0 14.♖ad1 ♗d6 15.♕e3 a6 16.♘e4 ♘xe4 17.♗xd8 ♘xf2 18.♕xf2 ♖xd8±) 11...♕c7±, Schoenwolff, K. – Sievers, S., Hamburg 1989;

C1b) 8.g4 (8.♗e3 – Game 10, 6.♗e3 c6 7.h3 ♗h5 8.♗e2; 8.♗g5 e6 9.♕d2 ♗e7 10.0-0-0 ♘bd7 11.♔b1 ♗xf3 12.♗xf3 ♘b6 13.♗f4 ♕b4 ½-½, Kalinin, A. – Gubnitsky, S., Kharkov 1966) 8...♗g6 9.♘e5

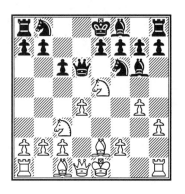

C1b1) 9...e6?! 10.♗f4 ♕b4 11.a3 ♕xb2 12.♘xg6 ♕c3+ 13.♗d2 ♕xa1 14.♕xa1 hxg6 15.♕b2 b6 16.♗f3 ♗e7 17.c4 0-0 18.h4 ♖c8 19.h5 gxh5 20.gxh5±, Annageldyev, O. (2483) – Hasangatin, R. (2416), Alushta 2005 or 10...♕d8 11.h4 ♗b4 (11...♘bd7 12.f3) 12.h5 ♗e4 13.f3 ♗d5 14.a3 ♗e7 15.♕d2 h6 (15...♘bd7 16.g5 ♘g8 17.♘xd5 exd5 18.0-0-0±; 15...♘fd7 16.0-0-0 ♘xe5 17.♗xe5 f6 18.♗f4±)

16.♘d1 c5 (16...b5 17.b3±) 17.dxc5 ♘bd7 18.c4 ♗c6 19.♘xc6 bxc6 20.b4±;

C1b2) 9...♘bd7 10.♗f4 (10.♘xg6 hxg6 11.♗e3 0-0-0 12.♕d3 e6 13.0-0-0 ♘b6=) 10...♘d5 (Franot, P. (2164) – Brun, P. (2122), France 2004) 11.♘xg6 ♕xg6 12.♘xd5 cxd5 13.♕d3± or 10...♘xe5 11.♗xe5 (11.dxe5 ♕b4 12.♗d2 ♘e4 13.♘d5 ♕xd2+ 14.♕xd2 ♘xd2 15.♘c7+ ♔d7 16.♘xa8 ♘e4∞) 11...♕d7 12.♕d2 e6 13.0-0-0 0-0-0±;

C2) 7...♗xf3 8.♗xf3 e6 (8...♘bd7 9.♗e3 0-0-0 10.♕e2 e6 11.0-0-0 ♘b6± or 9.0-0 0-0-0 10.♗e3 e6 11.♕e2 ♘b6 12.a4 ♘bd5±) 9.0-0 (9.♘e4 ♘xe4 10.♗xe4 ♘d7 11.0-0 ♘f6 12.♗f3 ♗e7 13.c4 0-0 14.♗e3 ♖fd8 15.♕b3 ♖d7±, Paglietti, N. (2293) – Garcia Palermo, C. (2445), Montebelluna 2006) 9...♘bd7 (9...♗e7 10.♘e2 ♕c7 11.c4 0-0 12.♕b3 ♘bd7 13.♗f4±, Rozentalis, E. (2619) – Brancaleoni, M. (2298), Genova 2004)

C2a) 10.a4 ♗e7 11.a5 0-0 12.♖e1; 10.♖e1 0-0-0 11.♗e3 ♕c7 12.♕e2 ♗d6 13.♕c4 ♘b6 14.♕b3±, Gallagher, J. (2514) – Cicak, S. (2543), Germany 2000 or 10.g3 ♘b6 11.a4 a5 12.b3 ♕d7 13.♗b2 ♗e7 14.♘e2 ♘bd5 15.♕d2 0-0 16.♖fd1 ♕c7 17.♖ac1 ♖fd8 18.c4±, Weeramantry, S. (2207) – Chahrani, I. (2308), Turin 2006;

C2b) 10.♘e4 ♘xe4 11.♗xe4 ♗e7 12.c3 0-0 13.♗c2 ♕c7 14.♖e1 ♗d6 (14...♘f6 15.♕d3 ♖fd8 16.♗g5 g6 17.♕f3 ♘d5±) 15.♕g4 ♖fe8 (15...♘f6? 16.♕h4 ♗e7 17.♗g5 h6 18.♗xh6 gxh6 19.♕xh6 ♖fd8 20.♖e3±) 16.♕h5 ♘f8 (16...g6!?) 17.♖e4 e5 (17...♘g6!? 18.♖g4? f5 19.♖g5 ♘h8 20.♕h6 g6±)

18.d×e5 (18.♖h4?! g6 19.♛d1 e×d4 20.♖×d4 ♖ad8∓) 18...♖×e5 19.♖×e5 ♗×e5±, Rogers, I. (2549) – Tao, T. (2319), Adelaide 2002.

Back to Hjartarson – Nevednichy.

7...♘bd7

After 7...e6, there are the following interesting possibilities for White:

A) 8.♘e5 ♗×e2 (8...♗f5? 9.g4 ♗g6 10.f4 h5 11.f5 e×f5 12.g×f5 ♗h7 13.♗c4 ♗g8 14.♗f4±)

A1) 9.♘×e2 ♘bd7 10.♗f4 (10.♘c4 ♛d5 11.♛d3 ♛e4 12.♛d2 ♘d5±) 10...♘×e5 11.♗×e5 (11.d×e5 ♛×d1 12.♖f×d1 ♘d5 13.c4 ♘×f4 14.♘×f4=) 11...♛d7 12.♘f4±;

A2) 9.♛×e2 ♘bd7 (9...♛×d4!? 10.♖d1 ♛c5) 10.♗g5 ♛×d4?! 11.♗×f6! ♘×f6 (11...g×f6? 12.♘×f7 ♚×f7 13.♖ad1 ♛c5 14.♖×d7+ ♗e7 15.♘e4 1-0, Bastian, H. (2360) – Mueller, G, Bad Neuenahr 1982) 12.♖ad1 ♛b6 (12...♛c5?! 13.♖fe1) 13.♘e4 (13.♖fe1?! ♗b4 14.♘×f7 ♚×f7 15.♛×e6+ ♚f8∓) 13...♗e7 14.♘×f7 (14.♘c4⩲) 14...♚×f7 15.♘g5+ ♚g6 16.♘f3∞ or 12...♛b4 13.♖fe1 ♗c5 14.a3 (14.♘×f7?

♚×f7 15.♛×e6+ ♚g6 16.♖d3 ♛f4∓) 14...♛f4∞;

B) 8.♗g5 (for 8.♗e3 – 7.♗e3 e6 8.0-0) 8...♘bd7 9.♛d2 (9.♗h4 ♛c7 10.♘e5 ♗×e2 11.♛×e2 ♗d6 12.♖fe1 0-0 13.a4 ♘d5±, Ivanov, V. (2238) – Shkola, V., Alushta 2004; 9.h3 ♗h5 10.♖e1 ♗e7 11.♛d2 ♛c7 12.♘e5 ♗×e2 13.♛×e2 0-0 14.♘e4 ♖ae8 15.♘×d7 ♘×d7 16.♗×e7 ♖×e7 17.c4 ♘b6±, Darban, M. (2341) – Mohammadi, H. (2267), Mashad 2003) 9...♛c7 10.h3 (10.♗f4 ♗d6 11.♗×d6 ♛×d6 12.♖ad1 ♖d8 13.♖fe1 0-0±, Kawaciukova, Z. (2050) – Nagrocka, E. (2140), Wuppertal 1994) 10...♗h5 11.♖fe1 ♗b4 12.♘b5 ♛a5 13.♘c7+ (Heinemann, D. (2240) – Nelki, H., Germany 1996) 13...♛×c7 14.♛×b4±.

We now return to Hjartarson – Nevednichy.

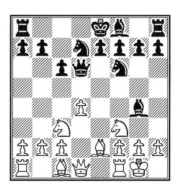

8.♖e1

8.♗e3 e6 9.♛d2 ♛c7 10.♗f4 ♗d6 11.♗×d6 ♛×d6 12.♛e3 (12.♖ad1 h6⇄, Doros, R. (1935) – Ardelean, G. (2475), Cluj 2008) 12...♗f5 (12...0-0=) 13.♗d3 ♘d5 (13...0-0 14.♗×f5 e×f5 15.♛d3 g6=) 14.♘×d5 ♗×d3 15.♘c7+ ♛×c7 16.♛×d3 0-0 17.♖fe1 ♖fd8⇄,

Muratovic, A. (2376) – Ardelean, G. (2461), Obrenovac 2004.

8...e6 9.♗g5

Other possibilities:

A) 9.h3 ♗h5 10.♗e3 h6 11.♕d2 g5 12.♘h2 (12.b4!?) 12...♗g6 13.♖ad1 ♗e7 14.♗d3 ♗h5 15.f3 (Vlasov, V. – Kulbachny, V., Serpukhov 2004) 15...0-0-0⇄ or 14...♗×d3 15.♕×d3 0-0-0⇄;

B) 9.♘e5 ♘×e5 (9...♗×e2 10.♕×e2 ♕×d4? 11.♘×f7 ♔×f7 12.♕×e6+ ♔g6 13.♘e2±; 10...♗e7±) 10.d×e5 ♕×d1 11.♗×d1 ♗×d1 12.♖×d1 ♘d7 (12...♘d5!? 13.♘e4 0-0-0) 13.♗f4 (13.f4?! ♗c5+ 14.♔h1 0-0-0 15.♘e4 ♘f6 16.♘d6+ ♗×d6 17.e×d6 ♘e4 18.♗e3 b6∓ or 14.♔f1 f5 15.e×f6 ♘×f6∓) 13...♗e7 14.♘e4 ♘b6 15.♖d3 ♖d8 16.♘d6+ ♗×d6 17.e×d6± or 13...0-0-0 14.♘e4 h6 15.♖d2 ♗e7±, Moroz, A. (2513) – Labensky, I. (2367), Rovno 2000.

9...♗f5

9...h6!?; 9...0-0-0 10.♕d2 ♕c7±.

10.♘h4 ♗g6 11.g3 ♗e7

11...0-0-0 (11...♕c7±) 12.♘×g6 h×g6 13.♗f4 ♕b4 (13...e5!?; 13...♕e7 14.a3 ♘b6 15.♗f3 ♕d7±) 14.a3 ♕a5 15.♕d2 (15.b4 ♕f5 16.b5?! g5! 17.♗e3 c5; 16.h4 ♘b6 17.♗d3 ♗e7⇄) 15...♕f5 (15...♘d5? 16.b4; 15...e5?! 16.b4 ♕c7 17.d×e5 ♘×e5 18.♕e3) 16.h4±.

12.♗f4 ♕b4 13.a3 ♕a5 (13...♕×b2? 14.♘×g6 h×g6 15.♘a4 +−) **14.b4 ♕d8**

15.♗f3 0-0 16.♘×g6 h×g6 17.♕d3 (17.b5!?) **17...♘b6 18.♘e2** (18.b5 ♘bd5 19.♗d2 ♘×c3 20.♗×c3 c×b5 21.♕×b5 ♖c8 22.♕b3 ♕c7⇄) **18...♘fd5 19.♗d2 ♗f6 20.c4 ♘e7 21.♖ad1±** (21.g4 g5 22.a4 ♘g6 23.♗e4 ♘h4 24.a5 ♘d7 25.a6 b6 26.f4 ♖c8±; 26.♗×c6? ♘e5; 23...♕d7!? 24.♗×g6 f×g6 25.a5 ♘c8 26.♕×g6 ♘d6 27.♖ac1 e5⧩) **21...♘f5 22.♗c3** (22.♗f4 a5 23.b×a5 ♖×a5 24.g4 ♘h4 25.♗e4 ♗g5∓) **22...♕c7 23.♗b2?!** (23.d5!?) **23...♖ad8?!** (23...a5 24.♕b3 a×b4 25.a×b4 ♖fd8=) **24.♕b3 ♖d7 25.♖d3 ♖fd8 26.♖ed1 ♘c8 27.a4?!** (27.♗c3!? e5 28.d5) **27...♘ce7** (27...a5!? 28.b×a5 [28.b5 c5 29.d5 ♗×b2 30.♕×b2 ♘b6∓] 28...♕×a5 29.♗c3 ♕a6 30.d5 c×d5 31.♗×f6 g×f6 32.c×d5 e5⇄) **28.a5 b6 29.a×b6 a×b6 30.g4 ♘h4 31.♗h1?!** (31.♗e4!?) **31...g5∓ 32.♗c1 ♘eg6?!** (32...b5!? 33.f4 g×f4 34.♗×f4 ♕a7) **33.♗e4 ♘f4 34.♘×f4 g×f4 35.d5?!** (35.b5!? c×b5 36.♕×b5 g6 37.d5±; 35...♖×d4 36.♖×d4 ♗×d4 37.b×c6 ♕e5⇄) **35...e×d5?!** (35...♕e5∓) **36.c×d5 c×d5 37.♗×d5** (37.♖×d5 ♖×d5 38.♗×d5 ♖d7=) **37...g5 38.♗b2?!** (38.b5!?) **38...♗×b2 39.♕×b2 ♘f3+ 40.♔g2?** (40.♖×f3 ♖×d5∓) **40...♘e5 41.♖c3** (41.♖d2 f3+ 42.♗×f3 ♘×f3 −+ or 42.♔h3 ♘×g4 −+; 41.♖d4 ♘×g4 42.♗f3 ♖×d4 43.♖×d4 ♖×d4 44.♕×d4 ♘e5±) **41...♕b8∓ 42.♕c2 ♖×d5 43.♖×d5 ♕a8 44.♖c6 ♕×c6 45.♕×c6 ♘×c6 46.♖×g5+ ♔f8 47.♖b5 ♖b8 48.g5 ♔g7 49.♔h3 ♘d4 50.♖d5 ♘e6 51.♔g4 ♖c8 52.h4 ♖c4 53.♖b5 f3+ 54.♔g3 ♘d4 55.♖×b6 ♘f5+ 56.♔×f3 ♘×h4+ 57.♔g3 ♘f5+ 58.♔f3 ♘d4+ 0-1**

Summary: After **1.e4 d5 2.e×d5 ♛×d5 3.♘c3 ♛d6 4.d4 ♘f6 5.♘f3 c6 6.♗e2**, neither 6.♗c4 (Game 1) nor 6.♗d3 (Game 13) is dangerous for Black, and in fact in some variations of these games White had definite problems with the d4-pawn. 6.♗e2 is a way to develop naturally, hoping to maintain small development advantage. Here, as in the Scandinavian with 3...♛d8 or 3...♛a5, the most popular moves are 6...♗f5 and 6...♗g4.

I consider 6...♗f5 somewhat better than 6...♗g4, because after 6...♗g4, White has more dangerous possibilities: 7.h3, 7.♗e3, 7.♗g5, 7.0-0. For example, after 7.0-0 e6 the line 8.♘e5 ♗×e2 9.♛×e2 ♛×d4 is very interesting.

Game 15
Wieczorek, O. (2200) –
Kulicov, O. (2405)
Marianske Lazne 2008

1.e4 d5 2.e×d5 ♛×d5 3.♘c3 ♛d6 4.d4 ♘f6 5.♘f3 c6 6.h3

6...♗f5

6...g6 (6...♘bd7 7.♗g5 ♘b6 8.♗d3 g6 9.♛d2 ♗g7 10.0-0 0-0 11.♗f4 ♛d8 12.♗h6 ♗e6 13.♖fe1±, Jaracz, P.

(2495) – Tiviakov, S. (2645), Bratto 2007; 7.♗c4!?)

A1) 7.♗e3 ♗g7 (7...♘d5!?) 8.♛d2

A1a) 8...♘d5 9.♘×d5 (9.♘e4!? ♛c7 10.♗h6) 9...c×d5 10.♗d3 0-0 11.0-0 ♘c6±;

A1b) 8...♗e6 9.♘g5 0-0 10.♗e2 ♗d5 11.♗f4 ♛d8 12.0-0 ♘bd7±, Svensson, B. (2432) – Jaderberg, B. (2307), Sweden 2001;

A2) 7.♘e5 ♗e6 (7...♘bd7!?) 8.♗f4

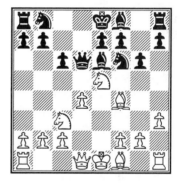

A2a) 8...♛d8 9.♛d2 (9.♗c4 ♗×c4 10.♘×c4 ♗g7±) 9...♗g7 10.0-0-0 0-0 11.♗h6 ♗×h6 12.♛×h6 ♘bd7 13.h4?! (13.♗c4 ♗×c4 14.♘×c4=) 13...♛c7 14.h5? (14.♘×d7) 14...♘×e5 15.d×e5 ♘g4∓ or 11...♘bd7 12.♗×g7 ♔×g7 13.f4 ♛a5 (13...♘d5!?) 14.♘×d7 ♘×d7 15.a3 ♘f6 16.g4 (16.♛e3!?) 16...♘d5 17.f5 g×f5 18.♛g5+ ♔h8 19.♘×d5 ♛×d5 20.♗d3∞, Bartel, M. (2585) – Muse, M. (2445), Germany 2007;

A2b) 8...♘d5 9.♘×d5 ♛×d5 10.♗e2 ♗g7 (10...♘d7!? 11.0-0 ♗g7) 11.♗f3 ♛b5 12.a4 ♛b4+ 13.♛d2 ♛×d2+ (13...♛×b2? 14.0-0±) 14.♔×d2± or 9.♘e4 ♛b4+ 10.c3 ♛b6 (10...♛×b2? 11.♘c4 ♛×a1 12.♛×a1 ♘×f4 13.g3

♘d5 14.♕b2 b6 15.♘g5±) 11.♘c4 ♕d8 12.♗g5 f6∓.

We return now to Wieczorek – Kulicov.

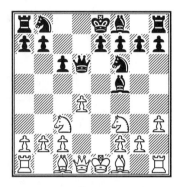

7.♗d3

7.♗c4 – Game 2. After 7.g4 ♗g6 8.♘e5 ♘bd7 (8...e6) 9.♗f4 or after 7.♘e5 e6 8.g4 ♗g6 9.♗f4, we have a position from Game 11 with the extra move ♘b8-d7 or e7-e6 by Black. After 7.♗e2 e6 8.g4 ♗g6 9.♘e5 ♘bd7 or 7.g4 ♗g6 8.♘e5 e6 9.♗e2 ♘bd7, we have a position from Game 14 with ♘b8-d7 or e7-e6 inserted. After 7.♗e3 e6 8.♗e2 ♘bd7 9.g4 ♗g6 or 7.g4 ♗g6 8.♗e3 e6 (8...♘bd7) 9.♗e2 ♘bd7 (9...e6), we have a position from Game 10 with ♘b8-d7 or e7-e6. I think 7.g4, 7.♗e2, 7.♗e3 and 7.♘e5 are safe for Black in other lines too:

A) 7.♘e5 ♘bd7 8.♘c4 (8.♗f4 ♘d5 9.♕d2 f6 10.♘xd7 ♕xf4 11.♘xd5 ♕xd2+ 12.♔xd2 ♔xd7=, Andriasian, S. (2225) – Aginian, N. (2305), Yerevan 2008) 8...♕c7 9.♕f3 (9.g4 ♗e6 10.♘e3 ♘b6 11.♗g2 0-0-0⇄, Lazetich, Z. (2198) – Schiller, E. (2172), San Francisco 2000) 9...e6 (9...♗xc2? 10.♗f4 ♕d8 11.♕e2+−) 10.♗f4 ♕d8 11.0-0-0 (11.g4 ♗xc2∓; 11.♘d6+ ♗xd6

12.♗xd6 ♗xc2 13.♖c1 ♗g6 14.♗e2 ♘b6∓) 11...♘d5±, Loeffler, S. (2463) – Kreindl, H. (2200), Vienna 2006;

B) 7.♗e2 ♘bd7 (7...e6 8.♘h4 ♗g6 9.♗g5 ♘bd7 10.♘xg6 hxg6 11.♕d2 ♘b6±) 8.0-0 (Kulaots, K. (2426) – Cicak, S. (2490), Gelsenkirchen 1999) 8...g6 9.♗d3 (9.a4 ♗g7±; 9.♗e3 ♗g7 10.♕d2 ♘d5 11.♘xd5 cxd5±) 9...♗xd3 (9...0-0-0? 10.♗xf5 gxf5 11.♘g5±) 10.♕xd3 ♗g7 11.♖e1 0-0 12.♗g5±;

C) 7.♗e3 ♘bd7 8.♕d2 h6 9.0-0-0 e6 10.♗f4 ♕b4

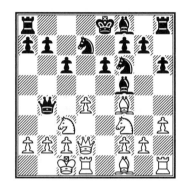

C) 11.♗c7 ♘b6 (11...♘e4!? 12.♘xe4 ♗xe4) 12.a3 ♕e7 13.♗e5 0-0-0 14.♗d3 ♗xd3 15.♕xd3 ♕d7±;

C) 11.♘e5 (Faber, H. (2162) – Kotronias, V. (2608), Kavala 2004) 11...♘xe5 12.♗xe5 (12.dxe5 ♘d5 13.♘xd5 cxd5 14.♕xb4 ♗xb4=) 12...0-0-0 13.a3 ♕a5 14.f3? (14.g4 ♗g6 15.♗d3 ♗xd3 16.♕xd3±) ♗xa3 15.bxa3 ♕xa3+ 16.♔b1 ♖d5! (16...♕b3+? 17.♔a1 ♗xc2 18.♖c1 ♕a3+ 19.♘a2±) 17.♘a2 (17.♘xd5 ♘xd5 18.g4 ♗g6 19.♗xg7 ♘c3+ 20.♕xc3 ♕xc3−+; 17.♗c4 ♕b4+ 18.♔a1 ♕xc4 19.♘xd5 ♘xd5∓) 17...♖a5 18.♗c4 ♖a4 19.♕e2 b5∓.

Back to Wieczorek – Kulicov.

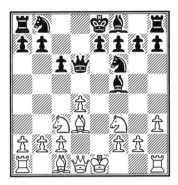

7...♗×d3

Other interesting possibilities for Black are 7...♗g6 and 7...g6:

A) 7...♗g6

A1) 8.0-0 ♘bd7 9.♗e3 e6 10.♛d2 ♗×d3 11.♗f4 (11.♛×d3 ♗e7∓, Djuric, N. – Randjelovic, S. Budva 2003) 11...♛b4 (11...♗×f1? 12.♗×d6 ♗×g2 13.♗×f8 ♗×f3 14.♗d6 ♘b6 15.♗e5 0-0-0 16.♗h2 ♘h5 17.♛e3 ♗d5 18.♛e5±) 12.♛×d3 ♗e7 13.a3 ♛b6∓;

A2) 8.♘e2 ♘bd7 9.0-0 e6 (9...0-0-0? 10.♗f4 ♛b4 11.♗×g6 h×g6 12.♘g5±) 8.0-0 ♘bd7 9.♗e3 e6 10.♛d2 ♗×d3 10.♗f4 ♛b4 11.c3 ♛b6 12.a4 a5 13.♗×g6 h×g6 14.♘d2 ♘d5 15.♘c4 (15.♗g5 ♛c7∓) 15...♛a6 16.♘d6+ (16.♛d3?! ♘7b6) 16...♗×d6 17.♗×d6 0-0-0± or 10.♖e1 ♛c7 11.c4 ♗×d3 12.♛×d3 (Malo Guillen, J. (2150) – Narciso Dublan, M (2390), Cordoba 1995) 12...h6 13.a4 (13.♗f4 ♗d6) 13...♗e7 14.♗f4 ♗d6 15.♗d2 0-0 16.c5 ♗e7 17.a5 ♘d5 (17...e5?! 18.♘g3) 18.♘c3 ♘7f6 19.♘e5 ♖ad8∓;

B) 7...g6

B1) 8.0-0 ♘bd7 9.♘e2 ♗×d3 10.♛×d3 ♗g7 11.♗f4 (11.♘g3 0-0 12.♗g5 h6∓) 11...♛b4 12.♗d2 (12.♖fe1 0-0 13.♘c3 ♖fe8 14.a3 ♛b6∓) 12...♛b6 13.♘f4 0-0 14.♖fe1 e6∓;

B2) 8.♗×f5 g×f5 9.♛d3 (9.♗g5 ♘bd7 10.♛d3 e6 11.0-0-0 ♖g8⇄; 10.0-0 0-0-0 11.♛d3 h6∓) 9...e6 10.0-0 ♖g8 11.♖e1 ♗e7 12.♘e2 ♘h5 13.c4 (13.♛b3 ♛b4) 13...♘d7 14.b3 0-0-0 15.a4 ♛c7⇄ or 12.♘e5 ♘bd7 13.♗f4 ♘d5 (13...♘×e5?! 14.♗×e5 ♛d7 15.♗×f6 ♗×f6 16.♛×f5) 14.♗g3 ♘×e5 15.♗×e5 ♛d7⇄.

Let's go back to Wieczorek – Kulicov.

8.♛×d3

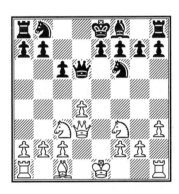

8...♘bd7 (8...e6!?) **9.♘e4**

Also worth consideration are **A)** 9.♗g5; **B)** 9.♗e3 and **C)** 9.0-0.

A) 9.♗g5 e6 (9...g6 10.0-0-0 ♗g7 11.♖he1 0-0 12.♔b1 ♖fe8 13.♘e4 ♛c7 14.♛d2 ♖ad8⇄, Hendriks, W. (2420) – Tiviakov, S. (2645), Trieste 2007; 12.d5 ♖fe8 13.d×c6 ♛×c6 14.♛b5 ♖ac8 15.♛×c6 ♖×c6∓) 10.0-0-0 ♗e7 11.♖he1 (11.♔b1 0-0-0 12.♖he1 ♛c7⇄) 11...0-0 12.♘e5 ♘d5

(12...♘b6 13.♗xf6 ♗xf6 14.♘e4±, Slobodjan, R. (2525) – Muse, D. (2410), Germany 2006) 13.♘e4 ♗xg5+ 14.♘xg5 ♘5f6⇄;

B) 9.♗e3 e6 10.a3 ♗e7 11.0-0 0-0 12.♖ad1 ♛c7 (12...♖fd8 13.♖fe1 ♛c7 14.♛c4 ♘b6 15.♛b3 (Cardoso Garcia, S. (2135) – Cabrera Peinado, M. (2180), Malaga 1999) 15...h6=) 13.♗g5 ♖fe8 14.♖fe1 ♖ad8 15.♛e2

B1) 15...♘d5 16.♘e4 (16.♗xe7!?) 16...♗xg5 17.♘exg5 h6 18.♘e4 e5 19.♛c4 b5 20.♛b3 exd4 21.♖xd4?! (21.♘xd4 ♖xe4 22.♖xe4 ♘c5 23.♛f3 ♘xe4 24.♛xe4 ♘f6 25.♛f3 a6=) 21...♘e5∓, Kovanova, B. (2330) – Lomako, A. (2300), Russia 2007;

B2) 15...h6 16.♗h4 (16.♗xf6 ♘xf6=) 16...♛b6 17.b4?! (17.♘a4; 17.♖b1) 17...a5 18.♘a4 (18.♖b1 axb4 19.axb4 ♖a8 20.♛c4 ♖a3∓) 18...♛b5 19.♛xb5 cxb5 20.♘c5 axb4 21.axb4 b6∓.

C) 9.0-0 e6

C1) 10.♖e1 ♗e7 (10...h6!? 11.♗d2 0-0-0⇄) 11.♗d2 0-0 12.a3 ♖fd8 13.♖ad1 h6 14.♛e2 ♛c7 15.♘e5 ♘xe5 16.dxe5 ♘d5=, Proehl, H. (2285) – Muse, D. (2295), Berlin 1994;

C2) 10.♘e2 ♛c7 11.♗f4 ♗d6 12.♗xd6 ♛xd6 13.♘c3 (13.♛b3 0-0 14.♖ad1 b5 15.♘g3 ♛d5=, Solovjova, V. (2265) – Mashinskaya, Y. (2386), Pardubice 2006) 13...0-0-0 14.a4 ♖ad8 15.♖fe1 a5 (15...♘b6!?) 16.♖a3 h6 17.♖b3 b6±.

C3) 10.♘e4 ♘xe4 11.♛xe4

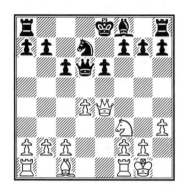

Compare this position with the French Defense, Rubinstein variation (1.e4 e6 2.d4 d5 3.♘c3 dxe4 4.♘xe4 ♗d7 5.♘f3 ♗c6 6.♗d3 ♘bd7 7.♛e2 ♘gf6 8.0-0 ♘xe4 9.♗xe4 ♗xe4 10.♛xe4 c6). Here, Black's queen is posted better. Now let's examine 11...♘f6 and 11...♛d5.

C3a) 11...♘f6 12.♛e2 (12.♛d3 ♛c7 13.♖b1 ♗d6 14.c4 0-0 15.♖e1 h6±) 12...♗e7 13.c4 (13.♖e1 0-0 14.c4 ♖fe8 15.♗e3 ♛c7=, Koustas, A. (2252) – Babaniotis, E. (2074), Korinthos 2002) 13...0-0

C3a1) 14.b3 ♖ad8 15.♗b2 ♖fe8 (15...♛f4!? 16.♖fd1 h6 17.♖d3 ♗d6) 16.♖ad1 ♛c7 (16...♛f4!?) 17.♖d3 ♘d7 (17...♘h5!? 18.g3 ♖d6) 18.♖fd1 ♘f8 19.♘e5 ♘g6 20.♘xg6 hxg6 21.♗c3 ♗f6 22.g3 (22.♛e4 ♗d7 23.♗b4 ♖ed8 24.a4±) 22...♗e7 23.♔g2 ♖ed7 24.h4 ♛b6 25.♛e4 ♛a6 26.♖1d2?! (26.a4 ♛b6 27.♗b2=) 26...b5∓, Manik, M. (2469) – Velicka, P. (2458), Passau 2000;

C3a2) 14.♗d2 ♖fe8 15.♗c3 (Kasparov, G. (2750) – Wirth, W., Zurich (simultaneous) 1988) 15...♖ad8 16.♘e5 ♘d7 17.a4 (17.♖ad1 ♘xe5 18.dxe5 ♛c7 19.b4 ♖xd1 20.♖xd1

♖d8±; 17.f4 ♘xe5 18.fxe5 ♛d7 19.♖ad1 b5 20.b3 bxc4 21.bxc4 ♖b8±) 17...♘xe5 18.dxe5 ♛d3 19.♛xd3 (19.♛g4?! h5! 20.♛xh5 ♛xc4) 19...♖xd3=.

C3b) 11...♛d5!?

C3b1) 12.♛d3 (12.♛xd5 cxd5 13.♗f4 ♖c8=) 12...♗d6 13.♖e1 (13.c4 ♛h5 14.♖e1 0-0-0± or 14...0-0±) 13...0-0 14.c4 ♛f5 15.♛xf5 exf5 16.c5 ♗c7 17.♖e7 ♖ad8 18.♗d2 (18.♘h4 f4) 18...♖fe8 19.♖ae1 ♔f8=;

C3b2) 12.♛e2 ♗e7

C3b2a) 13.♗f4 ♛f5 14.♗g3 h5 15.♖ad1 h4 (15...g5? 16.d5 cxd5 17.♛b5 g4 18.♛xb7 ♘b6 19.♘d4±; 15...0-0-0? 16.d5 cxd5 17.♘d4 ♛g5 18.♘c6±) 16.♗e5 0-0-0⇄;

C3b2b) 13.c4 ♛f5 14.♖d1 0-0-0 15.d5 (15.a4 h5 16.♗e3 ♘f6 17.♘e5 ♘d7 18.♘d3 ♗d6 19.b4 e5⇄; 15...g5!?) 15...♘c5 16.b4 (16.dxc6 ♖xd1+ 17.♛xd1 bxc6 18.♗e3 ♖d8 19.♛e2 ♗f6⇄) 16...♘a4 17.♘d4 ♛f6 18.♛c2 ♘b6 19.♗b2 ♛g6⇄.

Back to Wieczorek – Kulicov.

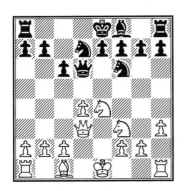

9...♘xe4 10.♛xe4 ♛g6

10...♘f6 11.♛e2 e6 12.0-0 see 9.0-0 e6 10.♘e4 ♘xe4 11.♛xe4 ♘f6 12.♛e2.

11.♛xg6 hxg6

We have an equal ending with four pieces and seven pawns on each side.

12.♗f4 e6 13.0-0-0 ♗e7

13...♘f6 14.♗e5 ♗e7 15.c4 0-0 (15...0-0-0 16.♘g5 ♖hf8 17.♔c2 b5⇄) 16.♖he1 b5 17.b3 ♖fd8 18.♔c2 ♖d7 19.a4 a6⇄.

14.♖he1 ♘b6

14...0-0-0 15.♖d3 ♘b6 16.♘e5 ♘d5 17.♗d2 ♖hf8 18.c4 ♘f6 19.♗c3 ♘d7 20.♘xd7 ♖xd7 21.♖ed1 ♗g5+ 22.♔c2 ♖fd8 23.b4 b5 24.c5 ♗f6 25.f3 g5 26.a3 a6 27.♗b2 ♖d5 28.♗c3 ♖8d7 ½-½, Klawitter B. – Jonovic,P., Internet 2003.

15.♗e5

15.b3 ♗a3+ (15...♗f6 16.c4 ♖h5 17.♔b2 ♖d8 18.♖e3 ♘f8 19.♗c7 ♖d7 20.♗b8 ♖a5 21.♖e4±) 16.♔b1 ♗b4 17.♗d2 ♗xd2 18.♖xd2 ♖d8 19.c4 ♖h5 20.♔b2 ♗e7 21.♔c3 a5 22.♘e5 ♘d7 23.♘d3 ♘f6 24.f3±.

15...♗f6 16.♖e4 ♚e7

16...0-0-0 17.b3 ♘d5 (17...♗×e5?!
18.♘×e5 ♖df8 19.♖f4) 18.♚b2 b6
19.c4 ♘e7 20.b4 ♚b7 (20...b5?
21.c×b5 c×b5 22.♖c1+) 21.a4 ♘f5
22.♚c3 a6=.

**17.♖d3 ♖hd8 18.♖b3 ♖d7 19.g4
♖ad8 20.g5 ♗×e5 21.♘×e5?!**
(21.♖×e5 f6 22.♖e1 ♘d5 23.♖a3 ♖h8
24.h4 b5=) **21...♖×d4 22.♖×d4
♖×d4 23.♖f3 ♖e4! 24.♘×f7 ♘c4
25.c3** (25.♘h8?? ♖e1 #) **25...♖e2**
(25...b5!? 26.b3 ♘e5 27.♘×e5 ♖×e5
28.♖g3 ♖e2∓; 28.h4 ♖e4 29.h5 g×h5
30.g6∞ or 28...♖e1+ 29.♚b2 ♖e2+
30.♚b1 a5∓) **26.b3 ♘e5** (26...♘a3?!
27.♘h8) **27.♘×e5 ♖×e5 28.h4**
(28...♖e4 29.h5 g×h5 30.g6 ♖e2
31.♖f7+ ♚d6 32.a4 b6 33.♚d1 ♖b2
34.♖×a7 ♖×f2 35.♖×g7 ♖g2 36.b4 h4
37.♖h7 ♖×g6 38.♖×h4=) **28...♖e2
29.a4 a5 30.c4** (30.h5?! g×h5 31.g6
♚d6 32.♖f7 b6 33.f4 ♖f2 34.♖×g7
♖×f4 35.♖h7 ♖g4 36.g7 h4∓)
**30...b6∓ 31.♚d1 ♖e4 32.♖h3
♚d6 33.♚d2 ♖g4 34.♖d3+ ♚e7
35.♖h3 ♚d6 36.♖d3+ ♚e7
37.♖h3 e5 38.♚e3 ♚e6 39.♖h1
♚d6 40.♖d1+ ♚e7 41.♖h1 ♚e6
42.f3 ♖g2 43.♖d1 ♖b2 44.♖d3
♚f5 45.♖c3 ♖h2 46.♖d3 c5
47.♖c3?!** (47.♖d6 ♖×h4 48.♖×b6∞)
**47...♖×h4 48.♖d3 ♖h1 49.♖c3
♖b1 50.♖d3 ♚×g5 51.♖c3 ♖d1
0-1**

Summary: After **1.e4 d5 2.e×d5
♛×d5 3.♘c3 ♛d6 4.d4 ♘f6
5.♘f3 c6 6.h3**, the move h2-h3, pre-
venting ♗c8-g4, is not very dangerous for Black. Also see, e.g., Games
2, 11, 19 and 30). As in those games,
Black should have an equal position

after **6...♗f5** or perhaps even after
6...g6.

After **6...♗f5**, White has many different continuations; for example, 7.♗c4,
7.g4, 7.♘e5, 7.♗e2, 7.♗d3, or 7.♗e3.
I think 7.♗d3 is the best.

After **7.♗d3**, Black has three good possibilities for an equal game: 7...♗×d3,
7...♗g6 and 7...g6. After **7...♗×d3
8.♛×d3 ♘bd7** (8...e6 is also possible), White has some interesting
moves; for example, 9.♗g5, 9.♗e3,
9.0-0 and **9.♘e4**. Preferable is 9.0-0
e6 when White has three reasonable
possibilities: **A)** 10.♖e1 ♗e7=; **B)**
10.♘e2 ♛c7=; and **C)** The line played
by Kasparov: 10.♘e4 ♘×e4 11.♛×e4.

Compare this position with that of the
French Defense, Rubinstein Variation,
after 1.e4 e6 2.d4 d5 3.♘c3 d×e4
4.♘×e4 ♗d7 5.♘f3 ♗c6 6.♗d3 ♘bd7
7.♛e2 ♘gf6 8.0-0 ♘×e4 9.♗×e4 ♗×e4
10.♛×e4 c6.

The 4...♗d7 line began to be played by
many well-known masters around
1990.Black's plan is to exchange off the
light-squared bishop via c6, and then
the pawn advance c7-c6 will give Black
a Caro-Kann set up without the bad
bishop. This line is very solid (it was

nicknamed the Fort Knox variation), but it is passive. If Black can play this position, with White to move, then the previous position should also be able to be played, probably even with greater success! For example, after 11...♛d5, Black can begin active play for the central light squares.

Game 16
Balogh, C. (2527) –
Dizdarevic, E. (2538)
Izmir 2004

1.e4 d5 2.e×d5 ♛×d5 3.♘c3 ♛d6 4.d4 ♘f6 5.♘f3 c6 6.♘e5 ♝f5

7.♝c4

7.♝e2 see Game 14. We will examine **A)** 7.♛f3; **B)** 7.♘c4; **C)** 7.g4 and **D)** 7.♝f4.

A) 7.♛f3 e6 8.♝f4 ♛×d4 (8...♛d8?! 9.g4 ♝g6 10.0-0-0 ♝b4 11.h4 ♝×c3 12.♛×c3±) 9.♖d1 ♛c5 (9...♛b6?! 10.♘c4 ♛c5 11.♝e3) 10.♝d3 (10.♘b5? (Michalczak, T. (2374) – Pytel, K. (2377), Skanderborg 2005) 10...c×b5 11.♛×b7 ♛b4+ 12.c3 ♛e4+ 13.♛×e4 ♝×e4 14.♝×b5+ ♚e7∓) 10...♘bd7 11.♘×d7 ♘×d7 12.0-0 0-0-0 13.♝e3 ♛a5 14.♝×f5 ♛×f5=;

B) 7.♘c4 This position also arises after 3...♛a5 4.d4 ♘f6 5.♘f3 ♝f5 6.♘e5 c6 7.♘c4.

B1) 7...♛c7

B1a) 8.♝g5 ♘bd7 9.♛f3 e6 (9...♝×c2? 10.♝f4 ♛d8? 11.♛e2+- or 10...e5 11.d×e5±) 10.♝f4 ♛d8± or 9.♛d2 ♘b6 10.♝f4 ♘×c4 11.♝×c4 ♛b6 12.d5 ♘e4 13.♘×e4 ♝×e4 14.0-0-0 ♝×g2 15.d×c6 ♝×c6 16.♖hg1 e6 17.♝e5⩲, Dutreeuw, M. (2415) – De Fre, W. (2031), Gent 2006;

B1b) 8.♛f3 e6 (8...♝g6?! 9.♝f4 ♛d8 10.0-0-0 e6 11.♝e2± or 10...♘bd7 11.d5±; 8...♝×c2 9.h4⩲; 8...♝g4 9.♝f4 ♝×f3 10.♝×c7 (Domon,t A. – Cassidy, J. (2415), Saint Vincent 2005) 10...♝h5±) 9.♝f4 ♛d8 10.♝d3 ♝×d3 11.♛×d3 ♘d5 12.♘×d5 c×d5 13.♘e5± or 12.♝e5 ♘×c3 13.♛×c3 f6 14.♝g3 ♘a6 15.0-0±;

B1c) 8.g3

B1c1) 8...g6 9.♝g2 ♝g7 10.♝f4 ♛c8 (10...♛d7) 11.h4 (11.0-0!? 0-0 12.♛e2) 11...0-0 12.♘e3 ♝e6 13.♛f3 ♘a6 14.0-0-0 ♘b4 15.a3 ♘bd5 16.♘c×d5 ♘×d5 17.h5 (Polgar, S. (2464) – Bitansky, I. (2297), Israel 2002) 17...a5 18.h×g6 f×g6⇄;

B1c2) 8...e6 9.♝f4 ♛d8 10.♝g2 ♝e7 11.0-0 0-0 12.♖e1 ♘a6 13.a3 ♘c7 (13...♘d5!?) 14.b4 (14.♘e3!?; 14.♘e5 ♘cd5 15.♘×d5 e×d5 16.c4 ♝e6 17.c5 ♖e8 18.b4 ♘d7 19.♘f3 ♝f5 20.♛b3 ♝e4 21.b5 ♝f6 22.♖ed1 h6 23.a4 ♛c8±, Zapata, A. (2543) – Tempone, M. (2437), USA 2003) 14...♘cd5 15.♝d2 (15.♘×d5 c×d5=) 15...♝g4 (15...♘b6!?) 16.♘e2 ♘b6 17.♘a5

(17.♘e5 ♗f5 18.b5 c×b5 19.♗×b7 ♖b8 20.♗f3±) 17...♕d7 18.c4⇄, Eliseev, A. (2439) – Utkin, A. (2382), Peterhof 2005;

B2) 7...♕d8

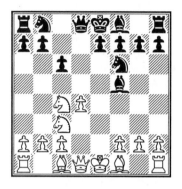

B2a) 8.♗e2 e6 (8...♘bd7 9.♗f3 e6 10.0-0 h6 11.♕e2 ♗e7 12.d5 c×d5 13.♘×d5 ♘×d5 14.♗×d5 ♕c7∓, Videki, S. (2465) – Muse, D. (2350), Split 1999) 9.g4 ♗g6 10.h4 ♗b4 11.h5 ♗e4 12.f3 (12.0-0!?) 12...♗d5 13.♘e3 h6 14.♔f2 (14.♕d3 ♕c7 15.♔f2 ♘bd7 16.♗d2 ♗×c3 17.b×c3 c5 18.♘×d5 ♘×d5 19.♖ab1±) 14...♘bd7 (14...0-0!?) 15.♗d3 0-0 16.♘c×d5 ♘×d5 17.♘×d5 e×d5±;

B2b) 8.♘e3 ♗g6 9.h4 h6 (9...h5!?)

B2b1) 10.h5 ♗h7 11.d5?! (11.♗e2 e6 12.0-0 ♘bd7 13.f4 ♗d6 14.f5 e×f5 15.♘×f5 ♗×f5 16.♖×f5 0-0 17.♕d3 ♖e8=) 11...c×d5 12.♘e×d5 ♘c6 13.♗b5 (13.♘×f6+ e×f6 14.♕g4 ♕d4 15.♕×d4 ♘×d4 16.c3 ♘c6∓) 13...♘×d5 14.♕×d5 ♕×d5 15.♘×d5 0-0-0 16.♗×c6 b×c6 17.♘e3 e5∓, Sutovsky, E. (2669) – Rogers, I. (2594), Nottingham 2005;

B2b2) 10.g4 e6 11.♗g2 ♗b4 (11...♗e7!? 12.h5 ♗h7 13.f4 ♘d5

14.♘c×d5 c×d5) 12.a3 (12.0-0 ♘bd7 13.♘c4 0-0⇄) 12...♗×c3+ 13.b×c3 ♘bd7 14.♘c4 (14.h5 ♗h7 15.a4 ♘e4 16.♗b2 0-0 17.♕e2 ♕g5⇄) 14...♕c7 15.a4 0-0-0⇄, Glek, I. (2590) – Hansen, C. (2630), Copenhagen 1995;

C) 7.g4 ♗g6 (7...♗e6!? 8.g5 ♘fd7 9.♘c4 ♕c7 10.♕f3 ♘b6 11.♗f4 ♕d7) 8.♗f4 (8.h4 – 5.♘f3 ♗g4 6.h3 ♗h5 7.g4 ♗g6 8.♘e5 c6 9.h4, Game 11; 8.f4!?) 8...♘d5 9.♕d2 ♘×f4 10.♕×f4 ♘d7 11.0-0-0 0-0-0 (11...f6!?) 12.♘×g6 (12.h4!?) 12...♕×g6 13.d5 e5 14.d×e6 (14.♕g3!?; 14.♕a4!?) 14...f×e6 15.♗c4 e5 (15...♗c5!?) 16.♕e4 (16.♕f5!?) 16...♗g5+?! (16...♗b4!) 17.♔b1 ♗b4? (17...♗c5‡) 18.♗a6 ♘c5 19.♗×b7+ ♘×b7 20.♕×b4±, Hatzidakis, M. (2201) – Babaniotis, E. (2069), Hania 2000;

D) 7.♗f4

After 7.♗f4 we examine **D1)** 7...♕b4; **D2)** 7...♕d8; **D3)** 7...♘g4 and **D4)** 7...♘bd7.

D1) 7...♕b4? 8.♘c4 ♘d5 (8...e6 9.♗d6 ♗×d6 10.a3 +−) 9.♗d2 (9.a3 ♘×c3 10.a×b4 ♘×d1 11.♘b6 e5 12.♔×d1 e×f4 13.♘×a8±, Geller, J. (2480) – Muse, D. (2407), Berlin 2006) 9...♘×c3

(9...♘b6 10.♘d5 +−) 10.♗×c3 ♕a4
11.b3 ♕b5 12.♘e3 +−;

D2) 7...♕d8?! 8.♗c4 (8.♗d3!? ♗×d3
9.♕×d3) 8...e6 9.g4 ♗g6 (9...♗e4
10.♘×e4 ♘×e4 11.♕e2 ♕a5+ 12.♔f1
♘d6 13.♘×f7 ♘×c4 14.♕×e6+ ♗e7
15.♖e1 1-0, Nagy, J. (2260) –
Outioupine, V., Pecs 1998; 11...♕×d4
12.♖d1 ♗b4+ 13.♔f1 ±; 11...♘d6
12.♗b3 or 12.♗d3 with better chances)
10.h4

D2b1) 10...♘bd7 11.♕e2 (11.♕f3!?
♘×e5 12.d×e5 ♘d7 13.h5 ♗×c2 14.♖c1
♘b6 15.♗e2 ♗a4 16.♕e4 ± or
12...♘d5 13.0-0-0 h5 14.♘×d5 h×g4
15.♕×g4 ±) 11...♗b4 12.0-0-0 (12.h5!?)
12...♗×c3 13.b×c3 ♗e4 (13...♕a5!?)
14.g5 ♗×h1 15.♘×f7 ♔e7 (15...♔×f7
16.♕×e6+ ♔g6 17.h5+ ♔×h5
18.♖×h1+ ♔g6 19.♗d3 #) 16.♘d6+
♔f8 17.g×f6 +−, Schuermans, R. (2235)
– Pytel, K. (2385), Le Touquet 2006;

D2b2) 10...♗e4 11.♘×e4 ♘×e4
12.♕d3 ♘d6 13.♗b3 ♘d7 14.0-0-0
♗e7 15.♔b1 a5 (15...♗×h4 16.♘×d7
♔×d7 17.d5 e×d5 18.♗×d5 ♗e7
19.♗×f7 ±) 16.a4 ♕b6 (16...0-0 17.h5
h6 18.c3 ♘f6 19.♗c2 ♕c7 20.g5 h×g5
21.♗×g5 ♘f5 22.♖dg1 ±) 17.c4 ♕a6
18.♕c2 ♖c8 19.c5 1-0, Lokasto, A.
(2330) – Safyanovsky, M. (2365), Moscow 1991;

D2b3) 10...♗b4 11.f3 ♕a5 (11...♘d5
12.♗×d5 ♕×d5 13.h5 ♗×c2 14.♕×c2
♕d4 15.♕d2 ±, Micalizzi, G. (2325)
– Spulber, C. (2345), Bucharest 1992)
12.♕d2 ♘bd7 13.h5 ♗e4 14.♘×d7
♔×d7 15.f×e4 ♘×e4 16.♕d3 ♘×c3
17.b×c3 ♗×c3+ 18.♗d2 ±;

D3) 7...♘g4

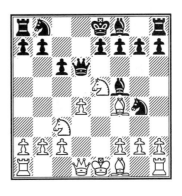

D3a) 8.♕d2 (8.♗c4 ♘×e5 9.♗×e5
♕g6 ∞ or 9.d×e5 ♕b4 10.♕d4 c5
11.♕d5 e6 12.♕f3 ♕×c4 13.♕×b7
♕×f4 14.♕c8+ ♔e7 15.♕×c5+ ♔e8
16.♕c8+ ♔e7 17.♕c5 with perpetual
check) 8...♘×e5 9.♗×e5 and now:

D3a1) 9...♕g6 10.0-0-0 ♘d7 11.f3
(11.♗c7!?; 11.♗e2!?) 11...0-0-0?!
(11...h5 12.♗c7 e6 ±) 12.♗f4 h5
(Djoudi, A. – Stuart, K., Internet 2003)
13.d5 e5 14.d×c6 e×f4 15.♕×f4
(15.c7!?) 15...♕h6 16.♕×h6 ♖×h6
17.c×d7+ ♖×d7 18.♗c4 ±; 12...e5
13.d×e5 ♗b4 14.g4 ♗e6 15.♗d3 ±;
12...♘b6 13.g4 ♗e6 14.♗d3 ♘c4
(14...f5 15.♖he1 ♗d7 16.d5) 15.♗×g6
♘×d2 16.♗×f7 ♗×f7 17.♖×d2 ±;

D3a2) 9...♕b4 10.a3 (10.0-0-0!?)
10...♕b6 (10...♕×b2? 11.♖a2 ♕b6
12.♗×b8 ♖×b8 13.♕f4 +−) 11.0-0-0
♘d7 12.♕f4 ♘×e5 13.♕×f5 ♘d7 14.d5
(14.♗c4 e6 15.♖he1 g6 16.♕f4 h5 ±)
14...g6 15.♕h3 0-0-0 ± or 15.♕f3
♖d8 ±;

D3b) 8.f3 ♘×e5 9.♗×e5 ♕b4 10.♗d3
(10.♖b1 ♘d7 11.♗c7 c5 12.d5 ♖c8 ⇄;
10.♕d2!? ♕×b2 11.♖b1) 10...♕×b2
11.♘a4 (11.♘e4?! ♘d7 12.♖b1 ♕×a2)
11...♕a3 12.♗×f5 ♕×a4 13.♕b1 e6

14.c3 (14.♛×b7? ♛b4+) 14...b6
15.♗d3 ♘d7 16.♗g3 ♘f6 17.0-0
♛a3∓;

D4) 7...♘bd7

D4a) 8.♛d2 (8.♗d3 ♗×d3 9.♛×d3
♘×e5 10.♗×e5 ♛d7 11.0-0 e6±)
8...♘×e5 9.♗×e5 ♛d7 (9...♛b4 10.0-0-0
0-0-0 11.a3 ♛a5 12.♗d3 ♗×d3
13.♛×d3 e6±) 10.0-0-0 0-0-0±;

D4b) 8.♘×f7 ♛×f4

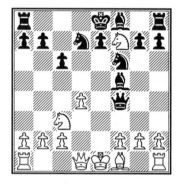

D4b1) 9.g3 ♛c7 10.♘×h8 e5 11.♗c4
e×d4 12.♛×d4 (12.♘e2? ♘e5) 12...0-0-0
13.♘f7 (13.♛f4 ♖e8+ 14.♘e2 ♛a5+
15.♛d2 ♛×d2+ 16.♚×d2 ♘e5∓ or
14.♗e2 ♗e6∓) 13...♖e8+ 14.♗e2
(14.♘e2 ♘b6∓) 14...♘e4 (14...♗c5!?;
14...♘d5!?) 15.♘×e4 ♖×e4 16.♛×a7
♗c5 17.♛a8+ ♘b8 18.0-0-0 ♛×f7
19.♗d3 ♖e7 20.♗×f5+ ♛×f5∓;

D4b2) 9.♘×h8 ♘e4 10.♘×e4 (10.♛e2
♘×c3 11.b×c3 g6 12.♛e3 ♛×e3+
13.f×e3 ♗g7 14.♘×g6 h×g6∓)
10...♗×e4 (10...♛×e4+ 11.♗e2?! ♛×g2
12.♗f3 ♛h3 13.♛e2 g6 14.0-0-0 ♗g7
15.♖he1 ♛h4∓; 11.♛e2 ♛×d4∓)
11.♛d2 (11.f3?! ♗d5 12.c4 ♗g8)
11...♛×d2+ (11...♛h4?! 12.♗c4)
12.♚×d2 g6 13.♗c4 ♗d5 14.♗×d5
c×d5 15.h4 ♗g7 16.♘×g6 h×g6±.

Back to Balogh – Dizdarevic.

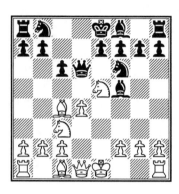

The same position arises after 6.♗c4
♗f5 7.♘e5.

7...e6 8.g4

Another interesting possibility is 8.0-0
(8.♗f4 – 7.♗f4 e6 8.♗c4) 8...♘bd7
9.♗f4 ♘×e5 (9...♛b4!?) and now:

A) 10.d×e5 ♛b4 11.♛e2 ♘d5 12.♗d2
♛×b2 13.♗×d5 (13.♖ab1? ♘×c3;
13.♘×d5!? e×d5 14.♗d3) 13...e×d5
14.♖ab1 ♛×c2 15.♖×b7 ♗d3?
(15...♛d3∓) 16.♛f3 ♗g6 17.♘×d5 0-0-0
18.♖fb1 ♛×b1+ 19.♖×b1 ♗×b1
20.♛c3 ♚b7 21.♛b2+ ♚c8 22.♛c1±;

B) 10.♗×e5

B1) 10...♛b4 (10...♛d7 11.♗d3 ♗g6±
or 11.♛e2 0-0-0±) 11.♗d3 ♗×d3
(11...♛×b2?! 12.d5 ♘×d5 13.♛e1)
12.♛×d3 0-0-0±;

B2) 10...♛d8 11.♗d3 ♗×d3
(11...♗g6!? 12.♗×g6 h×g6 13.♛f3 ♗e7
14.h3 ♛b6 15.a4 ♛a5± or 14.♘e4
♘×e4 15.♛×e4 ♗f6 16.c3 ♛d5=)
12.♛×d3 ♗e7 (12...♗d6?! 13.♛g3)

B2a) 13.f4 0-0 14.f5 (14.♖ae1 g6=)
14...e×f5 (14...♘g4!? 15.♖ae1 ♗d6

16.♗×d6 ♛×d6; 15...♘×e5!?) 15.♖×f5 (Gailleux, F. (2055) – Pytel, K. (2400), Bagneux 2006) 15...♘g4 16.♗g3 (16.♖h5? g6 17.♖h3 ♘×e5 18.d×e5 ♛b6+ 19.♚h1 ♖ad8 20.♛e2 ♛×b2 21.♖b1 ♛a3 22.e6 f5∓) 16...g6 17.♖f4 ♛d7 18.♖e1 ♖ae8=;

B2b) 13.h3 (13.♘e4 ♘×e4 14.♛×e4 0-0 15.♖fe1 ♛d5 16.♛g4 g6 17.h4±; 14...f6!? 15.♗g3 ♛d5 16.♖fe1 ♚f7) 13...0-0 14.♖fe1 (14.♛g3 g6 15.♖fe1±) 14...♘d5 15.♘e4 (15.a4 a5) 15...f6 16.♗h2 f5 17.♘c3 ♖f6±.

Let's return to Balogh – Dizdarevic.

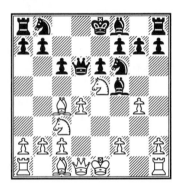

8...♗g6 9.h4

Another interesting possibility is 9.♗f4 ♛b4 (9...♛d8 10.h4 – 7.♗f4 ♛d8 8.♗c4 e6 9.g4 ♗g6 10.h4) 10.♗b3 ♘bd7 11.a3 (11.♘×g6 h×g6 12.♗c7 ♘d5 13.a3 ♛e7=; 11.♘c4 ♘d5 12.a3 ♘×c3 13.♛d2 ♛b5 14.♛×c3 ♘f6±) 11...♛a5 12.♘c4 ♛d8± or 10.♗d2 ♛×b2? (10...♛d6) 11.♘×g6 h×g6 12.♖b1 ♛a3 13.♖×b7 ♛d6 14.♛e2 14...♖×h2 (14...♛×d4 15.♖×f7 ♛×g4 16.f3 ♛g3+ 17.♚d1 ♛d6 18.♗×e6±) 15.♖×h2 ♛×h2 16.g5 ♘d5 (16...♛g1+ 17.♛f1 ♛×f1+ 18.♗×f1 ♘fd7 19.♗f4⩱) 17.♘×d5 ♛g1+ 18.♛f1 ♛×f1+ 19.♗×f1 e×d5 20.♖c7±.

9...♘bd7 10.♘×d7

Also worth consideration are 10.f4 and 10.♗f4:

A) 10.f4 ♘e4 (10...♘d5 11.♘×d5 c×d5 12.♗d3 ♗e7 13.f5 e×f5 14.h5 ♘×e5 15.d×e5 ♛×e5+ 16.♛e2 ♛g3+ 17.♛f2 ♛×g4 18.h×g6 f×g6∞) 11.h5 ♘×c3 12.b×c3 ♗e4 13.0-0 b5 (13...♘×e5 14.f×e5 ♛e7 15.♛e2 ♗d5 16.♗×d5 c×d5±) 14.♛e2 ♗d5 15.♗b3±;

B) 10.♗f4 ♘×e5 11.d×e5 (11.♗×e5 ♛b4 12.♗b3 h5∓)

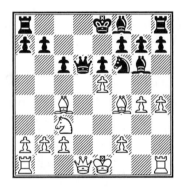

B1) 11...♛b4 12.e×f6 ♛×c4 13.♗e5 ♗b4 (13...♖d8? 14.f×g7 ♖×d1+ 15.♖×d1±) 14.♛e2 ♛×e2+ 15.♚×e2 g×f6 16.♗×f6 ♖g8 17.♖ac1 h6=;

B2) 11...♛×d1+ 12.♖×d1

B2a) 12...♘d5 13.♘×d5 c×d5 14.♗b5+ ♚d8 15.c4?! (15.♛e2 h5 16.♗d3=) 15...a6 16.♗a4 b5 17.c×b5 a×b5 18.♗b3 (18.♗×b5 ♖×a2) 18...h5∓;

Bb) 12...♘g4 13.f3 ♘h6 14.♘b5 ♖c8 15.♘×a7 (15.♘d6+ ♗×d6 16.e×d6 ♚d7) 15...♖d8 16.♗e3 ♗×c2 (16...♗e7=) 17.♖×d8+ ♚×d8 18.♗b6+ ♚e8 19.♚e2⩲.

10...♛×d7 11.h5 ♝e4 12.♞×e4 ♞×e4

13.♝e3

Alternatives are 13.f3, 13.c3 and 13.♛d3:

A) 13.f3 ♞f6 (13...♞d6!?) 14.c3 ♝d6 (14...0-0-0!?) 15.♛e2 ♝g3+?! (15...h6!? 16.♝d2 0-0-0 17.0-0-0 ♛c7=) 16.♚f1 (16.♚d1!? ♞d5 17.h6 or 16...0-0-0 17.f4) 16...♛d6 (16...♞d5!? 17.h6 g6 18.♚g2 ♝d6) 17.♚g2 (17.h6!?) 17...♝f4 18.♝×f4 ♛×f4 19.♜ae1 0-0-0 20.♛e5 ♛×e5 21.♜×e5 h6 22.♚g3±, Manik, M. (2380) – Sabol, M. (2302), Czech Republic 1995;

B) 13.c3 0-0-0 14.♛e2 (14.♛f3!? ♞d6 15.♝d3) 14...♞f6 15.♝d2 (15.h6!? g×h6 16.♝d2 ♜g8 17.f3) 15...♝d6 (15...h6!?) 16.0-0-0 (16.g5!?) 16...♜he8 (17.♛f3!? ♞d5 18.♝d3 h6 19.c4 ♞b4 20.♝e4 or 19...♞c7 20.♝c3) 17.f4 ♛c7 18.♛f3 c5 19.d×c5 ♝×c5 (19...♛×c5!?) 20.♚b1 (20.g5!? ♞d5 21.♝d3) 20...♛c6 21.♝×c6+ b×c6±, Svidler, P. (2684) – Adams, M. (2708), Frankfurt 1999;

C) 13.♛d3 ♞f6 (13...♞d6!? 14.♝b3 0-0-0) 14.g5 ♞d5 15.♝d2 ♞b4 16.♛b3 b5 17.♝e2 a5 (17...♛×d4 18.0-0-0≅)

18.c3 a4 19.♛d1 ♞d5 20.♛c2 (Borgo, G. (2445) – Sabol, M. (2260), Pardubice 1998) 20...♝d6 21.0-0-0 a3 22.b3 ♝f4±.

Returning now to Balogh – Dizdarevic.

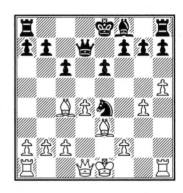

13...b5 (13...0-0-0 (13...♞f6!? 14.♛f3 ♞d5 15.0-0-0 h6) 14.♛f3 ♞d6 (14...♝b4+?! 15.c3 ♞×c3 16.b×c3 ♝×c3+ 17.♚e2 ♝×a1 18.♜×a1 f5 (Lutz, C. (2591) – Adams, M. (2708), Frankfurt 1999) 19.♛g3 ♜he8 ♛d6 20.♝f4 ♛e7 21.♛e3± or 20...♛d7 21.♛a3±) 15.♝d3 h6 (15...♞b5 16.0-0-0 ♞×d4? 17.♝×d4 ♛×d4 18.♝a6 ♛b6 19.♜×d8+ ♚×d8 20.♛×f7±) 16.0-0-0 ♝e7±) **14.♝b3** (14.♝d3!?) **14...h6 15.♛f3 ♞f6 16.a4** (16.0-0-0 ♞d5) **16...b4 17.a5 ♝e7 18.♜g1** (18.0-0-0 ♞d5 19.♚b1 0-0 ⇄ or 18.c4 b×c3 19.b×c3 ♜b8⇄; 18.♝c4 ♞d5 19.♛e4 ♛c7⇄) **18...♞d5 19.♝d2** (19.♝c4 ♛c7) **♝g5?!** (19...♛c7!? 20.g5 h×g5 21.♝×g5 ♜d8∓) **20.♝×d5** (20.♝×g5 h×g5 21.0-0-0 ♛c7⇄) **20...♝×d2+ 21.♚×d2 ♛×d5?** (21...c×d5 22.g5 ♜c8 23.g×h6 g×h6 24.♜g7 ♜f8=) **22.♛×d5 c×d5 23.♜a4 ♜b8** (23...b3!? 24.c×b3 ♜b8 25.♜g3 ♚d7 26.♜c3 ♚d6) **24.♜g3 ♚e7?!** (24...f5!? 25.g×f5 0-0 26.f×e6 ♜×f2+

27.♔d1 ♖f4±) **25.♖b3± ♖b5
26.♖a×b4 ♖×a5 27.♖b7+ ♔f6
28.♖f3+ ♔g5 29.♖f×f7 ♔×g4
30.♖×g7+ ♔×h5 31.♖b3 ♔h4
32.♖bg3 ♖a1 33.♖g2 ♖h1
34.♖7g6 h5 35.♖×e6 ♔h3 36.♖g5
h4 37.f4 ♖f1 38.♖e3+ ♔h2
39.♖e2+ ♔h3 40.♖e3+ ♔h2 41.f5
h3 42.♖e2+ ♔h1 43.♖e1 ♖×e1
44.♔×e1 ♖h4 45.c3 ♖f4 46.♔e2
h2 47.b3 a5 48.f6 ♖×f6 49.♖×d5
♔g2 50.♖g5+ ♔h3 51.♖×a5 ♖h6
52.♖a1 ♔g3 53.♔e3 h1♛
54.♖×h1 ♖×h1 55.d5 ♔g4
56.♔d4 ♔f4 57.b4 ♔f5 58.♔c5
♔f6 59.♔d6 ♖c1 60.b5 ♖×c3
61.b6 ♖b3 62.♔c7 ♖c3+ ½-½**

Summary: After **1.e4 d5 2.e×d5
♛×d5 3.♘c3 ♛d6 4.d4 ♘f6 5.♘f3
c6 6.♘e5**, the moves 6.♗d3, 6.♗e2
and 6.h3 are not dangerous for Black
(Games 13-15). The most significant
option is probably 6.♘e5, giving White
serious chances in some variations.

In Game 17 we will look at other alternatives, but **6...♗f5** looks very natural in many positions of the Scandinavian Defense. Unfortunately for Black,
after 6...♗f5, White often gets a strong
initiative after 7.♗c4 or 7.♗f4, followed
by an early g2-g4. But even here Black
can have interesting counterplay.

As far as Game 16 is concerned, please
note:

A) After 7.♘c4, we get well-known
positions from 3...♛a5 lines: 3...♛a5
4.d4 ♘f6 5.♘f3 ♗f5 6.♘e5 c6 7.♘c4. I
do not think 7...♛d8 is dangerous for
Black. As for 7...♛c7, Black can have
problems after 8.♛f3 ♗×c2 (8...e6 is
better).

B) After 7.♗f4, the continuation
7...♛b4 (or 7...♛d8) is dangerous for
Black. After 7...♘g4 or 7...♘bd7, Black
should have much better chances. In my
opinion, 7...♘bd7 is the best continuation.

C) After the forced line 7.♗c4 e6 8.g4
♗g6 9.h4 ♘bd7 10.♘×d7 ♛×d7 11.h5
♗e4 12.♘×e4 ♘×e4 White has a good
number of choices. I think 13.♛d3 is
the best.

Game 17
Anand, V. (2792) – Tiviakov, S. (2669)
Wijk aan Zee 2006

**1.e4 d5 2.e×d5 ♛×d5 3.♘c3 ♛d6
4.d4 ♘f6 5.♘f3 c6 6.♘e5 ♘bd7**

As we saw in different lines of Games
10, 11, 14, 15 and 16, in some positions
it is best for Black to try to eliminate
the e5-knight as quickly as possible.
Usually this idea is possible to realize
by ♘b8-c6, ♘b8-d7 or ♘f6-g4.

After 6...♗e6 (Black's bishop takes the
sting out of ♘c4 or ♗c4 ideas, and this
bishop also prepares a kingside
fianchetto)

we have the following continuations: **A)**
7.♘c4; **B)** 7.♗c4 and **C)** 7.♗f4.

A) 7.♘c4 ♕c7 (**7...**♕d8 8.♗e2 g6 9.0-0 ♗g7 10.♗g5 ♘bd7 11.a4 0-0 12.♕d2 ♘b6 ⇄ Gavrilakis, N. (2402) – Papaioannou, I. (2577), Aghia Pelagia 2004) 8.♗g5 (8.g3 g6 9.♗f4 ♕d8 10.♘e5 ♘bd7 11.♗g2 ♘b6 12.0-0 ♗g7 13.a4 ♘bd5 14.♘e2 ♘g4=, Geenen, M. (2334) – Tolk, P. (2244), Belgium 2001) 8...♘bd7 9.♕f3 g6 10.♘e3 ♗g7 11.h4 0-0 12.0-0-0 (Petrov, M. (2451) – Ibrahimov, R. (2404), Leon 2001) 12...♘b6 13.♗f4 ♕d7 ± ;

B) 7.♗c4 ♗xc4 (**7...**♘bd7!?) 8.♘xc4 ♕d8 (8...♗e6+!?; 8...♕c7 9.♕f3 ♕d7 10.♗e3 ♕g4 ½-½, Przedmojski, R. (2370) – Drabke, L. (2428), Netherlands 2004) 9.♗g5 e6 10.♕e2 ♗e7 11.♖d1 0-0 12.0-0 ♘bd7 13.♘e5 ♘d5 14.♗xe7 ♘xc3 15.♕f3 ♘xe5 16.♕xc3 ♕xe7 17.dxe5 ♖fd8=, Molner, M. (2335) – Gonzalez, R. (2505), New York 2008;

C) 7.♗f4

C1) 7...♕b4 8.a3 ♕a5 9.♗c4 (9.♕f3!? ♘bd7 10.♘c4 ♕d8 11.0-0-0) 9...♗xc4 10.♘xc4 ♕d8 11.0-0 e6 12.♖e1 ♗e7 13.♕d3 (13.♖e3!? 0-0 14.♖g3) 13...0-0 14.♖ad1 ♘d5 ± , Rogic, D. (2494) – Muse, D. (2407), Sibenik 2006; 14.b4!?

C2) 7...♕d8

C2a) 8.♕d2 g6 9.0-0-0 ♘bd7 10.d5!? ♗xd5 11.♘xd5 ♘xd5 12.c4 ♘e5 13.♗xe5 f6 14.♗g3 (14.cxd5 fxe5 15.♕c3 ♕c7 16.♔b1 0-0-0 ⇄) 14...♘b6 15.♕e3 (15.♕c2!? ♕c8 16.♗d3) 15...♕c8 16.h4 h5 17.♗d3 ♔f7 18.♖he1 ♗h6 19.f4 ♖e8 20.♔b1 f5 21.♕f3 e6 22.♗f2 ½-½, Zarnicki, P. (2497) – Soppe, G. (2448), Buenos Aires 1999; 9...♗g7!? 10.♗c4 (10.♗h6

♗xh6 11.♕xh6 b5 ⇄) 10...♗xc4 11.♘xc4 0-0 ⇄ ;

C2b) 8.♗e2 g6 (8...♘bd7 9.0-0 g6 10.♘xd7 ♕xd7 11.♗e5 ♗g7 12.♘e4 0-0 13.♘c5 ♕c8 ± , Popovic, P. (2495) – Muse, D. (2410), Germany 2006; 12...♘xe4!? 13.♗xg7 ♖g8 14.♗e5 0-0-0 ⇄)

C2b1) 9.h4 ♗g7 10.h5 (Borriss, M. (2455) – Muse, D. (2410), Germany 2006) 10...♘xh5 11.♗xh5 gxh5 12.♕xh5 ♕xd4 13.♕g5 ♗f6 14.♖xh7 ♖f8 15.♕g3 ♘d7 ∓ or 13.g3 ♘d7 14.♖d1 ♕b4 ∓ ;

C2b2) 9.♕d2 ♗g7 10.h4 h5 (10...♘bd7!? 11.h5 ♘xh5 12.♗xh5 gxh5 13.♖xh5 ♘f6 ⇄ or 11.0-0-0 ♘xe5 12.♗xe5 h5 13.d5 cxd5 ⇄) 11.0-0-0 ♘bd7 12.♕e3 (Tzermiadianos, A. (2370) – Papatheodorou, T. (2140), Athens 1997) 12...♘xe5 13.dxe5 ♘d7 ⇄ .

Back to Anand – Tiviakov.

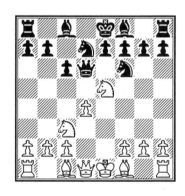

7.♗f4

Also worth noting are **A)** 7.f4 and **B)** 7.♘c4.

A) 7.f4 (Alexey Shirov's move) 7...♘b6 8.g4 (8.♗e2 g6 9.g4 ♗g7 10.g5 ♘fd5

11.♘e4 ♛d8 12.a3 0-0 13.c4 ♘c7⇄, Szalanczy, E. (2380) – Vegh, E. (2310), Budapest 2007; 8.♛f3 g6 9.♗d3 ♗g7⇄)

A1) 8...g6 (8...♘fd5 9.♘e4 ♛d8?! 10.♘g5 f6 11.♘gf7 ♛c7 12.♘xh8 fxe5 13.fxe5±, Delorme, A. (2375) – Vatter, H. (2325), Differdange 2008) 9.g5 ♘fd5 10.♘e4 ♛d8 11.c4 ♘c7 (11...♘b4!?) 12.♛e2 ♗g7?! (12...♘e6!?) 13.c5 ♘e6 (13...♘bd5 14.♘d6+!) 14.cxb6 ♘xd4 15.♛f2 ♗xe5 16.fxe5 ♛d5 17.♗g2 ♛c4 18.b3 ♛d3 19.♛d2 ♘c2+ 20.♔f2 ♛xd2+ 21.♗xd2 ♘xa1 22.♖xa1 axb6 23.♗e3 with better chances for White, Shirov, A. (2695) – Nisipeanu, L. (2690), Foros 2007;

A2) 8...h5 9.g5 ♘fd7 (9...♘g4? 10.♘f3)

A2a) 10.♗d3 g6 (10...♘xe5 11.dxe5 ♛c7 12.g6±) 11.♗e3 ♘xe5 (11...♛b4!?) 12.dxe5 (12.fxe5 ♛c7⇄; 12...♛b4!?) 12...♛b4 (12...♛c7⇄) 13.♛d2 (13.0-0 ♗h3⇄) 13...♘c4 14.♗xc4 ♛xc4⇄;

A2b) 10.♗g2 ♘xe5 11.fxe5 ♛g6 12.0-0 (12.♗e4 ♗f5) 12...♗f5 13.d5 ♖d8 (13...♗xc2?! 14.♛f3)

A2b1) 14.♛f3 ♗g4 (14...♗xc2?! 15.e6) 15.♛f2 cxd5 16.h3 ♗d7⇄ or 16.♗e3 e6 17.♘b5 ♖c8⇄;

A2b2) 14.♛e2 ♘xd5 (14...cxd5 15.♘xd5 ♘xd5 16.♛b5+ ♛c6 17.♛xc6+ bxc6 18.♖xf5 e6⇄) 15.♘xd5 cxd5 16.♛b5+ ♗d7 17.♛xb7 e6⇄ or 17.♛xd5 e6 18.♛xb7 ♛xc2⇄;

A2c) 10.♛d3 g6 11.♗d2 (11.♗g2 ♗g7 12.♘e4 ♛c7⇄; 11.♘e4 ♛c7 12.♗g2 ♘xe5 13.fxe5 ♗g7 14.0-0 ♗e6⇄ or 13.dxe5 ♗g4⇄) 11...♘xe5 12.fxe5 (12.dxe5 ♛xd3 13.♗xd3 ♗e6⇄) 12...♛c7 13.0-0-0 ♗f5⇄;

A2d) 10.♛e2 (10.g6?! ♘xe5 11.fxe5 ♛xg6; 10.♗e2 ♘xe5 11.fxe5 ♛g6 12.0-0 ♗f5⇄ or 12.♗d3 ♗f5⇄) 10...♛xd4 (10...♘xe5 11.dxe5 ♛g6 12.♗e3 ♗g4⇄) 11.♗e3 ♛b4 12.♘d3 (12.0-0-0?! ♘xe5 13.fxe5 ♗g4) 12...♛a5⇄;

B) 7.♘c4 ♛c7 The same position also arises after 3...♛a5 4.d4 ♘f6 5.♘f3 c6 6.♘e5 ♘d7 7.♘c4 ♛c7.

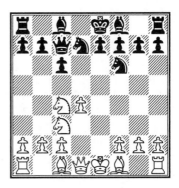

B1) 8.♗g5 h6 (8...b5!? 9.♘d2 e5 10.♛e2 ♗e7 11.♘f3 exd4 12.♘xd4 0-0 13.0-0-0 ♗b4=; 11.dxe5 ♛xe5=; 9.♘e3!?) 9.♗h4 ♘b6 10.♘e5 ♗f5 11.♗e2 (Espinosa, R. (2412) – Leon Hoyus, M. (2395), Mexico 2004) 11...e6 12.g4 (12.0-0 ♗d6=) 12...♗h7 13.♗g3 ♗d6 14.♛d2 0-0-0 (14...♘bd5!? 15.♘xd5 exd5) 15.0-0-0 ♘fd5⇄; 11.♗g3!? ♛d8 12.♗d3;

B2) 8.♗d3 b5 (8...g6 9.0-0 ♗g7 10.a4 0-0 11.♖e1 ♖e8 12.♛f3 ♘b6 13.♘e5 ♗e6 14.♗f4±, Reyes, J. – Pons Morro, P., Palma de Mallorca 1992; 8...e5!? 9.dxe5 ♘xe5) 9.♘e3 e5 10.d5 (10.♛e2 ♗b4 11.f4? e4 12.♘g4 0-0 13.♗xe4

♖e8 14.♘e5 ♘xe4 15.♛xe4 f6∓) 10...b4
11.dxc6 bxc3 12.cxd7+ ♗xd7 13.b3=;

B3) 8.g3 ♘b6 (8...♘d5!?)

B3a) 9.♗f4 ♛d8 10.♘e5 (10.♛d2 ♗e6
11.♘e5 g6 12.♗g2 ♗g7 13.0-0 0-0
14.♖fe1 ♘fd5 15.♗h6 ♘xc3 16.♗xg7
♔xg7 17.♛xc3 ♘d5 ½-½, Liwak, P.
(2340) – Malaniuk, V. (2539), Barlinek
2006) 10...♘bd5 11.♗d2 ♘xc3
12.♗xc3 ½-½, Oral, T. (2510)- Babula,
V. (2575), Olomouc 1998; 11.♘xd5
♘xd5 12.♛f3 ♗e6 13.♗g2 g6 14.0-0
♗g7 15.♗d2 0-0 16.♖ad1 ±, El Kher,
H. (2404) – Fries Nielsen, J. (2425),
Koge 2004;

B3b) 9.♘e5 ♗e6 10.♗g2

B3b1) 10...g6 (10...♘c4!? 11.♘f3 0-0-0
12.0-0 ♛a5 13.♛d3 ♘d6 14.♘e5
♘d7⇄) 11.0-0 ♗g7 12.♛e2 ♖d8
13.♗f4 (13...♖xd4? 14.♘xf7 ♖xf4
15.♛xe6 ♖f8 16.gxf4 ♖xf7±; 13...♘h5
14.♘xg6 ♘xf4 15.♘xf4 ♗c4 16.♛g4
♗xd4 17.♖fe1 e6 18.♖ad1±) 13...♛c8
14.♖ad1 0-0 15.♖fe1 ♖fe8 16.h4
♘bd5⇄, Vocaturo, D. (2440) – Borgo,
G. (2420), Cremona 2006;

B3b2) 10...♖d8 11.0-0 (11.♗f4 ♛c8
12.0-0 g6 13.♘e4 ♘xe4 14.♗xe4
♗g7⇄, Kojovic, D. (2405) – Drazic,
S. (2480), Belgrade 2007) 11...g6
12.♘e2 ♗g7 13.a4 (13.♗f4 ♛c8
14.♛d2 0-0 15.♛a5 ♛a8⇄) 13...0-0
14.a5 (14.♗f4 ♛c8 15.♛a5 ♘bd5
16.♗d2 ♘g4⇄) 14...♘c4 15.♘d3 a6
(15...♘h5!?) 16.♖a4 ♘d6⇄,
Nakamura, H. (2670) – Caspi, I. (2375),
England 2008;

B4) After 8.♛f3 ♘b6, a very popular
position is reached.

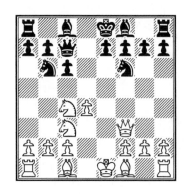

B4a) 9.♘e5 (9.h3 ♗e6; 9.♗g5 ♗g4)

B4a1) 9...♛d6 10.♗e3 (10.♗f4 ♛xd4
11.♖d1 ♛b4 12.♘d3 ♛a5∞) 10...♗e6
11.a3 g6 12.♗d3 (12.0-0-0!?) 12...♗g7
13.0-0 (13.0-0-0!? 0-0 14.♖he1) 13...0-0
14.♖fe1?! (14.♖fd1!? ♘fd7 15.♘g4)
14...♘fd7 15.♘xd7 ♛xd7∓,
Nevednichy, V. (2581) – Ardelean, G.
(2449), Timisoara 2006;

B4a2) 9...♗e6 10.♗f4 (10.♗d3 ♘bd7
11.♗f4 ♘xe5 12.♗xe5 ♛b6 13.0-0
♘d7 14.♘e2 ♘xe5 15.dxe5 h5 16.h3
g5⇄, Sax, G. (2568) – Brancaleoni, M.
(2314), Bratto 2005)

B4a2a) 10...♘bd5 11.♗g3 (11.♘g6?!
♘xf4 12.♘xh8 0-0-0; 11.♘xd5 ♗xd5
12.♛e2 ♛a5+ 13.c3 0-0-0 14.a4 ♗e6
15.g3 ♛d5 16.♖g1 ♛e4=,
Komliakov, V. (2440) – Ponkratov, P.
(2495), Russia 2008) 11...♛b6 12.0-0-0
g6 13.a3 ♗h6+ 14.♔b1 ♛a5 15.♘xd5
♗xd5 16.♛d3 ♘e4 17.f3 ♘xg3
18.hxg3 ♗g7 19.♛e3 0-0-0 ½-½,
Nataf, I. (2592) – Fontaine, R. (2518),
Besancon 2006) 11...♘xc3 12.♛xc3
♘e4 13.♛e3 ♘xg3 14.hxg3 ♛d6 15.c3
g6 16.♗e2 ♗g7 17.f4 h5=, Freitag, M.
(2410) – Kreindl, H. (2235), Austria
2006;

B4a2b) 10...♛d8 11.0-0-0 g6 (11...♘bd5 12.♘×d5 ♛×d5 13.♛b3 ♛e4 14.♛×b7 ♛×f4+ 15.♚b1∞, Zhigalko, A. (2530) – Vysochin, S. (2530), Warsaw 2006; 13.c4 ♛×f3 14.♘×f3±) 12.♗d3 ♗g7 13.h4 ♘bd5 14.♗c4 ♘×f4 (14...0-0!?) 15.♛×f4 ♗×c4 16.♘×c4 ♘d5 17.♛f3 ♘×c3 18.♛×c3 ♛d5=, Tirard, H. (2475) – Pytel, K. (2415), La Fere 2007;

B4b) 9.♗f4

B4b1) 9...♛d8 10.♗e5 ♗g4 (10...♗e6 11.♘e3 ♘bd7 12.0-0-0 ♛a5 13.♗×f6 e×f6 (Smeets, J. (2555) – Feygin, M. (2530), Netherlands 2007) 14.♚b1±; 10...♘bd5 11.♘×d5 c×d5 12.♘e3 ♘×g4 17.♛×g4 (Emms, J. (2502) – Ledger, A. (2430), Southend 2006) 17...♗f6 18.f4 g6±) 11.♛g3 h5

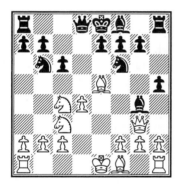

B4b1a) 12.h3 h4 13.♛f4 ♗e6 14.♘e3 (14.♘×b6 ♛×b6 15.0-0-0 0-0-0 16.♗e2 ♛a5⇄, Kravtsiv, M. (2530) – Nosenko, A. (2495), Alushta 2008) 14...♘bd5 15.♘e×d5 ♘×d5 16.♛d2 ♘×c3 (16...f6!? 17.♗h2 ♘×c3) 17.♛×c3 (17.b×c3 ♛d5 18.♘e3 ♗f5!?, Tiviakov, S.) 17...♗d5 18.♛d2 e6 19.c4 ♗e4=, Hossain, E (2460) – Tiviakov, S. (2669), Turin 2006;

B4b1b) 12.f3 (12.h4 ♘bd5 13.♘×d5 (Pavasovic D. (2600) – Skoberne J.

(2480), Nova Gorica 2008) 13...c×d5⇄; 12.♗d3 h4 13.♛f4 ♗e6 14.♘×b6 a×b6 15.♗c7 ♘d5 16.♘×d5 ♛×d5 17.0-0 (Landa, K. (2570) – Borgo, G. (2420), Reggio Emilia 2007) 17...g5⇄ or 17...h3⇄) 12...♗e6

B4b1b1) 13.♘e3 ♘bd5 14.♘c×d5 ♘×d5 15.♘×d5 ♛×d5 16.♗d3 (16.c3 f6 17.♗f4 (Vitoux, C. (2315) – Bednay, B. (2290), Budapest 2007) 17...g5 18.♗e3 0-0-0 19.h4 ♗h6∓) 16...f6 17.♗b8 h4 18.♛c7 ♚f7 19.♛×b7 c5 20.♛×d5 ♗×d5∓, Grischuk, A. (2719) – Tiviakov, S. (2669), Sochi 2006;

B4b1b2) 13.♗c7 (13.♘×b6 ♛×b6 14.0-0-0 0-0-0 15.a3 ♘d5⇄) 13...♛×d4 14.♗×b6 a×b6 15.♛c7 ♛d7 16.♛×b6 g6 17.♖d1 (17.♘e5 ♛c8∓) 17...♗d5 18.♗d3 ♗h6 19.0-0 ♗f4⇄.

B4b2) 9...♛d7 10.0-0-0 (10.♗e5 ♛g4 11.♛×g4 ♗×g4 12.♘e3 ♗e6 13.a4 ♘bd7 14.f4 ♘g4 15.♘×g4 ♗×g4 16.d5 ♘×e5 17.f×e5 0-0-0⇄, Ganguly, S. (2585) – Tiviakov, S. (2640), Khanty-Mansiysk 2007; 10.♘×b6 a×b6 11.0-0-0 e6 12.♗d3 ♘d5 13.♘×d5 ♛×d5 14.♛×d5 e×d5±) 10...♛g4 11.♛×g4 (11.♛e3?! ♘fd5) 11...♗×g4 12.f3 ♗e6 13.♘e5 g6 14.♘e4 ♘×e4 15.f×e4 f6 16.♘f3 ♗g7⇄, Zinchenko, Y. (2490) – Vysochin, S. (2520), Kharkov 2007; 13.♘a5 0-0-0 14.♗e5 ♗f5 15.♗d3 ♗×d3 16.♖×d3 e6⇄, Perez Candelario, M. (2535) – Caspi, I. (2410), La Massana 2008; 13.♘×b6 a×b6 14.a3 0-0-0 15.♗e2 g6 16.♗e5 ♗h6+ 17.♚b1 ♖he8⇄, Sanduleac, V. (2465) – Pytel, K. (2390), La Fere 2008 or 14.♗c7 b5 15.d5 ♗d7 16.a3 e6 17.d×e6 f×e6±, Brandenburg, D. (2430) – Lysyj, I. (2575) Hengelo 2007.

Back to Anand – Tiviakov.

7...♘d5

Another interesting possibility is 7...♘xe5 and now:

A) 8.♗xe5 ♕d8 (8...♕b4!? 9.a3 ♕b6 10.♗e2 ♗f5) 9.♗c4 ♗f5 10.♗xf6 (10.d5!?) 10...gxf6 11.d5 ♕c7 (11...♖g8!?; 11...♕b6 12.♕f3 ♗xc2 13.dxc6 bxc6 14.0-0≈) 12.0-0 (12.♕f3!? ♕e5+ 13.♔f1) 12...0-0-0 13.♕f3 e6 (13...♗g6?! (Kasparov, S. (2535) – Pytel, K. (2395), Metz 2007) 14.♖ad1 with strong pressure or 13...♗xc2?! 13.♖ac1) 14.dxe6 fxe6⇄;

B) 8.dxe5 ♕b4 (8...♕xd1+ 9.♖xd1 ♘d7 10.e6 fxe6 11.♘e4 ♘f6 12.♘g5 g6 13.♗c7 ♗d7 14.♗c4 ♘d5 15.♗e5 ♖g8 16.♘xh7 ♗h6 17.h4 0-0-0 18.♘g5 ♖df8 19.♗d3 ♗g7 20.♗xg7 ♖xg7 21.g3±, Larino Nieto, D. (2371) – Hasangatin, R. (2491), Pardubice 2006)

B1) 9.♗d2 (9.exf6 ♕xf4 10.fxg7 ♗xg7∓) 9...♘e4 (9...♘g4?! 10.f3 ♘e5 11.♘b5 ♕h4+ 12.g3) 10.♗e2 (10.♘d5?! ♕xd2+ 11.♕xd2 ♘xd2 12.♘c7+ ♔d8 13.♘xa8 ♘xf1 14.0-0-0+ ♗d7 15.♖hxf1 ♔c8 16.♖d4 g6 17.♖fd1 ♗h6+ 18.♔b1 ♗e6, Dilans, P.

– Melts, M., USA 1998; 10.♘xe4?! ♕xe4+ 11.♗e2 ♕xe5 12.0-0 ♗f5∓ or 11.♕e2 ♕xc2∓) 10...♘xd2 11.♕xd2 ♕xb2? 12.♖b1 ♕a3 13.♘b5!+–; 11.♗f5=;

B2) 9.♕d2

B2a) 9...♘d5 10.♘xd5 ♕xd2+ 11.♔xd2 cxd5 12.c4 ♗e6 (12...dxc4 13.♗xc4 e6 14.♗b5+ ♗d7 15.♗xd7+ ♔xd7 16.♖hd1 ♗c5±, Moldovan, D. (2450) – Burnoiu, N. (2415), Bucharest 2006) 13.cxd5 ♗xd5 14.♗b5+ ♔d8 (14...♗c6 15.♗xc6+ bxc6 16.♖ac1 0-0-0+ 17.♔e2 ♔b7 18.♖c4 e6 19.♖hc1 ♖c8 20.♖1c3≈) 15.♖hd1 e6 16.♖ac1 ♗xg2 17.♔e3+ ♗d5 18.♗g5+ ♗e7 19.♗xe7+ ♔xe7 20.♖c7+ ♔f8 21.♗e2≈;

B2b) 9...♘e4 10.♘xe4 ♕xe4+ 11.♗e2 ♕xg2 12.0-0-0 ♗e6 13.♕b4?! ♕xf2 14.♕xb7 ♕xf4+ 15.♔b1 ♖c8 16.♗b5 f5∓, Gharamian, T. (2471) – Pytel, K. (2396), France 2007; 13.♗c4 ♕h3 14.♗xe6 ♕xe6 15.h4 h5 16.♕b4≈ or 11.♗e3 (11.♕e3 ♕xc2∓) 11...♗e6 (11...♕xe5 12.0-0-0 ♗f5 13.♗c4 ♕c7 14.♖he1≈) 12.0-0-0 ♕a4 13.a3 h5! 14.♗d3 g6 15.f4 ♗g7∞.

Let's return to Anand – Tiviakov.

8.♘×d5

Also worth conderation are 8.♗g3, 8.♘×d7 and 8.♕f3:

A) 8.♗g3 ♘×e5 9.♗×e5 ♘×c3 10.b×c3 ♕a3 11.♕f3?! (11.♕d2!? ♕b2 12.♖d1 ♗e6 13.♗e2) 11...♗g4 (11...♕b2 12.♖d1 ♗e6 13.♗e2 f6 14.♗f4 ♗d5∓) 12.♕e3 ♕b2 13.♖c1 ♕×a2 (Skripchenko, A. (2461) – Marcelin, C. (2441), France 2006) 14.♗d3 f6 15.♗g3 ♕e6 ∓;

B) 8.♕f3 (8.♘×d7 ♕×d7 9.♗e5 ♘×c3 10.b×c3 ♕d5 11.f3 ♗f5 12.♗d3 ♗×d3 13.♕×d3 f6 14.♗g3 (Sedlak, N. (2543) – Benkovic, P. (2463), Subotica 2003) 14...0-0-0 15.0-0 h5⇄; 8...♗×f4!?) 8...♘×f4 9.♕×f4 f6 (9...♘×e5?! 10.d×e5 ♕c5 11.♗c4, Larrea, M. (2315) – Muniz, R. (2195), Montevideo 2007) 10.♘d3 ♕×f4 11.♘×f4 ♘b6⇄, Pedersen, J. (2215) – Lindestrom, T. (2225), Esbjerg 2007.

8...♕×d5

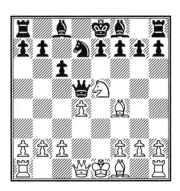

8...♘×e5 9.♘e3 (9.d×e5!? ♕×d5 10.♕×d5 c×d5 11.c4 d×c4 12.♗×c4) 9...♘d3+ 10.♕×d3 ♕×f4 11.d5 c×d5?! 12.♕×d5 e6 13.♗b5+ ♔e7 14.♕d2±, Gashimov, V. (2664) – Tiviakov, S. (2643), Reggio Emilia 2008; 11...♕b4+

12.c3 ♕×b2 13.♖b1 ♕×a2 14.♗e2∞; 11...e6!? ⇄; 11...e5!? ⇄.

9.♗e2

White has other possibilities here:

A) 9.♕d3 ♘×e5 (9...g5!? 10.♗g3 ♘×e5 11.♗×e5 f6 12.♗g3 ♗f5 or 11.d×e5 ♗e6=) 10.d×e5 ♕a5+ 11.c3 ♗e6 12.♗e2 g6 13.0-0 ♗g7 14.b4 ♕c7 15.♕e3 0-0 16.♗g3 (Kryvoruchko, Y. (2610) – Ivanov, O. (2475), Alushta 2008) 16...♕b6 17.♕×b6 a×b6 18.a4 ♖fd8∓;

B) 9.♘c4 ♕e4+ (9...♘f6 10.♘e3 ♕a5+ 11.c3 ♗e6 12.♗e2 g6 13.0-0 ♗g7 14.b4 ♕d8 15.c4 0-0 16.♗f3 (Hautot, S. (2335) – Pytel, K. (2410), Liege 2008) 16...♘d5 17.♘×d5 c×d5=; 12.♗d3 g6 13.0-0 ♗g7 14.♗e5±) 10.♗e3 ♘b6 11.♘d2 ♕g6 12.c4 ♗f5 13.♘f3 (Stevic, H. (2495) – Mrdja, M. (2395), Zagreb 2007) 13...e6⇄;

C) 9.♕f3 ♘×e5 10.♕×d5 c×d5 11.d×e5 ♗d7 12.0-0-0 e6 13.♗e3 ♗e7 14.f4 a6=, Velimirovic, D. (2452) – Sedlak, N. (2519), Zlatibor 2006; 9.♕d3 ♘×e5 10.d×e5±, Howell, D. (2515) – Tiviakov, S. (2645), Ottawa 2007; 9...g5!? 10.♗g3 ♘×e5 11.d×e5 ½-½, Inarkiev, E. (2625) – Dreev, A. (2665), Ermioni 2006; 9.f3 ♘×e5 10.♗×e5 (10.d×e5!?) 10...♗f5 11.c3 f6 12.♗g3 h5 13.♕b3 ♕×b3 14.a×b3 h4 15.♗f2 a6 16.♗c4 e6±, Ponkratov, P. (2465) – Lysyj, I. (2575), Saint Petersburg 2007;

D) 9.♘f3 ♘f6 (9...♘b6!? 10.♗e2 ♗f5 11.0-0?! ♕e4 12.♗g3 ♕×c2 13.♕×c2 ♗×c2, Airapetian, G. (2335) – Zablotsky, S. (2500), Voronezh 2007) 10.♗e2 and now:

D1) 10...♗g4 11.0-0 e6 12.c4 (12.h3!? ♗xf3 13.♗xf3 ♕d7 14.c4 with better chances for White, Ni Hua (2641) – Tiviakov, S. (2643), Reggio Emilia 2008) 12...♕d8 (12...♕e4?! 13.♗e3 0-0-0?! 14.♘e5± ; 13...♗e7 14.♕b3 0-0-0 15.♗d3+– or 14...c5 15.♗d3 ♕c6 16.♘e5±) 13.♕b3 ♕b6 14.♕xb6 axb6± , Garcia Garcia, R. (2285) – Vigil Alvarez, L. (2320), Leon 2006;

D2) 10...♗f5 11.c3 (11.0-0?! ♕e4; 11.♗e3 e6 12.0-0 (David, A. (2555) – Dutreeuw, M. (2390), Belgium 2008) 12...♘g4⇄) 11...e6 12.0-0 ♗e7 13.♘e5 (Lengyel, B. (2320) – Bednay, B. (2290), Budapest 2007) 13...♕e4 14.♗g3 ♕c2=.

Returning to Anand – Tiviakov.

9...♘xe5 10.♗xe5

10.dxe5 ♕xg2 (10...♕xd1+ 11.♖xd1 ♗f5 12.♔d2 ♖d8+?! 13.♔c3 e6 14.♗e3± ; 12...g6 13.♔c3 ♗g7 14.♔b3±) 11.♗f3 ♕h3 (11...♕g6?! 12.♕d2 ♗f5 13.0-0-0) 12.♕e2 (12.♖g1 ♗f5 13.♖g3 ♕h4 14.♕d4 ♖d8 15.♕b4 ♖d7∓) 12...g6 13.0-0-0 ♗h6 14.♗xh6 ♕xh6+ 15.♔b1 (Llaneza Vega, M. (2425) – Calzetta, M. (2285), Pamplona 2007) 15...♗e6 16.♗g4 ♕f4∓ .

10...♕xg2 11.♗f3 ♕g6 (11...♕g5!?) **12.d5**

12.♕e2 ♗e6 (12...♕e6!?; 12...♗f5 13.0-0-0 0-0-0?! 14.d5; 12...h5 13.h3 f6 (Szabo, K. (2505) – Kernazhitsky, L. (2335), Zalakarosi 2008) 14.♗f4∞ ; 13.0-0-0!? f6 14.♗c7) 13.d5 (13.0-0-0?! f6; 13.♗e4∞) 13...cxd5 14.0-0-0 (14.♕b5+ ♕c6 15.♕xd5 ♕xd5 16.♗xd5 f6 with better chances for Black) 14...f6 15.♗xd5 (15.♖xd5?! fxe5 16.♖hd1 ♕f6 17.♖d8+ ♔f7 18.♗d5+ e6∓ , Ivanets, S. (2205) – Smirnov, I. (2420), Ilichevsk 2007) 15...♕xe5 16.♕c4 e6∞ ; 16.♕b5+!? ♗d7 17.♕b3.

12...♗g4!

13.dxc6 (13.♗xg4? ♕e4+ 14.♔d2 ♕xe5 15.dxc6 bxc6 16.♔c1 ♕f4+ 17.♔b1 ♖d8∓) **13...bxc6 14.♕e2** (14.♖g1? ♗xf3–+) **14...♗xf3 15.♕xf3 ♖d8** (15...♕xc2 16.0-0 ♕g6+ 17.♔h1 ♖d8 18.♖ac1∞) **16.♖d1 ♕e6?!** (16...♕xc2 17.♖xd8+ ♔xd8 18.♗c3 ♕a4 19.0-0 f6 20.♖d1+ ♔e8 21.b3 ♕b5 22.♕e4 ♔f7 23.♖d7 h5 24.♗d2 a5 25.h4∞ or 16...♖xd1+ 17.♔xd1 ♕e6 18.♖e1 ♕d5+ 19.♕xd5 cxd5 20.♖e3 f6 21.♗d4 a5 22.♖b3 e5 23.♗c5 ♔f7 24.♖b7+ ♔g6 25.♖b8 ♔f7 26.a4∞ ;

16...h5! 17.♖×d8+ ♔×d8 18.♔d2 ♕g5+19.♗f4 ♕d5+ 20.♔e2 ♕×f3+ 21.♔×f3 g6 22.♖d1+ ♔c8 23.♖d3 ♗g7 24.♖b3 a5∓; 20...♕c4+!?; 18...♕e6!? 19.♗d4 ♖h6) **17.0-0 ♖×d1 18.♖×d1 h5 19.♕d3 ♕c8** (19...f6? 20.♕g6+ ♕f7 21.♖d8+ ♔×d8 22.♕×f7 +–) **20.h4! ♖h6 21.♔h2 ♖g6 22.♗g3 ♖g4** (with the idea ♖g4-b4-b7-d7; 22...e6!?) **23.a3 a6** (23...g6 24.f3 ♖a4 25.♕c3 ♕e6 26.♖e1 ♕d5∞; 24.b3 ♗g7 25.c3 g5 26.f3 g×h4 27.f×g4 h×g3+ 28.♔×g3 h×g4∓ but 26.♕h7! ♔f8 27.♕×h5 g×h4 28.♕×g4! or 27...♗e5 28.h×g5 ♗×g3+ 29.f×g3 ♔g8 30.c4±) **24.♖e1 c5 25.c3 ♖g6 26.♖e5 e6 27.♖×h5 ♖h6 28.♖×h6 g×h6 29.♕f3 c4 30.♗f4 ♕c5 31.♕a8+ ♔e7 32.♔g1 ♕f5! 33.♗g3** (33.♗d6+!? ♔×d6 34.♕×f8+ ♔d7 35.♕×h6 ♕b1+ 36.♔g2 ♕×b2 37.♕f6 ♕×a3 38.h5 or 37.♕g7 ♕×a3 38.h5 ♔e8 39.h6 ♕f8 40.♕g5 f5=, Tiviakov,S.; 34...♔e5 35.♕×h6 ♕g4+ 36.♔h2 ♔f5= or 35.♕c5+ ♔f6 36.♕×c4 ♕b1+ 37.♔g2 ♕×b2=) **33...♕b1+ 34.♔h2 ♕×b2 35.♕×a6 ♔f6** (35...♕×c3? 36.♕d6+ ♔e8 37.♕b8++ –) **36.♕×c4 ♕×a3 37.♕d4+ ♔e7 38.c4 ♔e8 39.♕b6 ♕c5 40.♕×c5 ♗×c5 41.h5 ♗d4 42.♔g2 ♔d7 43.♗f4 ♗g7 44.♗e3 ♔d6 45.♔f1 e5 46.♔e2 f5 47.f3 ♔c6 48.♔d3 ♗f8 49.♗c1 ♗g7 50.♗a3 ♗f6 ½-½**

Summary: As we saw in Game 16, after 1.e4 d5 2.e×d5 ♕×d5 3.♘c3 ♕d6 4.d4 ♘f6 5.♘f3 c6 6.♘e5 ♗f5, White has many alternatives, some of them rather aggressive and leading to critical and unclear situations difficult to evaluate. But, after 6.♘e5, Black has two other continuations, both safe enough and usually leading to positional play.

The first of these is 6...♘bd7, with the goal of removing White's knight from the active square e5. The usual continuations after 6...♘bd7 are:

A) 7.♗f4 ♘d5 (another interesting possibility is 7...♘×e5) 8.♘×d5 ♕×d5, which practice and analysis shows is not dangerous for Black;

B) 7.♘c4 ♕c7, which experience in the 3...♕a5 variation shows is not dangerous for Black either;

C) 7.f4 ♘b6 8.g4 h5 9.g5 ♘fd7, which analysis shows is also not dangerous for Black.

The second continuation is 6...♗e6. An important consideration here is that the bishop cannot be attacked by ♘f3-g5 because this knight is already on e5. But e6, blocking the e7-pawn, seems an unusual post for the bishop, and one might wonder how to develop the ♗f8. The answer is that after 6...♗e6 Black plans to develop his kingside by g7-g6, ♗f8-g7 and then 0-0. This is not a new idea; one finds the same idea in other well-known openings; for example, the Caro-Kann Defense: 1.e4 c6 2.d4 d5 3.♘c3 d×e4 4.♘×e4 ♘d7 5.♘f3 ♘gf6 6.♘×f6 ♘×f6 7.♘e5 ♗e6. This move appears to have originated with Yuri Razuvaev in 1971.

Game 18
Landa, K. (2640) – Bauer, C. (2610)
Nancy 2008

1.e4 d5 2.e×d5 ♕×d5 3.♘c3 ♕d6 4.d4 ♘f6 5.♘f3 a6 6.g3

6...♗g4

For 6...e6 7.♗g2 ♘c6 see 6...♘c6 7.♗g2 e6. We also examine **A)** 6...g6; **B)** 6...♘c6, **C)** 6...♗f5 and **D)** 6...b5.

A) 6...g6 7.♗g2 (7.♗f4 ♛d8 8.♘e5 ♗g7 9.♗g2 0-0 10.0-0 c6 11.♛d2 ♗e6 12.♖fe1 (Sakaev, K. (2660) – Kurajica, B. (2550), Istanbul 2003) 12...♘bd7 13.♗h6 ♘xe5 14.♗xg7?! ♘c4; 14.dxe5 ♘g4 15.♛xd8 ♖fxd8 16.♗xg7 ♔xg7 17.h3 ♘h6 18.♖ad1 ♘f5≠) 7...♗g7 8.0-0 0-0

A1) 9.♖e1 ♘c6 10.♗f4 ♛b4 (10...♛d8?! 11.d5 ♘b4 12.♘e5 e6 13.dxe6 ♗xe6 14.♗xb7 ♖b8 15.♗f3±, Nevednichy, V. (2505) – Kurajica, B. (2536), Ljubljana 1999) 11.♗xc7 ♗g4 12.d5 (12.♖b1 ♖ac8 13.♗f4 ♖fd8∞; 13.a3 ♗xf3 14.♛xf3 ♛xd4 15.♗f4 ♖fd8±) 12...♖ac8 13.dxc6 (13.♗f4 ♖fd8 14.h3 ♗xf3 15.♛xf3 ♘d4∞) 13...♖xc7 14.♛d4 (14.cxb7 ♖xb7∞) 14...♛xd4 15.♘xd4 bxc6 16.♘xc6 e6 17.♘b4 a5 18.♘c6 ♖fc8 19.♘xa5 ♘e8∞;

A2) 9.♗f4 ♛d8 10.♛d2

A2a) 10...♖e8 11.♖fe1 c6 12.a4 (12.♖ad1!?) 12...a5 13.♖ad1 ♗g4

(13...♘a6!?) 14.h3 ♗xf3 15.♗xf3 e6 16.♗g5 ♘bd7±, Arakhamia Grant, K. (2426) – Tiviakov, S. (2700) Birmingham 2005;

A2b) 10...♘bd7 11.♗h6 ♘b6 12.♗xg7 ♔xg7 13.♖fe1 c6 14.♘e4 ♘c4 15.♛c3 ♘d6!? 16.♘xd6 ♛xd6 or 15.♛b4 ♘xe4!? 16.♛xc4 ♗f5; 15.♛e2 (Vouldis, A. (2528) – Kurajica, B. (2557), Plovdiv 2003) 15...♘xb2 16.♘c5 (16.c3 ♘a4∓) 16...b6 17.♘b3 ♗g4 18.c4±;

B) 6...♘c6

We examine 7.♗f4 and 7.♗g2.

B1) 7.♗f4

B1a) 7...♛b4 8.a3 (8.♗xc7?! ♛xb2 9.♘a4 ♛a3 10.♘b6 ♛c3+ 11.♘d2 ♗g4∓) 8...♛b6 9.d5 ♘g4 10.♛d2 e5 11.dxc6 exf4 12.0-0-0 ♗d6 (Kasparov, S. (2485) – Ramon Perez, J. (2310), Balaguer 2008) 13.♛e2+ ♔f8 (13...♗e6 14.♘d4±) 14.♖xd6 cxd6 15.♘d5 ♛d8 16.c7±;

B1b) 7...♛d8 8.♗g2 (8.d5 ♘b4 9.♗c4 b5⇄) 8...e6 9.0-0 ♗e7 10.♛e2 0-0 11.♖ad1 ♘d5 12.♗c1 b5 13.♘e4 (13.♘e5!?) 13...♗b7 14.c3 ♛d7 15.♖fe1 (Spasov, V. (2585) – Kurajica,

B. (2545), La Laguna 2007) 15...♖ad8 16.♘c5 ♗×c5 17.d×c5 ♛e7 18.c4 b×c4 19.♛×c4 h6⇄ or 10.♛d2 0-0 11.♖fe1 ♘d5 (11...♘b4!?) 12.♗g5 ♗×g5 13.♘×g5 ♘×c3 (13...h6!? 14.♘ge4 ♘b6) 14.b×c3 h6 15.♘f3 ♖b8 16.c4 b5 17.♖ab1 (Kundin, A. (2417) – Gofshtein, L. (2523), Tel Aviv 2001) 17...♛d6 18.c3 ♖d8±;

B2) 7.♗g2

For 7...♗g4 see 6...♗g4 7.♗g2 ♘c6. After 7...b5? 8.♘e5, White is clearly better; for example, 8...♘×d4 9.♗f4 ♖a7 10.♘×f7 ♛e6+ 11.♗e3±; 8...♗b7 9.0-0 b4 (9...e6 10.♗f4±; 9...♖d8 10.♛e1 e6 11.♗f4±) 10.♘a4 ♘a5 (10...♖a7 11.♘×c6 ♗×c6 12.♗f4±) 11.♗×b7 ♘×b7 12.♗f4 ♛d8 (12...♛d5 13.c4 b×c3 14.♘×c3±) 13.c4 e6 14.♛f3±. After 7...g6?! 8.0-0 I do not like Black's position in many variations with ♗c1-f4 and d4-d5; for example, 8...♗g7 9.♗f4 ♛d8 10.d5 or 9...♛b4 10.d5; 8...♗f5 9.♗f4 ♛b4 10.d5 or 9...♛d8 10.d5. Let's look at 7...e6 and 7...♗f5.

B2a) 7...e6 8.0-0 (8.♗f4 ♛d8 – 6...♘c6 7.♗f4 ♛d8 8.♗g2 e6) 8...♗e7 9.b3 (9.♗f4 ♛d8 – 6...♘c6 7.♗f4 ♛d8 8.♗g2 e6 9.0-0 ♗e7) 9...0-0 10.♗b2

(10.♗f4!?) 10...♖b8 (10...h6!? 11.♛e2 ♖d8) 11.♘e2 b5 12.♘f4 (Glek, I. (2600) – Bronstein, D. (2435), Belgium 1995) 12...♘d5 13.♘d3 a5 14.♖e1 a4 15.♘c5 ♖d8±;

B2b) 7...♗f5 8.0-0 (8.♗f4 ♛b4 9.0-0 0-0-0 – 8.0-0 0-0-0 9.♗f4 ♛b4)

B2b1) 8...e6?! 9.♗f4 ♛d7 10.♘e5 ♘×e5 11.d×e5 ♛×d1 12.♖a×d1 ♘d5 13.♘×d5 e×d5 14.c4±; 9...♛d8 10.♘e5 ♘d5 11.♘×d5 e×d5 12.♖e1 ♗e7 13.♛h5 ♗g6 14.♘×g6 f×g6 15.♛×d5±, Tologontegin, S. (2270) – Arias, R. (2185), Turin 2006; 9...♛b4 10.d5 (10.♗×c7 ♖c8 11.♗f4 ♛×b2 12.♘a4 ♛b4 13.c3 ♛a5±, Zvara, P. (2395) – Gross, G. (2300), Prague 2008) 10...e×d5 (10...0-0-0!?) 11.♘×d5 ♘×d5 12.♛×d5 ♗e6 13.♖ae1 ♗e7 14.♖×e6 f×e6 15.♛×e6 ♖f8 16.♗×c7 ♛×b2 17.♘e5 ♘×e5 18.♗×e5±, Neubauer, M. (2468) – Dutreeuw, M. (2361), Gothenburg 2005;

B2b2) 8...0-0-0 9.d5 (9.♗f4 ♛b4⇄) 9...♘×d5 (9...♘b4? 10.♗f4 ♛c5 11.♘e5 ♗g6 12.♗e3 ♛d6 13.♘c4 ♛d7 14.♛d4 ♛g4 15.♛c5 e6 16.d6 ♗×d6 17.♘×d6+ ♖×d6 18.h3 1-0, Rohonyan, K. (2315) – Braunlich, T. (2175), Stillwater 2007) 10.♘×d5 ♛×d5 11.♛×d5 ♖×d5 12.♘g5 (12.♘h4 ♗e6 13.♗×d5 ♗×d5±, Colovic, A. (2418) – Almeida, O. (2452), Havana 2005) 12...♖d7 (12...♖c5!? 13.♘×f7 ♖g8 14.c3 h6) 13.♘×f7 ♖g8 14.♗e3 (14.♗f4?! ♘d4) 14...e6 15.♗×c6 ♖×f7±;

C) 6...♗f5 7.♗f4 (7.♗g2 ♘c6 – 6...♘c6 7.♗g2 ♗f5; 7...c6 8.0-0 e6 9.♗f4 ♛d8 10.♛e2 ♗e7 11.♖ad1 0-0 12.♘e5 h6±, Laznicka, V. (2446) – Jirovsky, P. (2400), Czechia 2004; 10...♗d6!?)

7...♕b6 8.♕d2 ♘c6 9.0-0-0 0-0-0 10.♗d3 ♗xd3 11.♕xd3 e6 12.a3 ♗e7= or 8...♕xb2 9.♖b1 ♕xc2 10.♕xc2 ♗xc2 11.♖xb7∞;

D) 6...b5?! (this move was very popular for a while) 7.♗g2 ♗b7 8.0-0

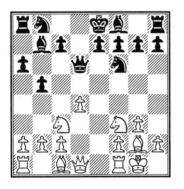

Black has the following possibilities: 8...c5, 8...b4, 8...♘bd7 and 8...e6.

D1) 8...b4 (8...c5 9.♗f4 ♕b6 10.♖e1 ♘bd7 11.d5 h6 12.a4 b4 13.♘d2 ♕a7 14.♘c4±, Tringov, G. (2420) – Donchev, D. (2520), Bankia 1991) 9.♗f4 ♕d8 (9...♕b6 10.♘a4 ♕a5 11.♘c5 ♗d5 12.a3±) 10.♘a4 ♘bd7 11.♘e5 ♗xg2 12.♔xg2 ♘xe5 13.dxe5 ♘d5 14.♕f3 e6 15.♖fd1± or 10...e6 11.c4 ♗e7 12.♘e5 ♗xg2 13.♔xg2 0-0 14.♕f3 c6 15.♖ad1±;

D2) 8...♘bd7 9.♗f4 ♕b6 10.d5

D2a) 10...c6 (10...g6 11.♘d4 ♗g7 12.♘c6±) 11.♘e5 ♘xe5 12.♗xe5 ♘xd5 13.♗xd5 cxd5 14.♘xd5 ♗xd5 15.♕xd5 ♖d8 (Visser, Y. (2451) – Konikovski, J. (2179), Ruhrgebiet 2003) 16.♕e4 with better chances for White; 10...c5 11.♘d2 h6 (11...g6 12.♖e1 ♘h5 13.♗g5 h6 14.♗xe7 ♗xe7

15.d6 ♕xd6 16.♗xb7 ♖a7 17.♘d5±) 12.h4 0-0-0 13.♖e1±;

D2b) 10...b4 11.♘a4 ♕a5 12.c4 bxc3 13.♘xc3 ♘xd5 14.♘xd5 ♕xd5 15.♕xd5 ♗xd5 16.♗xc7 ♖c8 17.♖ac1 e6 18.♘d4 ♗xg2 (18...♗c5 19.♗d6±) 19.♔xg2 ♗e7 (19...♗c5 20.♗d6±) 20.♖fd1 ♗f6 21.b3± or 16...e6 17.♖fd1 ♖c8 18.♖xd5 ♖xc7 19.♖a5 ♘b8 (Leary, P. (1845) – Shepley, J. (2114), Telford 2005) 20.♗f1 with better chances for White;

D3) 8...e6 9.♘e5!

D3a) 9...♕b6 10.d5 ♗c5 (10...b4 11.♗e3 ♕d6 12.♘xf7±; 10...♗d6 11.♗e3 ♕a5 12.♘xf7±; 10...b4 11.♗e3 ♕d6 12.♘xf7±; 10...exd5 11.♘xd5 ♘xd5 12.♗xd5±) 11.dxe6 fxe6 12.♘c4! bxc4 13.♘a4 ♕a7 14.♗xb7 ♗xf2+ 15.♖xf2 ♕xb7 16.♘c5 ♕d5 17.♕xd5 exd5 18.♗h6!±, Kurnosov, I. (2550) – Tzermiadianos, A. (2453), Warsaw 2005;

D3b) 9...♗xg2 10.♔xg2

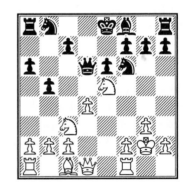

For 10...♗e7 11.♕f3 ♖a7 see 10...♖a7 11.♕f3 ♗e7. Alternatives include **D3b1)** 10...c5; **D3b2)** 10...c6; **D3b3)** 10...♘bd7; **D3b4)** 10...b4 and **D3b5)** 10...♖a7.

D3b1) 10...c5 11.♕f3 ♖a7 12.♗f4 ♕d8 13.d×c5 ♗×c5 14.♖fd1 ♕b6 15.♗g5 ♘bd7 16.♖×d7 ♖×d7 17.♗×f6± or 12...♕b6 (Langrock, H. (2402) – Kopylov, M. (2430), Hamburg 2005) 13.d×c5 ♗×c5 14.♘d3 ♘c6 (14...♗d4 15.♘e2±) 15.♘×c5 ♕d4 16.♘5a4 b×a4 17.♗e3 0-0 18.♖fd1 e5 (18...♖d7 19.♖×d4 ♖×d4 20.♖d1 e5 21.♘×a4±) 19.♗×d4 e×d4 20.♘×a4 ♕b4 21.♕c6±;

D3b2) 10...c6 11.♕f3 ♖a7 (11...b4 12.♗f4 see the line 10...b4 11.♕f3 c6 12.♗f4; 11...♕×d4 12.♗f4 ♘d5 13.♖ad1 ♕a7 14.♘×d5 c×d5 15.♖fe1 ♗b4 16.c3 ♗a5 17.♘×f7 ♕×f7 18.♕×d5+–, Godena, M. (2537) – Wong Meng Kong (2459), Turin 2006) 12.♗f4 ♘d5 13.♘e4 ♘×f4+ 14.♕×f± ♕c7 15.♖ad1 (15.♖fe1 f6 16.♘×f6+ g×f6 17.♕×f6 ♗g7 18.♕×e6+ ♔d8 19.♖ad1+– (Tzermiadianos, A.) 19...♖e8 20.♕g4 ♕d6∞) 15...f6 16.♕g4 f×e5 17.♕×e6+ ♔d8 18.d×e5+ ♘d7 19.♘g5 ♔c8 20.♘f7±;

D3b3) 10...♘bd7 11.♕f3 ♖c8 (11...♘b6 12.a4 b4 13.a5 ♘bd5 14.♘e4 ♘×e4 15.♕×f7+ ♔d8 16.♕f3±, Hossain, E. (2451) – Hossain, P. (2217), Dhaka 2003) 12.♗f4 ♕b6 (Pitl, G. (2380) – Jane Basora, J. (1885), Sants 2006) 13.♘×d7 ♘×d7 14.d5 ♗d6 15.d×e6 f×e6 16.♖ae1 0-0 17.♖×e6 ♕c5 18.♗×d6 c×d6 19.♕b7 ♘e5 20.♖e7± or 19...♖c7 20.♕×a6±;

D3b4) 10...b4 11.♕f3 c6 (11...♖a7 12.♘e4 ♕d5 13.♘×f6+ g×f6 14.♕×d5 e×d5 15.♘g4 ♘d7 16.♖e1 ♔d8 17.♗f4±, Szabo, Krl. (2475) – Paschall, W. (2374), Budapest 2006) 12.♗f4 (12.♘e4!? ♕d5 13.♖e1 ♘bd7 14.♗g5 with the initiative, Drazic, S. (2462) – Zelcic, R. (2576), Saint Vincent 2003)

12...b×c3 13.♘×f7 ♕×d4 14.♘×h8 c×b2 15.♖ad1 ♕c4 16.♗e5 ♘bd7 17.♗×b2 ♗e7 18.♘f7 ♕b5 19.♗×f6 1-0, Sax, G. (2584) – Heinzel, O. (2378), Bad Zwesten 2002;

D3b5) 10...♖a7 11.♕f3 ♗e7. This position may also be reached after 10...♗e7 11.♕f3 ♖a7 (11...b4 12.♘e4 ♕d5 – 10...b4 11.♕f3 ♖a7 12.♘e4; 11...c5 12.♗f4 ♕b6 – 10...c5 11.♕f3 ♖a7 12.♗f4; 11...c6 12.♗f4 – 10...c6 11.♕f3 ♖a7 12.♗f4) 12.♗e3 b4 (12...c5 13.♗f4 ♕b6/♕d8 14.d×c5 ♗×c5 – 10...c5 11.♕f3 ♖a7 12.♗f4 ♕b6/♕d8 13.d×c5 ♗×c5) 13.d5 ♕×e5 14.♗×a7± De Vreugt, D. (2498) – Gofshtein, L. (2580), Tel Aviv 2000.

We return now to Landa – Bauer.

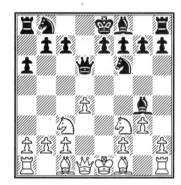

7.h3

We examine **A)** 7.♗f4 and **B)** 7.♗g2.

A) 7.♗f4 ♕b6 8.♘a4?! ♕c6; 8.♕d3 (Chernov, V. (2456) – Benkovic, P. (2431), Davos 2005) 8...♘c6 (8...♕×b2?! 9.♖b1 ♕a3 10.♘e5±) 9.♗g2 (9.0-0-0 0-0-0∓) 9...0-0-0 10.0-0-0 e6∓;

B) 7.♗g2 Let's look at the following possibilities for Black: **B1)** 7...e6; **B2)** 7...♘c6 and **B3)** 7...c6.

B1) 7...e6. After 8.♗f4, Black has 8...♕b4 (8...♕b6!?) 9.0-0 (9.♗xc7 ♕xb2 10.♘a4 ♕b5∓) 9...♘c6 – 6...♗g4 7.♗g2 e6 8.0-0 ♘c6 9.♗f4 ♕b4; 8...♕d8 9.h3 ♗xf3 10.♕xf3 (10.♗xf3 c6 – 6...♗g4 7.♗g2 c6 8.h3 ♗xf3 9.♗xf3 e6 10.♗f4 ♕d8) 10...c6 – 6...♗g4 7.♗g2 c6 8.♗f4 ♕d8 9.h3 ♗xf3 10.♕xf3 e6 or 9.0-0 ♘c6 – 6...♘c6 7.♗f4 ♕d8 8.♗g2 ♗g4 9.0-0 e6. Now **B1a)** 8.h3 and **B1b)** 8.0-0.

B1a) 8.h3 ♗h5?! (8...♗xf3) 9.g4 ♗g6 10.♘e5

B1a1) 10...c5 11.♗f4 ♕xd4 (11...♕b6 12.♘a4 ♕a5+ 13.c3 ♗e4 14.♗xe4 ♘xe4 15.♘c4 ♕d8 16.♕f3±; 12...♕a7 13.♗e3±; 13...♕b5 14.dxc5±) 12.♗xb7 ♖a7 13.♘c6±, Haslinger, S. (2465) – Littlewood, J. (2230), Liverpool 2007;

B1a2) 10...♕b6 (Chomet, P. (2405) – Bauer, C. (2490), Meribel 1998) 11.g5 (11.h4!? ♗b4 12.0-0) 11...♘fd7 12.♘c4 ♕b4 13.♕e2±; 10...♘bd7 11.♗xb7 ♖b8 12.♗c6± or 10...♘c6 11.♗f4 ♘xe5 12.dxe5 ♕xd1+ 13.♖xd1±;

B1b) 8.0-0

Now Black usually selects from: **B1b1)** 8...♗e7; **B1b2)** 8...♘bd7; and **B1b3)** 8...♘c6.

B1b1) 8...♗e7 9.h3 (9.♗f4 ♕b6 10.d5 ♕xb2 11.♕d4 ♕b4 12.♖ab1 ♕xd4 13.♘xd4 ♗c5 14.♘f3 ♖a7 15.♗xc7 ♘bd7±) 9...♗xf3 (9...♘h5? 10.g4 ♗g6 11.♘e5 ♘c6 12.♗f4) 10.♗xf3 c6 11.♘e4 ♘xe4 12.♗xe4 ♘d7 (12...g5!? 13.c3 ♘d7) 13.♗f4 ♕b4 14.♕d2 ♕xd2 15.♗xd2±, Nokes, R. (2330) – Sermek, D. (2526), Queenstown 2006;

B1b2) 8...♘bd7 9.♗f4 ♕b6 10.♕d2 (10.♕e1 ♗d6 11.♘e5 0-0 12.♘xg4 ♘xg4⇄) 10...0-0-0 11.♘g5 (11.♖fe1 ♗d6 12.♗e3 ♕a5 13.a3 h5 14.♘g5 h6⇄, Najbar, M. (2214) – Dziuba, M. (2310), Swidnica 1999) 11...♗h5 12.♕d3 ♗g6 13.♕c4 h6 14.♘ge4 ♘xe4 15.♗xe4 ♗xe4 16.♘xe4 ♘f6 17.♘xf6 gxf6⇄ or 9.h3 ♗h5 10.♗f4 ♕b6 11.♕d2 ♗e7 (11...0-0-0!? 12.a4 ♗xf3 13.♗xf3 e5) 12.♗e3 ♘d5 (12...0-0-0!? 13.♘e1 c5) 13.♘xd5 exd5 14.♘e5 (Gallagher, J. (2503) – Gouret, T. (2270), France 2002) 14...0-0-0 15.♗xd5 ♘xe5 16.dxe5 ♗c5⇄;

B1b3) 8...♘c6 9.♗f4 (9.h3 ♗xf3 10.♕xf3 ♕xd4∞ or 10.♗xf3 0-0-0⇄)

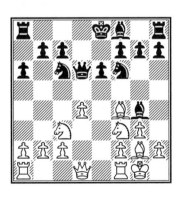

Now we examine 9...♕d7 and 9...♕b4.

B1b3a) 9...♕d7 10.h3 ♗xf3 (10...♗h5? 11.g4 ♗g6 12.♘e5) 11.♕xf3

B1b3a1) 11...♗d6 (Brandenburg, D. (2392) – Galego, L. (2528), Liverpool 2006) 12.d5 ♘xd5 13.♘xd5 exd5 14.♖fe1+ ♘e7 (14...♗e7 15.♕xd5 0-0-0 16.♕xf7±; 15...♕xd5 16.♗xd5±) 15.♕xd5 ♗xf4 16.♕xb7 0-0 17.gxf4± or 11...♖d8 12.♖ad1 ♗e7 13.d5 exd5 14.♘xd5 ♘xd5 15.♕xd5 ♕xd5 16.♗xd5 ♗d6 17.♖fe1+ ♔f8±, Varavin, V. (2515) – Vokarev, S. Ekaterinburg 1996;

B1b3a2) 11...♕xd4 12.♗xc7 ♗e7?! (12...♖c8!? 13.♖fd1 ♕c4) 13.♖fd1 ♕a7 14.♘a4 ♖c8 15.♗b6 ♕b8 16.c4 0-0 17.♖ac1±, Gerasimov, I. (2227) – Zemtsov, I. (2361), Kazan 2006 or 11...0-0-0 12.♖fd1 ♘d5? (12...♗e7!?; 12...♗d6!?) 13.♘xd5 exd5 14.c4 dxc4 15.♖ac1 ♗d6 16.♖xc4 ♔b8 17.♖dc1 ♗xf4 18.♕xf4±, Blauert, J. (2387) – Fries Nielsen, J. (2438), Germany 2002;

B1b3b) 9...♕b4

B1b3b1) 10.♗xc7 ♖c8 (10...♗e7? 11.a3 ♕xb2 12.♕d2 ♖c8 13.♖fb1±, Senff, M. (2469) – Pfleger, M. (2217), Bad Wiessee 2005) 11.♗f4 ♕xb2 12.♘a4 ♕b4 13.c4 (13.c3 ♕a5 14.h3 ♗h5 15.♕b3 b5⇄) 13...♖d8 14.♖b1 (14.a3 ♕xc4 15.♖c1 ♕a2∓) 14...♕xc4 15.♖xb7 ♘xd4 16.♕xd4 ♖xd4 17.♘xd4 ♕xd4 18.♗c6+ ♘d7∞;

B1b3b2) 10.a3

B1b3b2a) 10...♕xb2 11.♘a4 (11.♕d2!? ♗xf3 12.♗xf3 ♕b6 13.♗e3) 11...♕b5 12.c3 ♘d5 (12...0-0-0 13.♖b1 ♕d5 14.h3 ♗h5 15.♖e1⯑) 13.♖b1 ♕a5 14.♖xb7 ♘xf4 15.gxf4 ♗d6 16.♕c2⇄;

B1b3b2b) 10...♕b6 11.♘a4 ♕b5 12.c4 ♕xc4 13.♖c1 (13.♗xc7!? ♘d5

14.♖c1) 13...♕b5 14.♗xc7 ♖c8 11.d5?! 0-0-0 12.♗e3 ♕xb2 13.♖b1 ♕xc3 14.dxc6 ♕xc6 15.♕e2 e5 16.h3 ♗xf3 17.♗xf3 e4∓, Georgiadis, I. (2312) – Tzermiadianos, A. (2462), Litohoro 2006;

B2) 7...♘c6

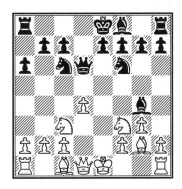

Alternatives now are **B2a)** 8.♗e3; **B2b)** 8.d5; **B2c)** 8.♗f4; **B2d)** 8.h3; and **B2e)** 8.0-0.

B2a) 8.♗e3 0-0-0 9.♕e2 (9.h3 ♗h5 see 8.h3 ♗h5 9.♗e3 0-0-0; 9.0-0 e5 10.dxe5 ♘xe5 11.♕xd6 ♗xd6 12.♘xe5 ♗xe5 13.♖fe1 ♖he8∓) 9...e5 10.dxe5 ♕b4 11.0-0 ♘xe5 12.♖ab1 ♗d6 13.♖fd1 ♕c4∓;

B2b) 8.d5 ♘e5 (8...♘b4!? 9.♗f4 ♕c5; 9...♕d7 – 8.♗f4 ♕d7 9.d5 ♘b4) 9.♗f4 ♗xf3 (9...♘xf3+ 10.♗xf3 e5 11.♗xg4 exf4 12.♕e2+ ♗e7 13.♗f3 0-0-0 14.0-0-0 ♖he8⇄, Gadacsi, M. (2099) – Czebe, A. (2489), Mindszentkalla 2002) 10.♗xf3 ♘xf3+ 11.♕xf3 e5

B2b1) 12.♗g5 ♘d7 (12...0-0-0?! 13.0-0 ♗e7 14.♕f5+ ♔b8 15.♖he1) 13.0-0-0 ♕g6 14.♗d2 f5 15.♖he1 0-0-0 16.♕e2 ♗d6⇄, Reppen, S. (2070) – Levin, F. (2500), Bygger 2006;

B2b2) 12.d×e6 (12.♕e2 ♘d7 13.0-0-0 0-0-0 14.♗e3 ♔b8 15.♔b1 ♕g6 16.a3 ♗e7 17.h4 h5∓) 12...♕×e6+ 13.♔f1 0-0-0 14.♔g2 ♗d6 (Torgersen, T. (2130) – Tolhuizen, L. (2255), Gausdal 2007) 15.♗g5 ♗e5 16.♖he1 ♖he8∓;

B2c) 8.♗f4.Now Black has **B2c1)** 8...♕e6+; **B2c2)** 8...♕b4; and **B2c3)** 8...♕d7.

B2c1) 8...♕e6+ 9.♗e3 (9.♕e2 ♕×e2+ 10.♘×e2 ♘d5 11.0-0-0 e6 12.h3 (Pasko, A. (2406) – Kovalenko, I. (2299), Dniepropetrovsk 2006) 12...♘×f4 13.♘×f4 ♗×f3 14.♗×f3 0-0-0∓; 9...0-0-0!? 10.♕×e6+ ♗×e6) 9...0-0-0 (9...♕c4?! 10.h3; 9...♘b4 10.♕e2 c6 11.a3 ♘bd5 12.♘×d5 ♘×d5∓, Sturua, Z. (2600) – Ye Rongguang (2535), Groningen 1998) 10.h3 ♗h5 11.0-0 ♕c4 12.g4 ♗g6 13.♘d2 ♕b4 14.♗×c6 b×c6 15.♕e2 (Delorme, A. (2206) – Nikolaidis, I. (2520), Cannes 2005) 15...♕b7 16.♘c4 e6⇄;

B2c2) 8...♕b4 9.0-0 (9.♗×c7 ♘d5?! 10.a3 ♘×c3 11.a×b4 ♘×d1 12.b5 with better chances for White, Kovanova, B. (2370) – Rogule, L. (2255), Plovdiv 2008; 9...♖c8!? 10.♗f4 ♕×b2; 9.h3 ♗h5 –7.h3 ♗h5 8.♗g2 ♘c6 9.♗f4 ♕b4; 9...♗×f3 10.♕×f3 0-0-0 11.0-0-0 ♘×d4 12.a3 ♕b6 13.♖×d4 ♖×d4 14.♗e3 e5∞, Kotan, L. (2289) – Ptacnikova, L. (2193), Olomouc 2006) and now:

B2c2a) 9...0-0-0 (9...e6 – 6...♗g4 7.♗g2 e6 8.0-0 ♘c6 9.♗f4 ♕b4; 9...♕×b2?! 10.♕d2)

Now let us take a look at 10.♘e2, 10.a3 and 10.d5.

B2c2a1) 10.♘e2 e6 (10...♗×f3 11.♗×f3 ♘d4 12.♘×d4 ♖×d4 13.♕e2 ♖×f4 14.g×f4 ♕×f4⇄, Doggers, P. (2192) – Gofshtein, L. (2518), Ghent 2001) 11.♗d2 (11.b3!? ♗d6 12.c3; 11.♕c1!?) 11...♕b6 12.c3 ♗e7 13.a4 a5 14.♖e1 ♗f5⇄, Mitkov, N. (2578) – Spraggett, K. (2526), Barreiro 2001 or 10...e5 11.♘×e5 ♘×d4 12.♘×g4 ♘e6 13.c3 (13.♕c1 ♘×g4 14.h3 ♘f6 15.a3 ♘×f4 16.♘×f4 ♕c4=) 13...♖×d1 (13...♕×b2?! 14.♘d4) 14.c×b4 ♖×a1 15.♖×a1 ♘×f4 16.♘×f4 ♘×g4 17.♘d3 ♘f6=;

B2c2a2) 10.a3

B2c2a2a) 10...♕×b2 11.♕d3 ♗×f3 (11...e5?! 12.♖fb1 ♕×a1 13.♖×a1 e×f4 14.g×f4; 11...♕b6?! 12.♖ab1 ♕a7 13.♘e5 ♘×e5 14.♗×e5) 12.♖fb1 (12.♖ab1 ♗×g2 13.♖×b2 ♗×f1 14.♕×f1 ♖×d4∞ or 14...♘×d4∞) 12...♕×a1 13.♖×a1 ♗×g2 14.♔×g2 ♖×d4∞;

B2c2a2b) 10...♕c4

B2c2a2b1) 11.♕e2?! (11.♕e1?! ♗×f3 12.b3 ♕e6 13.♕×e6+ f×e6 14.♗×f3 ♘d4 15.♗d1 g6∓, Koscielski, J. (2360) – Schmuecker, M. (2224), Dortmund 2005) 11...♕×e2 12.♘×e2 ♗×f3 13.♗×f3 ♘×d4 14.♘×d4 ♖×d4

15.♗e5 (Paragua, M. (2500) – Goh Koong Jong J. (2314), Ho Chi Minh City 2003) 15...♖d2 16.♖ac1 e6∓ or 15.♖ad1 ♖×d1 16.♖×d1 e6 17.g4 c6∓;

B2c2a2b2) 11.d5?! e6?! 12.d×c6! (similar to the idea in the line 10.d5 e6 11.a3 ♛×b2 12.♘a4 ♛b5 13.c4 ♛×c4 14.d×c6) 12...♖×d1 13.c×b7+ ♚b8 14.♖f×d1 ♗d6 15.♖×d6 (or 15.♗×d6 c×d6 16.♖×d6 ♛c7 17.♖ad1 ♘d5 18.♘×d5 ♛×d6 19.♘e3 ♛b6 20.♘×g4 with material advantage, Muzychuk, A. (2456) – Gara, A. (2349), Szeged 2006) 15...♗×f3 (15...c×d6 16.♗×d6+ ♚a7 17.♘e5+−) 16.♗×f3 c×d6 17.♗×d6+ ♚a7 18.♖d1 with a strong initiative, but 11...♘×d5! 12.♘×d5 ♖×d5 13.♘d2 ♗×d1 14.♘×c4 ♖c5 15.♖a×d1 ♖×c4 16.c3 e6, and Black has an extra pawn;

B2c2a2b3) 11.h3 ♖×d4 12.♛e1 ♗×f3 13.♗×f3 ♖d8 (13...♖×f4!? 14.b3? ♛×f1+; 14.g×f4 ♛×f4∞; 13...♖d7 14.♗g2?! e6 15.b3 ♛c5∓, Spasov, V. (2540) – Panbukchian, V. (2390), Bulgaria 1994; 15.b3!?) 14.b3 ♘d4 (14...♛c5!?) 15.♗×b7+ ♚×b7 16.b×c4 ♘f3+ 17.♚g2 ♘×e1+ 18.♖f×e1 e6⇄, Sanchez Romero, M. (2255) – Moreto Quintana, A. (2120), Spain 2008;

B2c2a3) 10.d5

B2c2a3a) 10...♛×b2 11.♛d3 ♘b4 12.♛c4 ♘f×d5 13.♘×d5 ♘×d5 14.♘e5 ♗e6 15.♖ab1±; 11...♛a3 12.♛e3 ♗×f3 13.♗×f3 ♘b4 14.♖ab1± or 10...e6 11.a3 ♛×b2 (11...♛b6 12.♘a4 ♛a5 13.c4 e×d5 14.b4±) 12.♘a4 ♛b5 13.c4 ♛×c4 14.d×c6 ♖×d1 15.c×b7+ ♚b8 16.♖f×d1 ♗d6 17.♖×d6 ♗×f3 18.♗×f3 ♛×a4 19.♖c6 ♘d5 20.♗×d5 e×d5 21.♖ac1 with better chances for White; for example, 21...♚b7 22.♖×c7+ ♚a8 23.♖×f7 ♛b3 24.♖g7 ♖e8 25.♖×h7 ♛×a3 26.h4±;

B2c2a3b) 10...e5 11.a3 (11.♗d2? ♘d4 12.h3 ♗×f3 13.♗×f3 ♛×b2∓, Klinova, M. (2407) – Gofshtein, L. (2513), Hoogeveen 2001 or 12.♘e2 ♗×f3 13.♗×b4 ♘e2+ 14.♚h1 ♘g3+ 15.h×g3 ♗×d1 16.♗×f8 ♖h×f8 17.♖a×d1∓, Longson, A. (2225) – Hanley, C. (2387), Edinburgh 2003; 11.♛e1?! e×f4 12.d×c6 b×c6∓) 11...♛×b2 (11...♛b6 12.♗e3) 12.♛d3 and now:

B2c2a3b1) 12...e×f4?! 13.♖fb1 ♗×a3 14.♖×b2 ♗×b2 15.♖×a6 ♚b8 16.♖×c6 b×c6 17.♘e5 ♖he8 18.♘×c6+ ♚c8 19.h3 ♖e1+ 20.♚h2 f3 21.♗×f3± or 15...b×a6 (15...♘b8 16.♖a7±) 16.♛×a6+ ♚d7 (16...♚b8 17.d×c6) 17.♛×c6+ with a winning attack;

B2c2a3b2) 12...e4 13.♛c4 (13.♘×e4!?)

B2c2a3b2a1) 13...e×f3?! 14.d×c6 b5 (14...f×g2 15.♖fb1±) 15.♖ab1 ♗e6 (15...b×c4 16.♖×b2 ♖d4 17.♖fb1 ♚d8 18.♖b8+ ♚e7 19.♖e1+ ♗e6 20.♗×f3±) 16.♗h3 b×c4 17.♗×e6+ f×e6 18.♖×b2 ♘d5 19.♖fb1 ♘b6 20.♗×c7 ♚×c7 21.♖×b6 ♖a8 22.♖b7+ ♚c6 23.♖1b6+ ♚c5 24.♖×e6±;

B2c2a3b2a2) 13...♘xd5 14.♘xd5 exf3 15.♗e5?! (15.♖ab1 fxg2 16.♖xb2 gxf1♛+ 17.♚xf1 ∞) 15...♛xe5 16.♛xg4+ ♚e6 17.♛xf3 ♘d4 18.♘e7+ ♗xe7 19.♛b7+ ♚d7 20.♖fe1 (20.♖ad1?! ♚e8∓, L'Ami, E. (2470) – Spoelman, W. (2193), Hoogeveen 2003) 20...♖b8 21.♖xe6 ♖xb7 22.♖xe7+ ♚xe7 23.♗xb7 a5∓;

B2c3) 8...♛d7

B2c3a) 9.h3 ♗xf3 (9...♗h5?! 10.g4 ♗g6 11.♘e5±, Kreiman, B. (2515) – Tare, M. Agios Nikolaos 1997) 10.♛xf3 ♛xd4 (10...0-0-0!? 11.0-0-0 e6) 11.♗xc7 ♖c8 12.♖d1 ♛c4 13.♗b6 (Vachier Lagrave, M. (2412) – Goh Koong Jong J. (2314), Chalkidiki 2003) 13...♘d7±;

B2c3b) 9.d5 ♘b4 10.♘e5 ♗xd1 11.♘xd7 ♗xc2 (11...♚xd7?! 12.♖xd1 a5 (13.a3 ♘a6 14.0-0±, Ahmed, S. (2321) – Abdul, M. (2233), Dhaka 2006 or 12...♗xc2+ 13.♚e2 a5 14.♗h3+ ♚d8 15.a3±) 12.♘f6+ exf6 13.♗c7 ♚d7 14.♗a5 ♗f5⇄;

B2d) 8.h3 ♗xf3 (8...♗h5 – 6...♗g4 7.h3 ♗h5 8.♗g2 ♘c6) 9.♛xf3 (9.♗xf3 0-0-0 10.d5 ♘b4 11.0-0 ♘bxd5 12.♘xd5 ♘xd5 13.♛e2⯳, Vasilkova, S.

(2355) – Danielian, E. (2480), Moscow 2008; 10...♛e5+! 11.♗e3 e6 12.0-0 exd5∓; 11.♚f1 e6 12.♚g2 ♘b4∓) 9...♛xd4 (for 9...0-0-0 10.♗e3 e6 11.0-0-0 – 7.h3 ♗xf3 8.♛xf3 ♘c6 9.♗e3 e6 10.0-0-0 0-0-0 11.♗g2) 10.0-0 (10.♗e3 ♛c4 11.0-0-0 e6∞, Dehaybe, A. – Vidalina, F., Internet 2003) 10...0-0-0 11.♖d1 ♛b6 12.♗e3 ♛xb2 (12...♛a5 13.♛e2⯳) 13.♘a4 ♖xd1+ (14...♚xd8?! 15.♘c5) 14.♛xd1 ♛a3 15.♗xc6 bxc6 16.♛d4 ♘d5 17.♛c4⯳;

B2e) 8.0-0. We now examine 8...e6 and 8...0-0-0.

B2e1) 8...e6 9.♘e2 (9.♖e1 0-0-0 10.♗f4 ♛d7⇄; for 9.♗f4 see 7.♗g2 e6 8.0-0 ♘c6 9.♗f4) 9...0-0-0 (9...♗e7 10.♗f4 ♛d7±, Vorisek, J. (2255) – Sleich, J. (2255), Czechia 2001) 10.c3 (10.♗f4 ♛b4 11.a3 ♛b6⇄) 10...e5 11.♖e1 (11.♛a4? e4) 11...exd4 12.♗f4 (12.♘exd4 ♘xd4 13.♛xd4 ♛xd4 14.♘xd4 ♗c5⇄) 12...♛c5 13.♘exd4 ♘xd4 14.cxd4 ♛b6∞;

B2e2) 8...0-0-0

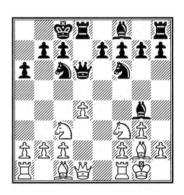

Alternatives now include **B2e2a)** 9.♗e3; **B2e2b)** 9.♘e2; **B2e2c)** 9.♗f4 and **B2e2d)** 9.d5.(9.h3 ♗xf3 10.♛xf3 ♛xd4 – 7.♗g2 ♘c6 8.h3 ♗xf3 9.♛xf3

148

♛×d4 10.0-0 0-0-0 or 10...e6 11.♗e3
– 7.♗g2 ♘c6 8.h3 ♗×f3 9.♛×f3 0-0-0
10.♗e3 e6 11.0-0; 9...♗h5 – 7.h3 ♗h5
8.♗g2 ♘c6 9.0-0 0-0-0.)

B2e2a) 9.♗e3 e5 10.d×e5 ♘×e5
11.♘×e5 ♗×d1 12.♘×f7 ♛d7 13.♘×d8
♗×c2 (13...♛×d8 14.♖a×d1 ♗d6
15.♗f4⩲, Khruschiov, A. (2415) –
Nadanian, A. (2435, Moscow 2002)
14.♘×b7 ♗b4 15.♘c5 (15.♖ac1 ♛f5∓)
15...♛f5 16.♗b7+ ♔b8 17.♘a6+
♔×b7 18.♘×b4 ♗e4 19.♘×e4 (19.f4?!
h5∓) 19...♛×e4∓ or 11.♛×d6 ♗×d6
(11...♘×f3+!?) 12.♘g5 h6 13.♘ge4
♘×e4 14.♘×e4 (Ivanov, A. (2257) –
Lysyj, I. (2470), Salekhard 2003)
14...♘f3+ 15.♗×f3 ♗×f3∓;

B2e2b) 9.♘e2 e5 10.c3 e4 (10...e×d4
11.♗f4∞) 11.♘g5 (11.♘d2 ♖e8 12.h3
♗h5 13.g4 ♗g6 14.♘c4∞) 11...♛d5
(11...♗h5?! 12.♛c2; 11...♖d7?! 12.♛c2;
11...♛e7 12.h3 ♗d7∞) 12.♖e1
(12.♘×e4!? ♘×e4 13.f3) 12...♖e8
13.♛b3 ♛a5⩱ or 9...♗×f3 10.♗×f3
♘×d4 11.♘×d4 ♛×d4 12.♛e2 e6
(12...e5 13.♗g5∞ or 13.♗e3∞)
13.♗e3 (13.♗f4?! ♗d6 14.♖fd1 ♛c5)
13...♛e5 14.♛c4 ♛b5 (14...♛f5!?
15.♗g2 ♘d5) 15.♛×b5 a×b5 16.a4 b4
17.a5∞;

B2e2c) 9.♗f4 ♛d7 (9...♛b4 – 7.♗g2
♘c6 8.♗f4 ♛b4 9.0-0 0-0-0; 10...♛f5?!
11.d×c6 ♖×d1 12.c×b7+ ♔×b7
13.♘d4+ ♔b8 14.♘×f5 ♖a1 15.♖×a1
♗×f5 16.♖d1 ♔c8 17.♗f1 ♔b7 18.♖d8
♘d7 19.♗d3±; 14.♖a×d1!?) 10.d5
♘×d5 11.♘×d5 ♛×d5 12.♛×d5 ♖×d5
13.♘g5 ♖f5 (13...♖b5 14.♘×f7 ♖g8
15.♗e4 g6 16.b3 ♗g7∞) 14.f3 14.f3
♖×f4 (14...♗h5 15.♗h3 e6 16.♗×f5
e×f5∞) 15.g×f4 (15.f×g4!?) 15...♗h5
16.♗h3+ e6 17.f5 ♗e7 18.♘e4 ♘d4

19.f×e6 f×e6∞, Michalczak, T. (2374)
– Horstmann, O. (2212), Hattingen
2005;

B2e2d) 9.d5 (after 9...♘×d5?! 10.♘×d5
♛×d5 11.♛×d5 ♖×d5 12.♘g5 Black
has a dangerous position; for example,
12...♖a5 13.♘×f7 ♖g8 (Lakos, N.
(2287) – Perez, R. (2435), Ortigueira
2002) 14.♗d2 ♖b5 15.♗c3 ♗f5
16.♖fd1 ♗c2 17.♖d2 ♗g6 18.♗h3+
♔b8 19.♗e6±). Main alternatives include:

B2e2d1) 9...♘b4 and **B2e2d2)** 9...♘e5.

B2e2d1) 9...♘b4?! 10.h3!

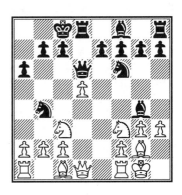

This position is dangerous for Black:

B2e2d1a) 10...♗×f3 11.♛×f3 ♘b×d5
12.♘×d5 ♛×d5 13.♛e3 ♛b5 14.c4
(14.♛a7!? ♛d5 15.♖d1) 14...♛b6
15.♛e2 e6 16.b4 ♛×b4 17.♗f4 ♛a4
18.♖ab1 ♗d6 19.♗×d6 ♖×d6
(Dimitrov, V. (2449) – Panbukchian, V.
(2312), Svilengrad 2006) 20.♗×b7+
♔d7 21.c5±;

B2e2d1b) 10...♗h5 11.♗f4 ♛c5/
11...♛b6 (11...♛d7 12.♛d4 ♗×f3
13.♛a7 ♛f5 14.♗×f3 g5 15.d6± or
14...♘×c2 15.d6±; 13...♘c6 14.d×c6

♛xc6 15.♗xf3+−; 12...♞c6 13.dxc6 ♛xd4 14.♞xd4 ♖xd4 15.cxb7+ ♚b8 16.g4 ♗g6 17.♖ad1±) 12.♗e3 and now:

B2e2d1b1) 12...♛a5 13.g4! (13.♛d4 ♞xc2 14.♛a7 ♞xe3∞)

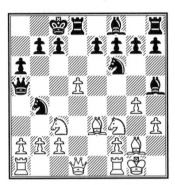

B2e2d1b1a) 13...♞bxd5 14.♞xd5 ♞xd5 15.♗d2 ♛c5 16.gxh5 ♞f4 17.♛e1 ♞xg2 18.♚xg2 ♛xh5 19.♗f4±, Shaw, J. (2445) − Vinas Guerrero, C. (2006), Caleta 2005 or 14...♖xd5 15.♗d2 ♖xd2 16.♛xd2 ♛xd2 17.♞xd2±, Kotronias, V. (2580) − Godena, M. (2480), Batumi 2002;

B2e2d1b1b) 13...♗g6 14.♞d4! (14.♛d4 ♞xc2 15.♛a7 ♞xe3∞; 14.♞e5 ♞xc2∞, Mikkelsen, N. (2290) − Reinderman, D. (2515), Gausdal 2007) 14...♞bxd5 (14...♖xd5 15.♞xd5 ♞bxd5 16.♞b3 ♛b5 17.a4 ♞xe3 18.axb5 ♞xd1 19.bxa6 bxa6 20.♖xa6+−, Wang Yu, A. (2385) − Tirto, (2425), Singapore 2006) 15.♞b3 ♛b4 16.♞xd5 ♞xd5 17.♗xd5 e6 (17...c6 18.♗d2±, Fossati, R. (2133) − McPhillips, K. (2225) Herceg Novi 2005) 18.a3 ♛b5 19.c4 ♛e8 20.♗xb7+ ♚xb7 21.♞a5+ ♚c8 22.♛f3±, Skripchenko, A. (2435) − Mamedjarova, Z. (2340), Crete 2007;

B2e2d1b2) 12...♛d6 13.♛e2! (13.♛d4 ♞xc2 14.♛a7 ♞xe3 (Sedlak, N. (2506) − Benkovic, P. (2469), Subotica 2003) 15.fxe3∞; 13.g4 ♗g6 14.♛d4 ♞xc2 15.♛a7 ♞xe3 16.fxe3 ♛b6∞, Ronchetti, N. (2402) − Pizzuto, S. (2219), Cremona 2005)

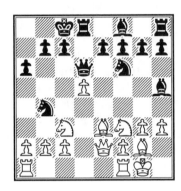

B2e2d1b2a) 13...e5 14.dxe6 ♛xe6 15.g4 ♗g6 16.♞d4 ♛e8 (16...♛e7 17.a3 ♞bd5 18.♞xd5 ♞xd5 19.♞c6 bxc6 20.♛xa6+ ♚d7 21.c4±, Zelcic, R. (2533) − Sermek, D. (2531) Sibenik 2005) 17.♖fe1 h5 18.♛f3 c6 (Fressinet, L. (2640) − Wong Meng Kong (2470), Mallorca 2004) 19.g5 ♞fd5 20.h4 ♗d6 21.a3 ♞c3 (21...♞xc2 22.♞xc2 ♗xc2 23.♞xd5 cxd5 24.♖ac1+−) 22.axb4 ♞e4 23.b5 axb5 24.♞f5 ♛e5 25.♞xd6+ ♞xd6 26.♗b6+−, Khalifman, A. or 13...♗g6 14.♖fd1 (14.♖ac1 e6!?) 14...♗xc2 (14...♞xc2 15.♗f4 ♛b6 16.♖ac1 ♛xb2 17.♞e5 ♛xc3 18.♞xg6 hxg6 19.♖xc2±) 15.♖d2 e6 16.♞g5 ♛e7 17.a3 ♗d3 18.♛f3 ♞bxd5 19.♖xd3±;

B2e2d1b2b) 13...♞bxd5 14.♞xd5 ♞xd5 15.♖ad1! (15.c4?! ♞e3 16.♛xe3 (Simon, O. (2400) − Garrel A. (2140), Condom 2006) 16...e6 with better chances for Black; 15.♖fd1 ♛e6 16.g4 ♞xe3 17.♖xd8+ ♚xd8 18.gxh5 ♞xg2∞, Ovetchkin, R. (2507) −

Hasangatin, R. (2501), Internet 2004) or 18.♘g5 ♕e5 19.♕×e3 ♕×e3 20.f×e3 ♗g6 21.♗×b7 e5 22.♗×a6 (Johansson, M. (1922) – Djoudi, A. (2274), Internet 2003) 22...h6∓)

B2e2d1b2b1) 15...♕f6 16.c4 ♘×e3 (16...♘b6 17.♖×d8+ ♔×d8 18.♖d1+ ♘d7 19.g4 ♗g6 20.♗g5 +– or 18...♔c8 19.c5 ♘d7 20.♕d3 +– ; 16...♘b4 17.♖×d8+ ♔×d8 18.♖d1+ ♔c8 19.♕d2 ♕d6 20.♕e1 ♕f6 21.g4±, Humphrey, J. (2245) – Aplin, C. (2020), Kuala Lumpur 2006) 17.♖×d8+ ♔×d8 18.♕×e3 ♗×f3 (18...♔c8 19.g4 ♗g6 20.♕a7 c6 21.♖d1 e6 22.g5 ♕e7 23.♘e5 +– ; 18...e6 19.g4 ♗g6 20.♕a7±) 19.♗×f3 ♕b6 20.♖d1+ ♔c8 21.c5 ♕b5 22.c6 +– ;

B2e2d1b2b2) 15...♕e6 (15...♕b4 16.c3 ♕a5 17.g4 ♗g6 18.♘e5 e6 19.♗g5 ♗e7 20.♘×g6 h×g6 21.♖×d5±) 16.g4 ♗g6 (16...♘×e3 17.♘g5 ♕e5 18.♖×d8+ ♔×d8 19.♕×e3 ♕×e3 20.f×e3 h6 21.♗×b7± or 20...♗g6 21.♗×b7 e5 22.♘×f7+) 17.♘g5 ♕e5 18.c4 (18.♖×d5!? ♖×d5 19.f4) 18...♘×e3 19.♗×b7+ ♔×b7 20.♖×d8 ♕×g5 21.♕f3+ c6 22.♖fd1±, Huerga Leache, M. (2315) – Navarrete Delgado, S. (2210), Mondari 2006;

B2e2d2) 9...♘e5!

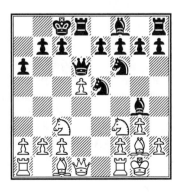

B2e2d2a) 10.♗f4 ♘×f3+ 11.♗×f3 ♗×f3 12.♕×f3 e5 13.d×e6 (13.♗g5 h6 14.♗e3 ♕d7 15.♖fd1 ♕g4 16.♕g2?! ♗b4, Mickiewicz, P. (2310) – Malaniuk, V. (2530), Krakow 2006; 16.♕g4+ ♘×g4 17.a3 f5 18.♔g2 ♘×e3+ 19.f×e3 ♗c5 20.e4 g6⇄) 13...♕×e6 14.♗g5

B2e2d2a1) 14...♗b4 15.♖fe1 ♕b6 16.♗×f6 g×f6 17.♘d5 ♖×d5 18.♕×d5 ♗×e1 19.♖×e1 ♕×b2 20.♕×f7 ♕b8 21.h4 ♕×c2 22.♕×f6 ♖g8 23.a3 ½-½, Pesotsky, V. (2335) – Bazarov, K. (2230), Lipetsk 2008; 15.♗×f6!?; 17.a3!? or 17.♖ad1!?;

B2e2d2a2) 14...h5 15.♗×f6 ♕×f6 16.♕×f6 g×f6 15.♖fe1 (17.♖ad1 ♗d6 18.♘d5 (Fernando, D. (2440) – Galego, L. (2501), Portugal 2005) 18...♖he8 19.♔g2 c6 20.♘e3 ♔c7±) 15...♕g4 16.♕×g4+ h×g4 17.♘e4 (17.♗×f6 g×f6=) 17...♘×e4 18.♖×e4 (18.♗×d8?! ♘d2 19.♗e7 ♘f3+ 20.♔f1 ♘×h2+) 18...f6 19.♗f4 f5=, Sedina, E. (2382) – Danielian, E. (2418), Elista 2004;

B2e2d2b) 10.♘×e5

B2e2d2b1) 10...♕×e5 11.f3 ♗e6 12.♖e1 (12.♗f4 ♕f5 13.♕d4 ♗×d5 14.♖ad1 e6 15.♘e4 b6∓) 12...♕f5 (12...♕h5!?) 13.f4 (13.♗f4?! ♘×d5 or 13.♕d4 ♗×d5 14.♖e5?! ♕×c2; 14.♕a7 e6 15.♗e3 ♗c6⇄) 13...♕g6 14.♕d4 (14.♖e5 ♗f5∞, Ninov, N. (2486) – Panbukchian, V. (2340), Pleven 2005) 14...♗×d5 15.♘×d5 (15.♕a7?! ♗×g2 16.♔×g2 ♘d7 17.♗e3 ♕c6+) 15...♘×d5 16.♗×d5 e6 17.♗×e6+ ♕×e6 18.♕×d8+ ♔×d8 19.♖×e6 f×e6 20.♗e3±

B2e2d2b2) 10...♗×d1 11.♘×f7

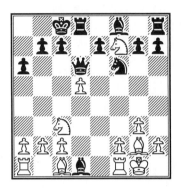

11...♕d7 (11...♗×c2 12.♘×d6+ e×d6 13.♖e1 ♖e8 (Ragger, M. (2365) – Nikolov, S. (2392), Kranj 2004) 14.♖×e8+ ♘×e8 15.♗d2 ♘f6 16.♖e1 with better chances for White)

B2e2d2b2a) 12.♘×d8 ♗g4 13.♘f7 ♖g8 14.♖e1 ♗h3 15.♗×h3?! (15.♘e5 ♕f5 ⇄) 15...♕×h3 16.♘g5 (Dimitrov, V. (2440) – Panbukchian, V. (2281), Pleven 2006) 16...♕h5 (16...♕f5!?) 17.♔g2 (17.♗f4?! h6 18.♘e6 g5 19.♗×c7 ♘g4∓) 17...h6 18.♘f3 g5∓;

B2e2d2b2b) 12.♖×d1 e5 13.♘×d8 ♕×d8 14.♗h3+ ♔b8 ⇄ or 14.♗e3 ♕d7 ⇄; 13.d×e6 ♕×d1+ 14.♘×d1 ♖×d1+ 15.♗f1 ♖g8 16.♘e5 ♗d6 17.♘c4 ♔b8∓ or 13.♘×h8 ♗c5 14.♖d3 ♖×h8 15.♗e3 ♗×e3 16.♖×e3 ♕f5 ⇄;

B3) 7...c6.

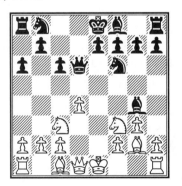

With this unusual move (why play c7-c6 after a7-a6?) Black pursues two goals: strong central control (the d5-square) and restriction of the light-squared ♗g2.

White's main alternatives are **B3a)** 8.h3; **B3b)** 8.0-0 and **B3c)** 8.♗f4.

B3a) 8.h3 ♗×f3 (8...♗h5!?) 9.♗×f3 e6 10.♗f4 ♕d8 11.♕d3 ♗b4 12.♗d2 (12.0-0-0 ♗×c3?! 13.♕×c3 ♘d5 14.♕b3; 12.0-0!?) 12...♘bd7 13.0-0-0 (13.0-0!?) 13...♕c7 14.♔b1 0-0 15.g4±, Ivanov, A. (2455) – Milanovic, D. (2515), Bucharest 2007 or 11...♗d6 12.0-0-0 ♗×f4+ (12...♕c7 13.♗×d6 ♕×d6±, Haslinger, S. (2423) – Parker, J. (2509), Swansea 2006; 13.♗d2!?) 13.g×f4 ♕d6 14.f5 (14.♕e3 0-0 15.♖hg1 ♘bd7±) 14...♕f4+ 15.♔b1 ♕×f5 16.♖×f5 e×f5 17.♖he1+ ♔f8 18.d5 g6 19.a4 ♖a7∞;

B3b) 8.0-0 e6

B3b1) 9.h3 (9.♖e1 ♗e7 10.♗f4 ♕d8 11.h3 ♗×f3 12.♗×f3 0-0 13.♕d2 ♘bd7 14.♖ad1 ♖c8 15.a3 ♘d5 ⇄, Mason, D. (2266) – Jones, G. (2416), Swansea 2006) 9...♗×f3 10.♗×f3 ♕c7 11.♘e2 ♘bd7 12.c4 ♗d6 13.♗e3 0-0 14.♗g2 ♖ad8 15.♕c2 ♖fe8 16.♖fd1 ♘f8 17.♖ac1 ♘g6±, Hou Yifan (2505) – Berg, E. (2585), Wijk aan Zee 2007;

B3b2) 9.♘a4 (9.♘e2 ♗×f3 10.♗×f3 ♕c7 11.c4 ♗e7 12.b3 0-0 13.♗b2 ♖d8 14.♕c2 ♘bd7 15.♗g2 ♘f8 16.♘f4 ♘g6±, Szabo, G. (2495) – Benkovic, P. (2430), Bucharest 2007) 9...♕d8 (9...♘bd7!? 10.c4 0-0-0 11.c5 ♕d5 or 10.♗f4 ♕b4 11.c3 ♕b5) 10.c4 ♘bd7 11.h3 (11.♕b3!? b5 12.♘c3) 11...♗×f3 (11...♗f5!?) 12.♕×f3 (12.♗×f3!? ♘b6

13.a4) 12...♗d6 13.b4 (13.♛b3!? ♖b8 14.♘c3) 13...0-0 14.♖b1 (Bologan, V. (2665) – Saric, I. (2545), Neum 2008) 14...e5±;

B3b3) 9.a4 a5 10.h3 ♗xf3 11.♛xf3 ♗e7 (11...♛xd4!? 12.♘b5 ♛d8 13.♖d1 ♘bd7⇄) 12.♗f4 ♛d8 13.♖ad1 0-0 14.♘e4 ♘xe4 15.♛xe4 ♘d7 16.c4±, Shabalov, A. (2605) – Gonzalez, R. (2440), Philadelphia 2004;

B3c) 8.♗f4

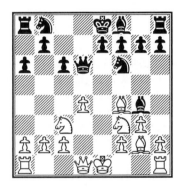

B3c1) 8...♛b4?! 9.0-0 ♛xb2 10.♛d3; 9...e6 (Brzeski, M. (2355) – Sergeev, V. (2485), Poland 2007) 10.a3 ♛a5 (10...♛b6 11.♘a4 ♛a5 12.c4 ♘bd7 13.♖e1 0-0-0 14.d5±) 11.h3 ♗h5 (11...♗f5 12.♘e5) 12.g4 ♗g6 13.♘e5 ♘bd7 14.♘c4 ♛d8 15.♖e1±;

B3c2) 8...♛d8 (8...♛e6+!? 9.♘e2 ♘bd7 or 9.♗e3 ♘bd7) 9.h3 ♗xf3 10.♛xf3 (10.♗xf3!?)

B3c2a) 10...e6 11.0-0-0 ♗e7 12.g4 ♘bd7 13.♔b1 ♘d5 (13...♘b6!? 14.♛d3 ♗d6) 14.♘xd5 (14.♗c1 b5⇄, Tiviakov, S.) 14...cxd5 15.c4 ♘b6 16.c5 ♘c4 17.♗f1 (17.b3!? ♘a5 18.h4 ♘c6 19.g5; 17...♗xh4 18.♛e3 ♗e7 19.g5 ♘c6 20.g6± or 19...g6 20.♛e5±)

17...♘a5 18.♛g3 ♗h4 19.♛e3 h6 20.♗e5 ♗f6 21.♗xf6 ♛xf6 22.f4 ♘c6 23.g5 ♛e7 24.h4 g6 25.♖h3 0-0-0 26.♗e2 hxg5 27.fxg5 e5 ½-½, Svidler, P. (2743) – Tiviakov, S. (2669), Turin 2006.

B3c2b) 10...♛xd4 11.0-0 (11.♗e3!? ♛d8 12.0-0 ♘bd7 13.♖ad1 e6 14.♘e4 ♘xe4 15.♛xe4∞, Tiviakov S.) 11...e6 (11...♘bd7!? 12.♖fd1 ♛b6)

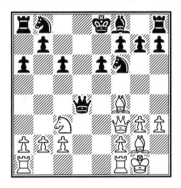

B3c2b1) 12.♖fd1 (12.♗c7 ♘bd7 13.♖fd1 ♛c5 14.♛d3∞) 12...♛b6 13.♗e3 (13.♘a4!?) 13...♛c7 (13...♛a5!?) 14.♘e4 (14.♗f4 ♛b6=) 14...♘xe4 15.♛xe4 ♘d7 16.♗d4∞, Tiviakov, S. ;

B3c2b2) 12.♖ad1 ♛b6 13.♘a4 (13.♗e3!?; 13.♖d2!?, Tiviakov, S.) 13...♛b5 (13...♛b4 14.b3 ♘bd7 15.♗d2 ♛a3 16.♗c3∞, Tiviakov S.) 14.b3 ♘bd7 15.c4 (15.g4 h6 16.h4 0-0-0±, Tiviakov, S.) 15...a5 16.g4 (16.♖d3!? Tiviakov, S.) 16...h6 17.♛g3 (Al Modiahki, M. (2564) – Tiviakov, S. (2668), Amsterdam 2006) 17...0-0-0 18.♛e3 (18.♖fe1?! ♗b4 19.♖e2 ♘c5∓; 18.♖d3?! ♗b4 19.♖fd1 ♘c5 20.♘xc5 ♗xc5∓) 18...e5 19.♗g3 ♖e8 20.♖fe1 (20.f4 exf4 21.♛xf4 ♖e6 22.♔h2 ♗e7 23.♛d4 ♗c5 24.♘xc5 ♛xc5∓) 20...♗b4 21.♖e2 ♘c5 22.♘xc5

(22.♗xe5 ♘fd7 23.♕f4 ♘xe5 24.♖xe5 ♖xe5 25.♕xe5 ♘xa4 26.♕xa5 ♗xa5 27.bxa4 ♖e8∓) 22...♗xc5 23.♕d3 ♖e6∓.

We return now to Landa – Bauer.

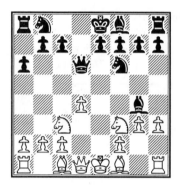

7...♗h5

7...♗xf3 8.♕xf3

A) 8...c6 9.♗e3 (9.♗f4 ♕xd4 10.♖d1 ♕b6 (Ivanov, A. (2455) – Benkovic, P. (2430), Bucharest 2007) 11.♗c4 e6 12.0-0∞; 10.♗d3!? ♘bd7 11.0-0-0⯑)

A1) 9...♘bd7 (9...♘d5 10.♗g2 e6 11.0-0 ♗e7 12.♘xd5 exd5 13.♗f4 ♕d7 14.♖fe1 0-0 15.h4 ♗f6 16.c3 a5 17.♔h2 ♘a6 18.♗h3 with initiative, Kalod, R. (2495) – Sermek, D. (2523), Turin 2006) 10.0-0-0 e6 11.♗f4 ♕b4 (Glek, I. (2553) – Kekelidze, M. (2512), Boeblingen 2000) 12.♗c7 (12.♗d3!?; 12.a3!?; 12.g4!?) 12...♘d5 13.a3 ♕e7 14.♘xd5 cxd5 15.♖e1 ♘f6 16.♗e5 or 15...♖c8 16.♗f4 with better chances for White;

A2) 9...e6

A2a) 10.♗g2 ♘bd7 11.0-0 ♗e7 12.♖fd1 0-0 (Hera, I. (2525) – Milanovic, D. (2510), Nova Gorica 2008) 13.♗f4 ♕b4 14.a3 ♕xb2 15.♖db1 ♕xc2 16.♖xb7⯑ or 14...♕b6 15.b3 ♘d5 16.♘xd5 cxd5 (or 16...exd5) 17.c4 with pressure;

A2b) 10.0-0-0 ♗e7 11.g4 ♕c7 12.g5 ♘d5 13.♘e4 b5 14.h4 ♘d7 15.♔b1 ♖f8 16.c4 bxc4 17.♗xc4 ♘7b6 18.♖c1 ♖b8 19.♗b3 a5 20.♘c5±, Sveshnikov, E. (2500) – Ponkratov, P. (2465), Chelyabinsk 2007; 10...♕c7 11.♔b1 ♘bd7 12.g4 b5 13.g5 ♘d5 (Brkic, A. (2454) – Kurajica, B. (2541), Solin 2004) 14.♘xd5 cxd5 15.h4 ♘b6 16.♗c1 ♘c4 17.h5 ♗d6 18.g6±;

B) 8...♘c6 9.♗e3 e6 (9...g6?! 10.0-0-0 ♗g7 11.♗f4 ♕d8 12.d5, Saric, I. (2287) – Plenkovic, Z. (2302), Split 2005) 10.0-0-0 0-0-0 (10...♘d5 11.♘e4 (Perunovic, M. (2334) – Chapliev, A. (2314), Ikaros 2002) 11...♕d7 12.c4 ♘xe3 13.fxe3±) 11.♗g2 ♗e7 (11...♕b4?! 12.♔b1 ♕a5 13.d5 exd5 14.♘xd5 ♖xd5 15.♖xd5 ♕xd5 16.♕xd5 ♘xd5 17.♗xd5 with a better ending for White, Stefansson, H. (2560) – Galego, L. (2525), Reykjavik 2008; 11...♘d5!? 12.♕xf7 ♘xc3 13.bxc3 ♘e5 14.dxe5 ♕xd1+) 12.d5 exd5 13.♘xd5 ♘xd5 14.♖xd5 ♕xd5 15.♕xd5 ♖xd5 16.♗xd5 ♘d8 17.♗d4 (Tarmak, M. (2333) – Konikowski, J. (2367), Internet 2000) 17...c6 18.♗b3 ♗f6 19.♗b6 ♘e6±.

Back to Landa – Bauer.

8.♗g2

After 8.♗f4 ♕b6 Black has no real problems; for example, 9.♖b1 (Koepke, C. – Nesterovsky, A., Internet 2003) 9...♘c6 (9...e6!? 10.♘a4 ♕c6) 10.g4

154

♗g6 11.g5 ♘h5 12.♗e3⇄ or 9.♗e2
♘c6 10.♘a4 ♛a7 11.c3 e6 12.b4
♗d6⇄.

Main alternatives include **A)** 8.♛e2 and
B) 8.g4.

A) 8.♛e2 ♘c6 9.♗e3 (9.♗f4? ♘×d4)
9...0-0-0 10.♗g2 (10.0-0-0?! ♘d5)
10...e6 (10...♘d5?! 11.♘×d5 ♛×d5
(Drobrzenski, J. – Al Khelaifi, S.,
Kemer 2007) 12.0-0 e6 13.g4 ♗g6
14.♘e5 ♘×d4 15.♗×d4 ♛×d4
16.♗×b7+ ♚×b7 17.♖fd1 ± or 12...e5
13.d×e5 ♘×e5 14.g4 ♗g6 15.♖ad1 ±;
10...e5 11.d×e5 ♘×e5? 12.g4 ♗g6
13.♘×e5 ♛×e5 14.f4 ♛e6 15.f5 ±, Sax,
G. (2520) – Drobne, M. (2102), Bled
2005; 11...♛b4!?)

A1) 11.0-0-0 (11.a3 ♘d5 12.♘×d5
e×d5⇄, Zelic, M. (2255) – Plenkovic,
Z. (2325), Split 2007) 11.♘d5 12.♘×d5
(12.♘e4!? ♛b4 13.g4 ♗g6 14.♘h4⇄)
12...♛×d5 (Drabke, L. (2433) – Pirrot,
D. (2398), Germany 2005) 13.c4 ♛a5
14.a3∓;

A2) 11.0-0

A2a) 11...♘b4?! 12.g4 ♗g6 13.♘e5
♘bd5 (13...♗e7 14.♘a4 ♘bd5
15.♘c5 ±; 13...♚b8 14.a3 ♘bd5
15.♘×d5 e×d5 16.f4 ± or 15...♘×d5
16.c4 ♘×e3 17.f×e3 ±) 14.♘×d5 e×d5
15.f4 ♘e8 16.c4 f6 17.c5 ♛e7 18.♘×g6
h×g6 19.f5 ±, Goloshchapov, A. (2550)
– Dutreeuw, M. (2380), Belgium 2006;

A2b) 11...♗e7 (11...♛b4!?; 11...♘d5
12.♘×d5 e×d5 13.c4 d×c4 14.♛×c4
♛b4 15.♖fc1 ♛×c4 16.♖×c4 f6⇄, Van
Oosterom, C. (2395) – Berg, E. (2600),
Maastricht 2008) 12.a3 ♘d5 13.♘e4
♛d7 14.b4?! (14.♘c5!?; 14.c4 ♘×e3

15.f×e3 f5 16.♘c3 ♗f6∓, Lane, G.
(2445) – Dragicevic, D. (2135),
Queenstown 2006) 14...f5 15.♘c5?!
(15.♘ed2∓) 15...♗×c5 16.b×c5 f4
17.g×f4 (Zelcic, R. (2514) – Sermek, D.
(2555), Sibenik 2005) 17...♘×d4
18.♗×d4 ♘×f4 19.♛e4 ♘×g2 20.c3 ♘f4
21.♘e5 ♘e2+ 22.♚h2 ♛d5∓;

B) 8.g4 ♗g6

9.♘e5 (9.♗g2 ♘c6⇄) 9...♘c6 and
now:

B1) 10.♗g2 ♘×e5 11.d×e5 ♛×e5+
12.♗e3 c6 13.♛e2 e6 14.f4 (14.0-0-0
♗c5) 14...♛d6! (14...♛c7 15.0-0-0
♗e7 16.♖hf1⯑, Sveshnikov, E. (2500)
– Belikov, V. (2525), Moscow 2006)
15.♖d1 (15.0-0 ♗e7∓) 15...♛c7 16.0-0
♗e7 17.♘a4 b5 18.f5 b×a4 19.f×g6
h×g6 20.♛f3 0-0 21.♛×c6 ♖ac8∓;

B2) 10.♘×c6 ♛×c6 11.d5 ♛d6
(11...♛b6!?) 12.♗g2 0-0-0 13.♗e3
(13.♛f3 e5 14.d×e6 ♛×e6+ 15.♗e3 c6
16.0-0 ♗d6∓, Deglmann, L. (2279) –
Radlovacki, J. (2400), Novi Sad 2002;
13.0-0 e6 14.♗g5 h5∓, Kuznetsov, V.
(2367) – Lysyj, I. (2470), Salekhard
2003) 13...e6 14.d×e6 (Soozankar, A.
(2250) – Hindermann, F. (2305),
Novokuznetsk 2008) 14...♛b4 15.♗d2

fxe6 16.0-0 ♕d4 17.♗e3 ♕xd1
18.♖axd1 ♖xd1 19.♖xd1 ♗xc2 20.♖d2
(20.♖c1 ♗g6 21.♗f4 ♘d7∓) 20...♗g6
21.g5 ♘d7∓ 22.♗xb7+?! ♔xb7
23.♖xd7 ♗d6 24.♖xg7 ♔c6∓;

B3) 10.♘xg6 (10.♗f4!?) 10...hxg6
11.d5 (11.♗g2 ♘xd4 12.♗xb7 ♖d8
13.♗g2 e5⇄) 11...♘b4 12.♗g2
(Manca, F. (2408) – Pizzuto, S. (2219),
Cremona 2005) 12...0-0-0 13.0-0 e6
(13...♘bxd5 14.♗xd5 ♘xd5 15.c4 ♘b4
16.♕b3⩱) 14.dxe6 ♕xe6 15.♗d2
(15.♕f3?! c6 16.♗f4 ♘xc2) 15...♗c5
16.♘a4 ♗d6 17.♕f3 ♘c6 18.♗c3 ♘xg4
19.hxg4 ♗h2+ 20.♔h1 ♗e5+ 21.♔g1
(21.♗h3? ♘d4 22.♗xd4 ♖xd4 23.♘c5
♕d5∓) 21...♗h2+ ½-½.

Returning to Landa – Bauer.

8...♘c6 9.♗f4

For 9.♗e3 0-0-0 10.♕e2 see 8.♕e2
♘c6 9.♗e3 0-0-0 10.♗g2 or 10.0-0 see
9.0-0 0-0-0 10.♗e3. Also worth consideration are **A)** 9.d5 and **B)** 9.0-0.

A) 9.d5 (9.♗e3 0-0-0 10.0-0 – 9.0-0
0-0-0 10.♗e3 or 10.♕e2 – 6...♗g4 7.h3
♗h5 8.♕e2 ♘c6 9.♗e3 0-0-0 10.♗g2)

A1) 9...♘e5 10.♗f4 (10.0-0!?)
10...♘xf3+ 11.♗xf3 ♗xf3 (11...e5!?)

12.♕xf3 e5 (12...♕b4?! 13.0-0-0 0-0-0
14.♖he1±, Samhouri, A. (2290) –
Abdulla, A., Dhabi 2006) 13.♕e2 ♘d7
14.0-0-0 ♗e7±;

A2) 9...♘b4 10.♗f4 (10.0-0 0-0-0?! –
6...♗g4 7.♗g2 ♘c6 8.0-0 0-0-0 9.d5
♘b4 10.h3 ♗h5; 10...♘bxd5!?∞ or
10...♘fxd5!?∞) 10...♕c5 11.♗e3 ♕a5
(11...♕d6 12.0-0 ♘bxd5!?∞ or
12...♘fxd5!?∞) 12.0-0 ♘bxd5 (12...0-0-0?!
– 6...♗g4 7.♗g2 ♘c6 8.0-0 0-0-0 9.d5
♘b4 10.h3 ♗h5 11.♗f4 ♕c5 12.♗e3
♕a5) 13.♘xd5 ♘xd5 14.♗d2 ♕a4
15.b3 ♕d7 16.g4 ♗g6 17.c4 ♘f6
18.♘e5⩱, Calistri, T. (2382) –
Chabanon, J. (2411), Clichy 2006;

B) 9.0-0 0-0-0

The main alternatives are **B1)** 10.d5;
B2) 10.♗e3 and **B3)** 10.♗f4.

B1) 10.d5?! Now this move is mistake.
10...♘xd5 (10...♘b4?! – 6...♗g4 7.♗g2
♘c6 8.0-0 0-0-0 9.d5 ♘b4?! 10.h3!
♗h5) 11.♘xd5 ♕xd5 12.♕xd5 ♖xd5
In the position with ♗g4, White, after
♘f3-g5, gets better game (f7-pawn).
Now White plays without sufficient
compensation for the pawn; for example, 13.g4 ♗g6 14.♘h4 ♖d8
15.♘xg6 hxg6 16.c3 e6∓, Saiboulatov,

156

D. (2410) – Grafl, F. (2410), Belgium 2007;

B2) 10.♗e3 e5 (10...e6!?; 10...♕b4? 11.a3 ♕b6 12.g4 ♗g6 13.b4± or 11...♕xb2 12.♕d2 ♕b6 (Emms, J. (2520) – Menacher, M. (2327), Port Erin 2003) 13.♖ab1 ♕a5 14.♘e5±) 11.dxe5 ♘xe5 and now:

B2a) 12.♕xd6 ♗xd6 13.♘xe5 (13.♘d2 ♖he8 14.♘de4 ♘f3+ 15.♗xf3 ♗xf3 16.♘xd6+ ♖xd6∓, Kotan, L. (2289) – Manik, M. (2460) Banska Stiavnica 2006; 14.♖ae1 ♗b4 15.f4 ♘c6 16.♘b3 (Morozov, E. (2275) – Zablotsky, S. (2500), Voronezh 2007) 16...♗xc3 17.bxc3 ♗d1) 13...♘xe5 14.f4 ♗xc3 15.bxc3 ♗e2 16.♖fb1 (16.♖f2?! ♗c4 17.♗d4 (Lengyel, B. (2339) – Schneider, V. (2195), Budapest 2006) 17...♖he8 18.g4 ♗d5∓) 16...♘d5 17.♗d4⇄, Ong, K. (2280) – Berg, E. (2570), Stockholm 2007;

B2b) 12.♘xe5 ♗xd1 13.♘xf7 ♗xc2 (13...♕d7 14.♘xd8 ♗xc2 15.♘xb7 ♗b4 16.♘c5 ♕f5 17.♗b7+ ♔b8 18.♘xa6+ ♔xb7 19.♘xb4 ♗e4 20.♘xe4 ♕xe4∓; 14...♕xd8 15.♖axd1 ♗d6 16.♗f4⩲) 14.♘xd6+ ♗xd6 15.♖ac1 ♗g6 16.♘a4 ♗e4 17.♘b6+ ♔b8 18.♘c4 ♗xg2 19.♔xg2 ½-½, Van den Doel, E. (2587) – Tiviakov, S. (2678), Leeuwarden 2005;

B2c) 12.g4 ♕xd1 13.♖axd1 ♖xd1 14.♖xd1 ♘xf3+ 15.♗xf3 ♗g6 16.g5 ♗h5 (16...♘d7?! 17.♗g4 ♗d6 18.♘d5 ♔d8 (Rudolf, A. (2275) – Gvetadze, S. (2415), Dresden 2007) 19.c4 f5 20.gxf6 gxf6 21.c5 ♘xc5 22.♗d4 ♖f8 23.♗xc5 ♗xc5 24.♘f4+ ♗d6± or 18...♖e8 19.c4 ♗c2 20.♘b6+ cxb6 21.♖xd6±) 17.♗xh5 (17.♔g2 ♗xf3+ 1/2-1/2, Perez

Candelario, M. (2511) – Gashimov, V. (2625), Kusadasi 2006) 17...♘xh5 18.♘d5 b5 19.♔g2 ½-½, Godena, M. (2490) – Zaitsev, V. (2411), Montecatini Terme 1999;

B3) 10.♗f4 ♕b4 (10...♕d7!? 11.d5?! ♘xd5 12.♘xd5 ♕xd5 13.♕xd5 ♖xd5 14.g4 ♗g6 15.♘e5 ♖xe5 16.♗xe5 ♘xe5 17.f4 ♘xg4 18.hxg4 ♗xc2∓ or 15.♘h4 ♖b5 16.♘xg6 hxg6 17.b3 e6 18.♖ad1 g5∓; 11.g4 ♗g6 12.♘e5 ♘xe5 13.dxe5 ♕xd1 14.♖axd1 ♘d7∞)

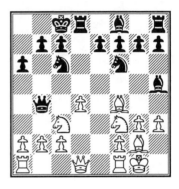

We examine **B3a)** 11.♘e2; **B3b)** 11.d5; **B3c)** 11.a3 and **B3d)** 11.g4.

B3a) 11.♘e2 ♗xf3 (11...♕xb2 12.♖b1 ♕xa2 13.♘e5 ♘d5 14.♘xc6 bxc6 15.♕d3 ♗g6⇄; 15.♖a1?! ♕c4; 15.♕d2?! ♕c4) 12.♗xf3 ♘xd4 (12...e5!?) 13.♘xd4 ♖xd4 14.♕e2 (Madl, I. (2369) – Borsuk, A. (2306), Mallorca 2004) 14...♖xf4 15.a3 ♕c4 16.gxf4 ♕xf4⇄;

B3b) 11.d5

B3b1) 11...e5

B3b1a) 12.a3? ♕xb2 13.♕d2 (13.♕d3 ♗g6) 13...♗xf3 14.♖fb1 (14.♗xf3 ♘d4∓) 14...♕xa1 15.♖xa1 ♗xg2 16.♔xg2 exf4∓;

B3b1b) 12.♗d2 e4 (12...♘d4!?) 13.♘xe4 ♕xe4 14.dxc6 ♕xc6 15.g4 ♗g6 16.♘e5 ♕d6 (16...♕c5 17.♖e1 ♗d6 18.♕f3 c6 19.♕c3 ♖he8±; 16...♕b5!? 17.♖e1 ♗c5) 17.♘xg6 hxg6 18.♗e3 (Khairullin, I. (2533) – Lysyj, I. (2523), Cheboksary 2006) 18...♘d5 19.♕f3 ♕f6 20.♕xf6 gxf6±;

B3b2) 11...e6 12.a3 (½-½, Tiviakov, S. (2700) – Almeida, O. (2462), Solsona 2005 – see the Introduction)

B3b2a) 12...♕b6 13.♘a4 ♕b5 (13...♕a5?! 14.c4 exd5 15.b4) 14.c4 ♕xc4 15.dxc6 ♖xd1 16.cxb7+ ♔b8 17.♖fxd1 ♕xa4 18.♖d4 ♕e8 19.♖c1 ♗d6 (19...♘d5 20.♖xd5 exd5 21.♖xc7±) 20.♖xd6 cxd6 21.♗xd6+ ♔xb7 (21...♔a7 22.♘e5±) 22.♘e5+ ♘d5 23.♖c7+ ♔b6? (23...♔a8 24.♘d7 ♕xd7 25.♖xd7±) 24.♘c4+ ♔b5 25.b3 a5 (25...♘xc7 26.a4#) 26.a4+ ♔a6 27.♗c5 ♘xc7 28.♘d6+- or 27...♕b8 28.♗f1+-;

B3b2b) 12...♕xb2 13.♘a4 ♕b5 14.c4 ♕xc4 (14...♕a5? 15.♗d2) 15.dxc6 ♖xd1 16.cxb7+ ♔b8 (16...♔xb7 17.♘e5+ ♕d5 18.♖fxd1 ♗d1 19.♖xd1 ♘e4 20.♖xd5 exd5 21.♘xf7 ♖g8 22.♘d8+ ♔c8 23.♘e6±) 17.♖fxd1

B3b2b1) 17...♗e7?! 18.♘b6 ♕e4 (18...♕b5 19.♖ab1 ♗xf3 20.♗xf3 ♕a5 21.♖dc1+- or 19...♕a5 20.♘d4 ♕c3 21.♖dc1+-; 18...♕xf4 19.gxf4 cxb6 20.♘e5±; 18...♕c5 19.♘e5 ♕xb6 20.♖db1±) 19.♘e5 ♕xg2+ 20.♔xg2 ♗xd1 21.♖xd1±;

B3b2b2) 17...♗d6 18.♖xd6

B3b2b2a) 18...cxd6?! 19.♗xd6+ ♔a7 20.b8♕+ ♖xb8 21.♗c5+ ♖b6 22.♗xb6+ ♔b8 23.♘e5 ♕xa4 24.♖c1 with a very strong attack; for example, 24...24...♗e2 (24...♘d5 25.♗xd5 exd5 26.♖c7+-) 25.♗c7+ ♔a7 26.♘c6+ ♔b7 27.♘d4+ ♘d5 28.♘xe2 ♕xa3 29.♗f4±;

B3b2b2b) 18...♗xf3 19.♗xf3 ♕xa4 (19...cxd6 20.♗xd6+ ♔a7 21.♖b1+-) 20.♖c6 ♘d5 (20...♘e8? 21.♖d1+-) 21.♗xd5 exd5 22.♖ac1 g5 (22...♔xb7?! 23.♖xc7+ ♔a8 24.♖xf7±) 23.♗xg5 ♖g8 (23...♔xb7 24.♖xc7+ ♔a8 25.♖xf7±) 24.♗e3 ♕e4∞;

B3c) 11.a3

B3c1) 11...♕b6 (for 11...♕c4 12.g4 ♗g6 see 11.g4 ♗g6 12 a3 ♕c4) 12.g4 (12.♗e3 ♗xf3 13.♕xf3 ♘d4 14.♗xd4 ♖xd4∞, Nyman, J. – Ottenweller, W.,

Internet 2003) 12...♗g6 13.♘a4 ♕a7 (13...♕a5? 14.c4±; 13...♕b5?! 14.b3 ♕d5 15.c4 ♕e4 16.♗e3), and White has the better chances;

B3c2) 11...♕×b2

B3c2a) 12.♕e1 ♗×f3 13.♖b1 (13.♗×f3?! ♘×d4) 13...♕×b1 14.♕×b1 ♗×g2 15.♔×g2 ♖×d4 16.♕b2 (16.♕b3 e6 17.♘e2 ♖d7 18.♖b1 ♘a5 19.♕a4 ♘c6 20.♕b3=) 16...e6 (16...e5!? 17.♗e3 ♖c4) 17.♖b1 b5∞, Zorko, J. (2310) – Nikolov, S. (2407), Nova Gorica 2004;

B3c2b) 12.♕d3 (12.♕d2?! ♗×f3 13.♖fb1 ♕×a1 14.♖×a1 ♗×g2 15.♔×g2 e5∓) 12...♗g6?! (12...♗×f3 13.♖fb1 ♕×a1 14.♖×a1 ♗×g2 15.♔×g2 ♖×d4⇄, Inkiov, V. (2520) – Dutreeuw, M. (2380), Paris 2006) 13.♕c4 ♕×c2 (13...♗×c2 14.♖fb1 ♗×b1 15.♖×b1 ♕×a3 16.d5 ♘×d5 17.♘×d5 e6 18.♘×c7 ♕d3 19.♕a2 ♕a3 20.♘a8 and White has a very strong attack) 14.♖fd1

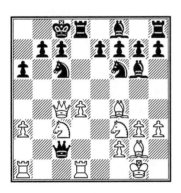

B3c2b1) 14...♘d5 15.♖ac1 ♘b6 16.♕f1 ♕b3 (Klimov, S. (2480) – Ginzburg, M. (2260), St. Petersburg 2008) 17.♘d2 ♕e6 (17...♕×a3 18.d5 e5 19.d×c6 e×f4 20.♘c4+– or 18...♘a5 19.♗×c7±) 18.♖e1 ♕f6 (18...♕d7

19.♗×c6 ♕×c6 20.♘ce4±) 19.d5 ♘a5 20.♗×c7±;

B3c2b2) 14...♘e4 15.♖ac1 ♕×f2+ 16.♔h2 ♘d6 17.♕a4 ♕b2 18.♘e5 e6 (18...♘×e5 19.d×e5±; 18...♕b6 19.♗×c6 b×c6 20.♘×c6 ♖d7 21.♖b1 ♗×b1 22.♖×b1 ♕×b1 23.♘×b1±) 19.♘×c6 b×c6 20.♕×c6 with a strong initiative;

B3c2c) 12.♘a4 ♗×f3 (12...♕b5?! 13.c4 ♕×c4 14.♖c1 ♗×f3 15.♗×f3 ♕×d4 16.♕c2 ♕d3 17.♗×c6 ♕×c2 18.♗×b7+ ♔×b7 19.♖×c2) 13.♕×f3 ♕×d4 14.♕b3 (14.♘c3?! ♕c4) 14...♘a5 and now:

B3c2c1) 15.♕b4 ♕×b4 16.a×b4

B3c2c1a) 16...e5 17.♗×e5 ♘c4 18.♗×f6 g×f6 19.♖fe1 (19.♘c5 ♗×c5 20.b×c5 c6 21.♖fb1 ♘e5∓, Neelotpal, D. (2448) – Hasangatin, R. (2485), Alushta 2004) 19...c6 20.♖e4 (Delchev, A. (2629) – Sulava, N. (2531), Hyeres 2001) 20...♘e5 21.f4 ♘g6 22.c3 ♔c7∓;

B3c2c1b) 16...♘c4 17.b5 (17...a×b5? 18.♘c5 ♘b6 19.♗×b7+ ♔b8 20.♗c6 ♘fd5 21.♖a5 ♘b4 22.♘a6+ ♘×a6 23.♖×a6+–) 17...a5 18.♘c5 ♘d5 (18...e5!? 19.♘×b7 e×f4) 19.♘b3 ♘×f4 20.g×f4 b6 21.♖a4 ♘d6 (21...♘d2? 22.♘×a5 b×a5 23.♗c6 ♘c4 24.♖×c4 e6 25.♖a1±, Zezulkin, J. (2529) – Danielsen, H. (2526), Germany 2002) 22.♘d4 e6 23.♘c6 ♘×b5 24.♘×d8 ♔×d8∓;

B3c2c2) 15.♗×b7+ ♘×b7 (15...♔b8 16.♕f3 ♘×b7 17.♖ab1 ♕d5 18.♕c3∞) 16.♖ab1 (16.♖ad1 ♕×d1 17.♕c4 ♕×f1+ 18.♔×f1 e5 19.♗×e5 ♗d6 20.♕×a6 ♔b8 21.♗d4 c5∓) 16...♘d6 17.♗×d6 ♖×d6 18.c4 (Liss, E. (2485)

– Gofshtein, L. (2515), Israel 2003)
18...♕a7 19.c5 ♖d5 20.♘b6+ c×b6
21.c×b6 ♕b7 22.♖fc1+ (Gofshtein, L.)
22...♔b8 23.♖c7 e6 24.♖×b7+
♔×b7∓;

B3d) 11.g4 ♗g6

B3d1) 12.♕e2 (12.♕c1 – 9.♗f4 ♕b4
10.g4 ♗g6 11.♕c1 0-0-0 12.0-0)
12...♕×b2? (12...e6!?) 13.♕e3 e6
(13...♗×c2?! 14.♖ac1 ♗g6 15.♘e5±)
14.♖ab1 (14.♘e5!? ♗b4 15.♘e2)
14...♕a3 15.♖b3 ♕a5 (15...♕e7
16.♘e5±) 16.♘e5 ♘d5 17.♘×d5 e×d5
18.♘×c6 b×c6 19.♖fb1±, Amesz, J.
(2185) – Van Beek, A. (2270)
Vlissingen 2000;

B3d2) 12.♘e5 ♘×e5 13.♗×e5 c6?!
(13...e6) 14.♕e2 ♘d7 15.♗g3 (15.d5!?
♘×e5 16.♕×e5) 15...e6 16.a3
(16.♘e4!?) 16...♕×b2?! (16...♕b6!?)
17.♕f3 ♘f6 18.♖fb1±, Neumeier, K.
(2283) – Kamaryt, T. (2103), Oberwart
2006; 12...♖×d4 13.♘×c6 b×c6 14.♗d2
(14.♕f3!? ♖×f4 15.♕×c6 or 14...♖c4
15.♗d2∞) 14...♕d6 15.♕e2 ♖×d2
16.♕×a6+ ♔d7 17.♖ad1 ♖d5 18.♕a4
e6 19.♖fe1∞; 12...♘×d4 13.a3 ♕b6
(13...♕c5 14.♖c1 e6 15.♘a4∞;
13...♕×b2? 14.♖b1 ♕×c3 15.♗×b7+)
14.♗e3 c5∞.

B3d3) 12.a3

B3d3a) 12...♕×b2?! 13.♕e1 (13.♕d2
♕×c2 14.♕×c2 ♗×c2 15.♘e5 ♘×e5
16.d×e5 ♘e8 17.♖a2 ♗g6 18.♖b2∞;
15...♖×d4 16.♗e3 ♘×e5 17.♗×d4
♘c4∓) and now:

B3d3a1) 13...♗×c2 14.♖a2 ♕b3
15.♕d2 ♗g6 (15...♗e4 16.♖b2 ♕×a3
17.♘×e4 ♘×e4 18.♕c2 ♘c3 19.♘e5±;
18...♘d6 19.♖×b7!) 16.♖b2 ♕×a3
17.♘e5 ♖×d4 18.♗×c6 b×c6 19.♕×d4
♕×b2 20.♘×c6± or 13...♕c2 14.♖c1
♕b3 (14...♕d3 15.♘e5 ♕×d4 16.♘e2
♕a4 17.♘×c6 b×c6 18.♖×c6±) 15.♘e5
e6 (15...♘×e5 16.d×e5 ♘e8 17.♕e3±;
15...♖×d4 16.♘e2 ♖e4 17.♘×c6 b×c6
18.♕a5±; 15...♖×d4 16.♘×g6 h×g6
17.♗×c7 ♔×c7 18.♕e5+ ♔d7
19.♖fd1±) 16.♘×c6 b×c6 17.♗×c6
♗d6 18.♕e2±;

B3d3a2) 13...e6 14.♖b1

B3d3a2a) 14...♕×a3 15.♘e5 ♗×c2
(15...♖×d4 16.♗×c6 b×c6 17.♗e3 ♖d5
18.♘×c6±) 16.♖a1 ♕b4 17.♗×c6 b×c6
18.♘×c6 ♕c4 19.♘d8 ♔×d8 20.♕d2
♗e4 (20...♗g6 21.♖fc1 h5 22.g5 ♘e8
23.♘e4 ♕d5 24.♘c5±) 21.♕b2 ♕b4
22.♕×b4 ♗×b4 23.♘×e4 ♘×e4
24.♖×a6±;

B3d3a2b) 14...♛×c2 15.♘e5 ♗d6
(15...♖×d4 16.♖×b7 ♚×b7 17.♘×c6
♖d5 18.♘d4 ♛b2 19.g5 ♚c8
20.♘×e6±) 16.♗×c6 (16.♖×b7 ♚×b7
17.♘×c6∞, Caruana, F. (2381) –
Strikovic, A. (2498), Lorca 2005)
16...b×c6 17.♛e3 ♘d5 18.♘×d5 e×d5
19.♖fc1 ♛×b1 20.♖×b1 ♗×b1 21.♛e2
♗×e5 22.♛×e5 ♖d7 23.♛e2± or
19...♛a2 20.♖b3 ♖he8 21.♛g3 ♗×e5
22.♗×e5 ♖d7 23.♛c3 c5 24.d×c5 with
a dangerous initiative;

B3d3b) 12...♛c4

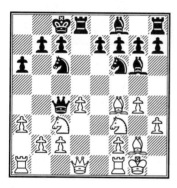

B3d3b1) 13.♘e5 ♘×e5 (13...♛×d4
14.♘×c6 b×c6∞) 14.♗×e5 e6 (14...c6?
15.♖e1 and then 16.♗f1) 15.♛f3 ♘d5
16.♘×d5 ♛×d5?! 17.♛c3 ♛d7 18.d5!
(18.♖ad1 f6 19.♗g3 ♗d6=,
Lintchevski, D. (2445) – Bazarov, K.
(2230), Sochi 2007) 18...e×d5 19.♗×d5
♗d6 (19...f6 20.♗e6+–; 19...c6
20.♖ad1±) 20.♗×g7 ♖hg8 21.♗f6
♖de8 22.♖fe1±; 16...e×d5 17.b3 ♛c6
18.c4 f6 19.c×d5 (19.♗g3 d×c4)
19...♛b6 20.♗g3 ♗d6⇄;

B3d3b2) 13.g5 ♘d5 (13...♘d7 14.♖e1
e5? 15.♗f1 ♛e6 16.d5±; 14...f6!?
15.♗e3 ♘b6) 14.♘×d5 ♖×d5
(14...♛×d5?! 15.♘e5 ♛b5 16.c4 or
15...♛×d4 16.♛g4+) 15.c3 (15.♘e5

♖×e5 16.♗×e5 ♘×e5 17.d×e5 e6
18.♛f3 c6 19.♖fd1 ♗e7∞) 15...♖d8
16.b3

B3d3b2a) 16...♛c3?! 17.d5! ♛c5
(17...e6 18.♗d2±; 17...a5 18.♘d4
♘×d4 19.♛×d4 f6 20.♛a7 with a strong
initiative or 19...♚b8 20.b4 ♛a4
21.♖fc1 e5 22.♗×e5 ♗d6 23.♗×d6
c×d6 24.♛×g7 ♛d7 25.♗c4±) 18.♘e5
♘×e5 19.♗×e5⯑;

B3d3b2b) 16...♛d3 17.♛c1 ♛c2
(17...e6 18.♖e1 ♗d6 19.♗×d6 c×d6
20.♖e3 ♛f5 21.c4 ♚b8=) 18.♛e3 e6
(18...♛×b3 19.d5 ♖×d5 20.♘d2 ♖×d2
21.♛×d2 e5∞ or 19.♘e5 ♘×e5
20.♛×e5 ♖d7∞) 19.b4 (Svidler, P.
(2725) – Tiviakov, S. (2665), Wijk aan
Zee 2007) 19...♗d6 20.♗×d6
(20.♖fc1 ♛d3=) 20...♖×d6 21.♘d2
♛a4 (21.♖fc1 ♛d3 22.♛f4?! h6∓;
22.♛×d3 ♗×d3=) 22.♘e4 ♗×e4
23.♗×e4 (23.♛×e4?! h6 24.g6 f5∓)
23...h6 24.♛f3 h×g5 25.♛×f7 ♛b3⇄
or 22.♘c4 ♖dd8 23.♖fe1 ♛b5
(23...h6?! 24.♗×c6 b×c6 25.♘e5)
24.♗f1 ♛a4 25.♗g2 (25.♖ad1?! h6∓)
25...♛b5=.

Returning to Landa – Bauer.

9...♛b4

161

9...♛d7?! 10.g4 ♗g6 11.♘e5±;
9...♛e6+ 10.♗e3 ♛c4?! 11.d5;
10...0-0-0!?; 9...♛d8 – 6...♘c6 7.♗f4
♛d8 8.♗g2 ♗g4 9.h3 ♗h5.

10.a3

Also coming under consideration are
10.0-0 and 10.g4:

A) 10.0-0 ♛×b2?! (10...e6!?; 10...0-0-0
– 7.h3 ♗h5 8.♗g2 ♘c6 9.0-0 0-0-0
10.♗f4 ♛b4) 11.♛d2 ♗×f3 (11...♗g6
12.♖ab1 ♛×c2 13.♛×c2 ♗×c2 14.♖×b7
with a strong initiative for the pawn;
11...0-0-0 12.♖ab1 ♛a3 13.♖b3 ♛a5
14.♘e5±; 11...♛a3 12.♖fb1 ♘a5
13.♘e5±) 12.♗×f3 ♛b4 (12...0-0-0
13.♖ab1 ♛a3 14.♖×b7 with a strong
attack) 13.♖ab1 ♛c4 (13...♛a5
14.♖×b7± or 13...♘×d4 14.♛d3±)
14.♗×c7 ♘×d4 (14...e6 15.♛d3±)
15.♗×b7 ♖c8 16.♗a5±;

B) 10.g4 ♗g6

Ba) 11.♛d2 0-0-0 12.0-0-0 e6 13.♛e3
(13.a3!?) 13...♛b6 (13...♘d5!? 14.♘×d5
♖×d5) 14.a3 ♗d6 (14...♘e7 15.♘e5
♘ed5 16.♗×d5 ♘×d5 17.♘×d5 ♖×d5
18.c4 ♖d8 19.h4 f6±) 15.♘e5 ♗×e5
16.♗×e5±, Maze, S. (2518) –
Gashimov, V. (2625), Montpellier 2006;

Bb) 11.♛c1 0-0-0 12.0-0 e6 (12...♘×d4
13.♘×d4 ♖×d4 14.a3 ♛c5 15.♗e3 e5
16.♘e2 ♛c4 17.♗×d4 e×d4 18.♛d2
♗c5∞, Zelcic, R. (2533) – Stevic, H.
(2514), Vukovar 2005 or 17.♘×d4 e×d4
18.♗f4 ♗×c2∞; 16.♖e1!?; 14...♛b6!?)
13.a3 ♛b6 14.♗e3 ♘d5 15.♘×d5 e×d5
16.c4 f6 (16...h5!? 17.c5 ♛b5 18.g5
♗e7⇄; 17.g5 ♗e4⇄; 17.c×d5 ♘e7
18.♘e5 ♘×d5 19.♗g5 ♘f6⇄) 17.b4
♘e7 (17...♗d3!? 18.c5 ♛b5 19.♖e1

h5⇄) 18.c5 ♛b5 19.♛b2 ♛a4
20.♖fc1 h5⇄, Abergel, T. (2515) –
Grafl, F. (2430), Belgium 2008.

10...♛×b2 (10...♛b6!?) 11.♘a4 ♛b5

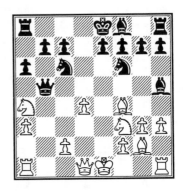

12.c4

12.c3?! e5 13.d×e5 ♘d5.

12...♛×c4 13.♖c1 ♛e6+

13...♛d5?! 14.0-0 ♖d8 (14...0-0-0
15.♖c5⩲) 15.g4 ♗g6 16.♗×c7±,
Butunoi, A. (2402) – Tober, G. (2318),
Austria 2006.

14.♗e3

14.♔f1 ♘d5 (14...0-0-0?! 15.g4 ♗g6
(15...♘d5 16.♘c5±; 15...♛e4
16.♗e5⩲) 16.♘e5 ♘×e5 17.♗×b7+
♔b8 18.♗×e5±) 15.♘c5 ♛c8 16.♛a4
b5 (16...♛b6!?) 17.♛b3 ♘×f4
18.g×f4∞.

14...♘d5 15.0-0

15.♘c5 looks good but after 15...♛c8
White cannot be happy; for example,
16.g4 (16.♛b3 e6 17.♘×b7 ♗b4+
18.a×b4 ♛×b7 with better chances for
Black) 16...♗g6 17.♘e5 e6 18.♗×d5

162

e×d5 19.♘×c6 ♗×c5 20.♖×c5 b×c6
21.♖×c6 h5 22.g×h5 ♖×h5 23.♕c1 ♔f8
24.♖×c7 ♕f5∓.

15...♘×e3 16.f×e3 ♕×e3+ 17.♔h1

Black has three extra pawns!

17...e6

After 17...0-0-0 18.g4 ♗g6 19.♖c3,
Black has problems:

A) 19...♕e6 20.♘c5 ♕d5 (20...♕d6
21.♘×b7 ♔×b7 22.♘e5±) 21.♘e5
♕×e5 (21...♕×d4 22.♕b3+−) 22.♕b3
♘a5 23.♗×b7+ ♔b8 24.d×e5 ♘×b3
25.♖×b3 ♔a7 26.♖f4+−;

B) 19...♕f4 20.♘c5 ♗e4 21.♕e2 ♗d5
22.♘×b7 ♘×d4 (22...♔×b7 23.♘e5)
23.♕×a6 ♗×b7 24.♕×b7+ ♔×b7
25.♘×d4+ ♔c8 26.♖×f4±;

C) 19...♖×d4 20.♘×d4 ♕×d4 21.♗×c6
♕×d1 22.♘b6+ c×b6 (22...♔b8
23.♖×d1 c×b6 24.♖d8+ ♔a7
25.♖d7+−) 23.♗f3+ ♔d7 24.♖×d1+
♔e6 25.♖d8 f5 26.♗d5+ ♔e5
27.♗×b7±.

18.g4 ♗×g4 (18...♗g6 19.♖c3 ♕h6
20.♘e5 ♘×e5 21.d×e5 ♖d8 22.♕f3

♗e7 23.♖×c7 ♕g5 24.♕×b7⯑;
22...♕g5 23.♖×c7? ♕×e5 24.♕×b7
♗d6 25.♗c6+ ♔f8 26.26.♗f×f7+ ♗×f7
27.♖×f7+ ♔g8−+ or 26...♖c×f7+ ♔g8
27.♖7f4 h5−+, but 23.♕×b7 23...♕e5
24.♗c6+♔e7∞) **19.h×g4 ♕h6+**
(19...0-0-0 20.♖c3 ♕h6+ 21.♔g1 ♗d6
22.♕b3 ♕f4 23.♖b1 ♘d4 24.♘b6+
♔b8 25.♘d7+ ♔c8 26.♘b6+ with a
draw or 24.♕×b7+ ♔d7 25.♕×a6
♕×g4∞; 22.g5! ♕g6 23.♕b3 ♕e4
24.♖e1 ♕f4∞, but 24.♖e3!? ♕d5
25.♘e5 ♕×b3 26.♖×b3 ♗×e5
27.d×e5± or 24...♕g4 25.♘c5 ♗×c5
26.d×c5 with better chances for White)
20.♔g1 (20.♘h2 ♗d6 21.♗×c6+ b×c6
22.♕e2 ♕h4 23.♕f2 ♕×f2 24.♖×f2
♗×a3 25.♖×c6 ♗d6⇄) **20...♗×a3**
(20...♕e3+ 21.♖f2 0-0-0?! 22.♖c3 ♕f4
23.♕c2; 21...♖d8 22.♖c3 ♕f4∞)
21.♖c3 (21.g5 ♕g6?! 22.♖×c6 b×c6
23.♘e5 ♕×g5 24.♕f3 0-0 25.♕×a3±;
21...♕h5 22.♘e5 ♕×d1 23.♗c6+ b×c6
24.♖c×d1 ♗d6∞) **21...♗b4**
(21...♗d6 22.g5 ♕h5 23.♘e5 ♕×d1
24.♗×c6+ b×c6 25.♖×d1 a5∞) **22.g5**
(22.♖b3 ♖d8 23.♘e5?! ♘×e5 24.♖×b4
♕e3+ 25.♔h1 h5 26.g5 ♘d3∓; 23.g5
♕g6∓) **22...♕h5** (22...♕g6!?)
23.♖c4 0-0 (23...a5!?) **24.♘e5**
♕×g5 **25.♘×c6 ♕e3+** (25...♗d2!?
26.♘e7+ ♔h8) **26.♔h1 ♕h6+**
27.♔g1 ♕e3+ 28.♔h1 ♕h6+ ½-½

Summary: After **1.e4 d5 2.e×d5
♕×d5 3.♘c3 ♕d6 4.d4 ♘f6 5.♘f3
a6 6.g3**, the move **6.g3** is one of the
most important of White's possibilities.
White pursues two goals: development
of the light-squared bishop at g2 (for
control of the diagonal a8-h1 and very
often for preparation of the advance
d4-d5) and development of the other
bishop at f4 with an attack on the
♕d6.

After **6.g3**, Black has many logical possibilities: 6...g6, 6...e6, 6...♘c6, 6...♗f5, 6...b5 and 6...♗g4. I cannot recommend 6...b5 for Black. Analysis indicates that Black has an equal game with counterplay after:

• **6...g6** – Black has a solid but sometimes passive position;
• **6...e6** 7.♗g2 ♘c6, transposing to the line 6...♘c6 7.♗g2 e6;
• **6...♗f5** with 7.♗g2 ♘c6 or 7...♘bd7 and 7...e6 8.0-0 ♘bd7;
• **6...♘c6** with 7.♗f4 ♕d8 or after 7.♗g2, 7...e6 (6...♘c6 7.♗g2 ♗f5) or 7...♗g4, transposing to the line 6...♗g4 7.♗g2 ♘c6.

As for 6...♗g4, Black can get an equal game with counterplay too. A few thoughts about this line:

1. After 6...♗g4 7.♗g2 c6, Black's chances are not bad at all. Black pursues two goals: stronger central control (the d5-square) and restriction of the light-squared ♗g2.
2. In some lines White plays ♗c1-f4 before 0-0. In this case Black can frequently answer ♕d6-e6+ with acceptable game.
3. Very often after 6...♗g4 White sooner or later plays ♗f1-g2 and then h2-h3. After ♗×f3 (it may not be safe for Black to play ♗g4-h5 since after g3-g4 and ♗h5-g6 White, may play ♘f3-e5, followed by h3-h4 or ♗c1-f4) White in some lines plays ♕×f3. After that Black may often accept the gambit by ♕×d4; for example, 6...♗g4 7.♗g2 ♘c6 8.h3 ♗×f3 9.♕×f3 ♕×d4; 6...♗g4 7.♗g2 ♘c6 8.♗f4 ♕d7 (8...♕d8) 9.h3 ♗×f3 10.♕×f3 ♕×d4; and 6...♗g4 7.♗g2 ♘c6 8.♗f4 ♕d8 9.0-0 e6 10.♖e1 ♗e7 11.h3 ♗×f3 12.♕×f3 ♕×d4.

Many lines after **6.g3** are minefields with many dangerous pitfalls for both sides!

Game 19
Wood, D. (2285) – Bronstein, D. (2445)
Hastings 1995

1.e4 d5 2.e×d5 ♕×d5 3.♘c3 ♕d6 4.d4 ♘f6 5.♘f3 a6 6.h3

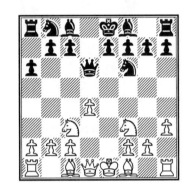

6...e6

As in the previous game, Black has considerable choice here. We examine **A)** 6...♘c6; **B)** 6...♗f5; **C)** 6...b5 and **D)** 6...♘bd7.

A) 6...♘c6 7.a3 (7.♗e3 – Game 21; 7.♗e2 – Game 23; 7.♗d3 – Game 30; 7.♗c4 – Game 26)

A1) 7...♗e6 (7...g6 8.d5 ♘e5 9.♗f4 ♘d3+ 10.♗×d3 ♕×f4 11.0-0 ♗d7±) 8.♗e3 g6 (8...h6!? 9.♕d2 g5) 9.♕d2 (De la Paz, F. (2437) – Arencibia, W. (2543), Clara 2001) 9...0-0-0 10.0-0-0 h6 11.♗f4 ♕d7 12.♗e2 ♗g7⇄;

A2) 7...♗f5

A2a) 8.d5 ♘e5 9.♗f4 (9.♘d4 9...♗d7⇄, Strachan, J. (2234) – Kovacik, E. (2204), Slovakia 2002)

9...♘xf3+ (9...♗xc2?! 10.♗xe5 ♗xd1 11.♗xd6 ♗xf3 12.♗e5 ♗h5 13.♗xc7 ♖c8 14.♗f4) 10.♕xf3 e5 11.♕e2 ♘d7 12.0-0-0 0-0-0 13.♗e3 h5 ⇄ ;

A2b) 8.♗d3 ♗xd3 (8...♗g6!?) 9.♕xd3 e6 10.♗e3 ♗e7 11.0-0-0 (11.0-0 0-0 12.♖ad1 ♖fd8 13.♖fe1 h6 14.♘e4 (Satta, V. (2218) – Cocchi, A. (2281), Porto San Giorgio 2002) 14...♘xe4 15.♕xe4 ♕d5 16.♕xd5 ♖xd5=) 11...0-0 12.g4 ♘d5 13.♘e4 ♕d7 14.♖dg1 b5 ⇄ ;

B) 6...♗f5

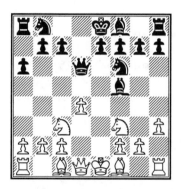

B1) 7.♗d3 ♗xd3 8.♕xd3

B1a) 8...e6 9.0-0 ♗e7 10.♗g5 (10.♘e4 ♘xe4 11.♕xe4 ♕c6 ±) 10...♘bd7 (10...♘c6!?) 11.♖fe1 c6 (11...0-0!? 12.♖ad1 h6) 12.♖ad1 0-0 13.♘e5 (Jirovsky, Petr (2340) – Jirovsky, Pavel (2340), Bayern 2002) 13...♕c7 ± ;

B1b) 8...♘c6 9.♘e4 ♘xe4 (9...♕e6!? 10.♘fg5 ♕d5) 10.♕xe4 (Hechl, G. (2250) – Hangweyrer, M. (2315), Austria 2003) 10...0-0-0 11.c3 e6= or 9.0-0 ♘b4 10.♕e2 e6 11.♗g5 (Matulovic, M. (2432) – Radlovacki, J. (2411), Pancevo 2003; 11.a3!?) 11...♗e7 12.♗xf6 gxf6 ⇄ ;

B2) 7.♗c4 e6 8.0-0 ♘c6 9.♖e1 (9.♘e2 ♗e7 10.♗f4 ♕d7 11.c3 0-0 12.♘g3 ♗g6 13.♘h4 ♘d5 14.♘xg6 hxg6 15.♗d2 ♖ad8 16.♗b3 ♘a5 17.♗c2 ♘c4 ⇄ Sluka, R. (2380) – Jirovsky, M. (2435), Czechia 1998) 9...♗e7 10.♗g5 ♖d8 11.♗xf6 (11.♕e2?! ♘xd4 12.♘xd4 ♕xd4 13.♖ad1 ♕c5 14.♖xd8+ ♗xd8∓, Deszczynski, A. (2348) – Gashimov, V. (2608), Warsaw 2005) 11...♗xf6 12.♘d5 ♘xd4 13.♘xd4 ♗xd4 14.♕xd4 0-0 15.♖ad1 exd5 16.♕xd5 ♕xd5 17.♖xd5 ♗e6=;

C) 6...b5

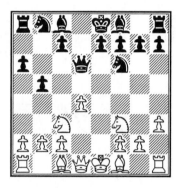

Alternatives include **C1)** 7.a4; **C2)** 7.a3; **C3)** 7.g3 and **C4)** 7.♗d3.

C1) 7.a4 b4

C1a) 8.♘a2 e6 (8...♘c6!?)

C1a1) 9.♗e2 (9.♗d3 ♘c6 10.0-0 ♗e7 11.♗e3 0-0 12.c4 ♗b7 13.♕d2 ♖ab8 ⇄) 9...♘bd7 10.0-0 ♗b7 (10...a5!?) 11.♖e1 ♕b6 12.♗f1 c5 (Jaenig, R. (2110) – Balinov, I. (2450), Dresden 2000) 13.♗f4 ♗e7 14.♘c1 (14.c4 cxd4 15.♘xd4 0-0 ⇄) 14...♘d5 15.a5 ♕a7 16.♗g3 ♖c8 ⇄ ;

C1b) 8.♘e2 ♗b7 9.♗f4 (9.♘f4 e6 10.c3 c5 ⇄ , Babiy, A. (2450) –

Miljutin, O. (2165), Ilichevsk 2007) 9...♛d8 (9...♛b6!? 10.a5 ♛e6 11.♗×c7 ♘bd7) 10.♘c1 (10.♘g3 e6 11.♗d3 ♗d6±) 10...e6 11.♘b3 ♗d6 12.♘e5 0-0 (Jelica, M. (2236) – Kaps, D. (2237), Rabac 2003) 13.♗d3 ♘d5 (13...♗×g2 14.♖g1 ♗d5 15.♗h6 g6 16.♗×f8 ♛×f8∞) 14.♗g3 ♘c6 15.0-0 f5⇄;

C2) 7.a3 ♗b7

C2a) 8.♗d3 (8.♗e3 ♘bd7 9.♛d2 e6 10.0-0-0 ♗e7 11.♗d3 b4 12.a×b4 ♛×b4⇄; 10.♗f4 ♛b6 11.0-0-0 ♗d6⇄) 8...e6 (8...g6 9.0-0 ♗g7 10.♖e1 0-0 11.♗g5 ♘bd7 12.♛e2±) 9.0-0 ♘bd7 10.♖e1 ♛b6 11.♗e3 c5 12.♗f1 ♖d8⇄, Timofeeva, G. (2116) – Agapov, S. (2232) Serpukhov 2003;

C2b) 8.♗e2

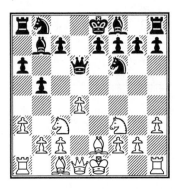

C2b1) 8...g6 9.0-0 ♗g7 (9...♘bd7!?) 10.♗g5 (10.♘e5!? 0-0 11.♗f4) 10...♘bd7 11.♛d2 0-0 12.♗f4 ♛b6 13.♖ad1 (Bodnaruk, A. (2275) – Lomako, A. (2300), Russia 2007) 13...♘d5 14.♘×d5 ♗×d5 15.♛b4 ♖fe8± ;

C2b2) 8...e6 9.0-0

C2b2a) 9...♘bd7 10.♘g5 (10.♗e3 ♗e7 11.♛d2 ♖d8 12.♖fd1 0-0⇄,

Zlatic, M. (2428) – Milanovic, D. (2480), Timisoara 2005) 10...♗e7 11.♗f3 ♗×f3 12.♛×f3 0-0 13.♖d1± ;

C2b2b) 9...♗e7 10.♗e3 0-0 (Doell, D. (2155) – Kopylov, M. (2465), Bad Wiessee 2006) 11.♛d2 ♘bd7 12.♗f4 ♛b6 13.♖ad1 c5 14.d×c5 ♗×c5 15.b4 ♗e7⇄ ;

C3) 7.g3 ♗b7 8.♗g2 e6 9.0-0 ♗e7 10.♘e5 ♗×g2 11.♔×g2 0-0 12.♛f3 c6 13.♗f4?! (13.♖d1) 13...♛×d4 14.♖fd1 (14.♘×c6 ♘×c6 15.♛×c6 ♖fc8∓) 14...♛c5∞ or 10.♗f4 ♛b6 11.a4 c6 (11...b4 12.a5 ♛a7 13.♘e2 ♘d5±, Burijovich, L. (2204) – Malajovich, S. (2090), Argentina 2006) 12.♘e5 0-0 13.a5 ♛d8 14.♘e2 ♘d5 15.♗d2 (15.c4!? b×c4 16.♛a4) 15...♘d7 16.c4 b×c4 17.♘×c4 c5⇄, Ardeleanu, A. (2405) – Nagatz, F. (2275), Dresden 2007;

C4) 7.♗d3 ♗b7

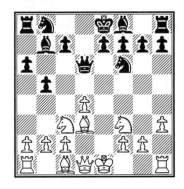

C4a) 8.0-0 e6 9.♛e2 (9.♖e1!? ♗e7 10.a4) 9...♗e7 10.a4 b4 11.♘e4 ♘×e4 12.♗×e4 ♗×e4 13.♛×e4 ♛c6± , Sulc, D. (2312) – Goric, E. (2346), Djakovo 2006;

C4b) 8.♛e2 e6 (8...♘bd7 9.♘e4 ♘×e4 10.♗×e4 ♗×e4 11.♛×e4 c6 12.0-0 e6

13.c3 ♛d5 ⇄, Rezonja, S. (2195) – Nikolov, S. (2415), Bled 1998; 9.0-0!? e6 10.a4) 9.♗g5 ♘bd7 10.a4 b4 11.♘e4 ♛d5 (11...♛c6!? 12.♘fd2 ♗e7) 12.c4 b×c3 13.♘×c3 ♛a5 14.0-0 (Gruenfeld, Y. (2520) – Kudischewitsch, D. (2373), Tel Aviv 2001) 14...♗d6 15.♖fe1 0-0 16.♗d2 ♛h5 ⇄ or 9...♗e7 10.0-0-0 (10.0-0!? ♘c6 11.♛e3) 10...♘bd7 (10...♘c6!?) 11.♖he1 b4 (11...0-0 12.d5!? ♘×d5 13.♗×h7+ ♔×h7 14.♘×d5) 12.♘e4 ♛d5 ⇄, Scholz, C. (2392) – Muse, D. (2443), Germany 2003;

C4c) 8.♗e3 ♘bd7 9.♛e2 (9.0-0 g6 10.♘g5 ♗g7 11.a4 b4 12.♘ce4 ♘×e4 13.♘×e4 ♛c6 14.f3 f5 15.♘d2 0-0 ⇄ or 10.0-0 (10.♛d2 ♗g7 11.♗f4 ♛b6 12.♖fe1 e6 13.♘e4 0-0 ⇄) 9...♘b6 (9...g6!? 10.0-0 ♗g7 11.♖fe1 0-0 12.♗g5 ♖fe8 ⇄) 10...e6 11.a4 b4 12.♘b1 ♘bd5 13.♘bd2 ♘f4 14.♗×f4 ♛×f4 (Brinck Claussen, B. (2325) – Zoltek, T. (2220), Spain 2007) 15.♗b5+ c6 16.♗d3 c5 17.♗b5+ ♔d8 18.♗c4 c×d4 ∞;

D) 6...♘bd7

7.g3 b5 8.♗g2 ♗b7 9.0-0 e6 10.♖e1 ♗e7 11.a4 b4 12.♗f4 ♛b6 13.a5 ♛a7 14.♘a4 ♘d5 15.♗d2 c5 16.c4 b×c3 17.b×c3 c×d4 18.♘×d4 0-0 19.♖b1

½-½, Bielczyk, J. (2359) – Hasangatin, R. (2482), Tatranske Zruby 2001 or 7.♗d3 c5 8.♗e2 (8.♗e3 e6 9.♛e2 – 6...e6 7.♗d3 ♘bd7 8.♛e2 c5 9.♗e3) 8...e6 9.♗e3 c×d4 10.♛×d4 (Olsar, J. (2334) – Hasangatin, R. (2463), Karvina 2001) 10...b5 11.♛×d6 ♗×d6 12.0-0-0 ♔e7 13.♘g5 ♗e5 14.♗f3 ♖b8 ⇄.

We return now to Wood – Bronstein.

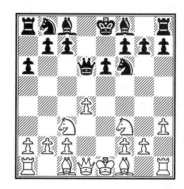

7.♗d3

7.♗e3 (7.♗e2 ♘c6 – 6.♗e2 ♘c6 7.h3 e6, Game 23) 7...b5 (7...♘c6!?) 8.a3 (8.♗d3 ♗b7 9.0-0 ♗e7 ±) 8...♗b7 9.♗e2 (for 9.♛d2 ♘bd7 – 6...b5 7.a3 ♗b7 8.♗e3 ♘bd7 9.♛d2 e6) 9...♘bd7 10.0-0 c5 (10...♗e7!? 11.♛d2 0-0) 11.d×c5 ♛×d1 12.♖a×d1 ♗×c5 13.♗×c5 ♘×c5 14.♘e5 ♔e7=, Ferguson, M. (2360) – Bronstein, D. (2445), Hastings 1995.

7...♘bd7

7...♘c6 – 5.h3 a6 6.♗d3 ♘c6 7.♘f3 e6, Game 30. Alternatives include 7...c5 and 7...♗e7:

A) 7...c5 8.d×c5 ♛c7 9.0-0 (9.b4!?) 9...♗×c5 10.♛e2 (10.♗g5!? ♘bd7 11.♛d2 0-0 12.♖fe1) 10...♘bd7

11.♗g5 h6 12.♗e3 b5 13.♘e4 (Trygstad, K. (2200) – Jamrich, G. (2235), Balatonbereny 1997; 13.a4!?) 13...♗b7 14.♘×c5 ♘×c5 15.♗×c5 ♛×c5∓;

B) 7...♗e7 8.0-0 0-0

B1) 9.♛e2 ♘c6 10.♘e4?! (10.♗e3±) 10...♘×d4 11.♘×d4 ♛×d4 12.♖d1?! (Pushkedra, F. (2293) – Schleifer, M. (2371), Guelph 2002; 12.c3!? ♛b6 13.♗e3) 12...♛e5 13.♘×f6+ ♛×f6 14.♗e4 c6 15.♖d3 g6, and White does not have sufficient compensation for the pawn;

B2) 9.♗g5 ♘bd7 10.♛d2 c5 11.♗f4 ♛b6 12.♗e5 c×d4 13.♗×d4 ♛c7 14.♖fe1 ♗c5 15.♗×f6 (15.♘e4!? ♗×d4 16.♘×d4) 15...♘×f6 16.♘e4?! (16.♖ad1 ♗d7 17.♘e5 ⇄) 16...♘×e4 17.♖×e4 (Dembo, Y. (2402) – Gvetadze, S. (2283), Chisinau 2005) 17...b5 18.♖h4 f5 19.♖e1 h6∓.

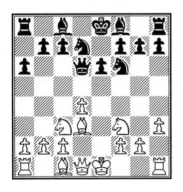

8.♛e2

8.0-0!? c5 (8...♗e7!?) 9.♗e3 ♗e7 10.♛e2 0-0 11.♖ad1 ♛c7

A) 12.♘e4 ♘×e4 13.♗×e4 ♘f6 14.♗d3 (14.♗g5!? ♘×e4 15.♗×e7) 14...b5

15.c4 (Kamstra, C. (2315) – Ye Rongguang (2535), Groningen 1998) 15...♗b7 16.d×c5 ♗×c5 17.♖c1 b4 18.♗×c5 ♛×c5∓;

B) 12.a4 c×d4 13.♗×d4 ♘c5 14.♗c4 ♗d7 15.♘e5 ♗c6 16.b3 ♖ad8 17.♖fe1 (17.♘×c6 ♛×c6∓, Muslija, I. (2237) – Plenkovic, Z. (2311), Omis 2003) 17...♗e4?! (17...♗d6; 17...♗d5) 18.♘×f7 ♖×f7 19.♗×f6 ♖×d1 20.♖×d1 ♗×c2 21.♛×c2 ♗×f6 22.♘e4±.

8...c5 9.♗e3 b5

A) 9...c×d4?! 10.♗×d4 ♗e7 11.0-0-0 ♘c5 12.♔b1 ♘×d3 13.♖×d3 ♛c7 14.♘e5 b5 (Miltner, A. (2330) – Mohrlok, D. (2425), Germany 1992) 15.♖g3 0-0 (15...b4 16.♘a4 0-0 17.♛f3 ♗b7 18.♖×g7+ ♔×g7 19.♛g3+ ♔h8 20.♘g6+ h×g6 21.♛×c7+−) 16.♘g4 ♘e8 (16...♘×g4? 17.♗×g7!) 17.♘h6+ ♔h8 18.♘f5 e×f5 19.♘d5±;

B) 9...♗e7 10.0-0-0 0-0 11.d×c5 ♛c7 12.♘e4 ♘×e4 13.♗×e4 ♘×c5 14.♗×c5 ♛×c5 15.♘e5 (Nakamura, H. (2364) – Arencibia, W. (2534), Ubeda 2001) 15...f5 16.♗f3 ♗f6 17.♖he1 ♖a7 18.♔b1 b5∓.

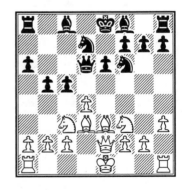

10.♘e4

10.0-0-0 c4 11.♗e4

A) 11...♘xe4? 12.♘xe4 ♛c6 (12...♛d5 13.♘c3 ♛f5 14.♘h4 ♛f6 15.♘e4 ♛e7 16.♗g5±) 13.♗g5 ♘b6 14.d5 ♘xd5 (14...♛c7 15.d6±) 15.♖xd5 ♛xd5 16.♖d1±;

B) 11...b4 12.♗xa8 bxc3 13.bxc3 (13.♛xc4?! ♛b8) 13...♘b6 14.d5 ♘xa8 (14...♘e4! 15.♗d4) 15.♛xc4∞.

10...♛c7 11.dxc5 ♗xc5

11...♘xc5 also looks playable, and now:

A) 12.♘xc5 ♗xc5 13.0-0-0?! ♗xe3+ 14.♛xe3 ♗b7 15.♘e5?! (Bielczyk, J. (2340) – Wagner, N., Marianske Lazne 2004; 15.♖he1 0-0 16.♘e5⇄) 15...♘d5 16.♛g5 (16.♛g3 f6) 16...g6∓; 13.0-0 ♗b7 14.a4 b4 (14...0-0 15.axb5 axb5 16.♗xc5 ♛xc5 17.♛e5±) 15.♖ac1 ♗xe3 (15...0-0 16.c3 b3 17.c4±) 16.♛xe3 ♘d5 17.♛d4 0-0 18.♛h4=;

B) 12.♘xf6+ gxf6 13.0-0-0?! (13.0-0!? ♗b7 14.♖fd1) 13...♗b7 14.♔b1 ♘d3 15.♖xd3 ♖d8 16.♗d4 ♗e7 17.♖hd1?! (Goossens, E. (2229) – Lendwai, R. (2416), Saint Vincent 2005; 17.♖c3 ♛d6 18.♗c5 ♛f4⇄) 17...e5 18.♗e3 ♖xd3 19.cxd3 ♛d7∓; 16.♖xd8+ ♛xd8 (16...♔xd8 17.♖d1+ ♔c8 18.a4 ♛c4 19.♛d2 ♗d5 20.b3 ♛b4 21.♛d3±) 17.♖d1 ♛c7 18.♘d4 h5⇄.

12.♗xc5 (12.a4!? b4 13.0-0) **12...♘xc5 13.♘xc5 ♛xc5 14.0-0** (14.a4!? b4 15.♛e5) **14...♗b7 15.a4 b4** (15...0-0!? 16.axb5 axb5 17.♖xa8 ♖xa8=) **16.♛e5** (16.♖ac1!? 0-0 17.c3) **16...♛e7** (16...♛xe5 17.♘xe5 ♔e7=) **17.♘d2** (17.♘d4 ♖d8 18.♖fe1 ♛d6

19.♘b3 ♗d5=; 17.♛g3 0-0 18.♖fe1 ♘h5 19.♛g4 g6=) **17...0-0 18.♖ae1?!** (18.♘c4 ♖ad8 19.♖ad1⇄) **18...♖fd8 19.f4?!** (19.♘e4 ♘xe4 20.♗xe4 ♗xe4 21.♛xe4 ♖ac8 22.♖d1 a5∓ or 19.♛g3 ♖ac8 20.♖e5 ♗d5∓) **19...♘d7! 20.♛e2** (20.♛d4 ♛c5 21.♛e3 ♛xe3+ 22.♖xe3 ♘c5 with the initiative) **20...♘c5 21.♘e4?** (21.♘c4!? ♘xa4 22.f5 ♛c5+ 23.♔h1) **21...b3?!** (21...♘xa4∓) **22.♘xc5 ♛xc5+ 23.♛f2 ♖ac8 24.♛xc5 ♖xc5 25.♖f2 ♔f8?!** (25...a5!?; 25...g6!?) **26.♖e3 bxc2 27.♗xc2 a5 28.♗e4 ♗a6 29.♔h2 ♖d4 30.♗c2 ♗b7 31.♔g3?!** (31.f5 e5 32.f6 gxf6 (32...g6?! 33.♖fe2) 33.♗xh7 ♘c6 34.b3∓) **31...h5 32.b3 h4+! 33.♔h2** (33.♔xh4 g5+ 34.♔g4 gxf4-+) **33...g6 34.♖e1 ♔g7 35.♖e3 ♗d5 36.♔g1 ♖c8 37.♔f1 f5 38.♔e1 ♔f6 39.♖ee2 ♖c3 40.♖d2 ♖b4 41.♖fe2 ♖xf4 0-1**

Summary: After **1.e4 d5 2.exd5 ♛xd5 3.♘c3 ♛d6 4.d4 ♘f6 5.♘f3 a6 6.h3**, we examined 6.h3 in Game 2 (after 5.♗c4 c6) and in Game 15 (after 5.♘f3 c6). As noted in the summaries of those games, I consider h2-h3 before ...♗c8-g4 as not all that dangerous for Black, and in my opinion, the best way for Black to equalize is 6...♗f5. The same applies here: Black can obtain an equal position after 6...♗f5. But Black has other alternatives offering equality and counterplay: 6...e6, 6...♘c6, or 6...b5, followed by 7...♗b7 and c7-c5 (with or without ♘b8-d7). David Bronstein showed how to employ several of these ideas: **6...e6, 7...♘bd7, 8...c5, 9...b5** and then **14...♗b7**. The legendary Bronstein played this game when he was 71-years old!

Game 20
Areshchenko, A. (2641) –
Gashimov, V. (2644)
Lausanne 2006

**1.e4 d5 2.e×d5 ♕×d5 3.♘c3 ♕d6
4.d4 ♘f6 5.♘f3 a6 6.♘e5**

6...♘c6

Alternatives include **A)** 6...♗e6; **B)**
6...♗f5; **C)** 6...♘bd7; **D)** 6...c5 and **E)**
6...e6.

A) 6...♗e6?! 7.♗f4 ♕b4 (7...♘c6 8.g3,
and, as shown in the line 6...♘c6 7.♗f4
♗e6 8.g3, Black has problems) 8.a3
♕b6 9.d5±; 7...♕d8 8.♕f3 c6 9.0-0-0±
or 7...♕b6 8.♘a4 ♕a5+ 9.c3±;

B) 6...♗f5?! 7.g4 (7.♕f3 ♘c6 8.♘×c6
♗g4∞ or 8.♕×f5 ♘×d4∞) 7...♗e6
(7...♗g6?! 8.♗g2 c5 9.♗e3 or 8...♘c6
9.♗f4) 8.g5 ♘fd7 (8...♘d5?! 9.♘e4
♕b6 10.c4) 9.♘c4 ♗×c4 (9...♕b4?
10.a3+–; 9...♕c6 10.d5+–) 10.♗×c4
♘c6 11.♗e3, and White has better
chances;

C) 6...♘bd7?! 7.♘c4 ♕e6+ (7...♕b4?
8.a3+–; 7...♕c6? 8.d5 ♕c5 9.♗e3+–)
8.♗e2 ♘b6 (8...g6? 9.d5 ♕f5 10.g4+–)
9.♘e5 g6 (9...c5?! 10.0-0) 10.0-0 ♗g7

11.♖e1 0-0 12.♗f3 ♕f5? (12...♕d6)
13.g4 ♕e6 14.♘×g6±;

D) 6...c5?! 7.♘c4 ♕e6+ 8.♗e3 c×d4
9.♕×d4 ♘c6 10.♕d2 ♗d7 (10...b5
11.♘b6 ♖b8 12.0-0-0 g6 13.♘cd5
♘×d5 14.♘×d5 ♕d6 15.♗c5 ♕d7
16.♕e3±, Ponizil, C. (2199) –
Rumjantsev, J., Herceg Novi 2006)
11.0-0-0 ♖d8 12.♗b6 g6 13.♗×d8±,
Stellwagen, D. (2561) – Werner, D.
(2376), Germany 2006;

E) 6...e6 7.♗f4 (7.♗e2 ♘c6!?) 7...c5?!
(7...♘c6!?) 8.d×c5 ♕×c5 9.♘c4 ♘bd7
(Tairova, E. (2415) – Hamrakulova, Y.
(2205), Yerevan 2006) 10.♗e2±;
7...♕b6?! 8.♘c4 ♕c6 (Claesen, J.
(2273) – Gouret, T. (2286), Belgium
2001) 9.♗e2 ♕×g2 (9...♘d5 10.♘×d5
e×d5 11.♘e5 ♕b6 12.0-0 ♘d7 13.c4±)
10.♗f3 ♕h3 11.♗×c7±.

We return now to Areshchenko –
Gashimov.

7.♗f4

7.♘×c6 ♕×c6 and now:

A) 8.♕d3 g6 (8...♗e6!?) 9.d5
(Slobodjan, R. (2550) – Sulava, N.
(2467), Arco 1999) 9...♕b6 10.♗e3

(10.♕e3 ♕d6 or 10...♗f5) 10...♕×b2 11.♖b1 ♕a3∓;

B) 8.♗e3 e6 (8...♗f5!?) 9.a3 (9.♕d2?! ♗b4 10.♗d3 ♕×g2 11.0-0-0 ♕c6∓) 9...♗d6 10.♗e2 (10.f3 0-0 11.♕d2 ♗d7 12.♗d3 ♘d5=) 10...♕×g2 11.♗f3 ♕h3 12.♕e2 h6 13.0-0-0 0-0 14.♖hg1 ♔h8 15.♖g2 ♖b8 16.♖dg1 ♖g8∓, Stoica, V. (2460) – Mozes, E. (2405), Herculane 1996;

C) 8.♗e2 ♕×g2 (8...♗f5 9.♗f3±) 9.♗f3 ♕h3 10.♗f4 c6 (10...♗g4!? 11.♗×g4 ♘×g4) 11.♖g1 (11.d5 c×d5 12.♘×d5 ♕e6+ 13.♗e3∞) 11...g6 (11...♗f5!? 12.♕e2 ♗×c2) 12.♘a4 (12.d5 c×d5 13.♘×d5⯑) 12...♖h6 (Brzeski, M. (2246) – Malaniuk, V. (2539), Mielno 2006) 13.♗c7 ♗f5 14.♘b6 ♖d8 15.♗×d8 ♔×d8 16.♕e2⇄;

D) 8.♗f4

D1) 8...♗e6 9.♕d3 0-0-0 10.0-0-0 g6 11.♗e2 ♗g7 (11...♕×g2 12.d5∞) 12.♗e5 (12.♗f3 ♘d5 13.♗g5 ♖he8⇄) 12...♖he8 (12...♕×g2!?) 13.♗f3 ♗h6+ 14.♔b1 ♕c4 15.♕×c4 ♗×c4 (Polgar, J. (2685) – Kurajica, B. (2548), Benidorm 2002) 16.♖he1±; 8...e6 9.♗e2 ♗b4 10.0-0 ♗×c3 11.b×c3 ♘d5⇄, Rasik V. (2460) – Jirovsky P. (2400), Czechia 2003 or 9.a3 ♗d6 10.♕d2 (Kosintseva, T. (2486) – Dushinok, A. (2263), Sochi 2005) 10...♘e4 11.♘×e4 ♕×e4+ 12.♗e3 ♗d7=;

D2) 8...♗g4 (8...♗f5!?) 9.f3 ♗f5 10.♗d3 ♗×d3 11.♕×d3 e6 12.0-0-0 0-0-0=, Jones, G. (2271) – Drazic, S. (2462), St. Vincent 2003 or 9...♗e6 10.♕d2 (10.♗d3 g6 11.♕e2 ♗g7

12.0-0-0 0-0 13.♔b1? ♘d5 14.♘×d5 ♕×d5 15.c4 ♕×d4 16.♗×c7 ♖ac8 17.♗a5 ♕c5∓, Zelic, M. (2308) – Horvath, C. (2519), Split 2000; 13.♗e5=) 10...0-0-0 11.♗e5 ♗c4 12.♗d3 e6 13.♘e2?! (13.♗×c4) 13...♗d6 14.♗×f6 g×f6∓, Ponomariov, R. (2585) – Hauchard, A. (2500), Belfort 1998;

E) 8.d5

E1) 8...♕b6 9.♗c4 (9.♗e2?! ♗f5 10.♗f3 0-0-0∓, Malbran, G. (2355) – Bianchi, G. (2430), Villa Martelli 1995) 9...♗f5 10.0-0 0-0-0 11.♗b3 e6 12.♕f3 (12.♗e3 ♕b4 13.♗g5 c6⇄, Inkiov, V. (2472) – Nikolaidis, I. (2522), Thessaloniki 2005) 12...♗g4 13.♕g3 ♗d6 14.♗f4 h5=;

E2) 8...♕d6 9.♗e2 (10.♕f4?! (Gunnarsson, J. (2425) – Duffy, S., Bunratty 2008) 10...e5 11.♕a4+ ♗d7 12.♗b5?! ♗×b5 13.♘×b5 ♕b4+; 12.♕b3 b5∓) 9...g6 (9...e5!?) 10.0-0 ♗g7 11.♗f3 0-0 12.♗e3 b5 13.a3 ♗b7 14.♕d2 ♖ad8 (14...e6!?) 15.♖ad1 ♖fe8 16.♕c1 ♕d7 17.♖fe1 ♕f5⇄, Berkvens, J. (2297) – Horvath, C. (2519), Budapest 2000.

Back to Areshchenko – Gashimov.

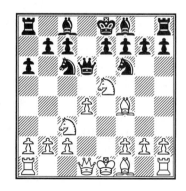

171

7...♘×d4

We examine **A)** 7...♘×e5; **B)** 7...♕×d4;
C) 7...♗g4; **D)** 7...♗e6; **E)** 7...♗f5 and
F) 7...♘g4.

A) 7...♘×e5?! 8.d×e5 (8.♗×e5 ♕b6
9.♕d2 ♗f5 ⇄) 8...♕b4 (8...♕×d1+
9.♖×d1 ±) 9.♕d2 ♘e4 10.♘×e4 ♕×e4+
11.♗e2 ♗f5 (11...♕×g2 12.0-0-0 ♗f5
13.♖hg1 ♕c6 14.♖g3 g6 15.♖b3 ♗g7
16.♗f3 ±) 12.0-0-0 g6 (12...c6 13.♗d3)
13.♗f3 ♕a4 14.♗×b7 ♖b8 15.b3 ♕b5
16.♗f3 ±;

B) 7...♕×d4?! 8.♘×c6 ♕×d1+ 9.♖×d1
b×c6 10.♗×c7 ♗b7 (10...♗f5 11.♗×a6
(Pisk, P. (2319) – Jirovsky, P. (2354),
Czechia 2005) 11...♗×c2 12.♗b7 ♗×d1
13.♗×c6+ ♘d7 14.♗×a8 ± or 10...♘d7
11.♗e2 e6 12.♗g3 ♘d5 13.♘e4 ±)
11.♗e2 e6 12.0-0 with an unpleasant
endgame for Black, Calzetta Ruiz, M.
(2281) – Vinas Guerrero, C. (2096),
Caleta 2005; 12.♘a4!? ♘d5 13.♗a5;

C) 7...♗g4 8.♗e2 (8.f3 ♗f5 9.♗c4
0-0-0 ∞; 8...♗e6!?; 8.♕d2 ♘×e5
9.♗×e5 ♕d7 10.h3 ♗e6 (Brunello, S.
(2234) – Borgo, G. (2423), Milan 2003)
11.♗e2 0-0-0 12.0-0 with better
chances for White; 8...♕×d4 9.♘×c6
♕×d2+ 10.♔×d2 b×c6 11.♗×c7 g6 ⇄)
8...♗×e2 (8...♕×d4?! 9.♕×d4 ♘×d4
10.♗×g4; 8...♘×d4?! 9.♗×g4 ♘×g4
10.♕×g4) 9.♘×e2 ♕e6 ±;

D) 7...♗e6 8.♗g3 (8.♘×f7?! ♕×f4;
8.♘g6?! ♕×d4; 8.♘×c6?! ♕×f4; 8.♕d2
♕×d4 9.♘×c6 ♕×d2+ 10.♔×d2 b×c6
11.♗×c7 g6 ∞, Klykow, L. (2160) –
Krysztofiak, M. (2410), Krakow 2004)
8...♕b4 9.♘×c6 b×c6 (9...♕×b2?!
10.♔d2 b×c6 11.♖b1 ♕a3 12.♕f3)
10.a3 ♕b6 (10...♕×b2?! 11.♘a4 ♕b8

12.♘c5 ♕c8 13.♗e2 g6 14.♗f3)
11.♗e2 with better chances for White;
for example, 11...11...♖d8 (11...g6
12.0-0 ♗g7 13.♘a4; 11...♗f5 12.♘a4
♕b7 13.0-0) 12.♘a4 ♕×d4 13.♗×c7;
8...♘×e5 9.d×e5 ♕×d1+ 10.♖×d1 ♘h5
(10...♘d7!?) 11.♗e2 (11.♗h4!?)
11...♘×g3 12.h×g3 ±;

E) 7...♗f5

8.♗c4 (8.♘g6?! ♕×d4 9.♘×h8 ♕×f4 ∓;
9.♕×d4 ♘×d4 10.0-0-0 h×g6 11.♖×d4
c6 ∓ or 8.♘×f7?! ♕×f4 9.♘×h8 ♘e4
10.♘×e4 ♕×e4+ 11.♕e2 ♕×e2+
12.♗×e2 ♘×d4 13.♗d1 g6 ∓; 8.♕d2
♕×d4 9.♘×c6 ♕×d2+ 10.♔×d2 b×c6
11.♗×c7 g6=)

E1) 8...♘×e5 9.d×e5?! (9.♗×e5 ♕b6
10.♕d2 ♗f5 ⇄) 9...♕b4 (9...♕c6?!
10.♕e2 ♕×g2 11.0-0-0, Arakhamia
Grant, K. (2425) – Mashinskaya, I.
(2300), Varna 2002; 10.♕d4!? ♖d8
11.♗×f7+) 10.♕e2 ♕×b2 11.0-0 ♕×c3
12.e×f6 g×f6 13.♖ab1 ♕c2 14.♕×c2
♗×c2 15.♖×b7 e5 16.♖×c7 ♔d8
17.♖×f7 e×f4 ∓ or 13.♖fd1 e5 14.♖ab1
♕c2 ∓;

E2) 8...e6 (8...0-0-0 9.0-0 e6 ⇄)
9.♘e2 (9.♘g6? ♕b4; 9.♘×f7?! ♕×f4)
9...♘×e5 10.d×e5 ♕b4+ 11.♕d2

♛xc4 12.exf6 gxf6 13.0-0-0 e5∓,
Filipowicz, H. – Demidowicz, A.,
Krynica 2001 or 9.♛f3 ♛xd4 10.♞xc6
(10.♜d1 ♛c5 11.♞xc6 ♝g4 12.♞e4
♝xf3 13.♞xc5 ♝xc6–+ or 11.♝b3
♞xe5 12.♛xb7 ♜d8 13.♜xd8+
♚xd8∓) 10...♛xc4 11.♞e5 (11.♞a5?!
♛b4 12.♛xb7 ♛xb7 13.♞xb7 ♜b8
14.♞a5 ♜xb2∓, Markholev, D. (2255)
– Panbukchian, V. (2425), Elenite 1993)
11...♛b4∞;

F) 7...♞g4?!

Andreas Tzermiadianos calls 7...♞g4 "a
strong GM Vasilios Kotronias novelty."
(*New in Chess Yearbook* #81, 2007). I
recommended this move in the first edition of this book, 2001, but see my new
analysis: 8.♞e4 ♛d5 (8...♛b4+?! 9.c3;
8...♛e6?! 9.♝c4 ♛f5 10.♝xf7+ ♚d8
11.♞xc6+ bxc6 12.♛f3 ♛xf7 13.♞g5)
9.♞c3 (9.f3 ♞gxe5 10.dxe5±)

F1) 9...♛xd4?! (9...♛e6?! 10.♝c4 ♛f5
11.♝xf7+ ♚d8 12.♝g3±) 10.♛xd4
♞xd4 11.♞d5! ♞e6 (11...♞c2+
12.♚d2 ♞xe5 13.♞xc7+ ♚d7/♚d8
14.♝xe5 ♞xa1 15.♞xa8±; 11...♞xe5
12.♞xc7+ with the same line) 12.♞xg4
c6 13.♞b6 ♞xf4 14.♞xa8 ♝xg4 15.f3
♝f5 16.0-0-0 e6 (or 16...e5) 17.g4 with
an unpleasant endgame for Black;

F2) 9...♛d6 10.♞d3 (10.♝c4!? ♞gxe5
11.dxe5 ♞xe5 12.♛e2 or 11...♛b4
12.♛d3)

F2a) 10...♛e6+ 11.♝e2 ♞xd4
(11...♛f5 12.h3 ♞f6 13.0-0 ♞xd4
14.♝xc7 ♞xe2+ 15.♛xe2 with better
chances for White; for example, 15...e6
16.♜ad1 ♝e7 17.♞e5 0-0 18.♝d6
♝xd6 19.♜xd6 b5 20.f4± or 15...b5
16.♜ad1 ♝b7 17.♞e5 e6 18.♞xb5±)
12.♞c5 ♛c6 (12...♛f6 13.♞d5)
13.♞xa6 ♜xa6 14.♛xd4 e5 15.♝xe5
♝c5 16.♝b5±;

F2b) 10...♛xd4 11.♝xc7 e5 (∓
Tzermiadianos, A.) 12.h3 ♝e6
(12...♞f6?! 13.♞xe5) 13.hxg4 ♜c8
14.♞xe5 ♛xd1+ 15.♚xd1! (15.♜xd1
♜xc7 16.♞xc6 ♜xc6 17.♝e2 ♝b4=)
15...♜xc7 16.♞xc6 ♜xc6 17.f3, and
Black does not have enough compensation for the pawn; for example,
17...♝b4 18.♞e4 0-0 19.♝d3 ♜d8
20.♚e2 or 17...♝d6 18.♞e4 ♝e5 19.c3
0-0 20.♚c2.

Let's return to Areshchenko –
Gashimov.

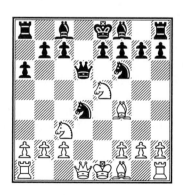

8.♝d3

White plays a real gambit!

Other alternatives: **A)** 8.♘×f7; **B)** 8.♘g6 and **C)** 8.♗c4.

A) 8.♘×f7?! ♕×f4 9.♘×h8 ♗f5 (9...g6 10.♗d3 ♗g4 11.♘×g6 h×g6 12.♗×g6+ ♔d7∞; 10...♘g4!?) 10.♗d3 (10.♘e2 ♘×e2 11.♕×e2 g6 12.f3 ♗g7 13.g3 ♕b4+ 14.c3 ♕b6∓; 11.♗×e2 ♕b4+) 10...♘g4 11.♕d2 ♕×d2+ 12.♔×d2 ♖d8 (12...♘×f2? 13.♗×f5 ♘×h1 14.♗×h7 ♘f2 15.♔e3+−, Belov, V. (2552) − Hasangatin, R (2474) , Internet 2004) 13.♘e4 g6 14.h3 ♗h6+ 15.♔e1 ♘e5∓;

B) 8.♘g6 ♕e6+ 9.♘e5 ♕b6 10.♘c4 ♕c5 (10...♕e6+ 11.♘e5 ♕d6 12.♘g6 ♕e6+ 13.♘e5 ½-½, Smith, R. (2290) − Sermek, D. (2545), Auckland 2000; 11.♘e3!?) 11.b4 ♕a7 12.♗e3 (12.♗×c7 ♗f5∞) 12...c5 13.b×c5 ♘f5 14.♕d2 e5∞; 10.♗e3 (10.♗c4!?) 10...c5 11.♘a4 ♕c7 12.♗×d4 c×d4 13.♕×d4 ♗f5 (13...♕×c2 14.♗d3 ♕c7 15.♘b6 ♖b8 16.0-0⩲) 14.♘b6 ♖d8 15.♕a4+ ♘d7 16.♘e×d7 ♗×d7 17.♘×d7 ♕×d7 18.♕×d7+ ♖×d7=;

C) 8.♗c4 ♗e6

C1) 9.♘e2 ♗×c4 10.♘×d4 (Ageichenko, G. (2343) − Zaitsev, V. (2412), Moscow 1999) 10...♕b4+ 11.♗d2 ♕×b2 12.♘df3 ♗d5∓; 9.♘g6 ♕c5 10.♘×h8 (10.♗×e6 h×g6 11.♗e3 ♖d8∓, Calzetta Ruiz, M. (2307) − Scharrer, P. (2210), Verona 2006) 10...♗×c4 11.♗e3 0-0-0∓; 9.♘×f7 ♕×f4 10.♗×e6 ♘×e6 11.♘×h8 ♖d8∓;

C2) 9.♗×e6 (9.♗d3 ♕b4 10.♕d2 0-0-0 11.0-0-0 g6 12.a3 ♕a5 13.♖he1 ♗g7 14.♗h6 ♗×h6 15.♕×h6 ♘g4∓, Timofeev, V. (2293) − Lysyj, I. (2523), Moscow 2006) 9...♘×e6 10.♕f3 ♘×f4 11.♕×f4

C2a) 11...g5 12.♕f5 (12.♕×g5?! ♖g8 13.♕e3 ♖×g2 14.♖d1 ♗h6∓; 13.♕f5 ♖×g2 14.♖d1 ♕e6 15.♕×e6 f×e6∓) 12...♕b4 (12...♕e6 13.♕×e6 f×e6 14.0-0-0 ♗g7 15.♖he1∞) 13.♖d1 ♗g7 (13...♗h6?! 14.♘d7 ♘×d7 15.♕×d7+ ♔f8 16.0-0⩲, Movsisyan, M. (2280) − Braunlich, T. (2195), USA 2007) 14.0-0 (14.♕×g5 ♕×b2 15.0-0 0-0 16.♖d3 ♘e4 17.♘×e4 ♕×e5 18.♕×e5 ♗×e5 19.♖d7 f5 20.♖×e7 ♖fe8∓) 14...0-0 15.♘d3 ♕h4 16.♕c5 ♖ac8∞;

C2b) 11...e6 12.0-0 ♗e7

C2b1) 13.♖ad1 ♕b6 (13...♕b4!?) 14.♘e4 (14.♘c4 ♕c5 15.♘e4 ♘×e4 16.♕×e4 0-0 17.b3 b6 18.♘e5 ♖fe8∓) 14...♕×b2 (14...0-0?! 15.♘×f6+ ♗×f6 16.♘d7) 15.♖b1 ♕×c2∓

C2b2) 13.♘e4

C2b2a) 13...♕d5 14.♖fe1 ♖d8 15.c4 (15.♘c3 ♕a5 16.a3 0-0 17.b4 ♕b6∓ or 16.♕f3 ♗d6 17.♘c4 ♕b4 18.b3 0-0∓) 15...♕d4 16.♘f3 (Mortensen, E. (2430) − Bronstein, D. (2445), Hastings 1995) 16...♕b6 17.b3 0-0∓;

C2b2b) 13...♕b4 14.♖fe1 0-0 (14...♕×b2 15.♖ab1 ♕×c2 16.♖×b7?!

0-0-0 17.♖bb1 ♖d4∓; 16.♖bc1 ♕xa2 17.♖xc7 ♕d5 18.♘xf6+ gxf6 19.♘d7 ♖g8 20.g3∞) 15.c3 (Perpinya Rofes, L. (2385) – Avila Jimenez, J. (2285), Spain 2008) 15...♕xb2 16.♖ab1 ♕xa2 17.♘xf6+ ♗xf6 18.♘d7 ♗xc3∓ or 15.♘xf6+ gxf6 16.♕g3+ ♔h8 17.c3 (17.♘d3 ♕c4∓) 17...♕xb2 18.♘c4 ♕b5 19.♕xc7 ♖fe8 20.♖ab1 ♖ac8∓.

Back to Areshchenko – Gashimov.

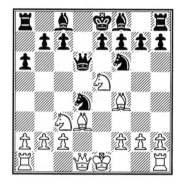

8...♗f5

Alternatives are **A)** 8...♘g4; **B)** 8...g5 and **C)** 8...♘e6.

A) 8...♘g4?! 9.♘e4 ♕b6 (9...♕d5 10.♘xg4 ♗xg4 11.♕xg4 f5 12.♕g5 ♕e6 13.0-0 fxe4 14.♖fe1±) 10.♘xg4 ♗xg4 (10...f5 11.0-0 fxg4 12.♗e3 c5 13.c3±) 11.♕xg4 f5 12.♕d1 fxe4 13.♗xe4 0-0-0 14.0-0 e6 15.c3 with an unpleasant position for Black;

B) 8...g5 9.♗g3 ♗f5 (9...♘f5 10.♕e2 ♘xg3 11.hxg3 ♗e6 12.0-0-0⯐, Mastrovasilis, D. (2568) – Skembris, S. (2434), Kavala 2004) 10.♘xf7 (10.0-0 ♕b6 11.♗xf5 ♘xf5∞ or 11.♘c4 ♕c5∞) 10...♕e6+ 11.♘e5 ♗xd3∞ or 10...0-0-0∞;

C) 8...♘e6

C1) 9.♕f3 (9.♘xf7?! ♕c6! 10.♘xh8 ♘xf4∓) 9...♘xf4 (9...g5 10.♗g3 ♘f4 11.♗xf4 gxf4 12.♕xf4 ♗e6∞) 10.♕xf4 g5 11.♕e3 (11.♕xg5 ♖g8 12.♕e3 ♖xg2 13.0-0-0 ♕b6∞) 11...♘g4 12.♘xg4 ♗xg4 13.♕xg5 h5∞;

C2) 9.♗g3 ♕b6 (9...♘c5!? 10.♕d2 g6 11.0-0-0 ♗g7) 10.0-0 (10.♕d2!? g6 11.0-0-0 ♗g7 12.♗c4) 10...g6 11.♔h1? (11.♘a4∞) 11...♗g7 12.h4 (12.f4 ♘h5 13.♗f2 ♕xb2∓, Andreev, E. (2440) – Lysyj, I. (2575), Nizhnij Tagil 2007 or 12.♘c4 ♕c5 13.f3 0-0 14.♗f2 ♕h5∓) 12...c6 13.♘a4 ♕a7 (13...♕d4!? 14.♘c4? b5 15.♘cb6 bxa4 16.♘xa8 ♕a7∓; 14.♕a5 ♕d5∞) 14.♕a5 b5 15.♗xg6?! (15.♘xc6 ♕b7 16.♘d8 ♕xg2⯐) 15...fxg6 16.♘xc6 ♗h6+ 17.♔b1 ♕b7 18.♘d8 ♘xd8 19.♖xd8+ ♔f7 20.♖xh8 bxa4∓, Kostenko, P. (2482) – Ovetchkin, R. (2557), Samara 2002.

We return now to Areshchenko – Gashimov.

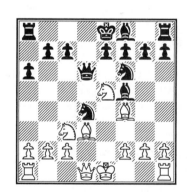

9.0-0

9.♗xf5!? ♘xf5 10.♕f3.

9...♗xd3

9...g5!? 10.♗g3 ♕b6.

10.♕×d3 ♘e6?!

Better was 10...♘c6 11.♕e2 ♘×e5 (11...♕b4!? 12.♕e3 e6 13.♘×c6 b×c6 14.♗c7 ♗e7=; 12.♘d3 ♕a5∞) 12.♗×e5 and now:

A) 12...♕e6 13.♖ad1 ♘d7 14.♗×c7 ♕×e2 15.♘×e2 ♖c8 16.♗a5 ♖c2? (16...e6±) 17.♖×d7 ♔×d7 18.♖d1+ and White wins or 13.♗×c7 ♕×e2 14.♘×e2 ♖c8 (Tzermiadianos ended his analysis of this line with ∓) 15.♗e5 ♖×c2 16.♖ac1 ♖×e2 17.♖fd1 e6 (17...♘d5 18.♖×d5 f6 19.♖c8+ ♔f7 20.♗c3±) 18.♖c8+ ♔e7 19.♖c7+ ♔e8 20.♖c8+ ½-½;

B) 12...♘c6 13.♖ad1 (13.♖fe1 0-0-0 14.♖ad1 ♖×d1 15.♖×d1 ♘d7 16.♕d3 f6∞; 14.♕e3 ♕b6 15.♕f4 g6∞) 13...e6:

B1) 14.♗×f6 g×f6 15.♖fe1 (15.♘d5 0-0-0 16.♘×f6 ♗g7 17.♖×d8+ ♖×d8 18.♘×h7 ♕d5 19.♕g4 ♗×b2∓) 15...h5 (15...♖g8!?) 16.♖d3 ♗d6 17.♘e4 0-0-0 18.♘×f6 ♕a4 19.♘e4 ♗e7⇄;

B2) 14.♖d3 ♗d6 15.♖g3 (Hommeles, T. (2384) – Dutreeuw, M. (2352), Belgium 2004) 15...♖g8 16.♗×d6 c×d6 17.♖d1 d5 18.b4 (18.♖gd3 0-0-0∓;

18.a4 ♕c5 19.♖gd3 0-0-0∓) 18...♕d6 19.b5 ♖c8 20.b×a6 b×a6 21.♖b1 g5∓; 15.♗×f6 g×f6 16.♘e4 (16.♕h5 ♕c5 17.♘e4 ♕×h5 18.♘×f6+ ♔e7 19.♘×h5 ♖ad8∓) 16...0-0-0 17.♘×f6 ♕a4 (17...h5!?) 18.♘e4 ♗e7⇄.

Let's return to Areshchenko – Gashimov.

11.♕f3 c6

11...♕b6 12.♖ad1 (12.♖fd1!?) 12...♘×f4 (12...♕×b2 13.♖b1 ♕a3 14.♕×b7±; 12...g6 13.♘d5 ♕×b2 14.♘c7+ ♘c7 15.♖b1 ♕d4 16.♕×b7 with a winning attack or 13...♘×d5 14.♗e3±) 13.♕×f4 e6 14.♘e4 ♗e7 15.♘×f6+ g×f6 (15...♗×f6 16.♘d7 ♕×b2 17.♕×c7) 16.♘d7 ♕×b2 17.♕×c7 ♕b5 18.♘b6 ♖d8 19.♕×b7 ♔f8 20.c4±.

12.♖ad1 ♕b4

12...♕c5 13.♖fe1 ♖d8 (13...♘×f4 14.♕×f4 e6 15.♘e4±; 13...g5 14.♘e4 ♘×e4 15.♕×e4 g×f4 16.♕f5+− or 15...♘×f4 16.♕f5+−) 14.♖×d8+ ♘×d8 15.♖d1 ♕b6 (15...♘e6 16.♕d3 ♕b6 17.♗g3) 16.♘c4 ♕c5 17.♕d3 ♘e6 18.b4 ♕h5 19.♗e5+− or 17...♘d5 18.♗e3+−.

13.♗g3 (13.♘d3!? ♕b6 14.♗e3)
13...♖c8

13...g6 14.♘×c6 ♕g4 15.♕×g4 ♘×g4 16.♘d4 (16.♘a5 h5 17.♘d5 h4∞) 16...♘×d4 17.♖×d4 17...♘f6 (17...f5 18.♘d5 ♔f7 19.f3 ♗g7 20.♖b4 ♘f6 21.♘×f6 ♗×f6 22.♖×b7, and White has an extra pawn) 18.a4 ♘h5 (18...♗g7 19.♖b4±) 19.♘d5 ♗g7 20.♖d3! (20.♖b4 ♖d8 21.♘c7+ ♔d7!±)

176

20...♖c8 21.♖e1 e6 22.♘c7+ ♔f8 (22...♔e7 23.♗d6+ ♔d7 24.g4 ♘f6 25.♗f8+) 23.♗d6+ ♔g8 24.♖b3 ♗f8 25.♗×f8 ♖×c7 26.♗h6 ♘f6 27.♖d1 ± or 26...f5 27.♖×e6±.

14.a3

14...♕b6?!

It may be difficult to believe, but after this move, Black is in a peculiar *zugzwang* with fourteen pieces and pawns!

14...♕×b2 15.♖d3

A) 15...♘c5 16.♖b1 ♘×d3? (16...♕×c2! 17.♕f5 – 15...♕×c2! below) 17.♖×b2 ♘×b2 18.♕e3 ♖d8 19.♕b6 ♘d1 20.♕b3 e6 21.♕×b7 ♘d7 22.♘e4 ♘×e5 23.♗×e5 ♖d7 (23...♘b2 24.♕×c6+ ♔e7 25.♗f6+ g×f6 26.♕c5+ ♔e8 27.♘×f6#) 24.♕a8+ ♔e7 25.♕×c6±;

B) 15...♕×c2! 16.♖b1 ♘c5 17.♕f5 ♕×b1+ 18.♘×b1 e6 19.♕f3 ♘×d3 20.♘×d3, and White's position is better but there does not appear a clear path to victory.

15.♘e4 (15.b4!?; 15.♕e2!?) **15...h5**

A) 15...♘d4 16.♕e3 ♘×e4 (16...c5 17.♘g5±; 16...♖d8 17.♘c4 ♕a7 18.♘ed6+) 17.♖×d4 ♘d6 18.♘d7!±;

B) 15...♖d8 16.♖×d8+ ♕×d8 17.♖d1 ♕b6 18.b4 h5 (18...♖g8 19.♕f5 c5 20.♘g5 g6 21.♕h3±) 19.♕d3 ♕d8 20.♕×d8+ ♘×d8 21.♖×d8+ ♔×d8 22.♘×f7+ ♔d7 23.♘×f6+ e×f6 24.♘×h8+−;

C) 15...♕×b2 16.♕f5 ♖a8 (16...h6 17.♘c5 ♕a2 18.c4 g6 19.♘×e6 g×f5 20.♖d8+ ♖×d8 21.♘c7#) 17.♖fe1 ♕b5 (17...♕×a3 18.♘×f6+ g×f6 19.♘×f7 ♕×f7 20.♕×e6+ ♔g6 21.♖e3 ♕c5 22.♗e5+−) 18.♕h3 ♘×e4 19.♖×e4 g6 20.♘×f7±.

16.h4 ♘d4 17.♕e3 c5 18.c3 ♘e6 19.♕f3 ♕b3 20.♖d3 ♖d8 21.♖fd1 ♖×d3 22.♕×d3 ♕a4 23.♘×c5+− ♕×d1+ 24.♕×d1 ♘×c5 25.b4 ♘cd7 26.♘×d7 ♘×d7 27.♕d5 ♖h6 28.♕×b7 e5 29.♗×e5 1-0

Summary: After **1.e4 d5 2.e×d5 ♕×d5 3.♘c3 ♕d6 4.d4 ♘f6 5.♘f3 a6 6.♘e5**, Black has a lot of possible moves. I think 6...e6 or 6...♘c6 is good for Black. I consider **6...♘c6** the best. Now White has two alternatives:

A) 7.♘×c6 ♕×c6, and here White has many interesting continuations; for example, 8.♕d3, 8.♗e3, 8.♗e2, 8.♗f4, and 8.d5. But after each of them, Black has a game with counterplay. The most dangerous for Black is 8.♗f4 ♗e6 9.♗e2 (there are many possibilities here where White retains the initiative although the lines are not that clear). But after 8.♗f4 Black can look to safer alternatives, 8...e6, 8...♗g4 or 8...♗f5. After 8.d5 I recommend 9...♛b6 or 9...♛d6 with good counterchances.

B) 7.♗f4 After this move (more aggressive than 7.♘xc6) Black has many interesting possibilities: 7...♘xe5, 7...♛xd4, 7...♗f5, 7...♘g4, 7...♗e6, 7...♗g4 and 7...♘xd4. I can recommend 7...♗f5 and the riskier 7...♘xd4. After 7...♘xd4 8.♗d3 (This is the best after 7...♘xd4), I recommend 8...♘e6 with good counterchances.

Game 21
Khakimov, T. (2380) –
Ginzburg, M. (2260)
St. Petersburg 2008

1.e4 d5 2.exd5 ♛xd5 3.♘c3 ♛d6 4.d4 ♘f6 5.♘f3 a6 6.♗e3 ♘c6

7.♛d2

For 7.♗e2 see Game 23; 7.♗d3, Game 25; and 7.♗c4, Game 28. Now there is **A)** 7.d5; **B)** 7.a3 and **C)** 7.h3.

A) 7.d5 ♘b4 8.♗c4 c6 9.dxc6 ♛xd1+ 10.♖xd1 ♘c2+ 11.♔e2 ♘xe3 (Holmsten, A. (2405) – Kiik, K. (2446), Espoo 2006) 12.fxe3 bxc6 13.♘e5 e6 14.♘xc6 ♗b7 15.♘a5 ∞;

B) 7.a3 e6 8.♗d3 ♗e7 9.0-0 (9.♛d2!? 0-0 10.♗f4) 9...0-0 10.♛d2 b5 11.♗g5

♖d8 12.♘e4 ♘xe4 13.♗xe4 ♗b7±, Koch, J. (2510) – Fressinet, L. (2440), Besancon 1999 or 7...♗g4 8.h3 ♗h5 9.g4 (9.♛e2 e6 10.0-0-0 0-0-0 11.g3 ♘d5 12.♘e4 ♛d7 13.♗g2 ♘xe3 14.♛xe3=, Gavrilov, A. (2465) – Perez Garcia, R. (2170), Seville 2007) 9...♗g6 10.d5 ♘e5 11.♘h4 (Scherer, H. (2250) – Koeller, O. (2345), Germany 1994) 11...♘e4 (11...0-0-0? 12.f4) 12.♘xg6 ♘xc3 13.bxc3 hxg6±;

C) 7.h3

C1) 7...e5 8.dxe5 (8.♗c4!?) 8...♘xe5 9.♘xe5 (9.♗f4!? ♘d3+ 10.♗xd3 ♛xf4 11.♛e2+) 9...♛xe5 10.♗c4 (Solomaha, A. (2384) – Vasiliev, M. (2213), Alushta 2005) 10...♗d6 11.♛e2 0-0 12.0-0-0 b5 ⇄;

C2) 7...♗f5

C2a) 8.♗c4 ♘b4 (8...e6 9.♛e2 ♘b4 10.♗b3 ♗e7 11.♖d1 ♘bd5 12.♘xd5 exd5 13.0-0 0-0 14.♖fe1±, Vang, F. – Westerinen, H. (2360), Torshavn 2003 or 11.♘e5 ♘bd5 12.♘xd5 ♘xd5 13.♗d2 (Groetz, H. (2299) – Brustkern, J. (2251), Kecskemet 2005) 13...♘f6±) 9.♗b3 e6 10.g4 ♗g6 11.♘e5 0-0-0 (11...♗e7!? 12.♘xg6 hxg6) 12.♛f3 ♗e7 13.0-0-0

♖hf8 14.♖he1 (14.♗f4!?) 14...♘bd5 15.♘xd5 ♘xd5 16.c4 ♘xe3 ½-½, Papa, S. (2411) – Benkovic, P. (2430), Winterthur 2004;

C2b) 8.a3 0-0-0?! 9.♘g5! (9.♕d2 e5=, Nakhapetian, P. (2226) – Krutko, A. (2324), Dagomys 2004) 9...♗e6 (9...♗g6 10.♗d3) 10.♕e2 g6 11.♘xe6 ♕xe6 12.0-0-0 ♗g7 13.♕f3 with better chances for White; 8...e5 (8...e6 9.♗c4 ♗e7 10.0-0 0-0 11.♕e2 ♘d5=, Muuss, K. (2010) – Schellmann, F. (2125), Dresden 2006; 9.♗d3!? 0-0-0 10.0-0) 9.dxe5 ♘xe5 10.♕e2 (10.♘d4 ♗d7 11.♕e2 0-0-0 12.0-0-0±, Pinter, P. (2150) – Bombek, P. (2240), Slovakia 2002) 10...♗e7 (10...0-0-0!?) 11.♖d1 ♘xf3+ 12.♕xf3 ♕e5 13.♗d3 ♗d7 14.♕xb7 0-0 15.♔f1 ∞.

We return now to Khakimov – Ginzburg.

7...♗g4

8.♗c4 – Game 26; 8.♗e2 – Game 23; 7...e5?! 8.♘xe5 ♘xe5 (Bogner, S. (2191) – Ivanov, M. (2453), Neuhausen 2004) 9.♗f4 ♘fd7 10.0-0-0; 7...♘b4!? 8.a3 ♘bd5 9.♘xd5 ♘xd5 10.c4 ♘xe3 11.♕xe3 ♕e6=, Solomon, S. (2465) – Xie, G. (2410), Parramatta 2008.

After 7...♗f5, we examine the following alternatives: **A)** 8.a3; **B)** 8.♘h4; **C)** 8.♗d3; **D)** 8.♗f4 and **E)** 8.0-0-0.

A) 8.a3 e6

A1) 9.♗c4 ♗e7 (9...♘e4!?) 10.♘h4 ♗e4 11.♘xe4 ♘xe4 12.♕d3 ♘c5 13.dxc5 ♕xd3 14.♗xd3 ♗xh4 ½-½, Rodriguez, K. (2440) – Reinhart, K. (2458), USA 2003;

A2) 9.h3 ♗e7 10.♗e2 0-0 11.0-0 ♖fd8 (11...♘d5!?) 12.♖fd1 ♖ac8 13.♖ac1 ♘d5 14.♘a4 ♘xe3 15.♕xe3 ♕d5 16.♘c3 ♕d6 17.♘e4 (17.d5 exd5 18.♘xd5 ♕c5 19.♘xe7+ ♕xe7 20.♕xe7 ♘xe7 21.c3 ♖e8=) 17...♗xe4 18.♕xe4 ♗f6 19.c3 g6 20.h4 h5=, Myo Naing (2394) – Goh Koong Jong, J. (2314), Ho Chi Minh City 2003;

B) 8.♘h4 ♗e6 (8...♗d7 9.♘f3 ♗f5, Zhang Zhong (2636) – Ye Jiangchuan (2670), Beijing 2000; 9.0-0-0!?)

B1) 9.0-0-0 0-0-0 10.♗e2 h6 11.f4 ♘b4 12.♔b1 ♘fd5 13.♘xd5 ♘xd5 14.♘f3 ♔b8 15.♘e5 f6 16.♘g6 ♖g8 17.♘xf8 ♖gxf8 18.♗f3 ½-½, Meier, V. (2280) – Grafl, F. (2411), Germany 2005;

B2) 9.a3

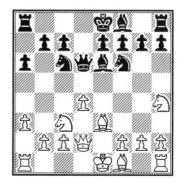

B2a) 9...0-0-0 10.0-0-0 (10.♘f3 h6 11.0-0-0 g5⇄) 10...♗g4 11.♗e2 ♗xe2 12.♛xe2 e6 13.♘f3 ♗e7 14.♖he1 ♖hf8 15.♗g5 h6 16.♗h4 ½-½, Hnatovsky, N. – Djoudi, A., Internet 2003;

B2b) 9...g6 10.0-0-0 0-0-0 11.♘f3

B2b1) 11...♗g7 12.♘g5 ♖d7 13.♘xe6 fxe6 14.♗c4 ♘a5 15.♗e2 ♛c6 16.♗f3 ♘d5 17.♗xd5 exd5 18.b3 ½-½, Fogarasi, T. (2446) – Narciso Dublan, M. (2544), Budapest 2001;

B2b2) 11...h6 12.♗f4 ♛d7 13.♘e5 ♘xe5 14.♗xe5 ♗g7 (Karolyi, T.) 15.d5! ♛e8 (15...♗f5 16.♛e3 ♚b8 17.♗xa6 bxa6 18.♛b6+ ♚c8 19.♛xa6+ ♚b8 20.♘b5+−) 16.♛d4 ♗xd5 17.♛a7 ♛c6 18.♖d3 e6 19.♘xd5 ♖xd5 20.♖c3 ♖xe5 21.♖xc6 bxc6 22.♗xa6+ ♚d7 23.c4±;

B2b3) 11...♛d7 12.♚b1 (12.♘g5 ♗h6 13.♘xe6 ♗xe3 14.♛xe3 ♛xe6 15.♗e2 ♖d6 16.♗f3 ♖hd8 17.♛xe6+ fxe6 18.♗xc6 ♖xc6=) 12...♘d5 13.♘g5 (13.♘xd5 ♗xd5 14.c4 ♗e4+ 15.♗d3 ♗xf3 16.gxf3 ♗g7⇄) 13...♘xc3+ 14.♛xc3 ♗d5 15.♗c4 e6=;

C) 8.♗d3

8...♗xd3 9.♛xd3

C1) 9...♘b4 10.♛e2 ♘bd5 11.♘xd5 ♘xd5 12.0-0 e6 13.♗d2 ♗e7 14.c4 ♘f6 15.♖fe1 c6 16.♖ad1 0-0±, Exizoglou, D. (2185) – Kulicov, O. (2400), Litohoro 2006;

C2) 9...e6 10.0-0-0 ♗e7 (10...0-0-0!?) 11.♚b1 0-0 12.♘e4 ♘xe4 13.♛xe4 ♛d5 14.♛xd5 exd5=, Zaw, W. (2497) – Goh Koong Jong, J. (2314), Ho Chi Minh City 2003.

D) 8.♗f4

D1) 8...♛d7 9.♗c4 e6 10.a3 ♗d6 11.0-0-0 0-0-0 12.h3 h6 (12...♘e4!?) 13.♖he1 g5 14.♗e5 ♗xe5 15.♘xe5 ♘xe5 16.♖xe5 ♛c6 17.♗f1=, Lorenzini, M. (2367) – Rosa Cintas, R. (2058), Alicante 2001;

D2) 8...♛b4 9.0-0-0 (9.♗xc7 ♛xb2 10.♖b1 ♛xc2 11.♖xb7 e6 12.♛xc2 ♗xc2 13.♚d2 ♗g6∞) 9...0-0-0 10.♗xc7 ♚xc7 11.♛f4+ e5 12.♛xf5 exd4 13.♘e4 ♖d5 14.♛f4+ ♗d6 15.♘xd6 ♛xd6 16.♛xd6+ ♖xd6=, Bellia, F. (2397) – Belotti, B. (2435), Milan 2003;

E) 8.0-0-0 ♘b4 (8...e6 9.♘h4 ♗g6 10.♘xg6 hxg6±, Gongora Reyes, M. (2454) – Almeida, O. (2452), Santa Clara 2005) 9.♗f4 ♛b6

E1) 10.♘e5?! (Biro, G. (2170) – Jaroka, S. (2293), Hungary 2004) 10...♗xc2 11.♘c4 ♛a7 12.♖e1 ♗g6 13.♗xc7 b5 14.♗a5 e6 15.♘e5 ♖c8∓;

E2) 10.a3 ♘xc2 (10...♘bd5!?) 11.♗d3 ♘a1 (11...♗xd3 12.♛xd3 ♘a1 13.b4 a5 14.♚b2 axb4 15.♛b5+ ♛xb5

16.♘×b5±; 12...♘×a3 13.b×a3 e6 14.a4±; 15...♛d8 16.a×b4±) 12.♔b1 ♘b3 13.♛c2 ♗e6 (13...♗×d3 14.♖×d3 ♘a5 15.♘a4 ♛c6 (Gamazo, J. – Brayman, N., Internet 2003) 16.♖c3 ♛e4 17.♗×c7 ♘c6 18.♘b6±) 14.♘a4 (14.♖he1!?) 14...♛a5 15.♘c5 ♘×c5 16.d×c5 c6∞.

Back to Khakimov – Ginzburg.

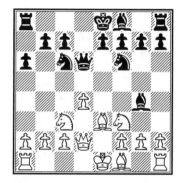

8.♘g5

8.♗f4 (8.♗e2 – Game 23, 6.♗e2 ♘c6 7.♗e3 ♗g4 8.♛d2.8.0-0-0 e6 9.h3 (9.a3 0-0-0) 9...♗×f3 10.g×f3 0-0-0±) 8...♛e6+ (8...♛d7?! 9.d5 ♘b4 10.0-0-0) 9.♘e5 (9.♗e2?! ♗×f3 10.g×f3 0-0-0 11.♗e3 ♘×d4 12.♗×d4 c5 13.♘b5 a×b5 14.♛c3 b6 15.♗e3 b4 with better chances for Black; 9.♛e3 0-0-0 10.0-0-0 ♛×e3+ 11.♗×e3 e6= or 10.♛×e6+ ♗×e6 11.0-0-0 g6⇄) 9...♘×e5 10.d×e5 g5 11.♗×g5 ♛×e5+ 12.♛e3 ♛×e3+ 13.♗×e3 0-0-0=.

8...♗f5

Other possibilities are **A)** 8...h6; **B)** 8...e6 and **C)** 8...e5.

A) 8...h6 9.♘ge4 ♘×e4 (9...♛b4?! 10.♘×f6+ e×f6 11.a3) 10.♘×e4 ♛g6

11.f3 (11.♗d3 ♗f5 12.♘c5?! 0-0-0∓) 11...♗f5 12.♗d3 (12.0-0-0!? ♗×e4 13.f×e4 ♛×e4 14.g3) 12...h5 (12...e5?! 13.g4, Johansson,M (1922) – Ochoa, A., Internet 2003) 13.d5 (13.0-0 0-0-0 ⇄ or 13.0-0-0 0-0-0⇄) 13...♘e5 14.♗f4 ♘×d3+ 15.♛×d3 0-0-0±;

B) 8...e6 9.f3 ♗h5 (9...♗f5 – 8...♗f5 9.f3 e6)

B1) 10.0-0-0 0-0-0 11.a3 ♘d5 12.♘ge4 ♛d7 13.♗f2 ♗g6 14.♗c4 (14.♗e2±; 14.♘c5?! ♗×c5 15.d×c5 ♛e7 16.♘×d5 ♖×d5 17.♛c3 ♖×d1+ 18.♔×d1 ♖d8+ 19.♔c1 e5∓) 14...♘a5 15.♗a2±;

B2) 10.♗e2 0-0-0 11.0-0-0 h6 (11...♘d5!?) 12.♘ge4 ♛b4 (12...♘×e4 13.♘×e4 ♛b4 14.c3 ♛a5 15.♗c4 ♗g6⇄) 13.a3 ♛a5 14.♘×f6 g×f6 15.d5 (15.♘e4 ♛×d2+ 16.♖×d2±) 15...♗g6 16.♗c4? (16.♗d3 e×d5 17.♗×g6 f×g6 18.♘×d5±) 16...♗×a3 17.♘a2 ♗b4 18.c3 ♗e7 19.b4 ♘×b4 0-1, Roiz Baztan, D. (2344) – Mellado Trivino, J. (2451), Cala Mendia 2001;

C) 8...e5 9.d5

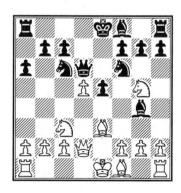

C1) 9...♘b4?! (9...♘e7?! 10.f3 ♗h5 11.0-0-0 0-0-0 (Hnatovsky, N. – Ochoa,A., Internet 2003) 12.g4 ♗g6

181

13.♘ge4 ♕b4 14.g5 ♘f×d5? 15.♗c5 ♕a5 16.♗×e7+−; 14...♘×e4 15.f×e4 ♔b8 16.♗e2 with strong pressure) 10.f3 ♗f5 11.♘ge4 ♕d7 12.0-0-0 c6

C1a) 13.d6

C1a1) 13...♘bd5 (13...♘fd5 14.♗c5 0-0-0 15.♗×b4 ♘×b4 16.♘a4+− or 14...♘×c3 15.♘×c3 ♘c2 16.♘a4±) 14.♗c5 (14.♘×d5 c×d5 15.♘×f6+ g×f6 16.♕×d5 ♖c8∞) 14...0-0-0 15.♗c4 ♘×e4 (15...♘×c3 16.♘×c3 ♗e6 17.♘a4 ♔b8 18.♕a5 ♗×c4 19.♕c7+ ♕×c7 20.d×c7+ ♔×c7 21.♗b6+ ♔c8 22.♖×d8#) 16.f×e4 ♘×c3 17.♕×c3 ♗×e4 18.♖he1 with a very strong initiative;

C1a2) 13.d×c6 ♕×d2+ (13...♘×c6 14.♘×f6+ g×f6 15.♕×d7+ ♗×d7 16.♘d5±) 14.♖×d2 ♗×e4 (14...♘×c6 15.♗c4 ♗×e4 16.f×e4 ♗e7 17.♘d5 ♘×d5 18.e×d5±) 15.♘×e4 ♘×c6 16.♘×f6+ g×f6 17.♗d3 0-0-0 18.♖hd1 ♔c7 19.c3 h5 20.♗f5 ♖×d2 21.♖×d2 ♘b8 22.h4 ♗h6 23.♗×h6 ♖×h6 24.a4±, Karpov, A. (2705) − Lutikov, A. (2515), Moscow 1979. After this game the move 8...e5 was adorned with the symbol "?!" in all publications. It is possible that this assessment has been incorrect all these years; see the next line.

C2) 9...♘d4!? 10.♗×d4 (10.f3 ♗f5 11.♗×d4 e×d4 12.♕×d4 ♗×c2∞ or 11.♘ge4 ♕b6 12.0-0-0 ♘×e4 13.f×e4 ♗g4∞) 10...e×d4 11.♕×d4 ♕b4

C2a) 12.♗c4 b5 13.f3 (13.h3 ♗h5 14.♕e3+ ♔d7 15.♗b3 ♖e8 16.♘e6 f×e6 17.d×e6+ ♔c6 18.g4 ♗g6 19.0-0-0 ♗c5∓) 13...♗c5 14.♗×b5+ (14.♕e5+? ♔f8 15.♕×c7 ♗d7 16.♗b3 ♖c8

17.♕g3 ♘h5 18.♘e6+ ♗×e6 19.♕g5 ♗d7 20.♕×h5 ♖e8+ 21.♔d1 ♗e3−+) 14...a×b5 15.♕×b4 ♗×b4 16.f×g4 ♗×c3+ 17.b×c3 0-0 18.0-0 ♘×d5∓;

C2b) 12.♕×b4 ♗×b4 13.f3 ♘×d5 14.0-0-0 (14.f×g4 ♘×c3 15.a3 ♗e7 16.♘×f7 ♔×f7 17.b×c3 ♖ae8∓) 14...♘×c3 15.b×c3 ♗a3+ 16.♔b1 ♗h5±.

Let's return to Khakimov − Ginzburg.

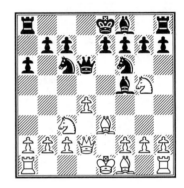

9.f3

9.♗c4 (9.0-0-0 h6 10.♗f4 (Parra, C. (2150) − Fels, B. (2120), Internet 2003) 10...♕d7 11.♘f3 e6 12.♘e5 ♘×e5 13.d×e5 ♕×d2+ 14.♖×d2 ♘d7=) 9...e6 10.♗b3 (Exizoglou, D. (2189) − Nikolaidis, I. (2522), Kirykos 2005) 10...h6 11.♘f3 0-0-0 12.0-0-0 ♗e7⇄ or 10.f3 ♘b4 11.♗b3 ♗e7 12.0-0-0 ♕c6⇄.

9...e6 10.♘ge4

10.0-0-0 ♘d5 (10...♕d7 11.♘ge4 ♘d5 12.♘×d5 e×d5 13.♘g3 ♗g6 14.♗d3 ½-½, Mastrovasilis, D. (2574) − Nikolaidis, I. (2527), Athens 2004)

A) 11.♘ge4 (11.♗c4 ♕d7 12.a3 0-0-0 13.♘×d5 e×d5 14.♗d3 h6 15.♗×f5 ♕×f5 16.♘h3 g5 17.♘f2 ♗g7 18.h4 f6

½-½, Hasurdzic, M. – Feuvrier, S., Patras 1999) 11...♛d7 12.g4 ♗g6 13.♘c5 ♗×c5 14.d×c5 0-0-0 15.♘×d5 (15.♗c4?! ♘×e3 16.♛×e3 ♛e7∓) 15...e×d5 16.♗d4 f6=;

B) 11.♘×d5 ♛×d5 12.c4 ♛d7 13.♗d3 ♗×d3 14.♛×d3 0-0-0 15.♘e4 (Baron Rodriguez, J. (2422) – Galego, L. (2496), Campillos 2005) 15...f5 16.♘c3 ♗c5 17.♗g5 ♗e7 18.♗×e7 ♛×e7 19.d5 ♖he8 20.♖he1⇄.

10...♛d7

10...♘×e4 11.f×e4 ♗g6 12.0-0-0±.

11.♘×f6+ g×f6 12.♘e4

12.♗d3 ♗×d3 13.♛×d3 0-0-0 14.0-0-0 ♗b4 (14...♘b4 15.♛e2 ♖g8 16.♔b1 h5=, Anka, E. (2487) – Fressinet, L. (2440), Bischwiller 1999) 15.♘e2 f5 16.a3 ♗e7 17.g4 (17.♘c3?! ♗f6 18.d5 ♘e7) 17...f×g4 18.f×g4=.

12...♗e7 13.0-0-0 0-0-0

14.c4 (14.a3 ♗g6 15.♗c4 f5 16.♘c3 ♗f6 17.d5 (Matjushin, G. (2302) – Ivannikov, V. (2420), St. Petersburg 2000) 17...♛e7±; 16.♘c5 ♛d6 17.d5 f4 18.♗f2 ♘e5± or 14...♖hg8

15.♔b1 ♛d5 16.♘c3 ♛a5⇄; if 15.h3?! e5 16.d×e5 ♛e6; 16.d5 ♘d4 17.♗×d4?! ♛×d5! or 17.d6 ♗×d6 18.♗×d4 ♗×e4 19.♗e3 ♗c6∓; 18.♘×f6 ♛e6 19.♘×g8 ♛a2 20.♛c3 ♗b4–+ or 19.♗×d4 ♛×f6∓) **14...♗g6** (14...♖hg8 15.g3 ♗g6⇄; 15.♘c5?! ♗×c5 16.d×c5 ♛e7 17.♛c3 h5 18.g3 ♖×d1+; 18.♖×d8+ ♖×d8 19.♗e2 e5 20.♖d1 ♘d4∓ or 18.b4 ♖×d1+ 19.♔×d1 ♘e5 20.♔c1 ♖d8∓) **15.h4** (15.a3?! f5 16.♘c3 f4 17.♗f2 ♘a5–+; 16.♘c5 ♗×c5 17.d×c5 ♛e7 18.♛c3 ♖×d1+ 19.♔×d1 ♖d8+ 20.♔c1 f4 21.♗f2 ♛g5 22.b4 ♛f5 23.♔b2 ♘e5∓; 15.g3 ♔b8⇄) **15...h5 16.♗e2?!** (16.♛f2 ♔b8⇄) **16...f5?!** (16...♗b4 17.♛c2 f5 18.♘c3 f4∓ or 18.d5 f×e4 19.d×c6 ♛×c6∓; if 17.♘c3 ♛e7 18.a3? ♘a5–+ or 18.♛e1 ♖d7 19.♛f2 ♗×c3 20.b×c3 ♛a3+ 21.♔d2 ♘×d4 22.c×d4 ♛b4+ 23.♔c1 ♘c3#; 22.♗×d4 e5∓) **17.♘c5 ♗×c5 18.d×c5 ♛×d2+** (18...♛e7 19.♛c3 e5 20.♖d5 ♖he8∓) **19.♖×d2 ♖×d2** (19...e5 20.f4 f6⇄) **20.♔×d2 f6 21.♖h3 ♛d7 22.♖g3 ♗f7 23.f4 e5 24.♔c3 ♔e6?!** (24...e4 25.b4 ♘d8⇄) **25.♖g7 ♘e7?!** (25...e4 26.b4 ♘d8 27.a4 ♔e7 28.a5 ♘e6=) **26.f×e5 f×e5 27.♗g5 ♘g6 28.c6** (28.g3!? a5 28.♗d1 ♘e7 29.♗c2) **28...b×c6 29.c5 ♘e7 30.♗×a6 ♘d5+ 31.♔d2 ♖b8 32.♔c2?** (32.♔c1) **32...♖b4??** (32...♘b4+) **33.♗c8# 1-0**

Summary: After **1.e4 d5 2.e×d5 ♛×d5 3.♘c3 ♛d6 4.d4 ♘f6 5.♘f3 a6 6.♗e3**, only **6...♘c6** was considered in this game; other alternatives (6...b5, 6...e6, 6...♗g4 and 6...♘bd7) will be discussed in Game 22.

7.♕d2 This continuation is more popular and logical than others (7.d5, 7.a3, 7.h3 and 7.♗e2). For 7.♗d3 see Game 25, and for 7.♗c4, Game 26 After both moves, Black has good chances.

After **7.♕d2**, Black has two main continuations: 7...♗f5 and 7...♗g4.

A) 7...♗f5, and now White has a number of choices (8.a3, 8.♗c4, 8.♗d3, 8.♘h4) but Black is safe enough in each of these lines;

B) 7...♗g4 Here White has two alternatives:

B1) 8.♗f4 but after 8...♕e6+ Black equalizes; and

B2) **8.♘g5**, as in Karpov-Lutikov (where after 8...e5 9.d5 ♘b4?! White had an advantage). As shown by practice and analysis, Black has improvements on Karpov-Lutikov: 9...♘d4 and (after 8.♘g5) 8...e6 or 8...♗f5 with equal chances.

Game 22
Gombac, J. (2295) – Sermek, D. (2530)
Nova Gorica 2007

1.e4 d5 2.e×d5 ♕×d5 3.♘c3 ♕d6 4.d4 ♘f6 5.♘f3 a6 6.♗e3

6...b5

For 6...♘c6 7.♕d2 (7.d5, 7.a3, 7.h3, 7.♗e2) see Game 21; 6...♘c6 7.♗d3 – Game 25; 6...♘c6 7.♗c4 – Game 26. Also possible are **A)** 6...♗g4; **B)** 6...♘bd7; **C)** 6...♗f5 and **D)** 6...e6.

A) 6...♗g4?! 7.h3

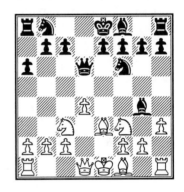

A1) 7...♗×f3 8.♕×f3 ♘c6 (8...c6 9.0-0-0 e6, and White has an extra tempo compared to Game 12) 9.0-0-0 0-0-0 (9...e6 10.♗f4 ♕d7 11.d5 with an attack) 10.d5 ♘e5 11.♕g3 (11.♕f5+ (Jovanovic, Z. (2482) – Vidackovic, B. (2006), Vukovar 2005) 11...♘ed7±) 11...♘ed7 (11...♘fd7 12.f4 ♘g6 13.♘e4 ♕b4 14.♘g5±) 12.♗f4 ♕c5 13.♗e2 ♘b6 14.♗g4+ ♘×g4 (14...♔b8 15.b4±) 15.♕×g4+ ♔b8 16.♗e3 ♕a5 17.a4 (17...♘×d5 18.b4+–) 17...h5 18.♕h4 g5 19.♗×g5 ♕c5 20.♖he1±;

A2) 7...♗h5 8.g4 ♗g6 9.♘e5 ♘d5 10.♕f3 c6 (10...e6 11.♗d3±) 11.♗d3 ♕f6 (11...♘×c3 12.♗×g6±) 12.♘×d5 ♕×f3 13.♘c7+ ♔d8 14.♘×f3 ♔×c7 15.♗×g6 f×g6 (15...h×g6 16.♘e5±) 16.♗f4+ ♔d8 17.0-0-0±, Godena, M. (2487) – Giua, F. (2138), France 2000 or 9...♘c6 10.♗g2 ♖d8 11.♕e2 ♘b4 (Drei, A. (2224) – Cocchi, A. (2311), Italy 2003) 12.♘×g6 h×g6 13.♗×b7±;

B) 6...♘bd7 7.♕d2 (7.♗e2 – 6.♗e2 ♘bd7 7.♗e3, Game 24) 7...b5

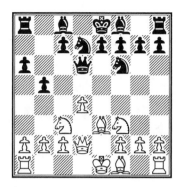

8.0-0-0 ♗b7 9.♗f4 (for 9.♗d3 e6 see 6...b5 7.♗d3 ♗b7 8.♕d2 ♘bd7 9.0-0-0 e6) 9...♕b6 10.♘e5 ♖d8 11.f3 e6 12.♗d3 c5 (12...♕xd4? 13.♘xf7) 13.dxc5 ♗xc5 ⇄, Groszpeter, A. (2502) – Szalai, K. (2277), Hungary 2004 or 12...♗d6 13.♗e3 (13.♖he1?! ♕xd4 14.♘xf7? ♗xf4–+) 13...0-0 14.♕f2 c5 15.♘xd7 ♘xd7 16.♔b1 f5 ⇄;

C) 6...♗f5 7.♘e5 (7.♕d2 ♘c6 – Game 21; 7.♗e2 ♘c6 – Game 23) 7...♘c6 8.g4 (8.♘xc6 ♕xc6 see Game 20) 8...♘xe5 9.gxf5 ♘eg4 10.♕f3 (Manca, F. (2350) – Sulava, N. (2516), Lido Estensi 2003) 10...0-0-0 11.♗c4 e6 12.fxe6 fxe6 13.0-0-0 ♘xe3 14.♕xe3 ♘d5=;

D) 6...e6 7.♕d2 (7.♗e2 – Game 23; 7.♗d3 – Game 25)

D1) 7...b5 8.a3 (8.♗d3 – 6...b5 7.♗d3 ♗b7 8.♕d2 e6) 8...♗b7 9.♗f4 ♕b6 (Bierbach, U. (2295) – Olbrisch, M. (2225), Dortmund 1992; 8...♘bd7!?) 10.0-0-0 ♗d6 11.♔b1 ♘bd7 12.♗d3 0-0= or 8.♗f4 (8.♗d3!? ♗b7 9.0-0) 8...♕d8 (8...♕b6!?) 9.♗d3 ♗b7

(Milliet, S. (2240) – Houska, J. (2386), Istanbul 2003) 10.0-0-0 ♗d6 11.♖he1 0-0±;

D2) 7...♗e7 8.♗f4 ♕b6 9.♗d3 (Schuh, D. (2261) – Ziegler, M. (2145), Boeblingen 2004) 9...0-0 10.0-0 (10.0-0-0 ♗d7 11.♘e5 ♗b5 ⇄) 10...♘c6 11.♖fe1 ♗d7 12.♖ad1 ♘b4 13.♘e4 (13.♘e5!?) 13...♘fd5 14.♘c5 ♗c6 ⇄ or 8.♗d3 0-0 9.0-0-0 (De Firmian, N. (2570) – Dzindzichashvili, R. (2540), Chandler 1997) 9...♘c6 10.♗f4 ♕d7 11.♔b1 ♖d8 ⇄.

We now return to Gombac – Sermek.

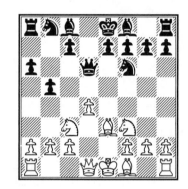

7.♗d3

White alternatives are **A)** 7.a4; **B)** 7.g3 and **C)** 7.♕d2.

A) 7.a4 b4

A1) 8.♘e2 ♗b7 9.♘g3 ♘bd7 10.c4 c5 (10...bxc3 11.bxc3 g6 12.♗d3 ♗g7 13.0-0 0-0=) 11.♕e2?! (11.♗e2 cxd4 12.♗xd4 g6 13.0-0 ♗h6=) 11...cxd4 12.♘xd4?! (12.♗xd4 ♖d8=) 12...e6 13.♖d1 ♖d8 14.♘b3 ♕c7∓, Rushton, D. – Wittal, W., corr. 2002;

A2) 8.♘b1 ♗b7 (8...g6 9.♘bd2 ♗g7 10.♘c4 ♕d8±, Zinchenko, Y. (2310) –

Sergeev, V. (2447), Simferopol 2003) 9.♘bd2 e6 10.♘c4 ♕d5 11.♘ce5 ♘c6 12.♗c4 ♕a5 13.0-0 ♘xe5 (13...♗d6!? 14.♗f4 0-0 15.♘xc6 ♗xc6 16.♘e5 ♗d5) 14.♘xe5 c5?! (Klasmeier, J. (2234) – Eismont, O. (2423), Germany 2003; 14...♗d6!?) 15.dxc5 ♗xc5 16.♗b5+ axb5 17.♗xc5 ♖d8 18.♕e1 ±; 12...♕d8 13.0-0 ♗d6 ±;

B) 7.g3 ♗b7 8.♗g2 ♘bd7 9.0-0 e6

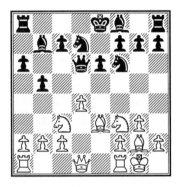

B1) 10.♖e1 (10.a4 b4 11.♘b1 c5 12.♘bd2 cxd4 13.♗xd4 ♗e7 14.♘c4 ♕c7=, Socko, B. (2554) – Krysztofiak, M. (2385), Dzwirzyno 2004) 10...♗e7 11.a4 b4 12.♗f4 ♕b6 13.a5 ♕a7 14.♘a4 0-0 15.c4 bxc3 16.bxc3 (Wendel, S. (2208) – Alber, H. (2387), Germany 2005) 16...h6 17.c4 ♗b4 18.♗d2 ♗xd2 19.♕xd2 ♖ab8 20.♘c3 ♕a8=;

B2) 10.♗f4 ♕b6 (In Game 18 we saw the same line, but with the pawn on e7.) 11.a4 b4 12.a5 ♕a7 13.♘a4 ♗d6 (13...♘d5 14.♗d2 (Heinemann, T. (2441) – Grafl, F. (2413), Germany 2006) 14...♗d6=) 14.♕d2 ♖b8 15.♗xd6 cxd6 16.♕f4 ♗xf3 (16...♕a8!? 17.♖fc1 g5 18.♕e3 g4) 17.♗xf3 ♕c7 18.c4 bxc3 19.♖fc1 e5 20.dxe5 dxe5 21.♕e3 ♕xa5 22.♘xc3 ½-½,

Hermansson, E. (2370) – Fries Nielsen, J. (2444), Stockholm 2003;

C) 7.♕d2 ♗b7 (8...♘bd7 8.♗f4 – 5.♗g5 a6 6.♘f3 ♘bd7 7.♕d2 b5 8.♗f4 in Game 36)

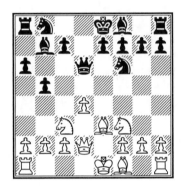

Alternatives include **C1)** 8.♘e5; **C2)** 8.0-0-0; **C3)** 8.♗f4 and **C4)** 8.♗e2.

C1) 8.♘e5 e6 9.f3 (9.♗f4 ♕b6 see 7.♕d2 ♗b7 8.♗f4 ♕b6 9.♘e5 e6) 9...♗e7 10.♗e2 (10.0-0-0 0-0 11.♗d3 c5⇄) 10...0-0 11.♗d3 (11.0-0 ♘c6 12.♘xc6 ♗xc6 13.♗f4 ♕d7=) 11...♘bd7 12.0-0 (Sirotine, K. (2410) – Bazarov, K. (2230), Sochi 2007) 12...e5 13.dxe5 ♘xe5 14.♗f4 ♕b6+ 15.♕e3 ♘xd3 16.♕xb6 cxb6 17.♗xd3 b4∓;

C2) 8.0-0-0 e6 9.♔b1 ♘bd7 (9...b4!? 10.♘a4 ♘bd7) 10.♗f4 ♕b6 11.♘e5 ♖d8 12.a3 (12.♗d3 c5 13.dxc5 ♗xc5⇄, Gonzalez, S. (2274) – Araque, R. (2388), Cali 2001) 12...♘xe5 13.♗xe5 ♘g4 (13...c5?! 14.♕f4) 14.♗g3 c5 15.♕f4 h5⇄;

C3) 8.♗f4 ♕b6 9.♘e5 (9.♗e2 e6 10.0-0 ♗d6 11.♘e5 ♘bd7⇄, Coenen, N. (2383) – Van Hul, C. (2181), Antwerp 1999) 9...e6 10.0-0-0 ♗b4 (10...♘c6!?)

11.♕e3 c5 12.d×c5 ♗×c5 13.♕g3 ♘h5 14.♕g5 ♘×f4 15.♕×f4 0-0 16.♘e4 f6 (16...♗e7!?) 17.♘×c5 ♕×c5 (Zaragatski, I. (2248) – Gofshtein, L. (2518), Willingen 2001) 18.♘d3 ♕b6 19.♕e3 ♕×e3+ 20.f×e3=;

C4) 8.♗e2 e6

C4a) 9.♗f4 ♕b6 (9...♕c6!? 10.0-0 ♗d6) 10.0-0 ♘c6 (10...♗d6 11.♗e3 0-0 12.d5 c5 13.d×e6 f×e6 14.♖ad1 ♗e7±, Espirito Santo, R. (2230) – Mary, P. (2267), Internet 2001) 11.d5 ♖d8 12.♗e3 ♗c5 (12...♕a5?! 13.d×c6 ♖×d2 14.c×b7) 13.♗×c5 ♕×c5 14.♕g5 ♘×d5∞;

C4b) 9.0-0 ♘bd7

C4b1) 10.♖fd1 c5 11.a4 b4 12.♘a2 (Schmidt, T. (2505) – Tarascio, G. (2384), Internet 2004) 12...♖c8 13.♗f4 ♕b6 14.c3 b3 15.♘c1 c4 16.♘e5 ♗d5= or 10.♖fe1 ♗e7 (10...b4!? 11.♘b1 ♗e7) 11.♗f4 ♕c6 (11...♕b6!?) 12.♗d3 0-0 13.♘e4 (Heimann, A. (2095) – Heinzel, O. (2402), Internet 2005) 13...♕b6 14.♘×f6+ ♗×f6 15.♕e2 c5 16.d×c5 ♗×c5 17.♘e5 ♖fd8⇄;

C4b2) 10.a4 b4 11.♘a2 ♗e7 (11...♘e4!? 12.♕d3 ♗e7) 12.♘c1 a5

13.♘d3 ♘d5 (13...♘e4!? 14.♕c1 0-0) 14.♘c5 ♘×c5 15.d×c5 ♕d8 16.♘e5 0-0 (Mazi, L. (2405) – Sermek, D. (2540), Bled 1999) 17.c6 ♗a6 18.♘d7 ♖e8 19.♗b5±.

Back to Gombac – Sermek.

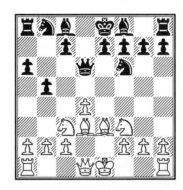

7...♗b7 8.♕d2

Alternatives include **A)** 8.0-0 and **B)** 8.♕e2.

A) 8.0-0 ♘bd7 9.♕e2 (9.9.♘d2!? e6 10.a4 b4 11.♘ce4) 9...e6

A1) 10.♘d2 ♗e7 11.f4 (11.a4!? b4 12.♘ce4) 11...c5 (11...0-0!? 12.f5 e5 13.♘de4 ♘×e4 14.♘×e4 ♕c6⇄) 12.♘de4 (Erashchenkov, D. (2400) – Rodchenkov, V. (2417), Essentuki 2003) 12...♕c7 13.d×c5 ♘×c5 14.♘×c5 ♗×c5 15.♗×c5 ♕×c5+ 16.♕f2 ♕×f2+ 17.♖×f2 0-0-0⇄;

A2) 10.♗g5 ♗e7

A2a) 11.♘e4 (11.♖fe1 0-0 12.♖ad1 ½-½, Popovic, P. (2495) – Milanovic, D. (2510), Zlatibor 2006) 11...♘×e4 12.♗×e4 ♗×e4 13.♕×e4 0-0 14.♗f4 ♕b6 15.♗e5 (Vavra, P. (2390) – Jirovsky, P. (2345), Czechia 2001)

15...♘f6 16.♗×f6 ♗×f6 17.c3 ♖ad8 18.a4 b4=,

A2b) 11.a4 b4 12.♘e4 ♕d5 (12...♕c6!?) 13.c4 (13.♘×f6+ ♘×f6 14.h3 0-0 15.♖fc1 h6⇄) 13...b×c3 14.♘×c3 ♕a5 15.♖ad1 (15.♘e5!? ♗d6 16.f4) 15...♖d8 16.♗h4 (16.♗f4 0-0=) 16...c5 17.♗e4 (17.♗b1 c×d4 18.♘×d4 ♕b4⇄, Goldin, A. (2620) – Stripunsky, A. (2533), San Diego 2004) 17...♘×e4 18.♘×e4 ♗×e4 19.♕×e4 ♗×h4 20.♕×h4 ♘f6=;

B) 8.♕e2

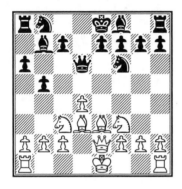

B1) 8...♘bd7 9.0-0-0 (9.0-0 – 8.0-0 ♘bd7 9.♕e2) 9...♘b6 (9...e6 10.♖hg1 ♘b6 11.♘e5 b4 ½-½, Herrera, I. (2432) – Garcia Martinez, S. (2380), Albacete 2003) 10.♗g5 b4 11.♘e4 ♘×e4 12.♗×e4 ♗×e4 13.♕×e4 ♕d5 14.♕×d5 ♘×d5 ½-½, Baramidze, D. (2535) – Sermek, D. (2532), Portoroz 2005;

B2) 8...g6 9.0-0-0 (9.0-0!? ♗g7 10.♘g5 0-0 11.a4 b4 12.♘ce4) 9...♗g7

B2a) 10.♗g5 0-0 11.♘e4 (Petrik, T. (2452) – Sermek, D. (2555), Steinbrunn 2005) 11...♕b6 12.h4 (12.♘×f6+ e×f6 13.♗f4 ♘c6 14.c3 ♖fe8 15.♕d2 b4⇄) 12...♘c6 13.c3 b4 14.♗×f6 e×f6 15.h5 b×c3 16.b×c3⇄;

B2b) 10.♔b1 ♘bd7 11.♖he1 0-0 12.♘g5 (12.♗g5 ♖fe8 13.♘e4 ♕b6⇄) 12...♘d5 (12...♕×h2 13.f3 ♕d6 14.♖h1 h5 15.♘ce4⩲) 13.♘×d5 ♗×d5 14.f3 ♖ad8 (14...♘b6!? 15.b3 ♖ab8) 15.♘e4 ♕c6 16.♘c3 ♘f6 17.♗f4 (17.♘×d5 ♘×d5 18.♗e4 ♕d6=) 17...♗e6⇄, Dolmatov, S. (2606) – Hasangatin, R. (2517), Toliatti 2003;

B3) 8...e6 9.0-0-0 (9.0-0 ♗e7⩱; 9...♘bd7 – 8.0-0 ♘bd7 9.♕e2 e6)

B3a) 9...♗e7 10.♘e5 (Deinert, W. (1951) – Stahl, M. (2165), Recklinghausen 2005) 10...b4 11.♘a4 ♘bd7⇄ or 11.♘b1 ♘c6⇄; 10...0-0 11.f4 ♘c6⇄ or 11.♗f4 ♕b6⇄;

B3b) 9...b4 (9...♘bd7 10.♖hg1 ♗e7 11.♘g5 ♘b6 12.♘ge4 ♘×e4 13.♘×e4 ♗×e4 14.♗×e4 ♘d5 15.♗d2 ♖d8 16.♔b1 0-0 17.g3 ♕b6 18.♗c1 b4 19.♕c4 ½-½, Stojanovic, D. (2459) – Goric, E. (2357), Brcko 2005; 11...0-0!? 12.♘ge4 ♕c6⇄) 10.♘b1 (Morozevich, A. (2707) – Kurajica, B. (2548), Bled 2002) 10...♗e7 11.♘bd2 0-0 12.♘c4 ♕d8⇄;

Let's return to Gombac – Sermek.

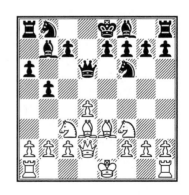

8...♘bd7

8...e6 9.♗f4 ♕b6 and now:

A) 10.0-0 (10.0-0-0!?; 10.♔e2 c5 11.d×c5 ♗×c5 12.0-0 0-0 13.♖ad1 ♘bd7⇄, Vujanovic, A. (2231) – Konikowski, J. (2404), Internet 1999; 10.a4 b4 11.♘e2 ♗×f3 12.g×f3 ♘c6⇄) 10...♗d6 11.♘e5 0-0 12.♘e2 ♘bd7 13.♘g3 (13.♘×d7 ♘×d7 14.♗×d6 ♕×d6=) 13...♖ad8 14.♖ad1 (Zumsande, M. (2381) – Heinzel, O. (2402), Internet 2005) 14...♘×e5 15.♗×e5 (15.d×e5 ♕c6 16.f3 ♗×e5 17.♗×e5 ♕c5+ 18.♕f2 ♕×e5∓) 15...♗×e5 16.d×e5 ♕c6 17.f4 (17.f3? ♕c5+) 17...♘g4 18.♖de1 ♕b6+ 19.♔h1 c5 20.♕e2 ♘h6⇄;

B) 10.♘e5 ♘c6 (10...♗×g2!? 11.♖g1 ♗b7) 11.♘×c6 (11.♗e3 ♘b4 12.0-0 ♘×d3 13.♕×d3 b4 14.♘e2 ♗d6 15.c4 b×c3 16.b×c3 ♗e4 17.♕d2 ♖b8⇄) 11...♕×c6 (11...♗×c6!? 12.0-0 ♕×d4 13.♗×b5 ♕×d2 14.♗×c6+ ♕d7=) 12.f3 0-0-0 13.♗e5 (Georgiev, V. (2326) – Panbukchian, V. (2336), Velingrad 2004) 13...♗d6 14.0-0-0 b4 15.♘e2 ♗×e5 16.d×e5 ♘d5=.

9.0-0-0 e6

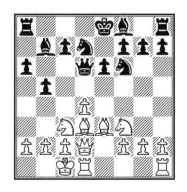

10.♖he1

A) 10.♘g5 (10.a3 ♗e7 11.h4 0-0 12.♗f4 ♕b6⇄) 10...♗×g2 11.♖hg1

♕c6 (11...♗b7 12.f3∞, Kett, T. (2240) – Zeidler, S. (2220), Cardiff 2008) 12.f4 ♗d5 13.♘×d5 ♘×d5 (13...♕×d5 14.♔b1 h6 15.♘h3 g6 16.f5!? g×f5 17.♘f4 ♕c6 18.d5 ♘×d5 19.♘×d5 ♕×d5 20.♕c3∞) 14.♘×h7 (14.f5?! e×f5 15.♗×f5 g6) 14...♘7b6 (14...♗b4!?) 15.♘×f8 ♔×f8 16.♕g2 g6⇄;

B) 10.♗f4 ♕b6 11.♖he1 ♗b4 (11...♗d6!?) 12.a3 ♗e7 (12...♗d6!?) 13.♘e4 0-0 (13...b4 14.a×b4 b4 14.a×b4 ♗×b4 15.c3±, Semcesen, D. (2190) – London, R., Malmo 2003 or 14...♘×e4 15.♗×e4 ♗×e4 16.♖×e4 ♘f6 17.♖ee1 0-0≝) 14.♘e5 (14.♘×f6+ ♘×f6 15.♘e5 ♖ad8 16.g4 ♘d5⇄) 14...♖ad8 15.♘×f6+ (15.♔b1 ♘d5⇄) 15...♗×f6 (15...♘×f6!? 16.g4 ♘d5) 16.c3 ♗×e5 (16...a5 17.♕e2⇄; 16...♗×g2!?) 17.♗×e5 g6 (17...c5? 18.♗×h7+ ♔×h7 19.♗×g7 e5 20.♗×f8 ♘×f8 21.d×c5±) 18.♕h6 ♘×e5 19.♖×e5 ♖d7⇄.

10...♗e7 11.♗f4 ♕b6 12.♘e5 ♖d8

12...0-0 13.♘×d7 ♘×d7 14.f3 ♘f6=.

13.♕e2 c5

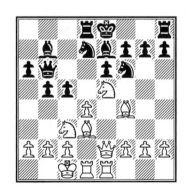

13...0-0 14.♘e4 ♘×e4 15.♗×e4 ♗×e4 16.♕×e4 ♘f6 17.♕f3 ♖×d4

(17...♘d5=) 18.♗e3 ♖×d1+ 19.♖×d1 c5 20.♛c6∞.

14.♘×f7 (14.d5 ♗×d5?! 15.♗×b5 a×b5 16.♘×d5 ♘×d5 17.♖×d5 e×d5 18.♘g6 ♛e6 19.♘×e7±; 14...♘×d5 15.♘×d5 ♗×d5 16.c4 b×c4 17.♗×c4?! ♘×e5 18.♗×e5 0-0; 17.♘×c4 ♛c6 18.♛c2⇄) **14...♚×f7 15.♗c7 ♛c6 16.d5** (16.♗f5?! ♖de8 17.♗×e6+ ♚f8 18.♗g3 c×d4 19.♖×d4 ♘c5 20.♗h3 b4∓ or 17.♛×e6+ ♛×e6 18.♗×e6+ ♚f8 19.d5 c4 20.d6 ♗d8 21.a4 ♗c6 22.f4 ♘c5∓) **16...♘×d5 17.♘×d5 ♛×d5 18.♗g6+** (18.♗×h7 ♖×h7 19.♖×d5 ♗×d5 20.♗×d8 ♗×d8 ⇄; 18...♛c6?! 19.♖d6!; 18...♛g5+?! 19.f4 ♛f6 20.f5 or 18...♛×a2 19.♛h5+ ♚f8 20.♗×d8 ♗×d8 21.♖×d7 ♛a1+ 22.♚d2 ♗a5+ 23.c3 ♛×b2+ 24.♚d1 ♛b3+ 25.♚e2 ♛c4+ 26.♚d1 ♛b3+ ½-½) **18...h×g6 19.♖×d5 ♗×d5 20.♗×d8 ♗×d8 21.♛g4?!** (21.a4 c4 22.a×b5 a×b5 23.♛e3 ♗b6∓) **21...♗c7∓ 22.h3 ♖h5 23.♛d1 ♖g5 24.g3 ♖f5 25.♛d2 ♘e5 26.♖d1 ♘c4 27.♛e1 ♗e5?!** (27...♘d6) **28.c3?** (28.b3 ♘d6 29.f4 ♗d4 30.♛a5⇄) **28...b4 29.f4 ♗f6 30.♖d3 b×c3 31.b×c3 g5 32.♛f2 g×f4 33.g×f4 ♗g5 34.♛×c5 ♗×f4+ 35.♚c2 ♘e3+ 36.♚b2 ♘c4+ 37.♚c2 ♗e3 38.♛c7+ ♚f6 39.♛d8+ ♚g6 40.♛e8+ ♚h7 41.♖d1 ♖f2+ 42.♚d3 ♗c5 43.♛h5+ ♚g8 44.♛e8+ ♖f8 45.♛h5 ♖f3+ 0-1**

Summary: After **1.e4 d5 2.e×d5 ♛×d5 3.♘c3 ♛d6 4.d4 ♘f6 5.♘f3 a6 6.♗e3**, in Game 21, only 6...♘c6 7.♛d2, 7.d5, 7.a3, 7.h3 and 7.♗e2; (6...♘c6 7.♗d3 – Game 25; 6...♘c6 7.♗c4 – Game 26) was examined. In this game, we examined 6...♘bd7,

6...♗f5, 6...e6, 6...♗g4 and 6...b5. As shown in the analysis, after 6...♗g4 7.h3, Black has problems. I recommend the continuations 6...♘bd7, 6...♗f5, 6...e6 and 6...b5. These alternatives can give Black good chances for equality and counterplay.

Game 23
Kozakov, M. (2445) –
Magem Badals, J. (2470)
France 2008

1.e4 d5 2.e×d5 ♛×d5 3.♘c3 ♛d6 4.d4 ♘f6 5.♘f3 a6 6.♗e2

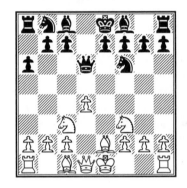

6...♘c6

Perhaps 6...g6 would also prove useful against 6.♗e2; 6...♗g4 – 5.♘f3 ♗g4 6.♗e2 a6, Game 10; 6...♘bd7 or 6...b5 – Game 24. We examine **A)** 6...e6 and **B)** 6...♗f5.

A) 6...e6

A1) 7.♗g5 b5 (7...♘bd7, Game 24) 8.a3 (8.0-0!? ♗b7 9.♘e5 ♘bd7 10.♗f3 or 9...b4 10.♗f3) 8...♗b7 9.♛d2 ♗e7 10.♗f4 ♛b6 11.♘e5 ♘bd7 12.♗f3 ♗×f3 13.♘×f3 0-0 14.0-0 c5⇄, De Louw P. – Eising H., Groningen 2002;

A2) 7.♘e5 ♘c6 (7...♘bd7?! 8.♘c4 ♕c6 9.0-0) 8.♗f4 (Weber M. (2305) – Schindler W. (2300), Germany 1992) 8...♘×d4 9.♘g6?! (9.0-0!?) 9...♕b4 10.♘×h8 ♘×e2 11.♗×c7 (11.♕×e2 ♕×f4 12.0-0 ♗d7 13.♖ad1 ♗d6 14.g3 ♕f5∓ or 12.g3 ♕h6 13.♖d1 ♗d7∓) 11...♗d7 12.a3 (12.♕×e2 ♕×b2 13.0-0 ♕×c3 14.♗e5 ♕c5∓) 12...♕c5 13.♕×e2 ♕×c7 14.0-0 (14.0-0-0 ♗×a3) 14...g6 15.♖ad1 16.♘×f7 ♔×f7∓;

A3) 7.0-0 ♗e7 (for 7...♘bd7 – Game 24; 7...♘c6 8.♗g5 ♗e7 9.♕d2 0-0±, Freitag M. (2383) – Grosar A. (2444), Austria 2004)

A3a) 8.a4 ♘c6 9.b3 0-0 10.♗a3 ♕d8 11.♗×e7 ♘×e7 (11...♕×e7 12.♗c4 ♖d8 13.♖e1 b6 14.♘e4 ♗b7⇄; 12.♕d2 ♖d8 13.♗d3 b6⇄) 12.♕d3 b6 13.♘e5 ♗b7 14.♖ad1 ♕d6 15.♗f3 ♗×f3 16.♕×f3⇄, Prizant J. (2483) – Johnson L. (2322), Dos Hermanas 2003;

A3b) 8.♘e5 ♘c6 9.♘×c6 ♕×c6 10.♗f3 ♕d6 11.♗e3 0-0 12.♕e2 ♖b8 13.g3 (13.♖ad1 ♗d7 14.♗c1 ♖fe8 15.♕e5 ♕b6 16.♖fe1 ♖bd8 17.♕e2 ♗c6 18.♗×c6 ♕×c6=, Tiviakov S. (2627) – Campanile A. (2174), Bratto 1999) 13...♗d7 14.♗f4 ♕b6 15.♖ab1 ♖fe8 16.♗e3 ♕a5⇄) 13...♘d5 14.♖fe1 (14.♘×d5!? e×d5 15.♕a5 c6 16.♗c7)

14...♘×f4 15.♕×f4 ♖b8 16.♖ad1±, Rozentalis E. (2605) – Bronstein D. (2455), Reykjavik 1996;

B) 6...♗f5

B1) 7.0-0 (7.♘h4 ♗d7 8.0-0 ♘c6 9.♗e3 0-0-0 10.♕d2 e5 11.d5 ♘e7 12.♖ad1 (Rahman, S. (2305) – Mohammed Abdul, M. (2305), Dhaka 2008) 12...♘g6 13.♘f3 h6⇄) 7...e6 (for 7...♘c6 see 6...♘c6 7.0-0 ♗f5) 8.♘h4 (8.♘e5 ♘c6 9.♗f4 ♕×d4∓ or 9.♘×c6 ♕×c6 10.♗f3 (Bryan J. (2200) – Russell H. (2119), Windsor Locks 2003) 10...♕b6⇄) 8...♗g6 9.♗f3 ♘c6 10.d5 ♘×d5 11.♘×d5 e×d5 12.♖e1+ ♗e7 13.♗×d5 0-0-0⇄;

B2) 7.♘e5 ♘c6 8.♘×c6 ♕×c6 9.♗f3 ♕b6 10.0-0 0-0-0 11.♗e3 e6 (11...♕×b2 12.♕e1∞, Zozulia A. (2360) – Weisenburger H. (2140), Bad Wiessee 2006) 12.♘a4 ♕a5 13.c3 b5 14.♘c5 ♗×c5 15.b4 ♗×b4 16.c×b4 ♕×b4 17.a4∞ or 9...♕e6+ 10.♘e2 (10.♗e3 0-0-0 11.0-0 h5⇄) 10...0-0-0 11.0-0 (Wegrowski H. – Dziuba M. (2310), Suwalki 1999) 11...♕b6 12.♗e3 e6⇄.

Let's return to Kozakov – Magem Badals.

7.a3

For 7.0-0 ♗f5 8.♗e3 see 7.♗e3 ♗f5 8.0-0; 7.0-0 ♗g4 8.♗e3 – 7.♗e3 ♗g4 8.0-0 or 8.h3 ♗h5 9.♗e3 – 7.♗e3 ♗g4 8.h3 ♗h5 9.0-0. We now look at 7.h3, 7.♗g5 and 7.♗e3.

A) 7.h3 ♗f5 (7...g6!?)

A1) 8.0-0 0-0-0 (8...♘b4!?; 8...e6!?) 9.♗e3 e5 (9...h6!? 10.a3 g5 11.♗d3 ♗×d3 12.♕×d3 e6⇄, Elamri L. (1921) – Goodger M. (2135), Gibraltar 2006) 10.d×e5 ♘×e5 11.♕c1 (11.♘×e5?! ♕×e5 12.♕c1 ♗d6 13.f4 ♕e7 14.♗f3 ♗c5∓) 11...♘×f3+ (11...♕e7 12.♘d4 ♗e6 13.♖d1±, Zaw W. (2497) – Goh Koong Jong J. (2314), Ho Chi Minh City 2003; 12...♕d7!?) 12.♗×f3 ♕b4⇄ or 11.♘d4 ♗d7 (11...♗e6 12.♕c1 ♘c4 13.♘×e6 ♕×e6 (Geher L. (2326) – Orosz A. (2255), Hungary 2005) 14.♗a7 ♘e5 15.♖e1±) 12.♕d2 c5 13.♘b3 ♕×d2 14.♘×d2 ♗f5⇄;

A2) 8.a3 0-0-0 (8...e6!?) 9.♗e3 e5 (9...h6!?) 10.d×e5 ♘×e5

A2a) 11.♘d4 (11.0-0?! ♘×f3+ 12.♗×f3 ♕e5 13.♕e2 ♗d6 14.g3 ♗×h3∓, Vidovic B. – Drobne M. (2042), Velika Gorica 2003) 11...♗g6 12.f4?! (Giakoumis I. (2025) – Nikolaidis I. (2522), Thessaloniki 2005) 12...c5 13.♘f3 ♘×f3+ 14.♗×f3 ♕e6 15.♕c1 ♖e8∓; 12.0-0 h5⇄;

A2b) 11.♕×d6 ♘×f3+ 12.♗×f3 ♗×d6 13.0-0-0 ♗e5 14.♘d5 ♖he8 15.♖he1 ♘×d5 16.♗×d5 ♗e6=, Le Kieu Thien K. (2320) – Aplin C. (2040), Singapore 2006 or 13...h6 14.♖he1 ♖he8 15.♔b1 ♗e5 16.♘d5 (Negi P. (2117) – Suvrajit S. (2391), Mumbai 2003) 16...♗e6=;

B) 7.♗g5 ♗f5 8.♕d2 0-0-0 9.♖d1 (9.♗f4?! ♕b4 10.d5 e6 11.♗d3 ♘×d5∓, O'Dwyer F. – Kaster M. (2140), Triesen 2007; 10.0-0-0 e6 11.h3 ♕a5 12.♘e5 ♘×d4 13.♘×f7 ♗b4 14.♗d3 ♘d5 15.♗×f5 ♗×c3 16.♕d3 ♘×f4 17.♕c4 ♕×f5 0-1, Simms G. – Van Meter L. (2285), Dallas 1999) 9...h6 10.♗e3 ♕b4 11.♕c1 ♘d5 12.♗d2 ♘×c3 13.♗×c3 ♕b6 14.0-0 e6= or 9.0-0-0 ♘e4 10.♘×e4 ♗×e4 11.c3 ♕e6 12.♕e3 h6 13.♗f4 f5 14.b3 g5 15.♗c4 ♕g6 16.♗e5 (Arnold L. (2408) – Varga Z. (2518), Budapest 2001) 16...♗g7 17.♗×g7 ♕×g7=;

C) 7.♗e3

Now Black has played **C1)** 7...♗g4 and **C2)** 7...♗f5.

C1) 7...♗g4

C1a) 8.0-0 e6 (8...0-0-0?! 9.♘g5 ♗e6 10.♗f3) 9.♕d2 (9.h3 ♗×f3?! 10.♗×f3 0-0-0 11.♕e2 ♗e7 12.♖fd1 ♖he8 13.a3 ♗f8 14.b4 with strong pressure, Al Modiahki M. (2555) – Othman A. (2315), Dubai 2007; 9...♗h5 10.♖e1 0-0-0 11.♘g5 ♗×e2 12.♕×e2 ♕d7⇄)

C1a1) 9...0-0-0?! 10.♖fd1 h5 (10...h6 11.a3 g5 12.b4 ♗g7 13.b5 a×b5

14.♘×b5 ♛d7 (Kamrla R. – Blaschke T. (2000), Willingen 2005) 15.♘e5 ♛d5 16.♘×f7±) 11.h3 ♝f5 12.a3 ♝e7 13.b4 ♘e4 14.♘×e4 ♝×e4 15.♝f4 ♛d7 16.c3 f6 17.♛e3 ♝f5 (Zagrebelny S. (2480) – Filippas S. (2145), Agios Kirykos 2007) 18.a4 g5 19.♝g3 with better chances for White;

C1a2) 9...♝e7 (9...h6!? 10.♖fd1 g5 11.a3 ♝g7 12.b4 ♖d8 13.♖ab1 ♝f5⇄, Finnie D. (2391) – Konikowski J. (2367), Internet 2000) 10.♝f4 (10.h3 ♝h5 11.♖ad1 ♖d8 12.a3 ♝g6 13.♛c1 (Lindner D. (2250) – Coates K. (2230), Sunningdale 2007) 13...0-0 14.♘h4 ♝h5⇄ or 11.♖fd1 ♖d8 12.a3 0-0 13.♝f4 ♛d7 14.♘e5 ♛e8 15.♘×c6 ♛×c6 16.♝×h5 ♘×h5 17.♝e5 ♘f6⇄, Manakov I. (2303) – Ivannikov V. (2420), St. Petersburg 2000) 10...♛d7 11.♖ad1 0-0-0!?⇄;

C1b) 8.♛d2 e6 (8...e5?! 9.♘×e5 ♘×e5 10.d×e5 ♛×e5 11.♝×g4 ♘×g4 12.0-0-0 ♝d6 13.♝d4 ♛f4 14.♖he1+ ♚f8±, Dervishi E. (2486) – Pizzuto S. (2137), Bratto 2004)

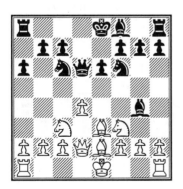

9.0-0-0 (9.h3 ♝h5 see the line 8.h3 ♝h5 9.♛d2 e6; 9.0-0 see the line 8.0-0 e6 9.♛d2; 9.♝f4 ♛d7 10.♖d1 0-0-0 11.♘e5 ♘×e5 12.d×e5 ♛×d2+ 13.♖×d2

♖×d2 14.♚×d2 ♝×e2 15.♚×e2 ♘d7 16.♘e4 ♘c5=, Novichkov V. (2419) – Zaitsev V. (2427), Zeleny Shum 2000) 9...0-0-0

C1b1) 10.♘g5 (10.♝f4 ♛b4⇄ or 10...♛d7⇄) 10...♝×e2 11.♘×f7 (11.♛×e2 ♛d7⇄) 11...♛d7 12.♘×d8 ♝×d1 13.♘×c6 ♛×c6 14.♖×d1 ♛×g2⇄;

C1b2) 10.a3 (for 10.h3 ♝h5 see 8.h3 ♝h5 9.♛d2 e6 10.0-0-0 0-0-0 or 10...♝f5 see 8.h3 ♝f5 9.♛d2 e6 10.0-0-0 0-0-0) 10...♛d7 (10...h5!?; 10...♝e7?! 11.♘g5 ♖df8 12.♘ge4 ♛d8 13.♘×f6 ♝×e2 14.♛×e2 ♝×f6 15.d5 e×d5 16.♘×d5±, Van Riemsdijk,H (2422) – Sermek,D (2545), Auckland 1999) 11.♘e5 ♘×e5 12.d×e5 ♛×d2+ 13.♖×d2 ♝×e2 14.♖×d8+ ♚×d8 15.♘×e2 (15.e×f6 ♝h5 16.g4 ♝g6 17.♖d1+ ♚c8⇄) 15...♘d7 16.♖d1 ♚c8 17.f4=;

C1c) 8.h3 ♝h5 (8...♝×f3 9.♝×f3 0-0-0 – 5...♝g4 6.♝e2 a6 7.h3 ♝×f3 8.♝×f3 ♘c6 9.♝e3 0-0-0, Game 10)

C1c1) 9.a3 (9.♘e5 ♝×e2 10.♛×e2 ♘×e5 11.d×e5 ♛×e5 12.0-0-0 e6 13.♛f3 (Collins S. (2390) – Coates K. (2240), England, 2008) 13...c6∞)

9...e6 (9...0-0-0?! 10.♘g5 ♗g6 11.♗d3 ♘d5 12.♕f3) 10.♕d2 ♗e7 11.0-0 0-0 12.♖ad1 ♖fd8 13.♕c1 ♕d7 14.♘e5 ♕e8 15.♗×h5 ♘×h5 16.♘f3 ♘f6=, Danin A. (2332) – Kurnosov I. (2543), St. Petersburg 2004;

C1c2) 9.0-0 ♖d8 (9...0-0-0?! 10.♘g5 ♗g6 (Osawa T. – Hauchard A. (2518), Shenyang 1999) 11.♗d3 h6 12.♗×g6 h×g5 13.♗×f7 ♘×d4 14.♗×g5± or 11...♘d7 12.♗×g6 ♕×g6 13.♕d3±) 10.♕d2 e6 11.♖ad1 ♗e7 (11...♕b4 12.a3 ♕×b2∞) 12.♗f4 ♕d7 13.♕e3 (Glinert S. (2278) – Spraggett K. (2541), Richmond 2002) 13...♕c8 14.♖fe1 0-0 15.♘e5 ♘b4⇄;

C1c3) 9.♕d2

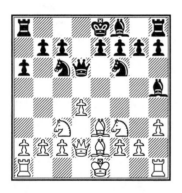

C1c3a) 9...0-0-0 10.0-0-0 (10.♘g5 ♗g6 (Grebenshikova T. (2090) – Kobzev D., Tula 2004) 11.♗d3 ♘d5⇄) 10...♗g6 (10...e6 – 9.♕d2 e6 10.0-0-0 0-0-0; 10...♕b4?! 11.♘g5 ♗g6 12.♗d3) 11.♘e5 ♘×e5?! (11...e6 – 9.♕d2 e6 10.0-0-0 0-0-0 11.♘e5 ♗g6) 12.d×e5 ♕×d2+ (12...♕d7 13.♕e1) 13.♗×d2, and Black has problems; for example, 13...♘d7 14.e6!; 13...♘d5 14.♘×d5 ♖×d5 15.e6! or 13...♘e4 14.♘×e4 ♗×e4 15.♗g5!;

C1c3b) 9...e6 10.0-0-0 (10.0-0 ♗e7 – 8.0-0 e6 9.♕d2 ♗e7 10.h3 ♗h5) 10...0-0-0

C1c3b1) 11.a3 ♗e7 12.♖he1 (12.♗f4 ♕d7 13.♘e5 ♘×e5 14.d×e5 ♕×d2+ 15.♖×d2 ♖×d2 16.♗×d2 ♘e4 17.♘×e4 ♗×e4=, Rooda K. (2145) – Dibala R. (2115), Hoogeveen 2006) 12...♕d7 13.♘e5 ♘×e5 14.d×e5 ♕c6⇄;

C1c3b2) 11.♘g5 ♗×e2 (11...♗g6 12.♗d3 ♕d7⇄) 12.♘×f7 ♕d7 13.♘×d8 ♗×d1 14.♘×c6 ♕×c6 15.♖×d1 (15.d5?! ♘×d5 16.♖×d1 ♗b4, Guido F. (2351) – Borgo G. (2417), Verona 2002; 15.♕×d1 ♕×g2∓) 15...♕×g2 16.d5 e×d5 17.♘×d5 ♘×d5 18.♕×d5 ♕×d5 19.♖×d5=;

C1c3b3) 11.♘e5 ♘×e5 (11...♗g6 12.h4 ♘×e5 13.d×e5 ♕×d2+ 14.♖×d2 ♖×d2 15.♗×d2 ♘e4 16.h5 ♘×c3 17.♗×c3 (Grigoriants S. (2553) – Galego L. (2493), Warsaw 2005) 17...♗f5 18.♗f3 h6 19.♖d1 ♗e7±) 12.d×e5 ♕×d2+ 13.♖×d2 ♗×e2 (13...♖×d2?! 14.♗×h5 ♘×h5 15.♗×d2 g6 16.g4 ♘g7 17.♗g5±) 14.♖×d8+ ♔×d8 15.e×f6 ♗h5 16.g4 ♗g6 17.♖d1+ ♔c8 18.♗d4 ♖g8 19.f×g7 ♗×g7 20.♗×g7 ♖×g7=;

C2) 7...♗f5

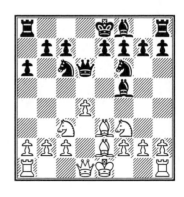

Now we examine **C2a)** 8.♛d2 and **C2b)** 8.0-0.

C2a) 8.♛d2 (8.a3 e6 9.0-0 ♝e7 10.♛d2 0-0 11.♖ad1 ♖fd8 12.♛c1 h6 13.♖fe1 ♘e4 14.♝f4 ♛d7 15.♘xe4 ♝xe4⇄, Klovans J. (2433) – Bauer C. (2599), Biel 2006; 9...0-0-0!?)

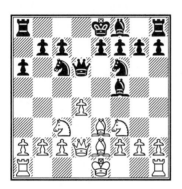

C2a1) 8...0-0-0 9.a3 (9.♘g5 ♝g6 10.♝d3 ♘g4=) 9...e5 (9...e6 10.0-0-0 ♘d5 11.♘g5 ♛d7⇄) 10.0-0-0 (10.dxe5?! (Toczek G. (2372) – Gashimov V. (2608), Warsaw 2005) 10...♛e6 11.♛c1 ♘g4 12.♝f4 ♝c5 13.0-0 ♘gxe5∓) 10...exd4 (10...♘e4?! 11.♘xe4 ♝xe4 12.dxe5 ♛xd2+ 13.♖xd2 ♖xd2 14.♝xd2 ♝xf3 15.♝xf3 ♘xe5 16.♝d5 with a difficult ending for Black, Chebotarev O. (2442) – Meshkov Y. (2396), Sochi 2004) 11.♘xd4 ♘xd4 12.♝xd4 c5=;

C2a2) 8...e6 9.0-0 (9.♘h4 ♝e4 10.0-0-0 0-0-0 11.♘xe4 ♘xe4 12.♛d3 f5 13.c3 ♝e7=) 9...♝e7 (9...h6!?) 10.♖fd1 ♖d8 11.a3 0-0 12.h3 ♘e4 13.♘xe4 ♝xe4 14.♛c1 (14.♝f4 ♛d7 15.c3±) 14...♝f6 (14...♛d5 15.c4 ♛f5 16.♛c3 ♝f6⇄) 15.c3 ♘e7 16.♘d2 ♝d5 17.♝f3 ♛c6 18.♖e1 ♘g6=, Bryzgalin K. (2435) – Voitsekhovsky S. (2503), St. Petersburg 2003;

C2b) 8.0-0

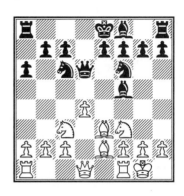

C2b1) 8...g6 (8...e6 9.♘h4?! ♝g6 10.♝f3 0-0-0∓, Battesti S. (1935) – Bauer C. (2630), Ajaccio 2007) 9.♛c1 ♝g7 10.♝f4 ♛d8 (10...♛d7!? 11.♖d1 0-0-0 12.♘e5 ♛e8) 11.♖d1 0-0 12.d5 (12.a3 e6 13.♛d2 ♛e7⇄) 12...♘b4 (12...♘a7!? 13.a4 ♘c8 14.♘d4 ♘d6) 13.♘e1 (Aseev K. (2591) – Pridorozhni A. (2415), St. Petersburg 2002) 13...a5 14.♝f3 ♘a6±;

C2b2) 8...0-0-0

C2b2a) 9.a3 (9.♛d2 e5⇄) 9...e5 10.dxe5 ♘xe5 11.♛xd6 (11.♛c1!?; 11.♘d4?! ♘eg4 12.♘xg4 ♘xg4 13.g3 ♘xe3 14.fxe3 ♝g6∓, Holusova T. (2153) – Vyskocil N. (2305), Stare Mesto 2004; 11.♝g5 ♛c5 12.♛c1 ♝d6∓) 11...♝xd6 12.♘d4 ♝g6 13.h3 ♝c5 14.♖ad1 (Bagirzada A. – Kantans T. (2015), Kemer 2007) 14...♖he8∓; 11...♘f3+ 12.♝xf3 13.♝xd6 14.♖ac1 ♘g4∓.

C2b2b) 9.♛c1

C2b2b1) 9...♘b4?! (9...h5!? 10.♘g5 ♘g4 11.♝f4 ♛g6 12.h3 ♘f6 13.♛e3 e6∓ or 10.♖d1 e6 ⇄) 10.♘e5 ♝g6 11.a3 (11.♝f4!?) 11...♘xc2 12.♘xg6 h×g6 13.♗f4 ♕×d4 14.♖d1 ♘×a1 15.♖×d4 ♖×d4 16.♘b5 ♖d7 17.♘×c7± or 11...♘bd5 12.♘×d5♘×d5 13.c4 ♘×e3 14.f×e3 c5 (Hansen L. (2330) – Pinazo Donoso J. (2175), Sitges 1997) 15.♘×f7 ♗×f7 16.♖×f7 c×d4 17.e×d4 ♕×d4+ 18.♔h1±;

C2b2b2) 9...e6 10.a3 h5 (10...♘g4 11.♗f4 (Losev, D. (2375) – Potapov, A. (2280), Kaluga 2007) 11...♕d7 12.♖d1 ♗d6 13.h3 ♘f6 14.♘e5 ♕e8 15.♗f3 ♘e7 16.♘e2 ♘g6 17.c4 ♘h4⇄) 11.♗f4 ♕d7 12.♖d1 ♔b8 13.♘e5 ♕e8 14.♘×c6+ (14.♕e3 ♗d6 15.♗f3 ♘e7⇄) 14...♕×c6 15.♗f3 ♕c4 16.♕d2 ♗d6⇄; 15...♕d7!? 16.b4 ♗d6.

Back to Kozakov – Magem Badals.

7...♗f5

A) 7...e5 8.d×e5 ♘×e5 9.0-0 ♗e7?! (9...♗f5?! 10.♘×e5 ♕×e5 11.♖e1±; 9...♗e6 10.♘g5 ♕×d1 11.♗×d1 0-0-0 12.♘×e6 f×e6 13.♖e1 with a better ending for White; 9...♗e6!?) 10.♘×e5 ♕×e5 11.♖e1 ♕c5 12.♗e3 ♕d6 (Shavtvaladze, N. (2407) – Tzermiadianos, A. (2250), Athens 2005) 13.♗f3 0-0 (13...♕×d1 14.♖a×d1 c6 15.♘a4± or 14...0-0 15.♗f4 ♗d8

16.h3±) 14.♕e2 with better chances for White;

B) 7...♗g4 8.d5 (8.♗e3 0-0-0 9.♘g5 ♗e6 10.♘×e6 ♕×e6⇄) 8...♘e5 9.0-0 ♗×f3 10.♗×f3 0-0-0 11.♗f4 ♘×f3+ 12.♕×f3 e5 (Frolov, D. (2350) – Zaitsev, V. (2425), Novosibirsk 1998) 13.♗g3 e4 14.♘×e4 ♕×d5 15.♕c3 ♕c6 16.♕×c6 b×c6 17.♘×f6 g×f6 with a better ending for White or 12...♕d7 13.♗e5 ♕g4 14.♕e3 ♔b8 15.♖ad1 with strong pressure;

C) 7...♗e6 8.♗e3 (8.h3 g6 9.♗e3 ♗g7 10.0-0 0-0 11.♕d2 ♖ad8 12.♖ad1 ♕d7⇄, Kotov, V. (2332) – Voitsekhovsky, S. (2492), Vladimir 2004) 8...0-0-0 (8...g6 9.♕d2 ♗g7 10.0-0-0 0-0? 11.♗f4 ♕d7 12.d5±; 10...0-0-0 11.♘g5 ♗h6 12.h4 ♕d7 13.♔b1±) 9.0-0 h6 10.b4 ♗g4 11.b5 ♗×f3 12.♗×f3 ♘×d4 13.♗×d4 ♕×d4 14.b×a6 b×a6 15.♕e2 ♖d6 (15...♕×c3? 16.♕×a6+ ♔d7 17.♖ad1+ ♔e8 18.♖×d8+ ♔×d8 19.♖d1+) 16.♘e4 ♘×e4 (16...♖e6?! 17.♖fe1) 17.♗×e4 e6 18.♖ab1⩱;

D) 7...e6 8.♗g5 (8.0-0!? ♗e7 9.g3) 8...♗e7 (8...h6!?) 9.♕d2 0-0 10.♗f4 (10.0-0 b5 11.♖ad1 ♗b7 12.♗×f6 ♗×f6 13.♘e4 ♕d8 14.♕f4 ♗e7 15.♘e5 (Berelovich, A. (2513) – Bakhmatov, E. (2276), Recklinghausen 2001) 15...f6 16.♘×c6 ♗×c6⇄) 10...♕d8 11.0-0 ♘d5 12.♗g3 ♘×c3 13.♕×c3 (13.b×c3!? ♗d6 14.♗d3) 13...♗d6 14.♖ad1 ♗×g3 15.h×g3 ♘e7±, Ni Hua, (2369) – Rainfray, A. (2422), Oropesa del Mar 1999.

Let's return to Kozakov – Magem Badals.

8.d5

8.b4 (8.♗e3 0-0-0 9.0-0 – 7.♗e3 ♗f5
8.0-0 0-0-0 9.a3 or 9.♛d2, 7.♗e3 ♗f5
8.♛d2 0-0-0 9.a3) 8...♖d8 9.♗e3 e5
10.d×e5 ♞×e5⇄, Grishchenko, M. –
Vasiliev, M. (2213) Alushta 2005.

8...♞e5 9.0-0

9.♞d4 (9.♞×e5!? ♛×e5 10.f4 ♛d6
11.g4) 9...♗e4?! (9...♗d7!?) 10.♞×e4
♞×e4 11.c4 e6 (Kulaots, K. (2499) –
Keskel, M. (2147), Tallinn 2000) 12.f3
♞f6 13.f4 ♞g6 (13...♞ed7 14.d×e6
f×e6 15.0-0 ±) 14.♛a4+ ♛d7
15.♛×d7+ ♚×d7 16.d×e6+ f×e6 17.0-0
with a better ending for White.

9...♞×f3+

9...0-0-0? (Tomcsanyi, P. (2235) –
Mozes, E. (2405), Hungary 1997)
10.♞×e5.

10.♗×f3 h6

10...0-0-0!? 11.♗e3 (11.♛d4 e5
12.♛a7 ♛b6 13.♛×b6 c×b6=) 11...e5
12.d×e6 ♛e5 13.♛e2 ♗×e6 ⇄.

11.♞e2

11.♗e3 g5 12.♖e1 ♗g7 13.♗d4 0-0-0?!
14.♗e5 ♛d7 (14...♛b6 15.♞a4)
15.♛d4 ♚b8 16.♞a4± ; 13...0-0
14.h3± .

11...g5 (11...0-0-0!? 12.♛d4?! ♞×d5
13.♛a7 ♛b6∓ or 12.♗f4 e5 13.d×e6
♛b6 14.♛e1 ♗×e6⇄; 12.c4 e5
13.♞g3 ♗g6 14.♖e1 ♖e8 15.♗e3 e4
16.♗e2 h5⇄ or 14.♗e3 ♛d7 15.b4
h5⇄) **12.♞g3** (12.c4!?) **12...♗g6**
13.c4 ♗g7 14.♗d2 (14.♖e1!?)
14...0-0 15.♖c1 (15.♗b4 ♛d7
16.♖e1 ♖fe8 17.h3 a5 18.♗c3 a4
19.♖c1±) **15...♖fe8** (15...♞d7
16.♗c3 ♞c5 17.♗×g7 ♚×g7 18.b4 ♞d3
19.♖c3 ♞f4 20.♗e3 a5∞; 18.♖c3 a5
19.b4 a×b4 20.a×b4 ♞d7 21.c5 ♛f4⇄)
16.♖e1 ♖ad8 (16...♞d7 17.♗c3 ♞c5
18.♗e4 ♞×e4 19.♞×e4 ♗×e4
20.♖×e4± or 16...a5 17.♗c3 a4
18.♗e5 ♛c5 19.♗d4 ♛a5 20.h3 ♖ad8
21.♗c3 ♛a6± ; 19...♛d6!?) **17.♗c3**
(17.c5?! ♛d7 18.d6 e×d6 19.c6 ♖×e1+
20.♗×e1 b×c6 21.♗×c6 ♛e7 22.♗a5
d5 23.♗b7 ♞e8 24.♛d2 ♛f6 25.b4
♞d6 26.♗×a6 ♞c4 27.♗×c4 d×c4
28.♛e3 ♛e5∓; 17.♗b4 ♛d7 18.h3 b6
19.♛b3 a5 20.♗c3±) **17...♛d7**
18.h3 b6 (18...b5!?) **19.♗e5 e6**
20.♛d4?! (20.d×e6 ♖×e6 21.♛×d7
♞×d7 22.♗×g7 ♖×e1+ 23.♖×e1 ♚×g7

24.♖d1 ♔f6=; 22.♗×c7 ♖×e1+
23.♖×e1 ♖c8 24.♗d6 ♗×b2 ⇄)
20...c5 21.♕d2 (21.♕c3 e×d5
22.♗×f6 d4 23.♕b3 ♗×f6 24.♕×b6
♖e6 25.♖×e6 ♕×e6 26.♕×c5 d3⩲ or
23.♖×e8+ ♖×e8 24.♕b3 ♗×f6 25.♕×b6
♗e5 26.♕×c5 d3⩲) **21...e×d5
22.c×d5 ♘e4 23.♗×e4 ♖×e5**
(23...♗×e5 24.♗×g6 f×g6 25.♖cd1
♗d4∓) **24.♗×g6 ♖×d5 25.♕c2
f×g6 26.♕×g6 ♖d6 27.♕e4**
(27.♕b1 ♖d2 28.♘f5 ♔h8 29.♖e7
♖d1+ 30.♖×d1 ♕×d1+ 31.♕×d1
♖×d1+ 32.♔h2 ♗×b2 33.♖e6 ♖b1
34.♖×h6+ ♔g8 35.♖g6+ ♔f8 36.♘e3
♔f7 37.♖×g5 ♗×a3 with a better ending for Black.) **27...♗×b2 28.♖b1
♗d4** (28...♗×a3 29.♘f5 ♖f6 30.g4
♗b4? 31.♖bd1 ♕c7 32.♕e5 +−;
30...♕f7 31.♘e3 ♖×f5 32.g×f5 ♗b4
33.♖ed1 ♖f8 34.♖a1 ⇄) **29.♘f5 ♖f6
30.g4 ♔h8** (30...b5!? 31.♖bd1 ♖df8
32.♔g2 ♖×f5 33.g×f5 ♖×f5 with a better ending for Black) **31.♖bd1 ♕d5
32.♕×d5 ♖×d5 ½-½**

Summary: After **1.e4 d5 2.e×d5
♕×d5 3.♘c3 ♕d6 4.d4 ♘f6
5.♘f3 a6, 6.♗e2** is one of the most
popular replies. In Game 23 we examined some of Black's alternatives,
except for 6...♘bd7 and 6...b5 (for
which see Game 24). Lines discussed
in Game 23 can sometimes transpose
to positions from Games 10, 22, 24
and 36.

Practice and analysis indicate that the
most solid continuations after 6.♗e2 are
6...e6, 6...♗f5 and 6...♘c6. After
6...♘c6, White has some interesting
possibilities (7.a3, 7.h3, 7.♗g5, 7.♗e3
and 7.0-0), but Black has counterplay
after each of these moves.

**1.e4 d5 2.e×d5 ♕×d5 3.♘c3 ♕d6
4.d4 ♘f6 5.♘f3 a6 6.♗e2 ♘bd7**

The actual move order in the game was
1.e4 d5 2.e×d5 ♘f6 3.♘f3 ♕×d5 4.♘c3
♕d6 5.d4 a6 6.♗e2 ♘bd7.

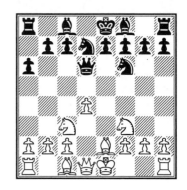

6...♗g4 – 5.♘f3 ♗g4 6.♗e2 a6, Game
10; 6...♘c6, 6...♗f5 and 6...e6 – Game
23.

7.0-0

Also worth consideration are **A)** 7.♗g5
and **B)** 7.♗e3.

A) 7.♗g5

A1) 7...b5 8.0-0 e6 (8...♗b7 9.♕c1 e6
10.♗f4 ♕b6 11.a4 b4 12.a5 ♕c6
13.♘a4 ♗d6 ⇄, Lengyel, B. (2302) –
Brustkern, J. (2258), Budapest 2005)

A1a) 9.♘e5 (9.♕d2 ♗b7 10.♗f4 ♕b6
– 7.♗g5 e6 8.♕d2 b5 9.♗f4 ♕b6 10.0-0
♗b7) 9...♘×e5 10.d×e5 (10.♗f4!? ♗b7
11.♗×e5) 10...♕×e5 11.♗f3 ♗d6
12.♗f4 (12.g3 ♖b8 13.♗c6+ ♗d7
14.♗×d7+ ♔×d7∓, Zolnierowicz, K.

(2340) – Sergeev, V. (2491), Prague 2000) 12...♛xf4 13.g3 ♛b4 14.♗xa8 ♛xb2 15.♗c6+ ♚e7⇄;

A1b) 9.♗xf6 (9.a3 ♗b7 10.♖e1 ♗e7 11.♛d2 0-0 12.♗f4 ♛b6⇄, Bauer, A. (2120) – Sattler, S. (2120), Bayern 1994) 9...gxf6 (9...♘xf6?! 10.♘e5 ♗b7 11.a4 b4 12.♗f3 ♘d5 13.♘e4) 10.♖e1 ♗e7 11.♛d3 ♗b7 12.♘d2 f5 13.♗f3 ♗xf3 14.♛xf3 0-0⇄, De Almeida, M. (2455) – Stephan, J. (2347), Internet 2002;

A2) 7...e6 8.♛d2 b5 9.0-0-0 (9.♗f4 ♛b6 10.0-0 ♗b7 11.a4 b4 12.♘d1 (Wegener, D. (2346) – Toberm G. (2318), Austria 2006) 12...♘e4 13.♛e3 ♗d6 14.♗d3 ♘ef6⇄) 9...♗b7 10.♘e5 ♘xe5 11.dxe5 ♛xd2+ 12.♖xd2 (Lopez Santana, O. (2210) – Hernandez Perez, X. (2075), Sant Boi 1998) 12...b4 13.exf6 bxc3 14.bxc3 gxf6 15.♗xf6 ♖g8⇄;

B) 7.♗e3 e6 8.♛d2 (8.0-0 – 7.0-0 e6 8.♗e3) 8...b5

9.a3 (9.♗f4 ♛b6 – 7.♗g5 e6 8.♛d2 b5 9.♗f4 ♛b6; for 9.0-0 ♗b7 – 6.♗e3 b5 7.♛d2 ♗b7 8.♗e2 e6 9.0-0 ♘bd7, Game 22; 9.0-0-0 ♗e7 10.♗f4 ♛b6 11.d5 0-0 12.dxe6 fxe6⇄; 9.♘g5 ♗b7

10.f3 c5 11.♘ge4 ♛c6⇄, Garbett, P. (2360) – Sermek, D. (2545), Auckland 2000) 9...♗b7

B1) 10.♗f4 (10.b4 ♘b6 11.0-0 ♛c6⇄, Okkes, M. (2297) – Borgo, G. (2430), Arco 2002) 10...♛b6 (10...♛c6!? 11.0-0 ♗d6) 11.b4 (11.0-0 c5 12.dxc5 ♗xc5 13.b4 ♗e7 14.♖fd1 ♖c8⇄, Pipitone, A. (2025) – Scharrer, P. (2220), Italy 2007; 11...♗d6!?) 11...♗d6 12.♗e3 ♘g4 13.♗d3?! (Schmidt, G. (2250) – Haehnle, B., Forchtenberg 2003) 13...0-0 14.♘e4 ♗xe4 15.♗xe4 ♖ae8 16.♛c3 ♘df6 17.♗c6 (17.♗d3 e5∓) 17...♘d5 18.♗xd5 exd5∓; 13.0-0 ♘xe3 14.♛xe3 0-0⇄;

B2) 10.0-0-0 ♗e7 11.♖ad1 (11.♖fd1 0-0 12.♗f4 ♛c6⇄, Hawes, J. (2155) – Brustkern, J. (2251), St. Helier 2005) 11...0-0 12.h3 ♖fd8 (12...♘e4!? 13.♘xe4 ♗xe4) 13.♛c1 (13.♗f4 ♛b6 14.♛e3 ♗d6⇄) 13...♖ab8⇄, Malbran, G. (2356) – Giaccio, A. (2458), Buenos Aires 2001.

Back to Griffin – Stepp.

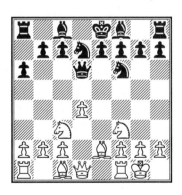

7...g6

Also worth consideration are **A)** 7...b5 and **B)** 7...e6.

A) 7...b5?! 8.♘g5 ♗b7 (8...e6 9.♗f3) 9.♗f3 ♗×f3 (9...c6 10.g3 e6 11.♗f4±, Vasquez, J. – Sharapan, D. (2150), Internet 2003) 10.♕×f3 ♖c8 (Pesola, J. (2040) – Hasangatin, R. (2515), Prague 2004) 11.♗f4 ♕b6 (11...♕b4 12.♕b7 ♖b8 13.♕×a6 ♕×b2 14.♕c6±) 12.♖ad1 e6 13.d5 e5 14.♗×e5 ♘×e5 15.♕f5 ♘ed7 (15...♘fd7 16.♖fe1 ♕f6 17.♖×e5+) 16.♖fe1+ ♗e7 17.d6±;

B) 7...e6

B1) 8.♗g5 ♗e7 (8...b5 – 7.♗g5 b5 8.0-0 e6; 8...c5?! 9.d×c5 ♘×c5 10.♕c1 ♗e7 11.♖d1 ♕b6 12.♘d2±; 9...♕×d1 10.♖a×d1 ♗×c5 11.♘d2 b5 12.♗f3 ♖a7 13.♘de4 ♘×e4 14.♘×e4±, Mascioni, V. (2299) – Winkler, T. (2390), Internet 1997) 9.♕d2 b5 10.♗f4 ♕b6

B1a) 11.♘e5 ♗b7 (11...♘×e5?! 12.d×e5 ♘d7 13.♖fd1 0-0 14.♗f3) 12.♘×d7 (12.a4 b4 13.♘d1 ♘×e5 14.♗×e5⇄, Dervishi, E. (2525) – Perez, R. (2429), Saint Vincent 2002) 12...♘×d7 13.♕d3 ♘f6 14.♗f3 (14.a4 b4 15.a5 ♕a7 16.♘a4 0-0 17.♕g3 ♘e4 18.♕e3 ♘f6=) 14...♗×f3 15.♕×f3 0-0 16.♖ad1 ♖ad8= or 12.♕e3 ♘×e5 13.♗×e5 0-0 14.a4 b4 15.a5 ♕a7 16.♘a4 ♘d7 (16...♗c6 17.♕g3 ♖fc8 (Forchert, M. (2400) –

Kayser, F. (2195) Bad Wiessee 2006) 18.♘c5 ♗×c5 19.d×c5 ♔h8 20.♗d4±) 17.♗×c7 ♗×g2 18.♗b6 ♕b7 19.♖fd1 ♗d5⇄;

B1b) 11.d5

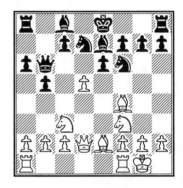

B1b1) 11...e×d5 12.♘×d5 ♘×d5 13.♕×d5 ♗b7 14.♕f5 ♕f6 (14...♘c5?! 15.♗e3 ♕g6 16.♕e5 f6 17.♕c3 Kuderinov, K. (2304) – Gorovets, A. (2356), Chalkidiki 2003) 15.♕×f6 (15.♗d3 ♘c5 16.♕×f6 ♗×f6 17.♖fe1+ ♘e6 18.♘g5 ♗d5± or 16...g×f6 17.♗f5±) 15...♘×f6 16.c4 (16.♗×c7!? ♖c8 17.♗a5) 16...b×c4 17.♗×c4 0-0±, Guido, F. (2303) – Drazic, S. (2508), Bratto 2000;

B1b2) 11...♘c5 12.d×e6 ♘×e6 (12...♗×e6!?) 13.♗e3 ♗c5 14.♗×c5 ♕×c5 15.♖ad1 ♗b7 16.♘d4 (16.♖fe1 0-0 17.♘d4 b4 18.♘a4 ♕a5 19.b3 ♖ad8 20.♕e3⇄) 16...0-0-0 17.♘×e6 f×e6 18.♗d3 (Dabo Peranic, R. (2341) – Sermek, D. (2577), Rabac 2003) 18...b4 19.♘e2⇄;

B2) 8.♗e3 b5 9.♘g5 (for 9.♕d2 ♗e7 10.♗f4 see 8.♗g5 ♗e7 9.♕d2 b5 10.♗f4 or 9.♕d2 ♗b7 – 6.♗e3 b5 7.♕d2 ♗b7 8.♗e2 e6 9.0-0 ♘bd7, Game 22) 9...♗b7 10.♗f3 ♘d5 11.a4 b4 12.♘×d5 (12.♘ge4 (Nijboer, F. (2586) – Spoelman, W. (2239), Zwolle 2004) 12...♕b6 13.♘×d5 ♗×d5⇄) 12.. ♗×d5 13.c4 (13.♘e4 ♕c6 14.♕d3 ♗e7 15.♖fe1 0-0⇄) 13...b×c3 14.b×c3 ♖b8 15.♗×d5 ♕×d5 16.♕h5 g6 (16...♕f5?! 17.d5 e×d5 18.♗a7) 17.♕e2 ♗e7 18.c4 ♕f5 19.g4 ♕a5 20.d5 e5 21.♘e4 0-0 22.g5±.

We return now to Griffin – Stepp.

8.♗g5

8.♖e1 ♗g7 9.♗g5 0-0 10.♕d2 b5 11.♗f4 ♕b6 12.♘e5 (12.b4!? ♗b7 13.a4; 12.♗d3!? b4 13.♘e4) 12...♗b7 13.♕e3 ♖ad8 14.♖ad1 b4 15.♘a4 15.♘c4?! ♕a7 16.♘b1 ♘d5∓, Op den Kelder, J. (2215) – Tiviakov, S. (2665), Dieren 2006) 15...♕a5 16.♘×d7 ♘×d7 17.b3 ♖fe8⇄.

8...♗g7 9.♕d2 b5 10.a3

10.♗f4 ♕b6 11.b4 ♗b7 12.a4 0-0 (12...♘e4?! 13.♘×e4 ♗×e4 14.a×b5 a×b5 15.♖a5 0-0 16.♖×b5±, Strikovic, A. (2535) – Tiviakov, S. (2680), Calvia 2006; 15...♖×a5 16.b×a5 ♕c6 17.♕b4±) 13.a5 ♕a7 14.♕e3 (14.♗×c7?! ♗×f3 15.♗b6 ♗×e2 16.♗×a7 ♗×f1 17.♖×f1 ♖×a7∓)

14...♖fe8 15.♖ad1 (15.♘e5 ♖ad8 16.♖fd1 ♘×e5 17.♗×e5 ♘d5⇄) 15...♘d5 16.♘×d5 ♗×d5⇄ or 13.a×b5 a×b5 14.♘×b5 ♗×f3 15.g×f3 ♘d5 16.♖×a8 (16.♗c4?! ♖×a1 17.♖×a1 ♘f4 18.♕×f4 c6∓) 16...♖×a8 17.♗c4 ♘7f6⊞.

10...♗b7 11.♗f4 ♕c6 (11...♕b6!?)

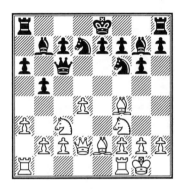

12.♖ad1 ♖d8

12...♘b6 13.♖fe1 (13.♗h6 0-0 14.♖fe1 ♖ad8⇄) 13...0-0 14.♗f1 ♘fd5 15.♘e5 ♕e6 16.♗g3 ♘×c3 17.♕×c3 ♖ac8 18.♗d3 ♕f6±.

13.d5

13.♕e3 0-0

A) 14.d5 ♕c5 15.♕×c5 (15.♕d2 ♘h5 16.♗e3 ♗×c3 17.b×c3 ♕×a3∓) 15...♘×c5 16.♗×c7 ♖d7 17.♗b6 (17.♗e5 ♘×d5 18.♘×d5 ♗×d5∓) 17...♘ce4 18.♘×e4 (18.♗d4 ♘×c3 19.♗×c3 ♘×d5∓) 18...♘×e4⇄;

B) 14.♕×e7 ♖fe8 15.♕b4 ♘b6 16.♗g5 (16.♖d2? ♘fd5; 16.♗e3?! ♘fd5) 16...♘fd5 17.♕b3 (17.♘×d5 ♘×d5 18.♕b3 f6 19.♗e3 ♕e6⊞; 17...♖×d5!? 18.♗e3 ♖h5) 17...♘×c3 18.b×c3

(18.♛×c3 ♛×c3 19.b×c3 f6 20.♗e3
♘d5⯑) 18...♖d5 19.♗e3 ♘c4⯑ or
16.♗e5 ♘e4 17.♘×b5 (17.♗×g7 ♘c3
18.♛×c3 ♛×c3 19.b×c3 ♖×e2 20.♗e5
♘d5∓) 17...♗f8 18.♛b3 a×b5 19.♗×b5
♛e6 20.♗×e8 ♗d5 21.♗×f7+ ♛×f7
22.♛b5 ♘c4 23.♗g3 (23.♖fe1 ♖a8∞)
23...c6∞.

13...♛b6 14.♗e3

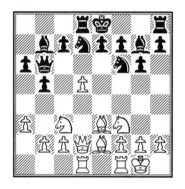

14...♛d6?

14...c5 (14...♛a5? 15.♘d4±)

A) 15.b4 0-0 16.♖b1 (16.h3 ♛c7
17.♗f4 ♛c8⇄) 16...♛d6 17.♗f4 e5
18.d×e6 ♛×e6⇄;

B) 15.d×c6 ♛×c6 16.♛d4 0-0 17.a4
b×a4 18.♛×a4 (18.♛b4 e6 19.♛×a4
♛×a4 20.♘×a4 ♘d5⇄) 18...♛×a4
19.♘×a4 ♘d5 20.♗g5 (20.♗d4?! ♘f4)
20...h6 21.♖×d5 (21.♗d2 ♗c6⇄)
21...♗×d5 22.♗×e7 ♖fe8 23.♗×d8
♖×e2∞.

15.♗f4? (15.♗×b5 a×b5 16.♘×b5+−;
15...0-0 16.♗f4 ♛b6 17.♗c4±)
15...♛b6 16.♛e1 (16.b4!?±;
16.♛e3!?±) **16...0-0 17.♘e5?!**
(17.♘g5 ♖fe8 18.♗f3 h6⇄; 17...h6!?)
17...♘×e5 18.♗×e5 ♘×d5

19.♗×g7 ♛×g7 20.♗f3 ♘×c3
21.♛×c3+ ♛g8 22.♖de1 (22.♗×b7
♛b7 23.♖fe1 ♖d6∓) **22...♖d7∓**
23.♗g4 f5 24.♗f3 ♖fd8 25.♛b3+
♛f8 26.♛c3 ♛f7 27.♛b3+ ♗d5
28.♗×d5+ ♖×d5 29.c4 ♖d3
30.♛a2 ♛f8 31.c×b5 a×b5 32.♖e6
♖8d6 33.♖e2 ♖d2 34.♖×d2 ♖×d2
35.♛b3 ♛c5 36.g3 ♛e5 37.♖d1
♛×b2 38.♛×b2 ♖×b2 39.♖c1 ♖a2
40.♖×c7 ♖×a3 41.♖b7 ♖b3
42.♛g2 ♛f7 43.♖b6 b4 44.f4
♖b2+ 45.♛f3 b3 46.h3 ♖b1
47.♛f2 b2 48.♛g2 e6 49.g4 h6
50.♛h2 g5 51.g×f5 e×f5 52.♛g2
g×f4 53.♖b3 f3+ 54.♖×f3 ♖g1+
55.♛×g1 b1♛+ 56.♛g2 ♛f6
57.h4 ♛e1 58.h5 ♛g5 59.♛h3
♛h4+ 60.♛g2 ♛×h5 61.♛g3
♛g4+ 62.♛f2 ♛×f3+ 63.♛×f3 h5
64.♛g3 h4+ 65.♛f3 h3 66.♛g3
h2 67.♛×h2 ♛f4 68.♛g1 ♛f3
69.♛f1 f4 70.♛g1 ♛e2 0-1

Summary: In this game, after **1.e4 d5**
2.e×d5 ♛×d5 3.♘c3 ♛d6 4.d4
♘f6 5.♘f3 a6 6.♗e2, we examined
6...♘bd7.

After 6...♘bd7, White has three interesting continuations: 7.♗g5, 7.♗e3,
and 7.0-0, but Black has counterplay in
each of these lines. Usually Black wants
to realize one of two plans:

1. After c7-c5, to exchange pawns on
d4. We can see same idea (with the same
pawn structure) in some variations of
the Caro-Kann and the French Defense.
Black ends up with an extra center pawn
as a result of this exchange. We also see
Black's 4-3 kingside majority with open
c- and d-files in the Sicilian Defence
after d7 (d6)-d5, e4×d5 with a piece
capture on d5.

2. b7-b5, followed by ♗c8-b7. I consider this safer and more solid than the first plan.

In Game 24 there is a new plan in the 5.♘f3 a6 6.♗e2 ♘bd7 line: after 7.0-0 g6 8.♗g5 ♗g7 9.♛d2 b5 10.a3 ♗b7, Black has a double fianchetto with counterplay.

Game 25
Vehi Bach, V. (2380) – Magem Badals, J. (2470)
Barcelona 2008

1.e4 d5 2.e×d5 ♛×d5 3.♘c3 ♛d6 4.d4 ♘f6 5.♘f3 a6 6.♗d3

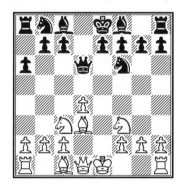

6...g6

We examine the alternatives **A)** 6...b5; **B)** 6...♘c6 and **C)** 6...♗g4.

A) 6...b5?! 7.a4 b4 8.♘e4 ♛e6 (8...♛b6 9.a5) 9.♘e5 ♘×e4 (9...♛d5 10.f3±) 10.♗×e4 ♖a7 11.0-0 ♗b7 (11...f6 12.♛h5+) 12.♗×b7 ♖×b7 13.♛f3± or 8...♛d5 9.♛e2 ♗b7 10.♘eg5 e6 (10...♛d6 11.♘e5 ♗d5 12.♗c4±) 11.♘×f7 ♔×f7 12.♗c4±;

B) 6...♘c6

B1) 7.♗e3 (7.h3 – Game 30) 7...♗g4 (7...g6 – 6...g6 7.♗e3 ♘c6) 8.♛e2?!

(8.0-0 – 6...♗g4 7.0-0 ♘c6 8.♗e3 or 8.h3 ♗h5 – 6...♗g4 7.h3 ♗h5 8.♗e3 ♘c6) 8...0-0-0 9.h3?! ♗×f3 10.♛×f3 ♘×d4 11.♗×d4 ♛×d4 12.0-0-0 ♛b6 13.♗e4 ♖×d1+ 14.♖×d1 c6∓; 8...e6 9.0-0-0 ♗e7 10.h3 ♗h5⇄, Nyysti, S. (2410) – Rocha, S. (2390), Bled 2002;

B2) 7.0-0 g6 (7...♗g4 – 6...♗g4 7.0-0 ♘c6) 8.♘e4 (8.h3 – 6...♘c6 7.h3 g6 8.0-0; 8.♗g5 ♗g7 – 6...g6 7.♗g5 ♗g7 8.0-0 ♘c6) 8...♘×e4 9.♗×e4 ♗g7 (9...♗g4 – 6...♗g4 7.0-0 ♘c6 8.♘e4 ♘×e4 9.♗×e4 g6) 10.c3 (Cicak, S. (2530) – Gallego Montes, A. (2040), Salou 2005) 10...♗f5 11.♗×f5 g×f5 12.♛d3 e6 13.b4 0-0-0 14.a4 ♘e5⇄;

B3) 7.♘e4 ♘×e4 8.♗×e4 ♗g4 (8...g6 9.0-0 ♗g7 10.c3 (Cicak, S. (2530) – Gallego Montes, A. (2040), Salou 2005) 10...♗e6 11.g3 0-0-0⇄; 8...e5!?) and now:

B3a) 9.♗e3 (9.0-0 – 6...♗g4 7.0-0 ♘c6 8.♘e4 ♘×e4 9.♗×e4; 9.h3 ♗h5 – 6...♗g4 7.h3 ♗h5 8.♘e4 ♘×e4 9.♗×e4 ♘c6) 9...f5 10.♗×c6+ (10.♗d3?! f4 11.d5 ♘b4) 10...♛×c6 11.d5 ♛f6 (11...♛d6 12.♛d4 ♗×f3 13.g×f3±, Pivovartsev, S. (2195) – Miljutin, O. (2165), Ilichevsk 2007) 12.0-0 0-0-0 13.h3 ♗h5 14.♖e1 ♖d7⇄.

B3b) 9.c3

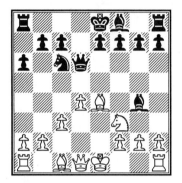

B3b1) 9...0-0-0 (9...e5?! 10.♛b3 0-0-0 11.dxe5 ♛d7 12.0-0±, Teran Alvarez, I. (2431) – Campora, D. (2549), Ayamonte 2004; 9...♛e6?! 10.♛d3 ♗f5 11.♘g5 or 10...0-0-0 11.♘g5 ♛f6 12.0-0) 10.h3 (10.0-0 – 6...♗g4 7.0-0 ♘c6 8.♘e4 ♘xe4 9.♗xe4 0-0-0 10.c3) 10...♗h5 11.♛c2 (11.0-0!?) 11...♗g6 12.♗e3 e6 13.0-0-0 (Cherin, D. (2301) – Nikolov, S. (2381), Nova Gorica 2006) 13...♗e7 14.♖he1 ♗f6=;

B3b2) 9...f5

B3b2a) 10.♗xc6+ (10.♗d3 e5 11.♛e2 0-0-0 12.h3 ♗xf3 13.♗xf5+ ♚b8 14.♛xf3 exd4) 10...♛xc6 11.0-0 ♗xf3 12.♛xf3 ♛xf3 13.gxf3 e6 14.♖e1 ♚f7 15.♗f4 (Stuart, K. – Hnatovsky, N., Internet 2003) 15...♗d6 16.♗e5 ♖hd8 17.f4 ♗xe5 18.fxe5 g5∓ or 18.♖xe5 ♖d5∓.

B3b2a) 10.♗c2

B3b2a1) 10...g6 11.h3 ♗xf3 (11...♗h5!? 12.0-0 0-0-0) 12.♛xf3 e5 13.dxe5 ♛xe5+ 14.♛e3 0-0-0 15.♛xe5 ♘xe5 16.♗g5 ♖e8 17.0-0-0± , Jaracz, P. (2485) – Vatter, H. (2327), Dresden 2006;

B3b2a2) 10...e5 11.dxe5 ♛xd1+ (11...♘xe5? 12.♛xd6 ♗xd6 13.♘xe5 ♗xe5 14.f3 ♗h5 15.♗xf5±) 12.♗xd1 0-0-0 13.♗f4 (Krutko, A. (2350) – Abramov, A. (2280), Nizhnij Tagil 2007) 13...♖e8 14.0-0 ♗xf3 15.♗xf3 ♘xe5=; 13.♗c2 ♖e8 14.h3 ♗xf3 15.♗xf5+ ♚b8 16.gxf3 ♘xe5 17.♚e2 ♗c5⯹ or 14.0-0 g6 15.♗e3 ♗xf3 16.gxf3 ♘xe5 17.♚g2 ♗d6⇄;

C) 6...♗g4

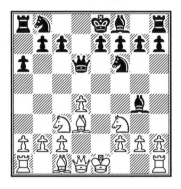

Now we consider the following alternatives: **C1)** 7.♘e4; **C2)** 7.h3 and **C3)** 7.0-0.

C1) 7.♘e4 ♘xe4 8.♗xe4 c6 (8...e6 9.c3 c6?! 10.♛b3 ♛c7 11.♘e5 Godena, M. (2502) – Pizzuto, S. (2219), Cremona 2005; 8...♘c6 – 6...♘c6 7.♘e4 ♘xe4 8.♗xe4 ♗g4) 9.0-0 (9.c3 ♘d7 10.♛b3 ♛e6 11.♛xe6 ♗xe6⇄, Nedev, T. (2516) – Sermek, D. (2523), Turin 2006) 9...♘d7 10.c3 (10.♛d3 e6) 10...♘f6 11.♗c2 (11.♗d3!?) 11...♛d5 12.♖e1 ♗xf3 13.♛xf3 ♛xf3 14.gxf3 e6± , Rogic, D. (2520) – Stevic, H. (2514), Vukovar 2005;

C2) 7.h3 ♗h5 (7...♗xf3?! 8.♛xf3 ♘c6 9.♗e3 0-0-0 10.0-0-0, Ansell, S. (2408) – Martin, A. (2433), West Bromwich 2005)

C2a) 8.♗e3 (8.0-0 ♘c6 – 6...♘c6 7.0-0 ♗g4 8.h3 ♗h5; 8.♗g5 ♘c6 9.g4 ♗g6 10.♗×g6 h×g6 11.d5 ♘e5 12.♛e2 ♘f×g4 13.0-0-0 ♘×f3 14.♛×f3 ♘f6 15.♗f4∞, Mikhaletz, L. (2458) – Jirovsky, P. (2400), Czechia 2004; 11...♘b4 12.♛d2 ♘f×d5 13.0-0-0 ♘×c3 14.b×c3 ♛×d2+ 15.♖×d2 ♘c6∓)

C2a1) 8...e6 9.♛e2 ♗e7 10.0-0-0 ♘c6 11.♔b1 (11.♘e4 ♘×e4 12.♗×e4 ♗g6 13.♗×g6 h×g6=, Manik, M. (2410) – Jirovsky, P. (2409), Czechia 2002) 11...♘b4 12.g4 (12.♘e4 ♛c6 13.g4 ♘×e4 14.g×h5⇄; 12...♘×e4!? 13.♗×e4 f5) 12...♘×d3 13.c×d3 ♗g6 14.♘e5 (Nyysti, S. (2410) – Rocha, S. (2390), Bled 2002) 14...0-0-0=;

C2a2) 8...♘c6 9.g4 (9.♛e2 0-0-0?! 10.g4 ♗g6 11.♗×g6 h×g6 12.♘g5±; 9...e6 10.0-0-0 ♗e7 11.g4 ♗g6 12.♗×g6 h×g6 13.♘g5 (Dumpor, A. (2309) – Medancic, R. (2290), Kostrena 2005) 13...♘b4=) 9...♗g6 10.♛d2 e6 11.0-0-0 0-0-0 12.a3 ♗e7 13.g5 ♘d5 14.♘e4 ♛d7⇄, Gouliev, N. (2572) – Milanovic, D. (2464), Hamburg 2005 or 10...♗×d3 11.♛×d3 e6 12.a3 0-0-0 13.0-0-0 h6⇄, Olsen, A. (2120) – Hernandez Castro, J. (1915), Copenhagen 2006;

C2b) 8.♘e4 ♘×e4 9.♗×e4 ♘c6

C2b1) 10.c3 ♗g6 (10...0-0-0 11.♛b3 ♗g6 12.♗×g6 ♛×g6 13.0-0 e6 14.♗f4 ♛f5⇄, Ellinger, P. – Duemmke, J., corr. 1991) 11.♛e2 e6 12.0-0 ♗e7 (Tsirulnik, M. (2095) – Golek, J. (1990), Sibenik 2007) 13.♘e5 (13.♗×g6 h×g6 14.♘e5 ♖h4⇄) 13...♗×e4 14.♛×e4±;

C2b2) 10.0-0

Now Black has 10...e6 and 10...0-0-0.

C2b2) 10...e6

C2b2a) 11.♖e1 ♗e7 12.c3 ♗g6 (12...0-0 13.b4 f5 14.♗c2 ♖ae8? 15.♖×e6±, Asensio Lisan, T. (2244) – Morejon Rodriguez, E. (2103), Mislata 2006; 14...♖f6 15.♗b3±; 13...♗g6!?; 13.♛d3!? ♗g6 14.♗×g6 h×g6 15.♛e4) 13.♘d2 (13.♗g5? ♗×e4 14.♖×e4 ♛d5 15.♛e2 ♗×g5 16.c4 (Krpelan, W. (2246) – Hangweyrer, M. (2347), Austria 2004) 16...♛d6 17.♘×g5 ♘×d4∓ or 17.d5 ♗f6 18.d×c6 ♛×c6∓) 13...0-0 14.♗f3 ♛d7±;

C2b2b) 11.c3

C2b2b1) 11...f6 12.♛b3 0-0-0 13.♖e1 ♗f7 (13...♛d7!? 14.c4 ♗g6) 14.c4 (14.♛c4!? ♛d7 15.b4 e5 16.♛d3) 14...♛b4 (14...g5? 15.c5 ♛d7 16.♗×g5! ♗g7±, Shirov, A. (2699) – Romero Holmes, A. (2524), Ayamonte 2002 or 16...f×g5 17.♘e5 ♛e8 18.♗×c6 b×c6 19.♛a4 ♔b7 20.♖e3 ♖a8 21.♖b3+ ♔c8 22.♛b4 with a very strong attack) 15.♗×c6 b×c6±;

C2b2b2) 11...♗g6 (11...♗e7 12.♛b3 ♖b8? (Hadzimanolis, A. (2281) –

Halkias, S. (2505), Patras 2001) 13.♗f4 ♛d7 14.d5 with a strong initiative or 13...♛×f4 14.♗×c6+ ♚f8 15.♘e5±; 12...♗×f3!?) 12.♗×c6

C2b2b2a) 12...♛×c6 13.♘e5 ♛b6 14.a4 0-0-0 (14...♗e7?! 15.a5 ♛b5 16.c4 ♛b4 (Todorovic, G. (2475) – Markovic, M. (2445), Zlatibor 2006) 17.♖a4 ♛d6 18.♗f4 with strong pressure) 15.♛f3 f6 16.♘×g6 h×g6±;

C2b2b2b) 12...b×c6 13.♘e5 f6 (13...♗e7?! 14.♗f4 ♛d5 15.♖e1 0-0 16.c4±; 15...0-0-0 16.♘×g6 h×g6 17.♖e5 ♛c4 18.♛f3±) 14.♘d3 ♛d7 (14...♗e7!?) 15.♘f4 ♗f7 (15...♚f7!? 16.♖e1 ♗d6) 16.♛g4 (16.♖e1!?) 16...h5 (16...e5!?) 17.♛g3 g5 18.♘d3 (Mitkov, N. (2561) – Garmendez, F. (2305), Mexico City 2006) 18...0-0-0 (18...♗g6!?) 19.♛f3 ♗e7 ⇄;

B2b3) 10...0-0-0 11.c3

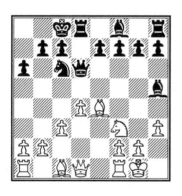

B2b3a) 11...e5?! 12.♛b3 ♗×f3 (12...e×d4 13.♘×d4 ♘a5 14.♛a4 ♛b6 15.♗e3±, Le Bail, C. (1950) – Bismuth, L. (2055), Guingamp 2007) 13.♗×f3 e×d4 14.c×d4 ♛×d4 15.♗e3 ♛b4 16.♛×f7± or 15...♛f6 16.♖ac1 ♖d6 17.♗c5±;

B2b3b) 11...e6?! 12.b4 (12.♛c2!? ♗e7 13.♖e1 ♗f6 14.b4) 12...♗g6 13.♗×g6 h×g6 14.a4 ♖h5 15.b5 a×b5 16.a×b5 ♖×b5 17.♗a3 ♛d5 18.♗×f8 ♖×f8 19.♖a8+ ♘b8 20.♛a4 1-0 Geller, J. (2484) – Ogloblin, N. (2447), Alushta 2004;

B2b3c) 11...♗g6 12.♗×c6 ♛×c6 13.♘e5 ♛d5 (13...♛f6!? 14.♛g4+ ♗f5 15.♛f3 ♗e6) 14.♗e3 e6 (14...f6?! 15.♛g4+ e6 16.♘×g6 h×g6 17.♛×g6 and Black does not have enough compensation for the pawn, Shirov, A. (2699) – Kurajica, B. (2548), Bali Benidorm 2002) 15.c4 ♛e4 16.♖e1 ♗c5 17.d5 (17.♘f3 ♗h5?! 18.♗g5; 17...♛c6 18.♛b3 ♗e7 19.♗f4 ♛b6 20.♛×b6 c×b6±) 17...♛×e5 18.♗×c5 ♛×b2∞;

C3) 7.0-0

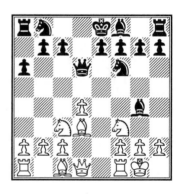

C3a) 7...♘bd7?! (Hoang Thi Bao Tram (2345) – Papadopoulou, V. (2246), Yerevan 2006) 8.h3 ♗h5 9.♖e1 0-0-0 (9...e6 10.g4 ♗g6 11.d5; 9...♗g6 10.♗×g6 h×g6 11.♘g5) 10.g4 ♗g6 11.♗×g6 h×g6 12.♘g5± or 8...♗×f3 9.♛×f3 0-0-0 10.♗e3 e6 (10...e5 11.♘e4 ♘×e4 12.♗×e4± or 11...♛c6 12.♘g5±) 11.♘e4 ♛e7 12.a4 ♘b6 13.c4 ♘×e4 14.♗×e4 c6 15.♖fc1±;

C3b) 7...e6 8.♘e4 ♘xe4 9.♗xe4 c6 10.c4 (10.c3 ♘d7 11.♕b3 ♕c7 12.♖e1 ♗e7⇄, Mitkov, N. (2520) – Gonzalez, R. (2419), USA 2004) 10...♘d7 11.♕b3 ♕c7 12.♘e5 ♘xe5 13.dxe5 (Fernandez Romero, E. (2435) – Rizouk, A. (2480), La Roda 2007) 13...0-0-0⇄.

C3c) 7...♘c6

C3c1) 8.♗e3 (8.h3 ♗h5 – 6...♘c6 7.0-0 ♗g4 8.h3 ♗h5; 8.♘e4 – 6...♗g4 7.0-0 ♘c6 8.♘e4) and now:

C3c1a) 8...0-0-0 9.h3 ♗xf3 10.♕xf3 ♘xd4 (10...e5 11.♘e4 ♘xe4 12.♗xe4 exd4 13.♖ad1 ♕c5 14.♗xc6 (Mnatsakanian, E. (2415) – Utasi, T. (2315), Budapest 1990) 14...♕xc6 15.♕xc6 bxc6∓) 11.♗xd4 ♕xd4 12.♗xa6 (12.♖ad1 ♕b6∞) 12...♕b6 13.♗c4 e6 (13...♕a5!?) 14.a4 ♕c5 15.♗d3 (Johansson, G. (2233) – Nikolov, S. (2399), Bled 2003) 15...♕h5 16.♕xh5 (16.g4 ♕a5⇄) 16...♘xh5 17.a5 ♘f4 18.a6 ♔b8 19.♗e4 c6∓;

C3c1b) 8...e6 (8.... e5 9.♗e2 ♗xf3 10.♗xf3 exd4 11.♗xc6+ ♕xc6 12.♕xd4 ♗d6 13.♖ad1 0-0 14.♗g5 ♗e7=, Pietruske, S. (2393) – Tarascio,

G. (2384), Internet 2004) 9.h3 ♗h5 10.♕e2 ♗e7 11.♘e4?! ♘xe4 12.♗xe4 (Ponkratov, P. (2360) – Lysyj, I. (2470), Chalkidiki 2003) 12...f5 13.♗xc6+ ♕xc6∓; 13.g4?! fxg4 14.♘e5 ♕g2+! 15.♔xg2 gxh3+ 16.♔xh3 ♗xe2∓.

C3c2) 8.♘e4 ♘xe4 9.♗xe4 and now:

C3c2a) 9...g6 10.c3 ♗g7 11.♕b3 ♖b8 12.♗g5 0-0 13.♖fe1 (Kobalia, M. (2618) – Hasangatin, R. (2485), Abu Dhabi 2004) 13...♖fd8 14.♗xc6 (14.h3!? ♗e6 15.♕c2) 14...bxc6 15.♗xe7 ♖xb3 16.♗xd6 ♖xb2 17.♗xc7 ♖c8 18.♗d6 ♗h6 19.♗b4 ♗xf3 20.gxf3 ♗f8 21.♗xf8 ♔xf8±;

C3c2b) 9...f5 10.♗xc6+ ♕xc6 11.d5 ♕d6 12.h3 ♗h5 13.♕d3 c6 (13...e6? 14.♖e1 0-0-0 (Gaudineau, E. (2320) – Delchev, A. (2548), Cannes 1999) 15.♗g5 ♖e8 16.♖xe6 ♖xe6 17.♕xf5±) 14.♕xf5 (14.dxc6 ♕xd3 15.cxd3 ♗xf3 16.gxf3 bxc6 17.♗f4±) 14...♕xd5 15.♘e5 (15.♕xd5 cxd5 16.♘d4 e5 17.♖e1 e4⇄ or 15.♕f4 ♗xf3 16.gxf3 e6 17.c4 ♕d7⇄) 15...♗g6 16.♕f4 ♗xc2 17.♗e3 (17.♖e1!?⩲) 17...g6 17.♕b4 ♕b5=;

C3c2c) 9...0-0-0 10.c3 (10.h3 ♗e6!? or 10...♗h5 – 6...♗g4 7.h3 ♗h5 8.♘e4

♘xe4 9.♗xe4 ♘c6 10.0-0 0-0-0; 10.♗xc6 ♕xc6 11.♘e5 ♗xd1 12.♘xc6 bxc6 13.♖xd1 (Kazakov, P. (2424) – Ovetchkin, R. (2573), Nefteyugansk 2002) 13...e5 14.♗e3 e4=)

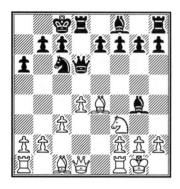

C3c2c1) 10...e6 11.♕a4 (11.b4!?; 11.h3!?) 11...♗xf3 12.♗xf3 ♘e7 13.♕b3 c6 14.♖d1 ♘f5 15.♗e4 g6±, Mikac, M. (2387) – Drobne, M. (2011), Bled 2003) 11...♘e5 12.h3 ♘xf3+ 13.♗xf3 ♗xf3 14.♕xf3±;

C3c2c2) 10...e5 11.♕b3! (11.♗xc6 bxc6 12.h3 ♗xf3 13.♕xf3 exd4 14.cxd4 ♕d5 15.♕e2 ♕b5 16.♕e4 ♕d5⇄, Dimitrov, P. (2169) – Nikolov, S. (2397), Sofia 2005) 11...♗xf3 12.♗xf3 exd4 13.cxd4 ♕xd4 14.♗e3! (14.♕xf7 ♘e5 15.♕f5+ ♔b8 16.♗e2 ♗d6⇄ or 16.♗g5 ♖e8⇄) 14...♕f6 15.♖ac1 ♖d6 16.♗c5⩲;

C3c2c3) 10...f5 11.♗c2 ♕d5?! 12.♗b3 ♗xf3 13.♗xd5 ♗xd1 14.♗e6+ ♔b8 15.♖xd1 g6 16.♖e1±, Hansen, S. (2551) – Wong Meng Kong (2470), Mallorca 2004; 11...g6!? 12.♗a4 ♗g7 13.h3 ♗h5⇄ or 11.♗xc6 ♕xc6 12.♘e5 ♗xd1 13.♘xc6 bxc6 14.♖xd1 e6 15.♖e1 ♔d7 16.♗f4 ♗d6 17.♗e5 ♖hg8±, Geller, J. (2500) – Peschansky, M. (2275), Voronezh 2007;

C3c2c4) 9...e6 10.c3 (10.h3 ♗h5 – 6...♗g4 7.h3 ♗h5 8.♘e4 ♘xe4 9.♗xe4 ♘c6 10.0-0 e6)

C3c2c4a) 10...♗e7?! 11.♕b3 ♗xf3 (11...0-0-0? 12.♘e5) 12.♗xf3 0-0-0 (12...♖b8 13.♗f4 or 13.g3) 13.♗e3 h6 (Beratti, H. (1115) – Johansson, M. (1922), Internet 2003) 14.c4 ♗g5 15.c5 ♕d7 16.♖ad1, and White has better chances;

C3c2c4b) 10...f5 (10...0-0-0 – 6...♗g4 7.0-0 ♘c6 8.♘e4 ♘xe4 9.♗xe4 0-0-0 10.c3 e6) 11.♗c2 (11.♗xc6+ ♕xc6 12.♘e5 ♗xd1 13.♘xc6 ♗h5 14.♘e5 ♗d6 15.♖e1 0-0-0 16.♘d3±, Salgado Lopez, I. (2420) – Galego, L. (2535), Soller 2007) 14...♗e7 15.♖e1 0-0-0 16.♘d3 ♗f7 17.♗f4 g5 18.♗e5 ♖hg8=) 11...0-0-0 12.h3 (12.♖e1!? ♖e8 13.b4) 12...♗h5 13.♕d3 ♗e7 14.♖e1 ♗f6 15.♘g5 ♖de8 16.♕g3 ♕d7 17.♗b3 ♘d8±, Stojanovic, D. (2465) – Nestorovic, D. (2400), Belgrade 2006.

Let's return to Vehi Bach – Magem Badals.

7.0-0

B1) 7.♗e3 ♘c6 (7...♗g7!? 8.0-0 0-0) 8.♕d2 ♘b4 9.♗e2 ♘bd5 10.♘xd5 ♘xd5 11.♗g5 ♗g7 12.c4 h6 13.♗h4 g5 (13...♘f6 14.♗g3 ♛d8 15.♗e5±, Gallagher, J. (2535) – Tukmakov, V. (2558), Lenk 2005) 14.♗g3 ♘f4⇄;

B2) 7.♘e4 ♘xe4 8.♗xe4 ♗g7 9.c3 (9.0-0 – 7.0-0 ♗g7 8.♘e4 ♘xe4 9.♗xe4) 9...♘d7 10.0-0 ♘f6 (10...c5 11.♗e3 cxd4 12.♗xd4 e5 13.♗e3 ♛c7±, Bajarani, I. (2352) – Sturua, Z. (2524), Dubai 2006) 11.♗d3 0-0 12.♖e1 ♗e6 13.c4 ♖fd8 14.h3 ♘d7 15.♗g5 ♗xd4 16.♘xd4 (16.♗xg6 ♘f6 17.♘xd4 ♛xd4 18.♗c2 ♛xc4⇄) 16...♛xd4 17.♗xe7 ♖e8 18.♗a3 ♖ad8⇄;

B3) 7.♗g5 ♗g7

B3a) 8.♛d2 ♘c6 9.0-0-0 ♗g4 10.♗f4 ♛b4 11.a3 ♛a5 12.♗e2 (12.♗c4 ♘h5⇄) 12...0-0-0 (12...0-0!?) 13.d5 (13.♘e5 ♘xe5 14.♗xe5±) 13...♗e6 14.♗c4∞, Petkov, V. (2512) – Panbukchian, V. (2312), Svilengrad 2006;

B3b) 8.0-0 ♘c6 (8...♗f5?! 9.♗xf5 gxf5 10.♛d3 e6 11.d5)

B3b1) 9.♛d2 ♘xd4 (9...0-0 10.♗f4 ♛d8=, Arias Rodriguez, S. (2140) – Gonzalez Menendez, I. (2260), Oviedo 2004) 10.♘xd4 ♛xd4 11.♖fe1 0-0 (11...♛c5!?) 12.♖xe7 ♗e6 13.♖xc7?! (13.♛f4 ♛xf4 14.♗xf4⇄) 13...♛b6 14.♖e7 (14.♗f4 ♘e8 15.♖e7 ♛xb2∓ or 15.♘a4 ♛d4∓) 14.♛b4 15.♖xe6 (15.♖c7 ♘e8∓) 15...fxe6 16.♖e1 ♖ae8∓;

B3b2) 9.h3 0-0 10.♛e2 (10.♗e3 ♘b4 11.♘e4 ♘xe4 12.♗xe4 f5 13.♗d3 (Movsesian, S. (2659) – Kurajica, B. (2551), Sarajevo 2003) 13...♗e6 14.♗e2 f4 15.♗d2 ♘c6 16.c3 ♗d5∓;

10.♗xf6 exf6 11.♘e4 ♛b4∓, Nevednichy, V. (2594) – Horvath, C. (2565), Sibenik 2005) 10...♗e6 11.♗c4 ♗xc4 12.♛xc4 b5 13.♛d3 ♖fd8⇄.

Back to Vehi Bach – Magem Badals.

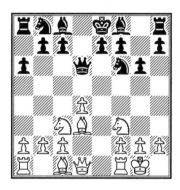

7...♗g7 8.♖e1

8.h3 (8.♗g5 – 7.♗g5 ♗g7 8.0-0) 8...0-0 9.♗e3 ♘f6 (9...♘bd7 10.♛d2 c5 11.♗f4 ♛b6 12.♘a4 ♛c6±, Annageldyev, O. (2458) – Hasangatin, R. (2485), Alushta 2004) 12.♗d3 ♖fd8 13.♖e1 c5⇄ or 8.♘e4 ♘xe4 9.♗xe4 ♘d7 (9...0-0 10.♗e3 ♘d7 11.c4 ♘f6 12.♗c2 b6 13.h3 ♗b7⇄, Coimbra, M. (2120) – Ruzic, S. (1915), Rijeka 2007) 10.c4 c5 11.♗e3 (Zigangirova, S. (2205) – Werner, D. (2349), Budapest 2004) 11...0-0 12.h3 cxd4 13.♗xd4 ♗xd4 14.♛xd4 ♛xd4 15.♘xd4 ♘c5⇄.

8...0-0

8...♘c6!? 9.♗g5 0-0.

9.h3

9.♘e4 ♘xe4 10.♗xe4 ♘d7 (10...♘c6 11.c3±, Mamedov, R. (2560) – Ptacnikova, L. (2190), Pardubice 2006)

11.c4 (11.c3 ♞f6 12.♝d3 ♝e6 13.c4 c6⇄) 11...♞f6 12.♝d3 c6 13.♛b3 ♝e6⇄.

9...♞bd7

9...♞c6 10.♝e3 ♞b4 11.♞e4 ♛b6 12.♞×f6+ ♝×f6 13.♝e4 ♜d8⇄; 12...f5 13.♝d3 ♞×d3 14.♛×d3 b5 15.♝g5 e6⇄.

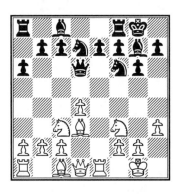

10.♛e2 e6 (10...♜e8!? 11.♝g5 ♞b6 12.♜ad1 ♝e6 13.♞e5 ♛b4 14.♝c1 ♜ad8⇄; 13.a3 ♜ad8⇄) **11.a4** (11...♝e3!? ♞b6 12.b3 ♞bd5 13.♞×d5 ♞×d5 14.♝d2 ♞f4 15.♝×f4 ♛×f4 16.♜ad1 ♜d8 17.c3± or 11...c5 12.♜ad1 ♛c7 13.d×c5 ♞×c5 14.♝d4) **11...c5 12.d×c5** (12.♝e3!?) **12...♞×c5 13.♝c4 b6 14.♞e5 ♞fd7** (14.♜d1 ♛c7 15.♛e5 ♛×e5 16.♞×e5 ♝b7⇄) **15.♞×d7** (15.♞g4 ♝b7 16.♝d2?! h5 17.♞e3 ♞e5 18.♜ad1 ♞c6∓; 16.♝h6 ♝×h6 17.♞×h6+ ♚g7 18.♞g4 h5 19.♞e3 ♜ad8⇄) **15...♝×d7 16.♝g5 ♜fc8 17.♜a3** (17.♜ed1 ♛e5) **17...♝c6 18.♝e3 ½-½**

Summary: After **1.e4 d5 2.e×d5 ♛×d5 3.♞c3 ♛d6 4.d4 ♞f6 5.♞f3 a6**, **6.♝d3** is very popular now. But Black has some good possi-

bilities for counterplay: 6...g6; 6...♞c6 and 6...♝g4.

6...g6 is an easier way for Black to get an equal game with counterplay. 6...♞c6 and 6...♝g4 are more aggressive and also more risky. Many games with 6...♞c6 will arrive at positions that are similar to those reached in the 6...♝g4 lines and transpositions between these lines are not uncommon.

Game 26
Kamsky, G (2686) –
Tiviakov, S. (2669)
Wijk aan Zee 2006

1.e4 d5 2.e×d5 ♛×d5 3.♞c3 ♛d6 4.d4 ♞f6 5.♞f3 a6 6.♝c4

6...♝g4

6...♞bd7 or 6...b5 – Game 27; 6...e6 or 6...♞c6 – Game 28. Also worth consideration is 6...♝f5.

6...♝f5 7.♞e5 (7.0-0!?; 7.h3 – Game 19; 7.♝e3 ♞c6 8.♛d2 e6 9.♞h4 ♝g6 10.♞×g6 h×g6 11.0-0-0 0-0-0 12.a3 ♞e7 13.g3 ♞ed5=, Timoshenko, G. (2565) – Dragicevic, D. (2195), Canberra 2007 or 9.0-0-0 0-0-0 10.♛e2 ♞d5 11.♞×d5 e×d5⇄, Paragua M.

(2500) – Yeo Min Yang E. (2202), Ho Chi Minh City 2003) 7...e6

A) 8.g4 ♘×g4 (8...♗×g4!? 9.♘×g4 ♛c6) 9.♘×g4 ♛c6 10.d5 (10.♖g1!? ♛×c4 11.♘e3 ♛c6) 10...♛×c4 11.♘e5 (11.♘e3 ♛f4) 11...♛b4 (11...♛h4 12.♛f3 ♗b4 13.d×e6 ♛e4+ 14.♛×e4 ♗×e4 15.e×f7+ ♔e7 16.0-0±) 12.a3 (12.♛e2 (Sorokina, A. (2120) – Houska, J. (2190), Elista 1998) 12...♗d6∓) 12...♛b6 13.b4 (13.0-0 ♗e7∓) 13...c5 14.♘a4 ♛c7∓;

B) 8.♗f4?! (8.♛e2!?; 8.0-0 ♘c6 9.♘×c6 ♛×c6 10.♗d3 ♗×d3 11.♛×d3 0-0-0 12.♗f4 ♗d6 13.♗×d6 ♖×d6∓, Lauk, U. (2333) – Keskel, M. (2147), Saaremaa 2000; 9.♖e1!? ♗g6 10.♗e3 0-0-0⇄) 8...♘c6! see the line 6.♘e5 ♘c6 7.♗f4 ♗f5 8.♗c4 e6 in Game 20.

7.h3

7.0-0!? (7.♗e3 ♘c6 – 6...♘c6 7.♗e3 ♗g4, Game 28) 7...♘c6 8.d5 (♗e3 – 6...♘c6 7.♗e3 ♗g4 7.0-0, Game 28) 8...♘a5 (8...♘e5 9.♗e2 ♘×f3+ 10.♗×f3 ♗×f3 11.♛×f3±; 9...h5!?) 9.♗e2

A) 9...♖d8?! (½-½, Pavlov, M. (2365) – Ciolac, G. (2323), Sovata 2000) 10.♛d4! b5 (10...♗d7 11.b4±) 11.♗f4 ♛b6 (11...c5 12.♛e3 ♛b6 13.b4 ♘b7 14.a4±) 12.♛×b6 c×b6 13.♗c7±;

B) 9...c6 10.d×c6 ♛×d1 (10...♘×c6 11.♛×d6 e×d6 12.♗f4 ♗f5 13.♖ac1 0-0-0±) 11.♖×d1 ♘×c6 12.♗f4 e6 13.h3 ♗h5±.

We return now to Kamsky – Tiviakov.

7...♗h5

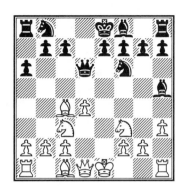

8.g4

8.♗e3!? and now:

A) In the game Rodriguez Uria, J. (2225) – Garcia Fernandez, C. (2360), Canete 1994, there was 8...♛b4?! 9.♗b3 ♘c6 10.♛e2 0-0-0 11.0-0-0 ♘a5 12.d5 ♘×b3+ 13.a×b3 ♛a5 14.♔b1 with strong pressure (14...♘×d5? 15.♖×d5 ♖×d5 16.b4±). After 10.d5!? Black also has problems; for example, 10...♘e5 (10...♘a5 11.a3 ♛d6 12.♗a2±) 11.g4 ♘×f3+ 12.♛×f3 ♗g6 13.0-0-0 0-0-0 14.♖d4 ♛d6 15.♖hd1±;

B) 8...♘c6 9.♛e2 0-0-0?! (9...♘a5 10.g4 ♘×c4 11.♛×c4 ♗g6 Black stands not bad, Marciano, D. (2480) – Prie, E. (2480), France 1996; 10.♗d3!?) 10.0-0-0

B1) 10...♘a5 (10...♘b4 11.d5 ♗g6 12.♗b3 ♘e4 13.♗×e4 ♗×e4 (Sveinsson, J. (1913) – Safarian, A. (2322), Internet 2003) 14.c3 ♘×d5 15.♘g5±) 11.♗d3 (11.g4 ♘×c4 12.♛×c4 ♗g6 (Richards, H. (2209) – Johansson, T. (2241), Gausdal 2002) 13.d5 with strong pressure) 11...♘c6 (11...♗×f3 12.♛×f3 e6 13.♘e4 ♛c6

211

14.♞xf6 ♛xf3 15.gxf3 gxf6 16.c3±)
12.g4 ♝g6 13.♝xg6 fxg6 14.♞g5±;

B2) 10...e6 11.g4 (11.d5!?) 11...♝g6
12.d5 ♞xd5 13.♞xd5 exd5 14.♝xd5
♛d7 (14...f6 (Gasik, A. (2065) –
Ivanova, T. (2155), Herceg Novi 2006)
15.♞h4 ♝e7 16.♞xg6 16...hxg6
17.♚b1±; 16.♜he1!?) 15.♝c4 ♝d6
16.♝xa6 bxa6 17.♛xa6+ ♚b8
18.♜d5+–; 16...♞b4 (Mamedov, N.
(2460) – Gashimov, S. (2333), Baku,
2003) 17.♞e5! ♛a4 18.♞xg6 fxg6
(18...♛xa2   19.♝xb7+   ♚xb7
20.♞xh8±) 19.♝c4 ♞xa2+ 20.♚b1
♞b4 21.♝b3±;

C) 8...♞bd7!? 9.♛e2 (9.0-0 0-0-0;
9.♝b3 e6 10.♛e2 ♝e7±, Maier, M. –
Olbrisch, M. (2225), Dortmund 1992;
10...0-0-0!?) 9...♞b6 10.♝d3 ♞bd5
11.♞xd5 (11.♞e4 ♞xe4 12.♝xe4 0-0-0)
11...♞xd5 12.g4 ♝g6±, Noble, W.
(1926) – Shchebenyuk, N. (2033),
Internet 2004.

Back to Kamsky – Tiviakov.

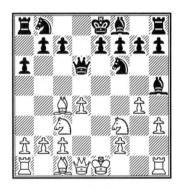

8...♝g6 9.♞e5?!

9.♝e3 ♞c6 10.♛e2 (10.♛d2 0-0-0
11.0-0-0⇄, Von Wantoch Rekowski,
D. (2110) – Danielian, E. (2420), Dresden

2007) 10...e6 11.0-0-0 (½-½, Stojanovski,
D. (2416) – Galego, L. (2521), Skopje
2002) 11...♞b4 (11...0-0-0?! 12.d5
exd5 13.♞xd5 ♞xd5 14.♝xd5 f6
15.♞h4±) 12.♝b3 (12.d5?! ♞fxd5
13.♝xd5 ♞xd5 14.♞xd5 exd5 15.♝f4+
♛e6 16.♛xe6+ fxe6∓ 17.♝xc7?
♜c8–+) 12...♞bd5 13.♞xd5 ♞xd5
14.♝d2 ♝e7 15.♞e5 ♝f6=.

9...♞c6 10.♞xg6

10.♝f4 ♞e5 11.dxe5 ♛c6 12.0-0
(12.♝d5 ♞xd5 13.♛xd5 ♛xd5
14.♞xd5 0-0-0∓) 12...♛xc4 13.exf6
♛xf4 14.♞d5 ♛c4 15.fxe7 ♝xe7
16.♜e1 0-0-0 17.♞xe7+ ♚b8∓,
Shkuran, D. (2313) – Sergeev, V.
(2478), Kiev 2002.

10...hxg6

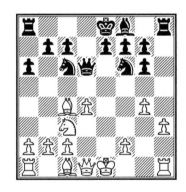

11.♝e3

11.g5 (!? Tiviakov, S.) 11...♛xd4 and
now:

A) 12.♛xd4?! ♞xd4 13.gxf6 ♞c2+
14.♚e2 ♞xa1 15.♞d5 ♜c8

A1) 16.fxe7 ♝xe7 17.♝d2 (17.♞xe7
♚xe7 18.♝d2 ♞c2 19.♚d3 b5 20.♝b3
♞b4+ 21.♝xb4+ c5∓) 17...♞c2

18.♔d3 (18.♗b3 ♘d4+) 18...b5
19.♔×c2 (19.♗b3 ♘b4+ 20.♗×b4
♗×b4 21.♘×b4 c5∓) 19...b×c4 20.♖e1
♔d7 21.♘×e7 (21.♖×e7+ ♔d6)
21...♖ce8 22.♗b4 ♖×h3 23.♖e4
♖h5∓;

A2) 16.♗f4 ♘c2 17.♘×c7+ (17.♔d3 e6
18.♘×c7+ ♖×c7 19.♗×c7 ♘b4+
20.♔e2 g×f6∓) 17...♖×c7 18.♗×c7
g×f6 19.♖d1 e5 20.♖d8+ ♔e7 21.♗d5
(21.♖b8 ♘d4+ 22.♔f1 b5 23.♗d8+
♔d7∓) 21...♘d4+ 22.♔e1 ♘e6∓;

B) 12.♕e2 ♘e5 (12...♘a5 13.♗d3 ♘d5
14.♘×d5 ♕×d5 15.♗e4 ♕b5∓;
12...♖h4!?) 13.♗b3 ♘h5 14.♗e3 ♕d7
15.♖d1?! ♕f5 16.♗d5 c6 17.♗e4 ♘f4
18.♗×f5 (18.♕f1? ♕×e4! 19.♘×e4
♘f3#) 18...♘×e2∓; 15.f4 ♘g3 16.♕g2
♘×h1 17.♕×b7∞.

11...e5

12.d5 (12.♕e2 0-0-0 13.d5 ♘d4
14.♕d3 ♘×g4 15.♗×d4 e×d4 16.♕×d4
♕e5+ 17.♕×e5 ♘×e5 18.♗e2 (Mocchi,
T. (2352) – Drobne, M. (2062), Nova
Gorica 2001) 18...♖h4 19.0-0-0 ♗c5∓
or 19.0-0 ♗b4∓ or 12.d×e5 ♘×e5
13.♕×d6 ♗×d6 14.♗e2 ♘f×g4∓;
13.♗b3 ♘e×g4 14.♕f3 ♘×e3
15.♕×e3+ ♕e7 16.♕×e7+ ♗×e7∓,

Wurm, T. – Djoudi, A., Internet 2003
or 15.♕×b7 ♖d8 16.♗a4+ ♔e7 17.f×e3
♖h5∓; 13.♗d5 0-0-0 14.♗g2 ♕b4
15.♕c1 ♘c4 16.a3 ♕d6 17.♘e2♖e8∓
or 17.♗f4 ♕e6+ 18.♔f1 ♗c5∓)
12...♘a5 13.♕e2?! (13.♗e2!? 0-0-0
14.♕d2 ♘×d5 15.0-0-0 ♘f6 16.♕e1
♕e6 17.♖×d8+ ♔×d8 18.g5 ♖;
15...♘b6 16.♗×b6 c×b6 17.♕e3 ♕e6
18.♖×d8+ ♔×d8 19.♖d1+ ♔c8
20.♘a4; 16...♕×d2+ 17.♖×d2 ♖×d2?
18.♗×a5 ♖d4 19.♘b1± or 17...c×b6
18.♖×d8+ ♔×d8 19.♘d5 b5 20.♖d1 ♖)
13...♘×c4 (13...♕b4?! 14.♗b3 ♕×g4
15.h×g4 ♖×h1+ 16.♔d2 ♖×a1 17.♗a4+
b5 18.♘×b5 a×b5 19.♕×b5+ ♔d8
20.♗g5 ♖c8 21.♗×f6 g×f6 22.♕e8+
♔b7 23.♕b5+ with a draw or
16...♘×b3+ 17.a×b3 ♖×a1 18.g5 ♘d7
19.♕c4 ♗d6 20.♘e4 ♔e7 21.♘×d6
c×d6 22.♕c7 b5 23.f4∞; 19...0-0-0
20.d6 ♗×d6 21.♕×f7∞; 19...♖c8
20.♘e4 b5 21.♕c6∞) **14.♕×c4 b5!**
15.♕d3 (15.♕e2 b4 16.♘b1 ♕×d5∓
or 15.♕c6 ♕×c6 16.d×c6 ♘×g4∓)
15...♘×g4∓ 16.0-0-0 ♘f6 17.f4
e×f4 18.♘e4 ♘×e4 19.♕×e4+
♗e7 20.♗d4 (20.♗×f4 ♖h4
21.♗×d6 ♖×e4 22.♗×c7 ♔d7∓,
Tiviakov, S.) **20...f5 21.♕f3 0-0-0**
22.♗×g7 ♖hg8 23.♗c3 b4
24.♗e1 g5?! (24...♖ge8!?, Tiviakov,
S.) **25.♕d3 ♖gf8 26.♗f2 ♔b7**
27.♖he1 ♗f6 28.♕f3 (28.♔c4
♖fe8 29.♗c5 ♔d7 30.♕×b4+ ♕b5
31.♕×b5 a×b5∓) **28...♖fe8 29.♖f1**
♖e4 30.♔b1 ♕e5 31.♕b3 a5
32.c3 ♕d6 33.a3 ♖a8 34.a×b4
a×b4 35.♖fe1 ♖ae8 36.c4 ♖×e1
37.♗×e1 ♖e2 38.♗×b4 ♕b6
39.c5 ♕b5 40.c6+ ♔b8
(40...♔c8?! 41.d6 ♖×b2+? 42.♕×b2
♗×b2 43.d7+ ♔d8 44.♗e7+) **41.d6**
♖×b2+ 42.♕×b2 ♗×b2 43.d7 ♗f6
0-1

Summary: After **1.e4 d5 2.e×d5 ♛×d5 3.♞c3 ♛d6 4.d4 ♞f6 5.♞f3 a6 6.♝c4**, Black has several possibilities for an equal game with counterplay: 6...e6, 6...♞c6, 6...♝f5, 6...♞bd7, 6...♝g4 and 6...b5. Of these, 6...♝g4 is the most aggressive plan with good chances for success.

Black often plays ...♝g4, followed by ♞b8-c6, with the idea of 0-0-0 or e7-e5. But if after **6.♝c4 ♝g4 7.h3 ♝h5** White plays 8.♝e3, Black needs to play 8...♞bd7 as after 8...♞c6 9.♛e2 0-0-0 10.0-0-0 the advance d4-d5 can be dangerous for Black in many lines.

Game 27
Nikac, P. (2355) –
Nestorovic, N. (2435)
Podgorica 2007

**1.e4 d5 2.e×d5 ♛×d5 3.♞c3 ♛d6
4.d4 ♞f6 5.♞f3 a6 6.♝c4 b5**

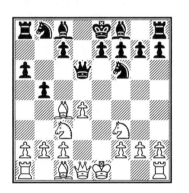

For 6...♝g4 or 6...♝f5 – Game 26; 6...♞c6 or 6...e6 – Game 28. Also worth consideration is 6...♞bd7.

7.0-0 b5 (7...e6 – Game 28) 8.♝b3 – 6...b5 7.♝b3 ♞bd7 8.0-0 or 8.♝d3 ♝b7 – 6...b5 7.♝d3 ♝b7 8.0-0 ♞bd7;

7.♛e2 b5 8.♝d3 ♝b7 – 6...b5 7.♝d3 ♝b7 8.♛e2 ♞bd7. We examine the following alternatives: **B1)** 7.a4; **B2)** 7.♝e3 and **B3)** 7.♝b3.

A) 7.a4 ♞b6 (7...e6 – 6...e6 7.a4 ♞bd7, Game 28; 7...c5?! 8.0-0 c×d4 9.♞×d4 ♞b6 10.♝b3 g6 11.♖e1 ♝g4 12.f3 ♝d7 13.♝e3 e6 14.♞×e6 ♝×e6 15.♛×d6 ♝×d6 16.♝×b6±, Kozhuharov, S. (2370) – Bratanov, J. (2393), Plovdiv 2003) 8.♝b3 ♝e6 9.a5 (9.♝×e6!? ♛×e6+ 10.♞e2) 9...♝×b3 10.a×b6 ♝e6 11.b×c7 ♛×c7 12.♞e5 (12.0-0!?) 12...g6 13.♛f3 ♝g7 14.♝f4 ♞h5 15.♞×g6?! ♛c6! 16.♛×c6+ b×c6 17.g4 h×g6 18.g×h5 ♖×h5∓;

B) 7.♝e3 e6 (7...b5 8.♝b3 ♝b7 (½-½, Kotan, L. (2372) – Boricsev, O. (2311), Hungary 2002) 9.♛d2 c5⇄) 8.♛d2 b5 9.♝b3 ♝e7 (9...♝b7!?; 9...b4!? 10.♞a4 ♞e4 11.♛d3 ♝b7⇄) 10.d5 e5 (10...♞c5!? 11.♝×c5 ♛×c5 12.d×e6 ♝×e6 13.♝×e6 f×e6) 11.♞g5 0-0 12.0-0-0 (Chan Yi Ren, D. (2135) – Kantans, T. (2015), Kemer 2007) 12...♞c5 13.♝×c5 ♛×c5 14.♖he1 ♝d6=;

C) 7.♝b3 e6 8.♛e2 ♝e7 (8...b5?! 9.d5!± ; 8...h6 9.0-0 ♝e7 10.♖d1 0-0 11.♞e5 ♞b6 12.♞e4 ♞×e4 13.♛×e4± , Zhelnin, V. (2484) – Zaitsev, V. (2412), St. Petersburg 1999) 9.♝g5 0-0 10.♖d1 c6 11.0-0 b5 12.♞e5 c5 13.♞×d7 ♛×d7 14.d×c5 ♛c6 15.♝e3 (15.♞e4 ♝b7) 15...♝b7 16.f3 ♝×c5 17.♚h1 (17.♛f2? ♞g4!-+, Hedric, H. – Wulfmeyer, J., Germany 1997) 17...♝×e3 18.♛×e3 ♖fd8=.

We return now to Nikac – Nestorovic.

7.♝e2

Also worth consideration are **A)** 7.♗d3 and **B)** 7.♗b3.

A) 7.♗d3 ♗b7

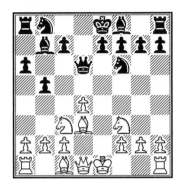

A1) 8.♛e2 ♞bd7 (8...e6 9.0-0 – 8.0-0 e6 9.♛e2; 9.♗g5 – 5.♗g5 a6 6.♞f3 ♞bd7 7.♛d2 b5 8.♗d3 ♗b7 9.♛e2, Game 36) 9.a4 (9.0-0 – 8.0-0 ♞bd7 9.♛e2) 9...b4 10.♞e4 ♞xe4 11.♗xe4 ♗xe4 12.♛xe4 c6 13.0-0 e6 14.c4 bxc3 15.bxc3 ♞f6 16.♛d3 ♛c7 17.♞e5 ♗d6 18.♖e1 0-0 (Hall, J. (2485) – Gausel, E. (2540), Munkebo 1998) 19.♗a3 ♗xa3 20.♖xa3± or 13...♛d5 14.♛e2 e6 15.c4 bxc3 16.bxc3 ♗d6 17.c4 ♛h5 18.♛e4 ♖c8±, Klima, L. (2357) – Hasangatin, R. (2474), Karvina 2002;

A2) 8.0-0

A2a) 8...♞bd7 9.♗g5 (9.♖e1 e6 – 8...e6 9.♖e1 ♞bd7) 9...e6 10.♖e1 (10.♛e2 – 6.♗e3 b5 7.♗d3 ♗b7 8.0-0 ♞bd7 9.♛e2 e6 10.♗g5, Game 22) 10...♗e7 11.♗h4 0-0 12.♗g3 ♛b6 13.♞e5 (Bensaid, A. – Vieillot, C., Calvi 2005) 13...♞xe5 14.♗xe5 (14.dxe5 ♞d5 15.♞xd5 ♗xd5⇄ or 15.♞e4 ♖ad8⇄) 14...b4 15.♞e4 ♞d7 16.♗f4 c5⇄;

A2b) 8...e6

A2b1) 9.♛e2 ♗e7 10.a4 (10.♗g5 – 8.0-0 ♞bd7 9.♛e2 e6 10.♗g5, Game 22) 10...b4 11.♞e4 ♞xe4 (11...♛d5?! (Crosa, M. (2384) – Giaccio, A. (2517), Montevideo 2002) 12.♛xd5 exd5 13.♗f4 ♞d7 14.♖fe1±) 12.♗xe4 ♗xe4 13.♛xe4 ♛c6 14.♛d3 (14.♛g4 0-0 15.♗h6 ♗f6 16.♖fc1 ♞d7⇄, Oechslein, R. (2220) – Wulfmeyer, J., Bayern 1995) 14...♞bd7 15.♖e1±;

A2b2) 9.♖e1 ♞bd7 10.♛e2 (10.♗g5 – 8...♞bd7 9.♗g5 e6 10.♖e1) 10...c5 (10...♛c6!? 11.a4 b4) 11.♞e4 ♛b6 12.c3 ♗e7 13.dxc5 ♞xc5 14.♞xc5 ♛xc5 15.♗e3 ♛h5⇄, Beganovic, E. – Dizdarevic, E. (2527), Bihac 1999;

B) 7.♗b3

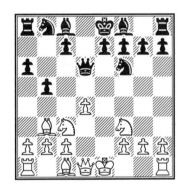

Black now has **B1)** 7...♞bd7; **B2)** 7...c5; **B3)** 7...e6 and **B4)** 7...♗b7.

B1) 7...♞bd7

B1a) 8.♞g5 e6 9.♛f3 ♖b8 (9...♖a7?! 10.♗e3 ♗b7 11.d5 with a strong initiative) 10.d5 (10.♗f4 (Santo Roman, M. (2382) – Gouret, T. (2248), France 2003) 10...♛xd4 11.♗xc7 ♖b7 12.♖d1 ♛g4 13.♛xg4 ♞xg4±) 10...♗b7 11.♗f4 e5 12.♗g3 ♛b6 13.0-0-0 ♗d6⇄;

B1b) 8.0-0

B1b1) 8...e6 (8...c5 9.a4 c4 10.♗a2 b4 11.♘e2 with better chances for White) 9.♖e1 (9.♘g5! ♗b7?! – 8...♗b7?! 9.♘g5 e6; 9...h6 10.♘ge4; 9...♗e7 10.♕f3 or 9...c5 10.♕f3) 9...♗e7 (9...c5 – 6.♗c4 e6 7.0-0 ♘bd7 8.♖e1 c5, Game 28) 10.d5 e5?! (Kuzmina, O. – Chuprikov, D., Internet 2006) 11.♕e2 with a strong pressure; 10...♘c5⇄;

B1b2) 8...♗b7?!

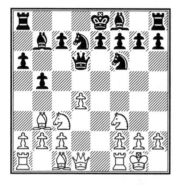

9.♘g5! e6 (9...♘d5 10.♘×f7 ♔×f7 11.♗×d5+ ♗×d5 12.♕h5+ g6 13.♕×d5+ ♕×d5 14.♘×d5 e6 15.♘c3±) 10.♖e1 ♗e7 (10...♘d5 (Nakamura, H. (2601) – Stripunsky, A. (2553), New York 2004) 11.♘ge4 ♕b6 12.♘×d5 ♗×d5 13.♗×d5 e×d5 14.♘d6+ ♔d8 15.♖e8#, Lane, G.) 11.♘×e6 f×e6 12.♖×e6 ♕b4 13.a3 ♕a5 14.♗d2 b4 15.a×b4 ♕f5 16.♕e2 ♘g8 17.♖a5! ♕f8 18.♘d5 ♔d8 (18...♗×d5 19.♗×d5 ♖b8 20.♘c6 ♔d8 21.♖×a6 ♘gf6 22.b5+−) 19.b5 ♗d6 (19...a×b5 20.♕×b5 ♖b8 21.♘×e7 ♘×e7 22.♗g5+−) 20.b×a6 ♗c6 21.♘b4 ♘b8 1-0, Ponomariov, R. (2616) – Fressinet, L. (2440), Batumi 1999;

B2) 7...c5 8.a4 (8.d×c5 ♕×d1+ 9.♔×d1 e6 10.♗e3 ♗b7⇄ or 9.♘×d1 e6⇄)

8...b4 (8...c×d4 9.♕×d4 ♕×d4 10.♘×d4 b4 11.♘d5 with the initiative; 8...c4 9.♗a2 ♗b7 10.a×b5 a×b5 11.♘×b5 ♕b4+ 12.♘c3 ♘e4 13.0-0 ♘×c3 14.b×c3 ♕×c3 15.♗e3 ♘d7 16.♕e2 ♘b6 17.♘e5±) 9.♘e2 e6 (9...♘c6?! 10.♗f4 ♕d7 11.♘e5) 10.♗f4 ♕d8 11.a5 ♗e7 12.d×c5 (12.♗×b8?! ♖×b8 13.♘e5 ♗b7 14.♗a4+ ♔f8 (Hamdouchi, H. (2541) – Kurajica, B. (2534), Villarrobledo 2000) 15.♗c6 ♕c7 16.♗×b7 ♖×b7 17.0-0 ♖b5⇄) 12...♕×d1+ 13.♖×d1 ♗×c5 14.0-0 0-0 15.♗d6 ♗×d6 16.♖×d6 with a better ending for White;

B3) 7...e6

8.♕e2 (8.♗g5 – 6...e6 7.♗b3 b5 8.♗g5, Game 28; 8.0-0 ♗b7 – 7...♗b7 8.0-0 e6 or 8...c5 – 6...e6 7.♗b3 b5 8.0-0 c5, Game 28; 8.♘e5 ♗b7 – 7...♗b7 8.♘e5 e6 or 8...♘c6/c5 – 6...e6 7.♗b3 b5 8.♘e5 ♘c6/c5, Game 28; 8.a3 ♗b7 9.0-0 c5⇄; 8.a4 b4 9.♘e2 ♗b7⇄) 8...♗b7 (8...c5/♗e7 – 6...e6 7.♗b3 b5 8.♕e2 c5/♗e7, Game 28) 9.♗g5 (9.♗e3 ♘bd7⇄ or 9...♗e7⇄; 9.♘e5 – 6...b5 7.♗b3 ♗b7 8.♘e5 e6 9.♕e2; 0-0 – 6...e6 7.♗b3 b5 8.♕e2 ♗b7 9.0-0, Game 28)

B3a) 9...b4 10.♘a4 ♘e4 11.♘c5 (11.0-0 ♘×g5 12.♘×g5 ♘d7 13.♖ad1 ♗e7

14.♘e4 ♗xe4 15.♛xe4 0-0⇄)
11...♘xc5 12.dxc5 ♛xc5 13.♗xe6
(13.0-0-0 ♗d6 14.♗xe6 0-0⇄)
13...♗e7 14.♗b3 ♘c6 15.0-0-0 0-0
16.♗xe7 ♘xe7 17.♖d7 ♘g6 18.♖e1
♗c6 19.♖dd1 ♖fe8 ½-½, Fercec, N.
(2494) – Sermek, D. (2603), Medulin
2002;

B3b) 9...♘bd7 10.0-0-0 (10.0-0 b4
11.♘a4 ♗e7⇄ or 11.♘b1 ♗e7⇄;
10.♖d1!? b4 11.d5)

B3b1) 10...c5?! 11.dxc5 ♛xc5 12.♗xe6!
fxe6 13.♛xe6+ ♗e7 (13...♗e7 14.♗xf6
♘xf6 15.♘e5 ♖f8 16.♖d7 ♗c8 17.♖xe7+
♛xe7 18.♛c6+ ♘d7 19.♛xa8±)
14.♛h3 0-0-0 15.♖he1 ♛c5 16.♘e5
♗c6 17.♘f7 ♗e7 18.♖e5 ♛b6
19.♖xe7±, Lupulescu, C. (2473) –
Svetushkin, D. (2501), Bucharest 2002;

B3b3) 10...♘d5 (10...♗e7?! 11.♖he1 0-
0 12.d5 ♘xd5 13.♖xd5 ♗xd5 14.♗xe7
♛xe7 15.♘xd5±, Mahia, G. (2427) –
Campora, D. (2552), San Luis 2006)
11.♘e4 ♛b6 12.♘e5 (12.♔b1 h6
13.♗c1 ♗e7 14.♖he1 0-0-0⇄, Zelcic,
R. (2554) – Kurajica, B. (2548), Spilt
2002; 14...0-0!?) 12...♘xe5 13.dxe5 h6
14.♗h4 ♗e7=, Medvegy, Z. (2456) –
Heinzel, O. (2402), Austria 2005;

B4) 7...♗b7

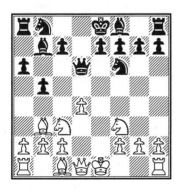

B4a) 8.♛e2 ♘c6 (8...e6 – 7...e6 8.♛e2
♗b7) 9.♗e3 e6 (9...0-0-0?! 10.♘g5;
9...♛a5 – 6.♘c6 7.♗e3 b5 8.♗b3 ♘a5
9.♛e2 ♗b7, Game 28) 10.0-0-0 ♘a5
(10...♘b4 11.♘e5 ♗xg2 12.♖hg1 ⯮)
11.d5 ♘xb3+ 12.axb3 ♘xd5 13.♘xd5
exd5∞;

B4b) 8.a4 b4 9.♘e2 ♗xf3 (9...e6!?
10.♗f4 ♛d8 11.0-0 ♗d6 12.♛d3 0-0
13.c4 bxc3 14.bxc3 ♘bd7⇄) 10.gxf3
e6 11.♗f4 ♛c6 12.♛d3 ♘bd7 13.a5
♗d6 14.0-0 0-0⇄, Tirard, H. (2401) –
Mellado Trivino, J. (2447), France
2002;

B4c) 8.♘e5 e6

B4c1) 9.♛e2 (9.0-0?! c5 10.♗f4 c4)
9...♗e7 (9...♛xd4? 10.♘xf7; 9...♘c6!?
10.♘xc6 ♗xc6 11.0-0 b4) 10.♗f4 ♛b6
11.0-0-0 0-0 12.d5?! (12.a3!? ♖d8⇄)
exd5 13.♘xd5 ♘xd5 14.♗xd5 ♗xd5
15.♖xd5 ♛e6 16.c4? (Sawatzki, F.
(2215) – Witthaus, J., Germany 1991)
16...♘c6 17.♖e1 ♗d6∓; 16.♛f3 c6
17.♖dd1 ♛xa2 18.c3⇄;

B4c2) 9.♗f4

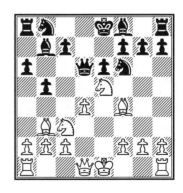

B4c2a) 9...♘c6 (9...♛d8 10.♛e2!;
9...♛b6 10.d5!) 10.♘g6 ♛xd4 11.♛xd4
♘xd4 12.♘xh8 ♗xg2 13.♖g1 ♘f3+
14.♔e2 ♘d4+ 15.♔d1! (15.♔e1 ♘f3+

16.♔e2 ♘d4+ 17.♔e1 ½-½, Tzermiadianos, A. (2300) – Georgiev, K. (2610), Katerini 1992) 15...♗f3+ (15...0-0-0 16.♔c1±; 15...♖d8 16.♔c1 ♘e4 17.♗xc7 ♘xc3 18.bxc3 ♗a3+ 19.♔d1 ♘xb3+ 20.♗xd8±) 16.♔e1 (16.♔c1 c5 17.♗e5 ♘c6⇄, Harkes, L. (2102) – Yee, L. (2232), Toronto 2001) 16...c5 (16...♗h5 17.♔f1 c5 18.a3 c4 19.♗a2 ♘xc2 20.♖c1 ♘d4∞) 17.♗e5 (17.♗e3 ♖d8 18.a4 b4∞) 17...♘f5 (17...♖d8 18.a4 b4∞) 18.a4 c4 19.♗a2 ♘g4∞;

B4c2b) 9...c5

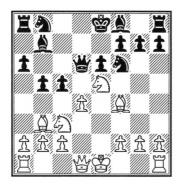

B4c2b1) 10.♘g6?! ♕xd4 11.♕xd4 cxd4 12.♘xh8 dxc3 13.bxc3 (13.♗e5 cxb2 14.♗xb2 ♗xg2 15.♖g1 ♗e4 16.0-0-0 ♘bd7∓) 13...g5 14.♗xg5 ♗g7 15.♘xf7 ♔xf7∓ or 10.♘xf7?! ♕xf4 11.♘xh8 (11.♗xe6 ♗xg2 12.dxc5 (Jossien, R. (2187) – Eliet, N. (2398), Bethune 1999) 12...♘c6∓) 11...c4 12.♕e2 ♕f5 13.♗xc4 bxc4 14.0-0-0 ♘d5 15.♕xc4 ♘d7 16.♖he1 ♗e7∓;

B4c2b2) 10.dxc5 ♕xd1+ 11.♖xd1 ♗xc5 12.0-0 ♘c6 13.♘xc6 ♗xc6 14.♗d6 ♗b6 (14...♗xd6 15.♖xd6 ½-½, Ramesh, R. (2443) – Mellado Trivino, J. (2493), Andorra 2000;) 15.♖d2 0-0-0∓, Ogloblina, L. (2150) – Lomako, A. (2280), Smolensk 2008;

B4d) 8.0-0

B4d1) 8...e6 9.♖e1 (9.♕e2 – 6...e6 7.♗b3 b5 8.♕e2 ♗b7 9.0-0, Game 28) 9...c5 10.♗xe6 (10.a4 b4 11.d5 bxc3 12.dxe6 ♕xd1 13.exf7+ ♔d8 14.♖xd1+ ♘bd7 15.bxc3⯊; 10...c4!? 11.♗a2 ♕c6 Boehnisch, M. (2354) – Jirovsky, M. (2450), Germany 2002) 10...fxe6 11.♘g5 ♗e7 (11...♕xd4!?) 12.♖xe6?! ♕d7 13.♕e2 (Alarcon, R. (2255) – Valido, C. (2305), Havana 2005) 13...cxd4∓ or 13.d5 0-0 14.d6 ♗d8∓; 12.♘xe6 ♔f7∞, Keserovic, M. (2225) – Lajthajm, B. (2464), Vrnjacka Banja 2006 or 11...♗c8 12.♕f3 cxd4∞, Flamant, J. – Boudre, J. (2384), Bethune 2001; 12.♘xe6!? ♗xe6 13.d5 ♗e7 14.♖xe6 ♕d7 15.♕e2⯊;

B4d2) 8...c5 (8...♘bd7 – 6...b5 7.♗b3 ♘bd7 8.0-0) 9.dxc5 (9.a4!?) 9...♕xd1 10.♖xd1 e6 11.♘e5 ♘c6 12.♗f4 (12.♘d3 ♘bd7 13.♘xc5 ♘xc5 14.♗f4⇄) 12...♗xc5 13.♘xc6 ♗xc6 14.♘e2 (14.♗d6 ♗xd6 15.♖xd6 ♖c8∓, Crut, A. (2303) – Mellado Trivino, J. (2460), France 2001) 14...0-0 15.♗d6 ♗xd6 16.♖xd6=.

Back to Nikac – Nestorovic.

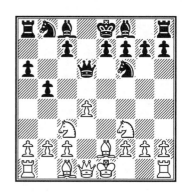

7...♗b7 8.0-0

8.♗g5 ♘bd7 9.0-0 e6 10.♖e1 (10.♕c1 ♗e7 11.♗f4 ♕c6 12.♘h4 ♘b6∓) 10...♗e7 11.♕d2 0-0 (11...b4!?) 12.♗f4 ♕b6 13.♖ad1 c5⇄, Buitelaar, J. – Van Beek, A. (2270) Hengelo 2000.

8...♘bd7

8...e6 9.♘e5 (9...♘c6 10.♗f4; 9.♗g5 ♘bd7 10.a4 b4 11.♘b1 ♘e4 12.♗e3 (Van Weersel, A. (2184) – Struk, J. (2237), Hoogeveen 2004) 12...♗e7=) 9...♗e7 10.♗f4 ♕b6 11.♗f3 0-0 12.♗×b7 ♕×b7 13.♖e1 ♖d8 14.♕f3 ♕×f3 15.♘×f3 c5=, Gorbov, A. – Kernazhitsky, L. (2370), Kiev 2007.

9.a4

9.♘g5 (9.a3 e6) 9...h6 10.♘h3 ♘b6 (10...0-0-0 11.♗e3 b4 12.♘b1 e5⇄) 11.♗e3?! (11.♗f4 ♕d7 12.♗e5 b4 13.♘b1 e6⇄) 11...g5 12.f3 (Dzhumaev, M. (2507) – Hossain, E. (2451), Dhaka 2003) 12...♗g7∓.

9...b4 10.♘b1 e6

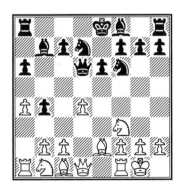

11.♘bd2

11.♗e3 c5 12.d×c5 (12.♘bd2 ♗e7 13.♘c4 ♕c7⇄) 12...♕×d1 (12...♗×c5

13.♘bd2 ♖d8 14.♘c4 ♕c7⇄) 13.♖×d1 ♗×c5 14.♗×c5 ♘×c5 15.♖d4 a5 16.♗b5+ ♔e7 17.♘bd2⇄.

11...c5 12.d×c5

12.♘c4 ♕c7 (12...♕d5?! 13.♘a5 c×d4 14.♘×b7 ♕×b7 15.♘×d4) 13.g3 ♘d5⇄.

12...♘×c5

12...♕c7!? 13.c6 ♗×c6 14.♘c4 (14.g3 ♗d5⇄; 14.♘d4?! ♗d5 15.♗f3 ♗c5 16.♗×d5 ♘×d5 17.♘e4 0-0∓) 14...♖d8⇄.

13.♘c4 ♕c7 14.♘fe5 (14.g3!?) **14...♖d8 15.♕e1 ♘d5**

16.♗f3 ♗e7 17.a5?! 0-0 (17...b3!? 18.♗d1 f6 19.♘f3 e5 with better chances for Black) **18.b3 ♖fe8** (18...f6 19.♘d3 e5 20.♗×d5+ ♗×d5 21.♘×b4 ♗f7∞; 18...♘c3 19.♗×b7 ♕×b7 20.♗d2?! ♘5e4; 20.♗b2 ♘d5 21.f4 f6 22.♘d3 ♖fe8∓) **19.♗b2** (19.♗d2 f6 20.♘d3 ♗c6 21.♖d1 ♕b7∓) **19...f6 20.♘d3 ♘×d3** (20...♔h8 21.♘×c5 ♗×c5∓) **21.♕×e6+ ♔h8 22.c×d3 ♗d6** (22...♗c8!? 23.♕e4 ♗c5 24.♕h4 ♘c3∞ or 23.♕f7 ♘f4 24.♖ae1 ♗f5

219

25.♗e5 f×e5 26.♕×f5 ♘×d3 27.♖e2
♖f8 ⇄; 23...♖f8!? 24.♕h5 ♘f4)
23.♕f5 (23.♕g4 ♗×h2+ 24.♔h1
♗f4 25.♖ae1 ♕f7 26.♗e4 ♗g5
27.♕h3 ♕g8 28.♕h2 ♗f4 29.♕h5
♗b8 30.g3±; 28... ♖e6 29.f4 ♗h6⇄)
23...♗c8 (23...♗×h2+ 24.♔h1 ♗f4
25.♖ae1 ♖×e1 26.♖×e1±; 24... ♘e7
25.♕g4 ♗×f3 26.♕×f3 ♗d6=)
24.♕h5 ♘f4 25.♕h4 ♘g6
(25...♘×d3?! 26.♗h5 ♘×b2 27.♗×e8
♖×e8 28.♘×b2 ♗e6 29.♖ac1 ♕×a5
30.♘c4 ♕c7 31.♘×d6 ♕×d6
32.♖fd1±; 27...♘×c4 28.♗g6 h6
29.♕×c4 ♗×h2+ 30.♔h1±) **26.♕h5
♘f4 ½-½**

Summary: After **1.e4 d5 2.e×d5
♕×d5 3.♘c3 ♕d6 4.d4 ♘f6 5.♘f3
a6 6.♗c4**, the topic for this Game 27
is the popular moves 6...♘bd7 and
6...b5.

After 6...♘bd7, White has many
continuations. After 7.a4, 7.♕e2,
7.♗b3, 7.♗e3 or 7.♗g5, Black is
usually able to complete development
without any particular problems. 7.0-0
b5 8.♗b3 ♗b7 transposes to a line
which is dangerous for Black, viz.,
6...b5 7.♗b3 ♘bd7 8.0-0 ♗b7;
preferable is 7...e6 – see Game 28.

After 6...b5, White has three possibilities: 7.♗d3, 7.♗b3 and **7.♗e2**.

1. After 7.♗d3 ♗b7, the chances are
equal.
2. After 7.♗b3 e6 or 7...♗b7, Black
has counterplay (7...♘bd7 8.0-0 e6
9.♘g5 or 7...c5 8.a4 is dangerous for
Black).
3. After **7.♗e2 ♗b7 8.0-0 ♘bd7**, the
chances are equal.

Cubas, J. (2445) – Crosa Coll, M. (2400)
Argentina 2007

**1.e4 d5 2.e×d5 ♕×d5 3.♘c3 ♕d6
4.d4 ♘f6 5.♘f3 a6 6.♗c4 e6**

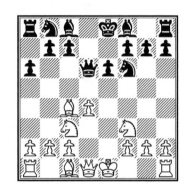

For 6...♗g4 or 6...♗f5 see Game 26;
6...b5, 6...c5 and 6...♘bd7 – Game 27.
Also worth consideration is 6...♘c6.
Then we examine the following continuations: **A)** 7.d5; **B)** 7.♘g5; **C)** 7.h3
and **D)** 7.♗e3.

A) 7.d5

A1) 7...b5 8.♗e2 (8.d×c6!? b×c4
9.♕×d6 e×d6 10.♗g5; 9.0-0!? ♕×c6
10.♘e5⯲) 8...♘b4 9.a4 b×a4
(9...♘f×d5?! 10.♘×d5 ♕×d5 (Fercec,
N. (2467) – Goric, E. (2385), Bosnjaci
2004) 11.c3 ♕×d1+ 12.♔×d1 ♘d5
13.a×b5 a5 14.c4 ♘b4 15.♗f4 c5
16.♗c7 a4 17.♘e5± or 14...♘f6
15.♗f4 ♖a7 16.♘d4±) 10.♖×a4 ♗b7
11.0-0⇄;

A2) 7...♘e5 8.♘×e5 ♕×e5+ 9.♘e2?!
(9.♕e2!?; 9.♗e3 b5 10.♗b3 ♗b7
11.0-0 0-0-0 12.♗d4 ♕f5 13.♕e2⇄)
9...♕e4 (9...♗h3!?) 10.♗b3 ♕×g2
11.♖g1 ♕×h2 12.♗f4∞, Baron

Rodriguez, J. (2413) – Serrano Aspa, X., Seville 1999;

B) 7.♘g5 e6 8.♗e3 h6 (8...b5 9.♗d3 (9.♗e2 ♗b7 10.♗f3 h6 11.♘ge4 ♘xe4 12.♘xe4 ♕d7 13.0-0 0-0-0⇄, Areshchenko, A. (2660) – Manik, M. (2450) San Marino 2006)) 9.♘f3 (9.♘ge4 ♘xe4 10.♘xe4 ♕b4+ 11.♘d2 ♕xb2∞) 9...♘d5 10.0-0 ♘xe3 11.fxe3 ♗e7 12.♕e2 0-0 13.♖ad1 b5 14.♗d3 ♕b4 15.♗e4 ♗b7⇄, Seret, J. (2348) – Rainfray, A. (2425), France 2000;

C) 7.h3 b5 (7...♗f5 8.♗e3 – 6.♗e3 ♘c6 7.h3 ♗f5 8.♗c4, Game 21; 8.0-0 e6 – 6.h3 ♗f5 7.♗c4 e6 8.0-0 ♘c6, Game 19)

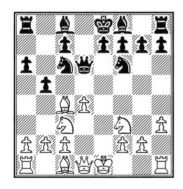

C1) 8.♗d3

C1a) 8...e6 9.0-0 ♗e7 10.♘e4 ♕d8?! (Jakubowski, T. (2220) – Hasangatin, R. (2460), Koszalin 1998) 11.a4 b4 (11...♗b7 12.axb5 axb5 13.♖xa8 ♗xa8 14.♘xf6+ ♗xf6 15.♗xb5±) 12.♘xf6+ ♗xf6 13.♗e4 ♗b7 14.♕d3 h6 15.♗f4 0-0 16.♖fe1 with pressure; 10...♘xe4 11.♗xe4 ♗b7 12.♘e5 ♗f6 13.♕e1 0-0 14.♗f4 ♗xe5 15.♗xe5 ♕d7± or 15.dxe5 ♕c5±;

C1b) 8...♗b7 9.♘e4 (9.0-0!? e6 10.♖e1 ♗e7 11.a4 b4 12.♘e4 ♘xe4 13.♖xe4 0-0 14.♗f4 ♕d7±) 9...♘xe4 10.♗xe4 e6 (10...0-0-0 11.c3) 11.c3 (Tikir, H. – Safar, A., Kemer 2007) 11...f5 (11...♗e7?! 12.♘e5) 12.♗d3 ♗e7 13.0-0 0-0 14.♖e1 ♘a5 15.♕e2 ♗d5 16.♘g5 ♖f6⇄;

C2) 8.♗b3 ♘a5

C2a) 9.♕e2 ♗b7 10.♗g5 e6 11.♗xf6 (11.0-0-0 ♗e7 12.♖he1 ♖d⇄; 11.0-0 ♗e7 12.♖fd1 0-0 13.♗xf6 ♗xf6 14.♘e4 ♗xe4 15.♕xe4 ♘xb3 16.axb3 ♖fd8⇄) 11...gxf6 12.0-0-0 0-0-0 (12...♘xb3+!? 13.axb3 ♕f4+ 14.♔b1 b4 or 14.♕e3 ♗h6) 13.♔b1 ♘xb3 14.axb3 ♖g8♯, Polivanov, A. (2393) – Kurnosov, I. (2527), Chalkidiki 2003

C2b) 9.0-0 ♗b7 10.♘e5 ♘xb3 11.axb3 ♖d8 (11...c5 12.♕e2 cxd4 13.♘xb5 ♕c5 14.♘a3 e6 15.♘ac4 ♗e7 16.♖d1 0-0 17.♖a5 ♕a7⇄) 12.♕e2

C2b1) 12...b4?! (12...c5?! 13.♘xb5 axb5 14.♕xb5+) 13.♕c4 (13.♘b5?! ♕b6) 13...♘d5 (13...e6 14.♘b5 axb5 15.♕xb5+ ♘d7 16.♕xb7 ♘xe5 17.dxe5 ♕xe5 18.♕c6+ ♔e7 19.♗e3±) 14.♘e4 ♕b6 15.♘c5 a5 16.♖xa5 1-0, Sukandar, I. (2213) – Fernandez, L. (1962), Marseille 2006

C2b2) 12...♘d7 13.♖d1 (13.♘f3 ♘f6 14.♗e3 e6 15.♘e5 ♘d7⇄) b4 14.♘xd7 (Acher, M. (2293) – Cornette, M. (2357), Hyeres 2002) 14...♕xd7 15.♘a4 (15.♘e4 ♕e6) 15...e6 16.♗f4 ♕c6 17.f3 ♗e7⇄;

D) 7.♗e3

For 7...♗f5 see Game 26. There are two main alternatives here: **D1)** 7...b5 and **D2)** 7...♗g4.

D1) 7...b5

D1a) 8.♗e2 ♗b7 (8...♗f5!? 9.0-0 g6 9.0-0 e6 10.♕c1 ♖d8 (10...♗e7 11.♗f4 ♕d7 12.♖d1 0-0 13.♘e5 ♘xe5 14.dxe5 ♘d5⇄) 11.♖d1 (Burns, C. (2015) – Goodhue, N. (2070), New Zealand 2007) 11...♗e7 12.♗f4 ♕d7 13.♘e5 ♕c8 14.♕e3 b4 15.♗f3 ♕a8⇄;

D1b) 8.♗d3 ♘b4 9.♗e2 (9.0-0!? ♗b7 10.♗g5) 9...♘bd5 10.♘xd5 ♘xd5 11.c4 bxc4 (11...♘xe3?! 12.fxe3 ♕b4+ 13.♔f2 ♕xb2 14.♕d3±) 12.♘e5!? (12.♗xc4 ♕b4+ 13.♘d2 e6⇄, Groszpeter, A. (2525) – Jones, G. (2442), Bratto 2005) 12...e6 13.♘xc4 ♕b4+ 14.♗d2 ♕b7 15.♘e5 (15.0-0 ♗b4±) 15...♗d7 16.♘xd7 ♔xd7 17.0-0 ♕xb2 18.♕a4+ ♔d8 19.♖fd1⧦;

D1c) 8.♗b3 ♘a5 (8...e6 9.0-0 ♗e7±; 9.♕e2 ♗b7 – 6...b5 7.♗b3 ♗b7 8.♕e2 ♘c6 9.♗e3 e6, Game 27);

D1c1) 9.0-0 ♘xb3 10.axb3 ♗b7 11.♘e5 ♘d7 (11...e6?! 12.♕d3 ♗e7 13.♘xb5 or 12...♕b6 13.♖fe1 ♗e7 14.d5) 12.♘d3 (12.♗f4 ♘xe5 13.♗xe5

♕g6 14.f3 0-0-0⇄) 12...e6 13.d5 (13.f3!? ♗e7 14.♘e4) 13...♗xd5 14.♗f4 ♕c6 15.♘xd5 ♕xd5 16.♗xc7 ♗e7 17.♕e2 0-0⇄;

D1c2) 9.♕e2 (9.♕d2 ♗b7 10.0-0-0 ♘xb3+ 11.axb3 e6=, Tan Lian Ann (2302) – Aplin, C. (1947), Kuala Lumpur 2005) 9...♗b7 10.0-0-0 (10.0-0 e6 11.♘e5 ♗e7 12.♘d3 ♘xb3 13.axb3 ♕c6 14.f3 0-0⇄, Kurenkov, N. (2393) – Ogloblin, N. (2429), Tula 2003) 10...♘xb3+ 11.axb3 b4 12.♘a4 ♗d5 13.♘e5 ♗xg2 14.♖hg1 ♗d5 15.♗f4 ♕d8 16.♘c5⩲, Matthews, S. (2223) – Juarez Flores, C. (2381) Turin 2006; 10.0-0-0!?; 13...e6!?;

D2) 7...♗g4 8.♕e2 (8.0-0 e6⇄, 8.h3 ♗h5 9.♕e2 or 9.g4 – 6...♗g4 7.h3 ♗h5 8.♗e3 ♘c6 9.♕e2 or 9.g4, Game 26) 8...e6 (8...♘b4 9.0-0-0 ♘bd5?! 10.♘xd5 ♘xd5 11.h3 ♗h5 12.g4 ♗g6 13.♘e5 0-0-0 (Darmin, D. (2177) – Kiselev, A. (2289), Ufa 2004) 14.h4 f6 15.♘xg6 hxg6 16.♗d2 with better chances for White; 9...e6±) 9.0-0-0 0-0-0 10.h3 ♗xf3 (10...♗h5 – 6...♗g4 7.h3 ♗h5 8.♗e3 ♘c6 9.♕e2 0-0-0 10.0-0-0 e6, Game 26) 11.♕xf3 ♘a5 12.♗d3 ♕c6 13.♘e4 ♗e7±.

Let's return to Cubas – Crosa Coll.

7.♗b3

7.♗g5 ♘bd7 8.♕e2 b5 9.♗b3 ♗b7 –
6...b5 7.♗b3 e6 8.♕e2 ♗b7 9.♗g5
♘bd7, Game 27 or 7...b5 8.♗b3 ♗b7
9.♕e2 – 6...b5 7.♗b3 e6 8.♕e2 ♗b7
9.♗g5, Game 27; 7.♕e2 b5 8.♗d3 ♗b7
9.♕e2 – 5.♗g5 a6 6.♘f3 ♘bd7 7.♕d2
b5 8.♗d3 ♗b7 9.♕e2, Game 36 or
8.♗b3 ♗b7 9.♗g5 – 6.♘c4 b5 7.♗b3
e6 8.♕e2 ♗b7 9.♗g5, Game 27. We
also examine the following continuations: **A)** 7.a4 and **B)** 7.0-0.

A) 7.a4

A1) 7...♘bd7 8.0-0 ♗e7 (8...c5?! 9.♖e1
♗e7 10.b3 cxd4 11.♗a3 ♕c7 12.♗xe7
♔xe7 13.♕xd4±, Azarov, S. (2530) –
Alekseev, V. (2409), Minsk 2003)
9.♕e2 0-0 10.♗g5 ♘b6 11.♗d3 ♘bd5
12.♘e4 (12.♘e5!? ♕b6 13.♘xd5 ♘xd5
14.♗xe7 ♘xe7 15.c3 with pressure)
12...♘xe4 13.♗xe7 ♕xe7 14.♗xe4±,
Claesen, J. (2285) – Schebler, G.
(2425), Belgium 1997;

A2) 7...♗e7 8.0-0 0-0 9.♖e1 ♘c6
(9...♘bd7?! 10.♗g5 c5 (Westphal, F.
(2159) – Heinzel, O. (2369), Duisburg
2000) 11.d5 ♘b6 12.♗a2 ♘bxd5
13.♗xd5 exd5 14.♘xd5 ♕xd5 15.♖xe7
with better chances for White) 10.♘e4

♕d8 11.♘xf6+ ♗xf6 12.c3 b6 13.♗f4
♗b7≐;

B) 7.0-0

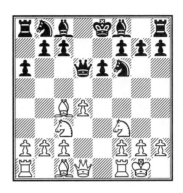

B1) 7...c5?! (7...b5 8.♗b3 ♗b7 – 6...b5
7.♗b3 ♗b7 8.0-0 e6, Game 27 or
8.♗d3 ♗b7 – 6...b5 7.♗d3 ♗b7 8.0-0
e6, Game 27) 8.♖e1 (8.dxc5 ♕xd1
9.♖xd1 ♗xc5 10.♗f4 b5 11.♗e2
♗b7±, Dojkova, G. (2005) – Shikova,
V. (2145), Bankia 1992) 8...b5 9.♗d3
♗e7 (Resika, N. (2210) – Jamrich, G.
(2310), Budapest 1998) 10.♘e4 ♘xe4
11.♗xe4 ♘c6 12.♗f4 ♕d7 13.♘e5±;

B2) 7...♗e7 (7...♘bd7!?) 8.♖e1 (8.♕e2
b5 – 6...e6 7.♗b3 b5 8.♕e2 ♗b7)

B2a) 8...b5 9.♗b3 (9.♗d3!? 0-0 10.a4
or 9...b4 10.♘e4) 9...b4 (9...♘c6 10.d5;
9...♗b7 – 6...b5 7.♗b3 ♗b7 8.0-0 e6
9.♖e1 ♗e7, Game 27; 9...♘bd7
10.♘g5! – 6...b5 7.♗b3 ♘bd7 8.0-0
♗b7 9.♘g5 e6 10.♖e1, Game 27)
10.♘e2 (10.♘e4!?) 10...♘bd7?! (10...0-0
11.♗f4 ♕b6≓ or 11.♕d3 ♘c6 12.♗f4
♕d7≓) 11.♘f4 ♘b6 (Belotti, B.
(2417) – Balinov, I. (2453), Charleville
2000) 12.a3 bxa3 13.♖xa3 0-0 14.c4
with strong pressure;

B2b) 8...0-0 9.♗b3 (9.d5 b5 10.♗b3
c5≓; 9.♗g5 b5 10.♗xf6 ♗xf6 11.♘e4

♛e7 ⇄, Perevoznik, O. – Kalinina, M., Evpatoria 2005) 9...♘c6 10.♗g5 ♘a5 (10...♖d8!?) 11.♗×f6 ♗×f6 12.♘e4 ♛d8 13.♘×f6+ ♚×f6 ½-½, Saric, I. (2432) – Goric, E. (2399), Umag 2004.

Back to Cubas – Crosa Coll.

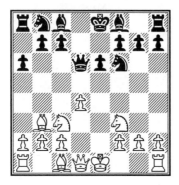

7...♗e7

After 7...b5 (7...♘c6 is interesting also; 7...♘bd7 8.♛e2 or 8.0-0 b5 – 6...♘bd7 7.♗b3 e6 8.♛e2 or 6...b5 7.♗b3 ♘bd7 8.0-0 e6, Game 27) there is: **A)** 8.♘e5; **B)** 8.♗g5; **C)** 8.0-0 and **D)** 8.♛e2.

A) 8.♘e5 ♘c6 (8.. ♗b7 – 6...b5 7.♗b3 ♗b7 8.♘e5 e6, Game 27; 8...c5 9.♛f3 c×d4 10.♛×a8 ♛×e5+ 11.♘e2 ♗b4+ 12.♚f1 ♛c7 13.♛f3 ∞; 9.♗f4 c4 10.♘g6 ♛c6 11.♘×h8 ♛×g2 12.♖f1 ∞ or 10.♛f3 ♘d5 11.♗g3 ∞) 9.♗f4 ♘×d4!? (9...♗b7 – 6...b5 7.♗b3 ♗b7 8.♘e5 e6 9.♗f4 ♘c6, Game 27) 10.♘g6 ♛c6 11.♘×h8 ♛×g2 12.♖f1 ♘f3+ 13.♚e2 c5 ∞ or 13...♗c5 ∞; 9.♘×c6 ♛×c6 10.0-0 (10.d5!?) 10...♗b7 11.d5 ♘×d5 12.♘×d5 0-0-0 ⇄;

B) 8.♗g5

B1) 8...♗b7 9.0-0 (9.♛e2 ♘bd7 – 6...b5 7.♗b3 e6 8.♛e2 ♗b7 9.♗g5

♘bd7, Game 27) 9...c5 (9...♗e7 10.♖e1 – 6...b5 7.♗b3 ♗b7 8.0-0 e6 9.♖e1 ♗e7, Game 27) 10.d×c5 (10.a4!?) 10...♛×d1 11.♖a×d1 ♗×c5 12.♘e5 ♘bd7 13.♘×d7 ♘×d7 ⇄, Boe Olsen, M. (2362) – Fries Nielsen, J. (2425), Koge 2004;

B2) 8...♘bd7 9.a4 (9.0-0!?; 9.♛e2 ♗b7 – 6...b5 7.♗b3 e6 8.♛e2 ♗b7 9.♗g5 ♘bd7, Game 27) 9...b4 10.♘e2 a5 [11.0-0 ♗b7 12.♖e1 (Grigoriants, S. (2413) – Dziuba, M. (2310), Litohoto 1999) 12...♗e7 13.♗f4 ♛b6 ⇄ or 10...♗b7 11.0-0 ♗e7 12.♗f4 ♛c6 13.a5 0-0 14.c4 b×c3 15.♘×c3 ♗d6 16.♗a4 ♛c4=; 15.b×c3 ♗d6 ⇄;

C) 8.0-0 c5 (8...♗b7 or 8...♘bd7 – 6...b5 7.♗b3 ♗b7 8.0-0 e6 or 6...b5 7.♗b3 ♘bd7 8.0-0 e6, Game 27) 9.a4 (9.d×c5 ♛×d1 10.♖×d1 ♗×c5 ⇄) 9.a4 c4 10.♗a2 ♘d5 (10...♗d7?! 11.♘e5 ♘c6 12.a×b5± or 11...♗e7 12.♗f4±) 11.♘e4 (11.a×b5 ♘×c3 12.b×c3 a×b5 13.♖e1 ♗b7 ∞ or 13.♘e5 ♗b7 14.♗f4 ♘d7 ∞) 11...♛c7 (11...♛b6!?) 12.♖e1 ♗e7 (12...♗b7!?) 13.b3 0-0 (13...c3?! 14.b4! ♘×b4 15.d5) 14.b×c4 b×c4 15.♛e2 ♗b4 ⇄;

D) 8.♛e2 ♗b7

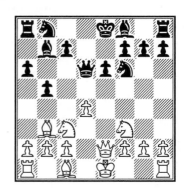

9.0-0 (9.♗g5 or 9.♘e5 – 6...b5 7♗b3 e6 8.♕e2 ♗b7 9.♗g5 or 6...b5 7.♗b3 ♗b7 8.♘e5 e6 9.♕e2, Game 27) 9...♗e7 10.♗g5 (10.♘e5 ♘c6 11.♘xc6 ♗xc6 12.♖d1 0-0=, Sokolov, D. (2409) – Ozgibcev, A. (2435), Sochi 2004)

D1) 10...♘bd7 11.♖ad1 (11.d5!? ♘xd5 12.♗xd5 ♗xd5 13.♘xd5 ♕xd5 14.♗xe7 ♔xe7 15.♖fd1 ♕c5 16.c4⯅ or 15...♕b7 16.♘e5⯅; 11...exd5 12.♖fe1⯅) 11...c5 (11...0-0?! (Vas, P. (2165) – Larsen, T., Copenhagen 2007) 12.d5!; 11...h6 12.♗h4 c5⇄) 12.dxc5 ♕xc5 13.♖fe1 0-0⇄, Rodriguez Gonzalez, I. (2244) – Martinez Perez, J. (2030) Mondariz 2005 or 13.♗xf6 gxf6⇄, Minhazuddin, A. (2325) – Mohammed Abdul, M. (2305), Dhaka 2008;

D2) 10...0-0 11.♖fe1 c5 (11...♘bd7?! 12.d5 – 6...b5 7.♗b3 ♗b7 8.0-0 e6 9.♖e1 ♗e7 10.♗g5 0-0 11.♕e2 ♘bd7?! 12.d5, Game 27; 11...♗xf3?! 12.♕xf3 ♘c6 13.♗xf6 ♗xf6 14.♘e4 ♘xd4 15.♘xf6+ gxf6 16.♕g4+ ♔h8 17.♖ad1 ±) 12.dxc5 ♕xc5 (12...♕c6?! 13.♘d5) 13.♗xe6 ♗xf3 (13...fxe6?! 14.♕xe6+) 14.♕xf3 ♕xg5 15.♗xf7+ ♔xf7 16.♕xa8 ♗c5⇄.

We return now to Cubas – Crosa Coll.

8.0-0

A) 8.♗g5 (8.♕e2 ♘c6 9.♗e3 0-0 10.0-0-0 ♘a5⇄ or 10.0-0 ♖d8 11.♖ad1 ♘a5⇄) 8...♘bd7 (8...0-0!? 9.♕d2 ♕b6 10.0-0 ♘c6) 9.♕e2 ♕b6 (9...h6 10.♗h4 0-0 11.0-0-0 b5⇄; 11.0-0 ♖e8 12.♖ad1 ±) 10.0-0-0 (10.0-0!? 0-0 11.♖fe1 a5 12.a4 ♗d7?! 13.d5±) 10...0-0 11.♘e4 ♘d8 12.♗xf6 ♗xf6 13.c3 (Kobalia, M. (2590) – Kantsler, B. (2507), Ohrid 2001) 13...♗e7 14.♘c5 a5 15.♗c2 a4⇄; 13.♘e5!? ♗e7 14.♘c5 a5 15.a4 ♘d5 16.♔b1 with pressure;

B) 8.♘e5 0-0 9.♗f4 ♕d8 (9...♖d8 10.♕f3 ♕xd4 11.♖d1 ♕c5 12.♖xd8+ ♗xd8 13.0-0 ♘bd7 14.♖d1 ♗e7∞) 10.0-0 (Zawadka, A. – Ciazela, A., Leba 2004) 10...♘c6 11.♘xc6 bxc6 12.♕f3 ♕xd4 13.♕xc6 (13.♖ad1 ♕b6∞) 13...♕xf4 14.♕xa8 ♘g4 15.g3 ♕h6 16.h4 (16.♕g2?! ♗b7 17.f3 ♘e3) 16...g5∞.

8...0-0

8...♘bd7?! (8...b5 9.♗g5 ♗b7 10.♕e2 – 6...e6 7.♗b3 ♗e7 b5 8.♕e2 ♗b7 9.0-0 ♗e7 10.♗g5 or 9.♖e1 – 6...e6 7.0-0 ♗e7 8.♖e1 b5 9.♗b3) 9.g3 (9.♖e1 b5 – 6...b5 7.♗b3 ♘bd7 8.0-0 e6 9.♖e1 ♗e7, Game 27) 9...♘b6 (9...0-0 10.♗f4) 10.♘e2 (10.♗f4!? ♕d8 11.♕d3) 10...0-0 11.c4 c5 12.♗f4 ♕d8 13.♕c2 cxd4 14.♘exd4 ♗c5 (Pinnamaneni, L. – Hoang Thi Nhu, Y., Tehran 2006) 15.♖ad1 ♕e7 16.♖fe1 ±.

9.♕e2

9.♖e1 – 6...e6 7.0-0 ♗e7 8.♖e1 0-0 9.♗b3.

9...♘c6

9...b5?! (9...♘bd7!? 10.g3 b5 11.♗f4 ♕b6) 10.a4 b4 (10...b×a4 11.♘×a4) 11.♘e4 ♘×e4 (11...♕d8!?; 11...♕c6 12.♘×f6+ ♗×f6 13.♖d1 ♖e8 14.a5 or 13...♖d8 14.d5 with strong pressure; 11...♕b6 12.♗g5 ♘bd7 13.a5 ♕a7 14.♘×f6+ ♘×f6 15.d5± or 14...♗×f6 15.♗e3 with strong pressure) 12.♕×e4 ♘c6 (12...c6 13.♗f4) 13.♗f4 f5 (13...♕d7 14.d5±) 14.♗×d6 f×e4 15.♗×e7 ♘×e7 16.♘g5±.

10.♖d1 ♘a5

10...♗d7!? (10...b5?! 11.d5) 11.d5 e×d5 (11...♘×d5?! 12.♘e4 ♕b4 13.c4 f5 14.♘c3 ♘f6 15.♖×d7±) 12.♘×d5 ♘×d5 13.♖×d5 ♕e6 14.♗e3 ♗d6 15.♖ad1 ♕f6 (15...♕g6!? 16.c4 ♗e6⇄ or 16.♘h4 ♕f6⇄) 16.c4 (16.c3 ♖ae8⇄) 16...♗g4 (16...♗e6? 17.♗g5 ♕g6 18.♘h4) 17.h3 ♗×f3 18.♕×f3 ♕×f3 19.g×f3 ♘e7±.

11.♗g5

11.♘e5!? ♘×b3?! (11...b5 12.♗f4 ♕b6 13.♗g5 h6 14.♗h4 c5⇄ or 14.♗×f6 ♗×f6 15.♘e4 ♗×e5 16.d×e5 ♗b7⇄) 12.a×b3 c5 (12...b6 13.♘b5 ♕d8 14.d5

♗d6 15.d×e6 ♗×e6 16.♘×d6 c×d6 17.♖×a6±) 13.♗f4 ♕b6 (13...c×d4 14.♘g6±) 14.♘a4 ♕a7 15.d×c5 ♗×c5 16.♘×c5 ♕×c5 17.c4 ♖e8 18.h4 Black is in *Zugzwang*! 18...b6 (18...♕e7 19.♖d4 ♖d8 20.♖×d8+ ♕×d8 21.♖d1 ♕e7 22.♗g5 h6 23.♗×f6 ♕×f6 24.♖d4 ♔h7 25.h5 a5 26.g3 a4 27.♖f4±) 19.♕f3 ♖a7 20.b4 ♕f8 21.b5 ♕c5 22.♕c6 ♕×c6 23.b×c6 ♖a8 24.c7±;

11...b6 12.♘e5 ♘×b3 13.a×b3 ♗b7 14.♖d3 ♖fd8 15.♖ad1 ½-½

Summary: In this game we examined 6...♘c6 and 6...e6 after **1.e4 d5 2.e×d5 ♕×d5 3.♘c3 ♕d6 4.d4 ♘f6 5.♘f3 a6 6.♗c4** as alternatives to 6...♗g4, 6...♗f5, 6...b5, 6...c5 and 6...♘bd7. As practice and analysis show, these can all produce interesting play with chances for both sides.

After 6...♘c6 7.d5 ♘e5, 7.♘g5 e6, 7.h3 b5 or 7...♗f5 and 7.♗e3 b5 or 7...♗g4, Black has a very playable game.

With **6...e6** Black wants to limit White's aggressive continuations; for example, as after 6...b5 7.♗b3 ♗b7, 7...♘bd7 or 7...e6. After 6...e6 White has many interesting possibilities (7.♗g5, 7.♕e2, 7.a4, 7.0-0) but Black should be fine with counterplay in each instance. In Game 28, White played the unusual **7.♗b3**. After 7...b5, Black needs to be ready to meet White's aggressive continuations (for example after 8.♘e5 or 8.♕e2). **7...♗e7** is more flexible and a safer move for Black, with good chances for counterplay.

Game 29
Parligras, M. (2490) –
Epishin, V. (2550)
Seville 2007

1.e4 d5 2.e×d5 ♛×d5 3.♘c3 ♛d6 4.d4 ♘f6 5.♘f3 g6

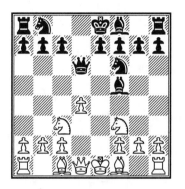

We examine the following alternatives:
A) 5...♗f5 and **B)** 5...♘c6.

A) 5...♗f5

A1) 6.♗d3 (for 6.♗e2 see 5.♗e2 ♗f5 6.♘f3 in Game 34) 6...♗×d3 7.♛×d3 e6 8.0-0 ♘bd7 9.♘b5 ♛b6 10.♗f4 ♘d5 11.♗g3 c6 12.♘d6+ (12.♘c3 ♗e7⇄, Roig Grau, J. – Garcia Gil, J., corr. 2003) 12...♗×d6 13.♗×d6 c5 14.d×c5 ♘×c5 15.♗×c5 ♛×c5 16.c4 ♘f6±;

A2) 6.♗c4

A2a) 6...♘c6 7.0-0 0-0-0 8.♘b5 (8.♗×f7 e6 9.♘h4 ♛e7 10.♘×f5 ♛×f7 11.♘e3 ♘×d4 12.♗d2 ♗d6∓; 8.♗e3 e6⇄, Hara, K. – Williams, D., Internet 2005) 8...♛d7?! (8...♛b4) 9.♗f4 ♘d5 10.♗×d5 ♛×d5 11.c4 ♛×c4 12.♘×a7+ ♘×a7 13.♖c1 ♛×a2 14.♖×c7+ ♔b8 15.♖c5+ ♔a8 16.♖×f5 g6 (16...♘c6 17.♛a1!) 17.♖c5 e5 18.♗×e5 ♗×c5 19.♗×h8 ♖×h8 (19...♛×b2 20.♗f6 ♖c8 21.♛a4 ♛b4 22.♛d7±) 20.d×c5 ♛×b2

21.♛d7 f5 (21...♖f8 22.♘g5±) 22.♘d4 ♖c8 23.♘e6 ♛e5 24.h3±;

A2b) 6...c6 7.0-0 (7.h3 – Game 2; 7.♘e5 – Game 16; 7.♗e3 – Game 35; 7.♗g5 – Game 36) 7...e6 (7...♘bd7!?) 8.♘e2 (8.♖e1 ♘bd7 9.♗g5±, Sdunzik, J. – Graffenberger, W., Ryck 1999) 8...♗e7 9.c3 0-0 10.♗f4 ♛d8 11.♘g3 ♗g6 12.♘e5 ♘bd7 13.♘×g6 h×g6±, Tiinanen T. – Aaltio E., Vantaa 2003;

A3) 6.♘e5 a6 (6...c6 – Game 16; 6...♘c6?! 7.♗b5; 6...e6?! 7.g4 ♗g6 8.♗g2 with strong pressure, Marholev, D. (2350) – Serra Vilaro, A. (2032), Castelldefels 2004) 7.♗c4 (7.g4!? ♗e6 8.g5 ♘fd7 9.♘c4 ♗×c4 10.♗×c4±; 7...♗g6?! 8.♗g2) 7...e6 8.0-0 ♘c6 9.♘×c6 ♛×c6 10.♗d3 ♗g6 11.a3 0-0-0 12.♗e3=;

A4) 6.♘b5 ♛d8 (6...♛b6 7.c4 c6 8.♘c3 e6 9.♗e2 ♗e7 10.0-0 0-0-0 11.♘h4 ♗g6 12.♘×g6 h×g6 (Gharamian, T. (2239) – Renard, S. (2026), La Fere 2003) 13.c5 with pressure; 8.c5!?) 7.♗d3 (7.♗c4 a6 8.♘c3 (Schlesinger, O. (2221) – Rack, M. (2093), Offenbach 2005) 6...♘c6 7.0-0 e6 8.♗f4 ♗d6=; 8...♛d6 – Game 26) 7...♗×d3 8.♛×d3 a6 9.♘c3 ♘c6 10.0-0 e6 11.♖e1 ♗e7 12.♗f4 0-0±;

B) 5...♘c6

B1) 6.d5 ♞b4 7.♞b5 ♛c5 8.c4 ♞g4 9.♛d2 (9.♞bd4 e5 10.d×e6 ♝×e6 11.a3 ♞c6 12.b4⇄) 9...♝d7 (9...♝f5? 10.♞bd4)

B1a) 10.a3 ♞×d5 11.b4?! (11.c×d5 ♝×b5 12.♛d4 ♛×d4 13.♝×b5+ c6 14.♞×d4 c×b5 15.♞×b5 0-0-0 16.h3 ♞f6=) 11...♛b6 12.♛×d5? (12.♞bd4 e5∓) 12...♛×f2+ 13.♚d1 0-0-0 14.♝d2 ♝×b5 15.♛×b5 ♜×d2+! 16.♞×d2 ♞e3+ 17.♚c1 ♛e1+ 18.♚b2 ♛×d2+ 19.♚b3 ♛c2#, Safonov, A. – Melts, M., Kharkov 1971;

B1b) 10.♞×c7+ (11.h3 ♞gf6 12.c×d5 ♝×b5 13.♛a5 a6 14.a4 b6 15.♝×b5+ ♚d8 16.♝e3 b×a5 17.♝×c5 a×b5∓; 12.b4 ♛b6∓) 10...♛×c7 11.♛×b4 e5 (11...e6? 12.d6!) 12.♛c3? (12.♛b3∞) 12...♛b6 13.♝e3 ♞×e3 14.♛×e3 ♛×b2 15.♛×e5+ ♛×e5+ 16.♞×e5 ♝b4+ 17.♚e2 ♝c3∓;

B2) 6.♞b5 ♛d8

B2a) 7.c4 (7.♞e5 a6 8.♞×c6 b×c6 9.♞c3±) 7...a6 8.♞c3 ♝g4 (8...e6!? 9.♝e2 ♝d6 10.0-0 0-0±) 9.d5 ♞e5 10.♝e2 ♞×f3+ 11.♝×f3 (Fernando, D. (2438) – Vitor, A. (2311), Santo Antonio 2003) 11...♝×f3 12.♛×f3 g6 13.0-0 ♝g7 14.♜e1 0-0±;

B2b) 7.d5 ♞b4 8.c4

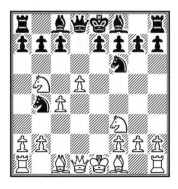

B2b1) 8...c6?! 9.d×c6 ♛a5 (9...b×c6 10.♛×d8+ ♚×d8 11.♞bd4 ♞g4 12.a3 e5 13.♝d2 c5 14.a×b4 e×d4 15.h3 ♞f6 16.♞e5 ♚e8 17.b×c5 ♝×c5 18.b4 ♝d6 19.♞c6± or 11...c5 12.a3 e5 13.a×b4 e×d4 14.♝f4±, Khalifman, A.) 10.♝d2 ♞e4 (10...b×c6 11.a3 c×b5 12.a×b4 ♛c7 13.c5±) 11.♝×b4 ♛×b4+ 12.♞d2 ♜b8 (12...♚d8 13.c×b7 ♝×b7 14.a3±) 13.♞c7+ ♚d8 14.♞d5 1-0, Bojkov, D. (2509) – Panbukchian, V. (2340), Pleven 2005;

B2b2) 8...e6 (8...♝d7!?) 9.♝f4 (9.a3 ♞a6 10.♛a4 c6 11.d×c6 b×c6 9.a3 ♞a6 10.♛a4 c6 11.d×c6 b×c6 ½-½, Filev, G. (2305) – Karakehajov, K. (2330), Sofia 2004; 9.d×e6 ♝×e6 10.♝f4 ♞a6 11.a3 c6 12.♞d6+ ♝×d6 13.♝×d6 ♞e4 14.♝f4 0-0⇄ or 10.♛×d8+ ♚×d8 11.♞bd4 ♝g4 12.a3 ♝×f3 13.g×f3 ♝c5 14.a×b4 ♝×d4⇄) 9...♞a6 10.d6

B2b2a) 10...c6 (Damaso, R. (2423) – Vitor, A. (2311), Santo Antonio 2003) 11.♞c7+ ♞×c7 12.d×c7 ♝b4+ 13.♚e2 ♛e7 14.a3 ♝c5 15.b4 ♝b6 (15...♞h5?! 16.♝e5 f6 17.b×c5 f×e5 18.♛d6±) 16.♝d6 (16.♛d6 ♛×d6 17.♝×d6 ♞e4 18.♝f4 c5∞) 16...♞e4 17.♝×e7 ♞c3+ 18.♚e1 ♞×d1 19.♝d8 ♞×f2 20.♜g1 ♝e3 21.♚e2 ♞g4 22.♜h1 ♝h6∞ or 20.c5 ♝×c7 21.♝×c7 ♞×h1∞; 19.♝h4!?;

B2b2b) 10...c×d6 11.♞×d6+ (11.♝×d6 ♝d7 12.♝×f8 ♜×f8 13.♞d6+?! ♚e7 14.♞×b7 ♛b6 15.c5 ♞×c5 16.♞×c5 ♛×c5∓; 12...♚×f8!?; 13.♛a4∞) 11...♝×d6 12.♝×d6?! ♞e4 13.♝a3 ♛a5+ 14.♞d2 ♝d7 15.♝d3 ♝c6∓ or 13.♝f4 ♛a5+ 14.♞d2 0-0 15.♝d3 ♞ec5∓; 12.♛×d6!?.

We return now to Parligras – Epishin.

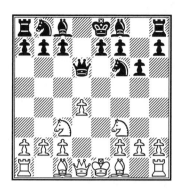

There are two other ways to arrive at this position; for example, 1.♘f3 g6 2.e4 d5 3.exd5 ♕xd5 4.d4 ♘f6 5.♘c3 ♕d6 or 1.d4 g6 2.e4 d5 3.exd5 ♕xd5 4.♘c3 ♕d6 5.♘f3 ♘f6.

6.♘b5

6.♘e5 (6.♗c4 ♗g7 – 4.d4 g6 5.♗c4 ♗g7 6.♘f3 ♘f6, Game 37; 6.g3 ♗g7 7.♗g2 c6 – Game 38 or 7...♘a6 8.♗f4 c6 9.♕d2 0-0 10.♘e5 ♗e6 11.a3 ♖d8 12.0-0-0 ♘h5 13.♘e4 (Guseinov, G. (2552) – Kurajica, B. (2541), Mallorca 2004) 13...♘xf3 14.♕xf4 ♘d7=). According to Khalifman after 5...g6 the most dangerous for Black is the plan with ♘f3-e5, then 0-0-0, followed by h2-h4-h5 (after Black castles short).

A) 6...c6?! (6...♗e6!?; 6...♗f5?! 7.♗c4 e6 8.g4; 6...♘bd7? 7.♘b5 ♕b6 8.♘c4 ♕c6? 9.d5 ♕c5 10.♗e3 +– or 8...♕e6+ 9.♗e2±; 6...♘c6?! 7.♘b5 ♕d8 8.♗f4 ♘h5 9.♘xc6 bxc6 10.♘xc7+ ♔d7 11.♗e5± or 8...♘d5 9.♗c4 ♘cb4 10.a3±) 7.♗f4 ♕b4 8.a3 ♕a5 9.♗c4 e6 10.♕f3 (10.0-0!? ♗g7 11.♗e2 0-0 12.♘c4) 10...♘bd7 11.♗d2?! (11.0-0-0!?) 11...♕d8?! (11...♘xe5) 12.♘e4 ♗g7? (12...♗e7) 13.♘d6+ 1-0, Berescu, A. (2510) – Matovic, P. (2200), Stara Pazova 2007;

B1) 7.♗e2 0-0 8.♗f4 ♘d5 9.♘xd5 ♕xd5 10.0-0 c5 (10...♘c6 11.♘xc6 ♕xc6 12.c3 ♗e6 13.♗f3 ♕b6 14.d5 ♖fd8 15.♕b3 ½-½, Ragger, M. (2525) – Almasi, Z. (2690), Crete 2007) 11.♗c4 (11.c3 cxd4 12.♗c4 ♕d6 13.♕xd4 ♕xd4 14.cxd4=) 11...♕xd4 12.♕xd4 cxd4 13.♖ad1 (13.♖fe1?! ♗xe5 14.♗xe5 ♘c615.♖ad1 ♗f5 16.♗b3 ♖fd8 17.f3 ♖ac8 18.♖d2 g5 19.♗a4 f6 20.♗xc6 ♖xc6 21.♗xd4 e5∓, Zakharstov, V. (2484) – Epishin, V. (2579), Elista 2001) 13...♘c6 14.♘xc6 bxc6 15.♖fe1 e6 (15...♗g4 16.f3 ♗f5 17.♖xe7 ♗xc2 18.♖d2 ♗f5 19.♗d6⯑) 16.♗e5 ♖d8 17.c3 c5 18.cxd4 cxd4 19.♗xg7 ♔xg7 20.♖e4=;

B2) 7.♗f4 (7.♗c4 0-0 8.0-0 a6 9.♖e1 ♘c6 10.♘xc6 ♕xc6⇄, Kinsiz, O. (2215) – Esen, B. (2450), Kocaeli 2008; 9.♗f4!? or 8...♘c6 9.♘b5 ♕d8 10.♗f4 ♘h5⇄) 7...♘h5 (7...♘d5!?) 8.♘b5 ♕d8 9.♕f3 0-0 10.0-0-0 c6 11.♘c3 ♘xf4 12.♕xf4

B2a) 12...♘d7 13.h4 (13.♘xd7 ♕xd7 14.♗c4 b5 15.♗b3 ♕f5∓; 13.♗c4 ♘xe5 14.dxe5 ♕c7 15.♖he1 b5 16.♗b3 a5⇄) 13...♘xe5 14.dxe5 ♕a5

15.♖e1 b5 16.h5? (16.a3 ♖b8∓)
16...b4 17.h×g6 h×g6 18.♘e4 b3∓;

B2b) 12...♗e6 13.h4 ♘d7 14.h5 ("White has a strong attack," Khalifman) 14...♘×e5 15.d×e5 ♛a5 16.♖e1 (16.♗c4 ♗×e5 17.♛h4 ♗f6∓; 16.h×g6 h×g6 17.♗c4 ♗×c4 18.♛×c4 ♛×e5∓) 16...♗×a2 17.h×g6 h×g6 18.♛h4 (18.♛h2 ♖fd8 19.♗d3 ♗e6∓; 18.♖e3 ♗e6 19.♗c4 ♗×c4 20.♛×c4 ♗×e5∓) 18...♖fe8 19.♗d3 ♗e6∓ or 17.♗d3 ♗e6 18.♛h4 ♖fe8 19.f4 ♛a1+ 20.♘b1 (20.♔d2 ♛×b2 21.♖b1 ♛a3 22.♖×b7 ♖ad8 23.♘e4 ♗c4∓) 20...♖ad8 21.h×g6 h×g6 22.g4 ♗a2 23.♔d2 ♛×b2∓.

Back to Parligras – Epishin.

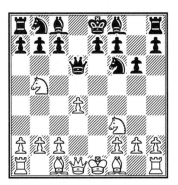

6...♛b6

6...♛d8 7.♗c4 (7.♗f4 ♘a6 8.c4 c6 9.♘c3 ♗g7 10.♗e2 0-0 11.0-0±, Kozak, V. (2245) – Smirnov, V., Yaroslavl 1995; 8.♗c4!?) 7...c6 (7...♗g7!? 8.♗f4 ♘a6) 8.♘g5 c×b5?! (8...♘d5; 8...e6) 9.♗×f7+ ♔d7 and White has a strong initiative; for example, 10.♘e6 ♛a5+ (10...♛b6 11.0-0 ♘h5 12.♛g4± or 11...♘c6 12.♛f3±) 11.c3 (11.♗d2 b4 12.a3 ♛f5) 11...b4 (11...♘c6 12.b4 ♛b6 13.♗f4±) 12.0-0 b×c3 13.b×c3 ♛×c3 14.♛a4+ ♛c6 15.♛b3 ♛b6 16.♛h3±.

7.c4

A) 7.♗f4 ♘a6 8.c3 (8.a4 ♗g7 9.a5 ♛c6 10.♗e2±, Adams, M. (2735) – Epishin, V. (2550), Catalan Bay 2007; 8...♘d5!?; 9...♛e6+!?; 9.♗c4 0-0 10.0-0 c6 11.a5 ♛d8 12.♘c3 ♗g4⇄) 8...♗g7 9.♛b3 ♗e6 (9...c6 10.♘c7+ ♘×c7 11.♛×b6 a×b6 12.♗×c7 ♗e6 13.♗×b6?! (Stuart, K. – Djoudi, A., Internet 2003) 13...♘d5 14.♗c5 b6 15.♗a3 ♘×c3∓; 13.a3 ♖fc8 14.♗e5 ♗d5±; 10.♘a3 ♘d5 11.♗g3 ♗f5=) 10.♘×c7+ ♘×c7 (10...♛×c7? 11.♗×c7 ♗×b3 12.♗×a6±) 11.♛×b6 a×b6 12.♗×c7 0-0 13.♗×b6 ♘d5 14.♗c5 b6 15.♗a3 ♘×c3⇄.

B) 7.♘a3 ♗g7 (7...♗e6!? 8.♘c4 ♛c6 or 8...♗×c4 9.♗×c4 ♛b4+) 8.♘c4 ♛c6 (8...♛e6+ 9.♘ce5 0-0 10.♗c4 ♛d6 11.0-0 ♘c6 12.♖e1 ♘d5⇄; 9.♗e2 ♘c6 10.0-0 0-0 11.♖e1 ♘d5±) 9.♗e2 0-0 10.0-0 ♘bd7 11.♖e1 ♘d5 12.c3 (Karpov, A. (2686) – Fernandez Garcia, J. (2452), Santurtzi 2003) 12...b5 13.♘a5 (13.♘e3 ♘f4 14.♗g4 ♘×e2+ 15.♛×e2 ♖e8 16.♘h6+ ♗×h6 17.♗×h6 ♗b7⇄) 13...♛b6 14.♛b3 c6 15.♛a3 ♗a6 16.♗g5±;

7...c6 (7...a6!?) **8.♘c3**

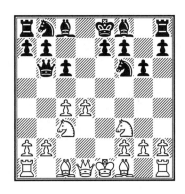

8...♗g4

8...♗g7

A) 9.♗e2 (9.c5 ♕c7 10.♘c4 b5 11.c×b6 a×b6 12.g3 0-0 13.♗f4 ♕b7 14.0-0 b5⇄ or 11.♗b3 0-0 12.0-0 a5⇄) 9...0-0 10.0-0 ♘a6 11.♘e5 (11.c5 ♕c7 12.♗c4 ♗f5 13.♕b3 b5 14.c×b6 a×b6 15.♘e5 e6=) 11...♘d7 12.c5 ♕c7 13.f4 ♘×e5 14.f×e5 ♗e6 15.♕a4 ♕d7 16.♗g5 ♘c7 17.♗f3 f6 18.e×f6 e×f6=;

B) 9.h3 0-0 10.♗d3 ♘a6 11.a3 (11.0-0 ♖d8 12.♖e1 c5 13.d5 e6⇄) 11...c5 12.♘a4 (12.d5 e6 13.0-0 ♖e8⇄) 12...♕c7 13.0-0 (13.♘×c5?! ♘×c5 14.d×c5 ♘d7 15.0-0 ♘×c5 16.♗c2 b6 17.♕e2 ♗b7∓) 13...c×d4 14.♘×d4 ♖d8 15.♘b5 ♕c6 16.♕e2 ♘c7⇄.

9.♗e2

9.c5!? ♕c7 (9...♕d8?! 10.♕b3) 10.♗c4 ♗g7 (10...♗×f3?! 11.♕×f3 ♗g7 12.♗f4 ♕d8 13.0-0-0 0-0 14.g4±, Shirov, A. (2713) – Kurajica, B. (2540), Sarajevo 2004) 11.h3 ♗f5 12.♘e5 (12.g4!?; 12.♘g5!? 0-0 13.♕b3) 12...0-0 13.♗f4 ♕d8 (13...♕a5? 14.♕b3±) 14.0-0 ♘bd7 (14...♘d5?! 15.♗×d5 c×d5 16.♕b3) 15.♖e1 ♘×e5 16.♗×e5 (16.d×e5 ♘d7 17.♕d4 b6 18.c×b6 ♘×b6⇄ or 17.b4 a5 18.a3 b6⇄)

16...b5 17.c×b6 (17.♗b3!?) 17...a×b6 18.g4 ♗c8 19.♕f3 ♗b7±.

9...♗g7 10.0-0 0-0 11.a3 ♖d8 12.♗e3 ♘bd7 13.b4 (13.h3!? ♗f5? 14.g4 ♗e6 15.d5± or 14...♗e4 15.♘g5±) **13...♕c7 14.h3 ♗×f3 15.♗×f3 ♘e8** (15...e5!? 16.♕c2?! e×d4 17.♗×d4 ♘g4 18.♗×g4 ♗×d4∓; 16.d×e5?! ♘×e5 17.♕e2 ♘×f3+ 18.♕×f3 ♘h5∓; 16.d5±) **16.♕b3** (16.b5 e5 17.b×c6 e×d4? 18.♘d5±; 17...b×c6⇄) **16...♘d6** (16...e5?! 17.d5) **17.♖ad1 ♘f5 18.♘e2 ½-½**

Summary: After **1.e4 d5 2.e×d5 ♕×d5 3.♘c3 ♕d6 4.d4 ♘f6 5.♘f3** we had examined Black's popular continuations 5...♗g4 (Games 10-12), 5...c6 (Games 13-17) and 5...a6 (Games 18-28). But there are other playable lines; for example, 5...g6, 5...♗f5 and 5...♘c6. These offer surprise value, and the first white mistake can result in equality or even an advantage for Black. Play may transpose into lines we have already examined, but in such cases White cannot hope for an advantage against best play. A more interesting situation arises when both sides look for theoretical novelties, and in such cases White has more chances for success.

Part IV 3.♘c3 ♛d6 4.d4 ♘f6

Games 30-36 cover lines after **1.e4 d5 2.e×d5 ♛×d5 3.♘c3 ♛d6 4.d4 ♘f6**, without 5.♗c4 or 5.♘f3.

In this section, we will examine 5.h3 (Game 30), 5.♘b5 (Game 31), 5.♘ge2 (Game 32), 5.♗d3 (Game 33), 5.♗e2 (Game 34), 5.♗e3 (Game 35) and 5.♗g5 (Game 36). Positions involving 5.g3 will be discussed in Part VI (Game 38), during the examination of the line 4.g3 ♘f6 5.d4.

Game 30
Klasan, V. (2220) – Ostojic, N. (2410)
Belgrade 2006

1.e4 d5 2.e×d5 ♛×d5 3.♘c3 ♛d6 4.d4 ♘f6 5.h3

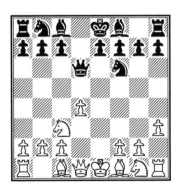

5...a6

Also worth consideration are **A)** 5...♗f5; **B)** 5...♘c6 and **C)** 5...c6.

A) 5...♗f5 6.♛f3 ♛e6+ 7.♗e3 c6 (7...♗e4 8.♘×e4 ♛×e4 9.♛×e4 ♘×e4 10.0-0-0 with a better ending for White) 8.0-0-0 ♘bd7 (Abbasi, R. – Mousavian, S., Teheran 2001) 9.g4 ♗e4 (9...♗g6 10.♘ge2 0-0-0 11.♘f4 ♗e4 12.♛e2 ♛d6 13.f3± or 11...♛d6 12.g5 ♘e8 13.♘×g6±) 10.♘×e4 ♛×e4 11.g5 ♛×f3 12.♘×f3 ♘d5 13.♗d2 with better chances for White;

B) 5...♘c6 6.♘b5 (for 6.♘f3 a6, see Game 19; 6.d5?! ♘b4 7.♘b5 ♛d7 8.c4 c6 9.d×c6 b×c6∓) 6...♛d8 7.♗f4 ♘d5 8.♛f3 ♘cb4 (8...e6!?) 9.c4 a6 (9...♘c2+?! 10.♔d1 ♘×a1 11.c×d5± or 10...♘×f4 11.♛×f4 g5 12.♘×c7+ ♔d7 13.♛×g5±) 10.c×d5 a×b5 11.♗×b5+ ♗d7 12.♗d3∞;

C) 5...c6

C1) 6.♗e3 (6.♗c4 – Game 2; 6.♘f3 – Game 15; 6.♗e2 g6!?; 6...♘bd7 – 5.♗e2 c6 6.h3 ♘bd7, Game 34 or 6...♗f5 7.♘f3 – 5.♘f3 c6 6.h3 ♗f5 7.♗e2, Game 15) 6...♗f5 (6...♘d5!?) 7.♘f3 ♘bd7 8.♘h4 (8.♗d3 ♗×d3 9.♛×d3 e6 10.0-0±; 8...g6!?) 8...♗e6 9.♛d2 (9.♗d3 g6 10.♘f3 ♗g7 11.0-0 0-0⇄) 9...♛b6 10.♗f4 (10.♘f3 0-0-0 11.♗d3 ♘bd5 12.0-0 ♘×e3 13.f×e3 g6 14.e4 ♛c7⇄) 10...♛b4 11.b3 0-0-0 12.♘f3 ♘bd5 13.♘×d5 ♛×d2+ 14.♗×d2 ♗×d5=, Wafzig, P. (2119) – Alber, H. (2319), Germany 2003;

232

C2) 6.g3 ♗f5 7.♗g2 ♘bd7 (7...♘a6 8.a3 0-0-0 9.♘f3 ♘c7) 8.♘ge2 (8.♘f3 h6 9.0-0 g5 10.♖e1 0-0-0 ⇄ or 9.♗f4 ♛b4 10.♛d2 0-0-0 11.g4 ♗h7 12.0-0-0 e6 ⇄) 8...♘b6 (8...0-0-0!? 9.0-0 e5) 9.a4 ♘bd5 (9...g6!?) 10.♘×d5 c×d5 (10...♘×d5!?) 11.c3 e6 12.0-0 ♗e7 13.g4 (13.♗f4 ♛b6∓, Kosa, P. (2104) – Szalai, K. (2185), Hungary 2003) 13...♗e4 14.f3 ♗g6 15.♘f4±.

We return now to Klasan – Ostojic.

6.♗d3

6.♘f3 – Game 19; 6.♗e3 – 5.♗e3 a6 6.h3, Game 35.

We examine the following alternatives: **A)** 6.g3; **B)** 6.♗c4 and **C)** 6.♗e2.

A) 6.g3 ♗f5 (6...♘c6 7.♘f3 e5?! 8.d×e5 ♛e6 9.♛e2 ♘d7 10.♗f4 h6 11.h4±, Vovk, A. (2500) – Aepfler, C. (2280), Pardubice 2007 or 8...♘×e5 9.♛e2 ♘fd7 10.♗f4 f6 11.♗g2 ♗e7 12.0-0 0-0 13.♖ad1±; 7...♗f5 ⇄) 7.♛f3 ♗d7 (7...♛e6+?! 8.♗e3 ♗e4 9.♘×e4 ♛×e4 10.♛×e4 ♘×e4 11.♗g2 Aranda Marin, C. (2298) – Labarta Gonzalez, I. (2099), Galapagar 2004) 8.♗f4 (8.♛×b7? ♛e6+ 9.♗e3 ♘c6) 8...♛e6+ (8...♛×d4?! 9.♛×b7 ♗c6 10.♛×c7 ♗×h1 11.♖d1

♘c6 12.♖×d4 ♘×d4 13.♗×a6 ♖d8 14.♘ge2±) 9.♛e3 ♘c6 ⇄;

B) 6.♗c4 b5 (6...e6!?; 6...♘c6 7.♗f1 ♛d6!?; 7...♛b6!?; 7...g6!?; 6...♘c6 7.♘f3 – 5.♗c4 a6 6.♘f3 ♘c6 7.h3, Game 28 or 7.♗e3 ♗f5 8.♘f3 – 5.♘f3 a6 6.♗e3 ♘c6 7.h3 ♗f5 8.♗c4, Game 21; 6...c5 7.d×c5 ♛×c5 8.♗b3 e6 9.♗e3 ♛a5 10.♘ge2 ♗c5±, Sutovsky, E. (2597) – Kudischewitsch, D. (2407), Israel 2000; 8.♛e2!?)

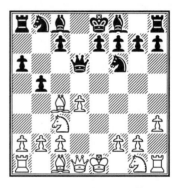

B1) 7.♛f3 ♖a7 8.♗f4 (Kuci, B. (2097) – Inhoven, S. (2231), Eppingen 2004) 8...♛×d4 9.♗b3 ♛b6∞; 7...♘c6!? 8.♗f4 ♛d7 9.♗b3 ♗b7 ⇄;

B2) 7.♗b3 (after 7.♗d3 ♗b7 8.♘f3 we have position from the line 5.♘f3 a6 6.h3 b5 7.♗d3 ♗b7 in Game 19, but with Black to move) 7...♗b7 8.♘f3 e6 7.♗b3 ♗b7 8.♘f3 e6 (8...c5!?) 9.♗e3 ♘bd7 10.0-0 c5 11.d×c5 ♛×d1 12.♖a×d1 (Hiermann, D. (2260) – Bawart, M. (2334), Oberwart 2006) 12...♘×c5 ⇄.

C) 6.♗e2 ♘c6 (6...b5?! 7.♗f3 ♘c6 8.♗f4) 7.♗e3 (7.♘f3 – 5.♘f3 a6 6.♗e2 ♘c6 7.h3, Game 23) 7...♗f5 8.a3 (8.♘f3 ♘b4 9.♖c1 g6 10.0-0 ♗g7=) 8...e5 (8...0-0-0!? 9.♘f3 e5) 9.d×e5

(Fossum, O. (2214) – Lyell, M. (2004), Calvi 2005) 9...♘xe5 10.♕xd6 ♗xd6 11.0-0-0 0-0-0 12.♘f3 ♖he8= or 12.g4 ♗e6=.

Back to Klasan – Ostojic.

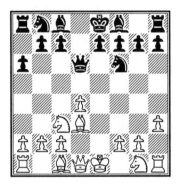

6...♘c6

Also coming under consideration are **A)** 6...b5 and **B)** 6...g6.

A) 6...b5 7.♕f3 (7.♘f3 – 5.♘f3 a6 6.h3 b5 7.♗d3, Game 19; 7.♘e4 ♕c6 8.♘xf6+ gxf6 9.♘f3 ♗b7⇄, Konstatinov, M. – Lindestrom, T. (2240), Esbjerg 2006;) 7...♖a7 (Marwan, A. (1983) – Mansour, A. (2018), Abu Dhabi 2005) 8.♗f4 ♕e6+ (8...♕xd4!? 9.♘ge2 ♕b6 10.0-0 ♘bd7∞ or 9.0-0-0 ♕b6∞) 9.♘ge2 ♗b7 10.d5 ♘xd5 11.♘xd5 ♕xd5 (11...♗xd5 12.♕g3) 12.♕e3 ♖a8 13.♘c3 ♕xg2 14.0-0-0⯲;

B) 6...g6 7.♘f3 (6.♘ge2 ♘c6 7.0-0 ♗g7 8.♗f4 ♕d8 9.♘c4 b5=) 7...♘c6 8.0-0 ♗g7 9.♗e3 (9.♗g5 – 5.♘f3 a6 6.♗d3 g6 7.♗g5 ♗g7 8.0-0 ♘c6 9.h3, Game 19)

B1) 9...0-0 (9...♘b4!?) 10.♕d2 b5 11.a4 b4 12.♘e2 a5 (12...♘d5!? 13.♗h6 ♗e6) 13.♗f4 ♕d8 14.c4 e6 15.♖ac1 ♗b7⇄,

(Niering, M. (2191) – Packroff, H. (2201), Germany 2005;

B2) 9...e5 10.dxe5 ♘xe5 11.♘xe5 ♕xe5 12.♘c3 (12.♗f4!? ♕xb2 13.♖b1 or 12...♕c5 13.♗e3) 12...0-0 (12...♗e6!? 13.♖e1 ♕c5 14.♗e3 ♕a5 15.♗c4 0-0 16.♗xe6 fxe6⇄) 13.♖e1 (13.♕f3!?) 13...♕a5 14.♕f3 ♗e6 15.♗d2 ♕b6 (15...♘d7!? 16.♘e4 ♕b6 17.♗c3 ♗d5⇄ or 16.♕xb7 ♖ab8 17.♕xa6 ♕xa6 18.♗xa6 ♖xb2⯲) 16.♗g5 ♘d7⇄, Hernandez Estevez, Y. (2238) – Ionescu Brandis, I. (2338), Leon 2001. Let's return to Klasan – Ostojic.

7.♘f3 (7.♘ge2 e5).

A position has arisen which may be reached via several different move orders; for example, 4...a6 5.♗d3 ♘f6 6.h3 ♘c6 7.♘f3; 4...♘f6 5.h3 a6 6.♗d3 ♘c6 7.♘f3; 4...a6 5.♘f3 ♘f6 6.♗d3 ♘c6 7.h3; 4...♘f6 5.♗d3 ♘c6 6.h3 a6 7.♘f3; or 4.d4 ♘f6 5.♘f3 a6 6.h3 ♘c6 7.♗d3 (this last was the move order in Klasan – Ostojic).

7...♘b4 (7...g6 – 6...g6 7.♘f3 ♘c6).

Black has the following alternatives: **A)** 7...e5; **B)** 7...b5; **C)** 7...h6; **D)** 7...e6; **E)** 7...♗e6 and **(F)** 7...♗d7.

A) 7...e5?! 8.dxe5 ♘xe5 9.♛e2 ♘fd7 10.♗f4 f6 11.0-0-0 ♛c5 (Antonio, R. (2521) – Goh Koong Jong, J. (2314), Ho Chi Minh City 2003) 12.♘e4 ♛a5 13.♘xe5 ♘xe5 14.♗c4 ♗e7 (14...♘xc4 15.♘d6+; 14...♗d7 15.♛h5+) 15.♖d5 ♛b4 16.♗xe5± or 11.0-0-0 ♛e6 12.♖he1 ♗d6 (Marasli, T. – Hamad, A. (2277), Istanbul 2006) 13.♗c4 ♛f5 14.♗h2±;

B) 7...b5?! 8.a4 b4 9.♘e4 ♘xe4 10.♗xe4 ♗b7 11.0-0 g6 12.c4 (12.♘e5!? ♗g7 13.♗f4) 12...♗g7 13.♖e1 0-0 14.c5 ♛d8 15.♗g5 ♖e8 (15...h6?! 16.♗xe7) 16.a5 (16.♛b3!?) 16...h6 17.♗f4 f5 18.♗xc6 ♗xc6 19.♘e5 ♗xe5 20.♖xe5±;

C) 7...h6 8.0-0 (8.♗e3!?; 8.♛e2 ♘xd4 9.♘xd4 ♛xd4∞; 8...g6!? 9.♗e3 ♗g7) 8...g5 9.♘e4 ♘xe4 10.♗xe4 g4 (10...♗g7!?) 11.hxg4 ♗xg4 (Veleska, V. – Safar, A., Kemer 2007) 12.♛d3 ♖g8 13.c3 0-0-0⇄;

D) 7...e6 8.0-0 ♗e7 (8...♗d7 9.♗e3 0-0-0 10.♖e1±) 9.♖e1 0-0 10.a3 (10.a4 ♘b4 11.♘e2 ♘xd3 12.♛xd3 c5 13.♗f4 ♛d8±, Williams, P. – Young, M. (1993), Catalan Bay 2004; 12...♘d5!? 13.c4 ♘b4) 10...b5 11.♘e2 (11.♗g5!? ♗b7 12.♗xf6 ♗xf6 13.♘e4 ♛d8 14.♘c5) 11...♗b7 12.c3 ♘d5 (Kulon, K. (2069) – Mitkovets, U., Herceg Novi 2005) 13.♘g3±;

E) 7...♗e6 8.0-0 0-0-0 9.♗e3 h6 10.♛e2 ♘b4 (10...g5!?) 11.♗e4 ♘bd5 12.♗xd5 ♘xd5 (12...♗xd5?! 13.♘xd5 ♛xd5) (Llobet Reus, P. (2151) – Mellado Trivino, J. (2447), Barcelona 2002) 14.b4 g5 15.c4 ♛f5 16.♘e5 ♛e6 17.♖ab1 with the initiative or 13...♘xd5 14.♘e5 ♛e6 15.c4 ♘xe3

16.fxe3 f6 17.♘g6 with better chances for White) 13.♘e4 ♛b6 14.♘c5 g5 15.c4 ♘xe3 16.fxe3 ♗g7⇄;

F) 7...♗d7 8.♘e4 (8.♗e3 e5 9.♛e2 (Semenova, I. (2312) – Albert, K. (2128), Zalakaros 2001) 9...0-0-0 10.dxe5 ♘xe5⇄ or 9.dxe5 ♘xe5 10.♘xe5 ♛xe5 11.♛d2±; 8.♘e2 e5 9.dxe5 ♘xe5 10.♘xe5 ♛xe5 11.♗f4 ♛xb2 12.0-0 ♗d6 13.♗xd6 cxd6 14.♖b1 ♛xa2 15.♖xb7∞, Zelcic, R. (2503) – Krumpak, H. (2115), Ljubljana 2001; 11...♛a5+!?; 12...0-0-0!?) 8...♘xe4 9.♗xe4 0-0-0 10.c3 e5 11.0-0 exd4 12.♘xd4 ♘xd4 (12...♗e6?! (Schnabel, M. (2067) – Ciolac, G. (2323), Bad Zwesten 2001) 13.♗xc6 bxc6 14.♛a4) 13.cxd4 f5 14.♗f3 ♗b5 15.♗g5⇄.

Back to Klasan – Ostojic.

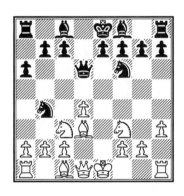

8.♗c4

8.♘e4 (8.0-0 g6 9.♗c4 ♗g7 10.♘e5 0-0 11.♗f4 ♘bd5 12.♗g3 ♛d8 13.♛f3 c6⇄) 8...♘xd3+ 9.♛xd3 (Batyte, D. (2176) – Brustkern, J. (2266), Budapest 2004) 9...♘xe4 10.♛xe4 ♛g6⇄

8...♗e6   9.♗xe6   (8.♗b3!?) **9...♛xe6+ 10.♗e3 ♘bd5** (10...♛f5

11.♖c1 e6 12.0-0 ♗d6 13.a3 ♘bd5 14.♘xd5 exd5=) **11.♘xd5 ♘xd5 12.0-0!?** (An interesting pawn sacrifice!)

12.♛d2 g6 13.0-0 ♘xe3 14.fxe3 ♗h6 15.♖fe1 (Torrecillas Martinez, A. (2372) – Narciso Dublan, M. (2529), Martinenc 2001) 15...0-0=.

12...♘xe3 13.fxe3 ♛xe3+

13...0-0-0 (13...♛b6?! 14.♘e5 f6 15.♛h5+; 13...♛e4!? 14.♛e2 f6 15.♘d2 ♛c6 16.c4 e6⇄ or 15.c4 0-0-0 16.♖ac1 e5⇄) 14.♛d3 f6 15.c4 ♛d7 (15...♛c6 16.d5 e5 17.a3 ♚b8 18.b4 ♗e7 19.e4 with pressure) 16.b4 e5 17.c5 exd4 18.♘xd4 with better chances for White.

14.♚h1

14...f6

A) 14...0-0-0? 15.♘e5 ♖xd4 (15...f6 16.♘f7±) 16.♘xf7 g5 (16...♖xd1 17.♖axd1±) 17.♛xd4 ♛xd4 18.♖ad1±;

B) 14...e6 15.♘e5 ♗d6 (15...f6?! 16.♛h5+) 16.♘xf7 0-0 17.♘xd6 cxd6 18.♛g4 (18.♖e1 ♛g5 19.♖xe6 ♖f2 20.♛g4 ♛xg4 21.hxg4 ♖c8 22.♖xd6

♖cxc2 23.♖e1 ♖xg2 24.♖e7 h5∓) 18...♖xf1+ 19.♖xf1 ♖f8 20.♖xf8+ ♚xf8=.

15.♖e1

15.c4!? 0-0-0 16.♛c2 ♚b8 [16...c6 ♖ae1 ♛h6 18.♖e6 ♚b8 19.♘e5?! ♛h5 20.♘f3 ♖d6; 19.♛b3⯪] 17.♖ae1 ♛h6 18.d5 g5 19.♘d4 [19.♖e6?! g4 20.♘g1 ♖g8 21.♛d3 ♖g5] 19...e5 20.♘e6 ♖c8∞.

15...♛f4 16.c4

A) 16.♖e6!? 0-0-0 17.♛e2 ♖d6 18.♖e4∞; 17...♚b8 18.c4∞ or 17...g5 18.♖f1∞;

B) 16.d5!? 0-0-0 17.♛e2 ♖d7 18.♖ad1 ♛b4 19.c4∞ or 17...g6 8.♖ad1∞.

16...0-0-0 17.♛e2?! (17.♛c2 e5 18.dxe5 ♗b4 19.♛e2 fxe5 20.c5⇄ or 19.♖e4 ♛f5 20.e6⇄; 17...c6 18.♖ad1 ♛c7 19.♛e4∞ or 18...e5 19.dxe5 ♗b4 20.♖xd8+ ♖xd8 21.♖e2⇄) **17...e5 18.dxe5 ♗b4 19.♖ed1** (19.♛e4 fxe5 20.♛xe5 ♛xe5 21.♖xe5 ♖he8 22.♖xe8 ♖xe8 23.a3 ♗c5 24.♖e1 ♖xe1+ 25.♘xe1∓ or 20...♖hf8 21.♖e2 ♛xe5 22.♖xe5 ♖f4 23.♖c1∓) **19...fxe5 20.♛xe5 ♛xe5 21.♘xe5 ♖de8** (21...♖he8!? 22.♘f7 ♖d7 23.♖xd7 ♚xd7 24.♖d1+ ♚e6 25.♘d8+ ♚e7 26.♘xb7 ♖b8 27.a3 ♖xb7 28.axb4 ♖xb4∓; 22...♖xd1+ 23.♖xd1 ♗c5 24.♚h2 c6∓) **22.♘d3 ♗d6** (22...♗e7!? 23.♖f1 ♗h4 24.♖f4 ♗f6 or 24.b3 ♖e2 25.♘f4 ♖d2; 23.♖ac1 ♗g5 24.♖c2 ♖hf8) **23.♖d2 ♗g3 24.♖f1 h5** (24...♖e3!? 25.♘c5 ♗d6 26.♘d3 b6) **25.♚g1 h4 26.♖f7?!** (26.♘f4? ♖hf8−+; 26.b3!?) **26...♖ed8?!** (26...♖e3!? 27.♖f3 ♖e4

28.b3 ♖d8; 27.♖×g7? ♖d8−+)
27.♖×g7?! (27.♔f1 ♖he8 28.♖e2 ♖f8
29.♖×f8 ♖×f8+ 30.♔g1∓) **27...♖d4
28.♖g4 ♖d7 29.♔f1 ♖e8 30.♖e2
♖f8+ 0−1**

Summary: After **1.e4 d5 2.e×d5
♕×d5 3.♘c3 ♕d6 4.d4 ♘f6 5.h3**
we had examined similar lines: 5.♗c4
c6 6.h3 (Game 2); 5.♘f3 c6 6.h3 (Game
15); 5.♘f3 a6 6.h3 (Game 19); 5.♘f3
a6 6.♗e2 ♘c6 7.h3 (Game 23); and
5.♘f3 a6 6.♗c4 ♘c6 7.h3 (Game 28).
In all these lines, Black equalizes.

In my opinion 5.h3 is without great independent significance. White's best
course is to transpose into one of the
aforementioned lines. If White does not,
analysis indicates that Black can obtain
an advantage.

Game 31
Gavric, M. (2398) – Kurajica, B. (2539)
Neum 2005

**1.e4 d5 2.e×d5 ♕×d5 3.♘c3 ♕d6
4.d4 ♘f6 5.♘b5**

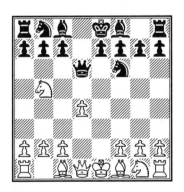

5...♕b6

The main alternative is 5...♕d8 and
now:

A) 6.c4

A1) 6...c6 7.♘c3 (this position is from
the variation 1.e4 d5 2.e×d5 ♘f6 3.d4
♘×d5 4.c4 ♘f6 5.♘c3 c6 but with Black
to move!)

A1a) 7...g6 8.h3 (8.♘f3!? ♗g7 9.♗d3)
8...♗g7 9.♘f3 ♗f5 10.♗e2 (10.♗d3!?)
10...♘a6 11.♗e3 0-0 12.0-0 (Moliboga,
V. (2295) – Tomashevich, G., Kiev
2002) 12...♕a5 13.a3 ♘e4 14.♘×e4
♗×e4 15.♗d3 ♗×d3 16.♕×d3 ♘c7
17.b4 ♕f5⇄;

A1b) 7...♗g4 8.♗e2 ♗×e2 9.♘g×e2 e6
10.0-0 ♗e7 11.♗e3 0-0 12.♕b3 ♕b6=,
Zivkovic, V. (2377) – Sermek, D.
(2571), Rabac 2003 or 8.f3 ♗f5 9.g4
♗g6 10.h4 h5 11.g5 (Najer, E. (2630)
– Kharitonov, A. (2520), Moscow 2008)
11...♘fd7 12.♕b3 ♕b6 13.♗e3 e5⇄;

A1c) 7...♗f5 8.♘f3 e6 9.♗e2

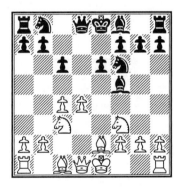

A1c1) 9...h6 10.♕b3 (Kupreichik, V.
(2468) – Antoniewski, R. (2523), Germany 2005) 10...♕b6 11.0-0 ♘bd7
12.c5 ♕×b3 13.a×b3 ♗e7 14.b4±;
11...♘a6!?; 10.0-0 ♗e7 11.♗d3 ♗×d3
12.♕×d3 ♘bd7 13.♗f4 0-0 14.♖fe1
♖e8 15.♘e4 ♘×e4 16.♕×e4 ♕b6=,
Leon Hoyos, M. (2490) – Tiviakov, S.
(2635), Lodi 2008)

A1c2) 9...♛c7 (9...♗e7 10.0-0 0-0
11.♘h4 ♗g6 12.♘xg6 hxg6 13.♗f3
♘a6 14.♗e3 ♗d6 15.♕b3± , Kurnosov,
I. (2590) – Tiviakov, S. (2635), Plovdiv
2008) 10.♘h4 ♗g6 11.♘xg6 hxg6
12.h3 ♘bd7 13.♕a4 (13.0-0!?)
13...♗d6 (13...e5!?) 14.0-0 0-0 15.♕b3
♖fe8 16.♖e1 e5 17.d5 (17.dxe5 ♖xe5
18.♗e3 ♖ae8=) 17...e4 (Demkovich,
A. (2426) – Buczak, K. (2246), Barlinek
2002) 18.♗e3 ♗c5=;

A2) 6...♘a6 (6...a6 7.♘c3 ♗f5 8.♘f3
e6 9.♕b3 (Maslak, K. (2405) –
Johnson, L. (2322), Internet 2003)
9...♘c6 10.♗e2 ♘b4 11.0-0 ♗c2
12.♕a3 ♗e7 13.c5 a5⇄) 7.♗f4 g6
8.♗e5 ♗g7 (8...c6!? 9.♘c3 ♗h6 10.♘f3
0-0⇄) 9.♗e2 0-0 10.♘f3 (Damjanovic,
M. (2320) – Muse, D. (2335), Medulin
1997) 10...c6 11.♘c3 ♕b6 12.♕d2 ♗f5
13.0-0 ♖ad8⇄;

B) 6.♗f4 ♘d5 7.♕f3 (7.♗g3 c6 8.♘c3
♗f5 9.♘xd5 ♕xd5=, Rozentalis, E.
(2575) – Jeffares, S. (2095), Dublin
2007)

B1) 7...♘xf4 8.♕xf4 ♘a6 9.0-0-0
(9.♗c4 e6 10.♘f3 c6 11.♘e5?! f6 12.0-0-0
♕b6 13.♘c3 fxe5; 11.♘c3 ♗d6±)
9...c6 10.♘c3 (Herb, S. (2065) –
Huebner, L. (2130) 10...♕d6 11.♕e3
(11.♕xd6 exd6=) 11...♘b4 12.a3 ♘d5

13.♘xd5 ♕xd5 14.♘f3 ♗g4 (14...♕a2?!
15.♘e5 ♕a1+ 16.♔d2 ♕xb2
17.♘c4+– or 15...♗e6 16.d5 ♗xd5
17.c4 ♗e6 18.♔c2±) 15.♕b1 0-0-0⇄;

B2) 7...c6

B2a) 8.♗c4?! ♘xf4 (8...♗e6 9.♗xd5
♗xd5 10.♘c7+ ♕xc7 11.♗xc7 ♗xf3 ½-
½, Williams, L. – Myers, H., USA 1982)
9.♕xf4 (9.♗xf7+ ♔xf7 10.♕xf4+ ♔g8
11.♘c7 e5! 12.♕xe5 ♗d6 13.♕e8+
♕xe8+ 14.♘xe8 ♗b4+ 15.c3 ♗a5∓,
Myers, H.) 9...cxb5 10.♕xf7+
(10.♗xf7+ ♔d7 11.♕f5+ ♔c7 12.♕c5+
♘c6–+, Myers, H.) 10...♔d7
(11...♔c7?! 12.♕c4+ ♘c6 13.d5 a6
14.♗a4 ♕d6 15.♗b3!) 11.♗xb5+ ♘c6
12.0-0-0 ♕c7 13.♘f3 ♕d6 14.♖he1
♕f6 15.♕b3 e6∓;

B2b) 8.♘c3 ♘xf4 (8...♗e6 9.♘ge2?!
♘d7 10.♘e4 ♘7f6 11.♗d2 ♘xe4
12.♕xe4 (Kuzmin, G. (2520) –
Spoelman, W. (2193), Hastings 2004)
12...g6 13.0-0-0 ♗g7 14.♘f4 ♘xf4
15.♗xf4 0-0∓; 9.♘h3 h6 10.0-0-0 ♘d7
11.♘xd5 ♗xd5 12.♕g3 ♕a5 13.a3
0-0-0 14.♗d2 ♕b6 15.♘f4±) 9.♕xf4
(Witt R. – Sohrabi, A., corr. 1991)
9...♕d6 10.♕d2 g6 11.♘f3 ♗g7
12.♗c4 0-0=.

We return now to Gavric – Kurajica.

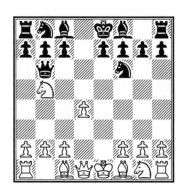

6.c4

6.♗f4 (6.♘f3!? c6 7.♘a3±; 6...♗g4!?)
6...♘d5 7.♛f3 c6 (7...♘xf4 8.♛xf4 ♘a6
9.0-0-0±) 8.♗d2 (8.♗e5? e6 9.c4 cxb5
10.cxd5 ♗b4+ 11.♔d1 f6∓, Beratti, H.
– Stuart, K., Internet 2003) 8...♘f6
9.♘c3 ♛xb2 (9...♘a6!? 10.♗c4 ♘b4)
10.♖b1 ♛a3 11.♗c4∞.

6...a6

6...c6 7.♘c3 e5 (7...♗g4 8.♗e2 ♗xe2
9.♘gxe2 e6 10.♗f4 ♗e7 11.0-0 0-0
12.a3 a5 13.♖b1 ♛a6 14.♛d3 a4=,
Batyte, D. (2138) – Holemar, D. (2285),
Brno 2005; 12.c5!? ♛a6 13.b4) 8.dxe5
(8.♛e2!? ♛xd4 9.♘f3) 8...♘g4 9.♛e2
(9.♘h3 ♗c5 10.♛c2 ♘a6∞) 9...♗c5
10.♘e4 0-0 11.♘xc5 ♛xc5 12.f4 ♛b4+
13.♛d2 ♘a6 14.a3 (Khruschiov, A.
(2400) – Sulava, N. (2526), Ohrid
2001) 14...♛e7 15.♘f3 (15.♛d6 ♛xd6
16.exd6 ♘c5⯗) 15...♘c5 (15...♖d8?!
16.♛c2 g6 17.b4) 16.h3 ♘h6
(16...♘b3?! 17.♛d1 ♘xa1 18.hxg4
♗xg4 19.♗e3) 17.♛c3 ♘f5⇄; 14.h3
♘e3 15.♛xb4 ♘c2+ 16.♔f2 ♘axb4
17.♖b1⇄.

7.♘c3 e5!?

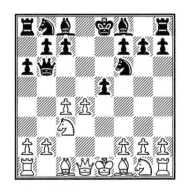

7...♗g4 (7...♘c6!?) 8.♘f3 e6 (8...♘c6!?
9.d5 ♘e5) 9.♗e2 (Tchernyi, A. (2174)

– Schmidt, D., Bad Zwesten 2005)
9...♘c6!? 10.c5 ♛a7 11.♗e3 0-0-0
12.♛a4 ♘d5 13.♘xd5 ♖xd5⇄; 9.c5!?

8.dxe5

8.c5

A) 8...♛b4 (8...♛a5? 9.♗d2 c6 10.dxe5
♘g4 11.♘e4±; 8...♛c6?! 9.♛e2 ♗e7
10.♛xe5 0-0 11.♘f3 ♖e8 12.♗e2)
9.dxe5 ♘g4 10.h3 ♘xe5 11.♛e2 ♘bc6
12.♘f3 (12.f4?! ♗e7 13.fxe5 ♗h4+
14.♔d1 ♗f5 with a very strong attack)
12...♛xc5 13.♘xe5 ♛xe5 14.♗f4
♛xe2+ 15.♗xe2 ♗e6 16.♗xc7=;

B) 8...♛e6 9.d5 ♛g4 (9...♛f5?! 10.♗e3
♘bd7 11.b4 a5 12.♘b5 ♔d8 13.d6
cxd6 14.cxd6 axb4 15.♖c1 ♖xa2
16.♘a7± or 14...♛e4 15.♘f3 ♛xb4+
16.♗d2 ♛e4+ 17.♗e2⯗) 10.♗e3
♛xd1+ 11.♖xd1 ♘g4 12.d6 cxd6
13.cxd6 ♘xe3 14.fxe3 ♗e6∓.

8...♘g4 9.♘h3

9.♛e2 ♘c6?! 10.♘d5; 9...♗c5 10.♘h3
– 9.♘h3 ♗c5 10.♛e2.

9...♗c5

9...♘xe5?! 10.♘d5 ♗b4+ 11.♗d2.

10.♛c2

10.♛e2

A) 10...0-0?! (10...♘c6?! 11.♘d5)
11.♘d5 (11.f3? ♘xe5 12.♛xe5 ♗xh3
13.gxh3 ♘c6⯗) 11...♛e6 (11...♛c6
12.b4±) 12.♘hf4 ♛xe5 (12...♗xf2+
13.♛xf2 ♘xf2 14.♘xe6 fxe6 15.♘c7
♘xh1 16.♘xa8±) 13.♘d3 ♛xe2+
14.♗xe2 ♗d4 (14...♗d6 15.c5±)
15.♘xc7 ♖a7 16.h3 ♘f6 17.♗f4±;

B) 10...♗e6 11.♘d5 (11.f3?! ♘e3) 11...♗×d5 (11...♕c6?! 12.f3 ♘h6 13.♗×h6) 12.c×d5 ♕b4+ (12...h5!?) 13.♗d2 ♕×b2 14.♖c1 ♗b4 15.♖×c7 ♕a1+ 16.♕d1 ♗×d2+ 17.♔×d2 ♕×a2+ 18.♔c1 ♕a1+ 19.♔c2 ♕a2+ with perpetual check.

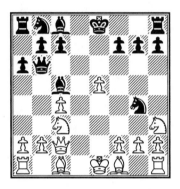

10...♘c6?!

A) 10...♘×e5 11.♘d5 (11.♕e4 ♗×h3 12.♕×e5+ ♕e6=; 11...0-0 12.♕×e5 ♗×h3 13.g×h3 ♘c6∞) 11...♕d6 12.♘g5 f5 (12...♗e6?! 13.♘e4 ♕c6 14.♘×c5 ♕×c5 15.♗e3 ♕c6 16.0-0-0±) 13.f4 ♘g4 14.♕e2+ ♔f8 15.h3 ♘f6 16.♗e3 ♗b4+ (16...♘×d5 17.♗×c5 ♕×c5 18.0-0-0) 17.♔f2 h6 18.♖d1 with pressure;

B) 10...♗e6!

B1) 11.♘a4 ♗b4+ 12.♗d2 ♗×d2+ 13.♕×d2 ♕c6 14.♘c3 ♘d7 15.♘f4 0-0-0 (15...♘g×e5 16.♘fd5 ♘g6=; 15...♘d×e5 16.0-0-0 0-0=) 16.♘fd5 ♔b8 17.f4 ♘b6 (17...f6!?) 18.h3 ♘×c4 19.♗×c4 ♕×c4 20.h×g4 ♗×d5 21.0-0-0 ♗c6∓ or 15.♘d5 (15.f4 0-0-0 16.♘d5 ♔b8 17.♗e2 ♘b6∓ or 17...f6∓) 15...♘d×e5 16.♘hf4 ♖d8 17.♕d4 ♕d6 18.0-0-0 (18.h3 ♗×d5 19.♘×d5 ♘f6∓) 18...♗×d5 19.♘×d5 0-0 20.♗e2 c6∓;

B2) 11.♘d5 ♗×d5 (11...♕c6!?) 12.c×d5

B2a) 12...♘d7 13.f4 ♗b4+ 14.♔d1 (14.♗d2 ♘e3 15.♕d3 ♗×d2+ 16.♕×d2 0-0-0∓) 14...0-0-0 15.♗e2? (15.a3 ♗c5 16.♗c4 g5 17.♕e2 h5∞) 15...♘d×e5! 16.♗×g4+ (16.♕f5+ ♔b8 17.f×e5 ♖d5+ 18.♔c2 ♘e3+ 19.♗×e3 ♕×e3∓; 16.f×e5 ♖d5+ 17.♗d3 ♘e3+ 18.♗×e3 ♕×e3–+) 16...♘g4 17.♕f5+ ♔b8 18.♕×g4 ♕d4+ and mate in a few moves;

B2b) 12...♘×e5 13.♕e4 (13.♗e2 ♘bd7 14.0-0 0-0-0∓) 13...♘bd7 (13...♕b4+ 14.♕×b4 ♗×b4+ 15.♗d2 ♗d6=; 13...0-0 14.♕×e5 ♘c6 15.♕g3∞) 14.f4 ♕b4+ 15.♕×b4 ♗×b4+ 16.♗d2 (16.♔f2 ♘g6∓) 16...♗×d2+ 17.♔×d2 ♘g6 18.♖c1 (18.♗d3?! 0-0-0; 18.♖e1+ ♘e7∓) 18...0-0-0 19.d6 ♘f6 20.♖×c7+ ♔b8 21.♖×f7 ♖×d6+ 22.♔c2 ♖c8+ 23.♔b3 ♖d2∞.

11.♘d5 ♘d4

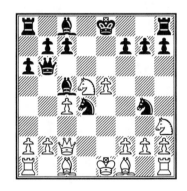

12.♕d1?!

12.♕a4+ (12.♘×b6?! ♘×c2+ 13.♔d1 ♗×b6 14.♔×c2 ♘×e5∓) 12...♕c6 13.♕×c6+ b×c6 14.♘×c7+ ♔e7 15.♘×a8 ♘c2+ 16.♔d1 ♘×a1 17.♗g5+ ♔e6 18.f3 ♘×e5 19.♗f4+ ♔d6

(19...♔f5 20.h4±) 20.♘d3 ♗f5
21.♘×c5 ♔×c5 22.♗e3+ ♔d6
(22...♔b4 23.♘c7±) 23.c5+ ♔e7
24.♗f4 ♘×f3 25.♘c7± or 17...f6
18.e×f6+ g×f6 19.♗f4 (19.♗d2!?)
19...♘e5 20.♔c1 ♗×h3 21.g×h3 ♖×a8
(21...♗×f2 22.♘c7±) 22.♔b1 ♗×f2
23.♔×a1 with better chances for White.

12...♕c6 13.♗e2?!

A) 13.♗f4 (13.f4?! ♗e6 14.♗e2 h5∓
or 14.♗d3 f5∓) 13...0-0 14.b4 (14.♗e2
♘×e2 15.♕×e2 f6 16.0-0-0⇄)
14...♗×b4+ 15.♘b4 ♕e4+ 16.♔d2
(16.♗e2?! ♘×e2 17.♕×e2 ♕×g2)
16...♘×f2 17.♘×f2 ♕×f4+ 18.♔c3 ♘f5
19.♕e1 ♕d4+ 20.♔b3 a5∞;

B) 13.b4 ♗f5 (13...♗×b4+? 14.♘×b4
♕e4+ 15.♔d2±) 14.b×c5 ♘c2+
15.♔d2 ♘×a1 16.♗b2 ♕×c5 (16...♘c2?!
17.♕f3 ♕d7 18.♗d3) 17.♕×a1 0-0-0
18.f3 (18.♗d4 ♕a5+ 19.♗c3 ♖×d5+
20.c×d5 ♕×d5+ 21.♔c1 ♖d8 22.♔b2
♘×e5∞; 21.♔e1? ♕e4+) 18...♖×d5+
19.c×d5 ♕×d5+ 20.♔e1 (20.♔c1? ♘e3
21.♗d4 ♘×f1 22.♖×f1 ♕c4+ 23.♔d2
♖d8∓) 20...♖d8 21.♔c1 ♘×e5 22.♘f4
♕a5+

B1) 23.♕c3 ♕a4 24.♗e2 (24.♕×e5?!
♖e8 25.♕×e8+ ♕×e8+ 26.♔f2 ♕a4
27.♘e2 f6∓) 24...f6 25.♕c1 ♕×a2±;

B2) 23.♗c3 ♕c5 24.♗d2 (24.♗e2 g5
25.♘h3 ♖e8 26.♔f1 ♗d3∓; 26...♘d3?
27.♕×g5) 24...♕b6 25.♗e3 ♕a5+
26.♔f2 ♕×a2+ 27.♔g3±.

13...♘×e5∓

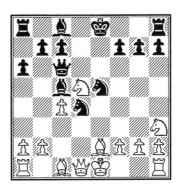

14.♗e3

A) 14.b4 ♘×c4 15.b×c5?! (15.♘hf4 ♗a7
16.0-0 ♗e6∓) 15...♕×d5 16.♕a4+ ♘c6
17.♕×c4 (17.♗×c4? ♕e5+; 17.♘f4 ♕d4
18.♖b1 ♗f5∓) 17...♕g2 18.♖g1
♕×h3∓;

B) 14.♗f4 (14.0-0?! ♗×h3 15.g×h3
♕g6+ 16.♔h1 ♕e4+ 17.f3 ♕×e2)
14...♗×h3 15.g×h3 (15.♗×e5? ♗×g2
16.♖g1 ♗×d5 17.c×d5 ♕×d5 18.♗×g7
♖g8∓) 15...♘g6 16.♗e3 (16.♗×c7?!
♘e7) 16...♘×e2 17.♕×e2 0-0-0
18.0-0-0∓.

14...♗×h3 15.♗×d4 (15.g×h3 ♗b4+
16.♔f1 ♘×e2 17.♕×e2 0-0∓)
15...♗×g2 16.♗×e5 (16.♖g1 ♗×d5
17.♗×e5 0-0-0 18.♕b3 ♗g2∓)
16...0-0-0?! (16...♗×h1 17.♘c7+
♔e7 18.♘×a8 ♕g2 19.♗d4 ♗b4+
20.♗c3 ♗×c3+ 21.b×c3 ♖×a8∓)
17.♕b3? (17.♗g4+ ♔b8 18.♗×c7+
♕×c7 19.♘×c7 ♖d1+ 20.♖×d1 ♗×h1
21.♖d7∓) **17...♗×h1 18.♗g4+
♔b8 19.♗×c7+ ♔a8** (19...♔a7!?)

20.♗×d8 ♖×d8 21.♖d1 ♕g6??
(21...♗×d5 22.♖×d5 ♖×d5 23.c×d5
♕g6∓) **22.♘e3??** (22.♘c7+ ♔a7
23.♖×d8+−) **22...♖e8 0-1**

Summary: After **1.e4 d5 2.e×d5
♕×d5 3.♘c3 ♕d6 4.d4 ♘f6
5.♘b5**, Black has two good replies:
5...♕d8 and 5...♕b6. White usually responds with one of two plans:

A) 6.c4 and after c7-c6 (usually a very
useful move in the 3...♕d6 system),
White's knight returns to c3. As practice and analysis show, Black can get
an equal game with decent counterchances.

B) 6.♗f4, trying to use a development
advantage. But here also Black has good
chances for an equal game with
counterplay.

In the game Gavric – Kurajica, after
5...♕b6 6.c4 a6 7.♘c3, Black played
a real gambit with **7...e5 8.d×e5 ♘g4**
with interesting chances for both sides.

Game 32
Ljubicic, F. (2395) – Sedlak, N. (2560)
Zupanja 2007

**1.e4 d5 2.e×d5 ♕×d5 3.♘c3 ♕d6
4.d4 ♘f6 5.♘ge2**

The main idea of this move is to support the bishop in the aggressive plan
♗c1-f4, ♕d1-d2 and 0-0-0.

5...c6

For 5...g6, see Game 37.

We examine the following alternatives:
A) 5...♘c6; **B)** 5...e6; **C)** 5...♗g4 and
D) 5...♗f5.

A) 5...♘c6 6.♗f4 ♕d8 (6...♕b4?! 7.a3;
6...e5 7.d×e5 ♘×e5 8.♕×d6 ♗×d6
9.♘b5 ♗e6 10.♘×d6+ c×d6±) 7.♕d2
♘b4 (7...♗f5?! 8.d5 ♘b4 9.♘d4)
8.0-0-0 (8.a3!? ♘bd5 9.♗e5) 8...♗f5
9.♘b5 ♘bd5 10.♘g3 ♗d7 11.♗e5
e6⇄, Rymskyy, A. (2095) – Kachur,
A. (2280), Odessa 2007;

B) 5...e6

B1) 6.♗f4 (6.♕d3 ♗d7 7.♗f4 ♕b6
8.0-0-0 ♘c6 9.♔b1 0-0-0⇄ Kosiorek,
M. (2378) – Malaniuk, V. (2511),
Kowalewo Pomorskie 2006) 6...♕b6
(6...♕d8 7.♕d3 ♗d7 8.h4 ♘c6 9.a3
(Weiss, C. (2429) – Horvath, C. (2542),
Saint Vincent 2005) 9...♗d6 10.0-0-0
0-0 11.♕f3 ♘e7⇄ or 8.0-0-0 ♗c6 9.d5
♗×d5 10.♘b5 ♘a6 11.c4 ♗c6
12.♕h3∞) 7.♕d2 (7.g3 ♗d6) 7...♗d6
(7...♗b4 8.0-0-0 (Petrossian, A. (2328)
– Fernandez, L. (1983), Marseille 2005)
8...0-0 9.a3 ♗d6±) 8.0-0-0 0-0 9.♗×d6
c×d6 10.♘f4 ♘a6 11.a3 ♗d7⇄;

B2) 6.g3 ♗d7 7.♗f4 ♕c6 (7...♕b6!?)
8.d5 e×d5 (8...♘×d5 9.♘×d5 ♕×d5
10.♕×d5 e×d5 11.♗×c7 ♘c6⇄) 9.♗g2
(9.♘d4!?) 9...♘a6 (9...♗e6 10.♘d4
♕b6 11.0-0⩲, Radovanovic, J (2360)
– Rogule, L. (2335), Brno 2007)
10.♘×d5 0-0-0 (10...♘×d5?! 11.♗×d5

242

♛b6 12.♗×f7+ or ♛f612.♗×b7) 11.♘d4 ♖e8+ 12.♗e3 ♛c4 13.♘×f6 g×f6⇄ ;

C) 5...♗g4 6.f3 (6.h3 ♗d7 7.♗f4 ♛b6⇄ ; 6.♛d3 ♘c6 7.♗f4 ♛d7 8.0-0-0 e6 9.h3 ♗f5 10.♛f3 0-0-0 11.g4 ♗g6 12.♗g2 ♘d5 13.♘×d5 ♛×d5 ½-½, Malinovsky, K. (2231) – Klima, L. (2432), Olomouc 2004; 8...0-0-0!?)

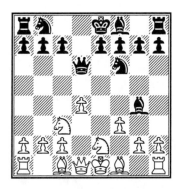

C1) 6...♗f5 7.♗f4 ♛d7 8.♘g3 (8.d5!?) 8...♗g6 9.♘ge4 ♘×e4 (Grigore, N. (2370) – Vajda, A. (2455), Predeal 2007) 10.f×e4 a6 11.♘d5± or 10...♘a6 11.d5 0-0-0 12.♗×a6 b×a6 13.♛e2 ♔b7 14.0-0-0± ; 7...♛d8 8.d5 a6 9.♘g3 ♗g6 (Feher, G. (2380) – Peredy, F. (2200), Heves 1997) 10.h4 h6 11.♗d3 ♗×d3 12.♛×d3 c6 13.d6 e×d6 (13...e6 14.0-0-0 with strong pressure) 14.0-0-0 ♗e7 (14...d5 15.♖he1+ ♗e7 16.♘f5+−) 15.♘f5 0-0 16.♘×e7+ ♛×e7 17.♗×d6± ;

C2) 6...♗d7 7.♗f4 (7.d5 e6 8.♗f4 e5⇄ ; 7.♘e4 ♘×e4 8.f×e4 e5=; 7.♘g3 ♛b6 8.♗e3 ♛×b2∞) 7...♛b6 8.♛d2 e6 9.0-0-0 (9.g4?! ♘c6 10.♗g2 (Reefat, S. (2478) – Abdul, M. (2233), Dhaka 2006) 10...♘×g4∓) 9...♘c6 10.♘a4 ♛b4 11.♛×b4 ♘×b4⇄ ;

D) 5...♗f5 6.♗f4

D1) 6...♛d8 (6...♛b4?! 7.♗×c7 ♘a6 8.a3 ♛×b2 9.♖a2 ♗×c2 10.♖×b2 ♗×d1 11.♗e5 or 7...♛×b2 8.♖b1 ♛×c2 9.♛×c2 ♗×c2 10.♖×b7 with the initiative) 7.♘g3 ♗e6 8.♛d2 (8.h4!? h6 9.h5 ♗h7 10.♗d3 ♗×d3 11.♛×d3 c6 12.0-0-0 , Kanovsky, D. (2368) – Ptacnikova, L. (2193), Olomouc 2006) 8...c6 9.♗e2 ♘bd7 10.0-0 g6 11.♖fe1 ♗g7 12.♖ad1 0-0± , Braun, P. (2305) – Nilsson, S. (2200), Marianske Lazne 2008; 7.d5!? c6 8.♘d4 ♗d7 9.♛e2;

D2) 6...♛b6 (8.♗d3 e6 9.♘ce4 ♘c6 10.c3 0-0-0 11.♛e2 ♘d5 12.♗d2 e5∓, Kanovsky, D. (2405) – Epishin, V. (2570), Czechia 2008; 8...♘c6!?; 6...♛d7 7.♘g3 ♗g6 8.♛f3 c6?! 9.0-0-0 e6 10.h4 h6 11.h5 ♗h7 12.♗×h6±, Potapov, A. (2315) – Paveliev, A. (2390), Dagomys 2008)

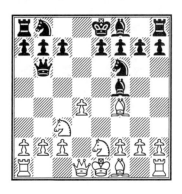

D2a) 7.♛d2

D2a1) 7...e6 (7...c6? 8.♗×b8 ♖×b8 9.♛f4+− or 8...♘e4 9.♘×e4 ♗×e4 10.0-0-0 ♖×b8 11.♛f4+−) 8.0-0-0 ♘c6 9.a3 (9.♘g3 ♗g6 10.♗d3 0-0-0 11.♗×g6 h×g6 12.♘ge2 e5 13.♗e3 e×d4 14.♘×d4 ♘×d4 15.♗×d4 c5 0-1, Ayas Fernandez, A. (2261) – Mellado Trivino, J. (2451), Cala Mendia. 2001) 9...0-0-0 10.♗e3 ♛a5⇄ ; 7.d5!?;

D2a2) 7...♘c6!? 8.a3 0-0-0 9.♘a4 ♕a5
10.♕xa5 ♘xa5 11.0-0-0 ♘e4 12.♗g3
(12.♗e3?! ♘c4) 12...g6 13.♘ec3 ♗h6+
14.f4 (14.♔b1?! ♘d2+) 14...♘xg3
15.hxg3 ♗g7 16.d5 c6∓ or 8.0-0-0
0-0-0 9.a3 e5 10.♗e3 ♕a5 11.♔b1
(11.g3?! ♗xa3 12.bxa3 ♕xa3+ 13.♔b1
♘b4∓; 11.♘g3?! exd4 12.♘a2 dxe3
13.♕xa5 ♘xa5 14.♖xd8+ ♔xd8
15.♘xf5 exf2∓) 11...h5∓;

D2b) 7.♘g3 (7.d5 e6 8.♕d2 ♗b4
9.dxe6 ♘c6 10.0-0-0 ♕a5∞) 7...♗g6
8.♘a4 ♕c6 (8...♕a5+ 9.c3 ♘c6 10.b4
♕d5±) 9.♘c3 ♕b6=.

Back to Ljubicic – Sedlak.

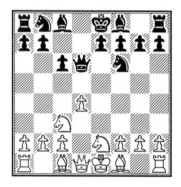

6.♗f4

6.g3 ♗f5 (or 6...♗g4) 7.♗g2, see Game
38.

6...♕b4

6...♕d8 7.♕d2 (7.g3 ♗g4 8.♗g2 e6
9.0-0 ♗d6±, Willemze, T. (2363) –
Papadopoulou, V. (2220), Stockholm
2006) 7...♗e6 (7...♗f5 8.♘g3 ♗g6 9.h4
h6 10.h5 ♗h7 11.♗d3 ♗xd3 12.♕xd3
e6 13.♘ce4 ♘bd7 14.0-0±,
Solodovnichenko, Y. (2514) – Pytel, K.
(2400), Rochefort 2005; 10.0-0-0 e6
11.♗d3 ♗xd3 12.♕xd3±, Van der

Weide, K. (2482) – Maes, T. (2179),
Oslo 2006) 8.0-0-0 g6 9.♗h6 ♗xh6
10.♕xh6 ♕d6=; 8...♘bd7!?; 8.g3 ♗c4
9.♗g2 e6 10.a3 ♗d6 11.♗xd6 ♕xd6
12.0-0 0-0=, Wedberg, T. (2540) –
Cicak, S. (2537), Skara 2002; 8...g6!?;

7.b3

There are other alternatives:

A) 7.♕c1 ♘bd7 8.a3 (8.♗c7 e6 9.a3
♕e7⇄) 8...♕b6 9.b4 (9.f3 g6=; 9.♗e3
♘g4=) 9...a5 (9...g6!?) 10.♘a4 ♕a7
([10...♕d8!?) 11.bxa5?! (11.b5!?)
11...♕xa5+ 12.♘ac3 e5∓, Fernandez
Calzada, J. (1925) – Epishin, V. (2575),
Sevilla 2008;

B) 7.a3 ♕xb2 8.♗c7 ♘d5

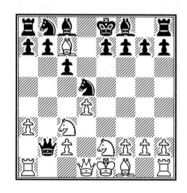

9.♘a4 (9.♗a5 ♗g4 10.♖a2 ♘xc3
11.♖xb2 ♘xd1 12.♖xb7 ♗c8∞)
9...♕b5 (9...♕a1 10.♕xa1 ♘xc7
(Hnatovsky, N. – Beratti, H., Internet
2003) 11.♘f4 with better chances for
White) 10.c4 (10.♘ec3 ♘xc3 11.♘xc3
♕g5∞, Saiboulatov, D. (2393) – Kalka,
A. (2401), Belgium 2005) 10...♕xc4
11.♘f4 ♘c3 12.♗xc4 ♘xd1 13.♖xd1
b5∞;

C) 7.♗c7 e6 (7...♕xb2? 8.♖b1 ♕a3
9.♖b3 ♕a6 10.♘c1 b5 11.♘xb5+–;

7...♘d5 8.a3 ♛×b2 – 7.a3 ♛×b2 8.♗c7
♘d5) 8.a3 ♛e7 9.♗e5 ♘bd7 10.♛d3
(10...g6!? 11.0-0-0 ♗g7 12.♛g3 ♘h5
13.♛e3 ♘hf6=; 12...0-0!? 13.♗d6 ♛d8
14.♗×f8 ♛×f8) 10...b6 11.♘g3 ♗b7
(11...♘×e5!? 12.d×e5 ♘d7) 12.♘ce4
(Landa, K. (2610) – Koenig, D. (2327),
Deizisau 2001) 12...0-0-0 13.♗d6
(13.♘d6+?! ♚b8 14.♘×b7+ ♘×e5
15.♛e2 ♘d3+ 16.♛×d3 ♛×b7∓ or
14.♘×f7+ ♘×e5 15.♘×e5 c5 16.♘e2
♛c7∓) 13...♛e8 14.♗×f8 ♛×f8⇄.

Let's return to Ljubicic – Sedlak.

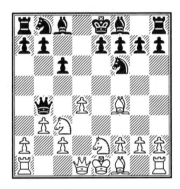

7...♗g4

7...g6!?; 7...♘a6!?; 7...♘bd7!?; 7...♛a5!?.

8.f3 ♗f5 9.♛d2

9.a3 ♛a5 (9...♛b6!?) 10.b4 ♛b6
11.♘g3 ♗g6 12.♗c4 ♘bd7 13.♛d2 e6
(13...♗×c2?! 14.♛×c2 ♛×d4 15.♛b3
♛×f4 16.♗×f7+ ♚d8 17.♘ce2 ♛c7
18.♗e6±) 14.0-0 ♗e7 (14...a5 15.b5
♗×c2 16.b×c6 b×c6 17.♘ge4⩲)
15.♘ge4 (15.♖fe1 ♘d5) 15...0-0⇄.

9...e6 10.g4

10.a3 ♛a5 11.♘g3 ♗b4 (11...♗g6
12.♘ge4±) 12.a×b4 ♛×a1+ 13.♚f2

♗g6 (13...♛a3? 14.♘×f5 e×f5 15.♗d6
♛d7 16.d5±) 14.h4 h6 15.♘b5 0-0
16.♘c7 ♘bd7 17.♘×a8 ♖×a8⇄;
10.♘g3 ♗g6 11.h4 h5⩲.

10...♗g6 11.♗g2

11.h4 h5 12.g5 ♘d5=; 11.0-0-0
♘bd7⇄.

11...♘bd7 12.0-0 (12.♗c7?! ♛a3∓)
12...♛a5 13.a3 ♗e7 14.b4 ♛d8
(14...♛a6!?) **15.♘e4?!** (15.♘g3!?;
15.h4!?) **15...♘b6** (15...♗×e4 16.f×e4
♘×g4 17.h3 ♘gf6 18.c4 0-0 19.♗e3
♘b6 20.♛c3 or 19...e5 20.d5 ♘b6
21.♖ac1 c×d5 22.e×d5∞; 15...♘×e4!?
16.f×e4 ♘f6) **16.♘c5?!** (16.♛d3!?
♘fd5 17.♗d2⇄ or 16...0-0 17.c4 h5
18.h3⇄) **16...♘c4 17.♛c3 b5**
18.♛b3 ♘d5 (18...♘b6 19.e5 ♘h5
20.♗e3 ∞; 18...a5 19.♗f3 a×b4
20.e5∞) **19.♗c1 h5 20.h3?!** (20.a4!?
♛c7 21.g5 0-0 22.a×b5 c×b5 23.f4⇄)
20...e5 (20...a5!?) **21.d×e5?!** (21.a4!?
e×d4 22.a×b5 c×b5 23.f4∞)
21...♗×c5+ 22.b×c5 ♛e7 23.♘f4
(23.♘d4 ♛×c5 24.♖d1 0-0-0∓)
23...♛×c5+ 24.♚h1 ♘×f4
25.♗×f4 0-0 (25...0-0-0!? 26.a4 ♖d4)
26.g×h5 (26.♖fe1 ♖fe8) **26...♗×h5**
27.♛c3 f6 (27...♖ad8!? 28.♖fe1 ♖fe8
or 28.♖fd1 ♖×d1+ 29.♖×d1 ♛×a3
30.♛×a3 ♘×a3 31.♗e3 ♖a8∓)
28.♖fe1 ♖ae8 29.e×f6 ♖×e1+
30.♖×e1 ♖×f6 31.♖e5 ♛f8
(31...♛f2 32.♗e3 ♘×e3 33.♛×e3 ♛×e3
34.♖×e3 a6∓) **32.♖×h5 ♖×f4**
33.♖g5?! (33.♗f1 ♛e7 34.♗×c4+
♖×c4 35.♛d3 ♖f4∓ or 33...♛f6
34.♛×f6 g×f6 35.♖c5 ♖×f3 36.♚g2
♖c3 37.♗×c4+ b×c4 38.♖×c6 ♖×c2+
39.♚f3 ♖c3+ 40.♚e4∓) **33...♛f6**
34.♛×f6 ♖×f6 35.f4 ♘×a3
36.♖c5 ♖×f4 37.♖×c6 a5 38.♖a6

a4 39.♗c6 ♖b4 40.c3 ♖b1+
41.♔g2 ♖b2+ 42.♔f3 ♖c2 43.c4
♖c3+ 44.♔f4 ♖×c4+ 45.♔g5 ♖c3
46.h4 ♔f8 47.♖a8+ ♔e7
48.♖a7+ ♔d6 49.♗×b5 ♘×b5
50.♖×a4 ♖g3+ 51.♔h5 g6+
52.♔h6 ♘c7 53.h5 ♘e6 54.♖a5
g5 55.♔g6 ♘f4+? (55...g4)
56.♔g7? (56.♔f5! ♘d5 57.h6 ♘e7+
58.♔f6 g4 59.h7 or 56...♘×h5 57.♖a6+
♔e7 58.♖g6 with a draw.)
56...♘×h5+ 57.♔g6 ♘f4+ 58.♔f5
♘h3 59.♖a4 ♔d5 0-1

Summary: White's idea after **1.e4 d5
2.e×d5 ♕×d5 3.♘c3 ♕d6 4.d4
♘f6 5.♘ge2** is to support the bishop
in the aggressive plan with ♗c1-f4,
♕d1-d2 and 0-0-0.

After **5.♘ge2**, Black has several sat-
isfactory continuations. Practice and
analysis indicate that all of these allow
Black an equal game with decent
counterchances, but I consider 5...c6,
5...e6 and 5...♗f5 to be the most solid
lines. In fact, after 5...♗f5 6.♗f4 ♕b6
7.♕d2 ♘c6, in my opinion, Black has
the better chances!

After 5...♘c6 6.♗f4 ♕b4 7.a3 or
6...♕d8 7.♕d2 ♗f5?! 8.d5, Black has
problems. Black also has an unpleasant position after 5...♗g4 6.f3 ♗f5
7.♗f4 ♕d7 8.♘g3 ♗g6 9.♘ge4 or
7...♕d8 8.d5.

Game 33
Jakimov, V. (2430) –
Vysochin, S. (2520)
Kharkov 2007

**1.e4 d5 2.e×d5 ♕×d5 3.♘c3 ♕d6
4.d4 ♘f6 5.♗d3**

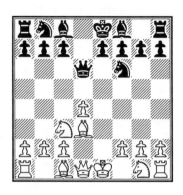

5...♗g4

Also worth consideration are **A)** 5...g6;
B) 5...c6; **C)** 5...a6 and **D)** 5...♘c6.

A) 5...g6 6.♘ge2 (for 6.♘f3 ♗f5, see
5.♘f3 ♗f5 6.♗d3 g6 in Game 29; 6...a6
– 5.♘f3 a6 6.♗d3 g6, Game 25;
6...♗g7!?) 6...♗g7 7.♗f4 ♕d8 8.♕d2
♘c6 9.0-0-0 0-0 10.♗b5 (10.h4 ♘b4
11.♗c4 c6 12.f3 b5 13.♗b3 a5⇄)
10...♘a5 (10...a6!? 11.♗×c6 b×c6
12.♗e5⇄) 11.♗h6 (11.h4!? a6
12.♗d3) 11...♗×h6 12.♕×h6 ♘g4
13.♕h4 (13.♕f4!? ♕d6 14.♖d2) 13...a6
14.♗a4 e5 (14...b5!? 15.♗b3 ♘×b3+
16.a×b3 ♘f6=) 15.♕×d8 ♖×d8 16.d×e5
♗e6 17.f4 c5⩲, Cabrera, A. (2491) –
Kurajica, B. (2558), Sauzal 2003;

B) 5...c6 6.♘ge2 (6.♘f3 – 5.♘f3 c6
6.♗d3, Game 13).

B1) 6...g6?! 7.♗f4 ♕d8 (7...♕b4
8.♗c7 ♘d5 9.a3 ♕×b2? 10.♘×d5
c×d5 11.♖b1 ♕×a3 12.♖b3 ♕a4
13.♘c3+− or 9...♘×c3 10.b×c3 ♕a4
11.♗e5±) 8.♕d2 ♗g7 (8...♘d5 (Jeric,
S. (2327) – Sax, G. (2520), Bled 2005)
9.♗e5 with better chances for White)
9.0-0-0 0-0 10.h4 ♘a6 (or 10...♗e6
11.h5 ♘×h5 12.♗h6) 11.h5 ♘×h5

12.♗h6 with a strong attack; White has better chances after 8...♗f5 9.♗×f5 g×f5 10.0-0 and after 8...♕a5 9.0-0 ♗g7 10.♗h6.

B2) 6...♗g4 7.f3 ♗h5 8.♗f4

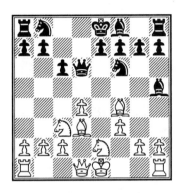

8...♕d8 (8...♕b4 9.♗c7 e6 10.a3 ♕e7 11.♗g3 ♕d8 12.♕d2 ♗e7 13.0-0-0 ♘bd7 14.♘f4 ♗g6± , Pavlov, S. (2415) – Sergeev, V. (2489), Kiev 2006) 9.♕d2

B2a) 9...e6 (9...♘bd7!? 10.♘e4 ♘×e4 11.f×e4 e5 or 11.♗×e4 ♘f6) 10.h4 ♗d6?! (10...♗g6!? 11.0-0-0 ♘bd7) 11.0-0-0 (11.g4 ♗g6 12.h5 ♗×f4 13.♘×f4 ♗×d3 14.♕×d3± , Mogranzini, R. (2400) – Borgo, G. (2420), Reggio Emilia 2007) 11...0-0 (11...♗×f4 12.♘×f4 ♗g6 13.♗e2± ; 11...♗g6 12.♘e4 ♘×e4 13.f×e4 ♗×f4 14.♘×f4 ♕×d4 15.h5 ♗×e4 16.♗×e4±) 12.g4 ♗g6 (12...♗×f4 13.♘×f4 ♗g6 14.♗c4±) 13.♗×g6 h×g6 14.h5± ;

B2b) 9...♗g6 10.♘e4 (10.0-0-0!?) 10...♘bd7 11.0-0 ♘×e4 12.f×e4 e5 13.d×e5!? (13.♗g5 ♗e7 14.♗×e7 ♕×e7 15.c3 0-0 16.♘g3 ♖ad8∓, Cappon, J. (2205) – Pytel, K. (2387), Proville 2006) 13...♘c5 (13...♕b6+ 14.♔h1 ♕×b2?! 15.a3 ♕b6 16.♖ab1 ♕d8

17.♖×b7± ; 14...0-0-0∞) 14.♘c3 ♗e7 15.♖ad1 0-0∞;

C) 5...a6 6.♘ge2 (6.♘f3 – Game 25)

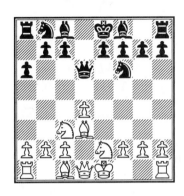

C1) 6...♘c6 7.♗f4 (7.♘e4 ♘×e4 8.♗×e4 e5 9.d×e5 ♕×d1+ 10.♔×d1 ♘×e5⇄, Krivec, J. (2315) – Bogut, Z. (2435), Cannes 2007) 7...♕d8 (7...e5 8.d×e5 ♘×e5 9.0-0 ♗e6?! 10.♘d4 0-0-0 11.♗×e5 ♕×e5 12.♘c6 ♖×d3 13.♘×e5 ♖×d1 14.♖a×d1± , De la Paz, F. (2442) – Campos, L. (2439), Albacete 2002; 9...♗d7!?) 8.♘e4 ♘×e4?! 9.♗×e4 e6 10.c3 ♗d6 11.♕d3 ♗d7 12.♕g3 with strong pressure, Vogt, L. (2475) – Richter, M. (2407), Zehlendorf 2006; 8...♘d5!?;

C2) 6...e6 7.♗f4 ♕d8 8.0-0 (8.♕d2 b5 9.0-0-0 ♗b7 10.f3 ♘bd7 11.♖he1 ♗e7 12.♘g3 0-0 13.♘ge4 c5 14.d×c5 ♘×c5⇄, Jeric, S. (2305) – Tratar, M. (2452), Portoroz 2004) 8...♗d6 9.♕d2 0-0 10.♖ad1 ♘c6 11.♘e4 ♗×f4 12.♕×f4 ♘d5 13.♕g3 f5 (13...♘db4?! (Pogonina, N. (2362) – Gunina, V. (2342), Nojabrsk 2005) 14.♘f4 ♕e7 15.c3 ♘×d3 16.♖×d3±) 14.♘g5 h6 15.♘f3 ♕d6 16.♕×d6 c×d6± ;

C3) 6...♗g4 7.f3 and now:

C3a) 7...♗d7 8.♗f4 (8.♘e4 ♕b6 9.c3 ♘c6 10.♘c5 0-0-0 11.♘xd7 ♖xd7⇄ or 9.a4 ♘c6⇄; 8.0-0 ♘c6 9.♗f4 e5 10.dxe5 ♘xe5⇄; 9.♘e4 ♘xe4 10.♗xe4 0-0-0⇄ or 10...e5⇄) 8...♕b6 9.0-0 (9.a4 ♘c6 10.♕d2 0-0-0 ⇄; 9.♕d2 ♘c6 10.♘a4 ♕a7 11.♘c5 0-0-0 12.♘xd7 ♖xd7 13.c3 e6⇄) 9...e6 (9...♘c6!? 10.♘a4 ♕a7 11.c3 e5⇄ or 10.♗e3 e5 11.♘a4 ♕a5⇄) 10.♔h1 ♗d6 (10...♘c6!?) 11.♕d2 ♘c6⇄, Bugalski, M. (2216) – Vyskocil, N. (2305), Stare Mesto 2004;

C3b) 7...♗h5 8.♗f4 ♕d7 (8...♕c6?! 9.d5; 8...♕d8?! 9.♕d2 e6 10.0-0-0 ♘bd7 11.g4 ♗g6 (Dembo, Y. (2441) – Milanovic, D. (2464), Hamburg 2005) 12.d5 or 9.♘e4!? ♘c6 10.c3)

C3b1) 9.♘e4 (9.♕d2 ♘c6 10.0-0-0 e6 11.g4 ♗g6 12.d5 ♘xd5 13.♗xg6 hxg6 14.♘xd5 exd5 15.♕xd5 ♕xd5 16.♖xd5 (Matta, V. (2280) – Ashwin, J. (2475), New Delhi 2007) 16...♗d6 17.♗xd6 0-0-0=) 9...♘c6 10.♘c5 (10.♘xf6+ gxf6=) 10...♕c8 (Rutkowski, M. (2295) – Cyborowski, L. (2535), Ustron 2006) 11.♘g3 ♗g6 (11...♘xd4?! 12.♗e5 ♘e6 13.♗f5) 12.0-0 e6 13.c3 ♗xc5 14.dxc5 ♘d5⇄ or 10.c3 ♘xe4 11.♗xe4 (11.fxe4?! e5) 11...e6 12.♕b3 0-0-0⇄;

C3b2) 9.d5! "A terrific idea which leaves Black with a grave risk that his Knight on b8 and Bishop on f8 will never emerge." – GM Ian Rogers

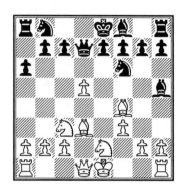

C3b2a) 9...♗g6?! (9...♘xd5?! 10.♗e4 ♘xc3 11.♘xc3, and according to Rogers 11...c6 12.♘a4 is extremely risky; but after 11...♘c6! 12.♕xd7+ ♔xd7 13.0-0-0+ ♔c8 the position is not clear. 10.♗f5 is much better for White; for example, 10...e6 11.♘xd5 ♕xd5 12.♕xd5 exd5 13.0-0-0 with a very strong initiative)

C3b2a1) 10.♕d2 c6 11.d6 (11.dxc6 ♘xc6 12.0-0-0 e5 13.♕e3 ♕e6⇄) 11...exd6 12.0-0-0 ♗e7 13.♖he1 0-0 14.♗xg6 hxg6 15.♗xd6 ♗xd6 16.♕xd6 ♕xd6 17.♖xd6 ♘bd7± or 10...♗xd3 11.♕xd3 c6 (11...g6?! 12.0-0-0 ♗g7 13.♕c4 c6 14.d6 0-0 15.♔b1 ♖e8 16.♘g3 (Kasparov, G. (2838) – Rogers, I. (2538), Batumi 2001) 16...b5⇄ or 15.dxe7 ♕xe7 16.♗d6 ♕e3+ 17.♔b1 ♖e8⇄; 12.♕c4!? c6 13.♖d1) 12.♗e5 ♘xd5 13.0-0-0 e6∞;

C3b2a2) 10.♗xg6 hxg6 11.♕d4 c6 (Rogers I.) 12.♘a4!, and Black may have problems; for example, 12...♘xd5 13.0-0-0 b5 14.♘b6 ♘xb6 15.♕xb6

♕c8 16.♗c7 ♘d7 17.♖×d7 ♕×d7 18.♖d1 ♕e6 19.♘f4 ♕c4 20.b3 ♕c3 21.♗e5+− or 12...♕×d5 (12...♕d8 13.♘b6) 13.♕b6 (13.♘b6 ♕×d4 14.♘×d4 ♘d5!?) 13...♘bd7 14.♕×b7 c5 15.♕c7 e6 16.♖d1 ♕c4 17.b3 ♕×c2 18.♕c6 ♖d8 19.♗c7± or 15...e5 16.♖d1 ♕×a2 17.♘ec3 ♕e6 18.0-0 ♗e7 19.♖fe1 0-0 20.♗×e5 ♖fc8 21.♗×f6 ♖×c7 22.♗×e6 ♘×f6 23.♖e5 with a better ending for White;

C3b3) 9...c6!?

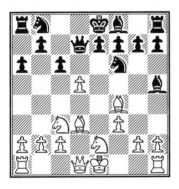

C3b3a) 10.♘a4 (10.d6!? e×d6 11.0-0 ♗e7 12.♘a4 or 12.♗e3) 10...♕d8 11.♕d2 (11.0-0 ♘×d5 12.♕d2 ♘d7⇄) 11...c×d5 (11...♘×d5 12.0-0-0≋) 12.0-0-0 ♘c6⇄;

C3b3b) 10.d×c6 ♘×c6 11.♘e4 (11.♘g3 ♗g6 12.♗×g6 h×g6 13.♕×d7+ ♘×d7 14.0-0-0 e5⇄; 11.0-0 e5 12.♗e3 ♗g6 13.♖c1 ♗e7⇄ or 13.♗×g6 h×g6⇄) 0-0-0 (11...♘d5?! 12.♘c5 ♕d8 (Wieczorek, O. − Swiercz, D. (2033), Urgup 2004) 13.♘×b7 ♕b6 14.♗e4 ♘f6 15.♗×c6+ ♕×c6 16.♘a5 ♕b6 17.♘b3 ♖d8 18.♘ed4 ♘d5 19.♗d2 e5 20.♕e2 with better chances for White) 12.0-0 e5 13.♗e3 (13.♘×f6?! ♗c5+ 14.♔h1 g×f6) 13...♘d5 14.♗f2 ♘cb4⇄;

D) 5...♘c6 6.♘ge2 (6.♗e3 a6 7.♘f3 g6 − 5.♘f3 a6 6.♗d3 g6, Game 25; 6...e5!?; 6...g6!?; 6.♘b5 ♕d8 7.♗f4 ♘d5 8.♕f3 e6 9.♗e4 ♗b4+ 10.c3 ♘×f4 11.♕×f4 ♗d6 12.♕f3 0-0=, Secer, A. (2305) − Citak, S. (2315), Ankara 2008; 8...♘cb4!?; 10...♗a5!? 11.0-0-0 a6 12.♘a3 f5; 6.♘f3 a6 see Game 25 or 6...♗g4!? 7.h3 ♗×f3 8.♕×f3 0-0-0 with a good game for Black)

6...e5 (6...♗g4 7.f3 ♗h5 − 5...♗g4 6.f3 ♗h5 7.♘ge2 ♘c6; 6...♗b4 7.♗f4 ♕d8 8.♗e5 e6± , Nijboer, F. (2529) − Tiviakov, S. (2678), Leeuwarden 2005 or 7...♕b6 (Owczarzak, J. (2380) − Toczek, G. (2339), Opole 2006) 8.0-0±)

D1) 7.0-0 ♘×d4 8.♘×d4 ♕×d4 9.♘b5 (9.♖e1 ♗d6 (Sokolov, A. (2582) − Nikolaidis, I. (2520), Athens 2005) 10.♘b5∞; 9...♗g4 10.♗e3 ♕×c3 11.b×c3 ♗×d1 12.♖a×d1 ♗e7∓)

D1a) 9...♕d8 10.♕e1 (10.♕e2!? ♗d6 11.f4) 10...♗d6 11.♘×d6+ c×d6 12.f4 ♕b6+ 13.♔h1 e4! (13...0-0?! 14.f×e5 d×e5 15.♗g5! e4 16.♗×f6 or 14...♘g4 15.♕h4 h6 16.e×d6 ♕×d6 17.♗f4 ♕d4 18.♖ae1 with a strong initiative) 14.♗×e4 0-0 15.♗d3 ♖e8⇄, Roschupkin, G. (2367) − Obukhov, G., Vladivostok 2006)

D1b) 9...♕b6 10.♕e2 ♗d6 (10...e4 11.♗f4 ♗d6 12.♘×d6+ c×d6 13.♗b5+ (Iordachescu, V. (2609) – Tzermiadianos, A. (2453), Warsaw 2005) 13...♔f8∞; 11.♗×e4!? ♗e7 12.♗f4 or 11...♘×e4 12.♗f4) 11.a4 (11.♗f4?! ♗g4; 11.♗e3 ♕a5∞) 11...0-0 12.a5 ♕c6⇄.

D2) 7.♘b5 (7.♗e3!?; 7.d×e5 ♘×e5 8.♗b5+ c6 9.♕×d6 ♗×d6∓, Manolov, I. (2257) – Panbukchian, V. (2343), Sunny Beach 2004 or 8.♗f4 ♘×d3+ 9.c×d3 ♕b6 10.0-0⇄, Blazek, M. (2106) – Orgon, D. (2034), Slovakia 2001)

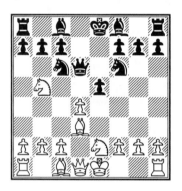

D2a) 7...♕d8 8.d×e5 ♘×e5 (8...♗b4+ 9.♗d2 ♗×d2+ 10.♕×d2 ♘×e5 11.0-0-0 ♕e7 12.♖he1 (Nakamura, M. – Paredes, C., Internet 2003) 12...0-0∞; 11.♕e3 ♕e7⇄) 9.♗f4 ♗b4+ 10.♘ec3 (10.♔f1 ♕e7⇄, Saldano Dayer, H. (2424) – Perez, R. (2449), Elgoibar 2003) 10...♘×d3+ (10...♗×c3+?! 11.b×c3, Safarian, A. (2322) – Sveinsson, J. (1913), Internet 2003; 11...♕e7+?! 12.♔f1 ♗a5 13.♘d6+ or 12...0-0 13.♘×c7) 11.♕×d3 ♕×d3 12.♘×c7+ ♔d7 13.c×d3 ♘h5 14.♗e5 f6 15.♘×a8 f×e5 16.0-0 (16.♖c1 ♘f4∞) 16...♗×c3 17.b×c3 ♘f4∞;

D2b) 7...♕e7 8.0-0 (8.d×e5 ♘×e5 9.♗f4 c6⇄, Macak, S. (2260) –

Kovacik, E. (2204), Slovakia 2003; 9...a6!?) 8...a6 (8...e4!? 9.♗c4 a6 10.♘bc3 ♗g4⇄) 9.d×e5 ♘×e5 10.♘bd4 (10.♘bc3 ♗g4 11.h3 ♗d7 12.♖e1 ♘×d3 13.♕×d3 0-0-0⇄, Dehaybe, A. (1925) – Pecotic, K., corr. 2005) 10...g6 11.♗g5 ♗g7 12.♘c3 0-0 13.♖e1 ♕d6⇄, Nay Oo Kyaw Tun (2431) – Goh Koong Jong, J. (2382), Bangkok 2004.

Back to Jakimov – Vysochin.

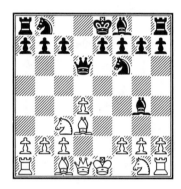

6.f3

6.♘ge2 ♘c6 (6...a6 – 5...a6 6.♘ge2 ♗g4 or 6...c6 – 5...c6 6.♘ge2 ♗g4) 7.♗e3 (7.f3 ♗h5 – 5...♗g4 6.f3 ♗h5 7.♘ge2 ♘c6) 7...e5 8.♘b5 (8.f3 ♗e6∞) 8...♕d7 9.h3 (9.d×e5?! ♘×e5 10.h3 ♗b4+ 11.♔f1 ♗h5∓ or 10.♗f4 ♘×d3+ 11.♕×d3 ♗b4+ 12.♔f1 0-0-0∓) 9...♗×e2 10.♗×e2 (10.♕×e2 e4 11.♗g5?! 0-0-0 12.♗c4 a6; 11.♗c4 a6 12.♘c3 ♗b4 13.a3 ♗a5⇄) 10...0-0-0 (10...a6?! 11.d×e5 ♘×e5 12.♕d4) 11.d×e5 ♕e6 12.♕c1 ♕×e5⇄.

6...♗h5 7.♘ge2 ♘c6

7...e6 (7...a6 – 5...a6 6.♘ge2 ♗g4 7.f3 ♗h5; 7...c6 – 5...c6 6.♘ge2 ♗g4 7.f3 ♗h5) 8.♗f4 ♕d7 9.♕d2 9.g4 ♗g6 (9...♘c6 – 7...♘c6 8.♗f4 ♕d7 9.♕d2

e6) 10.h4 ♗×d3 11.♛×d3 ♘c6⇄,
Hracek, Z. (2600) – Kantorik, M.
(2335), Pardubice 2002.

8.♗f4

A) 8.♘b5 ♛d7 9.♗f4 ♖c8 10.g4
(10.♛d2 e6 11.0-0-0 ♘b4 12.♘bc3
♗e7⇄, Rabeyrin, J. (2300) – Galyas,
M. (2455), Budapest 2008) 10...♗g6
11.♗×g6 h×g6 12.c4 e6 13.♛d2 ♗b4
14.♘bc3 ♘a5! 15.b3 b5∓, Marinkovic,
I. (2440) – Milanovic, D. (2510),
Zlatibor 2006;

B) 8.♘e4 ♘×e4 9.♗×e4 0-0-0 10.c3 e5
11.♛a4 (11.♗e3 ♗g6 12.♛a4 e×d4
13.♘×d4 ♘×d4 14.♗×d4 ♗×e4 15.f×e4
♛f4∓, Schwarz, D. (2203) – Lipka, J.
(2432), Slovakia 2003) 11...e×d4
12.♗f4 ♛c5 13.♗×c6 ♛×c6 14.♛×c6
b×c6 15.♘×d4 ♔b7⇄, Lerch, P. (2344)
– Libiszewski, F. (2458), France 2003.

Let's return to Jakimov – Vysochin.

8...♛d7

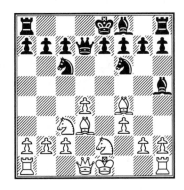

9.d5

9.♘b5 ♖c8 – 8.♘b5 ♛d7 9.♗f4 ♖c8.
We examine the following alternatives:
A) 9.♗g3; B) 9.g4 and C) 9.♛d2.

A) 9.♗g3 e6 10.♘b5 ♖c8 11.c3 a6
12.♘a3 ♗×a3 13.b×a3 ♘d5
(Narmontas, M. (2365) – Vysochin, S.
(2520), Warsaw 2007) 14.c4 ♘f6
15.♛b3 b6 16.d5 e×d5 17.c×d5±;
13...♗g6 14.♖b1 ♗×d3 15.♛×d3 ♖b8
16.0-0 0-0=;

B) 9.g4 ♗g6 10.h4 (10.g5?! ♘d5
11.♘×d5 ♛×d5 12.♗×c7 ♖c8 13.♗×g6
h×g6 14.♗f4 ♛×f3∓, Durao, J. (2150)
– Mellado Trivino, J. (2447), Seville
2002; 10.d5 ♘b4 11.♗b5 c6 12.d×c6
b×c6 13.♗a4 ♛×d1+ 14.♖×d1 ♗×c2
15.♖d4?! e5 16.♖×b4 ♗×b4 17.♗×c6+
♔e7 18.♗×a8 e×f4∓, Milliet, S. (2173)
– Dubois, M. (2049), France 2002;
15.♗×c2 ♘×c2 16.♔f2∞) 10...0-0-0
11.h5 (11.♗b5?! h5 12.g5 ♘d5∓, Jeric,
S. (2335) – Gombac, J. (2295), Nova
Gorica 2007) 11...♗×d3 12.♛×d3 ♘d5
13.♘×d5 ♛×d5 14.c4⇄;

C) 9.♛d2 e6 (9...♘b4 10.0-0-0 e6
11.♗c4 c6 12.h4 ♗g6 13.♗b3 h5⇄,
Atakisi, U. (2325) – Titova Boric, E.,
Antalya 2004; 11...♗g6 12.♗b3 0-0-0
⇄; 10.♗c4!? 0-0-0 13.♘b5; 10...e6
11.0-0 or 10...♗g6 11.0-0)

C1) 10.♗b5 a6 11.♗a4 0-0-0 12.0-0
(12.a3 ♗d6 13.0-0-0 ♗b4⇄, Elshani,
A. – Brunner, W. (2170), Kemer

2007)12...b5 (12...♗d6!?) 13.♘xb5 axb5 14.♗xb5 ♗d6 15.♗e3 ♘d5 16.♗f2∞; 11...♗g6 12.0-0 ♗d6 13.♖ad1 0-0 14.♗g5 b5 15.♗b3 (Sedina, E. (2382) – Danielian, E. (2418), Elista 2004) 15...b4 16.♘a4 ♖fd8⇄;

C2) 10.0-0-0

C2a) 10...♗b4 11.a3 ♗xc3 12.♘xc3 0-0-0 (12...♕xd4? 13.♘b5; 12...♘xd4? 13.g4 ♘xf3 14.♕g2 ♗xg4 15.♗b5) 13.♕f2 a6 (13...♕xd4?! 14.♕g3) 14.♗e5 ♕e7±; 11...♗a5 12.g4 ♗g6 13.♗xg6 hxg6 14.b4 ♗b6 15.d5 ♘d5 16.♘xd5 ♕xd5 17.♕xd5 exd5 18.♖xd5 ♖d8⇄, Jurkovic, H. (2400) – Sermek, D. (2601), Pula 2002;

C2b) 10...0-0-0 11.♗b5 (11.♘b5 ♘d5 12.c4 ♘xf4 13.♘xf4 a6 14.♘c3 ♗g6 15.d5 exd5 16.♘cxd5 ♗d6⇄ or 11.♘e4 ♗e7 12.c3 ♗g6⇄; 11...♘b4!?; 11...♔b8!?; 11...♗g6!?) 11...a6 12.♗a4 ♗b4 (12...♗g6!?) 13.a3 ♗a5 14.♗g5 ♗g6 15.h4 (Pavlov, S. (2306) – Kernazhitsky, L. (2371), Kiev 2004) 15...h5⇄.

We return now to Jakimov – Vysochin.

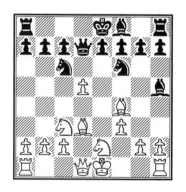

9...♘xd5 10.♘xd5

10.♗f5?! ♕xf5 11.♕xd5 ♕xd5 12.♘xd5 0-0-0 13.0-0-0 (13.♘xc7? e5) e6 14.♘dc3 ♗e7∓, Tscharotschkin, M. (2216) – Zeller, F. (2427), Germany 2004.

10...♕xd5 11.♗xc7 e5

11...♕d7!? 12.♗g3 e5 13.♗e4 ♗d6 14.♕d2 0-0-0 15.0-0-0 ♗g6⇄ or 12.♗f4 e5 13.♗e3 ♖d8 14.0-0 ♗e7 15.♗b5 ♗e6 16.♕e1 0-0⇄.

12.♗f5 (12.0-0? ♕d7) **12...♕xd1+ 13.♖xd1 f6** (13...♗c5?! 14.♖d5) **14.c3**

A) 14.♗d7+ ♔e7 (14...♔f7?! 15.c3 ♗g6 16.♖f1 ♗e7 17.f4)

A1) 15.♗d6+?! (15.0-0? ♘d4∓) ♔xd7 16.♗xf8+ ♔e6 17.♗xg7 (17.♗c5 ♖ad8 18.0-0 ♗g6∓; 17.♗a3 ♖hd8 18.♔f2 ♗g6∓) 17...hg8 18.g4 (18.♗h6?! ♖xg2 19.♖d3 ♘b4 20.♖c3 ♖d8∓) 18...♗xg4 19.fxg4 ♖xg7 20.h3 h5∓;

A2) 15.♔f2 (15.♘g3 ♘d4⇄; 15.♗xc6 bxc6 16.0-0 ♔e6⇄ or 16.♗d6+ ♔e6 17.♗xf8 ♖hxf8⇄) 15...♗e8 (15...♔f7?! 16.♘g3 ♗g6 17.c3 ♗c5+ 18.♔e2) 16.♗h3 (16.♗xe8 ♔xe8=) 16...♔f7 17.♗d6 ♗xd6 18.♖xd6 ♖d8 19.♖hd1 ♖xd6 20.♖xd6 ♔e7 21.♖d2 g6⇄;

B) 14.♘g3 ♗g6 15.♗d7+ ♔f7 16.c3 ♗e7 (16...♗c5 17.♘e4 ♗b6⇄; 17.♔e2!?) 17.♘e4 (17.♔e2 ♘b8 18.♗b5 ♖c8 19.♗d6 ♘c6⇄) 17...♘b8 18.♗xb8 (18.♘d6+ ♗xd6 19.♖xd6 ♘xd7 20.♖xd7+ ♔e6 21.♖xg7 ♖hg8⇄) 18...♖axb8 19.♔e2 ♖hd8⇄ or 18.♔e2 ♘xd7 (18...♗xe4!? 19.fxe4 ♘a6) 19.♖xd7 ♔e6 20.♖hd1 ♗e8 21.♖7d2 f5 22.♘d6 ♗c6⇄.

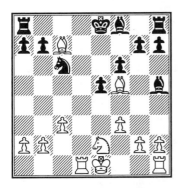

14...♗e7 (14...♗f7!? 15.b3 ♗a3∞ or 15...♗c5∞; 15.♗d7+ ♚e7 16.b3 ♗e6⇄) **15.♗d7+** (15.♘g3 ♗f7 16.♗d7+ ♚f8 17.b3 a5 18.♘f5 a4⇄) **15...♚f8** (15...♚f7!? 16.♘g3 ♗g6 – 14.♘g3 ♗g6 15.♗d7+ ♚f7 16.c3 ♗e7; 16.0-0 ♘b8⇄; 16.f4 e×f4 17.♗×f4 g5⇄) **16.f4** (16.♘g3 ♗f7 – 15.♘g3 ♗f7 16.♗d7+ ♚f8; 16...♗e8!?) **16.e×f4 17.♗×f4 ♗e8 18.0-0 ♖d8 19.♗g4 h5** (19...♗f7 20.♖×d8+ ♗×d8 21.♗d6+ ♗e7 22.♖d1 ♘e5 23.♗×e5 f×e5 24.♖d7 h5 25.♗f3 ♗×a2 26.♖×b7 ♖h6⇄) **20.♗f3** (20.♖×d8 ♘×d8 21.♗f3 ♗c6 22.♖d1 ♗×f3 23.g×f3 ♚e8 24.♗e3 ♘c6±) **20...h4?!** (20...♗f7 21.b3 ♗c5+ 22.♚h1 g5 23.♗c7 ♖×d1 24.♖×d1 ♚e7⇄ or 23.♖×d8+ ♘×d8 24.b4 ♗b6 25.♗d6+ ♚g7⇄) **21.♗e3 b6 22.♖×d8 ♗×d8 23.♘f4 g5 24.♘e6+ ♚e7 25.♘g7** (25.♘×d8!? ♘×d8 26.♖e1! ♚d6 27.♗d4 ♖f8 28.♗×f6±; 26...♚d7 27.♗g4+ ♚d6 28.♖f1 ♖h6 29.♗d4 ♚e7 30.♖e1+ ♚f7 31.♗×f6±; 26... ♘e6 27.♗d5 ♗d7 28.♗d4 ♖f8 29.c4 ♚d6 30.♗c3 ♘c5 31.b3 with better ending for White.) **25...♘e5 26.♘f5+ ♚e6 27.♗e4 ♗c7 28.♘g7+ ♚e7 29.♘f5+ ♚e6 30.♘g7+ ♚e7 31.♘f5+ ♚e6 32.♘g7+ ½-½**

Summary: Earlier we examined the lines 4.d4 ♘f6 5.♘f3 c6 6.♗d3 (Game 13) and 4.d4 ♘f6 5.♘f3 a6 6.♗d3 (Game 25). As we saw in those lines, Black has good chances for equality and counterplay. The same of course holds true if, after **1.e4 d5 2.e×d5 ♛×d5 3.♘c3 ♛d6 4.d4 ♘f6 5.♗d3**, both sides try to transpose back to one of those lines (for example after 5...c6 6.♘f3 or 5...a6 6.♘f3).

After 5...c6 6.♘ge2 ♗g4 the chances are equal. After 5...a6 6.♘ge2 ♘c6 7.♗f4 ♛d8 or 6...♗g4 7.f3 ♗d7 Black is usually able to complete development without any special problems. However Black has other good alternatives (5...g6, 5...♗g4, 5...♘c6) with good chances for equality and counterplay.

Game 34
Boskovic, D. (2465) – Stopa, J. (2410)
Richardson 2007

1.e4 d5 2.e×d5 ♛×d5 3.♘c3 ♛d6 4.d4 ♘f6 5.♗e2

5...c6

Also worth consideration are **A)** 5...g6; **B)** 5...♘c6; **C)** 5...♗f5 and **D)** 5...a6.

A) 5...g6

A1) 6.♘f3 ♝g7 (7.♘e5 – 5.♘f3 g6 6.♘e5 ♝g7 7.♝e2, Game 29) 6.♘b5 ♛b6 7.c4 c6 8.c5 (8.♘c3 ♝g7 9.♘f3 – 5.♘f3 g6 6.♘b5 ♛b6 7.c4 c6 8.♘c3 ♝g7 9.♝e2, Game 29; 6...♛d8!?) 8...♛d8 9.♘c3 ♝g7 ⇄;

A2) 6.♝e3 ♝g7 7.♛d2 c6 (7...0-0!?) 8.0-0-0 (8.♝f4!?) 8...♘d5 (8...0-0!? 9.♝f4 ♛d8) 9.♘xd5 ♛xd5 (9...cxd5!?) 10.c4 ♛d8 11.♔b1 (11.♘f3!? 0-0 12.h4) 11...♘d7 ±, Bittencourt, J. (2303) – Pinto, N., Brasilia 2003;

B) 5...♘c6

B1) 6.d5 (6.♘f3 a6 – 6.♝e2 ♘c6, Game 23) 6...♝b4 7.♘b5 ♛d8 (7...♛c5?! 8.c4; 7...♛b6?! 8.♝e3; 7...♛d7!?) 8.c4 (8.♘f3 a6; 8.♝f3 a6) 8...c6

B1a) 9.♛a4?! e5 10.dxc6 bxc6 11.♘a3 (Gonzalez de la Torre, S. (2420) – Vitor, A. (2294), San Sebastian 2002) 11...♘e4 12.♝e3 ♘c5 13.♝xc5 ♝xc5 14.♘f3 (14.♖d1 ♛f6∓) 14...e4 15.♘d2 ♝xf2+ 16.♔xf2 ♛xd2∓;

B1b) 9.dxc6 bxc6 10.♛xd8+ ♔xd8 11.♘a3 (11.♘d4?! e5) 11...♘e4 (11...♝f5 12.♘f3 e6 13.♝e3 ♝d6 14.0-0 ♔e7 ⇄) 12.♝f4 (12.♝e3 e5 13.♘f3 f6∓, Nevanlinna, R. (2343) – Kekki, P. (2273), Jyvaskyla 2003) 12...g5 13.♖d1+ ♝d7 14.♝e5 ♖g8 15.♝g4 e6 ⇄; 11...e5 12.♘f3 e4 ♝e6 14.♝f4 ♔c8 15.0-0 ♔b7∓;

B2) 6.♘b5 (6.♝e3 ♝f5 7.♘f3 e6 8.0-0 ♝e7 9.♘b5 ♛d7 10.c4 a6 11.♘c3 ⇄, Batsanin, D. (2298) – Vokarev, S. (2462), Novokuznetsk 1999) 6...♛d7 (6...♛d8 7.d5 ♘b4 – 5...♘c6 6.d5 ♝b4

7.♘b5 ♛d8) 7.♝f4 ♘d5 8.♝g3 a6 9.♘a3 e6 10.♘c4 (10.c4?! ♝b4+; 10.♛d2?! ♝b4 11.c3 ♘xc3 12.bxc3 ♝xa3) 10...♝b4+ (Bijaoui, M. (2197) – Hasangatin, R. (2523), Cappelle la Grande 2003) 11.c3 ♘xc3 12.bxc3 ♝xc3+ 13.♔f1 ♝xa1 14.♛xa1 ♘xd4 15.♝d6 ♘f5 16.♝b4 ♛d5 ⇄;

C) 5...♝f5

C1) 6.♘f3 e6 (6...c6 – 6.♝e2 ♝f5, Game 14; 6...a6 – 6.♝e2 ♝f5, Game 23; 6...h6 7.♘b5 ♛b6 8.a4 c6 9.a5 ♛d8 10.♘c3 e6 ⇄, Barbero Rodriguez, N. – Serra Vilaro, A. (1955), Barcelona 2007; 9.♘a3!? ♘bd7 10.♘c4) 7.0-0 7.0-0 ♘c6 (7...c6 – 6.♝e2 ♝f5 7.0-0 e6, Game 14) 8.♘b5 ♛d8 9.d5 exd5 10.♘fd4 ♘xd4 11.♛xd4 ♝d6 (11...c6?! 12.♛e5+; 11...♝e7?! 12.♛f4) 12.♘xd6+ ♛xd6 13.♝f4 ♛b6 14.♛xb6 cxb6 15.♝b5+ ♔d8∞;

C2) 6.♝f3

C2a) 6...c6 7.♘ge2 e6 8.♝f4 ♛d8 (8...♛b4 9.0-0 ♘bd7±) 9.♘g3 ♝g6

C2a1) 10.0-0 ♝d6 (10...♘a6!? 11.♘ge4 ♛b6 12.♘a4 ♛b5 ⇄ or 12.♘xf6+ gxf6 ⇄) 11.♘ce2 ♛c7 12.♛d2 ♘bd7=, Lupulescu, C. (2534) – Burnoiu, N. (2424), Bucharest 2006;

C2a2) 10.h4 h5 (10...h6 11.h5 ♗h7 12.♛d2 (Runic, Z. (2415) – Milanovic, D. (2475), Belgrade 2006) 12...♗d6 13.0-0-0 ♗×f4 14.♛×f4 0-0 15.♘ce4 ♘d5⇄) 11.0-0 ♘bd7 12.♛e2 (12.a4 ♗b4 13.♛e2 ♘g4⇄) 12...♛b6 13.d5 (13.♖ab1 ♛×d4) 13...c×d5 14.♘×d5 ♘×d5 15.♗×d5 ♗e7 16.♗f3 ♗×h4 17.♘×h5 0-0 18.♖ad1 ♖fd8 19.c3 ♗e7 20.♖fe1 ♖ac8⇄;

C2b) 6...♘c6 7.♘ge2 0-0-0 8.0-0 e5 (8...♘×d4!? 9.♘×d4 ♛×d4 10.♛e2 ♛b6 or 10.♛×d4 ♖×d4 11.♗e3 ♖b4) 9.d5 ♘b4 10.♗g5 (Naiditsch, A. (2657) – Dutreeuw, M. (2383), Belgium 2006) 10...♗×c2 11.♛d2 ♗g6 12.♘g3 (12.♖ac1 ♛a6∓) 12...♛a6 13.♗e2 ♛b6∓ or 9.♘g3 ♗g6 10.d×e5 ♘×e5 11.♗g5 (11.♗f4 ♛b4∓) 11...h6 12.♛×d6 ♗×d6 13.♗×f6 ♘×f3+ 14.g×f3 g×f6∓;

D) 5...a6 6.♘f3 – 5.♘f3 a6 6.♗e2, Game 23; 6.♗g5 ♗f5 (6...e6/♘bd7 7.♘f3 – 5.♘f3 a6 6.♗e2 e6/♘bd7 7.♗g5, Game 23) 7.♘f3 or 6...♘c6 7.♘f3 ♗f5 – 5.♘f3 a6 6.♗e2 ♘c6 7.♗g5 ♗f5 8.♛d2, Game 23. White now chooses from 6.♗e3 and 6.♗f3.

D1) 6.♗e3 ♘c6 (6...♗f5 7.♘f3 – 5.♘f3 a6 6.♗e3 ♗f5 7.♗e2, Game 23; 6...♘bd7 7.♘f3 – 5.♘f3 a6 6.♗e2 ♘bd7 7.♗e3, Game 24) 7.♛d2 (7.♘f3 – 5.♘f3 a6 6.♗e2 ♘c6 7.♗e3, Game 23; 7.♗f3 ♗f5 8.♘ge2 0-0-0∓ or 8.g4 ♗g6 9.g5 ♘d7 10.♘ge2 ♘b6 11.♗f4 ♛d7 12.♘e4 (Losada Carrera, F. (2199) – Almeida, O. (2458), Barbera del Valles 2006) 12...0-0-0∓; 10...0-0-0∓) 7...♗f5 8.a3 (8.♘f3 – 6...♘c6 7.♗e3 ♗f5 8.♛d2, Game 23) 8...0-0-0 9.♘f3 e5 (9...e6⇄) 10.d×e5?! (Balogh, M. (2198) – Vojtek, V. (2276), Slovakia

2002) ♛e6 11.♛c1 ♘g4 12.0-0 ♘g×e5∓; 10.0-0-0-0⇄;

D2) 6.♗f3

D2a) 6...h6 7.♘ge2 (7.♛d3 ♘c6 8.♗×c6+ ♛×c6 9.♘f3 ♗e6⇄ or 9...♗g4⇄; 9.d5 ♛d7⇄ or 9...♛b6!⇄) 7...g5 (7...♘c6?! 8.♗f4 ♛d8 9.d5 or 8...e5 9.♗×c6+)

D2a1) 8.♘e4 ♘×e4 9.♗×e4 ♘d7 10.h4 ♘f6 11.♗d3 ♖g8 12.h×g5 h×g5 13.c4 (Cosma, E. (2360) – Foisor, C. (2400), Predeal 2006) 13...e5⇄; 8.g3 ♘c6 9.h4 g4?! (Sasu Ducsoara, A. (2240) – Ionescu Brandis, I. (2338), Targoviste 2001) 10.♗g2 with better chances for White; 9...♖g8⇄

D2a2) 8.♗e3 ♘c6 9.♘g3 g4 10.♗e2 ♗g7 11.♛d2 h4 12.♘ge4 ♘×e4 13.♘×e4 ♛g6⇄, Hernandez, Y. (2225) – Titova Boric, E. (2284), Turin 2006; 10...♗g7 11.♛d2 (Solak, D. (2490) – Nadanian, A. (2413), Saint Vincent 2000) 11...♗d7 12.0-0-0 0-0-0⇄ or 12.0-0 0-0-0⇄;

D2b) 6...♘c6 7.♘ge2 ♗g4 (7...e5 8.♗×c6+ ♛×c6 9.d×e5 ♘g4 10.0-0 ♗c5 (Novikov, M. (2545) – Welling, G. (2370), Biel 2006) 11.♗f4±; 8...b×c6!?

or 7...♗f5 8.♗f4 ♛d7 9.0-0 e6 10.♖e1
0-0-0 11.♗e3 h6 12.a3 g5⇄,
Maljutina, Y. – Chudinovskikh, Z.
(1940), Smolensk 2008; 10.♘g3 0-0-0
11.♘xf5 exf5 12.d5 with pressure,
Roset, C. (2133) – Debray T. (2088),
Lyons 2004 or 10...♘xd4 11.♘xf5 ♘xf5
12.♗xb7 ♖b8 13.♗xa6 ♖xb2 14.♛f3
with the initiative)

D2b1) 8.♘e4 ♘xe4 9.♗xg4 e6
(9...♘f6!? 10.♗f3 e5∓; 10.♗h3 e6
11.0-0 0-0-0 12.c3 ♚b8⇄) 10.0-0
0-0-0 (10...♘f6 11.♗f3 ♗e7 12.♗f4
♛d7±, Bastian, H. (2400) – Vatter, H.
(2307), France. 2004) 11.c3 f5 12.♗f4
♛e7 13.♗f3 e5⇄;

D2b2) 8.♗xg4 ♘xg4 9.d5 (9.♗f4 e5
10.dxe5 ♘gxe5 11.♛xd6 ♗xd6
12.♗xe5 12.♘e4?! (Simonovic, A.
(2408) – Randjelovic, B. (2270),
Herceg Novi 2005) 12...♗b4+ with
better chances for Black) 9...♘ce5
10.♗f4 (10.f3!? ♘f6 11.♛d4) 10...♛b6
11.0-0 (11.♛d4!? ♛xd4 12.♘xd4)
11...g5 12.♗g3 (12.♗xg5 ♖g8 13.♛d2
♛g6∞) 12...♗g7 ½-½, Baramidze, D.
(2338) – Karpatchev, A. (2421), Kiel
2001.

Back to Boskovic – Stopa.

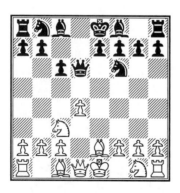

6.♗g5

There are other interesting possibilities
here:

A) 6.♘f3 (6.♘f3 – 5.♘f3 c6 6.♗e2,
Game 14; 6.♗e3 – 5.♗e3 c6 6.♗e2,
Game 35) 6...♘bd7 (6...g6!? 6...♗f5 –
5...♗f5 6.♗f3 c6) 7.♘ge2 e5 8.0-0
♗e7 9.♖e1 0-0 10.♗e3 (Erenska, H.
(2155) – Pytel, B. (2065), Augustow
1975) 10...♖d8 11.♛d2 ♘c5 12.♖d1
♛c7⇄;

B) 6.h3 ♘bd7 (6...♗f5 7.♘f3 – 5.♘f3
c6 6.h3 ♗f5 7.♗e2, Game 15) 7.♘f3
(Hoeing, J. (1993) – Broemmel, R.
(1919), Muensterland 2005) 7...g6
8.♗g5 ♗g7 9.♛d2 0-0 10.♗f4 (10.0-0
♘b6 11.♗f4 ♛d8 12.♗e5 ♗e6⇄;
10.0-0-0 ♘b6 11.♗f4 ♛b4 12.a3
♛a5⇄) 10...♛b4 11.0-0 (11.♖b1
♘b6) 11...♛xb2 12.a4 ♛b4 13.a5 e6∞
or 12...♛b6 13.a5 ♛d8∞.

6...♗f5 (6...h6!?) **7.♛d2**

7.♘f3, is also possible:

A) 7...h6 8.♗h4 ♘bd7 (8...♛b4!?)
9.♛d2 (9.0-0 e6 10.♗g3 ♛b4 11.♛d2
♛xb2 12.♖ab1 ♛xc2 13.♛xc2 ♗xc2
14.♖xb7 ♘e4∞ or 11.♖b1 ♗e7
12.♗c7 ♗d8 13.a3 ♛e7 14.♗g3
♗b6⇄) 9...e6 10.0-0-0 (10.h3 ♛c7
11.g4 ♗g6 12.♗g3 ♗d6 13.♗xd6
♛xd6 14.0-0-0 0-0-0=, Jeske, M. –
Chandler, P. (2238), Frankfurt 2001)
10...♗e7 (10...♛c7!?) 11.h3 (11.♗g3
♛b4 12.♗d3 ♛a⇄) 11...♛c7 12.g4
♗d6 13.♗g3 (13.♚b1 ♘e4 14.♘xe4
♗xe4⇄) 13...♗xg3 14.fxg3 ♘e4
15.♛e3 ♘xc3 16.♛xc3 ♗e4 17.♖hg1
0-0-0⇄, Tortosa, H. – Pott, B., Internet
2003;

B) 7...♘bd7 8.♛d2 and now:

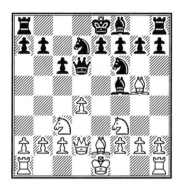

B1) 8...♘b6?! 9.♘e5 e6 10.g4 ♘e4 11.♘xe4 ♗xe4 12.f3 ♗g6 13.♗f4 ♛d8 14.c4 with pressure, Obodchuk, A. (2423) – Kuntz, P. (2200), Bled 2002 or 8...e5?! 9.0-0-0 e4 (9...0-0-0 10.dxe5 ♛xd2+ 11.♖xd2 ±) 10.♗f4 ♛b4 11.♘e5 ♘d5 (11...♘xe5 12.dxe5 ♘g4 13.♗g5 ♛a5 14.♘b5 ±) 12.a3 ♛a5 13.♘c4 ±, Roca Diaz, M. (2070) – Serra Vilaro, A., Sant Boi 1997;

B2) 8...e6?! 9.♘h4 (9.0-0 ♛c7 10.♘h4 ♗g6 ±, Nijboer, F. (2584) – Tiviakov, S. (2669), Hilversum 2006; 9...0-0-0!? 10.♘h4 ♘c5 ⇄ or 9.0-0 ♛c7 10.♘e5 ♗b4 ⇄, Ackermann, D. (2146) – Lorenz, K., Wuerttemberg, 1999) 9...♗g6 (9...♗e4 10.♗f4 ♛b4 11.a3) 10.♗f4 ♛b4 11.♘xg6 hxg6 12.a3 ♛a5 (12...♛xb2 13.0-0 ♛b6 14.♖fb1 ♛a5 15.♖xb7 ±) 13.0-0 ♘d5 (13...0-0-0 14.♘b5 ♛xd2 15.♘xa7#; 13...♗e7 14.♖fe1 0-0 15.h3 with better chances for White) 14.♘xd5 ♛xd2 15.♘c7+ ♚d8 16.♘xe6+ fxe6 17.♗xd2 ±;

B3) 8...h6 (8...0-0-0!? 9.♗f4 ♛b4 10.♘g5?! e5 11.♘xf7 exf4 12.♘xh8 ♗e6 with better chances for Black or 11.dxe5 ♘xe5 12.♛c1 ♗d6 13.♗xe5 ♗xe5 14.♘xf7 ♗f4∓; 10.0-0-0 h6

11.a3 ♛a5 12.♚b1 e6 ⇄) 9.♗f4 (9.♗h4 – 7.♘f3 h6 8.♗h4 ♘bd7 9.♛d2) 9...♛b4 10.0-0-0 e6 11.♗c7 ♘e4 (11...♘b6!? 12.a3 ♛a5 ⇄ or 12.♘e5 ♘a4 ⇄) 12.♘xe4 ♗xe4 13.♛e3 ♘f6 14.♗d3 ♗xd3 15.♛xd3 ♗e7 16.♖hg1 0-0 17.g4 (17.♗e5 ♘g4) c5 18.a3 ♛a4 19.dxc5 ♗xc5 20.g5 ⇄ or 18...c4 19.axb4 cxd3 20.♖xd3 ♘d5 ⇄.

Let's return now to Boskovic – Stopa.

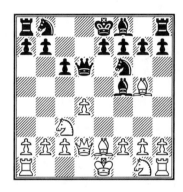

7...e6

7...♘bd7 8.♘f3 – 7.♘f3 ♘bd7 8.♛d2.

8.♗f3

Also worth consideration are:

A) 8.♘f3 h6 9.♗f4 ♛b4 (9...♛d8 10.0-0 ♗d6 11.♘e5 0-0 ⇄) 10.a3 ♛xb2 (10...♛b6?! 11.♘e5 ♘bd7 12.♘c4) 11.♖a2 ♛b6 12.0-0 ∞;

B) 8.♗f4 ♛b4 9.0-0-0 ♛a5 10.♗d3 ♘bd7 11.♗xf5 ♛xf5 12.a3 (12.♘ge2 ♗b4 13.f3 ♘d5 ⇄ or 13.a3 ♘e4 ⇄) 12...0-0-0 13.♘f3 ♘b6 ⇄; 10.a3 ♗xa3 (10...♘bd7!?) 11.bxa3 ♛xa3+ 12.♚b1 ♘d5 13.♘xd5 ♛b3+ with perpetual check or 8.0-0-0 ♘d5 (8...♘bd7!?)

9.♞×d5 ♛×d5 10.♔b1 ♞a6 11.♝f3 (11.♞f3? ♞b4; 11.a3? ♝×a3) 11...♛b5 ⇄; 9.a3 h6 10.♝e3 (10.♝h4? ♞×c3 11.♛×c3 ♛f4+) 10...♞d7 ⇄; 9.♞f3 h6 10.♝h4 ♞d7 11.♝g3 ♛b4 ⇄.

8...♞bd7

Also possible is 8...♞a6!? 9.♝×f6?! (9.a3 0-0-0 10.♞ge2 ♛c7 11.0-0-0 h6 12.♝f4 ♝d6 ⇄) 9...g×f6 10.♞ge2 (10.♝e4 ♝g6) 10...0-0-0 11.0-0-0 ♞b4 12.a3 h5 (12...♞×c2 13.♞e4 ♝×e4 14.♝×e4 ♞×a3 15.b×a3 ♛×a3+ 16.♔b1 ±) 13.♞e4 ♝×e4 14.♝×e4 f5 (14...♝h6 15.f4 ⇄) 15.♛×b4 ♛×b4 16.a×b4 f×e4 ∓.

9.♞ge2 h6 10.♝f4 ♛b4

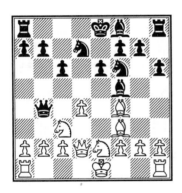

11.0-0?!

11.♞g3 ♝g6 12.0-0 0-0-0 ⇄; 12...♝d6!?; 12...♝e7!?.

11...g5 12.♝c7 ♞d5?!

Here 12...g4, looking for counterplay on the kingside, was necessary:

A) 13.♞g3 g×f3 14.♞×f5 f×g2 (14...♖g8?! 15.g3) 15.♖fe1 ♖g8 (15...♞d5?! 16.a3 ♛c4 17.♞e4)

16.♞×h6?! (16.a3) 16...♝×h6 17.♛×h6 ♛×b2 18.♛d2 (18.d5 ♛×c3 19.d×e6 f×e6 20.♖×e6+ ♔f7 21.♖ae1 ♖ae8 ∓) 18...♞b6 19.♖ab1 ♛a3 20.♝×b6 a×b6 21.♖×b6 0-0-0 ∓;

B) 13.a3 ♛c4 (13...♛e7?! 14.♞g3 g×f3 15.♞×f5 e×f5 16.♖fe1 ♞e4 17.♛f4 ♛g5 18.♛×g5 h×g5 19.♞×e4 f×e4 20.♖×e4+ ♝e7 21.♝d6 ±) 14.♞g3 g×f3 15.♞×f5 f×g2 (15...♖g8!?; 15...e×f5 16.♖fe1+ ♝e7 17.♝d6 ♞g8 18.b3 ♛a6 19.♝×e7 ♞×e7 20.♛e3 0-0-0 21.♛×e7 ∞) 16.♖fe1 ♖g8 17.♞e3 ♛a6 ∓.

13.a3 ♛e7?!

Preferable was 13...♛c4:

A) 14.♞g3 (14.b3 ♛a6 15.♞×d5 c×d5 16.♞g3 ♝g6 17.♝a5 ♝d6 ⇄ or 15.♝g3 0-0-0 16.♞×d5 e×d5 ⇄) 14...♞×c7 15.♝e2 ♝d3! ⇄;

B) 14.♝a5 ♝g7 (14...g4!?) 15.b3 (15.♖ad1 ♛a6 16.♞e4 0-0 17.♞2g3 ♝g6 ⇄) 15...♛a6 16.♞×d5 c×d5 17.♞g3 ♝g6 (17...♝×c2?! 18.♝e2 b5 19.a4)

B1) 18.♝e2 ♛c6 19.♞h5?! (19.c4 0-0 ⇄) 19...♝×h5 20.♝×h5 b6 21.♝b4 a5 22.♛c3 (22.♝c3 ♖c8) 22...♛×c3 23.♝×c3 ♖c8 ∓;

B2) 18.♞h5 (18.♝b4 ♛b6 19.♖ad1 a5 20.♝c3 0-0 ⇄) 18...0-0 19.♞×g7 ♔×g7 ±.

14.♝×d5 e×d5

14...c×d5 15.♞g3 ♝g6 16.♞×d5 ±.

15.♞g3 ♝e6

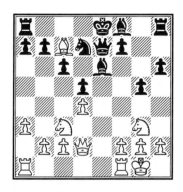

16.♖fe1?! (16.♞h5! ♞b6 17.♗e5
♞c4 18.♛e2 ♞×e5 19.♛×e5 f6
20.♞×f6+; 16...♖g8 17.f4 f5 18.♖ae1
♖g6 19.g4±; 17...g×f4 18.♖ae1 ♖c8
19.♗a5 b6 20.♗b4 c5 21.d×c5 b×c5
22.♗a5 with strong pressure or
19.♗×f4 ♛h4 20.♛e2?! ♖g4; 20.♞g3
♗e7 21.♛d3 ♖g6 22.b4 with better
chances for White.) **16...♞b6 17.♗e5**
(17.♗×b6!? a×b6 18.♖e3 0-0-0
19.♖ae1) **17...♞c4 18.♛d3**
(18.♛e2!? ♖g8 19.♞h5 or 19.♞a4)
18...♞×e5 (18...♞×b2?! 19.♛e2 ♖g8
20.♞b5) **19.♖×e5** (19.d×e5 0-0-0
20.♞ce2 c5?! 21.b4; 20...♛c7
21.♞d4 ♗g7 22.♛e3 ♖he8 23.♞h5
♗h8 24.♞f6 ♗×f6 25.e×f6 ♗d7∓)
19...0-0-0 20.♞a4 ♛c7 (20...b6!?
21.♞f5 ♛d7) **21.♞f5 ♖g8**
(21...♚b8 22.g3 ♗×f5 23.♖×f5 ♖e8
24.c4 d×c4 25.♛×c4 ♖e7 26.♖c1
♗g7 27.d5 ♛d7 28.g4 c×d5 29.♖×d5
♛c8=; 25...b5? 26.♖×b5+; 26...b5?!
27.♛b3 ♛d7 28.♖fc5) **22.♖ae1 b6**
23.♞c3 ♚b7 24.♞d1 (24.b4!? g4
25.f4 g×f3 26.♛×f3 ♖g5 27.♖f1⇄)
24...♖g6 25.♞de3 (25.b4!? ♗d7
26.b5; 25.a4 ♗b4 26.c3 ♗×f5
27.♖×f5 ♗d6 28.g3±; 25...♗c8
26.♞e7 ♖e6 27.♞×c8 ♖×e5 28.♖×e5
♖×c8⇄; 25...♗×f5 26.♖×f5 ♖e6
27.♖×e6 f×e6 28.♖e5 ♛f7 29.a5⇄;

28.♖f6 e5 29.d×e5 ♗g7?! 30.♖e6;
29... ♛×e5 30.♖f7+ ♚b8 31.♛a6?!
♛e1+ 32.♛f1 ♛e6 33.♖f3 ♛e4∓;
31.g3 ♗c5 32.♛h7 ♛e1+ 33.♚g2
♛e4+ 34.♛×e4 d×e4 35.♞c3 e3
36.f×e3 ♗×e3=) **25...♗c8 26.♞f1**
♖e6 27.♞1g3 ♖de8 28.♖5e3 ♛f4
½-½

Summary: After **1.e4 d5 2.e×d5
♛×d5 3.♞c3 ♛d6 4.d4 ♞f6
5.♗e2**, Black has counterplay and
good equalizing chances. In previous
games we examined 4.d4 ♞f6 5.♞f3 c6
6.♗e2 (Game 14) and 4.d4 ♞f6 5.♞f3
a6 6.♗e2 (Games 23, 24). That is also
the case after **5.♗e2** if there is a transposition (for example by 5...a6 6.♞f3
or 5...c6 6.♞f3). After 5...a6 6.♗e3
(6.♗f3) or 5...c6 6.♗g5 (6.♗f3, 6.h3)
Black is usually able to complete development without any particular problems. However, Black has other good
alternatives (5...g6, 5...♗f5 and
5...♞c6) with counterplay.

Game 35
Murariu, A. (2500) – Vajda, A. (2455)
Predeal 2007

**1.e4 d5 2.e×d5 ♛×d5 3.♞c3 ♛d6
4.d4 ♞f6 5.♗e3**

5...c6

We now look at: **A)** 5...♘c6; **B)** 5...♗g4 and **C)** 5...a6.

A) 5...♘c6?! 6.♘b5 (6.♘f3 a6 – Game 21; 6.♗c4 – Game 9) 6...♕d8 7.d5 ♘b4 (7...♘e5?! 8.♕d4 ♘g6 9.♕c5; 7...♘xd5?! 8.♕xd5) 8.c4 c6 9.dxc6 bxc6 (9...♘xc6 10.♕xd8+ ♚xd8 11.♘f3 h6 12.0-0-0+ ♗d7 13.♗d3±; 9...♕a5 10.♗d2 bxc6 11.a3 cxb5 12.axb4±) 10.♕xd8+ ♚xd8 11.0-0-0+ ♗d7 12.♘c3 with the better game for White or 8...e6 9.♗f4 ♘a6 10.d6 cxd6 11.♘xd6+ ♗xd6 12.♕xd6 ♕xd6 (12...♗d7 13.♘f3) 13.♗xd6 ♘e4 14.♗a3 with a better ending for White;

B) 5...♗g4 6.♗e2 (6.♘f3 a6 – Game 22) 6...♗xe2 7.♕xe2 c6 8.♘f3 ♘bd7 9.0-0 (9.0-0-0!?) 9...e6 10.♖fd1 ♗e7 11.♗g5 0-0 12.♘e5 ♘d5 (12...♕c7!?) 13.♘c4 (13.♘e4 ♕c7 14.♗xe7 ♘xe7±, Lindfeldt, J. (2293) – Jensen, J. (2113), Esbjerg 2005) 13...♕b8 (13...♕c7?! 14.♘xd5 cxd5 15.♗xe7 ♖fe8 16.♘e3) 14.♗xe7 ♘xe7 15.a4 ♕c7±;

C) 5...a6

C1) 6.♗d3 (6.♘f3 – Games 21, 22; 6.♗e2 ♘c6 7.♘f3 – Game 23 or 6...♘bd7 7.♘f3 – Game 24) 6...♘c6 7.♕d2 (7.♘f3 – Game 25) 7...♘b4 (7...e5!? 8.♘f3 exd4 9.♘xd4 ♘xd4 10.♗xd4 ♗e6 11.0-0-0 0-0-0=) 8.♘ge2 (8.♘f3 ♘xd3+ 9.♕xd3 g6!?) 8...g6 9.0-0-0 ♘xd3+ 10.♕xd3 ♗g7 11.♗f4 ♕b6⇄, Ciuksyte, D. (2255) – Xu Yuanyuan (2431), Moscow 2001;

C2) 6.h3 b5 (6...♘c6 7.♘f3 – 5.♘f3 a6 6.♗e3 ♘c6 7.h3, Game 21) 7.♗e2 ♗b7 8.♗f3 (Jakaityte, R. – Berdiugina, E.

(2166), Peniscola 2002) 8...♘c6 9.a4 b4 10.♘e4 ♘xe4 11.♗xe4 g6 12.♘e2 ♗g7 13.0-0 0-0⇄ or 7.♗d3 ♗b7 8.♘f3 ♘bd7 9.0-0 e6 10.♘g5 c5 11.♘ce4 (11.♘ge4 ♕c6⇄) 11...♕b6 12.c3 h6 13.dxc5 ♕c6⇄;

C3) 6.♕d2

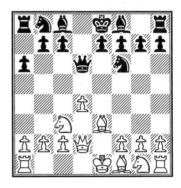

Now Black has the following possibilities: **C3a)** 6...♗g4; **C3b)** 6...♘c6 and **C3c)** 6...b5.

C3a) 6...♗g4?! (6...♗f5 7.♘f3 ♘c6 – Game 22) 7.♗f4 (7.♘f3 – Game 22; 7.h3 ♗h5 8.g4 ♗g6 9.♗g2 ♘c6 10.a3 0-0-0⇄, Alavi, S. (2485) – Saud, M. (2160), Dubai 2007) 7...♕b6 (7...♕d8 8.h3 ♗h5 9.g4 ♗g6 10.0-0-0 ♘c6 11.♗g2 e6 12.d5) 8.f3 ♗f5 9.g4 ♗g6 10.0-0-0 e6 11.d5 ♘xd5 12.♘xd5 exd5 13.h4 h5 14.♕xd5 ♗e7 15.♗d3±;

C3b) 6...♘c6 7.0-0-0 (7.♘f3 – Game 21)

C3b1) 7...♗f5 8.♗f4 (8.♘f3 – Game 21) 8...♕d7 9.d5 (9.♘f3 – 5.♗g5 a6 6.♕d2 ♗f5 7.♘f3 ♘c6 8.♗f4 ♕d7 9.0-0-0, Game 36) 9...♘b4 (the situation on the board has become very tactical, with better chances for White) 10.a3 (10.♘f3 ♗xc2 11.♘e5?! (Krug, S.

(2114) – Jirovsky, P. (2348), Bayern 2003; 11...♕f5 12.♖e1 ♘f×d5 13.♗c4 ♕×f4∓; 11.♖e1 ♗f5 12.♘e5 ♕d8 13.♗c4 b5∞) 10...♘×c2

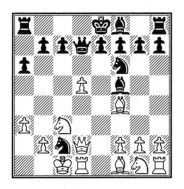

11.♘f3 (11.♗d3 ♘d4 12.♗c4 ♘b5∞, Llanos, G. – Bianchi, G. (2370), Pehuaj 1983; 11...♘a1!?)

C3b1a) 11...0-0-0 12.♘e5 ♘a1 (12...♕e8 13.♗d3 ♗×d3 14.♕×d3 ♘a1 15.♕c4±) 13.♗c4 b5 14.♘×d7 b×c4 15.♘c5 e5 16.♕e2 (16.♗×e5? ♗×c5∓) 16...♗×c5 17.b4±;

C3b1b) 11...♘a1 (11...♘h5 12.♘e5 ♕c8 13.g4) 12.♗c4 (12.♘d4?! c5) 12...b5 (12...♗c2 13.♘d4±) 13.♗a2 ♗c2 14.♘d4 ♗×d1 15.♖×d1±;

C3b2) 7...♘b4 8.a3 8.♗f4 (8.♗c4 ♗f5 9.♗b3 e6⇄; 8...♘bd5 9.♘×d5 ♘×d5 10.♗c4 (Pert, R. (2424) – Jones, G. (2442), Douglas 2005) 10...♗e6=) 8...♕b6 9.a3 (9.♘f3 ♗f5 10.♗c4 e6⇄) 9...♘bd5 10.♗c4 ♗e6⇄;

C3c) 6...b5

C3c1) 7.♗f4 (7.♘f3 ♗b7 – Game 22; 7.♗e2 ♗b7 8.♘f3 – Game 22 or 8.♗f3 ♘c6±) 7...♕b6 8.♗e2 (8.♘f3 ♗b7 – Game 22) 8...♗b7 9.♗f3

♘c6 (9...♘bd7 10.0-0-0 (Jansa, V. (2455) – Hettler, W., Hamburg 1992) 10...e6 11.d5 0-0-0 12.d×e6 f×e6 13.♗×b7+ ♔×b7⇄) 10.♘ge2 0-0-0 11.d5 ♘b4 12.a4 ♘f×d5 13.0-0 e6 (13...♘×f4?! 14.♗×b7+) 14.a×b5 a×b5∓;

C3c2) 7.♗d3 ♗b7 8.f3 (8.♘f3 – Game 22) 8...♘bd7 9.♘ge2 e6 10.♘e4 (10.0-0 c5 11.♖ad1 ♗e7?! 12.d×c5 ♕c7 13.b4±, Haslinger, S. (2410) – Hanley, C. (2322), Halifax 2003; 11...♕b6±) 10...♘×e4 11.f×e4 c5 12.c3 ♗e7 13.0-0 0-0 14.♖ad1 c×d4 15.c×d4⇄, Wedberg, T. (2530) – Fries Nielsen, J. (2444), Stockholm 2003.

We return now to Murariu – Vajda.

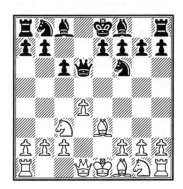

6.♕d2

Other possibilities are:

A) 6.♗c4 (6.♗d3 ♘a6 7.a3 g6±) 6...♗f5 (6...♗g4 7.♘f3 – 5.♘f3 c6 6.♗c4 ♗g4 7.♗e3, Game 1; 7.f3!?; 7.♘ge2!?) 7.♘ge2 e6 8.0-0 ♘bd7 9.♗f4 ♕b4 10.♗b3 (10.♗d3 ♗×d3 11.♕×d3 ♗e7 12.a3 ♕b6 13.a4 a5⇄; 12.♗c7 ♘b6⇄) 110...♕a5 11.♘g3 ♗g6 12.♖e1 (Jorgensen, E. (2459) – Stephan, J. (2347), Internet 2002)

12...0-0-0 13.♕f3 ♘b6 14.h4 h5
15.♖ad1 ♗e7=;

B) 6.♘f3 ♗f5 (6...♗g4 7.h3 ♗×f3
8.♕×f3 – 5.♘f3 ♗g4 6.h3 ♗×f3 7.♕×f3
c6 8.♗e3, Game 12 or 7...♘h5 – 5.♘f3
♗g4 6.♗e3 c6 7.h3 ♗h5, Game 10)
7.♘e5 (7.♕d2 – 5.♗e3 c6 6.♕d2 ♗f5
7.♘f3; 7.♗c4 – 5.♘f3 c6 6.♗c4 ♗g4
7.♗e3, Game 1; 7.♗d3 ♗×d3 8.♕×d3
♘bd7 9.0-0-0 e6 10.♖he1 ♗e7±,
Gitelman, O. – Melts, M., corr. 1989)
7...♘bd7 8.♘c4 ♕c7 9.♕d2 ♘b6
10.♗f4 ♕d8 11.0-0-0 e6 12.f3 ♘×c4
13.♗×c4 ♕a5 (13...b5!?) 14.♕e2 0-0-0
⇄, Kogan, A. (2565) – Vysochin, S.
(2520), Kemer 2007.

6...♗f5

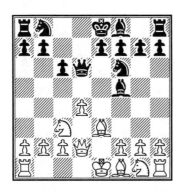

A) 6...♗g4?! 7.f3 ♗f5 8.♘ge2 ♘bd7
9.0-0-0 e6 (9...0-0-0 10.g4 ♗g6 11.h4
h5 12.♘f4 ♗h7 13.g5 ♘e8 14.d5±)
10.g4 ♗g6 11.h4 h5 12.♘f4 ♗h7 13.g5
♘d5 14.♘c×d5 c×d5 15.g6±, Kryakvin,
D. (2535) – Petrov, A. (2190),
Belorechensk 2007;

B) 6...♗e6 7.♘ge2 (7.♘f3!? ♘bd7
8.♗f4) 7...♗c4 (7...♘bd7!? 8.♗f4 ♕b4
9.0-0-0 0-0-0=) 8.0-0-0 (8.♗f4 ♕b4
9.b3 ♗d5 10.a3 ♕a5 11.♕b6±) 8...e6
9.f3 (9.♗f3 ♕b4 10.a3 ♕a5 ⇄) 9...♕c7

10.♔b1 ♘bd7 11.♗f4 ♕a5 12.♘c1
♗×f1 13.♖h×f1 ♗b4 14.♘b3 ♕a6
15.♗g5 0-0 16.a3 ♗×c3 17.♕×c3
♘d5=, Carlsson, P. (2433) – Cicak, S.
(2506), Malmo 2006.

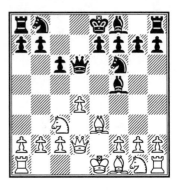

7.f3

Other interesting possibilities are **A)**
7.♗f4; **B)** 7.♘ge2; **C)** 7.♘f3 and **D)**
7.0-0-0.

A) 7.♗f4 ♕d8 8.♘f3 e6 9.a3 (9.0-0-0
♗b4) 9...♗d6 10.♘e5 (10.0-0-0 0-0-0±)
10...♕c7 (10...♘bd7!? 11.0-0-0 ♕c7)
11.♗e2 ♘bd7 12.♕e3 a6 13.♖c1?!
(13.0-0-0=) 13...c5 14.♘d3 ♗×d3
(14...c×d4!? 15.♕×d4 e5 16.♕e3 0-0
17.♗g3 ♗×a3) 15.♗×d6 ♕×d6
16.d×c5 ♘×c5 17.c×d3∓, Novotny,
M. (2235) – Kantorik, M. (2360),
Litomysl 2006;

B) 7.♘ge2 e6 8.♘g3 ♗g6 9.h4 h6
10.h5 ♗h7 11.♗d3 ♗×d3 12.♕×d3±,
Pavlovic, M. (2481) – Cicak, S. (2506),
Zuerich 2000; 7...♘bd7 8.♗f4 ♕b4
9.0-0-0 0-0-0 10.♘g3± or 8.♘g3 ♗g6
9.h4 h5 10.0-0-0 0-0-0±;

C) 7.♘f3 ♘bd7 (7...e6 8.♘e5 ♕d8 9.a3
♘bd7 10.♘×d7 ♕×d7=, Baramidze, D.
(2585) – Muse, M. (2440), Germany

2006; 8.♘h4 ♗g6 9.♘×g6 h×g6 10.♗f4±) 8.0-0-0 e6

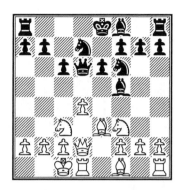

C1) 9.♗f4 ♛b4 10.♗c7 (10.♔b1 ♗e7 11.♘e5 ♘×e5 12.♗×e5 0-0-0⇄, Martin del Campo, R. (2407) – Garcia Correa, J. (2194), Merida 2003; 10.a3 ♛a5 11.♘h4 ♗g6 12.♘×g6 h×g6⇄) 10...♘b6 11.a3 (11.♘h4 ♘e4 12.♘×e4 ♗×e4⇄) 11...♛a5 12.♗d3?! (12.♘h4 ♘fd5⇄) 13...♗×a3! 13.b×a3 (13.♗×f5 ♗×b2+) 13...♛×a3+ 14.♔b1 ♘fd5 15.♘×d5 ♘×d5 16.c4 (16.♗×f5 ♘c3+ 17.♛×c3 ♛×c3∓) 16...♛b3+ 17.♔c1 (17.♔a1 ♘c3 18.♗d6 ♗×d3∓) 17...♘b4 18.♗×f5 ♘a2+ 19.♛×a2 ♛×a2 20.♗d3 ♛×f2∓;

C2) 9.♘h4 ♗g6 10.f3 ♛c7 11.♘×g6 h×g6 12.♘e4 0-0-0 (12...♘d5 13.♗f2 b5 (Enders, P. (2456) – Cicak, S. (2534), Germany 2005) 14.♗g3 ♛b7 15.♔b1 ♘7b6 16.b3 0-0-0±; 13...♛f4!?) 13.♗d3 (13.c3 ♘d5 14.♗f2 ♗e7 15.♗g3 e5 16.h4 f6⇄) 13...♘×e4 14.f×e4 e5⇄;

D) 7.0-0-0 e6 8.f3 (8.♘f3 ♛c7 9.♘h4 ♗g6 10.♘×g6 h×g6±; 8.♗f4 ♛d8 9.a3 ♗d6 10.♘f3±)

D1) 8...♛c7?! (8...♘bd7 9.♗f4 ♛b4⇄; 9.♘ge2 ♘b6±) 9.g4 ♗g6 10.♘ge2 h6?!

(10...♘a6!? 11.♘f4 ♘b4⇄) 11.♘f4 ♗h7 12.h4 ♘bd7 13.g5 ♘d5 (Parligras, M. (2510) – Burnoiu, N. (2415), Predeal 2006) 14.♘f×d5 c×d5 15.g×h6 g×h6 16.♗×h6 ♗×h6 17.♛×h6 0-0-0 18.♛e3±;

D2) 8...♘d5 9.g4 (9.♘×d5 ♛×d5 10.c4 ♛d7 11.♘e2 ♘a6 12.a3 0-0-0±; 9...c×d5!?) 9...♗g6 10.♘×d5 c×d5 (10...♛×d5!?) 11.♘e2 ♘c6 12.♘f4 ♖c8 13.♔b1 (Fedorchuk, S. (2577) – Cicak, S. (2530), Salou 2005) 13...♛b4 14.♛×b4 ♘×b4 15.♘×g6 h×g6 16.c3 ♘c6 17.h4±.

Back to Murariu – Vajda.

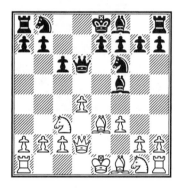

We had same position in the line 6...♗g4 7.f3 ♗f5 but now it is Black to move.

7...h5 8.♘ge2

After 8.0-0-0, Black has fine game; for example, 8...♘a6 9.♗×a6 (9.♗c4 ♘b4⇄; 9.♗f4 ♛b4⇄; 9.a3 ♘c7 10.♗f4 ♛d7 11.♗c4 e6 12.♘ge2 ♘cd5⇄;) 9...b×a6 10.♗f4 ♛b4 11.a3 ♛a5 (11...♛c4?! 12.b3) 12.♘ge2 e6 13.♘g3 ♗g6⇄.

8...h4 9.a3

9.0-0-0 e6 10.g4 h×g3 11.♘×g3 ♗g6
12.♘ce4 (12.♗f4 ♕d8 13.♘ge4 ♘bd7
14.♘d6+ ♗×d6 15.♗×d6 ♘b6 16.♗e5
♕e7⇄) 12...♕d8 13.♘×f6+ g×f6
14.♘e4 ♘d7 15.♗f4 ♕b6 16.♘d6+
♗×d6 17.♗×d6 0-0-0⇄ or 9...♘bd7
10.♗f4 ♕b4 11.♗c7 ♘b6 12.a3 ♕a5
13.g4 (13.♘f4 ♖c8 14.♗×b6 a×b6⇄)
13...♗d7 (13...h×g3!? 14.♘×g3 ♗g6)
14.h3 (14.♘f4!?) 14...♖c8 15.♗h2 ♘c4
16.♕d3 b5⇄.

9...g6 (9...♘bd7!?) **10.♖g1** (10.0-0-0!?)

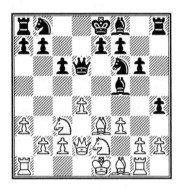

10...♘d5

Other interesting possibilities are:

A) 10...♘a6 11.g4 h×g3 12.♘×g3 ♗e6
13.♗f4 ♕d7 14.0-0-0 ♘d5 15.♘×d5
♕×d5 16.♘e4 ♗g7 17.♘g5 (17.♘c3
♕×f3 18.♗e2 ♕h3∞) 17...♕a2 18.♘c3
♗d5⇄;

B) 10...♘bd7 11.♗f4 e5 12.d×e5
♕×d2+ 13.♗×d2 (13.♔×d2 ♘h5
14.♖e1?! ♘×f4 15.♗×f4 ♗h6 16.g3 0-
0-0 17.♗d3 ♖he8∓; 14.♗e3 ♘×e5
15.♘d4 0-0 16.♔e1 ♗d7 17.♔f2⇄)
13...♘×e5 14.♗f4 ♘fd7 (14...♗d6?!
15.0-0-0 ♔e7 16.♗g5) 15.♘d4 ♗c5
16.0-0-0 h3⇄.

11.♘×d5 c×d5 12.♗f4 ♕d7

12...♕b6 13.0-0-0 ♘c6 14.♘c3 0-0-0
15.g4 (15.♗d3 ♗×d3 16.♕×d3 ♗g7
17.♘e2 ♗f6 18.♖ge1 e6⇄) 15...h×g3
16.h×g3 e5 17.♗g5 (17.♗×e5? ♘×e5
18.d×e5 ♕×g1; 17.♘a4?! ♕×d4
18.♕×d4 e×d4; 17.♗e3?! e×d4 18.♘a4
♕c7 19.♗f4 ♗d6) 17...♘×d4
(17...♖d6!?) 18.♗×d8 ♕×d8⇄. **13.g4
h×g3 14.h×g3 ♘c6 15.g4 ♗e6
16.♘c1** (Preferable perhaps was
16.0-0-0; for example, 16...♗g7
17.♔b1 0-0-0 18.♕e3 ♘a5?! 19.♘c3
♘c4 20.♗×c4 d×c4 21.d5 +− or 19...a6
20.b4 ♘c6 21.♘a4+−; 19...♖df8
20.♗b5 ♘c6 21.♘a4 b6 22.♖d3 ♔b7
23.♖c3 ♖c8 24.♕d3±; 22...♔d8
23.♖c3 ♗×d4 24.♕d3 ♗×c3 25.♕×c3
d4 26.♕×c6 ♕×c6 27.♗×c6±; 18...f6
19.♘c3 ♗f7 20.♘a4 e5⇄; 17...♕d8!?)
**16...♗g7 17.♘b3 ♕d8 18.♗b5
♕b6 19.♗×c6+ ♕×c6 20.0-0-0 b6
21.♖h1?!** (21.♖ge1 a5 22.♔b1 ♖c8=)
21...♔d7 (After 21...♖×h1!?
22.♖×h1 ♔d7 Black has better
chances: **A)** 23.♖e1 ♖c8 24.♔b1
(24.♗e5?! ♗h6) 24...♕c4 25.♗e5 f6
26.♗g3 (26.♗f4 g5 27.♗e3 ♗f7
28.♘c1 ♗g6∓) 26...f5 27.g5 f4
28.♕×f4 ♕×c2+ 29.♔a2 ♗f5∓; **B)**
23.♖h7 ♖h8 24.♖×h8 ♗×h8 25.♕h2
♗g7 26.♕h7 ♗f6 27.c3 ♕c4 28.♔c2
a5 29.♕h2 (29.♘d2 ♕c8 30.♔b1
♕h8∓) 29...♕c8 30.♕e2 a4 31.♘c1
♕c4 32.♕e3 ♗h4 33.♗g5 ♗×g5
34.♕×g5 ♕f1 35.♕e3 g5 36.♘d3
(36.♕d3 ♕×d3+ 37.♘×d3 f6∓)
36...f6 37.♘b4 ♕g2+ 38.♔b1 ♕h1+
39.♔a2 ♗g8∓; **C)** 23.♗e5 f6 24.♗g3
(24.♗f4 g5 25.♗g3 ♗f7 26.♖h7 ♖g8
27.♕d3 ♕c4 28.♕×c4 d×c4 29.♘d2
♔c6∓) 24...g5 25.♖h7 ♖g8 26.♔b1
♗f7 27.♘c1 ♗g6 28.♖h2 ♖h8
29.♖×h8 ♗×h8 30.♘d3 a5 31.f4 g×f4
32.♕×f4 ♕c4 33.b3 ♕c8 34.♔b2 ♗g7

35.a4 ♗e4∓) **22.♖he1 a5 23.♔b1**
♖ae8?! (23...♖ac8⇄) **24.♖e3 ♖c8**
25.♖de1 ♕a4?! (25...♕c4!? 26.♗e5
♗xe5 27.♖xe5 ♖h3) **26.♗e5 ♗xe5**
27.♖xe5 ♖c6?! (27...♕c6?! 28.♘c1
♔d8 29.♘d3 ♕c4 30.♘f4±; 27...♕c4!?
28.f4 ♗xg4 29.♖xe7+ ♔d6 30.♖xf7
♗f5 31.♖f6+ ♔d7∞) **28.f4 f6**
(28...♗xg4 29.♖xe7+ ♔d8 30.♖xf7
♗f5 31.♕g2±; 29...♔c8 30.♖xf7 ♗e6
31.♖f6±; 30... ♗f5 31.♕e2 ♖c4
32.♘d2 ♕xc2+ 33.♔a1±) **29.♖5e3**
♕c4 (29...♗xg4 30.♖xe7+ ♔d8
31.♕g2+−) **30.♖c3 ♕b5 31.a4**
♕xa4 32.♕e2 ♖h7 33.♖e3 1-0

Summary: After **1.e4 d5 2.exd5**
♕xd5 3.♘c3 ♕d6 4.d4 ♘f6
5.♗e3, Black has a variety of possible
responses – 5...♘c6, 5...♗g4, 5...a6 and
5...c6. The deployment of the ♗c1 with
the idea of quick development of the
queenside heavy pieces deserves serious attention. It allows White to de-
fer development of the kingside minor pieces until Black has decided on
the position of the ♗c8 (b7, e6, f5 or
g4), after which White can post the
♗f1 and ♘g1 to better advantage. For
example, if Black plays the ♗c8 to e6,
f5 or g4, White tries to exchange a
knight for this bishop and then decides
on a game plan.

5...a6 or 5...c6 is Black's best choice.
After the more usual 5...a6, White has
a number of choices, such as 6.♘f3
(Games 21, 22) or 6.♗e2 ♘c6 7.♘f3
(Game 23), while if 6...♘bd7 7.♘f3 see
Game 24. In that game we examined
moves 6.♗d3, 6.h3 and 6.♕d2. The
move 6.♕d2 looks more dangerous for
Black but after 6...b5 Black has good
chances with counterplay.

After **5...c6** White can play different
lines with 6.♘f3; for example, 6.♘f3
♗g4 7.♗c4 (Game 1), 7.♗d3 (Game
13), 7.♗e2 (Game 14) or 6...♗f5 7.♗c4
(Game 29). In Game 35, we examined
6.♗e2, 6.♗c4 and 6.♕d2. The move
6.♕d2 looks dangerous, but after
6...♗f5, Black has sufficient chances
for equality with counterplay.

Game 36
Ehlvest, J. (2625) –
Program Rybka 2.3.2a
Potomac 2007

1.e4 d5 2.exd5 ♕xd5 3.♘c3 ♕d6
4.d4 ♘f6 5.♗g5

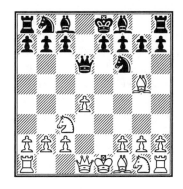

5...h6

Now we look at **A)** 5...♘c6; **(B)**
5...♗g4; **C)** 5...c6 and **D)** 5...a6.

A) 5...♘c6 6.♘b5 (6.d5 ♘b4 7.♗b5+
♗d7 8.♗xd7+ ♕xd7 9.♗xf6 gxf6 10.a3
♘a6 11.♕f3±, Khaetsky, R. (2375) –
Miljutin, O. (2165), Ilichevsk 2007)
6...♕d8 7.♗f4?! (7.d5!?) 7...♘d5 8.♕f3
♘cb4 9.c3 ♘xf4 10.cxb4 (10.♕xf4 ♘d5
11.♕e5 c6 12.♗c4 f6 13.♕e4 ♔f7∓)
10...a6 11.♕xf4 axb5 12.♗xb5+ c6
13.♗c4 e6⹁; 9.c4 a6 10.cxd5 axb5
11.♗xb5+ ♗d7 12.♗xd7+ ♕xd7

13.♕b3 ♕×d5 14.♕×d5 ♘×d5∓ or
9.♗c4 ♗e6 10.♗×d5 ♗×d5 11.♕e2
♖c8∓;

B) 5...♗g4 6.f3 (6.♕d2!? ♘c6 7.h3
Plaskett, J. ; 6.♗e2!? ♗×e2 7.♕×e2 or
6...♗f5 7.♘f3) 6...♗f5 (6...♗d7!?)
7.♕d2?! (7.♗c4 e6 8.♘ge2 ♗e7 9.0-0
0-0= McGeary, W.) 7...♘c6 8.♘ge2
♖d8 9.♕d2⇄; 8.♘b5?! ♕b4+) 7...♘c6

B1) 8.♘b5 ♕e6+ 9.♔f2 (9.♘e2 0-0-0∓;
9.♕e2 ♕d7∓) 9...0-0-0 10.g4 (10.c3
♕d7 11.♗c4 a6 12.♘a3 e5∓,
Gullaksen, E. (2354) – Guerrero, C.
(2073), Catalan Bay 2003) 10...♗g6
11.♗f4 ♘d5 12.c4 ♘×f4 13.♕×f4 ♕d7
14.d5 ♘b4∓;

B2) 8.0-0-0 (9.♘ge2 ♘×d4; 8.g4 ♗e6
9.0-0-0 0-0-0 10.♘ge2 h5 11.g×h5⇄)
8...0-0-0 9.♘ge2 e5 10.d×e5 (10.♘g3
♘×d4 11.♘×f5 ♗×f5 12.♗c4 ♕×d2+
13.♖×d2 ♖×d2 14.♔×d2 ♘d6, and
Black had an extra pawn in Landa, K.
(2542) – Hasangatin, R. (2458), St.
Petersburg 1999; 10.♗e3 ♕b4 11.a3
♕a5∓) 10...♕×e5 11.♕f4 ♗d6∓;

C) 5...c6

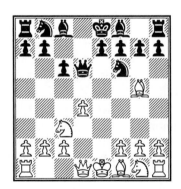

C1) 6.♗c4 (6.♗e2 – Game 34) 6...♗g4
(6...♗f5 7.♘ge2 ♘bd7 8.♕d2 ♘b6

9.♗b3 e6 10.0-0 ♗e7 11.♘g3 ♗g6
12.♖fe1 0-0=, Kalinin, A. – Melts, M.,
corr. 1990) 7.f3 (7.♘ge2 ♗×e2 8.♕×e2
♘bd7 9.0-0 e6 10.♖fd1 ♗e7±,
Schneider, H. (2213) – Alber, H. (2356),
Germany 2004; 8...♕×d4!? 9.♗e3 ♕d8
10.0-0 ♘bd7 11.♖ad1 e6 12.f4 ♕a5∞)
7...♗f5 8.♘ge2 e6 9.♕d2 ♗e7 10.h4
h6 11.♗f4 ♕b4 12.♗b3 ♘bd7 13.g4
♗g6 14.♗c7 ♘b6 15.♘f4 ♘fd5 16.a3
♕a5 17.♗×d5 e×d5 18.♘×g6 f×g6
19.♕d3 0-0⇄, Turishchev, A. –
Gubnitsky, S., Donetsk, 1968;

C2) 6.♕d2 ♗f5 7.0-0-0 (7.♗e2 – Game
34; 7.♘ge2 ♘bd7 8.f3 e5 9.0-0-0
(Tkachiev, V. (2630) – Gerard, N.
(2215) Paris 1997) 9...0-0-0 10.d×e5
♕×d2+ 11.♖×d2 ♘×e5±) 7...e6
(7...♘bd7 8.♘f3 h6 9.♗f4 ♕b4 10.d5
♘×d5 11.♘×d5 ♕×d2+ 12.♖×d2 c×d5
13.♘d4⊒, Smirin, I. (2677) – Fercec,
N. (2458), Pula 2000)

C2a) 8.♘ge2 e6 9.♘g3 ♗g6 10.h4 h6
(10...h5!?) 11.♗f4 ♕b4 12.h5 ♗h7
13.a3 ♕a5 14.♔b1 (14.♗c4? ♗×a3)
14...0-0-0 15.♘b5 ♕a4 16.♘c3 ♕a5
17.♗d3±, Stocek, J. (2555) – Konopka,
M. (2441), Slovakia 2002;

C2b) 8.♘f3 ♘bd7

C2b1) 9.a3 ♕c7 10.♘e5 ♗e7 11.f4 h6
12.♗×f6 (Svidler, P. (2723) – Cicak, S.
(2530), Rethymnon 2003) 12...g×f6
13.g4 (13.♘×d7 0-0-0 14.♘×f6 ♗×f6⊒)
13...♗h7 14.♘×d7 0-0-0 15.♘×f6 ♗×f6
16.♕e3 ♕d7⊒;

C2b2) 9.♔b1 ♕c7 10.♘h4 ♗g6
11.♘×g6 h×g6 12.g3 0-0-0 (12...♗b4!?)
13.♗g2 ♘b6 14.♘e4 ♘×e4 15.♗×e4
♗e7 16.♗×e7 ♕×e7=, Tirard, H. (2450)
– Nevednichy, V. (2575), La Fere 2006;

9.♘h4 ♗g6 10.♘×g6 h×g6 11.g3 (11.♗f4 ♕b4 12.a3 ♕a5 13.♗e2±) 11...♕c7 12.a3 ♘b6 13.♗g2 ♗e7±, Smirin, I. (2662) – Nevednichy, V. (2582), Turin 2006;

D) 5...a6

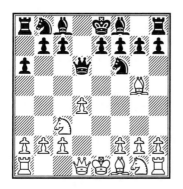

There are two main continuations here: **D1)** 6.♘f3 and **D2)** 6.♕d2.

D1) 6.♘f3 After this move we examine **D1a)** 6...♘c6; **D1b)** 6...b5; **D1c)** 6...♗g4 and **D1d)** 6...♘bd7.

D1a) 6...♘c6 7.d5 ♘e5 8.♗e2 (8.♕d4!? ♘×f3+ 9.g×f3 e5 10.♕c4) 8...♘×f3+ (8...h6!? 9.♗e3 ♗f5) 9.♗×f3 ♗f5 10.0-0 (10.♕e2!?) 10...h6 11.♗h4 0-0-0 12.♕e2 ♕d7 13.♗g3 g5?! (Collins, S. (2409) – McPhillips, K. (2210), Bunratty 2006; 13...♘b8!?) 14.♕e5 ♗g7 15.♘a4 ♔b8 16.♘b6 ♕d6 17.♕×f5 ♕×b6 18.c4 with strong pressure;

D1b) 6...b5 7.♗d3 ♗b7 (7...h6!? 8.♗e3 ♗b7 9.0-0 ♘bd7) 8.♕e2 ♘bd7

D1b1) 9.0-0-0 e6 10.♔b1 (10.♘e5!? ♕×d4!? 11.♗×b5; 10...♗×g2 11.♖he1 ⩲; 10...♗e7 11.♗f4) 10...♗e7 11.♘e5 0-0 12.f4 ∞, Peptan, C. (2471) – Galliamova, A. (2489), Istanbul 2003;

D1b2) 9.0-0 e6 10.♖ad1 (10.a4!? b4 11.♘e4) 10...♗e7 11.♖fe1 c5?! (11...h6!?; 11...0-0?! 12.d5 ♘×d5 13.♗×h7+ ♔×h7 14.♘×d5 ♗×d5 15.♗×e7 ♕×e7 16.♖×d5 with the initiative) 12.♘e4 ♕c7 13.♗×f6 g×f6 14.♘g3±, Zontakh, A. (2545) – Olenin, N. (2405), Sochi 2007; 12.♗e4!? ♘×e4 (12...♗×e4 13.♘×e4 ♕d5 14.♘c3) 13.♘×e4 ♗×e4 14.♕×e4;

D1c1) 8.♗e2 ♘bd7 (8...e6!?) 9.0-0 e6 (9...0-0-0!?) 10.♖e1 ♗e7 (10...0-0-0 11.♕d2 ♕b6±) 11.♘e5 (11.d5!? e×d5 12.♘h4) 11...♗×e2 12.♕×e2 ♘b6?! (Dougherty, M. (2213) – Gonzalez, R. (2419), USA 2004) 13.♕f3 c6 14.♘e4 ♕d8 15.♘c5±; 12...0-0 13.♖ad1 ♖ad8±;

D1c2) 8.♕d2 ♘bd7 9.♗e2 e6 10.0-0-0 0-0-0 (10...♗g6!? 11.♘e5 0-0-0) 11.♘e5 (11.g4 ♗g6 12.♕e3 ♕b6 13.♘e5 ♘×e5 14.d×e5 ♕×e3+ 15.♗×e3 ♖×d1+ 16.♖×d1 ♘d7 17.f4 h5=, Dragojlovic, A. (2400) – Milanovic, D. (2515), Bizovac 2007) 11...♘×e5 12.d×e5 ♕×d2+ 13.♖×d2 ♖×d2 14.♗×h5 ♖×f2 15.e×f6 ♖×g2 16.♗e3 (16.♘e4!? g×f6 17.♗×f6 ♗h6+ 18.♔d1) 16...g×f6 17.♗×f7 ♔d7 18.♗h5 f5±;

D1d) 6...♘bd7

After 6...♘bd7, White has played **D1d1)** 7.♗e2; **D1d2)** 7.♗d3 and **D1d3)** 7.♕d2

D1d1) 7.♗e2 b5 (7...h6!? 8.♗e3 e6 9.♕d2 b5 10.♗f4 ♕b6 11.0-0 ♗d6 12.♘e5 ♗b7 ⇄) 8.0-0 ♗b7 9.♕c1 (9.♕d2 b4 10.♘d1 ♘e4 11.♕e3 c5 ⇄) 9...e6 10.♗f4 ♕b6 11.a4 b4 12.a5 (Lengyel, B. (2302) – Brustkern, J. (2258), Budapest 2005) 12...♕a7 13.♘a4 ♘d5 14.♗g3 ♗d6 15.♕d2 0-0=;

D1d2) 7.♗d3 c5 (7...h6!?) 8.d5 b5 (8...♘xd5 9.♘xd5 ♕xd5 10.0-0 ⊒) 9.0-0 ♗b7 (9...c4?! 10.♗f5 ♘c5 11.♗xc8 ♖xc8 12.♖e1 ♖d8 13.♘e5 g6 14.♕f3 ♗g7 15.♘c6±, Lutz, C. (2587) – Kurajica, B. (2530), Pula 2000) 10.♖e1 b4 11.♘e4 ♕xd5 12.c4 ♕c6∞, Lutz, C. (2644) – Mellado Trivino, J. (2447), France 2002);

D1d3) 7.♕d2 b5 (7...e6?! 8.♗f4)

D1d3a) 8.a3 (8.a4 b4 9.♘a2 e6 10.♗f4 ♕b6 11.♗e2 ♗b7 12.0-0 ♗e7=, MChess Pro 5.0 – Bronstein, D. (2455), Maastricht 1996) 8...♗b7 9.0-0-0 e6 10.♘e5 ♘xe5 11.dxe5 ♕xd2+ 12.♖xd2 ♘d5=, Martin Alvarez, I. (2047) – Diaz Nunez, A. (2176), Ortigueira 2004;

D1d3b) 8.♗d3 ♗b7

D1d3b1) 9.♕e2 (this is the same position as in the line 6.♘f3 b5 7.♗d3 ♗b7 8.♕e2 ♘bd7 but with Black to move) 9...e6 10.0-0-0 (10.0-0 – 6.♗e3 b5 7.♗d3 ♗b7 8.0-0 ♘bd7 9.♕e2 e6 10.♗g5, Game 22) 10...♗e7 11.♖he1 ♘d5 (11...0-0 12.d5∞; 11...h6!?) 12.♘e4 (12.♗xe7 ♘xc3 13.♗xd6 ♘xe2+ 14.♖xe2 cxd6=) 12...♗xg5+ 13.♘fxg5 ♕e7 14.♕d2 h6 15.♘f3 (Van

den Doel, E. (2528) – Kurajica, B. (2541), Bugojno 1999) 15...0-0=;

D1d3b2) 9.0-0-0 e6 (9...b4 10.♘a4?! ♗c6 11.♗f4 ♕e6; 10.♘e2 e6±) 10.♖he1 (10.♘e5!?; 10.♗f4 ♕b6 – 6,♗e3 b5 7.♗d3 ♗b7 8.♕d2 ♘bd7 9.0-0-0 e6 10.♗f4 ♕b6, Game 22) b4 (10...♗e7 11.♘e5 (Grabarczyk, B. (2436) – Dziuba, M. (2454), Lubniewice 2002) 11...0-0 ⇄) 11.♘e2 ♗e7 12.♘g3 ♗xf3 (12...0-0 13.♔b1 ♖fe8 ⇄) 13.gxf3 ♕d5 (13...♕xd4? 14.♖xe6) 14.♔b1 ♕xf3∞;

D1d3c) 8.♗f4 ♕b6 9.a3 ♗b7 10.♗e2 e6 11.0-0 c5 (11...♗d6 12.♗xd6 cxd6=) 12.dxc5 ♗xc5 13.♖ad1 0-0 14.♗d6 ♗xd6 15.♕xd6 ♖ac8 16.♕xb6 ½-½, Dgebuadze, A. (2544) – Mellado Trivino, J. (2447), France 2002;

D2) 6.♕d2

D2a) 6...e5?! 7.dxe5 ♕xe5+ 8.♗e2 ♗b4 9.♘f3 ♗xc3 10.bxc3 ♕e7 11.0-0 ♘e4 12.♕d4 f6 (12...♘xg5 13.♕xg7 ♘xf3+ 14.♗xf3 ♖f8 15.♖fe1 ♗e6 16.♗xb7 ♖a7 17.♗d5 with a strong initiative) 13.♖fe1 ♘c6 14.♕d5 ♘c5 (14...♘xg5 15.♘xg5±) 15.♘d4 ♘e5 16.♗h5+ (16...♔f8 17.♖xe5 +– or 16...g6 17.♗xf6+–) 1-0, Ehlvest, J.

268

(2640) – Handoko, E. (2440), Dubai 2007;

D2b) 6...♘bd7?! 7.♗f4 ♛b6 8.0-0-0 (8.d5 e6 9.d×e6 f×e6 10.0-0-0 ♗b4 11.♛e1 0-0 12.♗c4 ♘d5⇄, Khachiyan, M. (2475) – Braunlich, T. (2195), Stillwater 2007; 8...♘c5!?) 8...e6 9.a3 (9.d5 ♗b4 10.d×e6 f×e6±, Fercec, N. (2433) – Sulava, N. (2526), Pula 2001; 9...♘c5!?) 9...♗e7 (9...c5 10.♘f3 c×d4 11.♘×d4 ♘c5 12.♗c4 ♗d7 13.♖he1±) 10.♘f3 0-0 11.♗c4 ♖d8 12.♖he1 with pressure;

D2c) 6...b5 7.f3 (7.♗f4 – Game 35) 7...♗b7 8.0-0-0 ♘bd7 (8...b4!? 9.♘a4?! ♘bd7 10.♗f4 ♛c6 11.b3 e6∓; 9.♘e4 ♘×e4 10.f×e4 ♗×e4 11.♘f3 ♛d5 12.♔b1 ♘c6⇄) 9.♗f4 ♛b6 10.♘h3 (10.♔b1 (Bednarek, S. (2321) – Sergeev, V. (2458), Warsaw 2005) 10...b4 11.♘ce2 e6 12.♘h3 ♗e7∓ or 11.♘a4 ♛a5 12.b3 ♘d5∓) 10...e6 11.♗d3 ♗b4 (11...♗e7!?) 12.a3 ♗e7 13.♔b1 b4 14.a×b4 ♗×b4 15.♘g5 0-0⇄;

D2d) 6...♗f5 7.0-0-0 (9.a3 e6 10.0-0-0 ♗e7 11.d5 e×d5 12.♘×d5 ♘×d5 13.♛×d5 ♛×d5 14.♖×d5±, Blanco, H. (2405) – Aguero, L. (2260), Havana 2007; 10...♗d6!? 11.♗c4 0-0 12.d5 e×d5 13.♘×d5 ♘e4 14.♛e3 ♖e8 15.♖he1 ♗c5⇄)

D2d1) 7...e6 8.♘f3 ♘bd7 9.♗d3 (9.♘h4 ♗g6 10.♘×g6 h×g6 11.♗f4 ♛b6 12.d5 e5 13.♗g3 0-0-0=) 9...♗×d3 10.♛×d3 ♗e7 11.♖he1 c6 (11...0-0-0 12.d5!?) 12.g3 b5 13.♗f4 ♛b4 14.♘g5 (Le Roux, J. (2496) – Marcelin, C. (2481), Besancon 2006) 14...♘b6 15.♔b1 0-0 16.a3 ♛c4 17.♛×c4 ♘×c4=;

D2d2) 7...♘c6 8.♗c4 (8.♗f4 ♛d7 9.♗d3 0-0-0 10.♘ge2 ♗×d3 11.♛×d3 e6⇄, Swathi, G. (2350) – MacKinnon, K. (2025), USA 2008) 8...0-0-0 9.♘f3 ♗g6 10.♖he1 ♛b4 11.♗b3 (11.a3!? ♛a5 12.♔b1 e6 13.d5) 11...h6 (11...e6 12.a3 ♛a5 13.♛e2? ♗×a3∓) 12.♗f4 e6=, Colovic, A. (2414) – Drazic, S. (2483), Mogliano Veneto 2000.

Back to Ehlvest – Rybka

6.♗h4

After 6.♗e3, we have a position from Game 35 with Black's pawn on h6.

6...♛b6 (6...♘c6!?) **7.♖b1**

A) 7.♗c4 (7.a3?! ♘c6 8.d5 ♛×b2 9.♘ge2 ♘d8 10.♗g3 c6 11.♗c7 ♘×d5 12.♗a5 ♗g4∓ or 12.♖a2 ♛×a2 13.♘×a2 ♘×c7∓) 7...♛×b2 8.♘ge2 ♛b4 9.♛d3 ♘c6 10.♖b1 ♗f5 11.♛×f5 ♛×c4 12.♗×f6 (12.♖×b7?! ♘×d4) 12...e×f6 13.0-0 b6∞;

B) 7.♛d2 ♛×b2 (7...♗f5 8.0-0-0 ♘bd7 9.♘f3 e6 10.♗d3 ♗×d3 11.♛×d3 0-0-0 ⇄) 8.♖b1 ♛a3 9.♘f3 e6 10.♖b3 ♛a5 11.♗×f6 (11.♗c4?! c6 12.0-0 ♘bd7 13.♖e1 ♗b4) 11...g×f6 12.♗d3 c6 13.0-0 ♘d7 14.a3 (14.♖e1 ♗b4) 14...♖g8 15.♖e1 ♛h5 16.♛e3∞.

7...♘a6

7...♘c6!? 8.d5 ♘d4 9.♗d3 (9.♘f3 ♘xf3+ 10.♛xf3 ♗g4 11.♛e3 0-0-0 12.♛xb6 axb6 13.♗c4 ♗f5 14.♖c1 ⇄) 9...♗d7 10.♘ge2 0-0-0 ⇄.

8.♗c4

8.♘f3!? ♗g4 (8...♗e6 9.b4±; 8...♗f5 9.♗d3 ♗xd3 10.♛xd3 ♘b4 11.♛e2 0-0-0 12.0-0±) 9.♗c4 0-0-0 10.0-0 ⇄.

8...♗f5

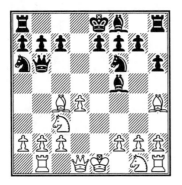

9.♘f3 (9.a3!? 0-0-0 10.♘f3 e5 11.d5±; 10...g5 11.♗g3 g4 12.♘e5 ♖xd4 13.♛e2 ♗g7 14.0-0 ⯬; 13...♘e4 14.0-0 ♘xg3 15.hxg3 ⯬) **9...♘b4 10.♗b3** (10.♖c1 0-0-0 11.0-0 e6 12.♛e2 ⇄) **10...0-0-0 11.0-0 e6 12.♛e2 g5 13.♗g3 ♘c6** (13...♗e7 14.♘e5 ♖h7=) **14.♘b5?!** (14.♖bd1!?) **14...a6 15.♗xc7** (15.♘xc7 ♘e4 16.d5 g4 17.♘e5 ♘d4 18.♛c4 ♗c5∓ or 17.♘a8 ♛a7 18.dxc6 gxf3 19.♛c4 b5−+; 19.cxb7+ ♚xb7 20.♛xf3 ♚xa8 21.♖fe1 ♛b7∓; 19.♛xf3 ♛xa8 20.♖bd1 bxc6∓) **15...♛xb5 16.c4 ♛b4**

17.♗xd8 ♘xd8 18.♖bc1 ♗g7∓ 19.♖fd1 ♘d7 20.c5 ♘c6 21.d5 exd5 22.♖xd5 ♗e6 23.♖d6 ♘xc5 24.♘e5 ♗xe5 25.♖xc6+ bxc6 26.♛xe5 ♖e8 27.g3 ♗d7 0-1

Summary: The primary objective of **5.♗g5**, after **1.e4 d5 2.exd5 ♛xd5 3.♘c3 ♛d6 4.d4 ♘f6**, is similar to that of 5.♗e3 in Game 35: early deployment of the ♗c1 to expedite development of the queenside heavy pieces. In some lines, thanks to ♗g5, White has tactical possibilities on the d8-h4 diagonal. However, 5.♗g5 is less flexible and less dangerous to Black than 5.♗e3 because a) after 5.♗e3 White has an extra defender for the d-pawn, and this is important in some lines; b) 5.♗e3 rules out certain possibilities for Black that 5.♗g5 does not; for example, 5.♗e3 ♗f5? 6.♛f3 or 5...♘bd7? 6.♘b5; and c) in some lines it is important to keep the g5-square open for the maneuver ♘f3-g5-e4.

After **5.♗g5**, Black has several possible continuations leading to good chances, 5...c6, 5...a6 and 5...h6. In the game Ehlvest vs. Rybka, after **5...h6**, Black equalized without much trouble and began to put pressure on White's d-pawn. Ehlvest reacted ambitiously with 14.♘b5 a6 15.♗xc7, giving up bishop and knight for rook and pawn while ripping open the cover around Black's king. In his post-game comments, he felt that White's chances should not be worse, but Black's pieces were well-placed and there did not seem to be much that White could do.

Part V 3.♘c3 ♕d6 4.d4

Game 37 covers lines after **1.e4 d5 2.e×d5 ♕×d5 3.♘c3 ♕d6 4.d4** without 4...♘f6.

In this section we will examine 4...g6, 4...a6 and 4...c6 (4...♘c6? 5.♘b5; 4...♗f5? 5.♕f3).

I think that 4...g6, 4...a6 and 4...c6, if they do not transpose to lines discussed earlier, are less important than 4...♘f6. These three possibilities are certainly playable, but do not really challenge White in the way 4...♘f6 does.

Game 37
Volokitin, A. (2650) – Kurajica, B. (2540)
Torrelavega 2007

1.e4 d5 2.e×d5 ♕×d5 3.♘c3 ♕d6 4.d4 g6

Let's also examine **A)** 4...a6 and **B)** 4...c6.

A) 4...a6 5.♘f3

A1) 5...♘c6?! (5...♗g4?! 6.h3 ♗×f3 7.♕×f3 ♘c6 8.♗e3 ♘f6 9.0-0-0 or 6...♗h5 7.♗e3 ♘f6 8.g4 ♗g6 9.♘e5 – Game 22; 5...♘f6 – Games 18-28) 6.d5

♘e5 7.♘×e5 (7.♗f4 ♘d3+) 7...♕×e5+ 8.♗e2 ♘f6 (8...e6 9.0-0 ♘f6 10.♖e1 ♕d6 11.♗f3 ♗e7 12.♕d4 with strong pressure) 9.0-0 ♕d6 (9...♗f5 10.g4 ♗d7 11.f4 ♕d6 12.g5±) 10.♗e3 ♗f5 11.♕d4±;

A2) 5...b5?! 6.♘e4 ♕d5 7.♗d3 ♘f6 8.♕e2 ♗b7 9.♘c5 ♗c6 10.a4 b×a4 11.c4 ♕d6 12.0-0 e6 13.b4 (13.♘×a4!? ♗e7 14.♖e1 0-0 15.d5 ♗×a4 16.♖×a4 ♘bd7 17.b4±) 13...♗e7 14.d5 e×d5 15.♖e1 d×c4 16.♗×c4 ♘d5 17.♗g5 f6 18.♗×d5⩲, Kovacevic, A. (2550) – Kurajica,B. (2550), Zadar 2007 or 6.♗d3!? ♘c6 7.a4 b4 8.♘e4 ♕d5 9.0-0 ♘f6 10.♖e1 ♗g4 11.h3 ♗h5 12.c4 (12.♘×f6+ g×f6 13.♗e4±) 12...b×c3 13.b×c3± or 10...♗f5 11.c4 b×c3 12.♘×c3 ♕d7 13.♗c4 ♗g4 (13...g6 14.♘g5 e6 15.d5±) 14.h3 ♗h5 15.♗f4±;

A3) 5...♗f5 6.♗d3 ♗×d3 7.♕×d3 ♘c6 (7...♘f6?! 8.♘e4 ♘×e4 9.♕×e4 ♘c6 10.♗f4 ♕b4+ 11.c3 ♕×b2 12.0-0; 8...♕c6 10.d5 ♕g6 11.♕×g6 h×g6 12.♗f4 or 8...♕e6 9.♘fg5 ♕b6 10.♗e3 ♕×b2 11.0-0) 8.0-0 ♘f6± or 8.♘e4 ♕g6±;

B) 4...c6

5.♘f3 (after 5.♘ge2 Black's best is probably 5...♘f6, tranposing to Game 32) 5...♗g4 (5...♘f6 – Games 13-17; 5...♗f5 6.♗d3 ♗×d3 7.♕×d3 ♘f6 – Game 29) 6.h3 (6.♗e3!?)

B1) 6...♗h5 7.g4 (7.♗e3!?) 7...♗g6 8.♘e5 (8.h4!?) 8...♘d7 (8...♘f6 – Game 11; 8...e6 9.h4 f6 10.♘c4±) 9.♘c4 ♕c7 (9...♕e6+ 10.♗e3 ♘gf6 11.f4±) 10.♕f3 f6 11.♗f4 e5 12.♗g3 0-0-0 13.0-0-0 with strong pressure;

B2) 6...♗×f3 7.♕×f3

B2a) 7...e6 (7...♘f6 – Game 12) 8.♗f4 ♕d8 (8...♕×d4?! 9.♘b5 ♗b4+ 10.c3 c×b5 11.♗×b5+ ♔f8 12.♗c7) 9.0-0-0 ♘f6 10.g4 (10.♗e2!? ♗d6 11.♗e5 0-0 12.♕g3) 10...♗e7 11.♔b1 ♘bd7 (Rasmussen, A. (2385) – Hansen, S. (2560), Aalborg 2007) 12.g5 ♘d5 13.♘×d5 c×d5 14.h4 with better chances for White;

B2b) 7...♕×d4 8.♗e3 (8.♘b5!? ♕d8 9.♗f4 ♘a6 10.♗c4 ♘f6 11.♖d1 ♕b6 12.♗e3 or 8...♕b6 9.♗e3 ♕a5+ 10.b4 ♕d8 11.♖d1 ♘d7 12.♗f4 c×b5 13.♗×b5 ♘gf6 14.♕×b7 with a strong initiative) 8...♕b4?! 9.0-0-0 ♘f6 10.♘b5; 8...♕d8 (Grabarczyk, B. (2439) – Cicak, S. (2527), Germany 2001) 9.♗c4 e6 10.0-0 ♘f6 11.♖fd1 ♘bd7 12.a3 ♗e7 13.♕g3⩲.

We return now to Volokitin – Kurajica.

As a result of GM Bojan Kurajica's successful use of 4...g6, this is not an uncommon position in modern chess praxis. This position may arise other ways; for example, 1.e4 g6 2.d4 d5 3.e×d5 ♕×d5 4.♘c3 ♕d6 or 1.d4 d5 2.e4 g6 3.e×d5 ♕×d5 4.♘c3 ♕d6.

5.♘ge2

Let's also take a look at **A)** 5.♗e3; **B)** 5.♘b5; **C)** 5.♗c4 and **D)** 5.♘f3.

A) 5.♗e3 ♗g7 (5...♘f6!?)

A1) 6.♕d2

A1a) 6...c6 7.0-0-0 (7.♘f3!? ♘f6 8.♗f4) 7...♘f6 8.♗f4 ♕b4 (8...♕d8 9.♗h6 0-0?! 10.h4 ♕a5 11.h5! with a strong attack as in the famous game Fischer, R. – Robatsch, K., Varna 1962: 3...♕d8 4.d4 g6 5.♗f4 ♗g7 6.♕d2 ♘f6 7.0-0-0 c6 8.♗h6 0-0?! 9.h4 ♕a5 10.h5! g×h5 11.♗d3 ♘bd7 12.♘ge2 ♖d8 13.g4 ♘f8 14.g×h5 ♘e6 15.♖dg1 ♔h8 16.♗×g7+ ♘×g7 17.♕h6 ♖g8 18.♖g5 ♕d8 19.♖hg1 ♘f5 20.♗×f5 1-0; 9...♗×h6 10.♕×h6 ♗e6 11.♘f3 ♕d6 12.♘g5 ♘bd7 13.♘×e6 ♕×e6±) 9.a3 ♕a5 10.♔b1 0-0 11.♗c4 ♗f5 12.♘f3 (12.♘d5 ♗×c2+!) 12...♘bd7 13.♖he1 ♕d8±;

A1b) 6...♗f5 (6...♘f6!? 7.0-0-0 0-0) 7.♘ge2 (Popovic, D. (2189) – Radovic, M. (2075), Internet 2004) 7...♘f6 8.♗f4 (8.0-0-0!?) 8...♕b6 9.♘a4 ♕c6 10.♘ec3 ♘e4⇄ or 9.0-0-0 ♘c6 10.♘g3 0-0-0⇄;

A2) 6.♘f3

A2a) 6...♘f6 7.♕d2 (7.h3 0-0 8.♗c4 a6 9.a4 ♘c6 10.♕d2 ♗f5 11.0-0 ♘e4⇄, Saez, N. (1980) – Fillon, D. (2160), Condom 2005; 9...♕b4!? 10.♗b3 ♘c6) 7...0-0 8.0-0-0 ♗f5 9.♗f4 (9.♘b5 ♕d8) 9...♕b6 10.♗d3 ♗g4⇄;

A2b) 6...a6 7.♕d2 ♘f6 8.♗f4

A2b1) 8...♕d8?! 9.0-0-0 0-0 10.♗h6 ♗×h6 (10...♘c6 11.♗×g7 ♔×g7 12.d5) 11.♕×h6 ♗g4 12.h4 ♕d6 13.h5 ♘×h5 14.♘g5 ♕f4+ (14...♘f6 15.♘ge4+–) 15.♖d2 ♘f6 16.♘d5+– or 13...g×h5 14.♗d3 ♘c6 15.♘g5 ♗f5 16.♔b1± or 13...♗×h5 14.♘g5 ♖d8 (14...♕f4+ 15.♖d2 ♘bd7 16.♗d3 ♖fd8 17.♖×h5 +–) 15.♖d2 ♘bd7 16.f3 ♘f8 17.g4±;

A2b2) 8...♕b6 (8...♕b4?! 9.♗×c7± ♕×b2? 10.♖b1 ♕a3 11.♖b3+–) 9.♗c4 (9.0-0-0 0-0 10.♘e5 ♘bd7 11.♘c4 ♕a7 12.♘e3 c6⇄) 9...0-0 10.0-0 (Kovalevskaya, E. (2457) – Kurajica, B. (2533), Solin 2005) 10...♘c6 11.d5 (11.♘a4 ♕b4 12.♕×b4 ♘×b4 13.♗b3 ♗g4 14.♘e5 ♗f5⇄ or 13.c3 ♘bd5 14.♗e5⇄) 11...♘c5 12.d×c6 ♕×c4 13.♘e5 ♕c5 14.b4 ♕b6 15.♘a4 (15.♗e3 ♕×b4 16.♖ab1 ♕d6 with better chances for Black) 15...♕b5 16.♘c3 ♕b6=;

B) 5.♘b5

B1) 5...♕d8 6.♗f4 ♘a6 7.♗c4 c6 (7...♘f6!?) 8.♕f3 (8.♘c3 ♗g7 9.♘f3 ♘f6 10.0-0±) 8...♘f6 (8...c×b5?! 9.♗×f7+ ♔×f7 10.♗c7+ ♗f5 11.♗×d8) 9.♕b3 e6 10.♗e5 ♗e7 11.♘c3 0-0 12.♘f3 b5 13.♗e2 b4 14.♗×f6 (14.♘a4 ♘c7±) 14...♗×f6 15.♘e4 ♗e7 16.0-0 ♕d5 17.♕e3 f6±;

B2) 5...♕b6 6.♗f4 ♘a6 7.♕e2 (7.a4 c6 8.♗c7?! ♘×c7 9.a5 ♕×b5 10.♗×b5 c×b5∓; 8.a5 ♕d8 9.♘c3 ♘b4⇄) 7...♗g7

B2a) 8.0-0-0 ♘f6 9.♘f3 ♘d5 10.♗d2 (10.♗e5 f6 11.♗g3 0-0⇄) 10...♗f5 11.♘e5 0-0 12.g4 ♗e6⇄;

B2b) 8.a4 ♘f6 9.♘f3 (9.a5 ♕c6 10.♘f3 0-0 11.♘e5 ♕d5⇄) 9...♗g4 (9...♘d5!? 10.♗e5 f6) 10.h3 ♗×f3 11.♕×f3 ♕e6+ (11...c6 12.♘c3 ♘b4 13.0-0-0 ♘fd5 14.♘×d5 ♘×d5 15.♗c4 ♘×f4 16.♕×f4 0-0=) 12.♕e2 (12.♗e2 c6 13.♘c3 ♘b4 14.0-0-0 ♘a2+ 15.♔b1 ♘×c3+ 16.b×c3 0-0⇄) 12...♕d7 (12...♕×e2+!? 13.♗×e2 ♘d5 14.♗g3 c6 15.♘c3 ♘ab4) 13.♗e5 0-0 14.c3 c6 15.♘a3 c5⇄, Jonkman, H. (2470) – Marcelin, C. (2441), Wijk aan Zee 2006;

C) 5.♗c4 ♗g7

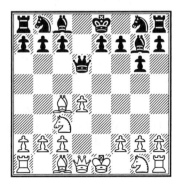

C1) 6.♘ge2 (6.♕f3 ♘f6 7.♘ge2 0-0 8.♗f4 ♕b6 9.0-0-0 ♘c6⇄; 8...♕b4!?)

C1a) 6...a6?! 7.♗f4 (7.0-0 ♘f6 8.♗f4 (Georgiadis, I. (2269) – Simeonidis, I. (2307), Athens 2006) 8...♕d8 9.a4 0-0±) 7...♕c6 8.♘d5 e5 (8...♕xc4 9.♘xc7+ ♔f8 10.♘xa8 ♘d7 11.♕d3±) 9.dxe5 ♕xc4 10.e6± ;

C1b) 6...♘f6 7.♗f4 ♕d8 (7...♕b6 8.0-0 0-0 9.♕d2 (Ljubicic, F. (2470) – Plenkovic, Z. (2370), Split 2008) 9...♘c6⇄) 8.♕d2 a6 (8...0-0!? 9.0-0 ♘c6) 9.a4 0-0 10.0-0 (Guo, X. – Farrington, E., Douglas 2005) 10...♘c6 11.d5 ♘a5 (11...♘b4!?) 12.♗a2 c5 13.♘g3 c4 14.♖fe1 ♖e8⇄ ;

C2) 6.♘f3 ♘f6 and now:

C2a) 7.h3 a6 8.♘e5 0-0 9.♗f4?! (9.0-0 ♘c6=) 9...♘c6 (9...♕d8 10.0-0± , Ermenkov, E. (2462) – Rowe, P. (2049), Turin 2006) 10.♘xg6 (10.0-0-0?! ♘h5 11.♗h2 ♘xe5 12.dxe5 ♗xe5; 10.♘xc6 ♕xc6 11.♗e2 ♖d8 12.0-0 ♗f5∓) 10...♕b4 11.♘e5 ♕xb2 12.♗d2 ♘xd4∓ ;

C2b) 7.♗g5 0-0 8.♕d2 (O'Shea, K. – Rowe, P. (2045), Grand Har 2006) 8...♘c6 9.♘b5 (9.0-0-0 ♕b4 10.♕e2 ♘a5 11.♗d3 ♗e6 12.a3 ♕d6⇄) 9...♕d8 10.♗f4 ♘e4 11.♕e2 ♘d6 12.0-0-0 ♗g4 13.c3 ♕d7=;

C2c) 7.0-0 0-0 (7...a6 8.g3 0-0 9.♗f4 ♕d8± ; 7...c6 8.g3 0-0 9.♗f4 ♕b4 10.♗b3 ♗g4 11.a3 ♕a5 12.♖e1 e6⇄) 8.♘b5 (8.h3 a6 9.♕e2 ½-½, Psakhis, L. (2611) – Epishin, V. (2567), Vissingen 2000) 8...♕d8 9.♗f4 ♘a6 10.d5 ♘d7 11.c3 ♘b6 12.♗b3 ♗d7 13.a4 ♗xb5 14.axb5 ♘c5 15.♗a2 a6⇄ ;

C2d) 7.♘e5 0-0 8.0-0 (Damljanovic, B. (2588) – Fernandez Garcia, J. (2468), Spain 2005) 8...♘c6 9.♘b5 ♕d8 10.♖e1 a6⇄ or 10.♗f4 ♘h5⇄; 8.♗f4 ♘h5 9.♗e3 ♗xe5 10.dxe5 ♕xe5 11.♕f3 ♘c6∞ ;

D) 5.♘f3 ♗g7 (6...♘f6 – 4.d4 ♘f6 5.♘f3 g6, Game 29)

This position may also arise from 1.♘f3 g6 2.e4 d5 3.exd5 ♕xd5 4.♘c3 (4.d4 ♗g7 5.♘c3 ♕d6) 4...♕d6 5.d4 ♗g7 or 1.e4 g6 2.♘f3 d5 3.exd5 ♕xd5 4.♘c3 (4.d4 ♗g7 5.♘c3 ♕d6) 4...♕d6 5.d4 ♗g7.

After 6.♗c4 ♘f6 we have a position from the line 5.♗c4 ♗g7 6.♘f3 ♘f6.Now possible are **D1)** 6.g3; **D2)** 6.♘b5 and **D3)** 6.♘e5.

D1) 6.g3

D1a) 6...♗f5?! 7.♗f4! (7.♗g2 ♕a6 8.♘e5 ♘d7 9.♘xd7 ♗xd7⇄, Avdic, A. (2304) – Kurajica, B. (2539), Neum 2005) 7...♕b6 (7...♕e6+ 8.♗e2 c6 9.0-0 ♘f6 10.♘e5 0-0 11.♖e1±) 8.♗b5+ ♘d7 (8...c6 9.♘d5±) 9.♘d5 ♕e6+ 10.♘e3± ;

D1b) 6...♘f6 7.♗f4 (7.♗g2 – 4...♘f6 5.♘f3 g6 6.g3 ♗g7 7.♗g2, Game 29)

7...♕b6 8.♕d2 0-0 9.0-0-0 c5 (9...♗g4!?) 10.♗g2 (10.d×c5 ♕×c5 11.♗g2 ♘c6⇄, Brkic, A. (2428) – Kurajica, B. (2557), Solin 2003; 11.♘e5!?; 11.♕e3!?) 10...♘c6 11.♗e3 ♘g4 (11...♕a5!? 12.d×c5 ♘e4 13.♘×e4 ♕×a2) 12.d×c5 ♕a5⇄;

D2) 6.♘b5

D2a) 6...♕d8 7.♗f4 ♘a6 8.♗e5 (8.♘c3 ♘f6 9.♗c4!? ♘b4 10.♕d2 ♘h5 11.0-0-0) 8...♘f6 9.♘c3 ♘b8 (9...0-0!?) 10.♗c4 0-0 11.♕e2 a6 12.0-0-0 b5 13.♗b3 ♘c6⇄, Radulski, J. (2501) – Kurajica, B. (2541), Zadar 2004 or 8.♗e2 c6 9.♘a3 ♘f6 10.0-0 ♘c7 11.♘c4 0-0 12.h3 ♘cd5 13.♗h2 ♗h6⇄, Kovacevic, A. (2556) – Kurajica, B. (2541), Zadar 2004;

D2b) 6...♕b6 7.♗f4 (7.♗c4 c6 8.♘c3 ♘h6 9.0-0 ♘f5 10.♘e2 0-0 11.c3 c5 12.♖e1 ♘c6⇄, Feletar, D. (2365) – Kurajica, B. (2550), Zadar 2007); 10...♘d6!? 11.♗b3 ♘d7) 7...♘a6

D2b1) 8.♕e2 ♗g4 (8...♘f6!? 9.0-0-0 ♗f5) 9.a4 (9.h3!?) 9...♗×f3 (Saric, I. (2456) – Kurajica, B. (2539), Sibenik 2005) 10.♕×f3 c6 (10...♘f6 11.♗c4 c6 12.♘c3 0-0 13.0-0-0±; 12...♕×d4? 13.♗×a6; 12...♕×b2? 13.♖b1 ♕×c2 14.♗×a6) 11.a5 ♕d8 12.♗d3 ♘f6 13.♘c3 ♘b4⇄;

D2b2) 8.a4 ♗g4 (8...c6 9.♗c7 ♘×c7 10.a5 ♕×b5 11.♗×b5 ♘×b5 12.a6 b6∓, Iturrizaga, E. (2470) – Moreno, J., San Cristobal 2008; 9.a5 ♕d8 10.♘c3± or 8...♘f6 9.♗c4 c6 10.a5 ♕d8 11.♘c3 ♘b4=) 9.♗c4 c6 10.a5 ♕d8 11.♘c3 ♘b4 12.0-0 ♘d7 13.d5 ♕f5⇄, Djingarova, E. (2290) – Kurajica, B. (2539), Santa Cruz de la Palma 2005;

D3) 6.♘e5

Alexander Khalifman analyzes this position in the book *Opening for White according to Anand 1.e4. Part 3*, and thinks 6.♘e5 is the best "...because other continuations do not give White an advantage."

D3a) 6...♗×e5?! 7.♘b5 ♕e6 8.d×e5 ♕×e5+ 9.♗e3 ♘a6 (9...♘c6?! 10.♕d5) 10.♕d4 ♕×d4 11.♗×d4⩲;

D3b) 6...♘f6 (again, this position may arise via 1.♘f3 g6 2.e4 d5 3.e×d5 ♕×d5 4.♘c3 ♕d6 5.d4 ♗g7 6.♘e5 ♘f6 or 5...♘f6 6.♘e5 ♗g7) 7.♗f4 ♘h5 8.♘b5 ♕d8 9.♕f3 0-0 10.0-0-0 c6 11.♘c3 ♘×f4 12.♕×f4 ♗e6 13.h4 ♘d7 14.h5 ("with a strong attack" – Khalifman) 14...♘×e5 15.d×e5 ♕c7. Black has counterchances here; for example, 16.♖e1 b5 17.♗d3 ♖fd8 or 16.h×g6 h×g6 17.♖e1 ♖fd8 18.♔b1 a5. 12...♘d7 13.♘g4 (13.h4 ♘×e5 14.d×e5 ♕a5∓) 13...♕a5 or 13...♘f6 is also not bad for Black;

D3c) 6...a6

D3c1) 7.♗c4 ♗×e5 8.d×e5 ♕×e5+ 9.♕e2 (9.♗e3 ♘f6) 9...♕×e2+ 10.♗×e2 ♗e6 11.♗f4 c6 12.0-0-0 ♘d7∞; 7.♘e4

♕d5 8.f3 (8.♘c3 ♕d6) 8...♗xe5 9.dxe5
♕xd1+ 10.♔xd1 ♘c6 11.♗f4 ♗f5
12.♔d2 0-0-0+ 13.♔c3 f6 14.exf6 ♘xf6
15.♘xf6 exf6= or 7.♗f4 ♘c6 8.♕d2
♕xd4 (8...♘xd4!?) 9.♘xc6 ♕xd2+
10.♔xd2 bxc6 11.♗xc7 ♗h6+
(11...♗e6 12.♗d3 ♘f6=) 12.♔e1 ♗f5
13.♗d3 ♗xd3 14.cxd3 ♘f6=;

D3c2) 7.♕f3 ♘f6 8.♗c4 0-0 9.♗e3
(9.♗f4?! ♕xd4 10.♖d1 ♕c5 11.♗b3
♘c6 12.♘xc6 ♗g4) 9...♘bd7 10.♘d3
♘b6 11.♗b3 ♗g4⇄ or 8.♗f4 ♕xd4
9.♖d1 ♕b4 10.c4 (10.♘d3 ♕b6)
10...0-0 11.a3 (11.♗b3 ♘c6 12.♘xc6
bxc6∞) 11...♕xb2 12.♘xf7 e6
13.♘h6+ ♔h8 14.♖d8 ♖xd8
(14...♕xa3 15.♘f7+ ♔g8 16.♘h6+
♔h8 17.♘f7+ with a draw) 15.♘f7+
♔g8 16.♘xd8∞.

Back to Volokitin – Kurajica.

5...♘f6

5...♗g7 (5...♗g4?! 6.f3!; 6.♗f4 ♕xf4
7.♘xf4 ♗xd1 8.♘xd1 e6 9.g3 ♘c6
10.d5 exd5 11.♘xd5 ½-½, Csoke, A.
(2235) – Horvath, J. (2245), Hungary
1993) 6.♗f4 ♕d8 (6...♕b6? 7.♘d5)
7.♕d2 (Jablonowski, C. – Brustkern, J.
(2250), Dresden 2005) 7...♘f6 8.0-0-0
0-0 9.d5 c6 10.d6 ♖e8⇄; 9.♘g3 ♘d5

10.♘xd5 ♕xd5 11.c4 ♕d7⇄ or 7.g3
♘f6 8.♗g2 0-0 9.0-0 c6⇄.

6.♗f4 ♕b6

6...♕d8!? 7.♘g3 ♗g7 8.♗c4 0-0 9.0-0
♘bd7⇄.

7.♕d2 ♗g7

7...c6 (7...♕xb2? 8.♖b1 ♕a3 9.♘b5)
8.0-0-0 ♗e6?! (8...♗g7) 9.♘a4 ♕b5?
(9...♕d8 10.♘c5 ♗c8) 10.♘c5 ♗c8
(10...♘bd7 11.♘xe6 fxe6 12.♘c3 ♕a5
13.♔b1±) 11.♗c7 b6 (11...♘a6
12.♘c3 ♕b4 13.a3+−) 12.♘g3 ♕a5
13.♕xa5 bxa5±, Mueller, M. (2325) –
Dassel, U., Germany 1996.

8.0-0-0 0-0

9.h4

9.♘a4 ♕b5 10.♘ec3 (10.♘c5 ♘a6
11.♘c3 ♕a5) 10...♕a5 11.a3 (11.♘c5
♘a6 12.♘xa6 bxa6 13.♗c4 ♖d8
14.♖he1 e6⇄) 11...c6 (11...♖d8?!
12.b4 ♕h5 13.♗xc7) 12.♖e1 ♕d8⇄
or 9.♘g3 ♖d8 (9...♘c6!?) 10.♗c4
(10.d5!? ♗e6? 11.♘a4; 10...♘a6
11.♗c4 ♘c5 12.♖he1 ♗d7⇄)
10...♗e6 (10...♘c6!? 11.♗e3 a6⇄)
11.♗xe6 ♕xe6 12.♗xc7±, Juarez

Flores, C. (2381) – Rowe, P. (2049), Turin 2006.

9...♖d8

9...♘c6 10.h5 ♖d8 (10...♘×h5?! 11.♘d5 ♕a6 12.♘ec3 ♕a5 13.♗×c7; 10...g×h5!?) 11.h×g6 h×g6 12.♘a4 ♕a6∞ or 9...♕a5 10.♘g3 ♘c6 11.♗c4 (11.h5 ♗g4 12.h×g6 ♗×d1 13.g×h7+ ♔h8 14.♕×d1∞) 11...♖d8 12.♕e2 e6 13.♘b5 ♘d5⇄.

10.♕e3?!

10.♘a4!? ♕c6 11.♘ec3 ♗f5 (11...♘h5 12.d5) 12.f3.

10...e5 (10...♗e6∓) 11.♗×e5?!

11.d×e5 ♖×d1+ 12.♘×d1 ♘g4 13.♕×b6 a×b6 14.♘ec3⇄.

11...♘g4 12.♕g3 ♘×e5 13.d×e5 ♖×d1+ 14.♘×d1 ♕a5∓

15.f4 (15.♘ec3 ♕×e5 16.♕×e5 ♗×e5 17.♘e3 ♘c6∓; 15...♗×e5!? 16.f4 ♗g7) **15...♕×a2 16.♘ec3 ♕a1+ 17.♘b1 ♘c6** (17...♗e6!? 18.♗d3 ♘c6 19.h5 ♘b4∓; 18.♕a3 ♕×a3 19.♘×a3 ♘c6∓) **18.♗c4 ♘d4?!** (18...♘a5!? 19.♕a3?! ♕×a3 20.♘×a3

♘×c4 21.♘×c4 ♗e6 22.♘de3 ♖d8 23.♖d1 ♖×d1+ 24.♔×d1 f6 with a difficult ending for White; 19.♗d3 h5 20.f5?! ♗h6+ 21.♘e3 ♗×f5 22.♗×f5 ♘c4; 20.♕g5∞; 19...♗e6 20.h5 ♖d8 21.f5? ♗h6+ 22.♘e3 ♖×d3 23.c×d3 ♘b3+ 24.♔c2 ♘d4+; 21.♘dc3 ♖d4 22.♕e3 c5∓) **19.♕d3 c5 20.♘e3 = ♗e6 21.c3 ♘b3+?!** (21...b5!? 22.♗×b5? ♘b3+ 23.♔c2 ♖b8 24.♖f1 c4 25.♗×c4 ♘c5−+; 22.c×d4?! b×c4 23.♕a3 ♕×a3 24.♘×a3 c×d4 25.♘e×c4 ♖d8 26.♖d1 ♗f8∓; 22.♗×e6 ♘×e6 23.♕×b5?! ♗×f4; 23.♘d5 c4∓) **22.♗×b3 ♗×b3 23.c4 ♕a4?!** (23...♗a2!? 24.♖d1 b5 25.c×b5 ♖b8⇄ or 24.h5 a5⇄) **24.♘d2 ♕a1+ 25.♘b1?!** (25.♕b1 ♕a4?! 26.♘×b3 ♕×b3 27.♕e4 ♖d8 28.♘d5 b5 29.♖d1; 25...♕×b1+ 26.♔×b1 ♗a4 27.♘d5±) **25...♕a4?!** (25...♗a2) **26.♘a3?!** (26.♘d2 ♕a1+ 27.♕b1±) **26...b5?!** (26...h5 27.♔b1 ♖e8∞) **27.♘×b5 ♕a1+ 28.♕b1 ♕a5 29.♘d6** (29.♘a3!? h5 30.♘d5) **29...♖d8 30.h5 ♕a6 31.h×g6 h×g6 32.♕d3 ♕a1+ 33.♕b1 ♕a6 34.g3 f5 35.♖h2 ♖×d6 36.e×d6 ♕×d6 37.♖d2 ♕a6 38.♖d3 ♕a4 39.♔d2 ♗d4 40.♕h1 ♗×c4 41.♕a8+ ♔g7 42.♘×c4 ♕b4+ 43.♔e2 ♕×c4 44.♕×a7+ ♔h6 45.♕b7 ♕c2+ 46.♖d2 ♕b1 47.♕f3 ♕c1 48.b3 ♗c3 49.♖d1 ♕b2+ 50.♔f1 ♗d4 51.♖e1 ♕c2 52.♖e2 ♕d1+ 53.♔g2 ♕g1+ 54.♔h3 ♕d1 55.g4 f×g4+ 56.♔×g4 ♕b1 57.♖h2+ ♔g7 58.♕b7+ ♔f8 59.♕c8+ ♔g7 60.♕h8+ 1-0**

Summary: Previously, after **1.e4 d5 2.e×d5 ♕×d5 3.♘c3 ♕d6 4.d4**, we had examined lines involving 4...♘f6, but Black does have other continuations, mainly 4...a6, 4...c6, and 4...g6.

I consider 4...a6 and 4...c6 less important than 4...♞f6 and on the whole inferior and more difficult, unless Black quickly transposes back to 4...♞f6 lines.

After 4...a6 5.♞f3 ♞f6, we have a position from Games 18-28. After 5...♞c6, 5...♝g4, or 5...♝f5, Black may have problems.

After 4...c6 5.♞f3 (after 5.♞ge2, Black's best chance is probably 5...♞f6,

transposing to a position from Game 32) 5...♞f6, we have a position from Games 13-17. After 5...♝g4 or 5...♝f5, Black may have problems.

4...g6 is certainly playable, but it does not really challenge White in the way 4...♞f6 does. After 4...g6, White has many good possibilities; for example, 5.♝e3, 5.♞b5 , 5.♝c4, 5.♞ge2 and 5.♞f3. After 5.♞f3 (This move is the best) 6...♝g7 (6...♞f6 – 4.d4 ♞f6 5.♞f3 g6, Game 29) White has three main continuations: 6.g3, 6.♞b5 and 6.♞e5 and each can be dangerous for Black.

Part VI 3.♘c3 ♕d6

Games 38-40 cover lines after **1.e4 d5 2.e×d5 ♕×d5 3.♘c3 ♕d6** without 4.d4.

After 3...♕d6, the most logical move is 4.d4, but here we will examine games without it. Of course, very often these can transpose to lines discussed earlier; for example, when Black refrains from e7-e5.

In practice White often plays 4.g3 (Game 38), 4.♗c4 (Game 39) and 4.♘f3 (Game 40).

What does White gain by renouncing an early d2-d4? First, when Black chooses ...♗g4, there is no target pawn at d4. Second, White can use a tempo for kingside development and castling; third, after d2-d3, White has control of the e4-square.

Games 38-40 show that after 4...e5, Black can have problems. In all these cases there is a good universal antidote for Black: 4...♘f6.

Game 38
Topalov, V. (2770) – Nisipeanu, L. (2690)
Sofia 2007

1.e4 d5 2.e×d5 ♕×d5 3.♘c3 ♕d6 4.g3

We will be looking at this move in conjunction with d2-d3 and ♘g1-e2, avoiding lines that transpose to positions from Game 18, and avoiding lines involving d2-d4 and ♘g1-f3, with the exception of 4.g3 ♘f6 5.d4.

4...♘f6

4...g6 is playable too; for example, 5.♗g2 ♗g7 6.♘ge2 ♘f6 (6...♘c6?! 7.0-0 ♘f6 8.d4, Djoudi, A. (2274) – Beratti, H. (1115), Internet 2003) 7.0-0 0-0 ⇄. We should also examine **A)** 4...e5; **B)** 4...c6 and **C)** 4...♘c6.

A) 4...e5 5.♗g2 ♘f6 (5...♘c6!?; for 5...c6 see 4...c6 5.♗g2 e5) 6.♘f3 a6 7.0-0 (7.♕e2 ♘c6 8.0-0 ♗g4 ⇄) 7...♘c6 (7...♗e7?! 8.d4 e×d4 9.♗f4 ♕b6 10.♕×d4 with strong pressure, Nechepurenko, R. (2340) – Tsoller, S., Oktjabrsky 2004) 8.♖e1 ♗e7 9.d3 ♗g4

279

10.h3 ♗×f3 11.♗×f3 0-0± or 6...♘c6
7.♘b5 (7.0-0 ♗g4 8.♖e1 0-0-0⇄,
Kolesnichenko, A. (2245) – Starostin,
G., Odessa 2000) 7...♕d8 8.0-0 a6
9.♘c3 ♗c5 10.♕e2 ♕e7 11.♖e1 0-0
12.d3 h6=;

B) 4...c6 5.♗g2

B1) 5...e5?! 6.♕e2 ♗e7 7.♘f3 f6 8.d4
e×d4 9.♘e4 ♕d8 10.♗f4 with a strong
initiative, Rossbach, K. (2060) –
Wulfmeyer, J. (2075), Bayern 2002 or
9...♕d5 10.0-0 ♗g4 11.♖d1 ♘d7
12.h3±; 6...♘d7 7.♘f3 f6 8.0-0 ♗e7
9.d4 e×d4 10.♗f4 ♕b4 11.♘e4±;
6...♗e6 7.♘f3 ♘d7 8.0-0 0-0-0 9.♘e4
♕c7 10.d4 ♘gf6 11.♘eg5± or 7...f6
8.0-0 ♘d7 9.d4 e×d4 10.♘×d4±;

B2) 5...♗f5 (5...♘f6 – 4...♘f6 5.♗g2
c6) 6.♘ge2 (6.♘f3 ♘f6 – 4...♘f6 5.♗g2
c6 6.♘f3 ♗f5; 6.d4 – 4...♘f6 5.♗g2 c6
6.d4 ♗f5) 6...♘f6 and now:

B2a) 7.b4 a6 8.a4 e6 9.♖b1 ♗e7 10.d3
(10.b5 a×b5 11.a×b5 0-0 12.0-0
♘bd7=, Meshkov, Y. (2385) – Belikov,
V. (2560), Sochi 2007) 10...0-0 11.0-0
♘bd7 12.h3 (12.♘e4 ♕c7=) 12...♖fd8
13.g4 ♗g6 14.f4?! (Barrientos
Chavarriaga, S. (2433) – Planas Ferret,
R. (2215), Barcelona 2005) 14...♘d5
15.♘×d5 c×d5∓; 14.♘f4 ♘b6 15.♘×g6
h×g6=;

B2b) 7.d3 (7.0-0 ♘bd7 8.a4 h5⇄)
7...♘bd7 8.0-0 e6 (8...e5!? 9.b4 ♗e7
10.f4 g6⇄) 9.h3 h6 (9...♗e7!? 10.♗e3
0-0=) 10.♖e1 g5 (10...♗e7 11.♗e3 0-
0 12.♘d4 ♗g6=) 11.♗d2 ♗g7 12.♘e4
♕c7 13.♗c3 0-0-0⇄, Jojua, D. (2125)
– Jirovsky, M. (2446), Batumi 2002;

C) 4...♘c6 5.♗g2

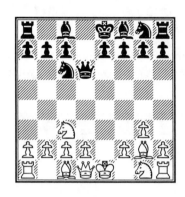

C1) 5...h5 6.♘f3 h4 7.♘×h4 g5 8.♘f3
g4 9.♘g1 (9.♘e4!? ♕e6 10.♘fg5 ♕g6
11.d4 ♗f5 12.♘c5) 9...♗f5 10.d3 0-0-0
11.♗e3 (11.♘ge2 ♗g7 12.♗e3 a6⇄)
11...♗h6 (11...♘f6!? 12.♘ge2 e5)
12.♕d2 (Lazic, M. (2485) – Vukovic,
Z. (2432), Vrnjacka Banja 2005)
12...♗×e3 13.♕×e3 ♘d4 14.0-0-0 ♘f6
15.♘ge2 e5⇄;

C2) 5...♘f6 and now:

C2a) 6.♘f3 ♗g4 7.h3 (7.d4 – Game 10;
7.0-0 ♘d4 8.d3 0-0-0=) 7...♗h5
(7...♕e6+ 8.♕e2 ♗×f3!? 9.♕×e6 ♗×g2)
8.g4 (8.d4 0-0-0 9.0-0 (Sveshnikov, E.
(2507) – Yegiazarian, A. (2537),
Stepanakert 2005) 9...♘×d4 10.♕×d4
♕×d4 11.♘×d4 ♖×d4 12.♗e3 ♖c4
13.♗×a7 e6 14.♗e3 ♗g6∓) 8...♗g6
9.d3 0-0-0 10.♗e3 e5 11.♘h4 ♘d4
12.0-0 c6⇄, Campora, D. (2522) –
Vitor, A. (2294), Lisbon 2002;

C2b) 6.♘ge2

C2b1) 6...e5 (6...h5!?; 6...♗g4 – 4...♘f6
5.♗g2 ♗g4 6.♘ge2 ♘c6) 7.d3 (7.0-0
♗g4 8.h3 ♗h5 (L'Ami, E. (2470) –
Gross, G. (2316), Germany 2004) 9.d3
0-0-0 10.♗e3⇄) 7...a6 (7...♗e6!? 8.0-0
♗e7) 8.h3 ♗e7 9.♗e3 0-0 10.0-0 ♗e6

11.f4 ♘d5 12.♘×d5 ♗×d5 ⇄, Joachim, S. (2471) – Muse, D. (2442), Germany 2003;

C2b2) 6...♗f5

C2b2a) 7.0-0 (7.b4?! ♘×b4 8.d3 (Bologan, V. (2585) – Hauchard, A. (2500), Belfort 1998) 8...0-0-0 9.♖b1 e5 10.0-0 ♗e7 11.♗a3 a5 12.♕d2 ♖he8∓)

C2b2a1) 8.a3 e5 9.d3 ♗h3 (9...♗e7!? 10.♗e3 0-0-0 11.b4 ♘d4) 10.♗e3 h5 (10...0-0-0!? 11.♕d2 ♗×g2 12.♔×g2 ♗e7 13.f3 h5 14.h4 ♕e6 15.♘e4 ♘d5∓) 11.d4 ♗×g2 12.♔×g2 0-0-0 13.d×e5 ♕f5 14.♕c1 (Novikov, S. (2498) – Chapliev, A. (2369), Serpukhov 2003) 14...♘×e5∓;

C2b2a2) 8.d3 e5 (8...0-0-0!? 9.♗e3 e5) 9.♗g5 (9.♗e3 0-0-0 10.a3 h5 11.b4 h4 12.b5 ♘d4∓) 9...♗e7 (9...0-0-0!?) 10.♗×f6 ♗×f6 11.♘d5 ⇄, Buchal, S. (2395) – Kayser, F. (2195), Bad Wiessee 2006.

We return now to Topalov – Nisipeanu.

5.♗g2

5.d4 ♗g4 (5...a6 6.♘f3 – Game 18; 5...c6 6.♗g2 – 5.♗g2 c6 6.d4; 5...♘c6

6.♘f3 ♗g4 – Game 10) 6.f3 (6.♘f3 ♘c6 – Game 10; 6.♗e2 ♗×e2 7.♘g×e2 ♘c6 8.♗f4 ♕d7 9.♕d2 0-0-0 10.0-0-0 e6=, Klemanic, E. (2248) – Lipka, J. (2389), Tatranske Zruby 2004 or 7.♕×e2 ♘c6 8.♘f3 e6 9.♗f4 ♕b4 10.0-0 0-0-0 ⇄, Angelov, A. (2220) – Panbukchian, V. (2333), Plovdiv 2003) 6...♗f5 and now:

A) 7.♗f4 ♕b6 8.♕d2 (8.♗d3 ♕×b2?! 9.♘ge2 ♗×d3 10.c×d3 ♔; 8...♗×d3 9.♕×d3 ♘c6 10.0-0-0 0-0-0 11.♘ge2 e6 ⇄) 8...♘c6 (8...♕×b2?! 9.♖b1 ♕c2 10.♕×c2 ♗×c2 11.♖×b7 ♔) 9.g4 (9.♘b5?! e5 10.d×e5 ♖d8 11.♕e2 ♘d5 ♔ or 10.♗×e5 ♘d5 11.0-0-0 0-0-0 ♔) 9...♗g6 10.g5 (Basagic, Z. (2366) – Sermek, D. (2590), Bled 2002) 10...♘h5 11.♗e3 0-0-0 12.0-0-0 ♘b4∓;

B) 7.♘ge2 (7.♗d3 ♗×d3 8.♕×d3 ♘c6 9.♗e3 ♘b4 10.♕d2 ♕e6∓, Koch, J. (2510) – Fressinet, L. (2440), Besancon 1999) 7...♘c6 8.♗e3 0-0-0 9.♕d2 (Solak, D. (2490) – Kovacevic, A. (2513), Novi Sad 2000) 9...♘b4 10.♖c1 e5∓ or 8.d5 ♘b4 9.♘d4 ♘f×d5 (9...♘b×d5?! 10.♘×f5 ♕e5+ 11.♕e2 ♕×f5 12.♕b5+) 10.a3 (10.♘×f5 ♕e5+ 11.♘e4 ♕×f5 12.a3 ♘c6 13.♗d3 ♕e6∓) 10...♕e5+ 11.♘ce2 (11.♔f2 ♘d3+) 11...♘c6 12.c4 ♘b6 13.♗f4 ♕f6 14.♘b5 ♖c8 15.♘×c7+ ♖×c7 16.♗×c7 ♕×b2 ♔;

C) 7.g4 ♗g6 8.♘ge2 (8.g5 ♘h5 9.♘e4 ♕b6=) 8...♘c6 9.g5 (9.♗f4 ♕d7∓) 9...♘h5 10.♘e4 (10.♗e3!?) ♕d5 11.c4 ♕×c4 12.♗e3 e6 13.♘2c3 ♕b4 14.a3 ⇄, Howell, D. (2515) – Parker, J. (2520), England, 2007; 12...0-0-0!?

Back to Topalov – Nisipeanu.

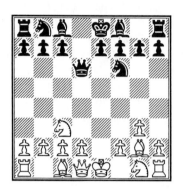

5...c6

5...♘c6 – 4...♘c6 5.♗g2 ♘f6; 5...e5 – 4...e5 5.♗g2 ♘f6. We now examine **A)** 5...h5 and **B)** 5...♗g4.

A) 5...h5 6.d4 h4 7.♗f4 ♕b6 8.♕d3 (8.♘ge2 c6 9.♕d3 ♘a6 10.a3 h×g3 11.f×g3±, Smirin, I. (2671) – Kurajica, B. (2541), Solin 1999) 8...h×g3 (8...♕×b2? 9.♖b1 ♕a3 10.♖×b7±; 8...♘c6!?) 9.h×g3 ♖×h1 10.♗×h1 ♗g4 (10...g6 11.0-0-0 ♗f5 12.♕c4±) 11.♘a4 ♕a5+ (11...♕e6+ 12.♔f1±) 12.♗d2 ♕×a4 13.♗×b7±; 6...c6 7.♗f4 ♕b4 8.♕d2 ♗f5 9.a3 ♕b6 (Caruana, F. (2373) – Mukic, J. (2328), Arco 2005) 10.0-0-0 ♘bd7 11.♘f3 e6±;

B) 5...♗g4 6.♘ge2 (6.♘f3 ♘c6 – 4...♘c6 5.♗g2 ♘f6 6.♘f3 ♗g4) 6...♘c6

B1) 7.d3 (7.d4 – Game 10; 7.d4 h5 – 4...♘c6 5.♗g2 ♘f6 6.♘ge2 h5 7.d4 ♗g4) 7...0-0-0 (7...e5!?) 8.h3 ♗h5 (8...♗f5!?) 9.♗e3 e5 10.♕d2 ♘d4 11.g4 ♗g6 12.f4 ♘×e2 13.♘×e2 (Brady, S. (2320) – McPhillips, K. (2225), Dublin 2005) 13...h5 14.f5?! (14.0-0-0∞) 14...♗h7 15.g5 ♘d5∓ or 10.0-0 ♕e6 (10...♘d4 11.g4 ♗g6 12.f4 ♘×e2+ 13.♕×e2 e×f4 14.♖×f4±, Praznik, A.

(2346) – Nikolov, S. (2394), Kranj 2005) 11.♕d2 ♗g6 12.♗g5 h6 13.♗×f6 ♕×f6 ⇄;

B2) 7.h3

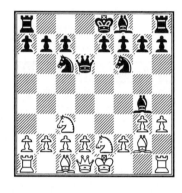

B2a) 7...♗×e2 8.♕×e2 ♘d4 9.♕d1 (9.♘e4!?) 9...♕e5+ 10.♘e2 0-0-0 11.c3 ♕×e2+ 12.♕×e2 ♘×e2 13.♔×e2 e5 14.d3±, Blatny, P. (2476) – Velicka, P. (2440), Czechia 1999;

B2b) 7...♗h5 8.0-0 (8.d4!? 0-0-0 9.♗f4; 8.g4 ♗g6 – 7...♗f5 8.g4; 8.d3 e5 9.g4 ♗g6 10.f4 – 4...♘f6 5.♗g2 ♗g4 6.♘ge2 ♘c6 7.h3 ♗f5 8.g4 ♗g6 9.d3 e5 10.f4 or 8...0-0-0 – 4...♘f6 5.♗g2 ♗g4 6.♘ge2 ♘c6 7.d3 0-0-0 8.h3 ♗h5) 8...e6 (8...e5!?; 8...0-0-0 9.d3 e5 10.♗e3 – 4...♘f6 5.♗g2 ♗g4 6.♘ge2 ♘c6 7.d3 0-0-0 8.h3 ♗h5 9.♗e3 e5 10.0-0) 9.d3 ♗e7 10.a3 0-0 11.g4 ♗g6 12.f4 (12.♘f4!?±) 12...♘e8 (12...♕c5+!? 13.d4 ♕b6) 13.♗e3 ♕d7=, Kovchan, A. (2515) – Smirnov, I. (2435), Kharkiv 2006;

B2c) 7...♗f5 8.d3 (8.g4 ♗g6 9.d3 e6 10.♗f4 ♕d7 11.♕d2 ♗e7 12.♗g3 (Schweiger, G. (2142) – Balinov, I. (2478), Passau 2000) 12...0-0-0 13.0-0-0 a6=) 8...e5 9.0-0 (9.♗e3 ♕d7 10.a3 0-0-0 11.g4 ½-½, Zavgorodniy,

S. (2409) – Danielian, E. (2400), Alushta 2003; 9...♗e7 10.♕d2 0-0-0 11.0-0-0 a6= or 10.0-0 0-0=) 9...0-0-0 10.♗e3 ♕d7 (Kokolias, K. (2185) – Nikolaidis, I. (2535), Litohoro 2006) 11.g4 ♗e6 12.f4 ♘d5⇄.

Let's retun to Topalov – Nisipeanu.

6.d4

6.d3 ♗g4 7.♘f3 – 6.♘f3 ♗g4 7.d3 or 7.♘ge2 – 6.♘ge2 ♗g4 7.d3; 6...♗f5 7.♘f3 – 6.♘f3 ♗f5 7.d3 or 7.♘ge2 – 6.♘ge2 ♗f5 7.d3. Now we look at **A)** 6.h3; **B)** 6.♘ge2 and **C)** 6.♘f3.

A) 6.h3 ♗f5 (6...g6!?) 7.d3 e6 (7...♘bd7!? 8.♗e3 e5 or 8.♘f3 g6) 8.♘f3 h6 9.0-0 ♘bd7 (9...♗e7 10.♖b1 0-0 11.b4 ♘d5⇄, Klenburg, M. (2331) – Bar, R. (2413), Tel Aviv 2002; 10.♗f4 ♕d8 11.♕e2 0-0±) 10.♗f4 ♕b4 11.♕d2 (11.a3 ♕×b2 12.♕d2 ♕b6 13.♖fb1 ♕a6 14.♘d4 0-0-0⇄) 11...g5 12.a3 ♕b6 13.♗e3 ♕c7⇄;

B) 6.♘ge2 ♗g4 (6...♗f5 – 4...c6 5.♗g2 ♗f5 6.♘ge2 ♘f6)

B1) 7.0-0 (7.d4 – 6.d4 ♗g4 7.♘ge2) 7...e6 (7...♘bd7!? 8.a4 0-0-0 9.a5 a6) 8.d3 (8.h3!? ♗f5 9.d4) 8...♘bd7 9.h3

(Musakaev, E. (2265) – Smirnov, I. (2435), Moscow 2007) 9...♗f5 10.♗e3 ♗e7 11.♘e4 ♕c7 12.♗f4 e5 13.♗g5 ♘×e4 14.♗×e7 ♔×e7 15.d×e4 ♗e6=;

B2) 7.h3 ♗h5 8.d3 (8.d4 e6 – 5...c6 6.d4 ♗g4 7.♘ge2 e6 8.h3 ♗h5) 8...e6 (8...♘bd7!?) 9.g4 ♗g6 10.♘f4 ♘bd7 (10...e5?! 11.♕e2 ♗e7 12.♘×g6 h×g6 (Delgado, N. (2541) – Gonzalez, R. (2424), Internet 2004) 13.♗e3 with better chances for White) 11.♕e2 0-0-0 12.♘×g6 h×g6 13.♗e3 ♕c7 14.0-0-0 ♗c5=;

C) 6.♘f3 ♗g4 7.0-0 (7.d4 – 6.d4 ♗g4 7.♘f3; 7.h3 ♗h5 8.0-0 e6 – 7.0-0 e6 8.h3 ♗h5) 7...e6

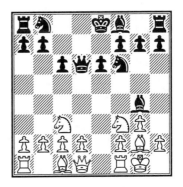

C1) 8.a4 (8.d4 – 6.d4 ♗g4 7.♘f3 e6 8.0-0) 8...a5 9.b3 (9.d4 ♘bd7?! 10.♗f4 ♕b4 11.♖a3; 9...♘a6!?) 9...♗e7 10.♕e1 (10.h3 ♗×f3 11.♕×f3 ♘a6±) 10...♘a6 11.♘e5 ♘b4 12.♘×g4 ♘×g4 (12...♘×c2? 13.♘×f6+ ♗×f6 14.♗a3±) 13.♕e2 h5=, Middelburg, T. (2415) – Tiviakov, S. (2665), Netherlands 2006;

C2) 8.h3 (8.d3 ♘bd7!? or 8...♕c7!?)) 6...♗f5 7.0-0 (7.d4 – 6.d4 ♗f5 7.♘f3) 7...e6 (7...h6 8.d4 e6 – 6.d4 ♗f5 7.♘f3 e6 8.0-0 h6) 8.d3 (8.d4 – 6.d4 ♗f5 7.♘f3 e6 8.0-0) ♗e7 9.a3 (9.♗f4!?)

9...0-0 10.♖b1 ♛c7 11.♛e2 ♞bd7 12.b4 a6 13.♗d2 ♖fe8 ½-½, Blehm, P. (2535) – Jirovsky, P. (2388), Czechia 2001.

We return now to Topalov – Nisipeanu.

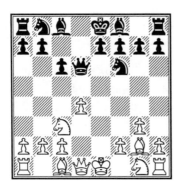

6...g6

Other interesting possibilities are **A)** 6...♗g4 and **B)** 6...♗f5.

A) 6...♗g4

A1) 7.♞ge2 e6 (7...♞bd7!?)

A1a) 8.h3 ♗h5 9.g4 (9.0-0!? ♞bd7 10.♗f4 ♛b4 11.♛d2 ♗g6 12.♖fb1) 9...♗g6 10.♞f4 ♞a6 11.♞×g6 h×g6 12.♞e2 (12.♛e2 0-0-0 13.♗e3 ♞b4 14.0-0-0 ♞bd5=) 12...♛c7 13.c3 ♗d6=, Veselovsky, S. (2419) – Voloshin, L. (2437), Czechia 2002;

A1b) 8.0-0 ♗e7 9.♗f4 ♛d8 10.♛d2 ♞bd7 11.h3 ♗h5 12.♖fe1 0-0 13.g4 ♗g6 14.♗g3 ♞b6 15.♞f4 ♞bd5 16.♞×g6 h×g6 17.♞×d5 ♞×d5 18.♖ad1 ♗h4 ½-½, Galkin, A. (2607) – Goncharov, V. (2310), Internet 2004 or 9.f3 ♗f5 10.g4 ♗g6 11.h4 (11.♗f4 ♛d8 12.♗g3 ♞a6 13.♛d2 ♛b6⇄) 11...h6 12.♗f4 ♛d8 13.♗g3 ♗h7 14.♞f4 (14.♛d2 ♞bd7 15.♖ad1 ♞b6∓, Shabalov, A. (2605) – Steinfl,

A. (2260), Las Vegas 2007) 14...♞bd7 15.♖e1 ♛b6 16.♖b1=;

A2) 7.♞f3 ♞bd7 (7...e6 – Game 40) 8.0-0 e6 9.♗f4 (9.a3 ♛c7 10.♗f4 ♗d6 11.♞e2 0-0 12.c4?! ♗×f4 13.♞×f4 e5 14.d×e5 ♞×e5 15.♛b3 (Managadze, N. (2444) – Nikolaidis, I. (2538), Kalamaria 2006) 15...♗×f3 16.♗×f3 ♛b6∓; 12.♖e1 h6 13.c4 ♖fe8 14.♛b3 e5⇄) 9...♛b4 10.♖b1 (10.a3 ♛×b2?! 11.♛d2 ♛b6 12.♖fb1 ♛a6 13.a4)

A2a) 10...♛a5 11.h3 ♗×f3 12.♛×f3 ♗e7 13.a3 0-0 14.b4 ♛f5 15.♛e2 ♞d5 16.♞×d5 c×d5 17.c4 (Azarov, S. (2570) – Zablotsky, S. (2500), Voronezh 2007) 17...♞b6 18.c5 ♞c4⇄;

A2b) 10...♗e7 11.h3 (11.a3 ♛b6 12.♛d2 0-0 13.♞e5 ♞×e5 14.d×e5 ♖fd8 15.♛c1 ♞d5∓, Van Delft, M. (2385) – Zatonskih, A. (2425), Netherlands 2005) 11...♗×f3 (11...♗h5!? 12.a3 ♛b6) 12.♗×f3 0-0 13.♞e2 (13.a3!? ♛a5 14.♛d3) 13...♗e2 14.♞c1 ♖fe8 15.a3 e5 16.b4 ♛c7 17.d×e5 ♞×e5 18.♞d3 ♗d6 19.♞×e5 ♗×e5 20.♗×e5 ♖×e5 ½-½, Lanin, A. (2465) – Lysyj, I. (2575), St. Petersburg 2007;

B) 6...♗f5 7.♞f3 (7.♞ge2 e6 8.♗f4 ♛b4 9.a3 ♛b6⇄) 7...e6 (7...♞bd7!? 8.0-0 e6) 8.0-0

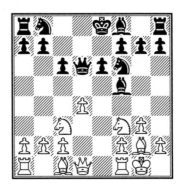

B1) 8...♘bd7

B1a) 9.♗f4 ♛b4 10.♛c1 (10.♖b1!?) 10...♗e7 11.a3 ♛b6 12.b4 0-0 13.♘a4 (13.♘h4 ♗g4 14.♛d2 ♘d5⇄) 13...♛a6 14.♘c5 ♘×c5 15.b×c5 ♘d5 16.♗d2 (Matvienko, I. (2240) – Stopa, J. (2440), Czechia 2008) 16...♛c4∓;

B1b) 9.♛e2 ♗e7 10.♖d1 (10.a3 ♛c7 11.h3 0-0 12.♘h4 ♗g6 13.♘×g6 h×g6 14.♖d1 ♖fe8 15.♗g5 ♖ad8±, Gutenev, A. (2280) – Stopa, J. (2440), Czechia 2008; 11...♘d5!?⇄) 10...h6 (Slovineanu, V. (2420) – Nevednichy, V. (2575), Predeal 2006) 11.♘e5±; 8...♗e7 9.♘e5 h5 10.h3 ♘bd7 11.♘c4 ♛b4 12.♘e3 (Vesselovsky, S. (2419) – Nedela, V. (2380), Czechia 2001) 12...♗g6 13.a3 ♛b6 14.♘c4 ♛a6=;

B2) 8...h6

B2a) 9.♗f4 ♛d8 10.a3 (13.♖e1!?; 13.♘e5!?) 10...♗e7 11.♖e1 ♘bd7 12.♛e2 0-0 13.♖ad1 (Mamedov, R. (2452) – Abbasov, F. (2443), Internet 2004) 13...♘d5 14.♘×d5 c×d5⇄;

B2) 9.♛e2 ♗e7 (9...♘bd7!?) 10.♗f4 ♛d8 11.♖ad1 0-0 12.♘e5 (Laznicka, V. (2429) – Nedela, V. (2378), Czechia 2004) 12...♘bd7 13.g4 ♗h7⇄ or 13.♘c4 ♘b6⇄;

B2b) 9.a3 ♗e7 10.♛e2 0-0 11.♗f4 (11.b3 ♛c7 12.♗b2 ♘bd7 13.♘e5 ♖ad8=, Palkovi, J. (2414) – Bachofner, A. (2326), Austria 2002) 11...♛d8 12.♖ad1 ♘bd7⇄, Murariu, A. (2441) – Ardelean, G. (2442), Bucharest 2006.

We return now to Topalov – Nisipeanu.

7.♗f4

A) 7.♘ge2 ♗g7 8.0-0 0-0 9.♗f4 ♛d8 10.♛c1 (10.b4 ♗e6 11.♛d2 ♘d5=) 10...♘a6 11.♗e5 ♘c7 12.♘f4 ♗h6 13.♛e1 ♗f5⇄, Marttala, T. (2260) – Cicak, S. (2530), Stockholm 2006;

B) 7.♘f3 ♗g7 (7...♗g4!? 8.♗f4 ♛e6+)

B1) 8.0-0 0-0 9.♗f4 ♛b4 (9...♛d8!? 10.♘e5 ♘a6) 10.♖b1 ♘d5 (10...♘a6?! 11.♖e1 ♖e8 12.d5 ♘×d5 13.♘×d5 c×d5 14.♛×d5 ♗e6 15.♖×e6) 11.♘×d5 c×d5 12.c3 (Filonenko, K. – Stanislavskaya, K., Alushta 2005) 12...♛b6 13.♛d2 (13.♘e5!?) 13...♘c6 14.♖fe1 ♗f5=;

B2) 8.♗f4 ♛b4 (8...♛d8!?) 9.♖b1 ♘d5 (9...♛c4?! 10.♘e5 ♛a6 11.b4 0-0 (Zimmermann, J. (2325) – Vovk, I. (2300) Gothenburg 2007) 12.b5 c×b5 13.♘×b5 ♘h5 14.♗d2 ♛b6 15.0-0 a6 16.♘c4 ♛d8 17.♗a5± or 12...♛a5 13.♛d2 c×b5 14.♖×b5 ♛a6 15.0-0±) 10.♗d2 ♛c4 11.b3 (11.♗f1 ♘×c3 12.♗×c4 ♘×d1 13.♖×d1 ♗f5) 11...♛a6 12.♘×d5 c×d5 13.♘e5 ♗e6=; 12.♗f1 ♛a3 13.♗c4 ♘×c3 14.♗×c3 ♘d7 15.0-0 0-0 16.♛e1 a5=.

7...♛b4

7...♕d8 8.♘f3 (8.d5 ♗g7 9.d×c6 ♕×d1+ 10.♖×d1 ♘×c6 11.♘f3±; 8.♘ge2 ♗g7 9.0-0 0-0 10.♖e1±, Ahmad, W. – Foudzi, J. (2078), Bikaner 2004) 8...♗g7 9.0-0 (9.♕e2!?) 9...0-0 10.♖e1 (10.♘e5 see the line 7.♘f3 ♗g7 8.0-0 0-0 9.♗f4 ♕d8 10.♘e5) 10...♘a6 11.a3 ♘c7±.

8.♘ge2 (8.♖b1!?)

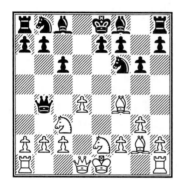

8...♗g7

8...♕×b2?! 9.♖b1 ♕a3 10.0-0 with problems for Black; for example, 10...♗g7 11.d5 ♘×d5 (11...0-0 12.♗×b8 ♖×b8 13.d×c6 with a strong initiative) 12.♗×d5 ♕a5 (12...c×d5 13.♘b5±) 13.♗b3 ♗×c3 14.♘×c3 ♕×c3 15.♖e1 0-0 16.♗h6 ♘d7 17.♖×e7±.

9.♕c1

9.0-0 0-0 10.♕d2 ♕×b2 11.♖ab1 ♕a3∞.

9...0-0 10.0-0 ♗g4

10...♗f5 11.a4 ♘bd7 12.a5 ♕c4 13.♖e1±; 11...a5 12.♖a3 ♕c4 13.♖b3 ♕a6⇄.

11.a3 ♕a5

11...♕b6 12.b4 ♘bd7 13.♖e1 ♖fe8=; 12.♗e3!? ♖d8 13.♘f4.

12.h3 ♗×e2

12...♗f5!? 13.b4 ♕a6 14.♖b1 ♕c4 15.b5 a5 16.b×c6 b×c6⇄.

13.♘×e2 ♘bd7 14.c4

14.♘c3 ♖fe8 15.♖d1 (15.b4 ♕d8 16.♕d2 ♘b6 17.b5 ♘fd5⇄) 15...♘b6 16.♕d2 (16.b4 ♕f5) 16...♘h5 17.♗c7 ♖ac8 18.b4 ♕a6=.

14...e5 15.b4 ♕c7

16.d×e5 ♘×e5 17.♕c2 a5 18.♖ae1 (18.♘d4!? ♘h5 19.♗e3±) 18...a×b4 19.a×b4 ♖fe8 20.c5?! (20.♘d4!? ♘h5 21.♗e3) 20...♘d5 21.♗d2 ♘d7 (21...♕d8 22.♖d1 ♕f6 23.♘f4 ♘c7 24.♗c3 ♘b5 25.♗a1 ♕g5⇄ or 24.♖fe1 ♘b5 25.♗c1 ♘d4⇄; 21...♖a3!?) 22.♕c4 ♘7f6 23.g4 (23.♘d4!?) 23...h5 24.♘g3 (24.g5 ♘h7 25.♗×d5?! c×d5 26.♕×d5 ♖ed8 27.♗f4 ♖×d5 28.♗×c7 ♘×g5 29.♔g2 ♘e6 30.♗g3 ♖a4 31.♖b1 ♗f6 with the better ending for Black; 25.b5 ♖ed8 26.b×c6 b×c6 27.h4 ♘f8 28.♘f4 ♘e7⇄) 24...h×g4 25.h×g4 ♕d7 26.g5 ♖×e1 27.♖×e1 ♘e8 (27...♘g4

28.b5 ♘e5 29.♛b3 ♘g4?! 30.b×c6 b×c6 31.♗h3; 29...♛g4 30.♖e4 ♖a1+ 31.♘f1 ♖b1 32.♛×b1?? ♘f3+ 33.♔h1 ♛h5+; 32.♛a3 ♖a1 33.♛b3 ♖b1=) **28.♗f3** (28.♘e4!? ♖a3 29.♖b1) **28...♘ec7 29.♗g4 ♛d8 30.♔g2 ♘b5 31.♖d1 ♖a1 32.♖×a1 ♗×a1 33.♗f3 ♗e5 34.♘e2** (34.♗×d5 ♛×d5+ 35.♛×d5 c×d5 36.f4 ♗b2=) **34...♘dc7 35.♗e3 ♘e6 36.♗g4 ♘bc7 37.♛e4 ♗g7 38.f4 ♛d1 39.♔f2** (39.♗f2 ♛d5 40.♔f3 ♛b3+ 41.♔g2 ♛d5=) **39...♗c3 40.b5?!** (40.♘×c3 ♛×g4 41.♗d2 ♛h3∓) **40...♛e1+** (40...♘×b5!? 41.f5 g×f5) **41.♔g2 ♘d5 42.b×c6?!** (42.♗c1 ♗d2 43.♗×e6? ♘×f4+; 43.♗×d2 ♛×d2 44.♗×e6 ♘×f4+ 45.♛×f4 ♛×e2+ 46.♔g3 ♛×e6 47.♛b8+ ♔g7 48.♛×b7 ♛e3+ with a draw.) **42...b×c6 43.♛d3?** (43.♗c1 ♗d2 44.♗×d2 ♛×d2 45.♗×e6 ♘×f4+ 46.♛×f4 ♛×e2+ 47.♔g3 ♛×e6 48.♛d4 with chances to save the game.) **43...♗d4!+− 44.♗×e6** (44.♗d2 ♛f2+ 45.♔h3 ♛f1+ 46.♔g3 ♗f2+ 47.♔h2 ♗g1+ 48.♔h1 ♗e3+ 49.♔h2 ♘e×f4+−; 47.♔f3 ♗g1+ 48.♔g3 ♛f2+ 49.♔h3 ♛h2#) **44...♘×e3+ 45.♔h2 ♛f2+ 46.♔h3 ♛f3+** (46...♛g2+ 47.♔h4 ♛h2+ 48.♗h3 ♛f2+ 49.♘g3 ♛×f4+ 50.♗g4 ♛×g4#) **47.♘g3 ♛g2+** (if 48.♔h4 ♛h2+ 49.♗h3 ♘g2+ 50.♔g4 ♛×h3+ 51.♔×h3 ♘×f4+) **0-1**

Summary: In this game, after **1.e4 d5 2.e×d5 ♛×d5 3.♘c3 ♛d6**, we examined **4.g3** with d2-d3 and ♘g1-e2, avoiding lines that transpose to positions from Game 18, and avoiding lines involving d2-d4 and ♘g1-f3, with the exception of 4.g3 ♘f6 5.d4. The move **4.g3** is not bad, and has sometimes

taken Black by surprise. However, practice and analysis both indicate that Black can equalize with counterplay after 4...e5, 4...c6, 4...♘c6 or 4...♘f6.

Game 39
Cicak, S. (2530) – Gofshtein, Z. (2520)
Sants 2006

1.e4 d5 2.e×d5 ♛×d5 3.♘c3 ♛d6 4.♗c4

In this game we examine ♗f1-c4 without an earlier d2-d4 and without transposition to other d2-d4 lines already reviewed.

4...♘f6

4...c6 or 4...a6 is also playable. Let's also examine **A)** 4...e5; **B)** 4...♘c6 and **C)** 4...♗e6.

A) 4...e5?! (as difficult as it may be to believe, after this move White has good winning chances!) 5.♘f3

A1) 5...♘c6 (5...♗e7 6.♘b5 ♛c6 7.♘×e5 ♛×g2 8.♗d5± or 6...♛c5 7.d3 f6 8.♗e3 ♛c6 9.♘×a7±) 6.0-0 ♘f6 7.♘b5 ♛e7 8.d4 a6 9.d×e5 a×b5 10.e×f6 ♛×f6 11.♖e1+ ♗e7 12.♗×b5 ♗g4 13.♗g5 ♛×g5 14.♘×g5 ♗×d1

15.♖a×d1±, Law, S. – Nemeth, L.,Internet 2003;

A2) 5...♘f6 6.0-0 ♗g4 (6...♗e6 7.♗×e6 ♕×e6 8.d4 e4 9.♖e1 ♗b4 10.♘g5 ♕f5 11.♘g×e4±) 7.♘b5 ♕c5 (7...♕c6 8.♘×e5 ♗×d1 9.♘×c6 ♘×c6 10.♖×d1±) 8.♕e2 e4 (8...♘a6 9.♗×f7+ ♔×f7 10.♘×e5+ ♔g8 11.♘×g4± or 8...a6 9.d4 ♗×f3 10.g×f3 ♕e7 11.d×e5 a×b5 12.e×f6±;

B) 4...♘c6 5.♘f3 (5.♘ge2 ♘f6 6.d4 ♗g4 – 5.♗c4 ♗g4 6.♘ge2 ♘c6, Game 9) 5...♘f6 6.d3 (6.d4 ♗g4 – 4.d4 ♘f6 5.♗c4 ♘c6 6.♘f3 ♗g4, Game 9; 6.0-0 a6 7.♖e1 ♗f5 8.d3 e6 9.♗g5 0-0-0⇄; 7...♗g4!? 8.h3 ♗h5) 6...a6 7.a3

B1) 7...g6 8.♘g5 ♕d8 9.♕e2 (9.♕f3!? ♗g4 10.♕g3 ♕×g3 11.h×g3 ♗g7±; 9.0-0!? ♗g7 10.♘f3 ♗g4 11.♘ce4±) 9...♗g7 10.♗d2 0-0 11.0-0-0 (11.0-0 ♘c6=) 11...b5 12.♗b3 ♘c6⇄, Godoy Bugueno, D. (2355) – Bianchi, G. (2425), Santiago 1995

B2) 7...♗g4 8.h3 ♗h5 9.g4 ♗g6 10.♗e3 (10.♘h4 e6 11.♗e3 0-0-0 12.♕d2 ♘e5∓ or 12.♕e2 ♘d5∓) 10...0-0-0 11.♕d2 ♘a5 12.♗a2 ♕c6 13.♕e2 (13.♔e2 ♕e8∓) 13...e5⇄;

C) 4...♗e6 5.♕e2 (5.♗×e6 ♕×e6+ 6.♘ge2 ♘f6 7.d4 (Kuehn, P. (2275) – Nelki, H., Germany 1994) 7...♕f5 8.♗f4 ♘a6 9.0-0 0-0-0 10.a3 ♘b8 11.♕c1 ♘c6 12.♖d1 e6⇄) 4...♗×c4 6.♕×c4 ♕c6 7.♕×c6+ ♘×c6 8.♘f3 ♘b4 9.♔d1 ♘f6 10.a3 ♘c6 (10...♘bd5 11.♘×d5 ♘×d5 12.c4 ♘f4 13.d4 ♘d3 14.♔e2 ♘×c1+ 15.♖a×c1±, Zoler, D. (2518) – Bitansky, I. (2377), Ramat Aviv 2004; 12...♘f6!?) 11.d3 e6 12.♔e2 h6=.

We return now to Cicak – Gofshtein.

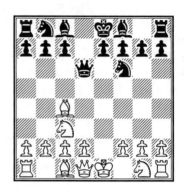

5.♘ge2

Also worth consideration are **A)** 5.♕f3; **B)** 5.d3 and **C)** 5.♘f3.

A) 5.♕f3 a6 (5...♘c6!? 6.♘b5 ♕d8 7.♕g3 e5) 6.d3 ♘c6 7.♗e4 (Prohaszka, P. (2265) – Galyas, M. (2444), Budapest 2005) 7...♕d7 8.♘×f6+ (8.♘e2 ♘e5 9.♕f4 ♘×c4 10.♘×f6+ g×f6 11.♕×c4 ♖g8∓) 8...g×f6 9.♘e2 ♘e5 10.♕e4 ♘×c4 11.♕×c4 ♖g8∓;

B) 5.d3 a6

B1) 6.♘f3 (6.♘ge2 – 5.♘ge2 a6 6.d3) 6...♘c6 (6...♗g4 7.h3 ♗h5 8.g4 ♗g6 9.♗e3 ♘c6 10.♕d2 0-0-0 11.0-0-0 ♘a5 12.♗b3 ♘×b3+ 13.a×b3 e6⇄, Gutierrez Jimenez, J. (2310) – Kantans, T. (2145), Pardubice 2008; 12.♕e2!?) 7.♗g5 ♗g4 8.h3 ♗h5 9.g4 ♗g6 10.♕e2 0-0-0 11.0-0-0 h6 12.♘e4 ♕d7⇄, Jaracz, B. (2256) – Nikolov, S. (2431), Nova Gorica 2005;

B2) 6.h3

B2a) 6...♘c6 7.♘f3 ♘a5 (7...♗e6!? 8.♗×e6 ♕×e6+ 9.♗e3 ♕d7 10.0-0 0-0-0=) 8.♗b3 (8.0-0!?) 8...g6

(8...♘xb3 9.axb3 g6 10.0-0 ♗g7 11.♖a4 ♗e6∓, Vancini, E. (2307) – Borgo, G. (2420), Bratto 2002) 9.0-0 ♗g7 10.♖e1 0-0 11.♗g5 ♘xb3 12.axb3 h6 13.♗e3 ♘d5 14.♘xd5 ♛xd5 15.♛d2 g5⇄;

B2b) 6...b5 7.♗b3 ♗b7 8.♘f3 ♘bd7

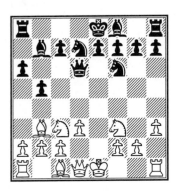

B2b1) 9.♗e3 e6 10.♛e2 ♘c5 11.0-0-0 (11.0-0!? ♗e7 12.d4 ♘xb3 13.axb3 0-0 14.♖fd1=) 11...♘xb3+ 12.axb3 ♗e7 13.♘e4 (13.♗g5!? 0-0 14.♔b1) 13...♛d5 14.♗g5 a5 15.♗xf6 gxf6∓, Szakolczai, P. (2285) – Brustkern, J. (2220), Budapest 2006;

B2b2) 9.♛e2 ♘c5 10.♗g5 e6 11.0-0 (11.♗xf6?! gxf6∓, Ledger, D. (2285) – Constantinou, P. (2170), London 2007) 11...h6 12.♗h4 ♗e7 13.d4 ♘xb3 14.axb3 0-0 15.♗xf6 ♗xf6 16.♘e4 ♗xe4 17.♛xe4= **or** 9...e6 10.♗g5 ♗e7 11.0-0 ♘c5 12.♖fe1 b4 (Klasmeier, J. – Heinzel, O. (2334), Essen Borbeck 1999) 13.♘a4 ♘xb3 14.axb3 0-0=;

B3) 6.a4 ♘c6 7.♘ge2 e5 (7...♗f5 8.♘g3 ♗g6 9.0-0 e6 10.♖e1 ♗e7 11.h4 (Kotan, L. (2361) – Vojtek. V. (2276), Slovakia 2003) 11...h5=; 7...g6 8.♗g5 ♗g7 9.♛d2 h6 10.♗h4 0-0 11.0-0 e5⇄, Diaz Rodriguez, J. (2130) – Vigil

Alvarez, L. (2320), Leon 2006) 8.♘g3 ♗e7 9.0-0 ♗e6 10.♘ge4 ♛d7 11.♗xe6 ♛xe6=, Kampman, T. – Stap, K. (2110), Dieren 2007;

C) 5.♘f3

5...♘c6 – 4...♘c6 5.♘f3 ♘f6. Other interesting possibilities are **C1)** 5...♗e6; **C2)** 5...c6 and **C3)** 5...a6.

C1) 5...♗e6 6.♘b5 (6.♛e2 ♗xc4 7.♛xc4 ♘c6 8.d3 e6 9.0-0 ♛b4 10.♛xb4 ♗xb4 11.♗d2 0-0-0 12.a3 ♗e7=, Bentsen, O. (2180) – Haugli, P. (2320), Norway 2007) 6...♛b6 7.♗xe6 ♛xe6+ 8.♛e2 ♛xe2+ 9.♔xe2 ♘a6∓;

C2) 5...c6 6.d3 (6.d4 – Game 1) 6...♗f5 (6...♗g4!? 7.0-0 ♘bd7 8.♖e1 e6) 7.♛e2 e6 8.h3 (8.♗g5 ♘bd7 9.♘e4 ♘xe4.dxe4 ♗g4 11.h3?! ♗xf3 12.gxf3 (Areshchenko, A. (2564) – Mastrovasilis, A. (2475), Moscow 2004) 12...♛e5! 13.f4 ♛xb2 14.0-0 ♛c3∓) 8...♗g6 (8...♘bd7 9.0-0 0-0-0 10.♗e3 ♘b6 11.♗b3∓) 9.♗b3 ♘bd7 10.a3 ♗e7 11.♗d2 ♛c7⇄, Areshchenko, A. (2641) – Wang Yue (2626), Lausanne 2006;

C3) 5...a6 and now:

C3a) 6.a4 (6.d4 – Games 26-28; 6.d3 – 5.d3 a6 6.♘f3) 6...♘c6 7.h3 h6 8.b3 ♗f5 9.♗a3 ♕d7 10.0-0 (10.a5 e5 11.♗xf8 ♖xf8 12.d3 0-0-0∓, Borges, Y. (2362) – Almeida, O. (2454), Santa Clara 2006) 10...e6 11.♗xf8 ♖xf8 12.♖e1 0-0-0 13.d3= or7...♗e6 8.♕e2 (8.♗xe6 ♕xe6+ 9.♘e2 0-0-0 10.d3 ♕d7 11.0-0 e5⇄) 8...♗xc4 9.♕xc4 (Trent, L. (2299) – Hanley, C. (2387), Millfield 2003) 9...e6 10.d3 0-0-0 11.♗f4 ♕c5 12.♕xc5 ♗xc5 13.0-0 ♘d5∓;

C3b) 6.0-0 b5 (6...♘c6!?; 6...♗g4!?; 6...♗f5!?) 7.♗b3 ♗b7

C3b1) 8.♘g5 e6 9.♖e1 ♕c6 10.f3 ♗e7 11.d4 h6 (11...0-0? 12.♘xe6 fxe6 13.♖xe6±) 12.♘xf7 (12.♘ge4 ♘bd7=) 12...♔xf7 13.♖xe6 ♕xe6 14.♗xe6+ ♔xe6 15.♗f4 (Pieri, T. – Busson, B. (2105), Provence 2003) 15...♔f7 16.♗xc7 ♘bd7⇄ or 15.a4 b4 16.♕e2+ ♔d7 17.♘e4 ♘c6⇄;

C3b2) 8.d3 (8.d4 – Game 27) 8...e6 9.♖e1 ♗e7 10.♘g5 (Nimko, N. – Stanislavskaya, K., Evpatoria 2007) 10...♕c6 11.f3 h6 12.♘ge4 (12.♘xe6?! fxe6 13.♖xe6 ♕d7 14.♕e2?! ♘c6 15.♗e3 0-0-0∓; 14.a4 b4 15.♘e4∓) 12...♘bd7 13.♗e3 0-0= or 9.♕e2 ♗e7 (9...♘bd7!? 10.a4 ♘c5) 10.a4 b4

11.♘e4 ♘xe4 12.dxe4 (Ivanovic, B. (2501) – Benkovic, P. (2469), Subotica 2003) 12...0-0 13.♖d1 ♕c6 14.♖d4±.

Back to Cicak – Gofshtein.

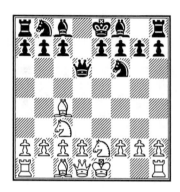

5...a6 6.0-0

There are two main alternatives here:

A) 6.a4 ♕c6 7.d3 ♕xg2 8.♖g1 ♕xh2 9.♗f4 ♕h5 10.♕d2 (10.♗xc7 ♕c5 11.♗f4 ♘c6 12.♕d2 ♗g4 13.0-0-0 h5∓) 10...♘c6 11.♖g5 11...♕h3 (11...♘d4!?) 12.0-0-0 (Petraki, M. (2094) – Kulicov, O. (2407), Athens 2006) 12...h6 13.♖g3 ♕d7∓;

B) 6.d3 (6.d4 – Games 5-6)

B1) 6...b5 7.♗b3 ♗b7 8.f3 (8.0-0 c5 – 5.♘ge2 a6 6.0-0 b5 7.♗b3 ♗b7 8.d3 c5; 8.♗f4?! e5 9.♗e3 ♗xg2) 8...♘bd7 9.♗f4 (9.♘g3 c5 10.♕e2 e6 11.a4 ♕b6⇄, Pinter, E. (2411) – Sergeev, V. (2451), Tatranske Zruby 2003; 9...♘c5!?; 10.0-0 e6 11.♗e3 ♗e7 12.a4 b4 13.♘ce4 ♕c7⇄) 9...♕b6 10.♕d2 e6 11.♗e3 c5 12.a4 ♗e7⇄, Heidrich, M. (2405) – Balinov, I. (2454), Nuernberg 2006;.

B2) 6...♘c6 7.0-0 (7.♗f4?! e5 8.♗g3 ♗e6 9.0-0 0-0-0∓) 7...♗g4 (7...♘a5!?

8.♗b3 ♘xb3 9.axb3 ♗g4) 8.f3 (Zhukova, N. (2465) – Aginian, N. (2370), Moscow 2005) 8...♗e6 9.♗b3 (9.♘e4!? ♘xe4 10.♗xe6 ♛xe6 11.fxe4) 9...0-0-0 10.♗e3 (10.♗f4 ♛c5+ 11.♔h1 ♗xb3 12.axb3 h5 13.♘e4 ♛f5 14.♛d2 e5 15.♗e3 h4 ∓; 14.♘g5 ♘d5∓) 10...g6 11.♛e1 ♗g7 12.♛f2⇄.

6...b5

6...♗g4!? (6...♘c6!?) 7.d4 ♘c6 8.f3 (8.♗e3 0-0-0 9.♗xf7?! e6) 8...♗f5 9.♗f4 ♛d7⇄.

7.♗b3 c5

Also possible is 7...♗b7; for example, 8.♘g3 (8.d4 – 7.♗b3 ♗b7 8.0-0, Game 6) 8...c5 (8...♘c6!?; 8...e6!?) 9.d3 ♛c6 10.f3 e6 11.♔h1 11.♗f4 (11.♛e2 ♗e7 12.♖e1 0-0 13.♗f4 ♘bd7 14.♘f5 ♗d8 15.♘d6? ♗c7 16.♘ce4 ♘h5∓; 11...♗e7 12.♛e2 0-0 13.♘ce4 ♛c7 14.♘xf6+ ♗xf6 15.♘e4 ♗e7=, Moreno Tejera, E. (2139) – Campos, L., Navalmoral 2000; 13...♘bd7!?) 11...♗d6 12.♛d2 ♗xf4 13.♛xf4 ♛b6 14.♔h1 0-0=.

e6 15.a4 ♗g7⇄, Kamenecki, S. (1930) – Jukic, Z. (2315), Sibenik 2007) 9...e5 (9...♛c6!? 10.f3 ♘bd7) 10.♗g3 (10.♗e3 ♘c6 11.♘g3 ♘d4 12.f4 ♘xb3 13.axb3 0-0-0 14.♛e2±) 10...♘bd7 11.f3 ♗e7 12.a4 ♛c6 13.axb5 axb5 14.♖xa8+ ♗xa8 15.♛a1 (Sig Vargas, M. (2112) – Tanco Salas, J., Spain 2004) 15...b4 (15...♗b7?! 16.♛a5 c4 17.dxc4 bxc4 18.♗a4 ♛c5+ 19.♛xc5 ♗xc5+ 20.♔h1 ♔e7 21.♗b5) 16.♘d1 0-0 17.♘e3 ♗b7±.

9...c4

9...b4!? 10.♘b1 ♘c6 11.♘d2 ♘a5 12.♘c4 (12.♗a2 g6⇄) 12...♘xc4 13.♗xc4 e6 14.♗f4 ♛c6 15.f3 ♗d6=.

10.dxc4 ♛c6 11.f3 bxc4 12.♗a2 ♘bd7

12...e5 13.♗g5 (13.♘g3!? ♘bd7 14.♛e2; 13.♛e1!? ♘bd7 14.♛g3) 13...♘bd7 14.♘g3 ♗b4 15.♘f5 0-0 (Cicak, S. (2532) – Mellado Trivino, J. (2388), La Pobla de Lillet 2006) 16.♛e2 h6 17.♗h4 ♖ac8 18.♖ad1±.

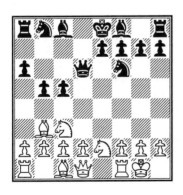

8.d3 ♗b7 9.a4

9.♗f4 (9.♘f4 ♘bd7 10.♖e1 g5 11.♘h5 h6 12.♛e2 ♛c6 13.♘xf6+ ♘xf6 14.f3

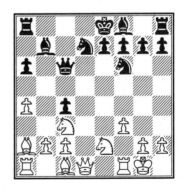

13.♘g3

A) 13.♗e3 (13.♛e1 e6 14.♘d4 ♛c7 15.♛e2 ♖d8⇄) 13...♘g4 (13...e5!?

14.♘g3 ♘g4) 14.♕d4 ♘xe3 15.♕xe3 e5 16.♔h1 ♗e7 17.♖ad1 ♕e6⇄;

B) 13.♘d4 ♕c7 14.♕e2 ♖c8 15.♘f5 (15.♖e1 e6 16.♘xe6 fxe6 17.♕xe6+ ♔d8 18.♔h1 ♘b6 19.♗xc4 ♕xe6 20.♗xe6 ♗d6∓ or 18.♗g5 ♕b6+ 19.♕xb6+ ♘xb6 20.♖ad1+ ♘bd7∓) 15...e6 16.♔h1 h5 17.♗g5 (17.♖d1?! ♘g4 18.fxg4 hxg4 19.♘h6 gxh6 20.♕xg4? ♘f6 21.♕f4 ♖g8∓) 17...♘c5 18.♗xf6 gxf6 19.♘e3 ♘e5 20.f4 ♗h6⇄.

13...e6 14.♕e2 ♖c8 15.♔h1 ♗e7 16.♖d1 0-0 17.♖d4 (17.♘f5?! exf5 18.♕xe7 ♖fe8 19.♕xb4 ♘e5∓) **17...♘b6 18.♘ge4** (18.a5 ♕c5 19.♗e3 ♕xa5 or 19.axb6 ♕xd4 20.♗e3 ♕d6 21.♗xc4 ♕b4∓) **18...♘xe4 19.♖xe4** (19.♘xe4 e5 20.♖d1 ♘xa4∓) **19...♕d7 20.♖g4 f5 21.♖xc4** (21.♗xc4? ♖c6 22.♖f4 g5∓; 21.♖g3 ♗h4 22.♖h3 ♗f6∓) **21...♘xc4 22.♗xc4 ♖c6 23.♗f4 ♗f6∓ 24.♖d1 ♕e7 25.♗b3 ♔h8** (25...♗c8 26.g3 ♖d8 27.♖xd8 ♕xd8∓; 26.♖e1 ♕b4 27.♗e5 ♗xe5 28.♕xe5 ♖d8∓; 27.♗d2 ♕c5 28.♗a2 a5 29.♘c1 ♖d8 30.♘d3∓) **26.♖e1 ♕c5 27.♘d1 e5?!** (27...♖d8∓) **28.♗xe5 ♗xe5 29.♕xe5 ♕xe5 30.♖xe5 ♖d6** (30...♖cc8∓) **31.♘f2 ♖d2?!** (31...♗c6) **32.♔g1 g6 33.♘d3± ♖d8 34.h4 ♗c6 35.♖c5 ♖d6 36.♖a5 ♗d7 37.♖e5 ♔g7 38.♖e7+ ♔f8 39.♖xh7 ♗e6 40.♗xe6 ♖xe6 41.♘f4 ♖c6 42.♔h2 ♖dxc2 43.b3 ♔g8 44.♖b7 ♖c7 45.♖b8+ ♖c8 46.♖b4 a5 47.♖d4 ♖2c6 48.♔g3 ♖b8 49.♖d7 ♖a6 50.♘d5 ♖xb3 51.♔f4 ♖b2 52.g4 fxg4 53.fxg4 ♖f2+ 54.♔g5 ♖f7 55.♖d8+ ♔g7 56.♖c8?? ♖e6 0-1**

Summary: After **1.e4 d5 2.exd5 ♕xd5 3.♘c3 ♕d6**, we examined **4.♗c4** without an earlier d2-d4 and without transposition to other d2-d4 lines. After **4.♗c4**, Black can respond with 4...♘c6 or 4...♗e6 (the natural-looking 4...e5 can bring trouble to Black). After the usual continuation 4...♘f6 (or 4...a6, 4...c6), White must decide what kind of position to play: a "normal" one with a pawn on d4, or an "original" one with the pawn at d3. In my opinion the latter course has more minuses for White than pluses.

Game 40
Alexikov, A. (2425) – Belikov, V. (2560)
Alushta 2007

1.e4 d5 2.exd5 ♕xd5 3.♘c3 ♕d6 4.♘f3

4...♘f6

Both 4...a6 and 4...c6 are also playable. Let's also look at **A)** 4...e5; **B)** 4...♘c6 and **C)** 4...g6.

A) 4...e5?! 5.d4 (the analysis of the position after 5.♗c4 shows an advantage for White) 5...exd4 6.♘xd4±; 5...♘c6 6.dxe5± or 6.♗b5±;

B) 4...♘c6 5.d4 (5.g3 ♗g4 6.♗g2 ♘f6 7.0-0 e5 8.♖e1 0-0-0⇄, Kolesnichenko, A. (2245) – Starostin, G. Odessa 2000; 5.♗b5 ♗g4 6.♕e2 ♘f6 7.d3 0-0-0⇄, Celis, G. (2335) – Bianchi, R., Buenos Aires 1995)

B1) 5...♗g4?! (5...♘f6 – 4.d4 ♘f6 5.♘f3 ♘c6 Game 29) 6.♘b5 ♕e6+ (6...♕d7 7.♗f4) 7.♘e5! ♕xe5+ (7...♘xe5 8.♘xc7+ ♔d7 9.♘xe6 ♗xd1 10.♘xf8+ ♖xf8 11.♔xd1±) 8.dxe5 ♗xd1 9.♘xc7+ ♔d8 10.♘xa8±;

B2) 5...a6?! 6.d5 ♘e5 (6...♘a7 7.♕d4 c5 8.♕h4 ♘f6 9.♗f4 ♕b6 10.0-0-0±) 7.♘xe5 (7.♗f4 ♘d3+ 8.♗xd3 ♕xf4±, Lutz, K. (2296) – Alber, H. (2387), Offenbach 2005) 7...♕xe5+ 8.♗e2 ♘f6 (8...♗g4 9.♗e3 ♗xe2 10.♕xe2 0-0-0 11.0-0-0 ♘f6 12.♕c4±) 9.0-0 ♗f5 10.g4 ♗d7 11.f4 ♕d6 12.g5 ♕b6+ 13.♖f2 ♘g8 14.♕d3 0-0-0 15.♗e3 ♕xb2 16.♖b1 ♕a3 17.♕d4±;

C) 4...g6 (this position may be reached several ways; for example, 1.♘f3 g6 2.e4 d5 3.exd5 ♕xd5 4.♘c3 ♕d6) 5.♗c4 (5.a4 5.♘f3 ♗g7 6.♗c4 ♗e6 7.♕e2 ♗xc4 8.♕xc4 c6?! 9.0-0 ♘f6 10.♖e1 0-0 11.b3 ♖e8 12.♗a3 ♕c7 13.♘e5 e6 14.♘b5±, Krstic, U, (2332) – Sermek, D. (2540), Pula 1999; 8...♘c6 9.0-0 ♘f6 10.♖e1 ♕b4 11.♕e2 0-0 12.♖a3 ♖ab8=) 5...♘f6

C1) 6.d3 (6.d4 – Game 29) 6...♗g7 7.0-0 0-0 8.♗g5 c6 (8...a6!? 9.♕d2 ♘c6 10.♖fe1 b5 11.♗f4 ♕d7 12.♗b3 ♗b7⇄) 9.♖e1 ♗g4 10.h3 ♗xf3 11.♕xf3 ♘bd7±, Okrajek, A. (2295) – Epishin, V. (2599), Werther 2002;

C2) 6.♘b5 ♕d8 7.♘e5 e6 8.d4 a6 9.♘c3 ♗g7 (9...♘c6 10.♘xc6 bxc6

11.0-0 ♗g7 12.♕f3 ♘d5±) 10.♗g5 h6 11.♗e3 (Hernandez, R. (2367) – Fernandez Garcia, J. (2468), Havana 2005) 11...♘c6 12.♘xc6 (12.f4 ♘d5 13.♘xd5 exd5 14.♗e2 ♕h4+ 15.g3 ♕e7⇄) 12...bxc6 13.♕f3 0-0 (13...♘d5!?) 14.♕xc6 ♖b8 15.0-0 ♘g4∞.

Let's return to Alexikov – Belikov.

5.g3

Other moves do not promise much:

A) 5.h3 (5.♗c4 – Game 39; 5.d4 – Games 10-29) 5...c6 (5...g6 6.♗c4 ♗g7 7.0-0 0-0 8.d3 ♘c6 9.a3 b6 10.♖e1 ♗b7 11.♗g5 ♖ae8 12.♕e2 e5 13.♗xf6 ♕xf6 14.♗d5 ♘d8 15.♗xb7 ♘xb7 16.♖ad1 ♕d6 ½-½, Galego, L. (2467) – Sulava, N. (2531), Lisbon 2001) 6.♗c4 ♗f5 7.♕e2 ♘bd7 8.d3 e6 9.♗d2 (9.0-0!? 0-0-0 10.♗e3) 9...♗e7 10.♗b3 ♘c5 11.♘e5 h6=, Galiana, J. (2290) – Tiviakov, S. (2680), Calvia 2006;

B) 5.♗e2 ♘c6 (5...a6!?; 5...c6!?; 5...g6!?; 5...♗f5!?) 6.d3 (6.d4 a6 – Game 23; 6...♗g4 see Game 10 or 6...♗f5 – 4.d4 ♘f6 5.♗e2 ♗f5 6.♘f3 ♘c6 in Game 34) 6...♗g4 7.0-0 e6 8.♗g5 ♗e7 9.♗h4 0-0 10.♗g3 ♕d7⇄, Marinsek, T. (2195) –

Nikolov, S. (2415), Pula 1998 or 6.♘b5 ♕d8 7.d4 a6 8.♘c3 ♗f5 9.♗f4 e6 10.0-0 ♗e7 11.h3 0-0=, Kosanski, S. (2365) – Nikolov, S. (2415), Radenci 1998.

5...♗g4

5...c6 6.♗g2 – Game 40.

6.♗g2 ♘c6

After 6...e6 (6...c6 7.0-0 e6 8.h3 ♗h5 9.b4 ♗e7 10.♖b1 0-0 11.d3 ♕c7 12.♗f4 ♗d6 13.♗xd6 ♕xd6 14.♘e4 ♘xe4 15.dxe4 ♕c7 ⇄, Varga,C. (2365) – Tiviakov,S. (2640), Hungary 2008) 7.d4 (7.d3 c6 8.♗f4 ♕d8±, Manet, E. (2000) – Bianchi, G. (2130), Proville 2007; 7...♘c6!? 8.0-0 0-0-0 ⇄) 7...c6 (7...♘c6!?) we have the following popular position.

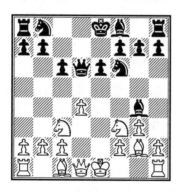

Also possible are 8.♗f4, 8.h3 and 8.0-0.

A) 8.♗f4

A1) 8...♕b4 9.♕d3 ♗f5 (9...♘bd7!? 10.0-0 ♗e7) 10.♕d2 ♘bd7 (Bluvshtein, I. – Zatonskih, A. (2445), Kapuskasing 2004) 11.♘h4 ♗g6 12.♘xg6 hxg6 13.a3 ♕b6 14.0-0 0-0-0?! (14...♗e7 15.a4 a5 16.♖fd1 0-0±) 15.♖fd1 ♗e7 (15...♘d5 16.♘xd5 exd5

17.h4) 16.b4 ♘d5 17.♘xd5 exd5 (17...cxd5 18.c4 dxc4 19.♖ac1) 18.♖e1 ♖de8 19.c3 ♘f6 20.a4±;

A2) 8...♕d8 9.h3 ♗xf3 10.♕xf3 (10.♗xf3 ♗e7 11.0-0 0-0 12.♕d3 ♘bd7 13.♖ad1 ♘d5 14.♘xd5 cxd5±, Murey, J. (2420) – Pytel, K. (2380), Saint Quentin 1998; 10...♗d6!? 11.♕d2 ♘a6±)

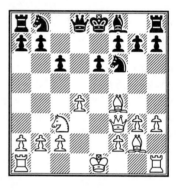

A2a) 10...♕xd4 11.♗e3 (11.♖d1 ♕b4 12.0-0 ♘bd7∞) 11...♕c4 (11...♕d8!? 12.0-0 ♘bd7) 12.a3 ♕a6 (12...♘bd7? 13.♗f1 ♘e5 14.♕g2) 13.♗f1 ♕a5∞;

A2b) 10...♗d6 (10...♗b4 11.0-0 0-0 12.♖fd1 12...♘bd7 13.♘e4 ♘xe4 14.♕xe4 ♘f6 15.♕e2±, Hermansson, E. (2387) – Jaderberg, B., Sweden 2003; 12.♕d3!? ♗d6 13.♗d2) 11.♗e5 (11.0-0-0 ♗xf4+ 12.♕xf4 0-0±) 11...0-0 (11...♗xe5!? 12.dxe5 ♘d5) 12.0-0-0 ♕e7 13.♕e2 ♘bd7 ⇄, Luukkonen, T. (2230) – Parkkinen, J. (2205), Helsinki 2006;

B) 8.h3 ♗h5 9.a3 ♗e7 (9...♕c7 10.0-0 ♘bd7 11.♖e1 0-0-0 12.b4 ♗d6 ⇄; 12.a4 ♕a5 ⇄) 10.0-0 0-0 11.g4 ♗g6 12.♘e5 ♖d8 13.♗e3 ♘d5 (13...♘bd7!? 14.f4 ♘b6 ⇄; 14.♘xg6 hxg6=) 14.♘xd5 cxd5 15.c4± , Sermek, D. (2523) – Sedlak, N. (2564), Turin 2006;

C) 8.0-0 ♗e7 (8...♘bd7 – 7...♘bd7 8.0-0 e6; 8...♛c7 9.h3 (Kovacevic, A. (2555) – Milanovic, D. (2490), Vogosca 2007) 9...♗h5 10.♘e2±)

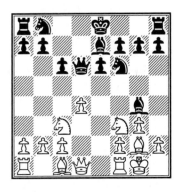

C1) 9.♖e1 (9.b3 0-0 10.♗b2 ♘a6 11.♛e2 ♖ad8 12.♖ad1 ♛c7 13.h3 (Rothuis, V. (2410) – Tiviakov, S. (2665), Netherlands 2007) 13...♗h5 14.a3 ♗d6 15.g4 ♗g6⇄) 9...0-0 10.♘e4 ♘xe4 11.♖xe4 ♗f5 12.♖e1 ♘d7 13.c3 ♛c7 14.♗f4 ♛b6 (14...♗d6 15.♗xd6 ♛xd6 16.♘h4 ♗g6 17.♘xg6 hxg6± , Godena, M. (2528) – Tiviakov, S. (2668), Saint Vincent 2006) 15.b3 h6 16.a4 a5 17.♘d2 ♘f6 18.♘c4 ♛d8=;

C2) 9.h3 ♗xf3 10.♗xf3 0-0 11.♘e2 ♘bd7 12.c3 (12.c4 ♖fd8 13.♗e3 e5 14.♛c2 exd4 15.♘xd4± , Cernousek, L. (2375) – Nedela, V. (2374), Czechia 2005; 12...e5!? 13.♗g2 ♖ad8) 12...♛c7 13.♛b3 ♗d6 (13...e5 14.♗g2 ♖fe8=) 14.c4 e5 15.dxe5 ♘xe5 16.♗g2 (Provotorov, I. (2380) – Faizrakhmanov, G. (2345), Sochi 2007) 16...♗c5 17.♗f4 ♖fe8 18.♖ad1 ♘h5=;

C3) 9.♗f4

C3a) 9...♛b4 10.a3 ♛b6 (10...♛xb2? 11.♛d2 ♗f5 12.♖a2 ♛b6 13.♖b1 ♛a6 14.♗f1 ♛a5 15.♘b5±) 11.♛d2 0-0

12.♘e5 ♗h5 13.b4 ♖d8 14.♗e3 ♘bd7 15.♘d3 (15.♘c4?! ♛a6 16.♘b2 ♘e5 17.♖fb1 ♘f3+ 18.♗xf3 ♗xf3∓ , Valsecchi, A. (2175) – Tiviakov, S. (2645), Bratto 2007) 15...♘g4 16.♘f4 ♘xe3 17.fxe3 ♗g6=;

C3b) 9...♛d8 10.♘e2 (10.♛d2 ♘bd7 11.♖fe1 0-0 12.♘e5 ♗f5 (Hadzimanolis, A. (2290) – Mateuta, G. (2469), Kavala 2004) 13.♘c4 ♘b6 14.♘e3 ♗g6=) 10...0-0 11.c4 ♘bd7 12.h3 ♗h5 13.♘c3 ♛b6 14.b3 ♛a5 15.♗d2 ♗b4 16.♛e1 ♛a3 17.♛e3 ♖ad8⇄ , Nestorovic, D. (2239) – Milanovic, D. (2434), Obrenovac 2004.

We return now to Alexikov – Belikov.

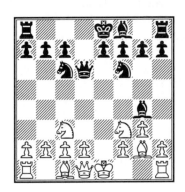

7.h3

7.d3 a6 (7...0-0-0 8.h3 ♗h5 – 7.h3 ♗h5 8.d3 0-0-0; 8.0-0!?; 7...♘d4 8.h3 ♘xf3+ 9.♗xf3 ♗xf3 10.♛xf3 c6± , Maciejewski, M. (2285) – Sygulski, A. (2400), Wroslaw 1987) 8.♗f4 ♛d7 9.♛d2± , Hansen, L. – Hughes, R. (2050), Gibraltar 2008; 8...e5!?.

7...♗h5 8.d3

8.d4 – 4.g3 ♘c6 5.♗g2 ♘f6 6.♘f3 ♗g4 7.h3 ♗h5 8.d4, Game 38.

8...0-0-0 9.♗e3

9.0-0 e5 10.g4 (10.♖e1!?) 10...♗g6 11.Nh4 (Stopa, J. (2460) – McPhillips, K. (2225), Herceg Novi 2005) 11...♘d4 12.f4?! (12.♘e2 ♘e6 13.♘c3 c6 ⇄ or 13...♘f4 14.♗×f4 e×f4 15.a4⇄) 12...♕b6 13.♔h1 (13.♘a4 ♕a6 14.f×e5 ♕×a4 15.e×f6 ♕×c2 16.♘×g6 h×g6∓) 13...e×f4 14.♖×f4 (14.♗×f4 ♕×b2 15.♘e2 ♘c6∓) 14...♖d7 15.♗e3 c5∓.

9...e5 10.g4 (10.0-0!?) **10...♗g6 11.♘d2**

After 11.♘h4 (11.♕d2?! e4), the chances are equal; for example, 11...♕e6 (11...♘d4 12.0-0 c6 13.♖b1 ♕c7 14.b4⇄, Campora, D. (2522) – Vitor, A. (2294), Lisbon 2002) 12.♘×g6 h×g6 13.g5!? (13.♕f3 ♗b4 14.0-0 ♗×c3 15.b×c3 ♘d5 16.c4 ♘×e3 17.f×e3=, Campora, D. (2506) – Araque, R. (2388), Cali 2001) 13...♘d7 (13...♘h5 14.♕g4 ♘d4 15.0-0-0=) 14.♗d5 ♕f5 (14...♖×h3?! 15.♔d2! ♕f5 16.♗g2 ♖×h1 17.♕×h1 ♕e6 18.♗d5 ♕f5 19.♗×c6 b×c6 20.♕×c6± or 15...♖×h1 16.♕×h1 ♕d6 17.♗×f7 ♘d4 18.♖f1 ♗e7 19.♕d5 with better chances for White) 15.♗e4 ♕e6 16.♕g4 ♘d4=.

11...♘d4 (11...♕e6!? 12.0-0 ♗b4) **12.♘ce4?!** (after this move, White experiences difficulties; 12.0-0!?) **12...♕a6** (12...♘×e4 13.♘×e4 ♕a6 14.0-0 h5∓; 13.♗×e4 h5?! 14.c3 ♘e6 15.♘c4∞; 14.♘c4?! ♕f6 or 13...♕a6 14.0-0 ♔b8 15.♗×d4 e×d4∓; 15.f4?! f5 16.g×f5 ♘×f5∓; 16.♗g2 e×f4 17.♗×f4 f×g4 18.h×g4 h5∓; 12...♘c6!? 13.c3 ♘e6∓) **13.♘×f6** (13.0-0 h5 14.g5 ♘e4 15.♘×e4 ♗e7 16.♕d2 f5 17.♘c3∓ or 14.♗×d4 e×d4 15.♘×f6 ♕×f6 16.♕f3 ♕×f3 17.♗×f3∓) **13...g×f6** (13...♕×f6 14.0-0 h5 15.g5 ♕a6∓) **14.♗e4** (14.0-0 h5 15.f4?! e×f4 16.♗×f4 h×g4 17.h×g4 ♗c5 18.♗e3 ♖de8∓; 15.♘b3 h×g4∓) **14...h5 15.♖g1 h×g4 16.h×g4 ♔b8** (16...♗×e4!? 17.♘×e4 ♕b5 18.b3 ♖h3 19.♗×d4 e×d4 20.♘×f6 ♗b4+ 21.♔f1 ♕c6⩲) **17.a3 f5** (17...♗c5!? 18.b4 ♗b6) **18.g×f5 ♘×f5 19.♕g4** (19.♕f3 ♘×e3 20.f×e3 ♗h5 21.♕f5 ♕h6 22.♕g5 ♕×g5 23.♖×g5 f6∓; 19...♕e6 20.♗×b7?! ♘×e3 21.f×e3 ♖h3; 20.♗×f5 ♗×f5 21.0-0-0∓) **19...♘×e3 20.f×e3 ♗h5 21.♕g3** (21.♕f5!?) **21...♕e6** (21...f6 22.♕f2 ♗b4 23.♗g6 ♗×g6 24.♖×g6 ♖h1+ 25.♖g1 ♖×g1+ 26.♕×g1∓ or 22...♕e6 23.♕f5 ♕f7 24.♘c4 ♖h6 25.♘a5 c6 26.b4 ♗d6 27.♔d2 ♗c7∓; 21...♗c5!? 22.♘b3 ♗d6 23.♔d2 c5) **22.♗f3 ♗c5 23.♗×h5 ♖×h5 24.♕f3** (24.0-0-0? ♖h3 25.♕g8 ♔c8∓) **24...♕h6 25.♘f1 ♖h4?!** (25...♖h3 [25...f5!? 26.0-0-0 f4] 26.♖g3 ♖×g3 27.♕×g3 ♕h5∓) **26.0-0-0 ♕e6** (26...f6∓) **27.♘d2 f5** (27...♖h3 28.♖g3 ♖×g3 29.♕×g3=; 27...♕h6 28.♘f1 f6∓) **28.♖g5 f4?!** (28...♕h6!? 29.♕×f5 ♗×e3 30.♖g2 ♖f8 31.♕×e5 ♖h1∓; 29.♖dg1 ♖g4 30.♖1×g4 f×g4

31.♕×g4 ♗×e3; 31.♖×g4 ♗×e3 32.♕e2
e4 33.♖×e4? ♕h1+ 34.♕d1 ♗×d2+
35.♔×d2 ♕e4−+; 33.♔d1) **29.e×f4
♖×f4**

30.♕e2= ♖e8?! (30...♕a2!? and
now: **A)** 31.♘b1? ♖f2 32.♕e4 ♗d4−+;
31.♕×e5? ♗d4 32.♕b5 ♕a1+ 33.♘b1
♗e3+ 34.♖d2 ♖f1#; 31.♖×e5?! ♗d4
32.♖b5 ♖f5 33.♖b4 a5∓ or 33.♖b3
♕a1+ 34.♘b1 ♖e5 35.♕g2 ♗e3+
36.♖d2 b6∓; **B)** 31.c3 ♕f6 32.♕×e5?
♗×a3 33.b×a3 ♖b6 34.c4 ♕×a3+
35.♔c2 ♕×d3+ 36.♔c1 ♕a3+ 37.♔c2
♕a4+ 38.♔c1 ♖b1+ or 33.♘c4 ♖f2
34.♖d2 ♖×d2∓; 32.♖×e5 ♗×a3

33.b×a3? ♕×a3+ 34.♔c2 ♕a2+ 35.♔c1
♖b6−+; 33.♘c4 ♗d6 34.♖a5 ♕b3=)
**31.♖e1± ♗d6 32.♔b1 ♕f6
33.♖g2 a6 ½-½**

Summary: After **1.e4 d5 2.e×d5
♕×d5 3.♘c3 ♕d6 4.♘f3**, Black has
more playable possibilities (4...a6,
4...c6, 4...g6, 4...♘c6, 4...♘f6) than
after 4.♗c4 (Game 39). 4...e5 is again
bad here; after 5.♗c4 we have a position discussed in Game 39. But **4.♘f3**
is more flexible than 4.♗c4, in keeping
with Lasker's old rule for the opening, "Bring out knights before bishops," as after **4.♘f3**, White keeps
open the option of playing the ♗f1 to
b5, c4, d3, e2 or g2. That can be very
important if White wants to play 5.d4.
As we saw before, the position of this
bishop can often influence the plans of
both sides.

In this game, we examined **4.♘f3 ♘f6
6.g3** without d2-d4. Practice indicates
that Black then has good chances for
equality and counterplay.

297

Index of Variations

5th Move Alternatives for Black

Index of Complete Games

Bibliography

Chess Informant 28/1979

Chess in the USSR 6/1968

Cook, William, *Synopsis of Chess Openings, a Tabular Analysis*, Robert Clarke & Co., 1884

Correspondence Chess Informator N1, Caissa Ltd. and M.Gluth, Fernschach-Verlag, 1992

Emms, John, *The Scandinavian*, The Chess Press, 1997

Emms, John, *The Scandinavian* (2nd edition), Everyman Chess, 2004

Freeborough and Ranken, *Chess Openings, Ancient and Modern*, Trubner, London, 1889

Grefe and Silman, *The Center Counter*, Chess Enterprises, 1983

Harman and Taulbut, *Winning with the Scandinavian*, Batsford, 1993

Hodges and Fischbein, *The Center Counter!*, R & D Publishers, 1994

Jakobetz, Somlai and Varnusz, *Skandinavisch*, Dreier Verlag, 1992

Karolyi, Tibor, *The Remarkable Shift Towards 6.g3*, New in Chess (NIC) Yearbook 70, 2004

Karolyi, Tibor, *Does Mikhail Melts thaw the Scandinavian Ice?*, NIC Yearbook 66, 2003.

Khalifman, Alexander, *Opening for White According to Anand, vol. 3* (Russian), Garde, 2005

Khalifman, Alexander, *Opening for White According to Anan,.vol. 3* (English), Chess Stars, 2004

Konikowski, Jerzy, *Die Skandinavische Verteidigung B01*, Beyer Verlag, 1996

Konikowski, Jerzy, *Panorama Szachowa* 4/1999

Land and Water, a weekly magazine published in London in the 19th century (absorbed in 1853 into another magazine well-known for its chess column, *The Field*)

Lane, Gary, *Ideas Behind Modern Chess Openings*, Batsford, 2005

Martin, Andrew, *Scandinavian Defence*, Trends Publications, 1991

Martin, Andrew, *The Scandinavian - The Easy Way* (DVD), ChessBase GmbH, 2005

McGeary, William, *The Myers Openings Bulletin*, 24/1982 and 25/1982

Melts, Michael, *Gubnitsky-Pytel Variation 3...Qd6!?*, *Chess Mail nos. 6, 7, 8, and 9, 1998*

Melts, Michael, *Gubnitsky-Pytel Variation 3...Qd6*, New in Chess Yearbook 48, 1998

Miller, Joseph W., *The American Supplement to the "Synopsis" containing American inventions in the chess openings, together with fresh analysis in the openings since 1882*, Robert Clarke & Co., 1884

Nielsen, Niels Jorgen Fries, *Skandinavisk*, Brabrand: Skakcentralens, 1982

Plaskett, James, *The Scandinavian Defence*, Batsford, 200

Polgar, Susan, *Center Counter with 3...Qd6*, Chess Life (May), 2005

Pytel, Krzystof, *Scandinawisch*, Echecs International, 1990

Pytel, Krzystof, *The Chess Player* 13/1977

Sawyer, Tim, *The Scandinavian Defense* (CD), Pickard & Son, 2000

Schiller, Eric, *Unorthodox Chess Openings*, Cardoza Publishing, 1998

Smith and Hall, *Winning with the Center Counter*, Chess Digest, 1991

Tesh, Rollie, *The Center Counter Game Rehabilitated*, Chess Digest, 1980

The Week in Chess (1-694), Chess & Bridge Ltd.

Tiviakov, Sergey, *Scandinavian with 3.;.Qd6,* Secrets of Opening Surprises, Vol.6, New In Chess, 2007

Tzermiadianos, Andreas, *The Scandinavian with 6...b5 - Completely Refuted!*, NIC Yearbook 76, 2005

Tzermiadianos, Andreas, *Sorry, no Advantage for White! - Part I*, NIC Yearbook 81, 2006

Tzermiadianos, Andreas, *Sorry, no Advantage for White! - Part II*, NIC Yearbook 82, 2007

Strategic Chess Thinking

A Strategic Opening Repertoire

2nd Edition

by Donaldson & Hansen   272 pages
ISBN: 978-1-888690-41-5   SRP:$29.95

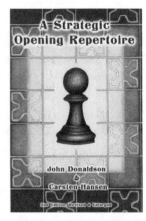

In 1998 a slim volume by International Master John Donaldson explored the crafting of a sophisticated but easily assimilated group of interrelated opening strategies intending to establish small but lasting advantages.
The result, *A Strategic Opening Repertoire*, was an instant success. Now this second edition, revised by Danish FM Carsten Hansen with the assistance of John Donaldson, is greatly expanded – twice the size – with many more games and detailed explanations.

How to Think in Chess

by Przewoznik & Soszynski   276 pages
ISBN: 1-888690-10-0   SRP: $24.95

What wins chess games? More than anything else, organized and efficient thinking. But chess thinking is specialized. Even Albert Einstein was a confessed chess duffer. *How to Think in Chess* teaches you practical ways of thinking to win. You'll see how to assess your thought processes during play and how to reorganize them in practice. You'll get exercises to increase your thinking skills. You'll see how to use elements of sports psychology in your preparation. *How to Think in Chess* gives you techniques to analyze and improve your own chess thinking; methods to foster creativity; over 200 specialized chess exercises to strengthen your game; advice on setting goals and coping with stress; and techniques to overcome mental blocks.

ChessCafe Puzzle Books

The ChessCafe Puzzle Book 1

by Karsten Müller   303 pages
ISBN: 1-888690-21-6   SRP:$19.95

Test and Improve Your Tactical Vision!

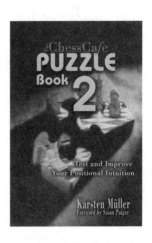

German grandmaster Karsten Müller combines
clear discussions of tactical themes with over 600
well-chosen positions to test, challenge and teach.
Although the classic combinations are not ignored,
the great emphasis is on positions from modern
tournament practice of the last decade.

"This book offers every type of tactical motif
imaginable, from the more common back rank
mates, pins, skewers, forks and the like up to and
including some of the most beautiful and rare combinations."
– From the Foreword by Women's World Champion, International
Grandmaster Susan Polgar.

The ChessCafe Puzzle Book 2

by Karsten Müller
ISBN: 978-1-888690-43-9   SRP: $24.95

Improve Your Positional and Strategic Intuition!

ChessCafe Puzzle Book 2 is a unique
instructional chess book that aims to help
intermediate and advanced players improve their
command of one of the most difficult aspects of
playing chess - strategy. It does so by offering a
large number of examples carefully selected by
the author, German Grandmaster Karsten Müller.

While there are many books and software
programs available to assist chess players in
improving their tactical ability, there are relatively
few that focus on strategic and positional
considerations. Working through these positions
and exercises is a great way to improve your positional understanding.

World Championship Matches

Tal-Botvinnik 1960

by Mikhail Tal   212 pages
ISBN: 1-888690-08-9   SRP: $19.95

One of the greatest books ever written about a
world championship match. Take a trip with the
'Magician from Riga' as he invites you to share
his thoughts and feelings as he does battle for
the world title.

International Grandmaster Andy Soltis: "Mikhail
Tal's splendid account of his world championship
match victory is one of the masterpieces of the
golden age of annotation – before insights and
feelings and flashes of genius were reduced to
mere moves and Informant symbols. This is simply the best book written
about a world championship match by a contestant. That shouldn't be a
surprise because Tal was the finest writer to become world champion."

Topalov-Kramnik –
2006 World Chess Championship

by Veselin Topalov & Zhivko Ginchev   220 pages
ISBN: 978-1-888690-39-2   SRP: $29.95

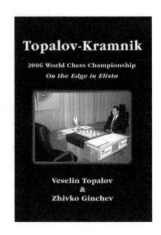

Two World Champions – in a class by
themselves. The profound Russian World
Champion Vladimir Kramnik, who had defeated
the seemingly invincible Kasparov to take the
"classical" world title in 2000. The brilliant
Bulgarian Challenger Veselin Topalov, ranked
No. 1 in the world, winner of the FIDE title in
2005. The immovable object versus the
irresistible force. This is Veselin Topalov's very
personal account of his 2006 world championship
match against the reigning world champion
Vladimir Kramnik. Complemented nicely by
almost 50 photographs.